10,000 Days in Alaska

Book One
1978-1989
(The First 12 Years)

Norman Wilkins

Copies of this book (volume one of three) can be ordered from Amazon or from the publisher. For additional information about the author, go to www.10000daysinalaska.com.

Books by Norman Wilkins:

Volume 1: 10,000 Days In Alaska Book One
Volume 2: 10,000 Days In Alaska Book Two
Volume 3: 10,000 Days In Alaska Book Three

ISBN: 1-886352-23-2
EAN 13: 978-1-886352-23-0

Published by
Cloud 9 Publishing
www.cloud9publ.wordpress.com

Volume one transcribed by Nadia Giordana, Cloud 9 Publishing.
Volumes two and three transcribed by Linda Law.
Technical advisor, Laura T. Behrendt.

Front cover photo: Norman's trap cabin. All photos are from the Wilkins' personal archives and include photos taken by family members and friends who have shared their prints.

All names of persons and places mentioned in this book are real; they have not been changed.

Copyright © 2010 Cloud 9 Publishing. No portion of this book may be reproduced, stored in a retrieval system or transmitted in any form-electronic, mechanical or other means without written consent of the publisher except in the case of brief quotations embodied in critical articles and reviews. All rights reserved. Primary and subsidiary rights include but are not limited to, electronic rights, motion picture and television rights, audio book rights, audiovisual rights, merchandizing rights and dramatic or performance rights and the creation of derivative works based on the copyrighted material.

Norman Wilkins makes a journal entry.

FOREWORD

Norman Wilkins and Slovenia-born Ladislava Kolenc (Sylvia to those who know her) met in postwar Gorizia Italy in 1946, marrying there in 1948. They moved to Iowa where Norman grew up, and farmed in several communities until 1957 when they moved to Motley, Minnesota and built the Tamarack Dell dairy farm. There, they raised their family and farmed until the late 1970s.

Norman had long felt the pull of the north, drawn to the mystique of Alaska—"The Last American Frontier" many said, and once the children were on their own, that desire to go north grew stronger. He made more than one hunting trip to Alaska before the 1978 expedition included in this book, and as the trips unfolded, so did Norman's desire to make Alaska his permanent home—to be a part of the expansive wilderness and yes, explore for gold!

Sylvia was not so enthusiastic in the beginning. (Bear in mind, those first few years they lived in a one-room, 12'x16' plywood cabin with no indoor toilet, no electricity and no running water.) Once, after they settled in Nelchina, Sylvia was asked how she liked Alaska, to which she replied, "I really like the people here, but you can take Alaska and give it back to the Eskimos!"

They *did* find gold in Alaska. They found it in the air, the mountains, the wildlife and especially in the people—the people they worked shoulder to shoulder with and shared their table with; each one weaving an independent piece of the tapestry of everyday life in the '70s, '80s, '90s and until 2005 along the Glenn Highway.

From their log cabin overlooking Scoter Lake at Nelchina, radiating outward to Glennallen, Anchorage, Copper Center, Tok, Palmer, Wasilla, Fairbanks, Denali, Matanuska, Susitna, Valdez, Cordova and other arctic communities, Norman Wilkins recorded daily journal entries throughout the entire 25+ years he and Sylvia spent carving out a life on the Alaskan tundra. The contents of this book have been transcribed from Norman's notebook-style pages as originally written with the exception of occasional edits and insertions for clarity.

Norman is well known as an honest man to the nth degree. Case in point—the title of this book; he questioned it, so I did the math. The 1978 trip (August 11 to October 29) took 79 days. Eight months of work and planning prior to moving to Alaska permanently, totaled 240 days. June 29, 1979 until May 3, 2005 (when they moved back to Minnesota) encompassed 9,066 days. That gives us 9,385 days (not including trips to Alaska prior to 1978). I think we're good with the numbers.

10,000 Days In Alaska is a three-volume documentary journal; all three books are available from the publisher and wherever books are sold.

Norman and Sylvia currently live in Minnesota, but a big part of Norman's heart remains in Alaska. I'm proud to call them my parents.

—Nadia Giordana, Cloud 9 Publishing

TABLE OF CONTENTS

1978—prospecting trip 7

1979—Alaska bound 19

1980—snow caves; gold rush; building trapper cabin 65

1981—accident at Old Man Lake; commercial fishing 117

1982—bear scare; staking claims; digging clams 161

1983—grizzly hunt; buffalo hunt; filing claims 201

1984—building permanent cabin 241

1985—prospecting near glaciers; rollogons across tundra 281

1986—exploring old mines; staking claims at Nelchina 323

1987—ore samples; crane hunting; goose hunting 369

1988—moose hunting; caribou hunting 415

1989—incident with a wolf 469

Dedicated to the memory
of my son, Paul Wilkins
1949-2008

Norman Wilkins

1978–prospecting trip

Friday, August 11, 1978–got a middle of the afternoon start. Took Highway 10 to Fargo, North Dakota, then No. 29 to Grand Forks, North Dakota, then Highway No. 2 west to Devil's Lake, which is 270 miles from my starting point in Motley Minnesota. Camped just north of Minot on No. 52.

Saturday, August 12, 1978–hit the road at 7:30 a.m. It's hills and flat land here. Cattle and grain country. The RCP had a shotgun road block about 40 miles east of Lloydminster. They checked us out and on we went. Drove into a very hard rain storm. In the town of Lloydminster, the rain and hail was so bad it stopped all traffic. I couldn't see past the hood of the truck.

Sunday, August 13, 1978–we left town at 7:30 a.m. We saw a buffalo herd just east of Edmonton–impressive. Had a tire failure. Rabbits were plentiful along the road. My brother (Jerry Wilkins) tried hunting for one but didn't get a shot.

Monday, August 14, 1978–got a real early start. The road was really bad. Sometimes I was in low gear for over 60 miles. It got better and we're making better time. Saw a wrecked and burned pickup and trailer in the ditch. Saw more rabbits and spruce hens. Another tire is going bad. We got as far as mile 747 on the Alaska Highway. Ed and Gloria Dolhan (Hunting Guide) live here. Had a nice visit this evening with them.

Tuesday, August 15, 1978–had breakfast with Ed and Gloria, then started for Whitehorse 114 miles away. The road was pretty good, then got wet and sloppy. Got to U.S./Canadian border and camped for the night.

Wednesday, August 16, 1978–started a little later this morning. Still seeing lots of rabbits. Made good time and got to Anchorage mid afternoon. Camped at Jerry Brandt's (a good friend of my brother, Jerry).

Thursday, August 17, 1978–got around late. Started running down leads on gold claims. Not much luck.

Friday, August 18, 1978–got to see Jim Davidson, made some plans.

Went to Chad & Trish's at Girdwood. Went to see Billie Goodpasture claims, but were not impressed with them. Jerry fished for salmon at Hope, but no luck.

Saturday, August 19, 1978—had appointment for J. Mull to show us his gold claim but he didn't show. We went to Anchorage to help J.D. with his airplane. My brother Jerry had an appointment with someone who didn't show. Went down to Jim D. He and Jerry took a sauna while I fixed supper. Talked to a fellow about mining and got a phone number of a guy who has claims for sale.

Sunday, August 20, 1978—helped Jim Davidson put the wings on his airplane. He got breakfast. Met Ray Snyder. He has a lot of gold claims and invited us moose hunting. Saw Jerry Brandt. Talked to a fellow with six claims above Petersville. Went to Chad's, had a salmon supper—very good.

Monday, August 21, 1978—went to Petersville and up into hill on the other side. Couldn't find the claims we were looking for. Stayed there that night.

Tuesday, August 22, 1978—drove back to Anchorage, then to Girdwood. Checked for mail. Jerry Wilkins voted. Went to Chad's. Jerry fell from the pony and hurt his groin. Partied that night.

Wednesday, August 23, 1978—Jerry is stiff and sore. Checked in with Jim, then went to Alaska Land Office. Didn't have any luck. Rested up, then Jim and I went over to Ray Snyder's and looked at pictures and listened to mining talk, hunting too. Ray seems like a nice guy.

Thursday, August 24, 1978—checked out some equipment and prices. Jerry made some phone calls. We stopped to see some friends of Jerry's. Bought groceries and gas and headed out for Kenai. No mail. Stopped at Chad's and borrowed a fishing pole. Went on down to Soldotna. Found Jan there. She had some friends there. Then went on out to the cabin.

Friday, August 25, 1978—got up late and went fishing. The salmon were not biting on the lures we had. Jerry did his laundry. Went to Soldotna, got salmon eggs and pixie lures. Jan and Chad W. came out and we went to the Kenai River. Chad and I each caught a salmon.

Norman Wilkins

Saturday, August 26, 1978—Jerry fixed breakfast, he is a good cook. I washed the dishes. I made a smoker out of a small cloth tarp and a few small poles and some rope. Went to Funny River. Chad caught a rainbow trout (a big one) and two nice Dolly Varden trout. Jerry got a nice Dolly and I got one humpy (pink salmon, also known as a humpback). Smoked some of the fish in the smoker and we ate all the rest. I cooked it.

Sunday, August 27, 1978—Jerry and Chad went fishing in Funny River and caught some more Dolly's. Lots of catch and release now. Chad and I went to Kenai River for silver salmon but didn't catch any. That evening Chad showed us the cabin he has in Ninilchek. It is a beautiful log cabin located in a perfect setting. Then we headed for Girdwood. Chad was driving his fast car. We came upon a huge grizzly in the other lane. We were all grateful it wasn't in our lane.

Monday, August 28, 1978—we got up late, Trish fixed us a good breakfast. Stopped at Jim Davidson's on the way to Anchorage. Went to Brandt's office, then over to Bertha M. (real estate). Met a fellow with nine claims on Cache Creek (past Petersville). Then met Ray at the "Time Out". Partied a little, then supper and to bed.

Tuesday, August 29, 1978—got up late, did our shopping and headed for the Patrician claims out of Petersville. (Note: When visiting gold claims, there aren't any roads. I am driving a Chevy 4x4 with a camper on it. It is slow going, especially when driving over rocks. If you get stuck, you get yourself out. There is help only if it happens to come by.) Met Peter on Gold Creek. Turned around there and went back up Cache Creek, then camped at an airstrip. Went hunting and missed a spruce hen and a squirrel.

Wednesday, August 30, 1978—drove over to the Bird Creek mine. Talked to Earl Ray, then walked over to the saddle in the mountain to the Patrician claims. Did a lot of panning and running gravel through the little sluice box. Did find some gold. It would take some pretty big machinery to work these claims.

Thursday, August 31, 1978—showered a little in the night. The air is so sweet here, as is the water. Got our act together by mid morning. On our

10,000 Days in Alaska Book One 1978-1989

way out on the dirt road closer to the highway, we came upon a large Winnebago that had slipped over into a mud hole. It was leaning a lot. The road was blocked. A 4x4 Ford tried and couldn't pull it out. Someone went out and got Alaska Highway State truck to come and pull the Winnebago out. We were held up two hours and got in to Anchorage late. Jerry got to see some friends. We had a hard time finding a campground that had room for us.

Friday, September 1, 1978–got up late. Worked on camper lights. Finally found the problem. Got a map. Saw Jerry Brandt. Went to Girdwood and got the mail. Stopped for a few minutes at Chad's, then back to Bird Creek campground for the night.

Saturday, September 2, 1978–went in to Anchorage to Ray S. and visited a while. Gretchen made a really nice breakfast. Ray described the claims that he and Jimmy Dale have on Tyone Creek. We played pool a while then fixed some batteries, etc., then back to Bird Creek campground.

Sunday, September 3, 1978–went down to Chad's and spent the day there.

Monday, September 4, 1978–stayed all day here at Chad's.

Tuesday, September 5, 1978–Left Chad's about noon. Stopped to see Jim D. Stayed at Bird Creek campground.

Wednesday, September 6, 1978–Up early, took Jerry to the doctor to look at a bruise. Dr. said it's okay. We did laundry, shopping, groceries and saw some people. Talked with Ray S. about going in to see his gold claims. There are more claims to be staked. Met the shop foreman, Don Anderson. Went to see Jerry Brandt. He is to set up a meeting tomorrow about some more gold claims.

Thursday, September 7, 1978–checked prices of lumber and steel to build a sluice box. Met Jerry Brandt, who took us over to see Charles Dick (professional realtor). He has 700 claims. Looked at most of the best of them.

Friday, September 8, 1978–had a battery to take care of, then to U.S.

Norman Wilkins

Geological Survey Office to research some of the creeks we are interested in. Didn't have real good luck, their information was not complete. The plan now is to take a couple days off, then get ready to hit the Eureka area. Been really studying the geological books.

Saturday, September 9, 1978—spent the day at Chad's.

Sunday, September 10, 1978—back in Anchorage late p.m. Can't make contact with Ray or Jim. Camped at Jerry Brandt's.

Monday, September 11, 1978—started out very late. Found out how to ship hand guns to Alaska. Jerry is closer to finding the man he is looking for. Ate supper and camped at Jerry Brandt's.

Tuesday, September 12, 1978—got up late and went to help Jim D. get his plane out of some mud. It was too muddy today. The weather is too bad to fly also. Went to Girdwood and camped at Bird Creek.

Wednesday, September 13, 1978—got up very early. Picked up Chad, went to portage to hunt ducks. It was a long walk. Jerry got five down. Chad got two shots and I got one. Then off to court on Ron Brandt's behalf. We camped at Chad's.

Thursday, September 14, 1978—got up early. Went to town to see Ray S. Went to State Land Office and got the latest information on Ray's area. Stopped at the real estate man, Jerry Brandt, then over to make plans with Ray S. to see his claims. Got that settled.

Friday, September 15, 1978—went looking for a 6x6 and trailer. Answered several ads and checked other places—no luck. Stopped at grocery store and map store.

Saturday, September 16, 1978—went over to Ray's and worked on his swamp buggy. Ran into some problems, but we did get the motor running.

Sunday, September 17, 1978—went over to work on swamp buggy and got quite a bit fixed up. Must get several parts Monday morning. Worked until afternoon, then went to Girdwood after equipment to go out into the bush.

10,000 Days in Alaska Book One 1978-1989

Monday, September 18, 1978—back to Ray's and worked on swamp buggy all day. Got the brakes and lights fixed. Still needs throttle.

Tuesday, September 19, 1978—Ray can't work on buggy this morning, so we shopped for supplies to go up in the mountains for three weeks at the claims.

Wednesday, September 20, 1978—bought more grub. Stopped at land office. Went over to Ray's and worked on the swamp buggy, then took Jim D. out to his plane, then back to Jerry Brandt's and camped.

Thursday, September 21, 1978—got a late start. Did more shopping, then over to Ray's. Worked on the 6x6 swamp buggy all afternoon. Got it finished, then did our laundry. Ate supper and camped at Jerry B's.

Friday, September 22, 1978—did some late shopping, then went over to Ray's and worked on the swamp buggy. Got them loaded and left town. Got as far as the State Weigh Station. Troopers red lined the truck and trailer with the buggy. We were able to get everything legal, finally. Got to the Little Nelchina River on the Glenn Highway and camped there for the night.

Saturday, September 23, 1978—got up fairly early, but a late start from camp. Went up the Little Nelchina River quite a ways and camped for the night. There was some ice in the river. Saw a small caribou bull. I drove for a while—the 6x6 is a S.O.B. to drive.

Sunday, September 24, 1978—got up early, it's warmer today. Went on up the river, hit the trail overland to Tyone Creek. Had one fiasco after another. Finally made camp at Tyone Creek. We saw many caribou today as well as a moose cow with calf. We broke two springs today.

Monday, September 25, 1978—got up fairly early and went fishing. Caught eight grayling, very easy. Jerry got four. Fried them for breakfast. Then Ray needed a hole on his Volkswagen motor to hang a spring on. He used my .22 rifle to make the hole—and blew a hole clear through his motor's oil cooler! Spent most of the day jury rigging that, then wound up blocking oil flow to the cooler. Jerry walked up the mountain and saw four bull moose and a caribou. He got three ptarmigan.

Norman Wilkins

Tuesday, September 26, 1978—went out to look at claims. Did some panning, and shoveled some through the small sluice box. Saw lots of fine colors. Once, Ray got badly stuck. Saw two claims I liked. Lots of caribou here.

Wednesday, September 27, 1978—Jerry and I went down the Tyone looking the claims over. Carrying guns, but no luck for ptarmigan. Saw four caribou and thirty six moose—thirty two in one bunch. Lots of grayling in the creek. They go down stream before freeze-up and winter in deeper water. This creek will soon be ice. Back at camp, I took a bath and shaved. This was a beautiful afternoon.

Thursday, September 28, 1978—went back up the Tyone as far as Red fox Creek. Panned on lots of the claims. Bill talon seems pleased with his claim. We did get nice colors there. Got back to camp at 3:30 p.m. Ate beans, then Jerry went out after ptarmigan. Bill and I checked out a chain that is jumping on the one buggy. There isn't any fix to it.

Friday, September 29, 1978—woke up to one inch of snow on the ground. We all decided to start for the highway. We got everything packed and loaded. Had to pull the 6x6 to get it started. Had good luck getting to Little Nelchina. We did have a rear wheel come loose. Bill and I got it tightened again, then a chain broke, got stuck, and had lots of trouble going down the Little Nelchina. We did have a nice place to camp.

Saturday, September 30, 1978—left camp in good time. Ice crystals in the river. The 6x6 had to be pulled a lot. Finally got out to the highway. Jerry and Bill hitched a ride down to get the pickup and drove in to Anchorage. It was late when we got there.

Sunday, October 1, 1978—slept late. Went to Girdwood, picked up mail. Called home from Jerry Brandt's. Camped at Chad's.

Monday, October 2, 1978—checked the legality of the Tyone claims in all the offices in Anchorage. Couldn't find Ray. Went to a garage to get the pickup oil changed. It was full. Ate supper, shot some pool, then to bed.

Tuesday, October 3, 1978—back to Anchorage. Got the runaround about the claim status. Spent all day going from office to office. Late in the day, went to Chad's and went fishing—no fish.

Wednesday, October 4, 1978—back to anchorage and in and out of offices until we finally got the information we wanted. Bill Tallon is building a retort for mercury recovery. Camped at Jerry Brandt's.

Thursday, October 5, 1978—went to Bill Tallon to see how his claim papers are coming. He isn't very far along with the retort. Went over to Ray S. to see the claim papers we are interested in. Jim Dale has them! We will have to wait until he gets to town!

Friday, October 6, 1978—down to State Lands Office again. More research. Pete Nelson at Natural Resources was not in. Went to a few radio and electronic people about emergency radios. Camped at Jerry Brandt's.

Saturday, October 7, 1978—got up late, it's a rainy morning. Will rest today. Showered and shaved. Tried to get a goose hunt together. No luck, will try again Sunday.

Sunday, October 8, 1978—Jerry got an airboat to use. Hooked it to the truck. Brandt has to do a tune up. Picked up Chad on the way. Had a time getting the boat out of the trailer. The Placer River is a swift current. Jerry drove the boat. The wind was strong. Went up stream at three to four MPH. At about a mile, we saw a few ducks, but no shooting. Had a hairy time getting boat back on the trailer—raining all the time. I was glad to get back to Chad's, eat and go to sleep.

Monday, October 9, 1978—still rainy this morning. Went to Anchorage. Weather was better there. Got an appointment with Mary Ried (real estate). She has a claim on Tyone Creek. Talked things over with her, then went over to Bill Tallon's and saw his retort. Camped at Jerry B's.

Tuesday, October 10, 1978—made calls this morning and got an appointment with Pete Nelson at Natural Resources—very informative session. Got a hold of Bill T. He will contact Mary R. and let us know.

Wednesday, October 11, 1978—got a late start. Went to look at two swamp buggy's and a trailer. Stopped at map office for a map of Daisy

Norman Wilkins

Creek. We did our laundry and shopped for groceries. Then on to Indian to help Jerry Brandt with some mechanical work on Stu's air boat and then Chad's pickup. Camped at Bird Creek.

Thursday, October 12, 1978—got a very late start. Checked on the air boat. Went on in to Anchorage for boat parts. Bill is not having any luck tumbling his fine gold. Couldn't find the needed boat parts. Camped at Jerry B's.

Friday, October 13, 1978—didn't work on the air boat till late. Got quite a bit done.

Saturday, October 14, 1978—got another late start on the air boat at Indian. Got more done.

Sunday, October 15, 1978—up early, went up Placer River with the airboat. Saw four swans, geese, and seven ducks. No shots. Got the airboat hung up a couple of times. The foot-feed broke, but we did get back in good time.

Monday, October 16, 1978—back to Anchorage to mining office to check status of Daisy Creek claims, then over to Ray S. He says he will go in to the office and straighten things out.

Tuesday, October 17, 1978—Alaska Day—State holiday, State offices are closed.

Wednesday, October 18, 1978—Lands and Mining Office tells us no change in Ray S. status on the claims. Talked to Bill Tallon and went to see Ray S. Nothing accomplished. We are disappointed.

Thursday, October 19, 1978—went to see PettyJohn about a claim on Jay Creek. Called all around town looking for an off road vehicle with no luck. Then out to work on the airboat for a while. Camped at Jerry Brandt's.

Friday, October 20, 1978—talked to PettyJohn, his claims appear to be in order. No luck finding off road vehicles. Called Mary Ried, she seems to be satisfied with Ray S. claims. My brother, Jerry Wilkins took sick with a pain in right side about 3:00 p.m. Took him to the hospital. They couldn't find anything wrong. Will watch it. Camped back at Jerry B's. Rained all night and snowed all day.

Saturday, October 21, 1978—didn't do much all day, lots of geese are flying in the night. My brother Jerry is somewhat better. I still can't get through on the phone to Sylvia.

Sunday, October 22, 1978—went down to Chad's, Sylvia called there. Camped at Chad's that night.

Monday, October 23, 1978—Jerry and I came to Anchorage and tried some equipment rental places. Took him to a doctor. He has two broken ribs. Stopped by Bill Tallon and compared notes, talked water rights, how he sells gold, as well as quit claim deeds, etc. Beans and ham for supper. Called Sylvia again.

Tuesday, October 24, 1978—did some shopping, picked up trousers being repaired. Left Anchorage for home about 2:00 p.m. Got to Tok Junction after 8:00 p.m. Ate supper and to bed.

Wednesday, October 25, 1978—finally got a call on the D4 Cat. It had been sold. Headed on out. Went through customs okay. Picked up a hitch hiking trapper (Fred Fink?). Very interesting to talk to. Saw a beautiful coyote cross the road, a spruce hen and a moose.

Thursday, October 26, 1978—started out at 4:00 a.m. Very sick. Got to Watson Lake at 7:00 a.m. Gassed the truck. Feel better now. Beautiful sunrise. The lakes and streams aren't frozen here to Whitehorse. Some flowing ice. Drove in one good snowstorm and several others before 7:00 a.m. Drove sixteen hours today and got to Fort St. John—a good 700 miles. Both shoulders are very tired. Have planned tomorrow's route, will eat and hit the sleeping bag.

Friday, October 27, 1978—started out before 7:00 a.m. Stopped 100 miles north of Edmonton. While I fried a hamburger, a squirrel hopped up on the camper step and looked at me. Traffic in Edmonton is terrible. Saw the Buffalo herd east of town. Stopped in Lloydminster and called Sylvia. Camped near a grain elevator in a little town.

Saturday, October 28, 1978—started out before sunup. Turned south at

Norman Wilkins

North Battleford. Saw a lake seven miles south of Elrose. Talked to a few farmers and got permission to hunt waterfowl. Saw four or five geese and lots of Mallard ducks, also two nice antelope and one jackrabbit. Fifty miles east of Moose Jaw, I saw so many geese, ducks and swans as to defy one's imagination. Crossed the border into N.D. at 10:00 p.m. Camped along the highway thirty miles later. Late supper tonight.

Sunday, October 29, 1978—started out at 5:00 a.m. Didn't see a single filling station last night. Ran out of gas thirty five miles from Minot North Dakota. Hitched a ride in to get gas. Got a can of gas and started walking. Walked several miles before someone pulled over and gave me a ride. It was a windy day today. Saw lots of geese in N.D. Got home about 5:00 p.m. Trip over.

Alaskan Highway indicating the 1979 detour route

10,000 Days in Alaska Book One 1978-1989

Roger Shequen and Norman Wilkins look over the 73,000 lb. rig.

Norman and Sylvia Wilkins—ready to go.

Norman Wilkins

1979–Alaska bound

Friday, June 29, 1979–after eight months of work and planning we leave Motley, Minnesota with a fully loaded rig. The truck is a 1964 Freightliner semi tractor with the frame extended. The bed on it measured 24 feet–and we were pulling a 20 foot pup trailer. The entire load of gear and equipment weighed 73,000 lbs. The welding work on the swamp buggy we were hauling (nicknamed the "mean machine") was done by Glen Peterson. We rushed all morning, then met Roger Shequen at the El Ray and had dinner. He has been a very big help. There were a lot of other people that gave me help and encouragement. My truck batteries were low and Roger pulled me with the truck he was driving. When we got to Wadena, we stopped and checked the load and tires. Everything was alright, just had to add a little air to a few tires. When we got near Detroit Lakes, it was raining hard. The heater hose broke, so I pulled over to the side of the road and cut the bad end off and re-clamped the hose into place. Then we started out again. Stopped on the west side of town, camped and slept in the cab of the truck.

Saturday, June 30, 1979–we left Detroit Lakes at almost 8:00 a.m. I soon noticed trouble with the truck lights and stopped at several towns along Highway 32 hoping to find someone to work on them with no luck so we continued on, crossing the border into Canada at 2:40 p.m. We had to wait there at the border for an hour until the Canadians came back from lunch to process us. The fella told me I should go back to the American side of the border and get documentation stating that I had the Caterpillar on my truck so I could get it back into Alaska without paying duty when we left Canada. Anyway, I walked back across the border and sure enough, they gave me the paper that I needed and we went on to Winnipeg and got on the Trans Canada Highway. We didn't get very far on the Trans Canada before we came to a car that had recently burned up along the road. Our truck ran well; no flats and the load seemed secure. A little farther on we saw a deer, and that evening we stopped at Brandon where Sylvia fixed us supper of fried steak out in the open over a Coleman stove (We have our camping gear and groceries with us on the truck). We met some really nice people there too. This was in a large open industrial area but it turned out to be a poor place to camp–there was lots of traffic noise and it ruined our sleep.

10,000 Days in Alaska Book One 1978-1989

Sunday, July 1, 1979—we needed some work done on the truck. Got that done, and then I had to fix a flat tire on the inside wheel of the trailer. After that, we only traveled about 40 miles (in the rain) before the fuel filter clogged up. May have been some bad fuel. We reached Saskatoon and parked at 10:00 p.m. and I took that opportunity to clean the fuel filter while Sylvia fried us a steak. I couldn't get a call through to Bill Tallon to let him know that we were on the road to Alaska. Some man where we were parked complained that Mike (our dog) barked. He is our guard dog. Sometimes he rode in the cab, but we had a box for him on the load and he rode there most of the time. It was rigged for him to be comfortable.

Monday, July 2, 1979—got up early (I'm usually up between 4:00 and 5:00 a.m.) and I serviced the truck while Sylvia fixed our breakfast. A tire on the trailer had gone down during the night so I got the spare out, put it on and we drove downtown to Saskatoon to have the flat fixed and found out it was a holiday (Canada Day usually falls on July 1st unless it's a Sunday, then it falls on July 2nd). Just our luck—they didn't have anyone on duty that could do tires. I eventually got both flats fixed but I had to do it myself. I adjusted the brakes on the truck, fixed a broken air line, and we started for Lloyd Minster, the next big town on the map. The truck was giving me trouble when I shifted. It just wasn't working like it should. I stopped for fuel and checked the wheels and tires and look the truck all over (something I do whenever I stop). The front seal on the left front tire is throwing grease. I have 20 ton jacks with me so I jacked that wheel up off the ground and looked at the bearings. They were tight so I gave it some more grease, thinking in all probability, the seal is leaking. We grabbed a hamburger and started for Edmonton. The truck is still giving me trouble when shifting. This was especially troubling because back at Motley, I took the truck to a mechanic that specialized in semis and big trucks. I had him go completely through the transmission. We shouldn't be having this problem. We soon ran into heavy winds and rain and the lights on the truck finally failed. We pulled over and had a snack for supper. It was too wet for Sylvia to cook outside on the camp stove. We slept there in the truck cab.

Tuesday, July 3, 1979—we got up ready to get an early start only to find that it was too foggy to drive so we sleep for another hour. We needed it anyway. When I tried the truck, it wouldn't start so I serviced it by greasing zerks, checked all the fluids and tires and waited, hoping for someone to come along who could give us a pull to get the truck started. A young Indian lad stopped with a full-sized pickup truck and offered to give it a try. We didn't know if he could pull it or not, as we were so heavily loaded. But he started out easy and snugged up the chain and I'll be darned, he got it done! So we went on into Edmonton. There was a particular station there I wanted to go to, but I didn't know exactly where to turn off the highway. By gosh, I went past the intersection where I should have turned, and I looked for that station thinking, "I know it's over on the left somewhere". That's when I came to where I could see its sign, but I was already past it. This was a four lane highway and when I came to another intersection, I decided to make a U-turn and go back. I got about halfway through the U-turn when, what do I see coming from my right, but the Canadian Mounties! Boy, my heart was in my throat and I'm thinking they aren't going to look on this maneuver very kindly. But there was no turning back, I was committed and finished the U-turn. To my happy surprise, the Mounties went right around me. They didn't even stop to talk to me about my driving. This was really early in the morning and there wasn't any traffic to speak of. Maybe they let me go for that reason. We went back to that intersection and the station I wanted and got some fuel for the truck and I serviced it again, checking everything. Some people there were helpful and told us the best way to get our outfit to Yellowhead Highway. I got out from there about six to eight miles and the shifting mechanism in the transmission of the truck failed. This is a 3x5 transmission meaning there are 15 gears in it. The first gear went out. After that happened, there was no hope of going on like it was so when I found a place where I could cross the four lane highway, I got clear over on the shoulder to my right and checked to see what was coming. The highway was open on both sides so I started across as tight as I could turn it. I barely made it on the right side of the highway going back towards Edmonton. It was a really hairy U-turn to make when using up what amounted to six lanes of road, but the ditch was wide and that helped. We went back to Edmonton.

    Trying to move around a city the size of Edmonton with a crippled truck is not easy. We finally were referred to a truck gear specialist who estimated the price to fix the transmission would be about $4,000 in Canadian. We are floored. I tried to find someone who would haul our equipment and gear to Alaska for us (I would have given them the truck and trailers in return). We found no takers and finally decided to have the truck fixed. This fellow that was going to do the work was a friendly sort of a guy and he let us camp there until we could get our truck in. It had been raining when we pulled into the yard in back of the shop. This is some kind of sticky, gooey red-like clay. I pulled in there with the truck and they wanted me to park my trailer down between two other semi trailers at a fence. I pulled up and got that truck and trailer lined up to back in there and I went out and locked the pin on the fifth wheel on the trailer and started backing. I looked over toward the shop and here are 10 or 15 guys that work there—and they are all watching me trying to back this trailer into a narrow space in four inches of muck. But by gosh, it went really well. I backed it right in on the first try! When I unhooked the trailer and drove the truck up to the shop, I walked in nonchalantly, like this was an everyday thing, no big deal.

They were pretty busy, but we got lucky and they had a cancellation. It was still going to be some time before they finished the work so the foreman of the shop helped us get our stuff out to a nearby campground and get set up. Mike the dog seems to be losing a little weight and we are concerned about him, but he has a break from riding in that box and we think this will help. He is enjoying these days more than we are. It was real nice and a little foggy the next morning. The last two mornings my back has been bad and I can barely stand up. We call the mechanics every day from the campground and the foreman stops to keep us informed how things are going.

Wednesday, July 4, 1979—the foreman stops to tell us that the truck should be fixed by the next morning. We called Roger Shequen, who looks after things of ours back in Motley, and talked to him.

Thursday, July 5, 1979—the foreman took us into the truck shop and the truck was done by noon that day. The bill didn't come to $4,000, it was $3,600 Canadian. That still left us short of money now for our trip. We were waiting for an insured check to come in to our bank and it hadn't arrived. The shop let me have the truck anyway with our promise that we would send the rest of the money from Whitehorse. The campground won't let us park our truck there when we went back to get ready to leave, so we picked up our tent and moved to a truck stop.

Friday, July 6, 1979—up early as usual. Sylvia fixed breakfast while I worked on the lights of the truck until noon. I didn't have much luck, they still weren't working right. I used a phone where we were staying and talked to the bank and they assured me the money was on the way. We went over to the bank we forwarded the money to, got it, and went to Edmonton Gear to pay them off. Stopped to talk to the fellas in the shop and a couple of those guys panned gold. It was really interesting talking to them. One guy, Lyle had been a real friend to us during this time (he hauled us around different times and wished us a good trip and wanted us to send a post card to the shop when we get to Alaska.) They were a really nice bunch of fellas.

Saturday, On July 7, 1979—we left Edmonton at 6:00 a.m. and the road was really hilly. We saw two deer and two large black bear. The bear we saw near McBride was very tall and thin. Both the bears we saw were big and it's not unusual to see them feeding along this highway. We learned a bridge was washed out on the normal road we would have taken to Alaska, so to get around it, we took a detour to Prince George and on up to Cassiar highway. Twenty miles east of Prince George we saw a two-year-old bull moose grazing in the ditch and one dead deer. We had a flat tire on an inside wheel of the truck near the top of a steep hill. I put blocks under the truck wheels and the trailer and changed it.

Coming in to Prince George there is a steep hill that goes down to the river there. Then you meet the railroad track and cross the river on a railroad bridge barely wide enough to accommodate a narrow road on each side of the tracks for vehicles. As I started down the hill, the heavy load we were carrying was pushing the truck hard. The engine is a Cummins 250 and it is to be run at 1,800 to 2,200 RPMs. If you push it over 2,200 RPMs the engine can fail. So as the RPMs increased, I would kick it up another gear to help save the engine—but we would run a little faster each time I did that. It was awfully windy and one of the mud flaps got to really flapping around, knocking the valve open on the air tank causing our brakes to overheat. Now we didn't have brakes. I knew once we get to the bottom of this hill, we were going to have to make an extremely sharp turn onto the bridge. I'm kickin' it up another gear—and another gear—and another gear. We are picking up speed alarmingly fast. Thinking we wouldn't make it, I told Sylvia to jump while she had the chance but she wouldn't do it. Instead, she said, "I'm ridin' it down with you." I have to give her a lot of credit she never even screamed. We were careening faster and faster down the hill and finally at the 15th gear, the truck reaches 2,800 RPMs. I expected it to blow any second. When we go to the sharp turn approaching that narrow, nine foot wide lane, we were looking right down into the river. I made up my mind I was gonna put that truck across the bridge. Going through the turn, our rig leaned dangerously out, threatening to go over, but it held. The trailer cracked the whip behind us and I put her right into that slot—never even touched a mirror on either side. There were only inches. Still moving much too fast, the trailer slid over and we blew out the two outside tires on the right side of it. Once across the bridge, we saw a dirt road straight ahead. We went down that for at least the equivalent of a couple of city blocks, finally coming to a stop. We pulled it over to the side and just sat there and talked a little bit to regroup ourselves. I said to Sylvia, "You know, I think maybe we should dig that bottle of whiskey out of the grub barrel. We haven't had a drink in a week. Maybe now's the time." She thought that was a good idea and we each had a drink. We stayed put and slept there at Prince George for the night.

Sunday, July 8, 1979—we got up and I decided I could get the outfit over to the truck stop and get these blown tires fixed. When I got over there and started working on it, I discovered that the frame on the fifth wheel of the trailer had broken loose coming down that turn as it was sliding. I got the tires all fixed, but the frame needed to be repaired. We decided that we couldn't continue with the trailer like it is. We had them fix all the bud wheels and tires for the trailer and rearrange both loads. We also got permission to leave the trailer and its load out in their parking lot and told them we'd be back in a week or so. We left the pup trailer. We got as far as Houston Campground that day.

Monday, July 9, 1979—started early and fueled the truck at Hazelton. Went up Highway 37, which at that time was a logging road owned by the logging company and they limited the times when other vehicles could be on the road. This road is very hard on the truck. We have to watch out for logging trucks all the time and several years ago in 1977, Sylvia and I was driving up this road when a logging truck *deliberately* came down the middle of the road and wouldn't get over. He ran us right off into the ditch. We had a flat and camped along the road. Took that wheel and tire off and put another on.

Tuesday, July 10, 1979—got up early again to get ahead of the logging trucks. We reached the Alaska Highway at 2:30 p.m. and stopped when we got to mile 747. Ed Dahlhan, the outfitter for hunting big game lives and operates out of here. (I hunted with him in 1977.) We had a nice visit with Ed and stayed overnight. A real nice family.

Wednesday, July 11, 1979—got a late start and had another flat just outside Whitehorse. Had both flats fixed. The young man working at that filling station would sit on the wheels when he was blowing them up. I suggested to him that was not a safe thing to do. They had a cage to put em' in to contain the tires because sometimes these blow right off the rims. He said, "We all gotta go sometime." Here he is only 18 or 19. After that, we went on through town and to the Yukon Territory weight station for trucks, we have to stop there and be weighed. I pulled onto the scale and the truck died. There are other trucks coming along every so often needing to be weighed. I had an extra set of batteries and the way this truck was set up it was two 12-volt batteries and part of the truck was on 24-volt and part was on 12-volt. I thought, well, my batteries are bad so I took those two batteries out and I put in two spare batteries I had with me— and it still wouldn't start. I am really embarrassed and don't know what to do. The scale man (Harvey) came out and he's real friendly. It turns out he's an old truck driver and had driven a 1964 Freightliner just like this one for 10 years. He said, "There's a Parallel switch on this truck. There's where your trouble is. You take that switch off and bring it in my office and I will show you how to fix it. Then, first truck that comes in, I'll have him pull you off over to the side". And that's what we did. I took the switch off (he told me to remember where every wire goes). When I got it off, I had 19 wires laid out and I need to remember where every one of those wires went when I get this fixed and go to put it back on the truck. I take it into his office and he opens the daily newspaper and lays it out on his desk. I took the switch apart out on his desk and when I got it apart he said, "Here's your problem." There were two copper spring-loaded connections that had been eaten out by the electricity shooting back and forth between them. I got them out and I was to file them off flat and get them so they fit to each other perfectly. I got that all done and he guided me in putting everything back like it was supposed to be. Then I take this thing out and I hook those 19 wires up—and it's not working. I got to thinking about this and I went back through it in my mind step-by-step and I thought, *It's gotta be that two wires are switched around. The only two that I wasn't so awfully sure about— it's gotta be that.* I moved each one and put those back on and by gosh, it worked—and it worked like it had never worked before. It was really good. No more having people pull the truck to get it started and the lights were working better too. So we thanked this man and we leave.

 We got about 80 miles from Whitehorse and came a cross a nice creek and a gravel pit. Sylvia says, "I need a bath, let's pull in here and I'll go down to the creek and take a bath." While she is down at the creek taking a bath, I check all the tires. And darn, I have a couple more flat tires. I was nearly done changing my flat tires when a motor home pulls in with a boat trailer behind it. This guy had broken a tongue out of his boat trailer. He had an axe with him and he had cut a tree down and tied the tree to the frame and to the tongue. He was dragging this off of the highway to see if he could do something about it. He and his family were going fishing at a lake and this was their holiday and this had happened. I told him, "Wait just a bit and I'll have this last wheel back on my trailer. Then you can pull up along the left-hand side of my outfit. I have a welder up there and we'll see if we can weld it". I got ready for him and he pulled along side the truck and we looked it over. I am gonna try to weld his tongue back into the boat trailer. He was concerned about what I might charge him. I told him I wouldn't charge him anything; I'd just do it for him. So we get started. At some time in its history, this trailer had been near salt water and the rust has eaten it out. It was extremely hard to try to get it welded. I had some extra steel for repairs on my trailers and truck and I had some steel that would work to weld this frame together. I get that stuff out and cut it and heat it and bend it and get it to fit his tongue and got it welded onto his frame and onto the tongue of his trailer. We get it all fixed up and he still wanted to pay me. I told him I didn't want any pay. I had mentioned to him that Sylvia being down at the creek taking a bath. He said, "Well you can have a bath here, we've got a shower in the motor home and you can have a nice hot shower." That sounded good. I took a nice hot shower and he gave me a bottle of beer. Then Sylvia comes walking in. She'd just had a cold bath in the creek. We all thought that was kind of comical. It turns out he was a railroad engineer for Whitehorse Railroad. He told us that anytime we were going through Whitehorse to be sure and stop and see him. Sorry to say, we never did do that.

Thursday, July 12, 1979—we got up early, the road was real good for a while and then it started raining. We drove through customs and later stopped in Tok, Alaska and waited until 2:00 am before we continued on.

Friday, July 13, 1979—we started at 2:00 a.m. and drove for four hours, stopped and slept for three hours, and drove on in to Eureka. We unloaded the swamp buggy from the truck and got the tires and repairs loaded. We piled and covered the lumber we had with us and left it there at Eureka. We still had some work to do on the truck and decided we'll camp here at Eureka tonight. We usually ate a couple of meals a day at the lodge and Sylvia would cook in our tent in between times.

Saturday, July 14, 1979–finished arranging things here and talked to Rex and two miners who were going back into the Talkeetnas about 15 miles west of us. We met another fella who takes care of the landfill. (At that time Eureka was hauling their garbage to the dump). We called with information about J. W., but we can't get hold of him. So we left for Tok. (We're on our way back to get the pup trailer we left behind in Prince George) On the other side of Glennallen we lost a wheel and tire for the pup. We turned around and went back to look in the bushes and see if we could find that wheel and tire, but with no luck. We turned around at the Richardson Highway and started back towards Tok. We got there at 10:00 p.m., stopped at a lodge and had dinner. Then we rested. While we rested, it rained quite a bit, but slacked off about 1:00 a.m. We went on through Tok and stopped and rested again later in the night.

Sunday, July 15, 1979–we woke up about 6:00 a.m. and got going. We stopped at Whitehorse, had a tire and wheel put together and got some fuel. (I have a 300 gallon fuel tank mounted in back of the cab in the bed of the truck. We carry that with fuel and we have a 60 gallon tank of fuel hanging under the frame of the cab of the truck.) We went on to Teslin Lake, getting there about 8:30 in the evening and camped for the night.

Monday, July 16, 1979–we left early in the morning and stopped at the Alaskan Highway at Cassiar Junction. Sylvia fixed bacon and eggs for breakfast. We found the Cassiar road to be very rough this trip, there are a lot of ore trucks that use this road and they drive fast. They have young Indian drivers and we were told they lose a lot of trucks and men every year. We saw a nice yearling moose and some horses along the road that probably belonged to Indians living there near Iskut. Shortly we saw two Indian boys herding horses back towards the village. Near the village, two Indian men were walking home, packing meat to the village. Not sure of this town, how to pronounce it, but we stopped at Kinasakaw Lake. We're really tired tonight.

Tuesday, July 17, 1979–I serviced the truck, checked all the tires, aired up those that needed it and drained the air tank on the brakes and we were on the way to the Yellow Head Highway. I make it a practice to look in the mirror every once in a while to watch in the back and suddenly I saw our dog Mike's box lying back there in the road! I got the truck stopped as quickly as I could and got out and ran around the truck to see what had happened. Somehow, the box had come apart. I had fastened the bottom of the box to the bed of the truck, but the rest of the box had come loose from the base and fallen off the side of the truck—that's what I had seen in the mirror. But when I got around to the back, here's Mike, standing there on the bed of the truck, really glad to see me. He was shaking he was so scared. He was alright though, not hurt or anything. I got his box back on the truck and refastened, but we put Mike in the front for a while. He sat there next to Sylvia, happy to be in the cab with us. He got over this shortly. Later we camped at the Houston campground at Yellowhead Highway off of the Cassiar. Again we serviced the truck and did all the necessary things to keep it running.

Wednesday, July 18, 1979—saw another black bear. We passed the seventh vehicle of the trip and got into Prince George about 10:00 a.m. and worked on the trailer all day; jacking the thing, straightening the 5th wheel out and getting it up into position to weld it back where it belonged. First, we had to get the Cat (Caterpillar brand of heavy equipment) off the pup trailer and onto the truck. I backed the truck up to the front end of the trailer, started the Cat and with it warmed up, put it into low gear. As the Cat tracks went from cross member to cross member, they broke through the deck. No time to stop and look at what has happened—it's moving, so I keep going. The Cat crawled up onto the truck bed. As it did, it started lifting the front end of the truck off the ground. With no chance of stopping and backing up, I kept going ahead knowing that the front end would come back down as the weight crossed the balance point, which it did with no problem—except now I had a wife that's been scared! The lesson here: put blocks under the rear truck frame! It goes without saying, "when the pressure is on, don't lose your nerve." Now we have the pup trailer unloaded and can work on it. I've got an acetylene torch and a welder on the load to do that.

Thursday, July 19, 1979—I get the 20 ton jack out and put a chain over it to each side of the trailer bed to jack this 5th wheel back into place so we could weld it. The jack is on top of the fifth wheel and we start cranking as far as the jack would go. It maxes out the 20 ton jack, but if I wait for a minute or so I can get another pull on the jack and take another bite with the load binder. I got some of it moved and then the jack reached its max and it had no more room to go so I backed it off and took another link on the chain and started jacking again. I'm waiting for the metal to slowly stretch and move and I tell Sylvia that this chain has got too much pressure on it and she should move out of the way. She was standing right in line with the chain. Sylvia said, "After the experience at the railroad bridge, I don't care, I'm ready to go." But I insisted and she moved. With the very next pump on the jack, the chain binder hook broke and the chain binder went flying like a missile. Had Sylvia not moved, she surely would have been hit. Most of the pieces went away from where she had been standing, but some pieces would have hit her. The load binder shot out over a high steel fence and hit a truck load of steel in that parking lot. It didn't do any damage to the steel of the truck or anything over there, but when that chain grazed my arm, (I had my shirt rolled up) it left a streak of rust right along my left bicep—just that close to taking my arm off. We were very lucky neither of us was hurt. I went over to the business next door and told them what happened and that I needed to get my load binder. They let me go out the back door and get it. We got everything back and finished our work on the trailer and got the 5th wheel up there where it belonged and welded into place.

Friday, July 20, 1979—I worked on the trailer lights, greased all the bearings and fueled the truck. We ate our dinner and went through the way station in Smithers and got groceries and reached Highway 37 (also called the Cassiar), just before 10:00 pm and camped for the night. We tried to travel when the logging trucks weren't running—they ran from 6 a.m. to 6 p.m. The road was owned by the lumber company and you didn't have any business being on the road in daylight—or at least during those hours.

Saturday, July 21, 1979—we camped at the Gulf station and left extra early to beat the logging trucks. Along the way, we had a flat tire and lost several things off the truck: the flat tire and another one, along with a load binder, the bar that Ed Teslick made for me, a piece of driveshaft tubing for the swamp buggy and parts of some chains for the truck. I had all this stuff chained down with load binders on the bed of the trailer, but it's hard to do that and get them to stay put. We saw a black bear dead along the road with patch of hair gone off of it—must have been hit by a vehicle. I ran over a poor little spruce hen, I just couldn't miss her. We saw a few rabbits and camped in the old "burn" area.

10,000 Days in Alaska Book One 1978-1989

Sunday, July 22, 1979—we pumped up a tire, then pumped one for a guy from Switzerland who was visiting Alaska and Canada and on a holiday. We passed five bicyclists on a long hill, had a flat tire and changed it between rain showers. We made it easily down the Stikine Hill. This hill is real steep, but I put the truck in low gear and we got down it in good shape. Once across the river bridge, we started up the other side. The truck was pouring smoke out of the stack and I'm going real slow. (We meet ore trucks every once in a while on the road and we dreaded meeting them in a position like this.) We got almost to the top of the hill and a large motor home was pulled off over on our side of the highway, stopped and were taking pictures of the Stickine river below. It's about a mile and a half climb up the hill in low gear and I had to get over on the other side of the road where I could potentially meet an ore truck head on. These people are on my side of the road in a very dangerous spot. I shook my fist at the guy at the steering wheel as I went around them. Luckily, no ore truck came. If there had been one, all three parties would have gone over the side...it really upset me.

Farther on, we saw a bear feeding on grass north of Pine Lake just south of the Cassiar. Some people that had followed us out of Prince George pulled into this camping site. We went over and introduced ourselves. They are Landed immigrants. (Canada had a plan at that time allowing immigrants to be in the country legally.) He has a job at the mine in Cassiar and his pay is $11.00/hour. He was originally from Sacramento. We visited with them for a while and then hit the sack.

Monday, July 23, 1979—we got up at 5:00 a.m. I serviced the truck while Sylvia fixed breakfast. I found the wood buffer between the frame and the bed had worked out. It took 2 hours to get the frame raised up and get that buffer back in and re-bolted. Got out on the road at 8:00 a.m. and drove hard all day. One wheel kept coming loose. We were on the Alaska Highway and a Mr. and Mrs. Berg from Staples waved us down about 80 miles from Whitehorse. Had a tire fixed and visited with them a while before continuing on. Earlier this same afternoon, we had a semi cut a curve coming at us; he barely got over on his side in time to miss our left front wheel on the truck. This Freightliner has a flat front. The driver and anyone in the cab sits right out there with no protection. It's been said that when you drive one of these, you're the first one at the accident. Anyway, we drove hard all day and we had a tire fixed in Whitehorse. Dave usually takes care of us there (We had previously picked out the friendlier places to fuel and to have tires fixed along the way). He filled us in on the news in that area telling us about a mining operation in Atland Canada that took out 1200 ounces of gold in 13 days, $1,500,000 worth. Everyone in the country was talking about it. We camped there in Whitehorse.

Tuesday, July 24, 1979—got up late, serviced the truck, went down to Whitehorse, shopped and got groceries and did laundry. While Sylvia was in after groceries, I was in the truck and a guy pulled up alongside, his name was Don. He was a silversmith. We got to visiting and he told me he goes in to Alaska and gets gold in the summertime with a dredge. Then he goes back outside to America and gets silver. (He does silver and gold work on jewelry.) He was an interesting man to talk to. We've seen the Gardenbergs again, they're from Minnesota. They bought coffee and we visited for a while. Then we saw the Swiss couple that I had pumped up a tire for and talked to them for a while. You meet lots of nice people along the road.

At the Yukon Weigh scale, Harvey advised us on how to service the truck to make it to Alaska. (He's the fellow that helped me before with the parallel Electrical switch.) When we went across the scale, he motioned me to stop and came out from his office. He didn't like the sound of my truck. He suggested that I go back downtown and get a case of #30 pure oil and put one quart in each 60 gallons of diesel fuel that I burn and that would help it make it to Alaska. So we limped back downtown and found the oil, bought it and put some in this 300 gallon diesel tank so that it would mix in there as we went down the road. We camped later about 35 minutes out of Haines Junction.

Wednesday, July 25, 1979—at Haines Jct., we got up at 4:00 a.m. and when I tried to start the truck, the fuel filter was plugged up. I had to get another one when we got into Tok Alaska, at 7:00 p.m. It was a long day. Don and his wife caught up to us here and bought coffee and we all visited.

Thursday, July 26, 1979—I had to wait for the State weigh scales, so I got up at 4:00 a.m. It's raining. Starting out, the truck was real tired it seemed like, and didn't have the snap that it should. I babied it into Eureka. (Eureka is at mile 128 on the Glenn Highway.) When we got there we parked the truck, put up the tent and tried to call my brother with no luck. We had a good rest and called a friend (Chad) and visited with him. Then another fella was going out to his claims, so we're going to haul him out there. He's going to call along about noon today.

Friday, July 27, 1979—one of the owners of the Eureka Lodge introduced us to a Tom and Betty. They lived just past the 40 Mile River Bridge. Tom was a State road maintenance man and he also looks after a Tom Reston's claims on Dunn Creek. It'd be a very good gold creek. They wanted to look at the swamp buggy I had built and were real interested in it, they were real fine people. I tried to start the Cat, the starting motor carburetor on it had to be removed and cleaned. Got that done and got the lumber unloaded and finally got to talk to my brother.

Saturday, July 28, 1979—worked on the truck lights, all the turn signals worked. Took a flat tire off, moved some tires around and repaired and serviced the equipment. Bill stopped by and we met a man named Rusty Miller and Shirley, I think it was. Rusty has lots of information on the area and is real friendly. He took us for a helicopter ride out over the Talkeetna Mountains. Sylvia really liked that. He went several miles out into the mountains and around showing us things. We saw two caribou and some old mine workings. It was sure nice up there looking down on everything.

Sunday, July 29, 1979—worked on the Cat in the morning and did some odd jobs. Studied the Cat engine book, studied some maps of the trail into Tyone Creek, the creek that Bill has his claims on. We did odd jobs around camp killing time while we waited for my brother. He showed up at 6:30. We had a sandwich and talked to him and made some plans and he went on to Anchorage. It's raining off and on and the tent leaks in a few places, much to Sylvia's consternation. It's not fun to be in a tent when it's leaking.

Monday, July 30, 1979—woke up to find out it is still raining—and the tent still leaks! This is the last day that Rusty will be working on this area with his helicopter we bought his lunch and visited a while then he left for Fairbanks. We just loafed around here all day. Jerry called and wants us to go into town to eat with him.

Tuesday, July 31, 1979—went into the lodge at Eureka and had pie and coffee. Then later, I cleaned the generator on the Coleman stove and let excess air out of the swamp buggy tires. I had those pumped up fairly tight for hauling up here from Minnesota but too tight for running on the ground. It's raining again and Sylvia bailed a little water out of the tent. Mike, the dog has an infection in his lip from a dog fight. He sure put the run on a big Doberman yesterday! He guards our property real well. Nobody came around us during this whole trip without him warning us that they were there.

Wednesday, August 1, 1979—worked on the Cat a little and it's raining yet. Then Bill and his brother-in-law, Jim, showed up with a 55-gallon drum to put fuel in. We moved the camp down to the Little Nelchina River. The river is high from all the rain we've been getting. We decided to take the equipment up the river. (In 1979, there were fewer restrictions on traveling and crossing rivers.) We'll move as soon as we can—between rain showers when the sun is shining. Washed the swamp buggy windows, hooked a few bluegills and puttered around until a fellow by the name of Bill Maitland came into camp. He hadn't had any luck dredging on the Oshetna Headwaters. We visited with him for a while, talking about prospecting gold.

Thursday, August 2, 1979—two natives, Dale and Ron Stevenson, asked to borrow two load binders. They're from Chugiak. They have claims on Daisy Creek and they need load binders to hold some of their load on the trailer so I let them have them.

Friday, August 3, 1979—Bill and Jim brought out some groceries; we cleaned the barrels out, got fuel and moved to Little Nelchina campground.

Saturday, August 4, 1979—the carburetor on the swamp buggy is giving us trouble. Took the buggy up river, waters over waist deep. The buggy worked well in the rocks and water, but the carburetor was still bad. Took it up to Nelchina gas station and discovered that the cross shaft is losing air. Henry, the owner, and Tim who works there, worked on it. (In the winter time, Henry traps up on Tyone Creek with Cal. Tim worked with Cal and Henry that summer mining on Alfred Creek.)

Sunday, August 5, 1979—Joe was here and worked on the plugs in his car. I started up the welder and used the generator to power the surface grinder to shape up bead breaker for tires. Mostly loafed and planned on going in to Anchorage to get a carburetor for the swamp buggy.

Monday, August 6, 1979—got up early and left for Anchorage. Bought almost everything we needed, lots of trouble finding a carburetor, got back just before dark.

Tuesday, August 7, 1979—we got up fairly early, worked all morning reloading supplies and equipment. Put the new carburetor on the buggy, ate dinner and went down to the river and started up stream. The swamp buggy front end wouldn't pull. After about 400 yards, I passed the swamp buggy with the Cat and pulled my load out onto a gravel bar, unhooked and backed down to the buggy. Hooked on to the buggy and pulled it up on the sand bar. There we discovered an allen screw and key were gone from the universal joint so we went downstream with it to the base camp. We just got there when Bob and Kahren Rudbeck and their daughter rolled in. We visited with them while fixing the key and checked the buggy over, found a bad plug and readjusted the carburetor and everything seemed okay. We tied our dog Mike so he would be under the trailer and out of any rain. We didn't want him running over to the campground and bothering anyone. Really tired tonight.

Wednesday, August 8, 1979—Sylvia fixed breakfast and then we headed up the river. Many large boulders at first. After the first two miles, the rocks were smaller. Many/muddy river crossings and gravel bar to gravel bar. Water is much deeper than last year. Water comes over the fenders of the Cat sometimes. We have to stand up on the Cat to drive it. The fan throws water at first and then the belt starts slipping. The Cat is overloaded, it's really working hard. Stop at noon for tea and sandwiches and to fuel the Cat, lots of trouble finding and picking a trail through the holes in the river. Silt, trees and so forth to deal with. Ran into one dead end, that's the but of a tree in the river, we got the Cat stuck. Got the buggy up to it and winced it out, then the buggy ran out of gas. At one really deep water hole, it was at least five feet deep and very slick. We worried if the buggy would get through it, but it made it. The trails are so the rocks roll out from under the track of the Cat when we cross the river. This is working the hell out of the Cat. Camped on a gravel bar and had a good supper and hit the sleeping bags. Very tired. One of the guys traveling with us was concerned about grizzlies coming in while we were sleeping, but none came. My hands cramp up at night so bad, I gave Bob the shotgun.

Norman Wilkins

Thursday, August 9, 1979—had a big breakfast. Jerry and I took the buggy up river to look the trail over, it was much better than yesterday, less rock and trees and it was washed out in some places. Came back and serviced our equipment, made dinner and started out. Trail was good for several miles, then lots of rock. Buggy trail was washed out in a lot of places, crossed the river many times from gravel bar to gravel bar. A lot of gravel was washed away by high water and we got into lots of rock. Lots of moose, wolf, one bear and some caribou tracks. There's grayling in this stream, they don't seem to pay any attention to our vehicles. We didn't have too awful much trouble, today. We came across two fellows traveling out from Daisy creek. I had met one of them in Eureka. He had been having lots of trouble. He had to get out and get an axel for his swamp buggy so he packed out on his back—no lazy people out here.

Friday, August 10, 1979—up early, started up the river, fairly good traveling, reached the trail to go over the White hill early afternoon. The Cat wouldn't pull the first big hill. Had to winch it for a ways. Jerry is learning to handle the swamp buggy in situations like that. Then we had to clean the plugs on it. Trail is too muddy and tough. Had to offload the plywood and some two-by-fours to get to the top of the trail. The rest of the trail is real bad too. Too much rain the last two months. At this time I decided to walk ahead to see what the trail was like. I walked ahead two miles and the trail is too bad—I decided we couldn't make it the rest of the way to Tyone Creek with the load that we had (gear and equipment). We left the trailer there, turned around, went back to the Little Nelchina and camped for the night. There we made plans to build a sled-like boat to haul the equipment and fuel in if the overland trail looks passable. I have steel back out at the highway that we can use to build the sled. The overland trail looks passable so this evening, Jerry and Bob fished for grayling. We are seeing caribou too. They come in close and they do this strange little bouncy run and they circle out about 75 yards. They really can't figure out what we are. Also there is some bear sign. Every once in a while we see something like that. I had to tighten my Cat tracks and pads today, so there must be some wear showing up there. We're camped where Flat Creek joins the Little Nelchina.

Saturday, August 11, 1979—loaded the things from the trailer that we need and went back down the Nelchina to the overland trail that goes to mile 130 on the Glenn Highway. We saw a helicopter and three men taking rock sample for rock dating. About a mile and a half from the trail over to Tyone. The overland trail is real steep. Later we came to a large swamp—buried the Cat in it. The buggy winched it out. Then Bob and I walked the swamp and he helped pick out a route over it. Then Jerry and Bob walked ahead while I backed the Cat across to the other side and then over lots more steep hills and small boggy spots. At Crooked Creek, had to put a pin back in the track. More steep hills. Three fellas and two Volkswagen buggies passed us. We also saw a caribou about three miles from the highway. Got the Cat stuck and threw a track in a bog hole. Tore up the come-along. (We were using it to pull the track together as we re-pinned it.) Getting very dark, so we got it out to the road, see a cow moose there, and we drive 8 miles to the Little Nelchina campground. Put up Jerry's tent. Sylvia had a big pot of beans cooked. Ate at Bob and Kahren's motor home, we share their fire and a couple of drinks and go to bed late and very tired.

Sunday, August 12, 1979—Bob and Kahren and Jackie leave for Kenai Peninsula to fish for silver salmon and visit friends. Chad and all come over to see the swamp buggy and Bill Talon walked out ahead of the Cat to call his brother-in-law to take him to Anchorage. Rested a lot today, worked on the buggy late in the afternoon, took a bath, ate and then we went up to Nelchina Lodge. They fix tires for us sometimes up there, gave us great service.

Monday, August 13, 1979—we worked on the buggy till after dinner. It still doesn't run right. Went down to mile 130 to the overland trail, drove to the Cat and got the track on and walked it out to the gravel pit, brought the buggy and Jerry's car back to the Little Nelchina campground and made supper. (We call our evening meal supper—which some people call dinner—and our "dinner" is what some people call lunch.)

Tuesday, August 14, 1979—we took the buggy to Nelchina to the Lodge and Henry and Betty offered us a chance to camp, so we moved here.

Wednesday, August 15, 1979—we tore part of the buggy motor down and unloaded the load onto the trailer.

Thursday, August 16, 1979—worked on the two room house Henry gave us to live in.

Norman Wilkins

Friday, August 17, 1979—worked on getting the gas stove hooked up in the house. Went into Palmer and Anchorage for parts. Henry and Ken had a going away party in the evening and we met several of the local people. Our dog Mike got three ducks (blue wing teal) in a little pond near the lodge here. The one duck dived down and hung on the bottom and Mike dived down and went completely out of sight and he found that duck and brought it back to us. These ducks have been eating blueberries and they were really tasty.

Saturday August 18, 1979—got up early and worked on the Cat for a while and then on the buggy and then on the Cat again—and then back to work on the buggy. Ed Farmer came by to give advice. We were trying to get the valves on the buggy adjusted. He and his brother are going hunting sheep. Wish I could go with them. We worked on the buggy until my back gave out leaning over that motor—suppertime anyhow. Betty and her kids, Doug and Denise, helped Sylvia get a nice mess of rose hips and cranberries. Mike from Sartell stopped by to visit for a little while.

Sunday August 19, 1979—up early, it was a nice day all day. Welded up the Cat every place that it needed it. Checked out the valve clearance on the swamp buggy. We think we've got that now. Put a chimney through the roof of the cabin that Henry is letting us live in. Jerry went to Anchorage. Called Roger Shequen in Minnesota to get the news from down there with the farm. He's looking out for a lot of things for us in Minnesota.

Monday August 20, 1979—worked on the Cat some more and got up some wood and worked on the Cat again.

Tuesday, August 21, 1979—Bob and Kahren and Jackie came by. Got the fan belt back on the Cat. It's quite a job to get that on there. There isn't much room between the fan and the radiator. My brother, Jerry Wilkins came back and we worked on the Cat and his car is giving him trouble, so we worked on it too.

Wednesday, August 22, 1979—Sylvia picked a lot of blueberries yesterday and picked rose hips today. She's very industrious like that. They are very good eating.

10,000 Days in Alaska Book One 1978-1989

Thursday, August 23, 1979—Sylvia picked more rose hips. Got the Cat back together and have some more welding to do yet.

Friday, August 24, 1979—went to Glennallen and registered to vote to establish our residency here. Sylvia got a few groceries and Jerry got his hunting license. We ate dinner and finished up the work on the Cat.

Saturday, August 25, 1979—Tim came over and adjusted the valves. Ate dinner and put the swamp buggy motor back together—still working on the darned thing. It still backfires. Sylvia found a few more rose hips and we are still eating fresh blueberries. They are very good.

Sunday, August 26, 1979—finished work on the Cat and the swamp buggy, showered and shaved, and took it easy the rest of the day.

Monday, August 27, 1979—we moved the Cat to a gravel pit at the trailhead and took the truck to Anchorage and sold it. The fella that bought it, I guess didn't know how to drive it and he had two of his workers ride with me in the truck and I showed them how to shift it and everything about operating it. Then we bought diesel fuel and we got back late to Nelchina.

Tuesday, August 28, 1979—we got up early and started organizing provisions and equipment and changed the oil and filter on the buggy. Jerry and Mary took the last of the afternoon off and rested up. We had a good roast for dinner and stew for supper, thanks to Sylvia. Sylvia made trail cookies they are really large and have lots of good things in them. The guys sure like 'em. She made some bread today and did the laundry and is tired tonight.

Wednesday, August 29, 1979—packed and loaded for the trail. We ate dinner at the lodge and it started raining. We hit the trail at 2:00 p.m. Saw a griz track in the trail. A little farther on, a wolverine, then moose and caribou had been walking in the trail. We saw a duck in the creek at Old Man Creek. We camped there for the night. Later Jerry saw four ducks.

Thursday, August 30, 1979—lots of hunting machines are traveling these trails now. The rain turned to snow—raining and snow at higher elevations. Tightened the tracks on the Cat and got stuck in a big bog.

Norman Wilkins

The buggy winched me out, we were lucky to have it with us. There was quite a bit of snow and blowing up on the ridges. We stopped at noon to boil tea and eat cookies. After all those hours on the Cat, the wind and the cold and the snow, I got really cold. Jerry opened the back of the swamp buggy and pulled out the Coleman stove and heated up tea and quick sandwiches and I got in the cab of the swamp buggy where the heater was and got warmed up. After a while then, we started moving toward the Little Nelchina down the trail. We saw several caribou and when we got to the Little Nelchina and the junction with Flat Creek. Saw several caribou and when we got to the trailer with the equipment and load on it, no one has really bothered it with the exception of somebody took a sack of charcoal briquettes. We got the Cat stuck crossing a small deep creek. Jerry tried to winch me out with the buggy and the fan got driven through the radiator. Of course we lost all our water and antifreeze in the radiator trying to winch that out so we camped there that night.

Friday, August 31, 1979—in the morning, we heard pans rattling outside the tent where we'd been cooking. Jerry, he rolled out of his sack. His tent has a zipper on the door and It had been raining and snowing and had frozen during the night and the zipper was frozen shut. Jerry wiggled it until he finally got it opened a little bit and he looked out at this grizzly bear and yelled, "Bear in camp!" I got out of my sleeping bag and grabbed the shotgun and looked out the window from my end. It was just getting light outside and I'm looking out the tent window just in time to see the bear come and pick up a chunk of ham and gobble it. He was standing about twelve feet away looking me in the eye. He was really a beautiful bear. He looked to be about three years old, didn't have the large head yet, and he appeared to have a long neck. (That tells a person that he's not a mature bear.) I've got every confidence in the 12-gage. Jerry yells at him and tells him to get out of there and he bounds over the hill towards Tyone Creek.

   I take the radiator out of the buggy and draw a picture and measure it and Jerry fixes breakfast—he's a good cook. I take a small lunch and a raincoat and start walking out to the highway (It's about 26 to 27 miles out there). I say so long to Jerry, from the top of the first hill. He has the flu and I tell him to sleep in the buggy in case the bear comes back. Flushed ptarmigan from off the trail and two miles later, two nice caribou bulls at about 200 yards. Then at three miles, a snow track, pulling a trailer, he had the tongue broke out. They planned to chain the tongue and the trailer and the snow track all together and continued to the hunt. I walk on to Little Nelchina and get a good drink of water and I tie my pant legs tight to my boots (loosened the boot strings and tied the pants tight to the boots) and then wade the river as fast as I can. That keeps most of the water from getting in my boots. It works real well. I get across the river and there's more bear droppings and the more along the river I walked, I see more. Two miles later the trail over Monument Mountain, I eat half of my food. Two thirds up the mountain, I smell carrion. I talk out loud and move on. (Talking helps avoid the possibility of startling a bear that might be in the vicinity.) No water here—small dip with snow and it doesn't taste good. I stop and rest a little coming down the other side of the mountain. Get a drink at Crooked Creek and I'm getting quite tired now.

I'm 4 ½ miles from the highway when a fellow gives me a ride. He's got a brand new Ranger track hunting vehicle and he's got a new trailer behind it. The guy is really thorough; he has built a ROP on it (rollover protection). When we come to the top of a big hill, I ask him if he wants me to get off and walk down the hill and he says, no, he thought it would be alright. We get down the hill about a third of the way and all of a sudden, the trailer hitch comes unhooked from the Ranger. It's a new outfit and he hadn't snugged up the bolt that keeps the hitch fastened to the Ranger and it ran ahead into the track and threw the track off of the Ranger. The Ranger went over on its side and on up on its top and is sliding down the trail, upside down. We didn't slide so awfully far, but it finally got stopped. He had safety belts on the seats and we were both strapped in and hanging upside down off of the seats. He asked if I'm all right. I told him yes, I was not hurt. So he undid his belt and dropped out and got out of the frame and I got mine unhooked and got out of the Ranger. We're standing there looking at it and telling each other how lucky we are we aren't hurt and I look at my rifle—it's got 4 inches of mud on the muzzle from where it had dragged in the trail coming down. There was nothing left to do but try to get the Ranger up on its tracks. He had a come-along with him and a really good strong rope. Luckily the rope reached some willows that were big enough to use as an anchor. It was a nylon rope and the darned thing stretched quite a bit. We had to unhook the come-along and re-hook and hook and re-hook. I'd hold the rope tight as I could while he would be changing it. We finally got the Ranger rolled upright—and it's crooked in the trail. We have to get it pulled around and blocked so it won't roll on down this hill. We get it jacked up off of the ground and we loosen the adjustments for the track and we get the track on there and then readjust the tracks. We discover what caused the accident when we went to hook it up to the Ranger; it was obvious that this bolt had gotten loose and let the whole thing happen. So we tightened that bolt. When he went to try to start the motor then, it wouldn't start. On closer inspection, we find that when the Ranger was rolling down the hill, it got to going really fast and he was using the gears and its compression to help with the brakes. It was going so fast that the pressure stretched the bolts that held the head on the motor. He did have a toolbox with all the tools he needed to work on it, so he re-tightened the head bolts. Then it started and ran well and we got out to the gravel pit at the highway (what everyone calls the trailhead). He had a vehicle there and gave me a ride to the Nelchina Lodge and then all that was left for the evening was to eat, drink and sleep. I was really tired.

Saturday, September 1, 1979—went into Glennallen and went to different places and I just couldn't find a radiator to match the drawing I had made of the buggy's radiator—it's still sitting out there in the boondocks. Finally I got back to Nelchina and Henry had one that he thought we could make work.

Sunday September 2, 1979—I talked to Dan Billman to see if he could fly me and the radiator out to Tyone Creek, but he can't fly me, he's booked up and we have to wait our turn. Chad and Charlie and I are there.

Monday, September 3, 1979—Dan had landing gear trouble. His wife Patti picked up tubing to fix it and brought it. Dan came in at noon and we work at fixing his landing gear.

Tuesday, September 4, 1979—Dan flew Chad, Charlie and I to the landing strip on Tyone Creek. Jerry wasn't in camp. I walked down to the stream and talked to some hunters. They thought he got a ride out to the road so we backpacked equipment over to the camp and put the radiator in the buggy. Dan flew Jerry back into camp about the time I was ready to go over and pull the Cat out of the Creek. We got up to Tyone Creek two or three miles and got the Cat out. I decided to turn around and go back in the Cat. Jerry and Chad proceed up the creek. The Cat threw a track—bad—and all the tools are in a swamp buggy with Chad and Jerry. I didn't have the proper wrench, so I gathered wood and slept near the fire overnight. It's a nice night and I drink lots of tea and decide to walk out the next morning.

Wednesday, September 5, 1979—I need a track pin punch. As I leave Tyone Creek, I get a real good drink of water and I got another drink of water at the Little Nelchina at the place where the trail leaves the river. The mountain I'm walking over is the White Mountain. I eat a little way up Monument Mountain and eat some snow (which tastes bad). I reached Crooked Creek and got a good drink of water there and walk slowly. I'm getting tired and the pack is heavy. A man hauls me the last mile on a two-wheel cycle. That darn thing upsets on a hill—I don't get hurt and he hauls me to Nelchina when we get out to the highway and I get something to eat and sleep. Really tired tonight.

Thursday, September 6, 1979—I make arrangements to have Dan fly me back in and then build a wrench with the torch and welder and the truck spring so I can repair the Cat out at Tyone Creek.

Friday, September 7, 1979—I get the tools made and Dan has problems and can't take me in.

Saturday, September 8, 1979—Dan has time today to fly me in to Tyone—but the swamp buggy was gone. So we check up and down stream and Yacko Creek, and the Little Nelchina and Monument Mountain. We don't know where Chad and Jerry have gone with it. So we came back to the cabin at 5:00 p.m. and Chad, Jerry and Charley come in with the buggy and they leave for Anchorage. So thankfully they are okay.

Sunday, September 9, 1979—I serviced the buggy and packed gear to take to Tyone Creek and get the Cat and other equipment. Tim Hurley is going along. Tim lives and works at the Nelchina Lodge. He's pretty knowledgeable and a good worker and he would like to go out on a trip like this. So he's going along to help and it's a hot day and the buggy is running quite hot. We meet three buggies coming out—some fellows are camped near the bend in the river. We pitched camp on a gravel bar. It was a beautiful evening. Tim fishes with no luck.

Monday, September 10, 1979—we're up early, beautiful morning. Cooked breakfast and Tim fished. We oftentimes like to have fish for breakfast, but he didn't have any luck. We met some nice people on the trail. We always talk about the trail when we meet people. Saw several buggies all traveling. We saw a cow moose feeding, and at one point on the Nelchina at the old town site (there's a steep bank there), Tim wanted to try driving the buggy up over that steep bank. He got to do it...that really tickled him. The buggy went right up that steep bank. It's quite a good rig. We then went over to the old town site and walked around. There was stuff at that time, several large freighting sleds and tin cans and cookware laying scattered all over. And the cabins, there was one that was partly up but all the other cabins had fallen down and rotted. The tundra had grown over them but you could still see the outline of the walls. Those cabins were built in about 1912 or 14, I think it was. We left there and traveled along the river. I saw a trap right out in the open. I suspected that it was Cal Gilcrist's. He trapped that area so I stopped and laid the trap out of sight, but at the same place so he could find it when trapping come winter. A little farther on we saw a cow moose feeding. Lots of people had been hunting here, but they weren't hunting cow moose, they were hunting the bulls. We reached the Cat on Tyone Creek just in time to set up camp. Everything was okay, no one had bothered it. It was really a fine evening.

Tuesday, September 11, 1979—got up early and it's cool up at that elevation. There is ice on the water bucket. We get the track back on the Cat, get the Cat stuck on the way to the trailer, and broke the winch on the swamp buggy and the cable. Got the swamp buggy chained to the Cat. We had lots of chain and he got out far enough ahead of me that he could pull and got the Cat out of this mud hole. We reached the trailer then after a few miles and hooked up to it and drove on down to the Little Nelchina river and camped on a gravel bar.

Wednesday, September 12, 1979—there are lots of parka squirrels here, and in the morning just as it was getting light, the ptarmigan visited us. They walked all around the tent and the whole area. They have a way of talking to each other—it's fun to listen to them. We got up and fixed breakfast and loaded our things. I was tying some gear on top of the buggy and while doing that, the darned rope broke and I fell six feet, landing on my head and shoulder. I broke or badly cracked my collar bone (It had been broken before.) and I sprained my thumb really bad. I had headaches, felt sick and dizzy and I had a bad nosebleed—but we're many miles from the road and there's nothing to do but go ahead. We loaded the lumber that I had there onto the trailer. We had five or six miles to go down river to get to Crooked Creek and the old Nelchina town site. I'm going down stream, pulling the trailer load and Tim's driving the swamp buggy ahead of me and right at the old town site, there is some deep water. The water came over the deck of the Cat and over the top of the tracks. This isn't a concern, we've done this before. This deep area is maybe about 20 or 30 feet long and then it starts gradually coming up. Just as I get up on the gravel and out of the water, the track on the right side of the Cat breaks! The Cat starts running ahead and I got it stopped before the track fell out. Otherwise, the Cat would have run off of the track and that would be really bad. So we leave everything sit just like it is and I get in the swamp buggy with Tim. (Boy, he really likes to drive this swamp buggy—and he's good at it.) We go over the land trail here out to Cal's on the highway. We're coming down a long grade to get to Cal's and it's really swampy. There's water in the trail—and it's dark. The lights on the swamp buggy aren't working, but the stars overhead are reflecting off the water in the trail and that's what he uses as a guide. We got out there at 9:00 p.m. and Cal invites us into the house (Cal and Mary are really nice people). We visit with them and use their phone to call Nelchina. Blake drove down to take us home so we can go to bed and get a good night's sleep, but I still have a nosebleed.

Thursday, September 13, 1979—we get up late and go to Cal's to get the buggy. The universal joint blew out, so we pull it to Nelchina. There, we built a reducer for Betty's furnace to pipe hot air into their well. Read last Sunday's newspaper.

Friday, September 14, 1979—I haven't felt very well for a few days. I suppose it's that head thing from the fall. Did a few odd jobs around the lodge. Tim went to Anchorage to get Cat and buggy parts to repair the Cat. It's still out at the old Nelchina town site.

Saturday, September 15, 1979—Tim came in late last night with the parts. I shortened the chain on their chainsaw, repaired the U-joints on the buggy and went hunting for spruce hens for an hour with no luck.

Sunday, September 16, 1979—spread gravel for the lodge and worked on a heat duct, carried in some wood and shot a spruce hen.

Monday, September 17, 1979—rebuilt the mounting for the winch on the swamp buggy and helped a little at the garage/lodge, sometimes fixing tires or helping with the gas station and odd jobs. Hunted spruce hens with no luck.

Tuesday, September 18, 1979—Henry got in last night from the Yukon gold camp where he'd been working. We'll get the Cat parts and go back to put it together. Henry has a wrecker and he got a call from a person who had a pickup stuck in the swamp, so I went with him back to this truck in the swamp, to help if needed. Lo and behold it turned out to be the son of a friend of mine by the name of Leonard Berg, and it's his son Jerry of Minnesota. Jerry had this 4-wheel drive pickup and he was gonna try to drive out this trail but it is too wet for a pickup. After we got back to the lodge, I worked on the buggy generator. It wasn't working correctly. I still don't feel good, but I leveled up the house. It was a house that had been moved in temporarily. No one had lived in it and it needed to be leveled.

Wednesday, September 19, 1979—helped Tim with his truck a little bit and give him a set of chains for it. I visited with him for a while. Mike and Lynette stopped by and left a chain saw muffler for me to weld. Later I went out and looked for a spruce hen, but no luck hunting. Went to the lodge in the evening and Dan Billman came in so I got to pay him for flying and had a good time with the fellows there.

Thursday, September 20, 1979—Henry and Tim took a dump truck and Cat tracks to Yukon Territory, so I took over the job of watching the gas station. In between times I roofed the well house and worked on the snowmobile. Fixed three tires and helped a fellow put an axel in a Travelall vehicle.

Friday, September 21, 1979—I made a storm window for the lodge, put visqueen plastic on the trailer windows and will tend bar tonight. It's been a beautiful day.

Saturday, September 22, 1979—weather was unsettled. Tim came back from the Yukon and I worked on reinforcing the oscillating part of the swamp buggy and got rained out of that job in the afternoon.

Sunday, September 23, 1979—finished working on the buggy and went with Tim to Mike Phillips' to put in a driveway.

Monday, September 24, 1979—cleaned the station and straightened things up. Roger Shequen called from Minnesota with good news. We always like good news.

Tuesday, September 25, 1979—I helped Tim haul trash from the lodge to the dump and moved three small piles of poles for our house heating stove. It's Mike Phillips' birthday.

Wednesday, September 26, 1979—didn't do much. The dump truck broke down for Tim and Mike. That had to be taken care of. Took swamp buggy to Slide Mountain and got stuck—and winched out and got part way up the mountain and then walked to an area of fossils. Picked up a few and came back. We'd wanted to go up and look for fossils for quite some time. It was known as Fossil Mountain until a few years ago when the state wanted to discourage people from picking fossils there, so they changed the name to Slide Mountain. The University has classes of students come out from Fairbanks and climb the mountain to see these fossils. There are areas where mountain literally 'slides' down and exposes the fossils. (Very few are found anymore.)

Thursday, September 27, 1979—cut up wood with a Swede saw and put some visqueen on the widows of the house we're in. It's getting cold enough to need things like that.

Friday, September 28, 1979—went with Tim to Brandt's to pick up a bus with the wrecker. This fella that had the bus used it to haul fresh vegetables and fruits around the country selling it out of this school bus. About a mile before we got the bus to Nelchina Lodge, a wheel came off and broke up through the floor of the bus. It took some doing to get it the rest of the way to the lodge.

Saturday, September 29, 1979—Tim and I get up early, fuel up, load grub and start for the Cat on Little Nelchina. We're driving the swamp buggy, and we get stuck in a swamp about two thirds of the way there. I had 280 feet of cable on the winch of the swamp buggy. Tim went out to the first tree that he thought might hold the buggy to winch it out, and when we winched, the tree pulled out! So we unhooked and ran the cable out almost to the end of it, found a good tree, and got ourselves out of this hole. We travel on out to the Nelchina river and we get up stream near the old town site to where the Cat is sitting—waiting for us to come and repair it. We discover that it's been cold enough up there that the pony engine has frozen and broken a cast plate in the bottom of the water jacket. It leaks badly. Then we had trouble driving in the track pin. I had made a tool to help with this. We were so glad to have it with us. We finally finished with the track pin. Since the old town site was nearby, we walked over to look at the ruins and junk that was there. It was late at that time and I cooked supper for us and went to bed about 8:00 p.m.

Sunday, September 30, 1979—got the Cat track on and went down the river. Saw a caribou hanging on a meat pole where some hunters had their camp during caribou season. We stopped there and Tim goes over and sniffs the meat and sure enough, it has spoiled. There was a sign posted there saying to take the meat if you want it, but of course, no one would want to eat that. We went on down the river, and just around the bend, near an old cabin, I had to clean the carburetor on the Cat pony motor before it would start. At lunch, where Old Man Creek comes into the Little Nelchina river, we stopped near a campground at the highway that goes to Nelchina Lodge. Henry and Ken get there a few minutes later. Henry's been working up on a gold claim in the Yukon and he's brought home mastodon tusks and bones from the Yukon. When we got to the highway, Ken loaded the Cat on the trailer and Tim drove the swamp buggy. We got the Cat up on the trailer and we were going down the highway when a state trooper pulled us over. He looked the whole outfit over and turned to us and asked whose outfit this was. I told him it was mine and he said, "I could fill out several tickets with everything I see that is wrong here." We asked him what we should be doing differently and he said, "Mud flaps on the trailer—you don't have mud flaps and the floor of that trailer is not in very good shape." I told him the Cat had busted the planks in the trailer and we're just coming out from the back country and I hadn't had a chance to replace the mud flaps that had gotten torn off traveling. He kind of accepted that, and this conversation went on over different things for a while and finally he told us, "Well, you can go on now." We got to Nelchina—glad this trip was over.

Monday, October 1, 1979—rested most of the day. It was quite windy. Then I went out, put a new fuel filter on the buggy, greased it and rearranged the load. Raining lightly this evening.

Tuesday, October 2, 1979—Libby Riddles and her helper with the dogs, Charlie, came down to the Nelchina Lodge and I got to meet them.

10,000 Days in Alaska Book One 1978-1989

Libby makes fur hats to help support her dog racing. She does a really fine job with them. (Later, in 1985, Libby Riddles became the first woman to win the Iditarod, an annual sled dog race where mushers and teams race 1,161 miles from Willow to Nome, Alaska.)

Wednesday, October 3, 1979—took the buggy down to Gunsight Mountain Trail (about 25 miles). Henry went with me. The trail there goes over Ballenger Pass. He had some guys mining back on Alfred Creek and when they were moving equipment out, his Cat broke apart in the rear end. They had to leave it behind. We are going in to pull his Cat out over the mountain and across a swamp to get it to the highway. Everything went well. Where the sun hadn't been shining, the trail was frozen and icy, but I had chained up all four tires on the swamp buggy, and it pulled this small Cat up the mountain. When we got down to the swamp, I really put the pedal down on the swamp buggy. Henry was riding the Cat back behind me, steering and trying to keep it in the trail, mud flying. It was quite a ride for him. We got through the swamp and down a steep hill to an old lodge where we had a trailer parked. We planned to load the Cat on it. We had chains and load binders with us. We worked the load binders one after the other, one length of chain at a time. It took us a long time—and was hard work. Henry and I were really tired by the time we got that Cat loaded and back to his lodge at Nelchina. (The next day, we were stiff and sore.) I did a few odd jobs around here at the lodge.

Thursday, October 4, 1979—Tim and I took Henry's Blazer to Anchorage—I pulled the wrecker (motor was kaput on it) and Tim's Datsun pickup as far as Sutton. Left the pickup at Sutton and pulled the wrecker on to Nelchina up over the mountains—quite a trip. Tim went back later and pulled the pickup to Nelchina.

Friday, October 5, 1979—went to Little Nelchina River with the buggy and pulled my trailer up to the lodge.

Saturday, October 6, 1979—unloaded the trailer and went back to the river and loaded the Cat on it, blew a hydraulic pump seal on the Cat doing that. Got up the highway about three mile and a trooper stopped me with lots of violations, but he let me off with a warning. Got home to Nelchina Lodge and unloaded the Cat.

Norman Wilkins

Sunday, October 7, 1979—took the hydraulic pump off the Cat. It's an all day job, because it's so difficult to get at the bolts that hold it on the front. This hydraulic pump sits in front of the radiator.

Monday, October 8, 1979—built a house for Mike, the dog. It's spitting snow this morning and rain this evening and real windy. Mike deserves a good, well insulated dog house. I put a piece of good strong, tarp in front so that it will swing back and forth when he goes in and out and it will shut off the cold from outside. My back is sore from yesterday.

Tuesday, October 9, 1979—it's raining this morning and windy. It stopped later. Tim took their loader and leveled a cabin building spot, and we got up some wood. I helped him cut some wood for the stove. They heat their shop with wood and I helped with that. Took the skill saw apart, the armature is burned on it.

Wednesday, October 10, 1979—Henry, Tim and I went to Anchorage. We all had parts to get for our equipment. It's 143 miles into town to buy parts. Got back about 10:00 p.m.

Thursday, October 11, 1979—I started building the plywood cabin to live in for the winter. This cabin is 12' x 16' with 8' walls and a plywood floor. Over the ceiling, we had a place for storage. I got the floor done today and got both ends done. A couple of fellas that were over at the lodge came and helped me. We turned it upside down and I put the insulation in the floor and nailed plywood over it. Then we flopped it back over on the skids.

Friday, October 12, 1979—got both ends of the cabin done (left a door opening on one end that would be on the south when the cabin is finished) and started one side.

Saturday, October 13, 1979—finished the framing and got the cabin sheeted. Really tired tonight. Geese have been flying all day. They are quite high, but that brings the work to a halt—wish I was hunting geese somewhere.

Sunday, October 14, 1979—worked on the cabin a little and Henry and I went to where the Cat was parked and loaded it on a trailer. We had to use load binders and pull in on a length or two at a time. We got back too late to put roofing on the cabin. It was a sunny day—would have been a good day to do that job. Saw trumpeter swans flying. They were quite high.

Monday, October 15, 1979—it was nice, but quite cool. We got the roofing on the cabin. I used roll roofing. Laid it out on a strip of blacktop from the old highway. The sun warmed it up, and I cut it into 16 foot strips to go over the roof of the cabin. The roof was 8 feet on each side and we had to "work like the dickens" to get the sealer where it joins and get the roofing nailed down, but we got it done.

Tuesday, October 16, 1979—went to Anchorage for some parts and insulation for the walls on the cabin. We also needed grub and other things.

Wednesday, October 17, 1979—worked on the Cat all day.

Thursday, October 18, 1979—put the insulation in and covered it up. The weather is very nice, 18-20 degrees above zero at night.

Friday, October 19, 1979—worked on the cabin putting in windows and making a door, a table and a bunk. We're really working hard to get everything done. Getting ready to go outside (to Minnesota).

Saturday, October 20, 1979—worked on the Cat, got it ready for winter. We packed our luggage to go to Minnesota and left Nelchina about noon. We met Kahren Rudbeck's friend at the airport in Anchorage and gave her their sleeping bags. Got on the plane at 6:45 p.m. Three hours later we were in Seattle. We had a three hour layover there, then 2 ½ hours later we were at Minneapolis/St. Paul Airport. Paul, my son and his wife Ruth came to meet us and we got to see Steven our grandson. He's a new grandson, we hadn't seen him yet. Later, my daughters Beverly Volk and Nadia, Darrell Breider (Nadia's husband) and my granddaughter Laura came over to Paul and Ruth's late. We had a nice visit. Of course we don't have a vehicle here in Minnesota, so Roger and Bridgette came down from Motley and drove us to our home here in Minnesota. Real tired.

Sunday, October 21, 1979—went to Brainerd and saw my daughter Theresa Austin and her son and daughter, Lee and Darcy and hubby

Norman Wilkins

Larry. Stopped to see Bob and Kahren Rudbeck who live west of Brainerd.

Monday, October 22, 1979—saw Lee, Roger, Taymond and Clara and Theresa's family and Everett gave me a tire, took Theresa's family out for supper.

Tuesday, October 23, 1979—went over to Ernie's and butchered that lamb that we were getting from him. We shopped in Staples, fixed some tires and took the pickup in to fix the heater. Roger and Bridgette went out to supper with us.

Wednesday, October 24, 1979—did some more shopping and cut up the lamb. Went to see the Rollins family. We have been friends for a long time and it was good to see them again.

Thursday, October 25, 1979—fixed tires on the pickup, put newer tires on. Shopped in Brainerd and Staples and visited Al and his mother.

Friday, October 26, 1979—Some time ago, I had gone to Iowa, cut some hickory logs and brought them up to Minnesota. I wanted them sawed so I could build a dog sled. They had been lying at a sawmill for a long time and hadn't been touched. I was disappointed about that. Roger knew of another sawmill we might use so we loaded up the untouched logs and hauled them to this other sawmill.

Saturday, October 27, 1979—we loaded some gear and did some visiting. Went grouse hunting and I made a nice shot on a grouse. They make a good meal.

Sunday, October 28, 1979—it's raining. I worked on my snowmobile trailer and then went to Brainerd and saw Theresa and family.

Monday, October 29, 1979—got some supplies and worked on snowmobile trailer some more, packed gear and did some farm business (rentals).

October 30, 1979 to Nov 1, 1979—no entries.

Friday, November 2, 1979—Sylvia doesn't want to go to Alaska for the

10,000 Days in Alaska Book One 1978-1989

winter so she went to Minneapolis to stay with Nadia's family there.

Saturday, November 3, 1979—deer season opened as I left for Alaska. I got up the road about a hundred miles and the tongue on the trailer broke at Thief River Falls. Every place was closed except one implement dealer. He had no one there to weld it, but he let me do the welding. I drove back to the farm in Cass County and slept for 12 hours.

Sunday November 4, 1979—got up well rested and got a better trailer tongue, (better metal and stronger). I left at noon, drove 435 miles (some ice on the road), got to Brandon Manitoba and slept in the truck on the seat.

Monday November 5, 1979—started out before daylight and had a flat tire on the trailer about noon. Saw a flock of swans and one of honkers near Defoe Saskatchewan. The tongue in that trailer gave more trouble. (I had loaned that trailer out one time, and this person that borrowed it had pulled a heavy load over a curb in town and tweaked the axel. It was never quite right after that.) I jury-rigged up the tongue and got going again, made it to Lloydminster a little after 9:00 p.m. (Minnesota time). Got a room in a motel there and got a good rest.

Tuesday November 6, 1979—got up at 6:30 and went downtown, gassed up and serviced the truck, headed for Edmonton. Lots of fog and light snow. Bought a few groceries in Edmonton and I had two more ruined tires on the trailer. I've got to stop and switch out a lot of spare tires and wheels. Every time one of them goes bad, it takes time to stop, jack it up and get another wheel and tire on. Bought more tires and had them mounted as spares for this doggone trailer. The trees are all white from an ice storm here around Edmonton. I reached Dawson Creek at 8:35 p.m. and got a room. It's too cold to sleep in the cab of the truck and I can sleep better in a bed, so that's what I did.

Wednesday November 7, 1979—I left at 7:30, saw a cow and a calf moose just outside Fort Nelson. There's lots of dust on the road here. I always think of the air cleaner on the pickup when I have to drive in dusty places. I'll have to watch the air filter in case it needs to be changed. Reached Watson Lake at 12:15 a.m. November 8th.

Thursday, November 8, 1979—left Watson at 7:05 a.m. Saw a moose right away on the highway. It's quite warm here, and more dust. It makes my sinus run and throat sore. Stopped at High Country Safaris (Ed Dolhan) for an hour—more dust there. Visited with them and then went on toward the Alaska border. I was out about 60 miles past Ed's and I stopped and slept for a while, then went on to customs. From there I went to Tok and slept a little and ate.

Friday, November 9, 1979—about 4:00 a.m. I left Tok and got to Nelchina just before the sun came up. It's great to be here. As I was driving down the road, I felt like I was going home. I really like Alaska. Unloaded the pickup and then went to a birthday party for Dan Billman. Met lots of new people, had a good time and got home late. The folks in the neighborhood all gather for this sort of thing and everyone always has a good time.

Saturday, November 10, 1979—left late and hauled in some wood with the snowmobile for me and for the shop at the Nelchina station. Then Henry and I went out making a trapline. Saw signs of fur—moose and caribou. Went to bed early.

Sunday, November 11, 1979—the Coleman lantern needed some fixing. I got that done and then cut up firewood for Henry. Then I boiled some traps in water and willow bark and later went to Dan's place. He flew us in the PA 12 out over the trapline and up over Slide Mountain. Saw about a hundred caribou up there. He showed me where two bulls had been fighting for two days. They had a large round-like area all beat down in the snow where they had been fighting. We did see a few moose. It was a great flight. You can see so much from the air. After we got back, helped Dan pump his well. Patti gave me a fresh loaf of bread—It tasted better than cake. Came back to Nelchina and built up the fire in the cabin and fixed supper. Mike, Henry, and John came over and talked trapping.

Monday, November 12, 1979—got up early and got gear loaded and Henry and I went out to set traps. Got a few set, lots of rough country and brush to try to set a trapline. We're using old seismic trails and the brush is beginning to grow back in them. It can be tough going in some places. We saw upwards of a hundred caribou, one was a huge bull up on top of Slide Mountain. We got back to Nelchina and hauled two loads of wood in for the lodge and then helped Tim with a small sled for trapping use. Tim finished up the barrel stove for my cabin today. It turned out very nice. He did all the welding. (We used this stove for more than 25 years. It was still in good shape and we continued to use it occasionally after that.) Got a spruce hen and ate her for supper.

Tuesday, November 13, 1979—serviced the snowmobile track and found the track adjusting bolt is lost. I have no replacement, so I drove over a 110 miles to Wasilla to get it and a spare belt and some material for the cabin and trapping license. Roads were icy and foggy. Got home late.

Wednesday, November 14, 1979—got up early and worked on the snowmobile, got trap gear ready, cut up some wood and Henry and I checked part of the trapline. Didn't find anything in any of the traps. Helped Tim haul logs with my snowmobile and sled. It was a beautiful sunset. It's dark enough here now that we need lights on the snowmobile after 4:00 p.m.

Thursday, November 15, 1979—while pulling a heavy load of wood out, I came to a turn and couldn't get around it quickly enough. I hung the snowmobile up on a spruce and I went out over the windshield and piled up over in the snow. Didn't get hurt. Things like that happen every once in a while. We went down to Cal's this evening to weigh out some gold. He'd gotten a black wolf already, and a nice wolverine, a mink and a martin so far on his trapline. He's doing very well. Checked my trapline and I had two rabbits in snares and one had been eaten by something. I set a snare for a lynx and then when I got back to Nelchina, worked on the cabin floor and started the door—been living without a door.

Friday, November 16, 1979—it started snowing and is still snowing lightly. We got about 8 inches, but the temperature is quite warm. I got wet getting a load of wood. Ate, then went out on the trapline, but no fur is moving in this weather. Picked up some sets that weren't producing and saw a cow moose and calf.

Saturday, November 17, 1979—last night was Jackie's birthday and Tim, Mike, Jim and Blake came over here for a while. Then we went over to the lodge for a small party. I tended the bar. Dan Billman was there. He had brought me back four dozen traps that he had gotten for me when he went into Anchorage.

Norman Wilkins

Sunday, November 18, 1979—I slept good and got up late. It's -01° and I worked on the cabin all day. Got the door hung and put in the stove and chimney. Felt good, hauled five loads of wood. Will work on the snowmobile after supper. (When that tree jumped out in front of me, it dented the snowmobile cowling.) Tim ran the trapline and there's still nothing on it. Someone else is trapping our area. He saw their tracks. It was -10 last night and zero most of the day.

Monday, November 19, 1979—Tim and I walked the fellow's line that has moved into our area. We picked up two of his traps and left a note to come to Nelchina to claim them. Worked on the cabin some more.

Tuesday, November 20, 1979—Tim and I went about half way up Slide Mountain. The snow was really deep, and it was rough going. He cut trail and I set five traps. Snowmobile got stuck several times. Gusts of wind blew snow off the trees and light snow coming down some of the time. We got back home to the lodge and my cabin, tired and pretty damp.

Wednesday, November 21, 1979—Tim and I went out on the upper part of the trapline and found nothing in the traps. It seems like there just isn't much fur here. Caribou have been in the area and they've walked the trapline too. We set two rabbit snares and establish a trail down off the mountain. When we get back to the lodge, I worked on the cabin. Got a bed, a bunk-like bed built and I put the door jam on. Dan Billman and Mike Phillips showed up. I helped put a heater on his car. It snowed most of the day.

Thursday, November 22, 1979—bright sunshine today. Built the counter and cupboards in the cabin. Mike and Tim came by on their snowmobiles. Mike had just caught a marten. Henry came over later to take pictures of the sunset. It was beautiful. I have a panoramic view of this beauty from the cabin. Snow was blowing from the mountain peaks in long streamers. I went to the lodge for Thanksgiving dinner. We had king salmon and king crab and all the trimmings. It was very delicious. I'm very tired tonight. Will boil tea, build a fire in the stove and sleep well. Woke up in the night with a toenail giving me hell. Took three aspirins and went back to bed.

Friday, November 23, 1979—another pretty day, but colder. Worked some more on the cabin then ran the trapline, nothing on it. Built the bench, table and a shelf in the cabin. My trapline up there on the mountain is short and doesn't take long to run it—as long as I don't have any trouble. Fixed supper just before midnight, quite tired.

Saturday, November 24, 1979—slept late. It's colder again this morning. Did dishes and got almost everything moved into my cabin. All went well. Will celebrate with steak, rutabagas and whiskey. Real happy tonight.

Sunday, November 25, 1979—slept late, hauled more things to the cabin. Cut up and split wood for the stove. Henry's son Doug helped me. Henry came to visit later. Mike and Tim stopped at the garage. Quite cold today, -15°. Tim and Ken came over and I traded them a 6-pack for a pair of arctic mitts—military surplus.

Monday, November 26, 1979—got the truck started. It starts really well in cold weather. Blake has to go to Glennallen to get Shelly tonight. Went to Gunsight Mountain Lodge to get gasoline. (The lodge here at Nelchina is out of gasoline.) Cut up and piled the poles I had sledded to the cabin. I'm boiling beef heart and rutabaga and onions for supper. Peter stopped by and ate supper with me and borrowed a sleeping bag and pad. Henry and Tim went to anchorage to buy a wrecker. They didn't get the wrecker as there was a lien against it. I went to Mike and Lynette's in Nelchina. Nelchina Sam was there. Later, after I got back to my cabin, Peter stopped in (it was 3:00 a.m.)

Tuesday, November 27, 1979—got up late, changed the plugs on the snowmobile. Tim and I went out to check the traps. Nothing there, no luck. I wiped out the windshield on the snow machine—rolled it over. Didn't get hurt. Bob Schmidt, Leo Ogilby, Lee Dudley and Mike Phillips were at the lodge. Fixed beef heart stew and noodles for supper.

Wednesday, November 28, 1979—I sure have a sore back today. Moved some more things from the little green house to the cabin. It snowed all night. It's nice to be in the cabin. At the green house, when I would get up in the mornings and walk over to the stove to build a fire, my feet would stick (freezing from the cold) to the floor. Here in the cabin, the floor is insulated and stays warm so my feet don't stick to the floor. After breakfast, I packed snow around the cabin and packed a trail to the wood area with the snowmobile. Worked on the clutch of the Ski-Doo. It's been giving me some trouble. Borrowed Dan Billman's draw knife. Mike gave me a mink carcass to use as scent and bait for the trapline. Then I put up a drying rack in the cabin. Lots of neighbors are at the lodge this evening.

Thursday, November 29, 1979—varnished the table and the counter in the cabin. Went out and cut the trees and hauled in two loads of wood from the wood lot. Then I ran the trapline (it's short and doesn't take very long). Had to move six—almost all the sets. The snow was really deep and I had to get them up out of the snow and recover them. The deep snow made traveling tough work. Today the weather was warm.

Friday, November 30, 1979—it's warm again today. I brought in three loads of wood. Snow was deep and we'll have to pack a trail down. It takes two days and nights for the snow to freeze up and get hard so that we can haul a load on the trail. Don McKee fixed the line from the propane tank to the regulator for my stove. He has done a lot of muzzle loader building and is involved with Rendezvous Days (Several historical rendezvous take place in Alaska each summer). It's fun to go to and watch these skillful muzzle loader shooters. (The Alaska State Muzzle

The original 12' x 16' temporary cabin

10,000 Days in Alaska Book One 1978-1989

Loading Association is an organization that supports responsible use and ownership of muzzle loading firearms. Rendezvous usually include muzzleloader shooting matches and other contests.) Don has built two log cabins. One is 25x32 and the other is smaller and he uses it for his gun building shop now. They both are nice buildings.

Saturday, December 1, 1979–blocked up some wood, split and piled yesterday's wood, and hauled in three more loads. It's 10° above today. Libby brought one of her racing sleds to the garage. We keep the garage heated night and day and she put it together there. It's a real good looking, light and very sleek sled, built for speed.

Sunday, December 2, 1979–moved Mike, our dog and his house, over to the cabin. He'll be much happier there. Hauled another load of things from what we call the green house (it was painted green). It's the house that Henry let us stay in when we first came here. I got that hauled over to the cabin and then I ran the trapline. Henry went along. This time though, there was nothing there. Saw a cow moose. Henry is leaving to go to California and work for a while. We had a party for him at the lodge, with lamb and buffalo to eat.

Monday, December 3, 1979–mailed some letters, filed the front sight down on the revolver. This revolver, I carry on the trapline and it shoots low. I filed the front sight down so it would shoot to where I was looking. I got the truck ready and took Henry to catch his flight in Anchorage. Charlie went along. We stopped for supplies and Charlie went to the doctor. We stayed at Charlie's cousin, Lisa's house. Met Tom also. Got back to Nelchina around 8:00 p.m.

Tuesday, December 4, 1979–It's great to be back here in my warm cabin. (The barrel stove Tim built me was made using an ex-compressor tank that was composed of ¼ inch steel.)

Wednesday, December 5, 1979–went to Libby and Charlie's. They needed some gas for Libby's pickup so we siphoned 5 gallons of gas out of mine–and for that, she gave me breakfast. I took Sam's plywood up to Ken and Jackie's for him and visited. Ken came in from hauling wood. Then I came home and worked on getting the cabin organized. Later Tim came by and we visited for a while. Then I ordered some knives and wrote Nadia a letter.

Norman Wilkins

Thursday, December 6, 1979—I went over to the green house and got some more gear that we had stored there and hauled it down to the cabin. Did the dished and then I worked on the heating stove at the Nelchina Lodge. Tim, he was there and helped. It's -20° here today. Sam came by to pay for his plywood that I had gotten him in town. We had a good visit and he left me two books to read. He invited me to his cabin to visit some time. Tim helped with the stove and we got it going.

Friday, December 7, 1979—finished moving to the cabin from the green house. Ran the trapline. It was -28° this morning and -25° at 3:00 p.m. There was nothing moving on the trapline. Cooked beans for supper and Dan Billman came down to the lodge. We worked on his snowmobile in the lodge garage, they keep it heated. We worked on that until 1:20 a.m. and we got everything done that was needed.

Saturday, December 8, 1979—Mike, our dog had a fight with the lodge's dog (named Bear). We got 'em separated. Neither dog was badly hurt. Tim and I each got one load of wood today out of the wood lot. It's warmer today. Cut up and stacked wood and moved the refrigerator into the cabin. That was one heck of a job—this is a big propane refrigerator. It is heavy and clumsy to handle. I went down to the wood lot and broke a new trail. When you break a trail out and you drive past the trees you're going to cut and make a circle out of it so you get back to the regular trail to haul the wood on. You widen this new trail out, so you can make the corners pulling the sled. Then the second day you drive over it again. By the third day, it would be reasonably frozen enough to haul a load of wood on.

Sunday, December 9, 1979—Cal and son Ernie stopped by and talked trapping. I put a windshield on the snowmobile. It's really windy today.

Monday, December 10, 1979—Mike gave me two muskrat carcasses to use for bait on my trapline. I called Lou, to send me some beaver castors and Libby brought pictures she had just gotten developed in town.

Tuesday, December 11, 1979—got up at 3:45 a.m. and got to Cal's at 5:00 a.m. He has invited me to ride in his snow track with him and his son Ernie on his trapline. It was such a day that trappers don't like. We didn't get any fur. I did get two ptarmigans and when I shot these ptarmigan, I walked over to pick them up and lo and behold there is overflow—on the ice. The snow is about a foot deep and the overflow wasn't obvious when I started for the ptarmigan. I got out on it and broke through a thin crust of ice and not knowing how deep the water was, I didn't want to overflow my Sorel boots and get my feet wet. It's very cold so I laid down on top of the snow which held my body in that manner and then I rolled off the area of the overflow—I did take the ptarmigans and rifle with me. We saw quite a few other ptarmigans but we didn't shoot any more. Saw some caribou and lots of moose, but we didn't see any bulls. But there may have been moose that had lost their horns and at a distance, it's hard to tell a bull from a cow and be positive about it—for me anyway. I really enjoyed the trip. It was fun and I thanked Cal for taking me along. His trapline is 73 miles out, and the temperature was -25° to -35° depending on the elevation of where we were at the time.

Wednesday, December 12, 1979—did some chores around the cabin and got the truck started. The lodge here at Nelchina wanted me to go down to Gunsight Mountain Lodge and get gas for them. While I was there at Gunsight, I listened to an amazing story told by a man named John and his wife. They had just walked over eight miles of the trail from Alfred Creek at -35° below zero to get here. The snow was very deep and they had no snowshoes. They had originally tried to drive out with a small Cat from the gold mine on Alfred Creek, but they couldn't get over the mountain and down the pass. The employer had left them there with too little food, promising to fly food in to them. This didn't happen and they ran out of food. It was such a hard walk, that he couldn't carry his wife. She became exhausted and he kept telling her that it's just a little farther, just a little farther... He coached her to stay with him and they eventually made it to Gunsight Lodge. Of course they had heat there and the lodge owner gave them food and a place to stay. It got down to -40° that evening. (Life in the bush demands fortitude.)

Thursday, December 13, 1979—put up some shelves in our cabin and put some more things away. Leo Ogilvy gave me a carving knife to use for carving horns. He comes around every once in a while to visit and have a few cups of coffee. Ran the trapline and re-baited and fixed some sets and—no fur again. I don't know why there isn't more fur here. Possible it's trapped out.

Norman Wilkins

Friday, December 14, 1979—it's -30°. Mike, Lynette and Lee came to the lodge later. Mark from Chitna showed up and we had a good discussion. (People in these parts know how to carry on a discussion).

Saturday, December 15, 1979—still cold Tim and Shelly went to Anchorage to do Christmas shopping. I just did small chores around the cabin and fixed one meal of pizza.

Sunday, December 16, 1979—didn't do anything, made a pie. Mike Phillips, he stopped by and we had a nice visit. Went over to the lodge and Lee Dudley and Mike and I talked guns.

Monday, December 17, 1979—straightened up the cabin, did dishes and some laundry. Tim came over for a little while. He got a Christmas tree for the lodge today. I only cooked one meal and carried water today.

Tuesday, December 18, 1979—it snowed 5 inched yesterday and last night. I shoveled snow and carried water and did more laundry. Mike came over, he needed a short rope. We talked gold and silver crisis. Cooked two meals. Mike had given me a moose steak, it was really good. I'm reading a book, and it's -15° tonight.

Wednesday, December 19, 1979—it's a little colder today, -30° this afternoon. Tim and I went out and got four loads of wood for his cabin.

Thursday, December 20, 1979—snowed all night and today. Warmed up to 10°. Roger Shequen called, had a nice visit. He brought me up to speed on things around Motley and about our property.

Friday, December 21, 1979—Betty, Shelly, Blake and I went to Glennallen. Denise and Doug were in a Christmas play at the schoolhouse. I went to Copper Center and got 200 gallons of fuel for the lodge. Betty tried to pay me for hauling the fuel, but I wouldn't take any money for that from them. Did some grocery shopping and got my Alaska driver's license. In the evening went to see Dan and Patti and we all went over to Mike and Lynette's for an evening of music.

Saturday, December 22, 1979—Peter brought back the sleeping bag and pad he had borrowed. I ran the trapline again. Nothing on it. No fur. Snow machine was acting up, went to Gunsight Mountain for gas for the lodge. Sam sent in a book for me to read. Later he came and Ken and Jackie stopped at the lodge. It was -32° at 6 p.m.

Sunday, December 23, 1979—worked on the chain saw today. Sharpened the chain and adjusted it. Worked on the snow machine, didn't quite get it finished. Mike, our dog is gaining some weight, so he's doing good in this weather. It's -35° this evening and I'm reading *The Education of Little Tree* by Forrest Carter. I like this book a lot. Mike Lynette, Dan and Patti and their two kids came at 10:00 p.m. and sang Christmas Carols. That was very thoughtful of them—and this was at 40 degrees below zero!

Monday, December 24, 1979—warmed up to -25° to -30° today. Did some sewing, worked on the lodge's chain saw. My snowmobile still isn't right. The carburetor on the lodge's snowmobile froze up today so we didn't get any logs out. Went to the lodge after supper, exchanged gifts and they gave me a beautiful beaver hat. (They had Libby Riddles make this hat for me.) I also got a bottle of whiskey and a package of Copenhagen.

Tuesday, December 25, 1979—went over to Bob and Margaret Schmidt's house party in the evening. Sylvia called, got to talk to Beverly, Nadia, Paul and Laura. It was really good to talk to the family, I miss them a lot. Betty at the lodge had a large Christmas Dinner.

Wednesday, December 26, 1979—slept late, loafed all day. Late in the afternoon Peter and I went to Mike and Lynette's. Ken stopped in there for a few minutes. Peter and I ate supper with them. Lee Dudley came a little later. I drove Peter to Mendeltna Creek and got back home early. Helped a little around the lodge, and then hauled two loads of cabin logs for the lodge. Read some out of the book and cooked supper and off to sleep.

Thursday, December 28, 1979—it warmed up in the night. The roof started to leak in one spot so I got up at 2:00 a.m. and pulled the snow off the roof and knocked the ice ledge off and the leak quit. Worked around the cabin until noon. Then Tim and Blake and I hauled firewood and logs all afternoon. We had lots of trouble with the last load—got stuck a lot as the trail had broken up. My right groin hurts tonight as well as my back.

Friday, December 29, 1979—did some chores, worked on the snow machine carburetor and fuel pump. Tim and Ken went with me on the trapline. Nothing on it. It's only -5° today. Remade all the sets. Saw a fox trail, followed that a little ways on the trail then came to a—call it a crazed moose trail. A moose ran down the mountain across my trapline. It was running so hard it was crashing into tree trunks. I followed that moose track on foot for some distance and I never saw any sign of wolf tracks chasing it or anything—it was just running! One of my trap sets is frozen in the overflow (the overflow is bad right now).

Saturday, December 30, 1979—it's colder today. Took one of Sam's books to Charley. Libby had been on an overnighter training for the Iditarod race. (On an overnighter, she runs the dogs and the sled out a long way from the cabin and camps out in the open.) Later I went up to Mike's to go fishing through the ice at Lake Louise—didn't catch any fish. We met a trapper named Andy Runyan. This man is a well known Kodiak bear guide.

Sunday, December 31, 1979—it's -30° this morning, stayed cold all day. Worked on the sled for log hauling (re-built the hitch, this time). Hauling logs in the tundra and deep snow is really hard on the sled. It was -40° at 6:00 p.m. Went to Lake Louise to party at Wolverine Lodge. The whole neighborhood is leaving in one group tonight. We hung around Wolverine Lodge for a while and then we decided to go into Glennallen. It was -47° at 11:40 p.m. when we headed for Glennallen. We saw small herds of caribou both coming and going. About half way down the Lake Louise Road towards the Glenn Highway, it was midnight and we all stopped our cars, got out, and wished each other Happy New Year. Then we went on to Glennallen to a roadhouse party and danced until 3:00 a.m. Then Dan Billman and Chris Ronning and I ran a hundred yard foot race in the parking lot. It was so cold that we didn't dare breathe—we ran the hundred yards without taking a breath. (You don't want to breathe under those circumstances when you are exerting yourself like that for fear of frosting your lungs.) We went back in the lodge and talked the cook into making breakfast for us. After breakfast, we went back to Nelchina. Chris Ronning came to the cabin about 5:00 a.m. the next morning. It was still -40° then.

10,000 Days in Alaska Book One 1978-1989

Left to right: Norman packs the stove into trap cabin; cabin door is hung with unwashed T-shirt providing "man-scent" to alert bears; Sylvia hauls a log with the puka sled; trap cabin window is rimmed with 12" log spikes pointing outward to discourage entry by bears.

Norman Wilkins

1980—snow caves, gold rush, building trapper cabin

Tuesday, January 1, 1980—fixed breakfast for Chris Ronning and I about 6:00 a.m. in the morning. We visited until early afternoon, then went to Charley and Libby's and after that, on to Chris's home. Took the battery out of his plane. He packed his clothes to take—he's going on a job up on the North Slope. Came back to Nelchina and he and another fella went on to catch a plane to the North Slope. I fixed supper and went to bed. It's -40° below zero.

Wednesday, January 2, 1980—got up about 9:00 a.m. and ate, worked a little on the sled, loafed mostly. It's warmed up to -15° today.

Thursday, January 3, 1980—had trouble with the cook stove. Tried to run the trapline and the snowmobile quit. Worked on it, but it still isn't working. Gold hit $635.00 dollars an ounce and dropped $25.00 by supper time.

Friday, January 4, 1980—did some laundry. Tim and I went to Copper Center to get heating oil for the lodge. I hauled it in the pickup in 50-gallon drums. Today is Betty's birthday; there was a small party at the lodge. Sam brought me three more books to read. I read lots of books.

Saturday, January 5, 1980—it snowed 3 inches last night and warmed up to about 15°. Sawed up some wood and baked a pumpkin pie. Gordon Johnson had sent me some beaver castors; they came in the mail today. I'm sharing them with some other trappers around here and today I gave some to Allen. (Beaver castor is made from the castor scent glands of a beaver and is used as a trapping lure.)

Sunday, January 6, 1980—Tim, Blake and I cut and hauled six loads of wood out of the wood lot, which is about ¾ of a mile away. It's 5° today. Sylvia called. I was in the woods and called her back when I came in and we had a visit. I'm reading *Coming Into The Country* by John McPhee.

Monday, January 7, 1980—blocked and split some wood. Ran the trapline, Tim and I each shot a ptarmigan. Put scent at each set and chopped two traps out of overflow ice. No catch today. Went to Cal's and gave him some beaver castor (scent). Beavers have a scent gland that lets other beavers know of their territory.

10,000 Days in Alaska Book One 1978-1989

Tuesday, January 8, 1980—did cabin chores, went snow shoeing and took beaver castor to Don McKee. They gave me two salmon filets. The wind is blowing tonight. It's been blowing so seldom, it's nice to feel it and hear it.

Wednesday, January 9, 1980—Tim adjusted the points on my snowmobile and it runs fine now. Went to Ken Kramer's and cut and hauled logs for wood and got gear ready to go to Tim's mother's cabin on Tyone Lake.

Thursday, January 10, 1980—we got up for an early start—it was -30°. I had bad feelings about this trip. I thought it was way too cold to go, but Tim really wanted to go. He wanted to get those metal bunks and bring them back to the lodge here. Hooked on to the trailer, loaded up the snowmobiles and sleds and went to Lake Louise. Unloaded the snow machines and checked the temperature there at the lodge and it was -45°. We got the machines started and went down the lake—it's maybe 20 miles or so to his mother's cabin on Tyone Lake. We stopped every couple of miles to look at one another's face, checking for frostbite. We had masks over our faces, but frost would still get through. We got to Tim's mother's cabin and my machine wasn't running right, seemed like there was still something wrong with the carburetor. When we got there, there was a little bit of daylight left so we went out looking for wood to use as fuel, but there was nothing but scrub, black spruce—it's very small. We found all the dead trees we could find from 6 to 8 feet tall. Got those up to the cabin and cut it up into stove wood and started to build a fire in the stove. This is a tiny, tin stove. Lo and behold, the stove is two thirds full of ashes. We dug the ashes out so there was some room and got a fire started. We didn't have very much light in there and we took turns sitting in front of the fire to thaw the masks off of our faces. We both have beards and our masks were frozen to our faces. By the time we got our masks off, it was warming up a little in there. We put a kettle on the stove and thawed out some beans for supper—tried to make a pot of coffee too. We ate the beans and cut up wood for the night, we were glad for that. We banked up the cabin with snow the best we could. Still, it was so cold in there that even later in the evening, we could sit back four feet and blow at the stove and see our breath. There is no insulation, it's just boards. In an effort to try and stay warm after we ate, we crawled in our sleeping bags. It was cold all night and we had a hard time getting any sleep.

Friday, January 11, 1980—(found out later that it had stayed -38° to -40° all night and we think that farther down at the lower elevation where we had been, it was probably even colder.) The snow machines were really cold the next morning. We fixed a good, big breakfast and I went out and took the carburetor off of my machine and brought it inside. That's a cold job with bare hands. I took the carburetor all apart and there was some ice in it—got it dry and put it back on. Then we loaded up our gear and those bunks and started out. I got a few white spots on my face from the frost, but we got back up to Lake Louise and to the lodge where we had our vehicles parked. We got things loaded up and got warm in the lodge and went back to Nelchina.

Saturday, January 12, 1980—Dan flew me over lots of the country around this area. We went up and looked at Botley Creek and all the way to Lake Louise. Saw quite a few moose and caribou, some fox tracks, several lakes and drainages that had muskrat pushups on them. (In winter, muskrats stay below the ice for long periods of time. They extend their feeding areas by making "pushups" which are piles of vegetation placed on top of the ice over an opening.) When we came back, there was a big party at Nelchina Lodge in the evening.

Sunday, January 13, 1980—melted water and cooked some food for my dog Mike then rested most of the day. I feed him hot food. He sleeps out in his house—he doesn't like the heat of the cabin, but he deserves a good hot meal every day. I melt snow in a 5-gallon bucket that I put on top of the heating stove.

Monday, January 14, 1980—did some laundry and Peter came over to visit. Unloaded gear and snowmobile.

Tuesday, January 15, 1980—slept late and straightened up the cabin. Peter came again.

Wednesday, January 16, 1980—Leo Ogilvy came and stayed most of the day, then Peter showed up and visited a while. Tim and Charlie came by too and Tim borrowed my acetylene torch to fix Peter's radiator in his vehicle. Ken came over to borrow a spark plug adapter to do something on his snowmobile. Then Sam came into the lodge and I gave him some beaver castor and returned some books that he had loaned me.

Thursday, January 17, 1980—carried water for the cabin from the lodge, did the dishes and laundry and carried traps to the cabin. Brit, Libby's friend from Norway stopped to visit a while.

Friday, January 18, 1980—Tim and I went to Ken Kramer's and plowed snow for Ken, helped Mike with his Volkswagen engine a little and worked on the snowmobile. Peter was here for supper. Tim and Shelley came down and talked about settling on some of the State land in the area that is up for homesteading.

Saturday, January 19, 1980—I did some chores around the cabin and helped Blake get in four loads of wood. It's very windy and warm, 20-30 degrees above zero.

Sunday, January 20, 1980—slept late, still warm and windy, it's even blowing down the chimney today, making it hard to start a fire. Made chili and pudding for supper and called Sylvia. Windy, warm and snowing now.

Monday, January 21, 1980—snow and raining. 30° to 32°. Put up a gun rack in the cabin, pulled snow off the roof and scooped snow off the lodge roof.

Tuesday, January 22, 1980—Henry and Betty and I went to Anchorage to tow Henry's Blazer back. The roads were snowy and icy and it was very windy. We hooked to the Blazer in Anchorage and I pulled it out of town on the Glenn Highway. When we got out on the flats, the wind was blowing so hard that sometimes it would blow me sideways off onto the shoulder. We couldn't travel at more than 20 MPH. It seemed that when we went faster, the wind could get a better push on us. Got up to Palmer and there is a grocery store outside of town there that had a nice parking lot. I chose to turn off the highway there to stop and put chains on the vehicle. Henry and Betty are riding with me and we turned down off the highway real slow and easy. I got down on that parking lot and what with the wind and slippery ice, the truck just kept going and kept going. There was a really fancy large, expensive car parked in the lot there and a cop car parked, facing that car. I'm sliding sideways right at that fancy car. It just kept slowing little by little and pretty soon I stopped. I was so close to that car that I couldn't open the door of my truck. I can just imagine those cops thinking, "Boy, we got a guy we can write up now!" But I got the truck away from there and Henry helped me put chains on all four tires and started out for Nelchina again. We were still about 98 miles from home. We didn't have any problem getting over the mountains with the truck chained up. Got his Blazer back to the lodge for him and all was well.

Wednesday, January 23, 1980—ran the trapline and there wasn't anything in it so I pulled the traps.

Thursday, January 24, 1980—went to Nelchina Sam's and had a nice visit. It was 0 to 10°. He has a nice trail broken in and the walk in there was nice. We usually walk with snowshoes when going to his place. He has a nice view of the Nelchina River.

Friday, January 25, 1980—Tim moved to Ken's

Saturday, January 26, 1980—got a load of wood. Henry is coming home from California and we're planning a welcome home party for him in the evening.

Sunday, January 27, 1980—rested most of the day. Betty has a bad knee and it's giving her trouble.

Monday, January 28, 1980—hauled a load of wood and visited Charlie and Libby—and Brit from Norway, then went on to Ken's. Mike was there.

Tuesday, January 29, 1980—slept late, did chores around the cabin, snowshoed two trails to get wood. Hauled one load and cut it up into stove lengths. A moose had walked in the trail. Took care of the bar while Henry took Betty to the doctor.

Wednesday, January 30, 1980—split wood, snowshoed the trail, cut lots of trees, hauled one load and got stuck. Blake got stuck twice. Strained my back getting these machines back on the trail. It's -20° and the loose snow is armpit deep. Last night it got to 10 degrees above and today bright sunshine.

10,000 Days in Alaska Book One 1978-1989

Thursday, January 31, 1980—hauled a load of cabin logs for Henry. We sort the wood and get the good cabin logs for Henry. Got one load of wood cut and split for me. Snowing and -50° today.

Friday, February 1, 1980—It's my birthday. Hauled more wood. Cut, split and stacked it and helped Henry around the lodge.

Saturday, February 2, 1980—hauled more wood, cut and split and stacked it. Repaired Henry's truck chains. Hauled a load of wood for him and cut up two more loads. Back is tired tonight.

Sunday, February 3, 1980—hauled and cut more wood and one load of Henry's cabin logs from out of the wood lot. Did laundry. Leo Ogilsvy came to visit. He likes his coffee, poor guy, he doesn't have much, can't buy coffee for himself.

Monday, February 4, 1980—quite warm last night some snow and wind, 20°. Started snowing hard and blowing early, slowed up at 2:00 p.m. and 25°. Went to Ken's to take him my meat saw. It's snowing big, wet flakes this evening.

Tuesday, February 5, 1980—16 to 18 inches of fresh snow this morning. 30° to 35° and sunny. Cleaned off the cabin roof, the woodpile and scooped paths. Snowshoed a trail out to the lodge. Tended the lodge in the morning and helped Henry and Dan fix tire chains.

Wednesday, February 6, 1980—it was a warm 25° day and cloudy. Scooped a little snow and did some cabin chores.

Thursday, February 7, 1980—a little cooler. I put up some driveway markers for the lodge. People can't see the edges of the driveway and it would be easy for someone to run off there and get stuck. Fixed the snowplow chains for the lodge.

Friday, February 8, 1980—did dishes and cabin chores. Cooked dog food for Mike. Snowshoed the trail to the wood lot, moose are feeding in that area. They like walking up and down on my packed trails.

Saturday, February 9, 1980—helped Henry around the lodge and garage. It's quite warm and rained a little in the evening.

Norman Wilkins

Sunday, February 10, 1980—Leo stopped for coffee. Didn't do much all day.

Monday, February 11, 1980—very warm, 51° and the sun is shining. Changed the oil and filter on the truck since I had such a nice day.

Tuesday, February 12, 1980—Lee and I snowshoed back to Sam's cabin on the Nelchina River. There was a young fella named Tommy there. He had walked in the 40 miles from where his parents lived out in the bush. He was quite a young fella but he was knowledgeable about the wilderness. Sam gave me three books to read and we had a good visit. I really enjoyed this afternoon.

Wednesday February 13, 1980—Henry and I tried to fix his jeep snowplow's spare transmission—didn't fit it. That was a disappointment.

Thursday, February 14, 1980—cut and hauled three loads of wood for the shop at the lodge.

Friday, February 15, 1980—Peter came to the lodge and I went with him and walked in to his cabin on Mendeltna Creek.

Saturday, February 16, 1980—stayed overnight at Peter's, had a good time. He has a very small, but nice tight cabin. The Northern Lights were exceptionally good. We saw a cow and calf moose.

Sunday, February the 17, 1980—did cabin chores and cooked food for Mike. Called Sylvia and she wasn't there. Called Bob Rudbeck and then Henry and I hauled wood for the lodge. Lee Dudley played a little guitar at the lodge

Monday, February 18, 1980—Jim, Mike, Lee and I went cross-country skiing. I'm the amateur and they're all experienced. We drove down to the summit near Eureka. We skied in six miles. It's really nice country in February and a good place to ski. We did climb and slide down some good hills. They weren't steep; they were something that I could handle. We had lots of fun. When we got ready to go back out to the highway, these guys all took off like a scared cat. I start coming along behind them, and these skis I'm on—I don't know much about turning them. I'm going faster and faster down this hill and there's a spruce tree coming up so I just sat down in the snow to put the brakes on. Then I walked around the tree and started out again and got down. Those guys all had a good laugh at that. Then we went out to the highway and over to Dan's in the evening.

Tuesday, February 19, 1980—went on snowshoes looking for wood to cut, found a nice stand and made a fresh trail to this new wood lot, packed it down and widened it out.

Wednesday, February 20, 1980—I rode the snowmobile on the trail for wood and packed it down some more. Then at the lodge we made plans for a cross-country, ski and camping trip.

Thursday, February 21, 1980—we cut and hauled two loads of wood for Blake, then worked on getting camping gear organized for this cross-country ski/camping trip.

Friday, February 22, 1980—it was -20°. We all gathered our gear at Nelchina Lodge, loaded up and left to go to Eureka Lodge. We unloaded our gear and left there about mid morning on skis. The skis I had were borrowed and they didn't work well on my boots. After a few miles, the guys could see I wasn't going to be able to keep up that way, so Jim had a pair of emergency snowshoes. He gave them to me to use. I could do a lot better on snowshoes than I could on those skis. We got out to Albert Dome and we used anything we could to move snow and dig a cave in the side of this dome up near the top. We had snowshoes and everything working at it. One of the things that I used was one of Sylvia's pet skillets—and I broke the handle off of it. It took quite some time and it was dark by the time we got the hole dug. This hole was back in a big drift. We dug it so it was bigger than a 12'x16' tarp that I had brought along to use as a ground tarp. Then we dug a little hole off of that, a little extra room for cooking. Dan, he suggested thinning the roof in one area in order to let in light through the snow, so the guys did that. Jim had a thermometer and kept track of the temperature in there. It would get warm enough from cooking that the warm air would go over to where they had made this shallowing in the roof of the snow cave and the water would drip down there. Dan had brought his dog along and Mike had brought his. Mike's dog was trained to pull a sled and she did really well. We had a place for the dogs to sleep up in the higher part of the snow cave. The snow cave dipped down and then went up so it preserved the heat inside. The heat didn't leak out into the outside air. We blocked the cave entrance too, to discourage heat loss. It was really nice, the temperature hung around 30° in there. We all had a good time. We slept late and we ate well.

Saturday, February 23, 1980—the guys, I believe it was Mike and Jim were fixing breakfast. We ate a huge breakfast of bacon and eggs—big enough that it took a big skillet to fry it for one person. We had a stack of pancakes and every one of us wanted the fat from their bacon poured over the pancakes, we wanted every drop of it. (Fat, when you're out in circumstances like this, is heat—it turns to heat when you eat it.) Anyway, we all had a big breakfast and then went out and decided to go exploring. There was a lot of fog. It was kind of "iffy". Dan and I didn't like the idea of going out in the fog. We kept within sight of the snow cave; there isn't much to identify it once you get too far away from it. We saw Jim and Mike take off on their skis, counting on the trail not drifting over before they came back. Then the fog lifted and Dan and I went too. We all went to Crooked Creek. I snowshoed and they skied. Along towards late afternoon while we were heading back, a white out came along—and a ground blizzard, but we found our way back to the snow cave.

Sunday, February 24, 1980—it was so nice in that cave, we just hated to leave. The weather had turned nice. We had told people at the highway that we would be coming out on the 24th. We started snowshoeing the eight miles back to Eureka. Those guys were ahead of me and when we were oh, about a half to three quarters of a mile away, and I just happened to look over and here was a small group of ptarmigan in amongst some real small spruce trees. The guys were skiing faster because they were getting close to Eureka and didn't look off to the side so they missed seeing them. Between them and the lodge, there was a person. It looked to be Patti Billman—and it sure was. She was walking out to meet us. She had big news. There had been a gold strike on the Nelchina Glacier. We were all excited about that and when we got into the lodge, there was a guy in the lodge that Dan knew really well. (We all knew this fella too) He walked up to Dan and he said, "Boy, where have you been?" So Dan told him where we had been. "Well", he said, "You should have been at the gold strike at Nelchina Glacier." Dan slapped this guy on his belly and said, "You couldn't go where we've been." Anyway, Eureka was full of people. We left and went to Nelchina to the lodge there.

10,000 Days in Alaska Book One 1978-1989

Monday, February 25, 1980—the US Geological Survey people are going to announce the location of a gold discovery in the Nelchina basin tomorrow morning—the gold rush is on! We found out the gold is near the Nelchina Glacier. Dan's brother, Denny had done some scouting in Anchorage and gained some other information that was helpful to us. The plan we had, Dan was going to fly us out and land us with his ski plane on the glacier.

Tuesday, February 26, 1980—Mike and I loaded our gear in the plane and we had some claim stakes. Dan stayed and helped with the measuring while Mike and I walked about 13 miles on snowshoes. That night, Dan flew in. It was getting quite dark and maybe -20°. Dan had Henry along and Henry was throwing out our duffle bags and sleeping bags and more stakes. When this stuff landed in the snow, it would get buried, so Mike and I hurried to where the drop area was and pulled everything on top of the snow that we could find. The star reflection on the snow gave us enough light that we could find them once they were up on top of the snow. There was one bundle of stakes we couldn't find, but we did find our sleeping bags and grub. We dug another snow cave, this one smaller, for two people. Mike fixed supper that night. We didn't have too bad a night, it was cool, but it was alright.

Wednesday, February 27, 1980—Dan flew in the next morning, and we staked six, forty acre claims. Then National Geographic and NBC News from Los Angeles California took pictures of us from their helicopter. My mother in California saw our pictures on the TV news. There was one helicopter (we didn't see this happen, but were told this later) tried to land and one skid went through the snow crust and damaged the helicopter. Then there was a light snowfall, but Dan was able to beat the darkness and fly us out to the Nelchina Lodge.

Thursday, February 28, 1980—got rested and dried, made plans to register our claims and ate supper with Henry and Betty.

Friday, February 29, 1980—sharpened Henry's chain saw and did the laundry and dishes.

Saturday, March 1, 1980—worked on year end bookwork. Got gear ready to go back to Nelchina Glacier. David Harding from NPR Radio in

Norman Wilkins

Anchorage interviewed all of us here at Nelchina Lodge about the gold rush.

Sunday, March 2, 1980—got up very early and Dan flew Henry and me to the Nelchina Glacier and we re-staked these claims and staked six more. It was a long day on snowshoes. At one time, I was walking ahead pulling a hundred foot steel tape. Henry was behind me and as I'm snowshoeing along, I suddenly hear the sound of running water. This is not good! I hollered at Henry and I very carefully walked backwards on my snowshoes. The Nelchina River runs out of the glacier winter and summer and I had walked right over where it was flowing. I had no idea how far it was to water, but I wasn't going to stay and find out!

Monday, March 3, 1980—we filled out the papers to file on the 12 claims. Dan, Mike and I went to Glennallen to file the claims.

Tuesday, March 4, 1980—did cabin chores, worked on income tax and got ready to go outside to Minnesota tomorrow.

Wednesday, March 5, 1980—Lynette invited me to have breakfast with her and Mike on the way past their place. Had a really good breakfast. It was pancakes with salmon in them—very tasty. Got as far that day as 80 miles or so past Whitehorse.

Thursday, March 6, 1980—woke up at 5:00 a.m. and started out. Saw a wolverine along the road and some ptarmigan—maybe the wolverine was hunting them. I caught the edge of a snow berm and the truck went into the snow, but not off the road. Having four-wheel drive, I could just back up and get lined up again. The road wasn't plowed or anything. Saw two moose—one was right in the road and I had to stop quickly for that one. Farther down the road closer to Fort Nelson, a pipeline truck came from behind at a high rate of speed and ran me off the road. They like to do that to people—they did it that time. He turned so sharp in front of me that I had to move out of his way. There again, I got really lucky and managed to hold the truck on the road and get back out in the trail.

Friday, March 7, 1980—slept four hours here in Dawson Creek. The roads are much better now.

Saturday, March 8, 1980—started out at 6:00 a.m. and it really felt cold this morning. The heater took care of that. The sun is bright, rode hard, got to Roger's (Shequen) about 7:00 p.m. and stayed the night.

Sunday, March 9, 1980—went to the farm and talked to the renter. We've had lots of problems with the renter. Got to see the house Roger was building.

Monday, March 10, 1980—got to Minneapolis about noon. Sylvia and Darrell were there. Beverly and Kevin (Volk) and Nadia and Laura and Vanessa (Beverly's daughter) all came later. It's a good time to be with family. We all had lots of talking to do.

Tuesday, March 11, 1980—rested up and Nadia and Darrell took us out for supper.

Wednesday, March 12, 1980—went over to Ruth and Paul's. Steve is sure growing. Went out looking for skis.

Thursday, March 13, 1980—Darrell, Sylvia and I went to Stoney's house and bought a lot of camping equipment (Stoney was a regular customer at Cloggy's in Minneapolis, a pub Nadia owned for a few years). Drove up to Roger and Bridget's.

Friday, March 14, 1980—helped Roger work on his house for a little while, and then we went out for drinks and supper. Their son, Randy is sure growing.

Saturday, March 15, 1980—helped Roger on his house again. Went to Staples and got a screwdriver to help speed up his drywall. Randy has a new tooth.

Sunday, March 16, 1980—snowed with large heavy flakes. Helped Roger on his house and visited with Taymond and Clara Hanson who lived on our other farm.

Monday, March 17, 1980—went to Kenneth's (Adams), Larry's (Adams), Harry's (McCoy) and did a little shopping for Roger. Washed the lawn mower.

Tuesday, March 18, 1980—went to Staples, then to Harold Hanson's, then Dick Peterson's and back to Roger's.

Wednesday, March 19, 1980—went to Allen Rollins's and Ernie Hengel's, then back to Roger's and then visited Peter Ackerman's in the evening. We're sure getting' around to see old friends.

Thursday, March 20, 1980—did some shopping and checked for sled runners and tried to find some thick inner tubes at the Vo-Tech school but was not able to. Went to Brainerd, partied at Motley in the evening and played pool.

Friday, March 21, 1980—put an ad in the paper and started emptying the mobile home (it's on a smaller acreage we have).

Saturday, March 22, 1980—showed the farm to a real estate agent. He's to look after things for us and try to sell the farm. Loaded some things to take down to Minneapolis. Lots of icy roads on the way down, slippery going.

Sunday, March 23, 1980—very few calls to rent the farm. Loaded the clothes and camping stuff we bought and got to visit Nadia, Paul and Beverly's families.

Monday, March 24, 1980—up early, drove to Motley, put an ad in the Staples World and picked up the income tax papers. We're staying at Roger and Bridgette's and their son Randy.

Tuesday, March 25, 1980—worked at cleaning out the mobile home, brought a davenport down to Roger and listed the farm to sell.

Wednesday, March 26, 1980—helped Roger remove the kitchen cabinets from the house. Larry H. is razzing, and talked to Bud and Roger Etsler. Bud would like to come up to Alaska and help with the gold mining.

Thursday March 27, 1980—hauled some more household goods from the mobile home down to Roger's house and did some shopping.

Friday, March 28, 1980—went to the farm. The renter paid some rent money. Went over to Scott Rollins', visited with them and cut out some rubber snowshoe bindings. Then went up to Roger's and helped him on

10,000 Days in Alaska Book One 1978-1989

his house after supper.

Saturday, March 29, 1980—Roger and I worked on his house and my silo room at the farm. We hauled the deep freeze down to Roger's from the mobile home.

Sunday, March 30, 1980—Roger and I worked on his house and my silo room again. We hauled the dryer from out of the mobile home and over to Roger's.

Monday, March 31, 1980—worked on the silo room and hauled two loads of household goods down to Roger's, then worked on his house.

Tuesday, April 1, 1980—we put an ad in the Staples World to rent out the mobile home and worked on the silo room again on the farm. The electric motor on the planer went bad.

Wednesday, April 2, 1980—we finished the silo room roof, then went to Roger's and worked more on his house.

Thursday, April 3, 1980—worked on the kitchen cabinets at Roger's house and talked with the real estate agent about selling our farm.

Friday, April 4, 1980—cleaned up around Roger and Bridgette's house. Bridgette's mother, Donna, came to visit.

Saturday, April 5, 1980—worked some on Roger's house and worked on the water line at the mobile home of ours.

Sunday, April 6, 1980—went to Minneapolis to visit the kids.

Monday, April 7, 1980—planed some lumber at Jim Nelson's and had Giza Plumbing go out to the mobile home to fix the water problem.

Tuesday, April 8, 1980—planed more lumber for the dog sled at Jim's.

Wednesday, April 9, 1980—Jim and Gwen, Ann, and Shirley, Roger, Bridgette, Sylvia and I went to the River Inn and partied.

Thursday, April 10, 1980—got things ready to put on the auction.

Norman Wilkins

Friday, April 11, 1980—the renter and son had their machinery auctioned.

Saturday, April 12, 1980—moved more junk.

Sunday, April 13, 1980—helped on Roger's house.

Monday, April 14, 1980—went to Buffalo Lake to see Ed and Pat, to see his dairy operation. We are considering renting our farm to them.

Tuesday, April 15, 1980—we were able to collect some more back rent from the renter.

Wednesday, April 16, 1980—worked on Roger's house (it's Roger Shequen's house we've been working on).

Thursday, April 17, 1980—went to the farm, checked things out and went to town with Roger and Bridgette and shot some pool.

Friday, April 18, 1980—hauled some more stuff from the mobile home to the chicken house on the east farm. We use this old chicken house for storage.

Saturday, April 19, 1980—up to the farm and then down to the city.

Sunday, April 20, 1980—we all went to a brunch at Mai Tai in Minnetonka. It was a really nice place; we had a good time there. Nadia and Darrell and others were there. We didn't get to see Theresa and family.

Monday, April 21, 1980—lots of grass and brush fires in the area east of Staples, Minnesota and the wind is driving it towards the house where Roger and Bridgette were staying. We got a water pump and hoses ready in case it came close to this house and we loaded important things into the vehicle so we could make a run for it if necessary. The wind shifted a bit and the fire went to the other side of the road—that saved the house. Later we went to St. Cloud for an appointment with the Federal Land Bank.

10,000 Days in Alaska Book One 1978-1989

Tuesday, April 22, 1980—worked up at the farm to get things squared around there. I got some post dated checks for the rest of the back rent that was owed on the farm.

Wednesday, April 23, 1980—Nadia's birthday. We worked at the farm and the trailer house. A fellow came to look at the farm.

Thursday, April 24, 1980—Ed and Pat came to look at the farm and negotiate terms of rental.

Friday, April 25, 1980—went to Brainerd on farm business and shopped for things we needed in Alaska. Stopped by Bob and Kahren's.

Saturday, April 26, 1980—worked at the farm, getting it in shape. Bridgette's horse got loose and we helped to hunt for it. Roger and Bridgette are having a kegger for us this evening.

Sunday, April 27, 1980—still working on the keg of beer and worked on Roger's house.

Monday, April 28, 1980—went to Brainerd to do some shopping and didn't get a chance to see the FHA.

Tuesday, April 29 through Thursday, May 1, 1980—no entries.

Friday, May 2, 1980—cleaned up around the farm and saw the real estate agent.

Saturday, May 3, 1980—cleaned some more around the farm and rented quite a bit of the farm out. Roger is having trouble with his well.

Sunday, May 4, 1980—helped Roger with his well all day.

Monday, May 5, 1980—went to St. Cloud with Ernie. (He plans to buy the 40 in section 30 of our farm.)

Tuesday, May 6, 1980—had to hurry, hurry to get things packed to go to Alaska.

Wednesday, May 7, 1980—ran errands and left for Alaska about 10:30

a.m. and camped outside Regina a ways at 10:00 p.m. Sylvia is with me this trip.

Thursday, May 8, 1980—started out for Regina at midnight, slept a couple of times and stayed at a hotel in Hythe, Alberta. Arrived at 10:30 in the night.

Friday, May 9, 1980—saw a dead horse and a dead moose alongside the road. They may have been struck by a truck or vehicle. Got to Watson Lake at 8:45 p.m. and drove on 80 miles or so and slept two hours and then drove on towards Whitehorse.

Saturday, May 10, 1980—got to Whitehorse at 8:00 a.m. and drove an hour and slept 35 minutes. Drove on to Tok and got a poor meal. It was pancakes and they were soggy. Shortly after that I had a tire failure. We reached Nelchina at 11:00 p.m.

Sunday, May 11, 1980—worked on getting settled, went to Mike and Lynette's and saw the pups I'm getting from them. I gave Lynette a treadle sewing machine. I also called my mother in California.

Monday, May 12, 1980—I got more work done getting settled and got the truck titled in Alaska. Henry, Sam, Peter and I went to Chitna. When we were there, we stopped in this bar and had a beer. We were sitting at a table (not standing at the bar). Nearby in front of us was a guy sitting on a stool at the bar and he had this gash across the back of his head and blood all caked on his hair, head, neck and after a while he turned and asked who we were and introduced himself. He told us that the night before, there had been a brawl in the bar. Somebody had hit him in the back of the head with a sledgehammer handle. We stopped at Squirrel Creek campground and loafed around there for a while on our way back to Nelchina.

Tuesday, May 13, 1980—went to Mike and Lynette's and brought the puppies home. Hauled the rest of our things from Henry's green house that we used to stay in down to the cabin.

Wednesday, May 14, 1980—one pup named Oscar, got loose and we just couldn't get him to come to us. We felt the need to tie him up so he wouldn't run out to the road and get hit by a car. Mike had to bring the mother (her name was Sheila) to help catch Oscar. He came to his mother and we got him caught and tied up again. Then I varnished my snow shoes and helped Henry work on his end loader.

Thursday, May 15, 1980—helped Henry move three small buildings at the lodge and visited Dan and Patti Billman in the evening. The pups are coming along nicely.

Friday, May 16, 1980—fixed two tires for the pickup. Went to Mendeltna (KROA campground) for a supper and a party.

Saturday, May 17, 1980—leveled up a building for Henry and helped around the garage with him. That darned Oscar got loose again. He pulls his head right through the strap and wriggles out of it. This time, he allowed me to catch him.

Sunday, May 18, 1980—Oscar and Mac are both loose from their collars. Their collars were for small pups and weren't strong enough as the pups got bigger, so I got new collars for them. Mike and Lynette came to visit and see the pups and how they're doing.

Monday, May 19, 1980—went to Anchorage for needed supplies. Saw three moose from along the road.

Tuesday, May 20, 1980—back home now, slept late, did a few chores. Went up to Hoffmans and emasculated two kid billy goats for Max and Irene. They gave us a couple quarts of milk and a dozen eggs.

Wednesday, May 21, 1980—I built four dog houses for the pups.

Thursday, May 22, 1980—worked on the gas refrigerator and helped Henry around the lodge. Mike and Lynette stopped a while.

Friday May 23, 1980—worked on the cabin, made sling and installed swivels on it for use on the shotgun. Ricked some wood in a pile.

Saturday, May 24, 1980—helped Henry fix the Winnebago at the lodge. Loaded the tank and hauled gas for the lodge. Changed the filter and oil in the pickup and ricked up some more wood. Leveled a spot for the greenhouse. (We decided we would build a greenhouse.)

Sunday, May 25, 1980—visited Max and Irene Hoffman. They have surplus milk and eggs and gave us some. Then we went over to Mike and Lynette's and visited with them. Lynette made salmon pancakes—they were very good.

Monday, May 26, 1980—started building the greenhouse. I got it framed up. It's very small. It's 8 feet square and 8 feet tall.

Tuesday, May 27, 1980—worked on the frame of the greenhouse again most of the day and went on a wrecker service call with Henry.

Wednesday, May 28, 1980—worked some more on the greenhouse. Leo Ogilvy and Mike both stopped to visit. Helped Henry this evening.

Thursday, May 29, 1980—put clear fiberglass paneling and some plywood on the lower parts of the greenhouse. Then I went to Dave's for a birthday party in the evening.

Friday, May 30, 1980—slept late, put the door on the greenhouse and did some other work on it. Mike stopped by. It's been quite windy most of the day and a light shower this evening.

Saturday, May 31, 1980—had to build benches in the greenhouse. We had a shower last night and half inch of snow and ice-like hail this afternoon.

Sunday, June 1, 1980—worked on the greenhouse and visited Lucky and Mary Beaudoin. Mike and Lynette stopped and Mike and I went shopping in a couple of the local dumps. That's always fun—sometimes you find something you really need.

Monday, June 2, 1980—went back to one dump that we had been to and picked up a wheel for the big trailer that I have. Allen Farmer gave me some black dirt and I went to his place and got it, and built some more flats for the greenhouse and put the black dirt in so we can plant vegetables in it.

Tuesday, June 3, 1980—worked on the greenhouse and went to Brandt's and got a drum of Diesel fuel for the lodge. Patti Billman brought cabbage plants and eggs to our place and Bob Schmidt gave us some pea seeds and flowers to plant.

Wednesday, June 4, 1980—we moved the last of the mining equipment to our cabin. Went to Mendeltna and did laundry and talked to Roy Beaver about the 40 mile claims. Roy stops in here at Nelchina quite often. He's a really great guy.

Thursday, June 5, 1980—stored the snow machine, straightened things up and made things look neater around the cabin. Got propane for the refrigerator and got it going and did a little work on the greenhouse. Last winter I lost the snowmobile light lens and I went into the woods where I thought I had lost it on the trail and looked for it.

Friday, June 6, 1980—worked on the swamp buggy. I asked Ed Farmer to come and help me. He figured out the troubles. He's a really good mechanic, very knowledgeable. Worked on one of Henry's buildings and went to the dump for some steel and roofing that I knew was there.

Saturday, June 7, 1980—a friend of Henry's by the name of Brian (people call him Custer) and a girlfriend of his, Amanda, came to Henry's. Had a good time with them.

Sunday, June 8, 1980—Roy Beaver stopped in at the lodge. He had a native lady by the name of Addy with him. We got to visit for a while. Then I worked on the Swamp buggy some more.

Monday, June 9, 1980—still working on the swamp buggy, but I went and helped Henry with the wrecker. This is our son Paul's birthday. Called, but he and Ruth were both at work.

Tuesday, June 10, 1980—went to Anchorage and did a lot of shopping. When we go into Anchorage like that, people who know we are going will ask us to pick up things for them. It works out well for all of us.

Wednesday, June 11, 1980—worked on the swamp buggy. Henry's brother Phillip, his wife, and Phil's friend, Dave are visiting from California.

Thursday, June 12, 1980—we're going on a prospecting trip so we worked on getting the gear together for that.

Friday, June 13, 1980—went to Peter's cabin and spent the day fishing. Caught whitefish and grayling in the stream there. Peter got a really nice grayling. Then Peter showed me some old, Indian dugout holes where they cached fish, covered it with moss to keep it fresh. The ground here is frozen and it keeps fish from spoiling when they put the tundra over it to insulate it. We had a good time exploring and fishing.

Saturday, June 14, 1980—took Henry, his brother Phillip and Bill Houser in the swamp buggy to Cal Gilcrist's gold claims on Alfred Creek. While there, we got a few nuggets—got stuck twice. Henry's always upbeat about things like that and it helps get the buggy out of the mud holes. The trail is wet and slippery. Had a good time, though. On the way back out, I was coming up this stream at Pass Creek and there was a big rock and the swamp buggy wouldn't climb over that big rock. The water was really deep and Henry's brother, Phillip was riding in the swamp buggy with me and Bill Hauser was up on top of it. When I couldn't go any further, Phil, he reached out with a cup and dipped it in the stream that was running by us and got himself a drink of water. Then I had to back a long ways down the stream before I could get out of there and get on the regular trail. When we got back to Nelchina in the evening, we had a party.

Sunday June 15, 1980—slept late and went to Gunsight Mountain Lodge and drove the swamp buggy home. Mike Phelps went with me.

Monday, June 16, 1980—I had lots of work to do on the swamp buggy and worked most of the day. It has water leaking from around two bolts.

Tuesday, June 17, 1980—had a few chores to do, then went to see Patti and Dan Billman. Went with Dan to look at a sawmill. Dick and Phyllis got here from Minnesota. It was really nice to see them. They are camping in their vehicle at our place. It's raining steady.

Wednesday, June 18, 1980—still raining. Did odd jobs around the cabin and Mike came to visit. It quit raining during the night. Dick and Phyllis, I'm sure would like to have the rain quit so they can enjoy their trip and visit with us.

10,000 Days in Alaska Book One 1978-1989

Thursday, June 19, 1980—got up early and Dick and Phyllis and Sylvia and I went into Anchorage and did some shopping. I got a gold dredge in the hopes we can do some dredging with it. From the highway, we saw Dall ewes and lambs on Sheep Mountain.

Friday, June 20, 1980—went fishing at Mike and Lynette's lake and hauled water for the greenhouse and got gear ready for our trip to Tazlina Lake to show Dick and Phyllis that area. I checked on the trail to the lake since I'd never driven it before.

Saturday, June 21, 1980—we got a late start for the lake and left the highway about noon got to the lake around 4:00 p.m. Had some trouble on the trail. It was wet and steep with water running down it. We had to cut a trail in the brush to go around some of the really bad spots. It's really nice here at the lake, nice trees, and big trees. Storms have driven a lot of driftwood out on the shores of the lake. This is close to where the Mendeltna Creek comes into Tazlina Lake. A fellow by the name of Barney has a cabin here. We camped away from his place and then walked over there to his place along the shore to go fishing.

Sunday, June 22, 1980—hooked two red salmon and lost them. There was another guy there who did catch one. Broke camp at 3:00 p.m. to go back out. Had to winch to get ahead on the trail at one place. We didn't get out to the highway until 7:30 in the evening.

Monday, June 23, 1980—went to KROA Campground at Mendeltna to do the laundry. On the way there, saw a bag along the highway. We stopped to pick it up—if it's trash, it goes in the trash. Lo and behold, it was a nice sleeping bag. Water was too high in the creek to fish at Mendeltna.

Tuesday, June 24, 1980—worked on the swamp buggy, dried some gear and did some odd jobs. Then went to mile 157 on the Glen Highway and pulled Harold and Barbara who live at Mud Lake out of a mud hole. Went sailing on Snowshoe Lake with Dan in the evening.

Wednesday, June 25, 1980—put a handle in Dan's hammer. I like putting handles in tools. I've done a lot of that and understand how it should be done. Took care of two other errands and went to look over the trail to Arizona Lake.

Norman Wilkins

Thursday, June 26, 1980—did odd jobs around the cabin and went fishing at Arizona Lake. Dick and I portaged the canoe about a quarter of a mile from the highway to the lake. We caught six grayling fishing from the west shore.

Friday, June 27, 1980—did more odd jobs and made dog training harness and visited Max Hoffman and hauled water and salvaged steel for the "long tom" sluice box and fixed the welder. We had rhubarb crunch for dessert. Phyllis spends a lot of time with Sylvia teaching her some school things.

Saturday, June 28, 1980—Dick and I welded on the long tom sluice. Max Hoffman and daughter Rhynell brought us some goat milk and eggs. Dan Billman gave us an air show with his 180 on floats. Dick has had some flying lessons and he watched Dan hang the float plane in the sky right over us and Dick said, "He can't do that!" but Dan understands what the topography of the ground does when you're that close to it and the sun is shining on it. It puts a current in the air that's rising and Dan was taking advantage of that.

Sunday, June 29, 1980—finished the long tom. Peter has been out on a kayak trip. He just got back from that and has pulled tendons in his right wrist. We visited and then it started raining in the evening. Saw a big bald eagle in the afternoon riding the air currents. Went to Dan's to talk about the trail to Barnett Creek. Hauled water for the greenhouse. It takes lots of water these days.

Monday, June 30, 1980—went to see Dan Billman to talk about Barnette Creek. Hauled more water for the greenhouse.

Tuesday, July 1, 1980—Dick, Phyllis, Sylvia and I went to Anchorage. We weren't able to get all that we needed. I worked at getting camping gear ready. (Dick and I are going to go up Slide Mountain to camp.)

Wednesday, July 2, 1980—got our gear all ready. Dick and I packed up Slide Mountain and camped at the top. We did see a young moose. That was all the wildlife we saw, but the view from up there is just wonderful. Dick likes to get around some of the country here and see it from off the highway. We had a good time.

Thursday, July 3, 1980—got up early and went over to a slide area to look for fossils. Didn't have much luck. We did see black bear tracks and some caribou horns and bones. Got back to the cabin in the afternoon.

Friday, July 4, 1980—Bob Schmidt gave us some fish and moose meat and also some that was freezer burned for the dogs. We all had a big buffet breakfast and lots of fireworks and singing and guitar playing—a day of celebration of the fourth.

Saturday July 5, 1980—went down to Nelchina River and walked and found some fossils down there. Dick and I picked up some of those. We saw the tracks of thirteen different bears on the sand bar there. I shot a porcupine. They come into where we live and then my dogs get a face full of porcupine quills, so I don't like them. Then we walked up the Nelchina River a ways, just exploring and looking at things. When we decided to head back home for supper time, Dick has got a real good sense of direction, so he led the way back through the trees and brush and we came right out at our cabin.

Sunday, July 6, 1980—I loaned my canoe to Danny Chapel and did a few things around here.

Monday, July 7, 1980—worked on the Cat all day.

Tuesday, July 8, 1980—went to Anchorage for parts and supplies.

Wednesday, July 9, 1980—worked on the Cat in the morning and helped Henry build a cache in the afternoon. Henry wants a real true cache sitting out across the driveway at his lodge.

Thursday, July 10, 1980—took the pony motor off the Cat and welded up the cracked water jacket on the bottom of it. I got most of it done. It's slow going welding a cast iron water jacket.

Friday, July 11, 1980—started putting the pony motor back on the Cat. There is one place there that I can't get my hand in to get nuts started on the bolts so I got Doug, Henry's son to come. He's got small hands, he's just a boy. He could get his hand in there and get the nut started. That was a big help to me. I got it back on and then put the dredge together and tested the pump. Met Jim and Rita and Greg at Dan's.

Saturday, July 12, 1980—backpacking gear together and left after dinner. Went to Summit Lake—claims turned out to be PettyJohn's on Indian land so we came back.

Sunday, July 13, 1980—worked on one of Henry's roofs and also his cache.

Monday, July 14, 1980—worked on the roof of another building, also the cache, and then went to mile 79 to get the Blazer started and bring it back. (Betty was driving it home from Anchorage and it quit at mile 79 on the Glen Highway and she got a ride to Nelchina and asked me to go get it). Dick went with me and we got down to the Blazer and I checked the battery cables. One cable was loose. We got that fixed and Dick drove my truck and I drove the Blazer and we got everything back to the lodge. We saw three moose along the road that day.

Tuesday, July 15, 1980—A cow and calf moose walked right by our cabin. I'm working on the roof of the cache again. Dick and Phyllis want to see more of Alaska, so they loaded their gear and took off to do that. We sure enjoyed their visit here. They are fun people.

Wednesday, July 16, 1980—worked on the track carrier roller on the Cat.

Thursday, July 17, 1980—still working on the Cat roller, fixed a tire and got propane for the lodge and modified the dog stakes.

Friday, July 18, 1980—helped Henry with his end loader and then hauled sand and welded on the Cat roller—I'm rebuilding it. Went to KROA for their anniversary party. Expected Roy to be there but he didn't show up.

Saturday, July 19, 1980—still welding on the Cat roller.

Sunday, July 20, 1980—Chris Ronning flew me in his plane out to Tyone Creek and Samona Creek, and Crater Lake. Then we went over to Rocky Lake and Black Lake and walked around there and did some exploring. He showed me some interesting things. Then we flew over and around the Little and Big Oshetna rivers and Grayling Lake. He had some camping equipment out there and we picked that up at Grayling Lake.

10,000 Days in Alaska Book One 1978-1989

We saw lots of moose, some eagles and fish. Swans were on a lot of lakes with their young. We saw quite a few ducks and there's mining operations working out there that we could see from the air. It was a beautiful day and a great flight. When we left Black Lake to go to Grayling Lake, the plane was laboring too hard to get up through a pass there with the way the wind was and his plane started to overheat, so he dropped back down in elevation and flew below the strong wind and flew through this slot in the mountains, resulting in a cooler engine. Saw lots of moose today.

Monday, July 21, 1980—worked on the Cat, welded two horseshoe puzzles and some D-rings for the dog harness. Went fishing, caught a trout and worked on a car at Henry's garage (sometimes when travelers have car trouble, the lodge will ask me to come up and see if I can help these people in some way). I am not much of a mechanic, but I can do some things.

Tuesday July 22, 1980—went fishing with no luck. Stopped and visited at Max and Irene's they're such nice people. Hauled water for the cabin and the greenhouse and got ready to take Henry to Homer to bring back his truck.

Wednesday, July 23, 1980—reached Homer about 5:00 a.m. (it's about and 8 hour trip). Got up at 8:00 a.m. and got his truck off the ferry—Henry drove it back. We started back to Nelchina—stopped to fish several times but didn't have any luck. Some friends, Chad and Trish, live in Birdwood. We stopped to see them, but they weren't home so we went on to Anchorage and camped there.

Thursday, July 24, 1980—got up early and got our business done in town and were back at Nelchina by 6:00 p.m. Got information on freighting equipment in to the gold miners—I'm thinking of trying that for a while.

Friday, July 25, 1980—did some odd jobs around here and put a fan belt on a pickup for Henry at the lodge garage. Started training the pups to pull a sled by pulling light weights around behind them.

Saturday, July 26, 1980—Mike and I went to Eureka and Gunsight to check out the fuel freighting trails. It's really wet this year and the trails are very poor. We talked to a fella that was operating a Cat for a gold miner and he said they are having a lot of trouble hauling fuel.

Sunday, July 27, 1980—helped Henry switch dry vans and reefers on two different trucks.

Monday, July 28, 1980—we got the reefer mounted on one truck and then worked on the swamp buggy. A surveyor stopped by and he brought the hole driller that I am to haul on the swamp buggy.

Tuesday, July 29, 1980—got up early. Doug and I test out the drill. This is to test for percolation on Slide Mountain for a proposed state land sale. We tested out the drill before we started up on the mountain to do that. It worked when it was properly mounted on the swamp buggy. Darrel got out here about 11:00 a.m. and we started for Slide Mountain. They hired me because of my equipment and my knowledge of the mountain. We didn't get started until about 12:00 noon and we quit at 7:00 p.m. We came down off of the mountain and Chad Wilson showed up that evening to visit.

Wednesday, July 30, 1980—we left the lodge at 8:00 a.m. to go up on the mountain. It was pretty tough going in this area. I had to winch once to get the swamp buggy out of a wet place with big hummocks. About 11:30 that morning, I'm crossing one of these bad places and I had an anti-roll bolt shear off in the articulation joint between the swamp buggy cab and front end and the back end. When this bolt sheared, the cab just laid over on its left side in the swamp. This fella that was with me, he is hanging on the window on his side at the door to keep from landing on top of me. We got his door open and got out of the swamp buggy. Neither one of us was hurt, but this was discouraging.

Thursday, July 31, 1980—I worked at getting the Cat ready to go up on the mountain to get the swamp buggy—I need the Cat to pull the swamp buggy back up to where all the wheels are on the tundra. Then Roy Beaver called about the prospecting trip to the Thirty Mile country. Later, Roger Shequen called. We talked a while. He watches over the farm and properties, takes care of things for us down there in Minnesota. He lived with us for 4 ½ years when he was still in public school.

Friday, August 1, 1980—I drove the Cat up Slide Mountain, pulled the swamp buggy back up on its wheels, and put a new shear bolt in the articulation and got back to the highway. Then Henry needed help with a couple jobs. He went with me up with the swamp buggy. We went up to the Cat, started it and he drove it down the mountain. Roy Beaver called again and we made some plans.

Saturday, August 2, 1980—Roy didn't come. We don't know what happened. Henry and I worked on the cache for his lodge. Charlie Trowbridge and another friend Steve, came to Nelchina. It was nice to see Charlie again.

Sunday, August 3, 1980—worked on Henry's cache for the lodge again. Blake got back yesterday. Mike, Lynette, Laura and Sylvia and I went to Don McKee's to the State Black Powder Jubilee that was held there this afternoon. It's real fun to walk around and see these mountain men, their tents and fires. They have competitions shooting, throwing axes, the usual things that the mountain men of yesteryear amused themselves with when they all got together.

Monday, August 4, 1980—worked on the swamp buggy again—seems like I'm always fixing something on it.

Tuesday, August 5, 1980—finished work on the swamp buggy. Roy brought Wyatt Towner up here to Nelchina. There's a gold area out of boundary that Roy's been telling me about. This Wyatt is a son of a friend of Roy's. He wants us to go up and check this out and probably stake it if it's good. Wyatt and I went to Tok and on the way we stopped and talked to Jim and Jimmy Fry. They have a station on the Alaska Highway where they fix tires and that sort of thing. They are very knowledgeable about the country around there.

Wednesday, August 6, 1980—talked to Jim Kato and then went to the Bureau of Land Management and got maps of where we were going. Then we went up to Taylor Highway to "Boundry". We stopped and talked to a miner who was prospecting the Sixty Mile and it looked futile. He wasn't having any luck finding gold so we went back down the road.

Thursday, August 7, 1980—waded across the South Fork River and prospected a creek there without any luck. So we went on to the town of Chicken, got gas and camped a few miles down the road from there and slept overnight. We found out that somebody had beaten us into the place we wanted to go and it was already taken.

Friday, August 8, 1980—we headed for home and came across a truck driver that was pulled over on this narrow dirt road. We stopped to see if he needed any help. He had a flat tire and couldn't get the wheel off of the truck and put a spare on alone, so the three of us got on this wheel wrench and we got the nuts loose and got the wheel changed for him. Previous to this, the doors on his trailer had opened and he had lost a lot of his load from out of the back end. I offered to take him down the road and we'd try to find things that he had lost. He had lost 18 tanks of oxygen and some gas and tools. We did find some stuff and we found empty boxes as though someone had come along and taken whatever happened to be in them and just left the boxes. Then we went back up to the truck with the things we had recovered and my truck we had offloaded onto his trailer and at that time he tells me that he's expecting the owner of this load to be coming along with his crew. They're going to start mining. He said "I hope they don't see your truck backed up to this trailer and we're moving his property. They'll think we're trying to steal it." But we got his stuff back in the truck and Wyatt and I leave to go to Tok. I had told this fella that I would look for more stuff along the highway and if I found it, I'd leave it at Roy's gas station and he could pick it up there. That was all right with him, he was happy. We got down the road a little ways and we were looking for stuff that might have rolled over the edge of the bank and here come several vehicles and 7 or 8 people. This guy comes over to me and said, "What are you doing?" I said "Some guy lost a bunch of stuff out of his truck" and I told him everything I found, I was going to leave at this filling station. He gets real upset at me and I didn't have a very long fuse and I put him in his place. I felt real bad that he didn't appreciate that we were trying to help and I told him so. Anyway, we got down to Tok and Henry had an El Camino there that he wanted pulled to Nelchina so we hooked on to it and started out. We got back as far as Jim Frye's and pulled in there to get a tire fixed. (We had a flat tire and he fixed it for us.) Then we left for Nelchina and got there that night.

Saturday, August 9, 1980—put away some of the gear and worked on the pickup. That night was Henry's birthday party (his birthday is tomorrow).

Sunday, August 10, 1980—went to Gunsight and hauled gas back for the lodge and rested up from the party.

10,000 Days in Alaska Book One 1978-1989

Monday, August 11, 1980–did laundry at Mendeltna and got hunting and trapping license at Tazlina.

Tuesday, August 12, 1980–went fishing in Mendeltna creek on Oilwell road. We got 20 salmon (We can the meat). Walked in to Peter's cabin to check it for him and it was okay.

Wednesday, August 13, 1980–went salmon fishing again and Scott, Doug and I, we got nine and we canned them that night. Nine fish made eleven quarts, canned.

Thursday, August 14, 1980–Chad, Trish and Frank Wilson came. Chad and family and Sylvia and I went to Lila Lake near Gunsight and caught a few grayling. Chad and I and the boys went across the lake to an outlet and fished there and the grayling were just thick! Mike P. tells me that fish and game stocked rainbows in his and other lakes in the area. Crater Lake for one, and Round Lake too, on the Lake Louise Road. In later years they maintained that and it is good fishing.

Friday, August 15, 1980–hauled more gas for the lodge. Chad went with us to Arizona Lake (it's a grayling lake) but today the fishing was poor. We stopped and visited Mike and Lynette on the way home.

Saturday, August 16, 1980–Went to see Dan Billman and helped kill eleven chickens. Sylvia is an old hand at butchering chickens. They wanted her there to show them how to do it. Met Denny Billman, Dan's brother, and his step-father Loyd. Dan's mother and step father own Anchorage Tank. Seemed like a really nice guy and we grew to be friends.

Sunday, August 17, 1980–Mike and Lynette needed help moving a refrigerator and a freezer.

Monday, August 18, 1980–helped at the lodge again and Sylvia picked a few blueberries. Sylvia was across the highway at the base of Slide Mountain on her hands and knees picking blueberries, engrossed in her work, when suddenly she feels something at her behind. She's thinking, "Oh my gosh, it must be a bear!" But when she turned, it was the lodge dog–whose name happened to be "Bear". It sure frightened her.

Tuesday, August 19, 1980—helped Mike and Lynette move. Stopped at Max and Irene Hoffman's and had a nice visit. Seems like they always give us something when we stop to visit them. They gave us five quarts of goat milk and two dozen eggs and they have strawberries from their garden, they gave us some of those. We really like these people; they're a long time in Alaska and homesteaded many years ago. Their homestead is 160 acres and they came up to this area from Florida, moved their household and everything they owned up here on a truck.

Wednesday, August 20, 1980—helped Henry fix seven truck tires. A contractor brought in these truck tires—that is quite a job all at one time. After we got that done, we pulled the rear end out of a bus that Henry had sitting along the shop. He's using the bus for parts storage. This bus will never be on the road again.

Thursday, August 21, 1980—went to Copper Center with Bob Schmidt to camp. He has permission to use a fish wheel and he's taking us with him. We got the fish wheel going and went to eat. While we were gone, we got some fish, some red salmon and one great big king. (He was over 50 inches.)

Friday, August 22, 1980—we got 47 salmon overnight including the one big king. We gave a lot of the fish away and watched the fish wheel catch two salmon, had coffee and started filleting salmon. We got done at 9:15 and went to check the other wheel. Someone had beaten us to it and we only got five salmon. Bob takes these salmon when I hand them up to him in plastic 5-gallon buckets. Sylvia canned salmon and some mushrooms.

Saturday, August 23, 1980—I helped Henry get his equipment repaired. The fuel pump is out on my truck and the radiator is leaking. They had live music down at KROA so we went to that.

Sunday, August 24, 1980—I worked at getting gear on the swamp buggy ready for a sheep and caribou hunt combined with some prospecting.

Monday, August 25, 1980—finished getting ready for the hunting trip. Mike and I left at 3 p.m. We got to Crooked Creek and the Little Nelchina confluence at 8 p.m. and camped for the night. I got stuck and had to winch out once. We saw a caribou, but it was so early in the hunt, we didn't want to shoot it. We expect to be out here for about three weeks.

Tuesday, August 26, 1980—up at 6 a.m., broke camp at 9:00, reached Flat Creek at 11:00 and went on to McDougal creek. Went up McDougal 3.5 miles, prospecting on the way and glassed for sheep and camped. Saw one caribou.

Wednesday, August 27, 1980—went up a mountain of rotten rock, held together with very little moss. We got up on the shoulder of that mountain and sat down to rest for a while. We were looking the country over and we saw a wolf—this wolf had a white tail tip, much like that of a red fox. We watched this wolf and he seems to be going somewhere, but he's hunting as he goes along. Pretty soon we see him get very cautious and he circles around, finally he goes in to feed on a caribou that a bear has killed—but he's always looking around in fear that the bear will come along, but it doesn't show up. He fed for a while until he took the antlers in his teeth and dragged them off for a ways and kind of worked at that. The last we saw of him that day he was going off to the north. Then we went on up the mountain. We had to cross—I guess you'd call it a slice or crack in the mountain. The rocks are rotten here. This kind of rock, when exposed to oxygen, gets rotten, and it's so steep there, it rolled down this chute. We crossed on the upper end of it on snow and we get over to the other side and crawl up there. We can see a lot of country out there. All we saw was ewes and lambs, no rams. We decided there was no sheep to hunt here, so we back off and get back to this chute and we want to cross it but the snow is no longer frozen and it's soft from the heat of the day. We had a little trouble getting around it and we got across it to the other side and we climb out and we go over to the shoulder of this mountain and we start to go down that shoulder and it does not feel good to us. The rocks are rotten. Didn't give us any trouble climbing up but, going down—and it's so far down that if one of us slipped and fell, we'd roll for a long ways. So we went back up on top of the shoulder to decide what to do. We went back over to this chute and I tested the rocks along the side we were on. I could pull them loose and drop them and they'd roll down this chute. But out in the middle of this chute there was solid rock. I told Mike, "I'm going out on that and see what it looks like from out there." I went out on that and it was solid and after a few minutes of mulling this dilemma over, I told Mike I thought we could go down this chute (the loose rock was something like a couple

Norman Wilkins

feet deep or so) and I thought I could walk down it, sliding all the time, of course, and the rock's going to be moving and we'd have to keep our feet moving and not fall. It took Mike some time to decide he wanted to do that and we decided to go. I started down in the center of this. I would pull my foot up and take a great big long step and then the next foot and all the time sliding, a pack on my back and a rifle. It went really well and I could see down there that there was a bulge out from the mountain and this chute makes a slight turn there and I aimed my downward movement to come to that bulge so I could stop there and look things over. Mike, he's coming down and when I got to that bulge, why it looked good from there on down so I continued on down. Then Mike came down. It turned out fine.

Thursday, August 28, 1980—this day we decided to go through the pass to the west and, by gosh we saw this gray wolf with the white tipped tail again. He was hunting on a mountain over in that area. We got out to the end of the pass and it's a vertical drop to the little creek on that side. We didn't go down—no way for a man to get down there. We glassed for game for a while and watched the country, really nice there, but we didn't see any game—no sheep.

Friday, August 29, 1980—we got the dredge off the top of the swamp buggy and put it to work in two places on McDougall Creek. We got some gold, but it's fastened to a darker material-tried a magnet on it and decided it was mixed with iron and could be magnetized. We did catch one grayling.

Saturday, August 30, 1980—Mike and I dredged again in McDougall Creek and today again, we had poor luck finding any gold. The gray wolf fed on the bear kill again. Charlie had a pilot fly him over us. They landed down at the confluence with the Little Nelchina where the pilot let Charlie off. Mike and I went to meet him. I broke a wheel on the swamp buggy at Flat Creek. It was pretty dark by the time we got Charlie to our camp—good to see him.

Sunday, August 31, 1980—Mike left for Gunsight Mountain to get my welder so we could fix the wheel on the swamp buggy. Meantime, Charlie and I hunted caribou. Saw three and didn't shoot.

Monday, September 1, 1980—I saw a large bull and cow, but it was too far to shoot. Charlie saw a cow and a calf but didn't want to shoot those. We sighted in his rifle. It rained and blew hard and then a few flakes of snow. It's pretty cold up in these mountains tonight.

Tuesday, September 2, 1980—up early and hunted off to the north. We walked up a creek there quite some distance. Brought our lunch with us. Saw a pinnacle of rock—an outcropping quite tall and it had lots of white eagle pooh on it. An eagle was sitting up there looking the country over. We walked a little farther and there was an esker (gravel esker) sticking up not too awfully high and it had a really sharp peak on its top. I decided to walk down this. Charlie followed me. We were walking along and I saw this interesting rock—it's been broke in two. It was a three-toed dinosaur track. This rock was made out of mud, water and pressure at some time in the distant past. I picked up the two pieces that make the dinosaur track and put them in my pack. We ate our lunch and headed south and east. We saw some more caribou that were too far away to shoot. We shot some ptarmigan, boiled it up and ate the meat. We boiled everything on this ptarmigan, all the little bones and we drank the broth from that—really was good. (One day when we were out hunting ptarmigan, I had a 12 gage shotgun and Charlie carried a rifle. We'd switch off shooting. When I shot a ptarmigan, why then I'd give him the shotgun and I'd take his rifle and he's shoot the next ptarmigan and so on. We were walking up through the willows and we came upon a six foot grizzly. All I saw at first was just his head. He had heard us coming and was looking at me. Then he stood up and I said "Bear!" to warn Charlie that there was a bear close by. Charlie couldn't tell from that whether or not the bear was coming at us, so he was backpedaling. When the bear stood up and saw there was two of us, the thing reeled and ran. Charlie said afterwards he was concerned that he was handling a strange gun and was wishing he had his familiar .30-06 in his hands when I hollered "bear". Here I am holding his .30-06, not familiar with it—and I wished I had my shotgun! But nothing came of it and we got back to camp and dressed out the ptarmigan and had our supper.)

Wednesday, September 3, 1980—Charlie had breakfast and walked out to the strip on the Little Nelchina to meet Whitey, the pilot. Whitey will fly him out to the highway. He's sorry to have to leave us, but he must. I hunted ptarmigan and got five. Mike came back in the early afternoon. He had made arrangements to have a fellow with a swamp buggy bring the welder to us.

Norman Wilkins

Thursday, September 4, 1980—did camp chores, then Mike and I walked the six miles to Little Nelchina airstrip. We were waiting for Ray to show up with the welder. On the way I saw three ptarmigan. He didn't come, so we walked back to camp with our packs.

Friday, September 5, 1980—we rested up some and tied the dredge up on top of the buggy. Dug a garbage hole, buried our garbage, did some target shooting, carried in wood and caught four trout and two graylings.

Saturday, September 6, 1980—swamp buggy isn't here with the welder and it's been several days. We're wondering where it's at, so I left camp at 11:30 a.m. and walked 27 miles looking for Ray, not knowing just exactly what trail he might have taken to get to us. The last hour of walking was in the dark and as I came up on a long swamp, all I could see is the water in each track (vehicle track) shining from the stars. I decided to camp along the trail. I'm carrying a pack, sleeping bag, hip boots and some grub. I lay down along the trail on a small piece of canvas (in my sleeping bag) and pull the canvas around over the top of my sleeping bag (in case we get a shower in the night) and go to sleep. During the day I had seen a two cow moose, and one calf and a very large bear track, along with lots of broken down ATV's and swamp buggies. (There are lots of hunters traveling now and this country is hard on vehicles.)

Sunday, September 7, 1980—I was up real early and walked the last three miles out to the highway and hitched a ride to Nelchina. At Nelchina, I got reorganized and went to Gunsight Lodge. Whitey flew me to the confluence of the Little Nelchina and Flat Creek, where I waited again for Ray for several hours. While I'm waiting, I'm walking around this large gravel bar that Whitey landed his plane on and I found a rock that is called a thunder egg. I kept looking and found eight of them. If you cut these rocks in half, they are beautiful in the center. I gather these all up and I have them ready right beside my pack so I can take them with me when Whitey comes, but somehow I didn't pick them up and take them when I left. When I got to the camp at Flat Creek, the welder had already been delivered.

Monday, September 8, 1980—got up real early and welded the buggy wheel back together, mounted it on the buggy and loaded up our camp.

10,000 Days in Alaska Book One 1978-1989

Mike feels that his wife would like to have him back home now. On the way out to the highway we saw three caribou. On the Nelchina, there was a huge piece of petrified tree (I had seen it previously) that I thought I could lift and put on the back of the swamp buggy to take back with us. As we went down the trail, I lost track of where it was and we got past it, so I didn't turn around to go back and look for it again. It was going to be dark anyhow. Even so, it got quite dark on the trail the last hour that we were coming out. When we got out to Cal's, Ray Kole was there. Ray is the man that brought the welder out for me. We visited there for a while.

Tuesday, September 9, 1980—went to Gunsight and saw Sylvia. (She's been working there and rather than drive the 20 mile back and forth each way, she would stay overnight and work another day.) Then we stopped at Cal's and drove the buggy home. Mike and I unloaded the gear and got him ready to go home. Dan Billman stopped by and then I went back to Gunsight and stayed the night with Sylvia.

Wednesday, September 10, 1980—went to Billmans, then to the Hoffmans and got Max's mower going. He has a mower for his tractor and I've farmed for so many years, I know something about mowers. I helped him with a few little jobs there and stayed for supper and they gave me some milk and eggs to take home.

Thursday, September 11, 1980—got up early and worked with the dogs, getting in some training. Helped at the garage until afternoon, then built a stove and a tub to heat water out of a 55-gallon drum. I'm going to heat my hickory lumber for the sled runners to get a bend in them at the front. Then when that's done, I'll boil and dye traps in the tub for trapping this winter. Saw Charley T. for a while today and Sylvia.

Friday, September 12, 1980—boiled the hickory sled runners all day and worked at the lodge. Made a form for the runners and went and got Sylvia.

Saturday, September 13, 1980—finished steaming the runners. The wood was so dry, it was hard to get them to the point where they would bend. Possibly I boiled them too long. Then I boiled the traps in dye and fixed the tire for the trailer for the swamp buggy. Waxed the traps, and it's raining. Did laundry at Mendeltna and visited people there. Then I took my swamp buggy up another creek and trail. I came across another swamp buggy that had gotten badly stuck. They pulled the winch so tight that they couldn't get the cable loose. I had to pull them ahead into the swamp farther so that the cable could be loosened and get if off of this tree and pull them out of the swamp. Then I had the winch to work on. They were hunters going out moose hunting.

Sunday, September 14, 1980—went to Dennis and Sally's cabin on Tazlina Lake. Pretty nice cabin. I also went to look at Bob Schmidt's cabin on the same lake, then Sylvia had to go back to work at Gunsight, so I took her over there. I came across Ray Kole's. His machine was broken down and he had two other hunters with him. I took him and these other fellows back to Gunsight and then went home and worked on the dog sled.

Monday, September 15, 1980—bent more hickory for the dog sled and sighted in the .338 rifle. Did cabin chores and started getting gear together to fly out in the bush to hunt and look for a trapline cabin site.

Tuesday, September 16, 1980—bent more wood for the sled and got laundry dry. Went to Dan's with my gear and he flew me over lots of the area looking for trapper cabin sites. Landed me at Nye Lake. (I plan to hunt moose and caribou here). Got my tent up and made camp.

Wednesday, September 17, 1980—got up early and went out. Came close to a bear that was feeding. I heard him first and backed away. Saw over 20 caribou, but nothing nice or in range. Saw two caribou bull fights, saw an owl and spruce hens and two eagles. Dan flew over to check and see that I was all right. There was a beautiful sunset, and two moose fighting at that time.

Thursday, September 18, 1980—I saw three caribou a quarter mile from camp, but they winded me and left. Saw some loons on this lake and a few duck, and a real pretty hawk. It's very windy, though nice in the sun. Walked quite a ways today and discouraged tonight. There is lots of bear sign in this area and I'm not getting any hunting done with game so scarce.

Friday, September 19, 1980—got up early and went out hunting. Ran into a fella (Bill) who was looking for another guy that was lost. I showed him the area where I was camping and hunting and where I'd heard a bear and they checked all that out and didn't find this man. Scott, Chris, Henry and Dan flew in. Scott wanted to stay and hunt, so he and I went hunting. We didn't have any luck hunting, but I found a place that I think will be a great spot to build a trapper cabin. I like the country there.

Saturday, September 20, 1980—got up early, it's a really nice day. Scott and I hunted and we got a spruce hen and missed one. Saw some ducks and came across two wolf dens, but no other big game. Went to Maxom Lake and Bill (the man who was looking for a friend) found out that the friend had walked out to the highway. That turned out okay.

Sunday, September 21, 1980—it snowed in the night one inch and then snowed and some rain during the day. We hunted a little and waited for Dan Billman to pick us up. He came and got us and we were back at Nelchina about 7:00 p.m. Went on down to Gunsight to see Sylvia and stayed over night.

Monday, September 22, 1980—it drizzled all night and day and the dogs are getting muddy. I had wet gear from the trip and it took all day to dry that stuff out.

Tuesday, September 23, 1980—cleaned up around here and started getting ready for winter. It's not too early to do that now.

Wednesday, September 24, 1980—got four pickup loads of wood for Libby Riddles. She wants this wood and in return, will let me use a lead dog to help train my pups. Charlie came along on the last load and helped me with it. That happened to be the load we got stuck. Had to unload the wood and Henry came to pull me out but had no luck. Tired tonight.

Thursday, September 25, 1980—got the pickup winched out with the swamp buggy, then went to Anchorage for materials and supplies. Charlie and Judy Phillips went along. I came back alone and stopped at Gunsight and stayed the night with Sylvia.

Friday, September 26, 1980—getting ready for winter, getting gear organized and materials ready to take to the bush to build a cabin.

Norman Wilkins

Saturday, September 27, 1980—Mike and Lynette's wedding today—Reception and party afterwards.

Sunday, September 28, 1980—picked up and got things ready here for winter and rested up.

Monday, September 29, 1980—worked on getting supplies and gear and so forth ready to go to build the cabin.

Tuesday, September 30, 1980—still working on getting the gear ready—made some stretcher boards.

Wednesday, October 1, 1980—sawed plywood sheets in half lengthways ready to be loaded on the pontoons of a super cub airplane, and got some of the gear loaded in the pickup.

Thursday, October 2, 1980—started building the dog sled and near sundown, I cut some grass hay for dog bedding. It snowed southwest of us along the mountain. With the sun shining through, the snow looked like a fire—really beautiful.

Friday, October 3, 1980—worked on the dog sled. It snowed and rained today. I called Jim.

Saturday, October 4, 1980—pretty nice today and I worked on the dog sled again. We're going to the Pollack party at Tolsona creek at Blackie's. Paul called; Lee and Barb want to rent a house from us there in Minnesota.

Sunday, October 5, 1980—worked on the sled and got the mortise and tenon joints done and the planeing and tied six joints with rawhide.

Monday, October 6, 1980—worked on the sled until 10:30. Ronning called to fly us to the trap cabin site. Sylvia is going there with me. We hurried to pack, started to fly at 2 p.m. with three loads. I made four packs to camp and set up a tent. Sylvia saw caribou and moose.

Tuesday, October 7, 1980—I packed seven loads from Hole Lake from where Chris had unloaded it. He flew in with another load while I was packing these in to where the cabin will be built. This is a steep grade, at least 100 feet above Hole Lake and a little more than a quarter mile of tundra and brush to get through after that. The stove was one of the last things—it was very clumsy and heavy to pack for our camp. It rained last night, but it's very nice today. It's too windy though at Snowshoe Lake for Chris to fly in the plywood.

Wednesday, October 8, 1980—I packed four more loads from Hole Lake to our camp, saw 12 caribou, decided on the cabin site and the cache site and packed 2 more loads. Got pretty well along with the cache.

Thursday, October 9, 1980—just finished the cache and it started snowing. I rushed to build a tarp lean-to and put gear into it for a cook camp. Set up the airtight stove and put extra food up in the cache. It's 12 feet up off the tundra. Then we got a snowstorm of 4 inches.

Friday, October 10, 1980—started sawing the base logs and the chain saw quit, and then broke the mill attachment for sawing lumber. It just popped so easy. Got the saw fixed so it runs and I packed a can of gas in the morning from Hole Lake and then Chris flew in the plywood towards evening. I ran over to Hole Lake to meet him and help unload the plywood and I packed a can of gas back to the camp and I carried one bag of traps up to the top out of Hole Lake and cached it in a clump of black spruce. It was borderline flying for Chris, but he got our plywood to us before freeze-up. I told him how grateful I was that he was able to get this done for me. I really like Chris.

Saturday, October 11, 1980—it was a beautiful sunrise and 1° all day. We dragged the foundation logs to the site and got them into position and got seven floor joist mortised into them. Sylvia still has a sore throat. Cleared some brush and sided logs. I lost my tape measure somewhere.

Sunday, October 12, 1980—up early, beautiful day, hunted caribou (they evaded us). Saw a martin, mink, fox and porcupine tracks. Packed eight of the half sheets of plywood to camp (two packs), and finished the floor joists and nailed the plywood floor down. It's turned cloudy.

Monday, October 13, 1980—I two-sided 14 logs, peeled 9 and cut 15 more. Cut firewood and packed in eight, 2 x 8 sheets of plywood from Hole Lake. I'm very tired. Sylvia's cold is a little better. Luckily I found the tape measure and I won't have to guess—I can measure my logs and lumber. It's cloudy and the geese are flying south at night—we can hear them.

Tuesday, October 14, 1980—I went hunting and saw a cow moose and calf. Caribou had been near camp, there were more martin track and Sylvia's cold is much better. No luck hunting.

Wednesday, October 15, 1980—up early, warmer and sunny. Cut lots of trees today, sawed lumber for a door, table and so forth—and two-side logs.

Thursday, October 16, 1980—peeled and hauled logs to the cabin with the little puka sled. Sylvia hauls the logs from the wood lot where I'm cutting them. I cut them down and two-side them. They're six feet long. I put two in the puka and she has a rope that goes over her chest. She pulls these logs to the cabin and unloads them and comes back for the next two. This one time, she's just ready to start out and I clicked my cheeks on my teeth and (like you do when you tell a horse to start and pull). Sylvia, she stopped, turned, looked at me, stuck her finger at me and said, "Don't do that again!". I didn't. I shot a spruce hen for supper and there were more geese flying south. We can hear them especially at night. Two wolves were howling this morning, they sounded really close. They must have been young wolves and didn't know what we were. They weren't very far from our camp, knew we were there and were howling. We put up a wall of the cabin today.

Friday, October 17, 1980—breakfast was over by daylight. Put up another wall, cut a window and put up a few logs on the next wall. I don't have a drill to drill holes and I have to drive the logs together with these big log spikes with a three pound hammer. Cut 30 more logs. (It's partly cloudy and a nice temperature to work.) Cut and trimmed most of the rafters, light snow this evening.

Saturday, October 18, 1980—up early, two-sided logs until 3 p.m., then spiked some to the cabin. Occasional light snow, really a warm and nice day. Sylvia pulled all of today's logs in on the puka sled.

Sunday, October 19, 1980—two-sided more logs and finished the walls and cut another window, sawed boards for the door, and put the plates on top of the logs. It's been a nice warm day.

Monday, October 20, 1980—finished putting up the end logs, the ridgepole and started the rafters. We put the plywood sheeting on the rafters as we went along. Finished the roof on the east side and got three rafters and two plywood sheets on the west side. Sylvia really likes the cabin shaping up. One night when we were sleeping in the tent, we could hear something walking around outside it. She was really concerned about what might be walking towards the tent. Listening, I knew it was a porcupine. If you've ever seen a porcupine walk, you'll know what it sounds like in the snow.

Tuesday, October 21, 1980—finished the roof on the east side and got three rafters and two plywood sheets on the west side. Chris Ronning flew in and landed with wheels on our little lake. It's frozen over now. I got in some firewood while he went after oil and insulation for us. (He brought back a bottle of whiskey.) Then he took off just as it was getting really dark. Before he left, he asked me to cut down two trees farther out, away from the lake in the landing line and take off strip.

Wednesday, October 22, 1980—I packed in more plywood, finished putting up the rafters, and ceiling, built the door and put in the windows. We moved the stove here and moved into the cabin to sleep. I am more pleased with it every day. We had a beautiful sunset. Sylvia is very glad to have solid walls to sleep behind.

Thursday, October 23, 1980—got up late, nice to be in the cabin. Got the press plates tarred and put onto the roof—these press plates are aluminum sheets that the newspaper press in Anchorage has left over when they publish their daily paper. I tarred in between the plates as I put them on the roof. Then we got some firewood in, cut and stacked up. After that, we chinked on the inside of the cabin until 11:30 p.m. We have a Coleman lantern so we have light at night.

Friday, October 24, 1980—chinked more logs, packed plywood and sawed lumber and built the kitchen, bunks and went hunting. Saw a small hawk, and huge bear tracks (measured two inches longer than my shoes). Saw no game today and chinked more logs in the evening by the light of the Coleman lantern.

Norman Wilkins

Saturday, October 25, 1980—we had breakfast before daybreak. It's frosty and foggy and I went hunting for a while with no luck. Built a bench and table. Put some finishing touches on the inside and out of the cabin. Hunted up some more trees to cut for firewood. Chinked some more tonight.

Sunday, October 26, 1980—foggy and frosty again. Cut eight dead trees and cut up and stacked the wood. Saw a big hawk. We chinked on the cabin and built a sawbuck to buck up wood for heating. Put metal guards around the trees that the cache is in to keep varmints from crawling up and getting inside. I have two 55-gallon drums up there on the cache to put food and other things—protect them from the weather and varmints.

Monday, October 27, 1980—took Sylvia to a hill to see the great view from there. Cut and stacked more wood and built five dog houses and put up the cable to tie the dogs (bedded down with spruce boughs). Really tired tonight.

Tuesday, October 28, 1980—I did a few finishing touches and Chris flew in this morning to fly us out. Sure hate to leave the cabin. We landed at Billman's, ate dinner and then went to Nelchina. Partied this evening.

Wednesday, October 29, 1980—went to Bob Schmidt's, he gave Henry and I some deer hides and some venison. Did not get much else done.

Thursday, October 30, 1980—got up early, worked on the skis and the dog sled. The truck won't start. Dan Chappel dropped me off at Billman's and I sawed out two more slats for the sled.

Friday, October 31, 1980—went to Anchorage for supplies and brought a sled for Mark out from Nelchina.

Saturday, November 1, 1980—measured the dogs for harness and borrowed Billman's scale to weight them. Got water at Cache Creek and got a load of wood from nearby at Old Man Lake Trail. Went to Dennis and Sally's cabin on Tolsona Lake for a party.

Sunday, November 2, 1980—slept until noon and went to Hoffman's and butchered a billy goat for them. The meat is so strong they gave the meat to me for dog food. We had supper with them.

10,000 Days in Alaska Book One 1978-1989

Monday, November 3, 1980— it snowed an inch and a half. Cut up the goat meat and put rawhide on the dog sled to tie the joints together and put slides on the runners and side rails and so forth.

Tuesday, November 4, 1980—we voted. Put rawhide on the driving bow and brush bow and tied the driving bow on the sled. Made false stanchions for the front part of the runners and steamed wood to laminate the front of runners. Varnished the sled.

Wednesday, November 5, 1980—worked on the sled—nearly finishing now. Weather is still quite warm.

Thursday, say November 6, 1980—went to Jackie and Ken's. They will pick up supplies and dog harnesses for me in Anchorage when they go to town. Stopped at Dan and Patti's and worked more on the sled. Mike and Lynette got back from Minnesota, Peter from Germany, and Charlie from Texas.

Friday, November 7, 1980—got a kidney stone obstruction in the middle of the night. It was quite painful. Sylvia dressed and went up to Henry's and woke him up at the lodge and asked if he would drive me to the hospital in Glennallen. I was sick with this all day and night there at the hospital.

Saturday, November 8, 1980—in the morning, I felt somewhat better. They took x-rays. I decided to go home. Henry brought Sylvia in to town and the hospital let me go home with them. On the way home, we stopped at Lake Louise Junction at Cora's (she has a restaurant and a filling station). I went to the outhouse there to take a leak and I passed the stone. Good!

Sunday, November 9, 1980—it was -17° this morning. Took care of some dog meat and varnished the dog sled. (I'm working on the sled up at the lodge in their shop.)

Monday, November 10, 1980—went with Henry, Sam, Scott and Charlie to get logs for the new lodge for Betty. We cut seventy five lodge logs and some others for firewood. Henry bought Sylvia and me a drink and our supper—tired tonight.

Norman Wilkins

Tuesday, November 11, 1980—Henry, Charlie, Scott and I cut a lot more logs. I brought a load of wood home.

Wednesday, November 12, 1980—cut and stacked the wood, got the trailer ready for Henry to use. Went to Glennallen and licensed the trailer and did a little shopping for us and for Charlie. There is a party here for Mike and Lynette tonight and we stopped to visit Ken and Jackie Kramer.

Thursday, November 13, 1980—just before dark, we went to the wood lot and loaded logs and firewood and hauled them home. Sam gave me *When Alaska Was Free* by Knut Peterson. Very good book.

Friday, November 14, 1980—put a handle in the single bit ax, cut and stacked a pick-up load of wood. Put the bridle on the dog sled, looked the trail over to run the dogs and made up six pair of snow shoe bindings. Ken stopped by with some money for us.

Saturday, November 15, 1980—hitched and ran some of the dogs. Mac and Oscar did really well. Went to Dan Billman's birthday party this evening and came home fairly early. Had a good time. It's snowing.

Sunday, November 16, 1980—slept late, took one of the snow machines and made a trail for the dogs to follow. We got about three inches of snow and it's quite warm today. Took Sylvia to Gunsight Lodge to work again.

Monday, November 17, 1980—I ran Fear, the lead dog, Oscar, Mack and Chrissy twice today—three miles each time. They are doing pretty well. Weather is nice, a low of zero degrees to a high of 10 above. Called Nadia, Ernie H. and Jim R.

Tuesday, November 18, 1980—ran the dogs again today, Lefty helped. Mack got loose and tore up two harnesses. Henry hauled logs. I called George S. to sell corn and Jim Phillips stopped in this evening.

Wednesday, November 19, 1980—ran the dogs—lots of tangle and trouble. Hauled a load of wood home. Visited the Hoffmans, they gave me yarn and eggs. Went with Ken and Sam to Tazlina Lodge to shoot some pool.

Thursday, say November 20, 1980—slept late. Cut and stacked some wood here, then went to Max and Irene Hoffman's and cut up some wood for them. Stopped at Schmitz with some eggs I got from Hoffmans, cut up more wood and fed the dogs and fixed supper. There is a beautiful sunset this evening.

Friday, November 21, 1980—cut and split more wood and tried running the dogs and it was a total disaster. Lead dog Fear wouldn't run and screwed up the other dogs.

Saturday, November 22, 1980—didn't do much all day George S. called to say he sold the corn. I went to Gunsight and listened to a recital of Robert Service poems, then Sylvia and I went to Tazlina Lodge to a dance.

Sunday, November 23, 1980—sewed up the harness that Fear chewed up. Did some reading—it's been a beautiful day. Called Ernie in Minnesota and the loan will go through. (He is buying some land from us.)

Monday, November 24, 1980—tried to run the dogs, Fear chewed her harness again so no go this time. Split wood and did chores. Helped Charlie T. put a handle in a splitting mall. (I happened to have a handle on hand.)

Tuesday, November 25, 1980—up early. Sylvia stayed at Gunsight and I went on in to Anchorage to get plane tickets and a few other things. Got a couple of inches of snow on the way home.

Wednesday, November 26, 1980—Charlie T. helped run the dogs—turned out fairly well. I built a snow hook and a new brake claw for the dog sled. Repaired the dog harnesses. Fixed supper, did some reading and went to bed.

Thursday, November 27, 1980—Charlie helped me run the dogs again today. Things didn't go well. This is discouraging. Fear, the lead dog just isn't strong headed enough to lead the dogs.

Friday, November 28, 1980—cut up firewood for the lodge garage, their saw is broke down so we used my saw. Did chores and took care of the dogs and ran Sylvia to Gunsight to help Nancy at the lodge. Mike was here and visited for a while.

Saturday, November 29, 1980—didn't do much all day, it's getting colder tonight. Dan didn't get home from a flight he was out on. We're worried.

Sunday, November 30, 1980—killed some time building a fire in the shop of the lodge and repaired one dog harness. Ray brought Sylvia home from Gunsight where she had been working. Ray from Gunsight lodge brought his water hauling pickup to Nelchina and I helped him put a clutch and it. Dan is okay, the plane is stuck in snow. -20° this evening. The water system froze up here at the lodge.

Monday, December 1, 1980—up early, took Sylvia to Gunsight, helped Ray a little then came back and hitched the dogs to the sled and took them to Libby Riddles place (three miles). She put a dog called Phantom in my team. Had a good run, lots of excitement. Broke my brake on the grade off of Snowshoe Lake so I turned back for home to make repairs.

Tuesday, December 2, 1980—Ray brought his water hauling pickup to Nelchina and I helped him work on mounting a tank and a topper on it.

Wednesday, December 3, 1980—helped Ray with his water tank again and finished mounting it on his pickup. Then helped Henry put an engine on his pickup in the evening.

Thursday, December 4, 1980—Ray and Nancy are in Anchorage shopping. Not much to do here at Gunsight. Sylvia and I, and Ray and Nancy's daughters are taking care of the lodge while Ray and Nancy are Christmas shopping.

Friday, December 5, 1980—still taking care of the lodge, Ray and Nancy stayed overnight. I don't do very much, just mainly need to be here. Ray and Nancy got back real late in the evening. We went home to our cabin. It is -10° this evening.

Saturday, December 6, 1980—cut and hauled a pickup load of wood. Cut, split and piled it up. There was a party at KROA that we went to at

10,000 Days in Alaska Book One 1978-1989

Mendeltna Creek.

Sunday, December 7, 1980—slept late, did some leather work and made a gun sling and holder for my dog sled. Also made a snow hook for a brake on the dog sled. It was -30° today—all day.

Monday, December 8, 1980—finished up the leather work and fixed up some rope for tug line repairs on the dog sled—it's still -30°. Henry's furnace ran out of fuel. I got fuel pumped into it and Betty got it going. Henry is in Anchorage.

Tuesday, December 9, 1980—it's -37° this morning. I glued the heels of my Sorel boots where they were weakening. Took my dogs on a training run in the afternoon at -40°. At supper time, Mike P. called.

Wednesday, December 10, 1980—put the snow hook holder that I made out of leather onto the dog sled, allowing me to more safely carry the snow hook when I'm driving the dogs and the sled. I put some oil in the front differential of the pickup and cut up some logs for Henry. It was -35° all day and dropped to -40° this evening.

Thursday, December 11, 1980—I read late last night and slept late this morning. Henry's water system froze up and I helped get it thawed and back in service. Took dog collars and a chain and a snow hook back that I had borrowed from Libby Riddles. Now I have my own equipment. It's -45° today.

Friday, December 12, 1980—hitched up the dogs this morning at -48° and took pictures in front of the cache here at the lodge of the dogs and sled. I tried to run them, but Fear, the lead dog that I got from Libby just wouldn't lead. The pups sure wanted to go. It's discouraging—maybe she thought it was too cold. Dan's wife Patti had asked him to bring his van down for me to take into Anchorage. He did it, but didn't understand why Patti wanted me to drive it into Anchorage. Unbeknownst to him, Patti had made arrangements in Anchorage for his van to have a new paint job. She wanted to surprise him for Christmas.

Saturday, December 13, 1980–got up early to get ready to go "outside" to Minnesota. Got all packed and started in Dan's van. It was -45° and the wind was blowing the snow. It's not fun driving around on mountain roads in these conditions, but we got into Anchorage in time to catch the plane. The airline had to deplane two people who were giving trouble to the crew, so we were late taking off. We had quick connections in Seattle and arrived in Los Angeles and my Mother was there to meet us. Our luggage was lost.

Sunday, December 14, 1980—our luggage was delivered to us before bedtime. Having a nice visit with Mother, but I'm getting sleepy as I write this.

Monday, December 15, 1980—slept late and went to the VA park to see the plaque mother's chapter of the DAR had presented—it's very nice, liked the looks of it there. We did some shopping.

Tuesday, December 16, 1980—we said goodbye to Mother, left Los Angeles, and arrived in Minneapolis late and went to Nadia's home.

Wednesday, December 17, 1980—we called the FLBA office in St Cloud and set up an appointment to meet with those people.

Thursday, December 18, 1980—just enjoyed loafing here and visiting.

Friday, December 19, 1980—we went over to Beverly's and visited with her. Theresa's family came over and we had a really good time visiting with them.

Saturday, December 20, 1980—we went to the Nutcracker Fantasy—beautiful symphony music and all that goes with it as guests of Nadia and Darrell.

Sunday, December 21, 1980—good time here at Nadia's. Went to a program at their church.

Monday, December 22, 1980—met with FLBA in St Cloud and did business with them.

Tuesday, December 23, 1980—talked to the FHA in Brainerd and the lawyer in Staples, working at getting our business here in Minnesota squared around.

10,000 Days in Alaska Book One 1978-1989

Wednesday, December 24, 1980—took care of farm business in the morning and then on to Minneapolis in the afternoon. Visited with Kevin's family in the evening.

Thursday, December 25, 1980—they had a Christmas dinner here at Nadia and Darrell's. She has a beautiful large table and everything was so nice. My gifts were shirts and books. They were really nice—I read lots of books and of course, wear lots of shirts.

Friday, December 26, 1980—took a short walk. Up early every day and we did a lot of visiting with Nadia and Darrell.

Saturday, December 27, 1980—we went over to Paul and Ruth's and spent time with them.

Sunday, December 28, 1980—we're having a good time here at Paul and Ruth's and went to REI and shopped there.

Monday, December 29, 1980—drove up to Motley to stay with Roger and Bridgette.

Tuesday, December 30, 1980—had some farm business in the evening and we found out Bridgette's mother had died.

Wednesday, December 31, 1980—we did some farm business. Ernie H. and I butchered two lambs and I took them in to the locker plant in Staples.

Norman Wilkins

Left to right: Sylvia butchers a caribou outdoors in the snow; Nelchina Lodge circa 1980's; Norman and dogs next to the cache he helped Henry Johnson build for Nelchina Lodge; The dogsled Norman built by hand; and Norman and his guard dog, Mike.

10,000 Days in Alaska Book One 1978-1989

Sylvia pans for gold.

Norman Wilkins

1981—accident at Old Man Lake, commercial fishing

Thursday, January 1, 1981—didn't do much all day, up late last night at a party.

Friday, January 2, 1981—I was a pall bearer for Donna Hendricks (Bridgette's mother). After the funeral we went to see Russell Shequen at the Staples hospital.

Saturday, January 3, 1981—ran all over doing farm business.

Sunday, January 4, 1981—hurried around to go to Minneapolis. Roger and Bridgette (with their son Randy) are driving us down to Minneapolis. There we saw most of our children and will stay at Theresa's place now.

Monday, January 5, 1981—slept late here at Theresa and Earl's and played with the grand kids.

Tuesday, January 6, 1981—went over to Nadia and Darrell's where we enjoyed a good supper. Kevin and Beverly came over and we got to visit with them too.

Wednesday, January 7, 1981—got on the plane about 10:00 a.m. to go to Anchorage. We arrived there 12 hours later and got home at 12 p.m.

Thursday, January 8, 1981—visited Henry, Betty and Jane all morning, did a few jobs around the cabin, then went to see the dogs. Charlie has been taking care of them at Billman's.

Friday, January 9, 1981—went to visit Hoffmans (Max's home). Irene is in Anchorage and I brought the dogs home from Billman's place today.

Saturday, January 10, 1981—Max and Irene dropped 2 dozen eggs off at our place while on their way to get water. I worked with the dogs getting them used to the harness and driving commands. They love to run and are eager to go.

Sunday, January 11, 1981—built a snow rake to pull the snow off the cabin roof and put storm windows on the cabin to help keep it warm.

10,000 Days in Alaska Book One 1978-1989

Mike and Lynette came to the lodge so we went up there to visit with them.

Monday, January 12, 1981—did some small repair to the gang line for the dogsled, hitched them up and tried to lead them. I have to lead them across the highway for fear traffic will come and hit us—they didn't want to do that. Very nice sunny day.

Tuesday, January 13, 1981—put Mac and Niki on the sled and ran them. That worked out pretty well. Then Sylvia had to go to Gunsight to work and I had a lot of trouble getting her there. The truck quit before we even got to Eureka. Eventually I got her there so she could help Nancy at the lodge.

Wednesday, January 14, 1981—it's snowing. We got my pickup out of the ditch (I had hit a snow berm and went in the ditch). I went on to Gunsight to fill the truck with gas and left Sylvia's suitcase. Helped Charlie a little with his Volkswagen that was giving him trouble.

Thursday, January 15, 1981—cleaned snow off my roof and part of the lodge and shoveled trails to the wood pile and part of the dog yard. Pulled Charlie back on to Billman's driveway. Blake stopped in to pick up a motor at the shop.

Friday, January 16, 1981—finished shoveling snow from the dog yard—big job.

Saturday, January 17, 1981—ran the dogs with Mac in the lead, then Fear in the lead, hoping she would get comfortable with being up front and leading. Doug helped me with the dogs this time. Went to Gunsight to get Sylvia and partied there and at Nelchina.

Sunday, January 18, 1981—rested all day.

Monday, January 19, 1981—got up late, read the Sunday paper and went to visit Billmans at their place. His brother-in-law, John will give me two sled dogs.

Tuesday, January 20, 1981—took a bath and read, Will called with an offer for the farm and I called him back with a small counter offer. It's not such a great deal, but hopefully good for the farm.

Wednesday, January 21, 1981—didn't do much all day except some reading. Gave a little advice to Charlie on preparing hides for tanning. Libby Riddles stopped to have me repair a sled brake.

Thursday, January 22, 1981—repaired brake for Libby's sled. Telephoned "Borstead", visited Charley. I'm reading *Hanta Yo* by Ruth Beebe Hill, very good book. Ran the trapline—nothing, so I pulled the traps.

Friday, January 23, 1981—didn't do much all day. Went to get Sylvia at Gunsight, then went to see movie, "Mountain Men" at the Glennallen movie house.

Saturday, January 24, 1981—went to Dan Billman's. John, Patti's brother was there. He had brought two dogs he was giving me.

Sunday, January 25, 1981—had the flu today.

Monday, January 26, 1981—still have the flu, just too sick to do anything—this is a bad one.

Tuesday, January 27, 1981—went to Glennallen and had the farm lease and purchase agreement notarized. Went on to Mike and Lynette's place and stayed overnight and had a good time.

Wednesday, January 28, 1981—drove home, built a fire in the cabin—flu hangs on.

Thursday, January 29, 1981—still quite sick. This is Jim C.'s birthday. He got a little upset and broke up the party. Mike P., Sylvia, James and I went to Tazlina Lodge and played pool.

Friday, January 30, 1981—worked on a pair of gaiters to keep snow out of my boots.

Saturday, January 31, 1981—rested a lot and tried to make friends with Judy (one of the new sled dogs that John gave me). It's very warm. Went to KROA at Mendeltna.

10,000 Days in Alaska Book One 1978-1989

Sunday, February 1, 1981—Dan and Patti came to wish me a happy birthday. I rested most all day. It's nice warm weather now. The Northern Lights are bright at night. Still making friends with the new dogs.

Monday, February 2, 1981—I still have the flu. Called the bank and the insurance people about the farm business and rested most of the day.

Tuesday, February 3, 1981—went to see Dan Billman and helped him a little in the afternoon. He had a snowfall that crushed a tent. We took Dan and Patti and the kids to supper.

Wednesday, February 4, 1981—still quite sick. Some Bavarians with a dog team stopped in at Nelchina in a motorhome. They want to run their dogs in this area. Sylvia went to Gunsight for a while to work.

Thursday, February 5, 1981—did a few chores and helped Yourg, Lawrence and Peter with their dogs and pictures. They've been hanging around the lodge in the evenings. They are from Austria.

Friday, Friday, February 6, 1981—fed Libby's dogs and went to Tazlina for a beer and had a good time, got back late.

Saturday, February 7, 1981—fed Libby's dogs in the morning and went to Gunsight and got Sylvia. She's been working there for a while. James and I went on two wrecker calls. While on this wrecker call, I had a piece of cable with loose steel go through my mitt and bloodied up my hand and when the blood dried, it got hard and ruined my mitt. It might not have happened if it had been daylight, but I was clumsy in how I handled the cable.

Sunday, February 8, 1981—put bindings on snowshoes. Sylvia has the flu now, and a sore throat. Read all day, Betty came over to visit for a while.

Monday, February 9, 1981—Sylvia is quite sick. Took a Sunday paper to the Hoffmans. They have a newborn little kid goat and it was doing well (there had been a problem when it was born). They gave us some eggs and citrus for Sylvia in hopes that it would help her throat.

Tuesday, February 10, 1981—did chores around the cabin and James

Callahan went with me to snowshoe a trail to run the dogs on. The trail is all blown in and we have to make a new trail. James is pretty good on snowshoes. It's bright and sunny today and very beautiful. Sylvia is still pretty sick with this flu.

Wednesday, February 11, 1981—it turned warm and cloudy and Sylvia is okay today. Did some more snowshoeing on the trail and went with James on a wrecker call. Started feeding the goat to the dogs (the one that Hoffmans lost in birthing). I give the dogs a portion of it for each meal.

Thursday, February 12, 1981—no entry.

Friday, February 13, 1981—no entry.

Saturday, February 14, 1981—Fear started having her pups. She had seven of them. This may have been part of her problem with running lead this winter. Jim, Andy, James and I went to Tazlina to shoot pool.

Sunday, February 15, 1981—visited with Andy and Connie from Anchorage and their daughter Angela. It's -30° this morning.

Monday, February 16, 1981—it's cold. Cut up some wood for Henry. My back is giving me trouble and hurts.

Tuesday, February 17, 1981—visited at Ken Kramer's. It is Lee D's birthday and at Nelchina, Sam's party for Lee at the Lodge.

Wednesday, February 18, 1981—it's Beverly's birthday. I slept till noon, worked on the dog stuff, loaded the snowmobile and getting ready to go to Anchorage.

Thursday, February 19, 1981—we found out the bank had sent our check back to Minnesota. We didn't get all our shopping done. Got quite upset with this bank. Stopped at Andy and Connie's and Andy was working. He has a business.

Friday, February 20, 1981—Mike P. is working on his Volkswagen engine and brought information about the claim on Nome Creek. Doug and brothers and Andy and Dave were at the lodge.

10,000 Days in Alaska Book One 1978-1989

Saturday, February 21, 1981—worked on the Coleman lantern. They require service every once in a while.

Sunday, February 22, 1981—ran the dogs and helped Mike P. with his Volkswagen. Went to Tazlina and shot pool.

Monday, February 23, 1981—slept late, helped Mike again with his Volkswagen.

Tuesday, February 24, 1981—ran the dogs—James helped me get them across the road. They followed him on the trail. We saw a ptarmigan and fox tracks and also wolverine.

Wednesday, February 25, 1981—went to Anchorage for supplies.

Thursday, February 26, 1981—unloaded the supplies from the truck and a bunch of people here went skiing up on Slide Mountain.

Friday, February 27, 1981—ran the dogs and Mike did just great the first time out—not so good the second time.

Saturday, February 28, 1981—did chores around here and ran the dogs and played 3-ball at Tazlina. Dennis and Sally showed up here at Nelchina.

Sunday, March 1, 1981—Mike and Lynette visited.

Monday, March 2, 1981—took Sylvia to Gunsight to help Nancy and gave Scotty a knife holster that I made. Ran three dogs and they did well.

Tuesday, March 3, 1981—ran the dogs again today, five of them and they did quite well. Went to see Hoffmans—met Max Junior then came home and ate. Fed the dogs and went to Gunsight Lodge.

Wednesday, March 4, 1981—ran the dogs with Mac in the lead, Chrissy second, then Judy, Micky, Niki and Oscar. They all did quite well.

Thursday, March 5, 1981—we went to Gunsight for Ray's birthday. Betty, Doug and Denise and James went too. We had a good time. We got to see Mike and Sue McKinley, they were there too. Mike is the guy that does my serious snowmobile repairs.

Friday, March 6, 1981—tried to run the dogs to Cache Creek, but I didn't get all the way there. Back home, then I sharpened my knife and hatchet and machete.

Saturday, March 7, 1981—I started making hatchet sheaths. Mike called, then Dan called and offered to fly me to Blue Lake so I can stay at my trap cabin a few days. His new plane is very nice.

Sunday, March 8, 1981—left Dan's about noon. Sam flew with us. We looked over the country. It was really nice, we could see so much of the land—then we landed at Blue Lake and broke trail to the cabin. On the way there, we had no trail. I had to go by where I thought the cabin was. It's a little over a mile through the brush and trees and I led them to within a few yards of the cabin. The guys were quite surprised how I did that and I just passed it off as an everyday thing. Dan and Sam were on skis and I was on snowshoes. The cabin was just as I had left it. It was a nice day and we had a really good time there. I really appreciated Dan taking me.

Monday, March 9, 1981—a marten has been in my cache here at the trap cabin. He likes noodles and butter. I dried my frosty gear and worked on the dog tie-outs. Went snowshoeing, saw tracks of caribou, wolf, moose and martin. I'm really enjoying being out here at the trap cabin.

Tuesday, March 10, 1981—slept late, don't feel good. Snowshoed a trail to Blue Lake for the snow machine. Light snow last night, marten visited the cabin. Sunny today. Put out two lines of spruce boughs on the little lake to mark a landing strip for Dan's plane to land here at the cabin.

Wednesday, March 11, 1981—dressed fur stretching boards last night and more today. Snowed two inches of wet stuff, windy and clearer later this afternoon.

Thursday, March 12, 1981—bright and sunny, got ready to leave. The marten was back in the cache. I ran him away. He scolded much like a squirrel—I imitated him—he scolded more. Dan didn't show up with the plane to pick me up—something must have delayed him.

10,000 Days in Alaska Book One 1978-1989

Friday, March 13, 1981—up very early. Fixed a good breakfast and snowshoed to the trap cache at the west lake, then south to pick up a trap, then back to cabin. Chris R. flew in to visit and Later Dan landed on Blue Lake. He had Mike P. with him. They skied the mile or two to my cabin. After coffee, Dan flew us to his place on Snowshoe Lake. I welded Dan's Okio (a style of sled often used for freighting). Hauling firewood is hard on sleds.

Saturday, March 14, 1981—resting up today, Sam stopped by. We had coffee and visited.

Sunday, March 15, 1981—I am an early riser, so I often see the sunrise. There was a beautiful one today—and it lasted all day. Ran snow machine over a trail that I use for training the dogs. Judy is still in heat, so I only ran Mac, Micky and Oscar. Oscar likes me; he stands with his front paws on my shoulders out of pure joy. It does the both of us a lot of good.

Monday, March 16, 1981—Charlie T.'s birthday. Ran three dogs, gave two females away. Sam went with me on a wrecker call. We couldn't get a van pulled back up on the highway. It will take a bigger wrecker than this one.

Tuesday, March 17, 1981—up early, went to Anchorage. Sam W. from Nelchina went along. Did lots of shopping and got a pair of touring skis and boots. Stopped at Gunsight on the way home.

Wednesday, March 18, 1981—took Sam to his trailhead. He had a lot of supplies so I packed a load of groceries in to his cabin for him. Lee Dudley put his skis on and came along. It's only a couple of miles to Sam's cabin. We all were on skis. Lee and I came back by way of the lake and out to the highway.

Thursday, March 19, 1981—very nice day. Ran four dogs, and then went cross-country skiing. Cut up a tree that blew down across dogsled trail. Went to see Hoffmans, had supper there. Saw a large flock of snowbirds.

Friday, March 20, 1981—called Mike Phillips and we made plans to go to my cabin by snow machine to haul trapping gear back here to take on a ratting trip.

Saturday, March 21, 1981—I came down with a bad sinus flew during the night so we didn't go to the trap cabin. Worked a little on equipment for the ratting expedition.

Sunday, March 22, 1981—called Mike and told him I was sick, put off the trip to cabin.

Monday, March 23, 1981—still a little sick, got some things ready to go back to the trapping cabin. I think I sold the Taymond Hanson 160 acres in Minnesota to a neighbor.

Tuesday, March 24, 1981—Mike came over and we left for trap cabin to get traps for the ratting expedition in another area. Ski-Doo is giving me engine trouble. Hauled wood. Put two 55-gallon drums up on the platform Cache. I will store things in them over summer. Put sharp spikes around both cabin windows to discourage bears from trying to get in. Quite tired tonight. It's really great to be out here at the trap cabin. I think Mike likes it out here too, he is a woodsman at heart.

Wednesday, March 25, 1981—after breakfast, we went to the trap cache and brought the rat traps back here to the cabin. Had lunch and loaded everything we needed to take out to the highway on our sleds. Left the cabin after dinner some time—I was leading on my Ski-Doo pulling a heavy load on the sled behind me. About four miles out, I was going up a short rise in the trail and gave it more gas. I don't know how it happened, but I got knocked off my snow machine and landed butt down on a 5-gallon can of gas. My right leg was dragging in the trail in front of the runner of the sled I was pulling when the runner caught on a tree, pinning my leg in between. The Ski-Doo and sled dragged on around the tree and I went airborne and landed in a low place six or eight feet down off the trail. When Mike arrived, we took my Sorel boot off and all the socks so I can feel my lower leg and find out how badly I was hurt. The right leg lower small bone was broken, knee twisted, and same for the ankle. It was -25° or thereabouts so we wasted no time getting the socks and boot back on. We decided Mike would drive my outfit and I would drive his smaller machine with no load. I got my right foot tucked on the running board and it wasn't too bad until we got close to Old Man Lake. Mike couldn't get my Ski-Doo to pull the sled up a short, but steep rise up off a small lake we were crossing. He worked hard and tried everything he knew. The sun slipped down below the trees taking the temperature even lower. Mike came out to me on the lake to see what I wanted to do. He was concerned about leaving a sled load of gear sitting here. I told him I was cold from just sitting and he should move the sled out of the way so I can drive by and we would go on to Dan and Patti's, which was about 18 miles from where we were. He did that and we had just gotten out onto Old Man Lake when a local pilot spotted us and taxied over. Mike walked over to him and told him what was up. This pilot offered to fly me to the airport at Gulkana. It was a small two passenger plane and I dreaded trying to get that bum leg stuffed into the close quarters of that plane, and then out again at Gulkana so I refused his kind offer. When I got to Billman's place, Patti saw me drive up and came out, took my left arm over her shoulder and helped me into the house. Mike came in on my Ski-Doo a little later and drove me to the little hospital in Glennallen. I have one broken bone, crushed muscle and a wrenched knee and ankle. This of course, wrecked the rat trapping expedition.

Thursday, March 26, 1981—I sure don't like being in the hospital. Mike and Sylvia came to get me in the evening and when we got home, Charlie came to visit for a while.

Friday, March 27, 1981—Peter and Sam came to visit. It's sun shiny today and I'm recuperating, but slow. Sylvia went to a movie with Betty and the kids in Glennallen. There isn't much for TV here and the movie house in Glennallen is about all we have.

Saturday, March 28, 1981—my knee is red so we went to the doctor and he said it's okay. He put a walking splint on my leg and I'm walking now—carefully. Went to KROA at Mendeltna for an Italian feed. The lady that owns it is Italian and a good cook. We had a good time there that evening.

Sunday, March 29, 1981—I hobbled up to the lodge once and back home I slept a little and read one book—I read lots of books. It's a favorite pastime for me.

Monday, March 30, 1981—I laid around most of the day, babying my leg.

Tuesday, March 31, 1981—went to the doctor to take the splint off.

Norman Wilkins

Wednesday, April 1, 1981—went and spent a few hours up at the lodge. The leg bothered me after a while up there later in the night.

Thursday, April 2, 1981—I got up early, I couldn't sleep well. The leg is quite sore and the tailbone also. I slammed my tailbone down on that 5-gallon bucket and it sure was hard.

Friday, April 3, 1981—laid around all day. Mike and Mark stopped at the lodge to eat and then we all went to see the movie, "Jeremiah Johnson" in Glennallen that evening. Everyone here likes that sort of movie. Saw three caribou along the highway.

Saturday, April 4, 1981—the leg sure is sore. I'm sick in my guts most of the night and day. Real sunny, down around zero at night and up to 30 above in the daytime.

Sunday, April 5, 1981—nice day. I'm still sore and stiff. Ken Kramer stopped to visit and Chuck Tangen called. Then I called Ernie H. I did go out and split some wood.

Monday, April 6, 1981—nice all day and about 30°. Relieved the fore end pressure on the model 70, .338 Winchester rifle. Split some wood. Helped James with the wrecker a little. Fixed a flashlight that needed some attention. Henry got back home from work tonight—good to see him.

Tuesday, April 7, 1981—got up at 4 a.m. Leg hurts, had Charlie T take me to Anchorage to the clinic to have it looked at. Got groceries and came home late. Really tired from that trip.

Wednesday, April 8, 1981—it's a really nice day and the swelling in the leg has started to go down. I read again all day.

Thursday, April 9, 1981—another nice day, read more. Called Chuck T. about the land and also Daniel on farm business.

Friday, April 10, 1981—beautiful day.

Saturday, April 11, 1981—nice again today.

10,000 Days in Alaska Book One 1978-1989

Sunday, April 12, 1981—Mike P. and Dan B. came to visit and Sam Weaver came later in the evening. Oftentimes we trade out books.

Monday, April 13, 1981—another day of beautiful weather. Leg is swelled up again. By noon I was sure tired of this. Jim brought the mail down and then we went to Gunsight in the evening.

Tuesday, April 14, 1981—it was a little cloudy and light snow on the Slide Mountain, and cooler. Visited James and Peter at the lodge.

Wednesday, April 15, 1981—got up early, the leg is bad. Charlie T. stopped by with books that Sam sent along for me. Tom is going to Anchorage to pick up medicine. It's a beautiful day though.

Thursday, April 16, 1981—another beautiful day. It's 35° in the day and zero at night. The leg is feeling better. Tom Smayda stopped in with medicine from town. We watched the Iditarod 81 on TV at the lodge. Our realtor in Minnesota called about farm business.

Friday, April 17, 1981—went with Charlie T. to drive his Volkswagen back to the lodge and spent some time with Dan Billman talking about putting his sawmill together.

Saturday, April 18, 1981—snow in the evening on Slide Mountain and Heavenly Ridge. It often has a way of snowing on the mountains and we don't get any down where we live.

Sunday, April 19, 1981—bright and sunny, Henry brought me a bale of straw for dog bedding. Sam came later in the evening and Dan and Patti Billman came to visit.

Monday, April 20, 1981—it was sunny and windy. Silt was blowing down on the river bed and over towards us. Read for a while and cleaned two guns. Sylvia went to Gunsight.

Tuesday, April 21, 1981—another nice day just lying around resting and reading.

Wednesday, April 22, 1981—it's a beautiful day. Snow is going fast now.

Norman Wilkins

Thursday, April 23, 1981—not much doing, very nice weather. This is Nadia's birthday.

Friday, April 24, 1981—another nice day and I'm reading all the time.

Saturday, April 25, 1981—laid around and read most of the day again. Lee wasn't home and too muddy here to target shoot.

Sunday, April 26, 1981—Charlie and I went to Lee's and shot my .338.

Monday, April 27, 1981—partied all day at Ronning's

Tuesday, April 28, 1981—I rested all day, James stopped by in the evening for a while. We planned to quit drinking.

Wednesday, April 29, 1981—Sylvia's birthday, another beautiful day for it. Worked on the cabin door jam and went to the lodge for a while to celebrate Sylvia's birthday.

Thursday, April 30, 1981—another perfect day, down near 30° at night and 50° in the daytime. There was a barbeque for everybody at the lodge.

Friday, May 1, 1981—went to Glennallen on business, then to Copper Center for groceries and to visit Mike and Lynette. Mike wasn't home but we got to see Lynette. Weather is nice but a little windy.

Saturday, May 2, 1981—another beautiful day and mild wind. Will called, and I called Charles—and Roger Shequen.

Sunday, May 3, 1981—cloudy, then sunny later. Saw eight eagles while raking the dog yard. Great fun. This time of year the Eagles come up from down south and warmer climates, they're locating their nests.

Monday, May 4, 1981—cloudy all day and 40°. Knee hurts, read most of the day and helped James a little. James borrowed my pickup.

Tuesday, May 5, 1981—changed oil and filters on the truck. Nadia called to tell me that Roger Shequen had been killed in an auto accident. James will drive us to the airport to go to Minnesota for the funeral.

10,000 Days in Alaska Book One 1978-1989

Wednesday, May 6, 1981—we didn't have any cash on us so we gave Roy a check and he gave us cash to pay for the airline tickets. James drove us to the airport and Anchorage. We arrived in Minneapolis at 1:00 p.m. and went to Beverly's first, later to Nadia's.

Thursday, May 7, 1981—up at 4:30 a.m., went to the funeral for Roger. This was a very stressful time for us. We paid our respects to Roger's family and parents and then while we were near Motley, we stayed with Taymond and Clara Hanson that night. (We had bought their farm from them some years ago).

Friday, May 8, 1981—we got up early and went to the bank and did farm business all day. Stayed at the motel.

Saturday, May 9, 1981—we were up early and did farm and rent business all day and drove to Minneapolis in the evening.

Sunday, May 10, 1981—Beverly and Theresa and their families were all at Nadia's for Mother's day. Paul's family went to Leader to be with Ruth's family.

Monday, May 11, 1981—went back up to the farm, looked up the renters and so forth all day. Took Ernie H. and his wife Diane out for supper. Sold some hay that I had for sale. Returned to Minneapolis at 3:00 a.m. on the 12th.

Tuesday, May 12, 1981—up early and still tired, made some calls and went over to Paul and Ruth's and back to Nadia's. Beverly and Vanessa came over for supper.

Wednesday, May 13, 1981—Nadia's husband, Darrell gave me a book on wilderness living. That was thoughtful of him. Flew home to Alaska. James met us at the airport and we did some shopping for groceries. Then we went to Nelchina. It's great to be home again.

Thursday, May 14, 1981—straightened and arranged some of the cabin.

Friday, May 15, 1981—put a different carburetor on a truck and cleaned the dog yard. Visited Hoffmans and Billmans. Came home and Henry

Norman Wilkins

came down from the lounge to visit.

Saturday, May 16, 1981—Henry wants to dig a new basement for the lodge. I built some protection for my dog sled and Jeff came up from Anchorage for a couple of hours.

Sunday, May 17, 1981—helped haul trash to the dump for the lodge. Watered everything in the greenhouse. Finished reading the book, *Creek Mary's Blood* by Dee Brown. I really enjoyed that book. Henry and Mike visited for a while.

Monday, May 18, 1981—went to Anchorage to get some things for James and Henry. Visited Andy Boyle and Jeff (known as "fat man"). I did some shopping in town there and then James and Doug and I went home.

Tuesday, May 19, 1981—rested up most of the day and read some, unloaded the truck, then wrote letters.

Wednesday, May 20, 1981—peeled a burl for Henry's mailbox post. James took my pickup to Copper River and Lisa stopped in to ask me to care for her dogs. Planted some garden and Gary stopped (the trucker that I had helped out on Taylor Highway—I believe this was the time that he was leaving Alaska and going back to the lower US). He told us that after Thursday, we could have anything they hadn't sold on the yard sale.

Thursday, May 21, 1981—went to Gunsight for a beer.

Friday, May 22, 1981—worked some on the mailbox post for Henry

Saturday, May 23, 1981—Andy and Joyce, and Rob and Barb came to visit James. Henry tuned up his pickup and set the mailbox post.

Sunday, May 24, 1981—we planted the peas in the garden.

Monday, May 25, 1981—rested all day and did some reading and glued patches on two shoes.

Tuesday, May 26, 1981—went to Lake Louise Junction to get gas. Had dinner with the Hoffmans. Denise and I picked up trash around the lodge and I helped her with some schoolwork. Radish and lettuce is

10,000 Days in Alaska Book One 1978-1989

coming up in the garden.

Wednesday, May 27, 1981—my right leg is really bad today. Betty and Henry took my pickup to Palmer and James and I worked on Henry's pickup and gave it a tune up, then James took Doug to baseball practice in Glennallen. Charlie Trowbridge stopped in late in the evening and we had a good visit.

Thursday, May 28, 1981—Charlie and I went to Anchorage. Gary Leach, the trucker, gave me a lot of mining hose and fittings as he had promised. Charlie helped me get that stuff all loaded in the truck. Some of the bundles were quite heavy. Charlie had errands to do also. On the way home, we caught a horse for John (we recognized the horse and got it tied up for him). He came and got it then.

Friday, May 29, 1981—nailed up a doghouse for the lodge's dog named "Bear" and I started a knife sheath for James. Henry went back to Delta, he runs a Cat there clearing land for a farmer.

Saturday, May 30, 1981—started cleaning the fuel and tank for Betty's mobile home at the lodge. Switched the front tires on the truck and adjusted the emergency brake. Betty had a birthday party for Zoe.

Sunday, May 31, 1981—rained last night a little, slept lake and loafed all day. Sunny and breezy today. Called a fella about a gold claim yesterday.

Monday, June 1, 1981—I put a seal in the front differential of the truck and the front drive line needs repair. Went to Dan's and also to Doug's ball game and saw the movie "Night Hawk".

Tuesday, June 2, 1981—got a late start to Anchorage and stayed at Andy, Connie and little Angela's.

Wednesday, it is June 3, 1981—ran all around town getting supplies and talking to Ken Harris about the claim on Bonanza Creek in the Brooks Range.

Thursday, June 4, 1981—didn't do much today.

Friday, June 5, 1981—fixed the drive line on the truck. It rained and

Norman Wilkins

hailed and I went to Tazlina with Henry to get gas.

Saturday, June 6, 1981—wasted most of the day.

Sunday, June 7, 1981—helped Henry a little and went to Tazlina to see Darrel. Charlie stopped in for a little while.

Monday, June 8, 1981—burned out the paint barrel to haul water for the greenhouse and got some gear ready for the trip. Henry and James borrowed my canoe.

Tuesday, June 9, 1981—Sylvia called to tell me that mother has had a stroke (she's been in Minneapolis). Later James and I went to borrow a trailer to help Henry but couldn't get it.

Wednesday, June 10, 1981—helped tar the lodge roof and replanted some rhubarb.

Thursday, June 11, 1981—left Nelchina at noon and went to Mike's and to Ten Mile on the Denali road. Charlie and Ellen are doing salmon reproduction work for the state of Alaska. We stayed there overnight. It's interesting to watch how they handle the eggs and prepare them for the winter. They have spring water running through the beds with rock to simulate conditions the eggs would have if they were in the wild.

Friday, June 12, 1981—ate breakfast at the Cherokee in Delta with Bill and George and Henry. I went to the farm where they're working and looked at a land claim. Went through Fairbanks and took the road out to Livengood. Got to the north fork of Bonanza Creek 10 miles past the Arctic Circle (beautiful country). As you go north on what's called the "haul road", the land changes slowly. It's all looks different, but it's all beautiful.

Saturday, June 13, 1981—along the road, I stopped at a fella with some equipment and (Leonard and Loretta, the folks there that I talked to) he asked me to help him move some mining equipment to claims on Fish Creek. He had a D8, Terex bucket loader and a sluice. We went to pump #5 to get permission to park the truck and couldn't find the gate key where he told us it was. We looked for the trail to the claims on the north fork with no luck. Discouraged tonight.

10,000 Days in Alaska Book One 1978-1989

Sunday, June 14, 1981—I was up early left for Nelchina and saw a nice black bear ten miles north of the Yukon River I stopped in Livengood for lunch and talked to the fella there. Went on then through Fairbanks to Delta and I got a hunting, fishing and trapping license there. Henry and I did some dump picking.

Monday, June 15, 1981—stopped again near Paxson and watched Charlie and Ellen plant salmon fry and went with him up to dump some in a lake and looked the hatchery over. Then when I got down to Copper Center, I went to Mike's and talked mining and stopped at Tazlina to see Darrel and BS'ed and played pool and stayed the night.

Tuesday, June 16, 1981—I brought James to Nelchina. He and Scott then went on to Anchorage.

Wednesday, June 17, 1981—Darrel and I went to Anchorage and took papers and maps back to Ken Harris (When I went to look at his claims on the Hall road, I didn't like the looks of having to climb the mountain with my Cat and get equipment over to that creek that he wanted to lease out, so we aborted that plan). Stayed at Andy's, Birdie was there.

Thursday, June 18, 1981—finished our shopping and got home late. Took Darrel and his provisions to Tazlina Lodge. We partied there and brought Doug and Denise home.

Friday, June 19, 1981—worked a little on the Cat and other small things around here.

Saturday, June 20, 1981—went to Dan and Patti's and brought my snowmobile home. It had been there since I got laid up with my leg. Went to Mike and Lynette's and picked 12 salmon from a fish wheel. Met Harry Billum who is a well-know and very good trapper in this area. Went to Paxson with Mike and Lynette.

Sunday, June 21, 1981—slept late, picked 13 salmon out of the fish wheel. Came home and gave away some salmon and packaged some for here.

Monday, June 22, 1981—no entry.

Norman Wilkins

Tuesday, June 23, 1981—no entry.

Wednesday, June 24, 1981—no entry.

Thursday, June 25, 1981—went to Tazlina, Lloyd Ronning came with me. We hung around there for quite a while.

Friday, June 26, 1981—Steve Brooks who lives across the highway from the lodge—it's his birthday and they had a party for him.

Saturday, June 27, 1981—went to Dan Billman's. Denny, his brother was there. He got his truck stuck—came to see me about skidding logs for him. Denny is hauling house logs to build with.

Sunday, June 28, 1981—Denny and I went to KROA to shoot pool and did some finger pulling using a plastic strap-like with the holes in it. I have strong hands and did well.

Monday, June 29, 1981—Charlie brought my canoe back this morning that he'd been using. Re-nailed the roof on the shop for the lodge, measured out the new lodge. Rusty gave me some steel and I worked on the swamp buggy doors. The greenhouse is doing great.

Tuesday, June 30, 1981—went to see Billmans. Denny is in town. Left some lettuce for Dan and Patti and worked on the door of the swamp buggy. Rain in the morning and sunny and wind in the afternoon. Mike asked me if I wanted to go to Egegik with him. His sister Judy had tendonitis and she needed help with her commercial fishing netting and I agreed to go.

Wednesday, July 1, 1981—I got packed after 2 a.m. on July the first. Mike and I drove to Anchorage and stopped at a store where I bought some gear to go commercial fishing at Big Creek, Judy Phillips' site at Egegik. We arranged for our tickets and caught a WEIN flight to King Salmon. We transferred to a smaller plane for a flight to Big Creek and landed on the beach there. The tide needs to be out so the plane can land on the hard sand. It was fishing time when we arrived that day and we jumped right in, pulled our hip boots on and helped Judy pick fish in her net. We got 360, six pound fish (red salmon—beautiful). Met Scott,

10,000 Days in Alaska Book One 1978-1989

who fishes and Claudia who fishes, they both fish nearby. Claudia is also Mike's landlady back in Copper Center. We set up the tent in a strong wind and were really tired, but slept real well.

Thursday, July 2, 1981—it's very windy, sand blows into everything. Wind blows on the tent so hard, it just pops and sometimes it lays down right on our face. We have it tied off to a plane that has been wrecked on the beach. That anchors our tent and keeps the wind from blowing it away. We went over twice to "Andy's" fish buying. Judy sells to him. We met several people that work on the beach fishing. Judy needed more help and some guys helped carry her nets all around the sand dunes. Saw a dead seal—teeth looked old. Then I went over to another fish camp north—it's bigger. Five skiffs and some bigger boats fish out of there. On the way back to Judy's the wind picked up to 40+ miles per hour and we guyed the tent down some more. It sure pops in this wind. Met a guy by the name of Mike and two girls. We slept well after a great supper. I filleted fresh caught, sea run salmon for our supper. Excellent repast!

Friday, July 3, 1981—got up at 6:45 a.m. The wind has dropped some. Judy's net had gotten partially buried in the mud last night and we only got 87 fish. We were all disappointed. She and a friend of hers canned salmon tonight.

Saturday, July 4, 1981—ate a little rice and went out to pick the net. Got 547 fish—nice, big red salmon. It was a high tide and she's repairing holes in the net now. We'll set in deep water for tonight's tide. Didn't get enough tide, one net had very few fish. Sunny day, nice in that respect. C-119's and DC3's haul most of the fish from this camp.

Sunday, July 5, 1981—up early, just as the tide is going out. Got a bite to eat and coffee, picked the fish out of the net. We got 500. We loaded them on the camp truck and reset the nets and got 247 this evening. Saw a small, dead, spotted seal. It was a beautiful day and a beautiful sunset.

Monday, July 6, 1981—went out with Scott to help him—half his net is tore up. Judy and Mike got 289. It was a little windy, but sunny. We did some beachcombing and then on the evening tide, we got 129 more salmon.

Tuesday, July 7, 1981—it's blowing and a light rain, 489 fish in the morning. It rained all day and we got only 130 fish that evening.

Wednesday, July 8, 1981—it's blowing pretty hard, cloudy. We got 240 fish. It's sunny today. Later in the day we went beachcombing and found a glass ball, wood, and plastic floats. Saw one bear track, one dead seal. Got only 150 fish. The net got rolled by the tide and consequently we didn't get very many fish.

Thursday, July 9, 1981—a very good day. We got 1107 fish this day. Judy is very happy. It's rainy and nearby is Ed's place. Ed is sick and Claudia asked me if I would take his place fishing. So I'm pulling fish over there now. I got a 130 fish outta the net I picked and I get paid for picking salmon here. One of the men who worked on a fishing boat got an infection of some kind in a wound and got very sick. His body actually stiffened out. They phoned out for a plane to come and fly him to medical help. Surprisingly, he was back in a few days and went to work. In between fishing periods and tides, we walked along the beach looking for things that had washed up on the beach. Occasionally a seal would tear a big hole in the net, and Judy would repair it. What with the carrion washing up on the beach, attracting bears, we paid close attention to our surroundings, especially in the darkest part of the night. This is quite an experience for us—me a Minnesota farmer.

Friday, July 10, 1981 through Thursday, July 16, 1981—no entries.

Friday, July 17, 1981—skidded logs for Denny who is building a log house.

Saturday, July 18, 1981—took the swamp buggy to Tolsona Lake and retrieved two vehicles (for a guy by the name of Mike) that were stuck in a real bad mud hole in the swamp near Dennis's cabin. Went to a dance at KROA.

Sunday, July 19, 1981—Rusty, James, Scott and I hung out at the lodge in Tazlina until late.

Monday, July 20, 1981—loaned my pickup to the lodge to haul gas and peeled logs for Dan B.

10,000 Days in Alaska Book One 1978-1989

Tuesday, July 21, 1981—skidded more logs for Denny and he took me and a girlfriend of his out for supper and to play pool.

Wednesday, July 22, 1981—finished skidding logs for Denny—it came to 327 logs. Henry came home from the work up at Delta.

Thursday, July 23, 1981—did some things around here, Darrel and I went to Tolsona Lake and I Bar F in Glennallen. Saw Laurie P. at that I Bar F. She used to work at the Nelchina Lodge. Came back to Tazlina later.

Friday, July 24, 1981—got to Tazlina at 5:00 a.m. The place is pretty littered with broken glass and bullet holes in the glass of one cabin. I felt sorry for Darrel. He was managing the lodge and alone there in that respect. This fella who had come to the lodge, got rowdy and (I don't know the name of the guy) Darrel put him to sleep in one of the cabins and then this guy took to shooting out the windows and carrying on. When the owner comes back, it will be a mess, But Darrel did manage to get this fella under control.

Saturday, July 25, 1981—helped Henry with repairs on his wrecker and went to Tazlina to see how things are going on there. Visited for a while. Charlie Trowbridge came back home here to Nelchina today.

Sunday, July 26, 1981—Charlie and I went to the dump and we found four big wheels with tires on them. I could use those, they fit my big trailer. Brought them home and helped Henry with the wrecker repair some more. Charlie and I went to look at a cabin on Snowshoe Lake for him to live in. Some people owned some land there and they had one cabin that sits some distance from the main group of cabins and he was looking for a place.

Monday, July 27, 1981—we did some things around here and over at the lodge.

Tuesday, July 28, 1981—drove Henry to Anchorage for a job. Andy Boyle, Henry and I went out on the town late. Saw Nubie—he had done some gold mining, talked with him and later hauled some things in the pickup that Andy wanted moved.

Wednesday, July 29, 1981—I checked on some Coghill River claims

Norman Wilkins

records with the state of Alaska and got all my shopping done and Henry rode home with me.

Thursday, July 30, 1981—I did some things at the cabin and lodge and moved the scoop mobile to the RCA building site. Worked on my swamp buggy. Dennis, Sally and Mike showed up and we visited Hoffmans.

Friday, July 31, 1981—I took Henry to this RCA building and just got started when the machine quit. So we came back home and I thinned out some of the garden and picked some coral mushrooms (they're good eating). Charlie, Lee and Clint Meyers showed up and I did the laundry after they left.

Saturday, August 1, 1981—helped Henry a little, saw Lloyd and Chris Ronning at Tazlina Lodge.

Sunday, August 2, 1981—Charlie and I canoed across Snowshoe Lake a ways to a cabin that he has permission to use and is getting ready for the winter. Today is Henry and Betty's 12th wedding anniversary. Tom and Lorraine came down to the lodge in the evening.

Monday, August 3, 1981—I did cabin chores, wrote letters and fixed a package to send to Minnesota. It rained a lot. Roy Beaver stopped by—always good to see and talk to him.

Tuesday, August 4, 1981—helped Henry with his loader, hauled trash and so forth. Andy is out to visit. Andy and I went to Tazlina and stayed late.

Wednesday, August 5, 1981—tarred the roof on the lodge, went to Tazlina again and played pool, danced. Lots of people at a party there.

Thursday, August 6, 1981—slept late and loafed all day. Tom and Darrel came down and later Zoe.

Friday, August 7, 1981—didn't do much all day, Dennis Billman called.

Saturday, August 8, 1981—worked on the dryer at the lodge. It had a belt that sometimes would get out of line and come off its pulley—it's a simple thing to put it back on. Then it would run again for quite some time and be all right. Then I worked on the swamp buggy for a while and later on the D4 Cat and got it running. Helped Henry with a car that he's working on. Went to Mendeltna Creek on Oil Well Road to show Jerry J. the salmon that come in there and lay their eggs this time of year. They aren't to be fished or anything. This is a perfect gravel area for salmon to lay eggs in so it's protected. The bears don't pay any attention to that; they feed on the salmon just the same. Helped Charlie T. put a roof on his cabin at Snowshoe Lake. He had a friend, Dennis that was there and he helped also. Went in to Gulkana to State Bureau of Land Management and applied for a remote parcel of land. The state is starting a promotion so people can claim remote parcels of land. Henry and Tom Murdock are going to Delta for construction work. Went to Dan about flying an area named Green Acres that will be open for staking. Then went to see Hoffmans and on to Tazlina to see Darrel. He was asleep. Darrel came down later.

Sunday, August 9, 1981—helped Charlie T. We put a roof on his cabin at snowshoe Lake. His friend Dennis helped us.

Monday, August 10, 1981—went into Gulkana to the Alaska State Office, Bureau of Land Management and applied for a remote parcel of land. Henry and Tom Murdock are going to Delta for construction work.

Tuesday, August 11, 1981—went to see Dan Billman about flying Green Acres, and then on to Hoffmans later to see Darrel, he was asleep and came down later.

Wednesday, August 12, 1981—helped Betty sort her things out in the black shed that was used for storage. Did some laundry, fixed a propane leak in the darned regulator.

Thursday, August 13, 1981—went to Anchorage for a supplies, maps and so forth. Stopped at Gunsight to visit, then to Tazlina.

Friday, August 14, 1981—loafed all day, visited with Bob and Margaret Schmidt in the afternoon. Margaret is a real nice lady. She and Sylvia always got along really well.

Saturday, August 15, 1981—helped Charlie get his cabin ready to move in to. Henry came home from his job up there at Delta in the evening.

Sunday, August 16, 1981—helped Charlie some more, this time insulating the cabin and put visqueen on the ceiling to make the cabin easier to heat.

Monday, August 17, 1981—Hoffmans decided to wait to butcher the goats so I worked on the left front hub of Henry's car and did lots of things around the cabin.

Tuesday, August 18, 1981—went to Gunsight with the buggy and hauled some gear for two young people to back to Fossil Creek and met some other people there (they have a small dredge in operation on that creek).

Wednesday, August 19, 1981—left Fossil Creek about 1 p.m. and winched the swamp buggy back on the trail. Up near the top of Ballinger Pass, is another fellow that has claims and mines gold back there. Got back to Nelchina about 6:00 p.m.

Thursday, August 20, 1981—got gear ready for Doug and me to go caribou hunting. His dad wants Doug t go out with me to the trap cabin and hunt. He'd like to see Doug get a caribou. Prior to this, I had taken Doug out with my 20 gage shotgun and introduced him to shooting. He did real well with the shotgun; he could hit whatever he aimed at with it. He didn't have cartridges for the rifle that he was going to use, so before we went in to hunt, I took him with me to Anchorage and got cartridges. Had a tire fail on the way into town. Chris Ronning flew me out first and the hunting looked good around my cabin, saw a moose and caribou and a few good bulls. We got to the cabin about 5 p.m. Doug is real interested in the cabin and the area out here. We got a little rain, then it rained hard after dark. We're grateful for the cabin as opposed to camping in a tent tonight. The cabin is in fine shape, no varmint damage at all.

Friday, August 21, 1981—we got up early, had a good breakfast, hunted to the south, came back for lunch and then we went north and I showed Doug an old bear den. A while later we saw a caribou at 500 yards—only for a second. Too far and no chance for a shot. We saw one nice flock of ducks on a lake. Then we came back to the cabin and Doug fixed some blueberries. Dan and Chris both flew their planes over the cabin this evening and we went out again for an evening hunt. No luck. Did some cabin chores and cleaned up around the place—covered some old sawdust piles. Doug fixed his own chocolate drinks. He does well for a boy his age.

Saturday, August 22, 1981—we got a good night's sleep, got up early, it's a beautiful day. Ate a big breakfast and started walking up to Nye Lake. The climb from Hole Lake up to Nye Lake is steep. I showed Doug how to take deep breaths to get more oxygen into his lungs. Thus, more power in his legs. When we got there, we spotted four caribou and two legal moose bulls, one was 40+ inches at a hundred yards and another boo that I wasn't quite able to get Doug in position to shoot. There is a gravel esker in that area that wolves use for whelping pups in the spring. I put Doug on top of one end of the esker and I went to the other end. We hope the height will help in spotting game. After some time, a nice bull caribou appears out of the brush walking in our direction. I wanted Doug to have the shot, so I slipped down the other side of the esker and over to Doug. He gets ready for the caribou but it doesn't show up! Evidently a current of air had taken our scent to the caribou and he just disappeared into the brush. That afternoon, Doug didn't get a chance for a shot. Then we saw another moose that was too far for shooting and then a light colored moose cow and another moose nearby—they weren't legal. Walked back to Hole Lake, just as Chris was looking for us to see how we were doing. He over-flies people to see if they're okay. He stopped and told us of several moose that he had seen that day. We got back about 4:00 in the afternoon and did some cabin chores. Then a medium-sized bull caribou and two others came up to the cabin and laid down 12 feet away from the back side of the cabin. I just happened to go outside and saw them. I quietly went back in the cabin and we got the guns and got out of the cabin and got Doug in position. They got up and ran so I took a shot at the running bull but missed him. Doug didn't get a chance to shoot.

Sunday, August 23, 1981—got up, ate breakfast, took off for Nye Lake—first I walked down to Hole Lake and left a note for Chris there. Then went on to Nye Lake to hunt. Saw six cows and a bull caribou soon after we got there. They were passing the spot where I wanted to hunt. We stayed at that spot a long time, then climbed a knoll—20 minutes later, a big, bull boo walked by right where we had been previously. Doug didn't get a chance to shoot at that one either. We aren't having very good luck.

Chris was to meet us at 3:15 p.m., but he didn't stop. Something he must have had to do. We went to another knoll at the other end of the lake and no luck there. Saw another bull go by (one horn) that good crossing. Chris flew by again. Then we started for Hole Lake and he flew over again. Doug was ready to go home by this time. I twisted my knee going down to Hole Lake. We waited there for Chris for quite some time. We saw a loon take off the lake and circle it and a hawk that was hunting—and lots of fish rising in that lake. Chris didn't show up so then on to the cabin. We were really tired tonight. it had been a beautiful day though. then Chris and Brent Myer flew in just at dusk and dropped a smoke signal canister. They landed and parked the plane down on the lake and came up from Hole Lake to the cabin and had coffee with us.

Monday, August 24, 1981—Chris had Doug and me out to Tazlina by noon and we stopped at the outlet of Old Man Lake to watch the red salmon spawn. Saw lots of ducks and swans from the air too. Chris is a really good pilot. When he came to pick us up this morning, the temperature was warming up fast. He was going to be taking off out of Hole Lake so he thought it would be better to take Doug down to Blue Lake and come back and pick me up to get out—too much weight with both of us. Doug was a little apprehensive about being at Blue Lake all alone. I told him that it wasn't likely that a bear would be around there and we would be there shortly. Chris came back and I got in the plane. Chris started down Blue Lake and the temperature had warmed up even more—with warm air, the plane doesn't get the lift that it needs to take off. We're getting down there towards the end of the lake and it's not looking good. Chris aborts the take-off. We turned around and went down to the other end of the lake and he went deeper into the lilies and turns the plane and we start down the lake again and it's looking like we're going to make it and the plane DOES lift off the water. Chris then lands at Blue Lake and we pick up Doug (that's when we stopped at the outlet of the lake to watch the red salmon spawn). There's lots of ducks and swans on Old Man Lake, really a neat area. There are a number of old cabins around there and we know three owners that have cabins there.

Tuesday, August 25, 1981—did laundry, a beautiful day, helped around the lodge. Denny came up from Anchorage. I had supper there at Dan's place—grilled Halibut and then we went to KROA. Sam Weaver is back now. He's been off on a job.

10,000 Days in Alaska Book One 1978-1989

Wednesday, August 26, 1981—I took Sam to mile 149 so he could go to his cabin. Took care of the lodge today. It's so very nice, 78°. This is very unusual at this time of year.

Thursday, August 27, 1981—no entry.

Friday, August 28, 1981—Henry had told me to come up to Delta Junction if I wanted to work. They needed help. So I drove up to Delta Junction. On the way found two truck wheels at a pull off that would fit my good trailer that someone had ditched as junk. They were old and rusty. I got up to Delta Junction and hired on to help build a grain storage facility. First off, they put me to falling trees. Then they skid them out to a sawmill. I worked the first day until after 4:30 p.m. and then did some carpenter work on Jack's house. Then met Bob, Al, Clint and Norman. It's hard to find a place to sleep but I slept in a little trailer.

Saturday, August 29, 1981—they sent Al and me out to do finish work on Jack's house. We got our part done.

Sunday, August 30, 1981—moved from the trailer on John and Bob's farm to one close to the job site. Pat somebody owns it. Rained this afternoon.

Monday, August 31, 1981—went to work at 7:00 a.m., set up the screening plant, then went to the log area and cut trees. The wind was so bad I couldn't control where the trees would land. It was too dangerous to continue cutting so I came back to the building site and piled lumber and so forth. I worked 13 hours today. Got to see a ruffed grouse.

Tuesday, September 1, 1981—I cut more trees and Clint who's running the skidder, he tore a valve stem off the tractor, caught it on a stump or log or something. They got the wheel and tire off and I took it in my truck to Delta Junction trying to find somebody to fix it.

Wednesday, September 2, 1981—this day I took a tractor tire into Delta to be fixed and after dinner, took it to the woods. A fella by the name of Norm and I put it on equipment, then I headed for home.

Thursday, September 3, 1981—did a bunch of things around here since

Norman Wilkins

I've been gone for a while. In the evening, Charlie and I go to Eagle River to Betty's and we stay overnight there.

Friday, September 4, 1981—we went on into Anchorage from Betty's place and did a lot of shopping. Missed picking up the dog at Patti's and got home, loaded up books and beds for Betty and Henry came home and we drove to Betty's at 4:30 a.m.

Saturday, September 5, 1981—we did our shopping and went to see Andy Boyle and then back to Betty's and picked up the dog, Fisher from Patty, friend of Charlie's.

Sunday, September 6, 1981—moved the dog yard to put a gravel pad where they were.

Monday, September 7, 1981—No entry.

Tuesday, September 8, 1981—got my gear all ready to fly out to my cabin and hunt. Chris will fly us. He flew Dennis out to Blue Lake first and then he flew me out. It was dark when I got to the cabin. Dennis and I made a supper and got our gear arranged and ready to hunt the next morning. Got a good night's sleep.

Wednesday, September 9, 1981—we got up and I made breakfast and we took the gear we need for the day. Dennis has never been here and I made a circle, hunting—and we didn't see a thing! Then I made a circle to the south in the evening. We didn't have any luck there either. It was getting dark going back to the cabin.

Thursday, September 10, 1981—made a larger circle to the north—only saw some ducks. Came in and ate lunch. Went back out and went to the west and south this time. We didn't see anything again. Got back to the cabin and I had a little time so I started digging a hole (will build a toilet over it). Dan and Chris both flew their planes over us today. It was a nice day.

Friday, September 11, 1981—after breakfast, we walked over to Nye Lake, which was a pretty good walk, then along the bench and crossed back to the cabin side of the bench and came in to camp from that direction. We didn't see any game.

10,000 Days in Alaska Book One 1978-1989

Saturday, September 12, 1981—Chris flew over early. We hunted the east side of Blue Lake. We did see two caribou cows and heard the bull, but we couldn't see him. We did see two caribou skulls and horns. (Later that winter, Darrel and I were coming up through that draw on the snow machines. I knew where these skulls and horns were and I swung over there and dug them out of the snow and hauled them back to the trap cabin and later nailed them up on the cabin). Anyway, we did see one moose there, and one spruce hen. Chris and another plane flew over this evening. We really worked hard today. It was a nice day, but we're sure tired tonight.

Sunday, September 13, 1981—Chris flew in and picked Dennis up about 10:30 a.m. and Dan came and got me and we were out before noon.

Monday, September 14, and Tuesday, September 15, 1981—no entries.

Wednesday, September 16, 1981—Darrel and I are going out with the swamp buggy. We got the gear packed, but didn't get started until late. We got about a half mile off the road and stopped for the night.

Thursday, September 17, 1981—the next morning we were up early and we drove the seismic trails on our way to Ranger lake and we were climbing a small knob with the "mean machine" (also known as the swamp buggy) and as we got up to the top, the brush is all torn up and piled. We realize that this is where a grizzly has made a kill. We aren't too worried in the machine we're in. We looked the place over and there was part of a yearling moose that still hadn't been eaten. Later we saw a pretty darned nice, bull moose swim the lake just south of Ranger Lake. We walked around Ranger Lake and were not overly impressed. We're looking for land to claim in this "Green Acres" that the state is putting up for people to claim for cabins and land of their own. We did see ducks, two swans and a flock of large geese fly over. This was before I knew that the geese nested and raised young in this part of Alaska. Quite a few geese were nesting in this area.

Friday, September 18, 1981—cloudy early then the sun tried to shine. Got a late start, ran seismic trails looking for a way to Old Boot Lake. Generator quit. Camped for the night at a starting place to walk to Old Boot Lake in the morning. Raining, tent got wet, slept in swamp buggy.

Saturday, September 19, 1981—got up early ate breakfast but got a late start. Saw wolf, caribou and moose tracks and sign. Walked right to Old Boot Lake across country from another seismic trail. It's a very nice lake. Looked it over and also stopped at other small lakes. Quite windy all day. Got back to camp close to dark. Darrel and I each found 40 acres that we would like to get from the state in this "Green Acres". They happen to be side by side. He has one along one lake and I have one on Old Boot Lake itself. I chose Old Boot Lake and Darrel chose the lake right next to Old Boot Lake. Later he named it "Satiety".

Sunday, September 20, 1981—got into Tazlina at Noon and went on home to Nelchina.

Monday, September 21, 1981—I rested and put gear away and got the Cat started.

Tuesday, September 22, 1981—put more gear away and Henry and Dennis and Sally went to Anchorage and I tried to use the Cat and the controller rod for the hydraulic broke. Roger and Todd Pike came at 10:00 p.m. in the evening.

Wednesday, September 23, 1981—Roger and Todd are still here.

Thursday, September 24, 1981—I slept late and tried to move gravel with the D-4 and the clutch handle shattered in my hand. I did get the hydraulic rod fixed though, and it started snowing.

Friday, September 25, 1981—I made a clutch handle out of a shovel handle and got it on the lever for the D-4. It's snowing again today and I built part of the pad that Henry wants for a building site.

Saturday, September 26, 1981—last night and this morning, I got ready for winter, in the afternoon I finished the work Henry wanted and went to Tazlina for a Moose supper. Met Zoe's mother, Gerry. Zoe had come down to ask me to come to this dinner. She had Lloyd Ronning there too. Her mother Gerry had brought up a whole sack of things like fresh sweet corn from Oregon and other goodies that are hard to come by here. We had a really good meal and enjoyed their company.

10,000 Days in Alaska Book One 1978-1989

Sunday, September 27, 1981—still working at getting ready for winter. Put new tires on the front of the truck and serviced it. Took the rubber off of the two truck rims I found.

Monday, September 28, 1981—Henry and I went to Delta. We went with Allen in his pickup. We pulled an engine from Henry's truck that he had there at Delta and had been using it on the project. We stayed overnight at Ernie's and met a fella by the name of Ray.

Tuesday, September 29, 1981—we got the rest of Henry's business done in Delta. We got home late in the afternoon and Andy and I went to Tazlina and found another truck rim on the way.

Wednesday, September 30, 1981—doing more things to be ready for winter.

Thursday, October 1, 1981—shoveled some gravel up around the cabin, re-staked the dogs in new places, pumped some fuel and got the furnace in the trailer going for the lodge.

Friday, October 2, 1981—helped Dan for a bit, putting bigger tundra tires on his Super Cub. Chris and Dan are going buffalo hunting down on the Copper River.

Saturday, October 3, 1981—went to Hoffman's to work on their barn and in the evening went to Polack Days at the Ranch House at Tolsona Creek. They always have good food there and lots of people we know. It's a fun thing to participate in.

Sunday, October 4, 1981—slept late. Put a drive line in the pickup. Henry and I went to Eagle River.

Monday, October 5, 1981—took Henry's engine over to a fella to have it overhauled.

Tuesday, October 6, 1981—we went back to Ron's and he called around for engine parts.

Wednesday, October 7, 1981—Henry and I did some shopping for ourselves and came home. Darrel's pickup had broken down and he wanted me to pull it to Tazlina for him and I did that.

Thursday, October 8, 1981—rested all day and read a book. It's snowing this evening.

Friday, October 9, 1981 through Sunday, October 18, 1981—no entries.

Monday, October 19, 1981—got the Cat ready and loaded on Dan's truck. We graveled the road to his new place and graveled the air strip.

Tuesday, October 20, 1981—I took the Cat up to Hoffman's place and unloaded it off the truck and landscaped around their barn before moving over to the gravel pit to load gravel for Dan.

Wednesday, October 21, 1981—we loaded gravel all day with only small breakdowns.

Thursday, October 22, 1981—loaded gravel again this day.

Friday, October 23, 1981—finished loading and hauling gravel to Dan's at Snowshoe Lake.

Saturday, October 24, 1981—worked on the lights on the pick-up and I was lifting a barrel and hurt my back.

Sunday, October 25, 1981—went down to Dan's and got some of my tools I had left there.

Monday, October 26, 1981—my back is really bad.

Tuesday, October 27, 1981—my back is still sore—cloudy and cool today.

Wednesday, October 28, 1981—my back is feeling better and I did things around home here. I got the Cat started and moved to Hoffman's. They gave me dog food and a dozen eggs.

Thursday, October 29, 1981-no entry.

Friday, October 30, 1981—Darrel and I took my snowmobile to Gunsight. There is a good snowgo mechanic here. (Snowgo is local slang used to denote any snow machine, snowmobile, snowsled, etc. regardless of make or model.)

Saturday, October 31, 1981—went to the Ranch House for a Halloween party and took Sally and Chris along.

Sunday, November 1, 1981—Sylvia called. It's been a while since we talked over the phone.

Monday, November 2, 1981—Sylvia called to give me her plane arrival time.

Tuesday, November 3, 1981—went to Anchorage to pick up Sylvia. James went along and Jeff stopped at the lodge to visit.

Wednesday, November 4, 1981—we got some shopping done before we went out to Nelchina. The road was slippery all the way home.

Thursday, November 5, 1981—it was -5°. Helped Rusty move some things from the shop to another building and worked on the chain saw. Sylvia is busy cleaning around the cabin.

Friday, November 6, 1981—cut up stove wood, built two dog houses, Rusty and I took the pickup to the wood lot and got one load. It's a nice day this morning, -5°.

Saturday, November 7, 1981—cut and hauled a load of wood, split and stacked it, some other chores too. Of course, I've got the dogs to take care of every day. Went to Tolsona Lodge for the Polack party. They had lots of good food, lots of people we knew and we had a fine time.

Sunday, November 8, 1981—Sylvia did the laundry; I changed the oil in the truck and got it ready for winter. We went to Tazlina. Saw Lloyd Ronning and Leo Zura. Leo gave us some smoked salmon. Leo's a real fine man.

Monday, November 9, 1981—went to Tom & Lisa's and showed Sylvia Dan and Patti's new place and we visited them. Went back home and drained the anti-freeze from the Cat at Hoffman's and put a tank heater on Max Hoffman's tractor. He wasn't familiar with how to do that. They gave us two dozen eggs and some gloves.

Tuesday, November 10, 1981—went to Glennallen and saw Lorrie at I-Bar F.

Wednesday, November 11, 1981—Mark and Clyde stopped in.

Thursday, November 12, 1981- didn't do much, called our real estate agent in Minnesota. Went to Gunsight and got the snow machine and went to Tazlina and worked on the snowmobile sled.

Friday, November 13, 1981—slept late, got things ready for the trapline. Split kindling wood for Sylvia.

Saturday, November 14, 1981—got more trapping gear ready. There was a skating party for Dan Billman's birthday and we went to that. Lots of people were there.

Sunday, November 15, 1981—went up to look at the Eleven-Mile Trail off of the Lake Louise Road and another one at 13 Miles. Patti's brother John gave me two dogs named Fluffy and Smokey.

Monday, November 16, 1981—it was -25°. Got up early and loaded the gear and the snowmobile on the truck and drove to the Eleven-Mile Trail on the Lake Louise Road. Jackie and Ken came twice and Jackie drove their truck back to her home. We unloaded my truck and trailer at Jan's on Lake Louise Road. Ken and I then drove the snow machines and sleds to the end of the seismic trail, which was about six miles. Then we broke out our own trail to my cabin. We hung up a few times, especially on one steep hill. It was a heck of a time to get up to the top of that. It was getting towards dark and I felt the pressure of finding the cabin. I go in the general direction that I think the cabin is. Ken was breaking trail for me and I was pulling a real heavy load on my sled behind the machine. We broke out into a more open place and I recognized it and knew exactly where the cabin was. I tried to holler at Ken to catch his attention. He got to be about a hundred yards away from me before he stopped and I waved him over and pointed towards where the cabin would be and he started breaking trail in that direction. We got there just as it was getting dark. Sure glad to have plenty of wood split and ready to go in the stove. We got a fire started and it took a while to warm the cabin up. We were so grateful to have hot water to make coffee, get warm and I had Chili to thaw out so we could have something to eat. We were very hungry. We ate the first batch of chili. I could tell Ken was really hungry yet and I could use some more. The next package of chili filled us up. He thought it was a really nice cabin. The evening temperature was running -12° to -15°. Did a few things in the cabin and built a trap carrier for the snow machine. Today was a pretty day and it also had kind of a rainbow in the sky. Very unusual.

Tuesday, November 17, 1981—it was -10°. After breakfast, we got ready and I went with Ken half way to the end of the seismic trail to make sure he got headed out on the trail with no problems. We said our good-byes and he went out to the road. His wife was to pick him up and take him home. I headed back to the cabin. When I got to the upper end of Blue Lake, I set two martin traps and I got a ptarmigan for supper.

Wednesday, November 18, 1981—Rested all day.

Thursday, November 19, 1981—it was -18° when I woke up and it was cloudy with some ice fog. I found I was really stiff and sore today. I got a slow start. I got out on the trapline and made an otter set and some fox and martin sets south and west of Blue Lake. Saw a few ptarmigan tracks and rabbit tracks but no spruce hens. Nothing much near here, only moose and caribou tracks and some martin and fox. Went hunting for bait, didn't get anything. Ice fog setting in this evening and it's -15° tonight. I could see the seismic trail from a high hill west of Blue Lake. I must tell Ken that would make a landmark to follow. Not enough snow for good snowmobiling, it's really rough.

Friday, November 20, 1981—it was -20°. Slept late, need the rest. Lots of frost in the snowmobile gas, I suppose because of the foggy nights. Broke another trap trail to the north, then east, then south, then back home. Set four martin and otter. No fox bait with me. Saw fox and martin tracks and some caribou, otter and moose. Saw a beautiful small lake today. It was really nice out there. It's -15° at dark. Fixed supper, read and rested. The Coleman lantern lights the cabin in the evening and I cook on the airtight stove. (A type of wood burning stove.) It's a medium sized airtight. It's a really nice stove for a remote cabin like this. I've got a big firewood pile that I put up last spring just before snow left. I'll do that again this coming spring so that I'll have dry wood to use through the winter.

Saturday, November 21, 1981—it got warmer. I made a short trail. There are no fresh tracks of any kind, so I put up insulation in the ceiling of the cabin. It only took 2 ½ hours, but it sure made a difference in the wood it takes to keep the cabin warm. I sharpened my knives here at the cabin too. It's -10° this evening.

Sunday, November 22, 1981—it was -10° in the morning and 0° at noon. Very bright and sunny, no wind. Measured the ice on the cabin lake. It's 13 inches with 4 inches of snow on top. I made two sets on the ridge back of the cabin. No new game or fur tracks anywhere. It was really nice all day, but it looks like snow clouds 20-30 miles to the north by east, I can see some really nice peaks from in the higher ridges. This country right through here has little high places. When you get up on them, it's about 2700 elevation and often times, you get a real nice view. It helps keep track of where you are in the country too, once you learn what it looks like. The cabin stays lots warmer now and heats with less wood since I insulated the ceiling. It's -10° this evening.

Monday, November 23, 1981—it's 5° above zero with a light dust of snow falling overnight. It was 8° at noon. I ran both lines today—no fur. Did see a cow and calf moose though. It seems to be much warmer. There is a lot of overflow and water that comes up through the ice and soaks the snow. Plan to go out to the road tomorrow.

Tuesday, November 24, 1981—had a good run out to the road, saw 32 caribou on the trail. When I parked at Jan's, I met Jay, Jan's father. The trip took two hours coming out from the trap cabin (about 16 miles). The next day, went to Hoffmans for dimmer. Met George. He's an announcer at the local radio and his family was there. They're friends of the Hoffmans. Then we went to Tazlina in the evening.

Wednesday, November 25, 1981—snowed 2 inches last night. Charlie stopped to talk dogs. He wants to run them for me. I don't have them trained well enough nor do I have the trails for them to run on the trapline. We went into Glennallen to get some supplies that we needed.

Thursday, November 26, 1981 through Saturday, November 28, 1981—no entries.

10,000 Days in Alaska Book One 1978-1989

Sunday, November 29, 1981—we flew into Old Boot Lake and got camp set up. We're planning on staking and claiming some land in what the state has called Green Acres.

Monday, November 30, 1981—Curt called to tell us he couldn't fly today. We looked the land over and Curt flew me to Tolsona Lake and I drove home.

Tuesday, December 1, 1981—I started for the trapline and there was a van on the road ahead of me. These people suddenly stopped to look at far off caribou. I was following another car behind the van and the snow was flying up. The car ahead of me ran in the ditch and missed the van, but it was too late for me, I bumped his bumper. This all made it too late to make the run out to the cabin.

Wednesday, December 2, 1981—I didn't go to the cabin today but got gas ready and most of the gear I needed to take out there.

Thursday, December 3, 1981—it was 15° and snowed six inches last night. I went to Jay's and saw Lloyd Ronning's pickup was in the ditch, so I pulled him out with my pickup. It snowed heavy all afternoon.

Friday, December 4, 1981—I got up early, had breakfast and gathered supplies, went to Tazlina and went to John's place. Loaded the snowmobile and drove the machine back to Eleven-Mile Trail and then went 4 miles to the upper lake above Old Boot Lake. We have a tent camp there on Old Boot Lake. The snow was really deep and when I would come down the hills the snow would flow about six feet ahead of the machine. I'm going down hill that way and it flows out and along the sides. My heart in my throat, I'm hoping that I don't get stuck. When I get there, Daryl and his dog, Rufus are doing okay. He had been flown in to the cabin site with this tent that is a military—army tent. It's designed for winter camping.

Saturday, December 5, 1981—the days are really short, so we got what we would call a late start and it's really cold. We got some compass bearings and paced off some land and shoreline. We did see over a hundred caribou yesterday, their tracks are all over. Saw two moose cows with calves and two fox track. When we get up on the higher places of these properties, there are some nice views.

Sunday, December 6, 1981—it was a nice day, but pretty cold. Cut firewood. We've got 720 feet of land boundary measured. We've got a hundred foot steel tape that we used. Then we took some time and looked at building sites. Building sites must be a hundred feet set back from the shoreline of the lake. Saw a few rabbit tracks and a place where ptarmigan or a spruce hen had dived in the snow to sleep—it's pretty warm under the snow. We sure liked the nice views from around here. Darrel isn't feeling very well.

Monday, December 7, 1981—I'm sick and what we picked up, we don't know, but I snowmobile out—woke up sick in the night, didn't get much sleep. Both the carburetor and steering froze up on the snow machine. Finally got it going. I had a big heavy screwdriver on the snow machine and a hatchet and I would hammer on that screwdriver handle and chip the ice out so I could get the steering so it would move. I got to Jan's about noon. Then went home and later went to the land office in Glennallen, and then shopped for groceries. After that I went to Mike's with a message from Henry.

Tuesday, December 8, 1981—I'm still sick.

Wednesday, December 9, 1981—I slept late. It's a nice warm day but I don't feel good this morning. I decide to go back in and I'm pulling the sled. Broke more trails and set six traps. Got a red fox thawed out, skinned and stretched him. He had two porcupine quills in him—so they meet porcupines and get a quill once in a while. Got things ready for the trip out, saw two moose, had a camp robber and a rabbit in the traps. An owl ate the rabbit. I made one fox set, caribou had been moving around.

Thursday, December 10, 1981—we do some more measuring on Old Boot and also across the middle lake and land dividing it from Upper Lake and another part of that lake. This is the area that Darrel has chosen. We're expecting a plane so we snowmobiled an airstrip on the lake. Made four, square posts with the chain saw to mark our post corners with.

Friday, December 11, 1981—chipped the ice out of the steering on the snowmobile again this morning. Took two stakes with us to Darrel's 40.

10,000 Days in Alaska Book One 1978-1989

Rufus has died. He had some kind of kidney problem and Darrel wanted Rufus over on his 40. We put in the stakes and chopped two lines and flagged them. Then we went to my 40 acres and staked and flagged one line and measured my lakeshore. It was getting close to dark so we get in stove wood for the night.

Saturday, December 12, 1981—we looked at what would make a building site and evaluated the lines of the sides of the 40 and then packed up to leave. Chris came in on our landing strip to fly Darrel out just before dark. I went out with the snowmobile pulling an empty sled. Then we celebrated at Nelchina.

Sunday, December 13, 1981—rested all day, went to Gunsight for gasoline and oil for the snowgo.

Monday, December 14, 1981—we unpacked the Green Acres gear and packed to go out to the traplines.

Tuesday, December 15, 1981—I had a tough time getting in to the cabin. The trail was not good all the way to Blue Lake. I lost the trail entirely—deep snow. I knew where Blue Lake was and I was trying to get there and I came up over a small ridge. Just as I got to the top, there was no place to go but a bunch of alders. I got stuck in them and then the darned Ski-Doo wouldn't start. I tried to cut some of the alders out from under the machine so I could get going but the machine just would NOT start. There was nothing to do. It was right at dark, so I started walking towards the cabin. It's probably two miles to the cabin from where I'm stuck. The bunny boots sure got heavy! Soon it's dark, but there were stars shining. They gave enough light so I could follow the trail—especially when you know it. When I get here, the cabin is in fine shape. I had wood split and ready to build fire. I get a fire going. It's been dark for some time, walking on the trail. I got here three hours after dark. Saw a caribou, moose cow and a calf and three ptarmigans today.

Wednesday, December 16, 1981—I got up early, had breakfast, walked back to the snowmobile and got it un-stuck and off of the brush. It started then and I went back to the cabin and ran some of the trapline. Got a nice marten. Then I got lost from the trail and came out by the highway by way of Old Man Lake.

Norman Wilkins

Thursday, December 17, 1981—finished fixing the truck, shopped and went to Nelchina, unloaded supplies, then to Tazlina and unloaded more. Lost a hundred pound propane tank. Stopped to ask Blake to feed the dogs and pack for the trip to Minnesota.

Friday, December 18, 1981—picked Darrel up and started out at 12:30 a.m. Arrived at Hanes Junction late in the morning. Whitehorse, we had supper, Watson Lake, we got there at midnight. The roads are snow covered and ice under the snow.

Saturday, December 19, 1981—we arrived at Dawson Creek at 6:30 p.m. and ate supper. The roads are very bad. Darrel took turns driving my pickup. Sylvia sits in between us. It's not comfortable sitting in the middle, this truck has a gear shift, it's not automatic—but she's not complaining.

Sunday, December 20, 1981—at 6:00 a.m. in Edmonton, the roads are very bad and it's blowing snow. It's tiring to drive.

Monday, December 21, 1981—we got to Saskatoon at noon. The roads are still bad and blowing snow. We kept on going and ate supper in Winnipeg.

Tuesday, December 22, 1981—Arrived in Fargo at 5:00 a.m., dropped Daryl off at the bus station where he met a friend to drive him to South Dakota. We went on to Motley and then to Cushing and stopped at the real estate agent, then to Little Falls to sign the sale papers for the west 80, then to Minneapolis to Darrell and Nadia's. The kids came over to visit us. I slept a lot, trying to catch up.

Wednesday, December 23, 1981—no entry.

Thursday, December 24, 1981—here at Nadia's, lots of visitors. Visited Kevin's relatives in the evening.

Friday, December 25, 1981—nice Christmas day with the kids and friends.

Saturday, December 26, 1981—it was snowing, we went out shopping and then we went out again for supper.

Sunday, December 27, 1981—went over to Beverly's for supper and a movie.

Monday, December 28, 1981—went to the farm and visited some people and got some things that we had in storage over at the chicken house on the east farm. Got back to Nadia's late.

Tuesday, December 29, 1981—did some shopping and visited Beverly, Kevin and Vanessa.

Wednesday, December 30, 1981—we did more shopping and played with Vanessa and it's snowing and warm. We have plans to go to Theresa's for supper this evening. Had Minnesota venison for supper and a good time.

Thursday, December 31, 1981—had goose for dinner and a nice visit all day. Went to Paul and Ruth's in the evening.

Norman Wilkins

The trap cabin and its interior

10,000 Days in Alaska Book One 1978-1989

Norman using a moose call he made from a coffee can and cord.

Norman Wilkins

1982–bear scare, staking claims, digging clams

Friday, January 1, 1982–visited with Paul, Ruth and Steve all day and had a good time.

Saturday, January 2, 1982–went to Nadia's. Darrell helped me get loaded and ready for the trip back to Alaska. We left there and went to the farm, and then from the farm, we drove to Fargo, North Dakota. The roads were snowy and icy. We got there at 9:30 p.m. and waited for Darrel to arrive. Soon, Darrel, Larry and Doug arrived at 12:30 a.m. We all visited for a while and then we left for Alaska.

Sunday, January 3, 1982–still traveling. Roads are better though, but it's cold. It was -40°. More of the same, shopped in Fort Nelson–more cold.

Monday, January 4, 1982–when I we got to Watson Lake today, it was -56°. No one was shutting off their vehicles if they expected to drive them. Our truck is stiff, mechanically. For instance, the brake and the clutch feel strange when you use them. The doors on the truck have shrunk up and they rattle. The cold air blows in; the heater barely keeps it so we can stay in it.

Tuesday, January 5, 1982–blowing snow and icy roads and very cold. We had a detour from Jakes, Corner to Carcross and then to White Horse. We did a little shopping and then had ice fog and snow and high winds and more cold all the way to the border. A distance before the border, in the night, Darrel was driving and I saw vehicle tracks that appeared to me that they went over in the other lane of the highway and gone off into the ditch. So I asked Darrel to turn around and go back so we could look to see if there was somebody in the ditch. We got back to this place and I got out and walked around and I had a flashlight. I could see where this vehicle had left its lane and left the highway, over the end of a culvert and into the ditch, over on its top and gear and cans of fuel and lots of stuff was lying around in the snow. The vehicle was destroyed; it's a brand new Ford ¾ ton pickup. I walked the perimeter looking for tracks of anyone who might have been stunned and walked or maybe wandered out on the snow and brush–I found no tracks out there. We hadn't seen a vehicle in hours. Those folks must have been really lucky that someone came along and picked them up–of course we'll never know what happened to them.

10,000 Days in Alaska Book One 1978-1989

Wednesday, January 6, 1982—we arrived home about 7:00 a.m. and rested all day. The temperatures here at home are running -40° to -55°.

Thursday, January 7, 1982—got up late and it's still -55°.

Friday, January 8, 1982—unloaded part of the pickup, visited Jackie—Blake wasn't home. Had supper with Bob and Margaret Schmidt.

Saturday, January 9, 1982—went to Glennallen grocery shopping. Mike P. and Ken K. stopped in and brought Judy back and told us of a dead moose along the highway east of us. We called it in to fish and game and they came out and looked at it and said I could have it for dog food. Henry pulled it home with his wrecker. That really worked well. He could winch it out to the road, and pulled it right down the highway into the lodge parking lot. When I butchered this moose, I found it was pregnant.

Sunday, January 10, 1982—no entry.

Monday, January 11, 1982—put a handle in an ax and visited with Sam.

Tuesday, January 12, 1982—cut quarters off moose with an ax. Dan Billman stopped by and we had a visit.

Wednesday, January 13, 1982—pulled two quarters of the moose to a place where I would be cooking it for the dogs. Lee Dudley and Darrel G. came to the lodge and we played cards and dice games and visited. We have a game called Ship Captain & Crew....We all like to play that.

Thursday, January 14, 1982—cut up some wood. Cleaned snow off half the cabin roof and did cabin chores.

Friday, January 15, 1982—I don't feel good today, didn't do much. Read the book, *Chesapeake*. It's -40°.

Saturday, January 16, 1982—it's -35° to -40°. I still don't feel good, but it's a nice sun shiny day.

Sunday, January 17, 1982—read again today. It's nice, but a really cold

Norman Wilkins

day. I bedded the dogs to keep them warm.

Monday, January 18, 1982 and Tuesday, January 19, 1982—no entries.

Wednesday, January 20, 1982—Henry hauled the rest of the moose carcass to Tazlina for dog food for Darrel's dogs.

Thursday, January 21, 1982—nice day, but cold. Cut up and split wood, read most of day.

Friday, January 22, 1982—no entry.

Saturday, January 23, 1982—messed around here, read and had a great night's sleep. The Northern Lights were fantastic—sort of yellow and looked like a gently curving river flowing in the sky.

Sunday, January 24, 1982—split wood, visited Blake and Jackie. Paid them fore feeding and caring for the dogs while we were in Minnesota. They gave us two moose t-bone steaks. Boy, were they good.

Monday, January 25, 1982—went to Tazlina for a few hours and came home at 7:00 p.m. It was -41°.

Tuesday, January 26, 1982—nice day but cold. It stays at -40° below zero at night. Cut up more wood.

Wednesday, January 27, 1982—went to Tazlina Lodge in the evening and got home late.

Thursday, January 28, 1982—went to Anchorage to shop and bring James and Zoe back to Nelchina. Stayed at Andy and Connie's while we were in Anchorage. Angela, the daughter is in the hospital and Connie stays there with her. Andy was in Fairbanks. He has a business and has a job there to do.

Friday, January 29, 1982—there was a party for James and Zoe at Tazlina. Got home early.

Saturday, January 30, 1982—didn't do much all day.

10,000 Days in Alaska Book One 1978-1989

Sunday, January 31, 1982—cut up wood and read a lot. Slightly foggy today, warmer these days. It's -20° below this evening.

Monday, February 1, 1982—my birthday, Sylvia fixed a good dinner. I don't feel good today. Worked on a large knife scabbard for James. He's building a very large knife and I'm making a scabbard for it. It was cloudy and warmer today.

Tuesday, February 2, 1982—went to Tazlina Lodge with Chris Ronning and played Ship, Captain Crew.

Wednesday, February 3, 1982—Darrel gave us some breakfast sausage. Talked to Mark. He thinks he'll stop in Sunday. Quite warm today.

Thursday, February 4, 1982—Brit and her friend from Norway visited in the afternoon. We visited Charlie T. and had supper at Hoffman's. Allen Farmer stopped in there. Took our trash to the dump and took the finished knife sheath and books to James.

Friday, February 5, 1982 and Saturday, February 6, 1982—No entries.

Sunday, February 7, 1982—rested all day. Brit and Heidi stopped in to say good-bye. They're going back home to Norway.

Monday, February 8, 1982—Bob Schmidt got a call early of a road kill caribou. Henry and I went with him to load it. I skinned and cleaned it out. Cut and split firewood and bedded the dogs and other chores around the cabin.

Tuesday, February 9, 1982—took the snowmobile to Jan's, visited with Jay and his wife, stopped at Tazlina, didn't get home until late.

Wednesday, February 10, 1982—No entry.

Thursday, February 11, 1982—resting up, Sylvia doesn't feel good today.

Friday, February 12, 1982—Sylvia feels okay today. Denny B. and Mike stopped by in the evening.

Saturday, February 13, 1982—slept late, James Callahan and I switched wheels and tires around on my pickup and then went to get his step van. I put chains on my 4-wheel-drive pickup and pulled his van to Nelchina.

Sunday, February 14, 1982—got some gear ready to go in to the cabin on the trapline. Darrel stopped to visit, he had been to Hoffman's, they had a goat die in birthing a kid and Darrel brought it to us to use for dog food.

Monday, February 15, 1982 and Tuesday, February 16, 1982—No entries.

Wednesday, February 17, 1982—Darrel and I hauled Henry's Ski-Doo to Jan's, fueled up, and loaded the sled and started for the cabin. Saw a few wolf tracks, and fox and caribou and moose. Got the sled hung up in some trees and the trail is lost, can't find it. I got into some trees and got stuck. He saw my trouble and stopped his machine and came up to help me get mine out. It was actually stuck between two trees. We came back to Jan's and went home disappointed.

Thursday, February 18, 1982—got up early, went to Jan's, fueled the machines again, tried to make a new trail to the cabin and had trouble finding a good trail. Eventually got to the cabin, built a fire, and went back to make the trail but couldn't find a decent one. Went back to the cabin. We'll try again tomorrow. It's a nice day, -15° tonight and I'm tired.

Friday, February 19, 1982—it's -22°. Split wood here at the cabin, did chores, went to break trail to get the sled in to the cabin. Saw a nice moose at the upper end of Blue Lake and went to the sled where we'd left it yesterday. On the way back, got stuck and found a big skull and rack from a bull caribou. Got back to the cabin at 4:00 p.m. It's still cold. Only saw one bird, a raven. Not much game moving now, nor fur. It's a nice day and glad to be out here at the cabin.

Saturday, February 20, 1982—left for trap cabin at noon. Saw moose and two wolves on the way out to the road. Went over to Old Boot Lake and then back out to the road and to Jan's and from there we went home. KROA is having a party this evening. Everyone takes pot luck food and they have music. Lots of people were there.

Sunday, February 21, 1982—didn't do much all day.

10,000 Days in Alaska Book One 1978-1989

Monday, February 22, 1982—Sylvia went over to see Blake and Jackie and their baby. Sam and Darrel came by in the evening.

Tuesday, February 23, 1982—we went to Glennallen grocery shopping and visited Ken and Jackie Kramer and stopped at Tazlina lodge on our way back.

Wednesday, February 24, 1982—Sylvia and I have the flue I suppose. We picked it up in town or something. It's a beautiful day, cold and a little windy.

Thursday, February 25, 1982 through Friday, March 5, 1982—No entries.

Saturday, March 6, 1982—slept late this morning, we are all sick. Darrel and I and James went up Lake Louise Road to Eleven-Mile Trail. And down this trail about less than a half a mile to the east to look at a cabin for Darrel to live in. The lodge where Darrel has been working changed hands and he's got to try to find a place to live.

Sunday, March 7, 1982—tried to get Darrel's snow machine running.

Monday, March 8, 1982—Darrel has decided to make that place livable so we helped him move to this cabin east of the Eleven-Mile Trail. This isn't much of a cabin, it's quite old, and the roof sags a lot.

Tuesday, March 9, 1982—Charlie Trowbridge came to visit. Still don't feel well.

Wednesday, March 10, 1982—did chores and read. Zoe and James came and visited and gave us a chair. This flu sure hangs on.

Thursday, March 11, 1982—warm and bright.

Friday, March 12, 1982—no entry.

Saturday, March 13, 1982—butchered out a small moose calf that Fish & Game gave Bob Schmidt. They had called him to come and get it. Bob needs help with something like that.

Norman Wilkins

Sunday, March 14, 1982—didn't do much all day. James and Zoe visited.

Monday, March 15, 1982—cut up our share of the little moose.

Tuesday, March 16, 1982—James brought some of his guns over to store here. We all went over to KROA for a while and then back here to our place.

Wednesday, March 17, 1982—James and Zoe left for Palmer this afternoon on his motorcycle.

Thursday, March 18, 1982—Sylvia, Sam and I went to Darrel's and then on to Tolsona and then home. Darrel stayed with us tonight.

Friday, March 19, 1982—Sylvia, Darrel and I went to Lake Louise Junction and worked on his snowgo. It still wasn't running. He went to his place and Sylvia and I went to Old Boot Lake. She wasn't too impressed with Old Boot Lake. The rough snowmobile ride probably didn't help.

Saturday, March 20, 1982—sick today, and it's windy. Sam and Peter stopped to visit. We had supper at Max and Irene Hoffmans.

Sunday, March 21, 1982—Sam visited. Really nice day, sick all day.

Monday, March 22, 1982—beautiful day, did things around the place.

Tuesday, March 23, 1982—went to Glennallen and did laundry. Bob Moore wasn't back in his forestry office.

Wednesday, March 24, 1982—went to Dimmick's. Harold and Rachel are in Nome so stopped at Blake and Jackie's. Baby Jessica sure is cute. Jackie fixed supper for Sylvia and I, and I split some wood for her.

Thursday, March 25, 1982—it's snowing. Darrel came out from the cabin, (I read most all day).

Friday, March 26, 1982—no snow this morning, went to Darrel's and then decided not to go to the cabin. I don't feel well.

10,000 Days in Alaska Book One 1978-1989

Saturday, March 27, 1982—still have this flu. It's a nice day.

Sunday, March 28, 1982—Charlie stopped in on his way to Anchorage and work, he'll work out of Cordova for Fish & Game.

Monday, March 29, 1982—real nice day, a little cooler. Worked on the income tax. Went to Dimmick's, Harold and Rachel aren't home yet. Henry came over from his work this evening. We still have the flu.

Tuesday, March 30, 1982—No entry.

Wednesday, March 31, 1982—loaded some gear and went to Darrel's and loaded the snow machine sled. Darrel and I went to Old Boot Lake and fixed up our camp there, looked over our staking problems and spent the evening reading regulations and making decisions and plans. It's been a real nice day, a little windy here. A small herd of caribou was near our camp as we drove up.

Thursday, April 1, 1982—another nice day, very windy. Saw four caribou and ptarmigan while we were making Darrel's back property line. We got lots of measuring done today.

Friday, April 2, 1982—we've been working the last few days trying to get the land we're claiming on Old Boot Lake lined out. It's 40 acres and I have to cut trail around it ¼ mile by ¼ mile, by ¼ mile and we're having a lot of trouble with the back lines to get through the brush and keep it straight. I snowmobiled out to feed Darrel's dogs and came home for a few things we need. Nice day, but it was cold.

Saturday, April 3, 1982—it's a very nice day up early, went to Dimmick's they were not home. Went to Darrel's and we all went to Old Boot Lake. We got a lot of work done this afternoon.

Sunday, April 4, 1982—we worked on the property lines at Old Boot and Satiety Lake. Got the corner posts and lines in on my 40 acres. Saw a spruce hen. Some really nice trees here. I had a burbot set out, but didn't catch one. Came out to the road in the evening.

Monday, April 5, 1982—slept late, then worked on paperwork for remote parcel, 40 acres. Did cabin chores, then visited Henry. Sam came to visit and stayed the night.

Tuesday, April 6, 1982—visited Henry, called land office and went to Dimmick's. We ate muktuk, a traditional Inuit/Eskimo meal of frozen whale skin and whale blubber, dried seal, fish and seal oil, then visited Dan and Patti Billman. It was a warm day.

Wednesday, April 7, 1982—nice day, up all night, couldn't sleep. But handle in double bit ax and made a sheath for it. Did a multitude of other little jobs. Full moon tonight.

Thursday, April 8, 1982—did maintenance work on truck and dog chores. Nice day, light snow and evening. Put a ground on the radio.

Friday, April 9, 1982—nice day, I put a handle in a hatchet. Went to Glennallen to the State Lands office. Stopped by Ken and Jackie Kramer's and had supper with them. Mike and Lynette Phillips were there.

Saturday, April 10, 1982—another nice day. Betty came yesterday; she is still at the lodge. Went to see Don McArthur, but he wasn't home.

Sunday, April 11, 1982—up early, drove the snowgo to my trapping cabin, got things all done there then went to Old Boot Lake and took pictures of the corner posts. Cut up some trees at a ditch on the seismic trail near the fifth line on Old Boot Lake that Henry stakes. Saw moose caribou, bear, fox, martin, tracks. Parked the truck up to Jay's place and got to see him and his wife at mile 16 on the Lake Louise Road. Visited Max and Irene Hoffman and did a lot of odd chores around here it was a pretty nice day.

Monday, April 12, 1982 through Tuesday, May 4, 1982—No entries.

Wednesday, May 5, 1982—went into Old Boot Lake and painted Henry's stakes. Saw moose caribou, bear, fox, and marten tracks. Visited Jay and his wife at mile 16 on the Lake Louise Road.

Thursday, May 6, 1982—took canoe behind Ski-Doo into Old Boot Lake. Trail is soft. Darrel went with us to Glennallen. Stopped to visit Dennis and Sally at Tolsona Lake.

Friday, May 7, 1982—No entry.

Saturday, May 8, 1982—visited Max and Irene Hoffman. Did a lot of odd chores around here. Very nice day.

Sunday, May 9, 1982—Tom and Lisa stopped to visit and then we went to Darrel's and got the chain saw, sled and Ski-Doo. Pulled his car to his place and stopped at KROA for pizza.

Monday, May 10, 1982—we had a little snow and rain, hauled a load of wood to Max Hoffman—Irene looks better. Got another load of wood to take to Andy Boyle. Had to work on the chain saw, ordered some parts for it.

Tuesday, May 11, 1982—up early and read. Henry came over later and Peter and Tom. Did a few things here and called the real estate agent for our properties in Minnesota from Blake and Jackie's. Read some more and then went over to visit Bob and Margaret Schmidt. They asked us out for supper.

Wednesday, May 12, 1982—wrote Bill Wolf and Paul Norris. Did lots of chores around here and at noon, Henry and I went to feed "Coyote Ugly's" dogs, then went to Glennallen, then to Dennis and Sally's, ate supper with them and came home late.

Thursday, May 13, 1982—went to Anchorage to do grocery shopping and business and stayed with Andy and Connie.

Friday, May 14, 1982—finished shopping and got home before dark.

Saturday, May 15, 1982—went to Tolsona Lake to Dennis and Sally's.

Sunday, May 16, 1982—went to Valdez, Dennis and Sally went along. Sylvia was keeping her eyes out for mushrooms and sometimes we went walking and looking for them.

Monday, May 17, 1982—stayed overnight at Dennis and Sally's—didn't do much, just visit and hung out.

Tuesday, May 18, 1982—went to Hoffman's and butchered a billy goat for them. Henry and Darrel stopped in and Jackie and baby stopped in for a while. Sylvia always likes to see the baby. A guy stopped in and left a doghouse with us. Did a lot of service work on the truck and did some things around here.

Wednesday, May 19, 1982—Henry, Sally, Dennis, Sylvia and I went to a party. Henry goes to work at Slate Creek tomorrow evening.

Thursday, May 20, 1982—painted signs for Henry. He and Dennis and Sally showed up a while. Peter stopped at noon and ate with us. I called Digiovanni and Borders and real estate agent looking out for our properties. Visited Billmans and met a guy there (Leo?) Sylvia started planting garden.

Friday, May 21, 1982—went to Hoffman's place to work on the Cat and went to Glennallen to get an O ring for a hydraulic hose leak.

Saturday, May 22, 1982—picked up trash off the highway ditches for two hours in the morning. (We have a dedicated one mile where we pick the trash up.) Then we went to Hoffman's and got the Cat started and came home. Did things around here and called Ernie H. Then Rodney Borders called us at Blake's. Later we went to KROA to a farewell party.

Sunday, May 23, 1982—nice day, a few snow showers. I straightened up the brown storage trailer. This was a trailer that was abandoned at the lodge here. Someone had broken the axel and left it there and Henry gave it to me to use. Made storage for a bunch of 5-gallon cans, dog food and Blazo. James, (a friend of Rusty) came to get the Ranchero.

Monday, May 24, 1982—used the bucket on the cat to load gravel for Dan. Sylvia felt sick today. We had some rain showers and two Canadian geese were at Snowshoe Lake; also saw a loon and duck and five caribou. (Their horns are in velvet now.)

Tuesday, May 25, 1982—loaded more gravel. Dan got stuck. Took swamp buggy and winched him out.

Wednesday, May 26, 1982—hauled garbage for Bob Schmidt and stopped at Dan's, then later Darrel came and stayed overnight at our place.

Thursday, May 27, 1982—Darrel got a job, so he bought pizza and beer at KROA for Jackie and us. He is glad to be working again.

Friday, May 28, 1982—worked on the big trailer in the morning and feel sick this afternoon. Light shower this evening.

Saturday, May 29, 1982—Blake and Jackie came over then Betty and kids came up from Eagle River and got a load of their things. Helped Blake a little in the afternoon. There was a bad rollover on the highway near mile 142.

Sunday, May 30, 1982—Darrel and I walked to Old Boot Lake to look for a survey monument. We did not find one. Saw two Canadian geese along Lake Louise Road. Sometimes they do their pairing up along small lakes there, but I've never seen that they've hatched eggs there. Darrel borrowed money and dog food until payday. Sylvia went to Lucky and Mary's for movies. She likes to go down and visit with Mary, they're good pals.

Monday, May 31, 1982—worked at things around here. Blake and Jackie and baby were here for a Moose rib supper. It was hot and sunny today.

Tuesday, June 1, 1982—visited Max and Irene Hoffman, then went to see Lucky and Mary and watched two movies. Real nice day. Lucky and Mary are always friendly. We watch TV there sometimes. (We do not have electricity at our place.)

Wednesday, June 2, 1982—worked on the welder. It doesn't want to start. Went with Bob and Margaret to KROA. Two light showers and cooler today.

Thursday, June 3, 1982—worked on the welder. Had to get Ed Farmer to find a short in it, and it runs now. Worked on the chain saw also and Sylvia sowed greens in the greenhouse today.

Friday, June 4, 1982—Dan stopped in and we made plans to go prospecting. Went to Hoffman's and tightened the tracks on my Cat. Went to KROA for gasoline, visited Blake and Jackie and called Ron

Brandt and Melissa answered. Ron is on a job in the field and will be back in two weeks.

Saturday, June 5, 1982—the Billmans aren't home, Welded and repaired the snowgo sled, started building the snowgo toboggan sled and went to Lucky and Mary's for movies in the evening. It is cool and windy but nice today. Darrel was here while we were gone.

Sunday, June 6, 1982—worked on an aluminum trap carrier to mount on the snowgo. Went to Dan Billman and borrowed a saber saw to help cut this aluminum. Very windy and blowing glacial dust off of Nelchina River with gusts over 30 mph. Sunny, light clouds.

Monday, June 7, 1982—go like hell getting the rest of the gear ready to go to Coghill Lake. Windy here. Watching the weather, hope it will let us get there. Dan with his 185 Cessna will fly his brother Denny and me to prospect in the Coghill River and Lake Area.

Tuesday, June 8, 1982—up early, left Snowshoe Lake late, got to Coghill Lake and made camp. It rained with some fog. It was a great trip over the glaciers to Prince William Sound. We saw five black bears near where we camped, one was a monster! When we landed the plane there, we found a rubber raft that a bear had bit and put holes in it, leaked the air all out. We saw lots of ducks and swans and lots of beavers. We prospected most of the night. It got real late.

Wednesday, June 9, 1982—we prospected several creeks and got a small amount of gold. It will take a more expensive effort to see if this is worthwhile. We saw another black bear from the air. It's still raining. The first night, Dan tied the plane up along the shore. He slept in the plane and Denny and I each had tarps. We crawled in our sleeping bags and wrapped up in our tarps. These were really tall trees and it was rainy. In the morning we discovered that where Denny had chosen to sleep, the darned water had run in underneath his tarp and he and everything in there was wet. Dan tried to start a fire but we couldn't get the wood to burn—it was all too wet. Dan would drain off AV gas and we'd try to pour that on the wood to get it to burn, but it just wouldn't burn. After a few failures like this, we got in the plane and flew over to near Coswell Lake and we got ourselves in to a forester cabin over there. There was dry wood and we got a fire going and got dry. Then we went out and got more wood and brought it is so it would dry out overnight from the heat from the stove. Denny, he chose to sleep up in the loft. This cabin was an A-frame and there were bunks on each side of the a-frame against the outside of the roof.

Thursday, June 10, 1982—I woke up looking a big black bear square in the eyes at two feet with the window between us. He was reared up with paws on the window and was looking at me. When I saw him, I yelled, "Bear! Get the hell outta here!" Dan, he heard that and he happened to be faced towards the side of the A-frame. He rose up so quickly, he hit his head on the A-frame. Then he had to flop around in the bunk and in the sleeping bag to get rolled over so he could see something. His brother Denny, up in the loft, slammed the door shut and stood on it so the bear wouldn't get up there at him. (These two guys were thinking the bear was in the cabin.) But when they looked around, they saw there was no bear inside. We got all dressed and went out and we could see where the bears claws had gripped the edge of the porch (this is an overhanging lip over the porch) and the bear made a leap off of the porch and it was about 3.5 feet to the ground—he landed on all four feet, 18 feet—six big steps from the porch. You could see where he went running out through the grass and brush and stuff. So we had breakfast and then Denny and I took guns and went out looking for the bear. A bear that time of year would make awfully good eating. We walked around and we saw paths that the bear had made walking through the grass and stuff. It was trying to rain all the time, but it was easy to track him. But we couldn't get up to him. Finally later in the day we decided we would go to Whittier and out over Portage Pass in Anchorage. Dan is a pilot and he knows the ways and just how and where to go safely.

Friday, June 11, 1982—Denny, Chris and I were at the lodge and we met Herb Farmer he's from down in the lower 48 and has spent lots of years up in Alaska also.

Saturday, June 12, 1982—rested most of the day. Sylvia helped with a spaghetti party to raise money for the Glennallen hospital. Bob Schmidt asked me to go to Chet's fish wheel tonight. Bob and he are good friends and Bob likes to get salmon out of the fish wheel. Good of him to invite us along.

Sunday, June 13, 1982—left for the fish wheel. We stayed in a cabin there and went around the town of Copper Center. Bob got permission to use another fish wheel from a fella he knew. About 1:00 a.m., we got about 200 red salmon, all first class fish. One of the salmon was a king salmon. It was one of the first fish we got. All the way home from there, we gave lots of fish to all the neighbors. We offered them all they might want. Then Bob and Sylvia and I shared what was left. We got our share all cleaned and were sure tired that next evening. But it had been a very good day—the small mosquitoes were out today.

Monday, June 14, 1982—Sylvia canned salmon. She really is good at that, and likes to put up meat and food. I went to Dan's for a while.

Tuesday, June 15, 1982—went to Anchorage and did shopping and so forth. Some light rain.

Wednesday, June 16, 1982—got a fairly late start, but got seven loads of gravel loaded and hauled to Dan's. Fairly heavy rain. Went to see Hoffmans for a while.

Thursday, June 17, 1982—got up early to a light rain. Loaded and hauled gravel for Dan all day. Prospected in the evening. Found some very interesting gold in Cache Creek. Saw a moose swim across Snowshoe Lake.

Friday, June 18, 1982—it's raining, but we prospected anyhow. We got farther up Cache Creek and found more gold. Tom came for his dog that had been staying with us.

Saturday, June 19, 1982—got up early, then cleaned the cabin and made more bookcases. Rodney Borders called with farm business. Andy Boyle called about a commercial fishing ad.

Sunday, June 20, 1982—got some things ready to prospect Cache Creek. Dennis, Sally and son Chris visited. Dennis and Bob Schmidt and I celebrated father's day at KROA.

Monday, June 21, 1982—Dan and Patti Billman, Sylvia and I staked four 40 acre claims on Cache Creek—really tired tonight. We had a good fish supper.

10,000 Days in Alaska Book One 1978-1989

Tuesday, June 22, 1982—went to Glennallen, lots of things to do. Saw Darrel and talked to him a little. Went to the Ranch House. A fellow by the name of Bill wants me to prospect for him later in the summer. I may or may not do that.

Wednesday, June 23, 1982—nice sunny day, Sylvia didn't feel well all night, feeling much better this evening. Jackie and baby were here for supper. Sylvia went to Mary's for a home movie. Lots of mosquitoes out now.

Thursday, June 24, 1982—got up early and went to Dan's. We sent in our application for caribou and bison hunts. Worked on the Cat and a grease gun. Had lunch at Hoffman's, worked on the pickup. It's really hot for here, got up to 80° today and real sunny.

Friday, June 25, 1982—worked for Dan all day, got his truck stuck. He had to haul a load of logs to town. Very sunny and hot, 80° again.

Saturday, June 26, 1982—got Dan's dump truck out and then hauled gravel all day. Hydraulic pump went out on the Cat late in the evening. Went to Chet's fish wheel with Bob Schmidt and he gave me some rhubarb—got home late.

Sunday, June 27, 1982—worked all day on the Cat are taking the hydraulic pump off. Boy that is one heck of a job. Some of the bolts that hold it in there, I had to cut a wrench in half in order to get it in there and then work it with another wrench. Got the job done though. It was sunny and breezy today.

June 28, 1982—the hydraulic pump is now off the Cat, took it to Ken Kramer at Glennallen. He has done work like that. I wanted him to repair it. Visited with Darrel on the way home and had supper at KROA and had good pickings at the dump, found some things we needed. Sunny, winds up to 35 mph.

Tuesday, June 29, 1982—up early and went to Dan's to move a fuel tank. That was a heck of a job too, but we got it moved to a new position. The women helped, just like we did. Nadia called from Seattle. She's coming up to see us. Dan flew Patti, Sylvia and I to Fire Lake at Birchwood to meet Nadia. She came in on the plane and a lady (Billman's relation) picked her up and drove her to Fire Lake to Dan's plane. After Nadia got here, Dan took off with the plane. He wanted to show Nadia things on the way. It's over a 130 miles of flying from Fire Lake. He showed us moose, swans and salmon, the trap cabin, and Old Boot Lake. He would have flown us up the Nelchina Glacier, but as he rounded the corner to go there, he met winds that he did not want to fly in. As a smart pilot, he did not go there. We then went for pizza and had Dan and Patti with us.

Wednesday, June 30, 1982—went to Dan and Patti's and loaded the stand for a gas barrel and moved it from their old place. This was a 500-gallon one. We moved it down to their new property and put the tank up on this stand. Then we went to KROA and then the Ranch House and had supper. We came home early. Really a nice evening, we sure enjoy having Nadia here.

Thursday, July 1, 1982—slept late and then loaded the dredge, went to Cache Creek and I showed Nadia how the dredge is set up and worked and how to pan gold with it. We ran the dredge but didn't get much gold at all. Then we went to Ken and Jackie's for supper and to see how the pump repair was coming along. It's a real nice day and Nadia had a good time—and we with her.

Friday, July 2, 1982—up early and took Nadia to Anchorage for the plane. Sure wasn't much traffic on the streets of Anchorage at 3:00 a.m. Did lots of research for prospecting at Coghill while in town that day. Got some parts, gas and grub, got home at 8:30 p.m. and went to Dan's and called Ken about the Cat pump repair.

Saturday, July 3, 1982—went to Dan's to phone for Cat parts. Couldn't talk to a parts person about it. Hauled water for the greenhouse. Panned some black sand and worked on our radio. Blake and I visited. Dennis, Sally and Chris left their dog (and Henry's) with us. They are going to Michigan to visit relatives.

Sunday, July 4, 1982—some fellow stopped by wanting to go to Daisy Creek. I suggested they fly it first and then I will take them. Went to KROA. Sylvia and I met Bob and Claire from Lake Louise Road. Talked trade and manufacturing sites to establish property and the use of it. Came home and did chores and ate supper.

10,000 Days in Alaska Book One 1978-1989

Monday, July 5, 1982—did odds and ends around here. Sure a nice day, but windy.

Tuesday, July 6, 1982—went to Dan's and called for Cat parts. Built an aluminum box for carrying things on the snowmobile. Called Teresa and then Beverly called us back. Another sunny day, windy and 72°.

Wednesday, July 7, 1982—not as windy, hot and sunny, 80+ degrees. Went to Dan's fishing Creek—it was low, lots of bugs and too hot to fish. Did lots of jobs around here and started on the gasoline water pump. We have to get repairs for it. Visited Bob and Margaret Schmidt for a while.

Thursday, July 8, 1982—went to see Hoffmans and visited, then to Dan's. Patti hadn't gotten back from Anchorage with parts yet. She stopped later with the parts at our place. Sylvia went to Mary Beaudoin's to see a movie. It's cooler today. Got the radio going.

Friday, July 9, 1982—worked on the snowgo carrier and the Homelite water pump. Checked on Federal State status on lands at Glennallen to no satisfaction. Left Cat parts at Ken's and came home early. He's working on the hydraulic pump.

Saturday, July 10, 1982—read *All Creatures Great and Small* by James Herriot most of the night and again this morning. 50°, some light rain, cloudy all day. Went over to Bob and Margaret Schmidt's for drinks and grayling supper.

Sunday, July 11, 1982—rested most of the day, then went to Glennallen and picked up the hydraulic pump for the Cat—thank you, Ken. Cool and rainy today.

Monday, July 12, 1982—cool and rainy again. Worked on the Cat all day. Almost got the hydraulic pump and the rest of that part of the Cat back together.

Tuesday, July 13, 1982—finished Cat, trouble getting dump truck running. Got five loads hauled and two buildings moved. Dan, Patti, and Jason Sylvia and I went to Kianna Creek in Dan's 185 Cessna. Dan's got one large king salmon and Sylvia caught one large, and one small king salmon—about 100 pounds of fish.

Wednesday, July 14, 1982—up early, hauled seven loads, then napped two hours. Helped Dan put his new boat in the lake and ran it a while. Came home for two hours and went back for an hour to watch him water ski, then went to KROA.

Thursday, July 15, 1982—up real early and hauled gravel for Dan until 6:00 p.m. Sylvia did laundry at KROA until 11:00 p.m. Haven't been sleeping well these last evenings.

Friday, July 16, 1982—hauled gravel, got stuck late in the day. I had to use a Snatch Block to get the truck out and snapped the cable on the swamp buggy. Hope Bob Sanders can go prospecting on Coghill River. Raining all day.

Saturday, July 17, 1982—slept late, and rested most of the day, light rain and partly cloudy. Greased the dump truck and part of the swamp buggy.

Sunday, July 18, 1982—some rain. Visited Hoffmans, drained oil in the Cat and greased it. James and Zoe stopped in for a while. Beautiful sunset.

Monday, July 19, 1982—beautiful day, hauled four loads of gravel to the Hoffmans, and several to Dan's. Broke one side of a link on the Cat track. Tom did a lot of shopping in Anchorage for us.

Tuesday, July 20, 1982—went to small claims court for Ray Lawrence (Gunsight), judge ruled against my charge for swamp buggy. Bought lunch for Ray, Nancy and Kim. Talked to Darrel and dispense evening at Dan's and KROA. Had a good time.

Wednesday, July 21, 1982—warm and mostly sunny—worked on the Cat track day.

Thursday, July 22, 1982—warm and sunny. Worked on the cat and got one load hauled and then got stuck in the lane. Tore up the Snatch Block. Patti and I shoveled a load off, then the engine on the truck blew up—so goes some days.

Friday, July 23, 1982—Henry is back from his work. Took Cat to Dan's and started putting pad in and spreading gravel. Pretty nice day, a little cloudy.

Saturday, July 24, 1982—sent in an order for snowmobile parts and chain saw sharpener. Spread and smoothed the gravel at Dan's and moved an outhouse for him.

Sunday, July 25, 1982—dug drainage ditch at Dan's and moved the generator building and leveled the pad for the wind generator. There was a light earthquake tremor at 8:00 p.m. tonight. Mostly a nice day, one light shower.

Monday, July 26, 1982—some folks from Minnesota came up to visit. Worked at Dan's straightening log buildings, moved the generator. Dan took us all salmon fishing. Flew us out to this good spot. We only got one red salmon—got home at 12:30 in the morning.

Tuesday, July 27, 1982—got gear ready to prospect—Dan and Bob and I flew to Coghill Lake. Saw many Dall sheep, salmon, seals, and boats fishing. Located a quartz outcrop on College Fjord and another on Coghill River—yet another above the glacier. We saw two black bear catching salmon.

Wednesday, July 28, 1982—slept late, visited with Bob and Kahren Rudbeck and took them hiking up Slide Mountain looking for fossils— found a few and a wolverine skull. Nice day, beautiful view, good time.

Thursday, July 29, 1982—went to Dan's. A couple of people had over-staked our claims (claim jumpers). We called a trooper, and then told them to pull their stakes and flagging and to get off our claims. Went to Glennallen and filed amended claim forms.

Friday, July 30, 1982—Sylvia is canning the 12 salmon that Darrel brought last night. Went to the dump, got a bee sting. Bob and Kahren left for Soldotna at 2:00 p.m. Rained after they left.

Saturday, July 31, 1982—went to Dan's for a little while. Visited at Hoffman's. A nice day, getting dark earlier and now.

Sunday, August 1, 1982—did a little work on the Cat and visited Herb

Farmer. Dan, Lisa and Jason were here for supper. Another nice day.

Monday, August 2, 1982—went early to Dan's and worked on the Cat front idlers. Got quite a bit done on them. Tired tonight. Very nice day, small rain shower, Sylvia got two more squirrels. Herb Farmer helped on the Cat, he's an excellent welder, knows lots of machinery and heavy equipment.

Tuesday, August 3, 1982—real nice day, Herb helped on the Cat again today. I finished it late. We had supper over at Bob Schmidt's.

Wednesday, August 4, 1982—worked on Hoffman's barn. Charlie was back and worked with me. It was a nice day over there working on the barn—one light shower. Had supper at Bob Schmidt's.

Thursday, August 5, 1982—worked on Hoffman's barn again. Charlie helped all morning and we got quite a bit done. Two light showers, a nice day and supper again at Bob's.

Friday, August 6, 1982—worked on the barn again—got the floor joists in and some bridging. Went to KROA to pick up things (they had shopped for us) and drove up Lake Louise Road. Visited Bob and Claire, got two hot showers. Beautiful yellow rainbow this evening.

Saturday, August 7, 1982—talked with Dan and then on to Hoffman's to work on the barn—one rain shower today, cloudy and cool. Finished the bridging and got a fourth of the floor nailed down.

Sunday, August 8, 1982—cloudy and rainy most of the day. Dan and two sheep hunters came to Hoffman's and we've got three quarters of the sub floor on. (This country is great for people volunteering their help and labor). Ran out of nails and we don't have enough lumber.

Monday, August 9, 1982—walked some of Cache Creek claim lines, rested most of the day. Partly cloudy and a light shower.

Tuesday, August 10, 1982—visited with the Billmans.

Wednesday, August 11, 1982—spent most of that day just visiting with friends and did things around the neighborhood. Sally came to get their dog, Hippo, while we were gone. We missed seeing her. Rainy most of the day.

Thursday, August 12, 1982—bright and sunny all day. Worked on Hoffman's barn then went over to Billman's place and moved a log building. Tore up stiff leg on swamp buggy. The woodshed collapsed when we tried to move it. Dan took us all out to the Ranch House for dinner.

Friday, August 13, 1982—beautiful day today, even hot. Moved another building for Dan, it was a tough one. Very nice evening.

Saturday, August 14, 1982—pulled another building for Dan and Patti, then started digging the basement for a house—long day, warm and sunny.

Sunday, August 15, 1982—went to Dan's and chased around for a culvert to put in for a well. We hit permafrost while digging the hole, but did get down about four feet. Hope it will be enough. Visited Hoffmans, Tom and Lisa got back from the Yukon River float trip. Bob and Kahren Rudbeck are back.

Monday, August 16, 1982—went to Tolsona Lake with Bob and Kahren to look at land. Visited Dennis and Sally. Sylvia worked at KROA and we went back there later.

Tuesday, August 17, 1982—Don Taylor stopped in wanting me to do some swamp buggy work. I looked the job over, but it looked too risky.

Wednesday, August 18, 1982—hurried around all morning getting ready to go to Anchorage and Homer later. We plan to go clam digging and silver fishing and Halibut fishing. Had a flat tire on the way to town. Stayed at Andy's and Bob's camper. It was a nice day.

Thursday, August 19, 1982—did business and shopping around town. Bought new tires for the pickup. Met Clarence W. and his wife in the afternoon. Nice day, went to Birdie's at mile 142.5, which is south of Ninilchek—got there at 10:00 p.m.

Norman Wilkins

Friday, August 20, 1982—up early to catch the tide. Birdie went with us to dig clams at mile 144. I dug eight big clams and we had a big clam feed—others got clams too. We tried for silvers at Ninilchek but didn't have any luck. It was very nice weather, went looking for fossils too.

Saturday, August 21, 1982—got some clams far down on the Ninilchek beach. Jeff and Birdie were there, Bob and Kahren Rudbeck fished. I'm passing blood in my urine—I got real sick and went to the Soldotna hospital. Then I got even more sick at Homer and went to the hospital there.

Sunday, August 22, 1982—still very sick and in intensive care at the Homer Hospital. I had lost a lot of blood. I got several blood transfusions and so forth that goes with this. Bob and Kahren went fishing on a charter boat

Monday, August 23, 1982—still very sick. Doctor Sayer looked in my stomach. He sees where the blood is coming from. He recommends no more alcohol for me. I took his advice. (As of August 2008, it has been 26 years since I last took a drink.)

Tuesday, August 24, 1982—got out of the hospital at noon and went to Anchorage and stayed at Andy's and Connie's.

Wednesday, August 25, 1982—shopped all day in Anchorage, got some new tires on the truck, I like them. Got home at 10:30 p.m.

Thursday, August 26, 1982—went to visit the Hoffmans and also visited Sandy Farmer. It's a nice day and I rested a lot.

Friday, August 27, 1982—took some garbage to the dump near KROA and then went to Billman's and worked on the swamp buggy. It's been a nice day, but a little cool. Had a bad setback with my stomach.

Saturday, August 28, 1982—a real nice day, had a little ice on the dog pan this morning. Don Taylor rented my swamp buggy. Darrel works for him and is going to drive it. Sylvia went with Schmidt's to visit some lodges and I repaired a tarp. Tom and Lisa stopped by to visit and Hoffmans brought another quart of milk. Dan Billman stopped in.

10,000 Days in Alaska Book One 1978-1989

Sunday, August 29, 1982—woke up early, pretty sick. Tom and Lisa and everyone else convinced me to go to Anchorage to get checked out. Darrel took the swamp buggy to pull phone poles out at Gunsight. Stopped to see how they were doing. It was raining in Palmer when I got there. Saw the doctor and stayed overnight with Andy.

Monday, August 30, 1982—rained all day, shopped all day. Went to hospital at 4:00 p.m. Test was okay, got home at 8:30 p.m. and fed Tom's dog.

Tuesday, August 31, 1982—worked on tarps, visited Billmans and Hoffmans, it's Max's birthday. Also went to Bob Schmidt's. It's a nice day with a few little showers.

Wednesday, September 1, 1982—it was a nice day with a few showers again. Mailed a lease to Rodney B. Bob and I went up Lake Louise Road hunting moose and caribou then went flying with Dan and flew over the trapper cabin. Saw caribou there.

Thursday, September 2, 1982—Rhynell brings milk every morning—goat milk, for my stomach. Worked around here till mid afternoon, stopped at Hoffman's and on to a movie at Glennallen.

Friday, September 3, 1982—put two shovel handles in, did some work on the swamp buggy. Ken Kramer visited. I went over to Danny Chappel's. Shot a spruce hen with my 30-06, took the head off, and didn't wreck any meat. Visited Dan Billman in the evening.

Saturday, September 4, 1982—up early, washed three of my winter jackets and tried to get the water pump for the swamp buggy fixed. It broke. Sylvia sewed a tarp for me. Very nice day, pretty, full moon and cool this evening.

Sunday, September 5, 1982—went to Dan's and did some Cat work, then up to Hoffman's and cleared some land and dug a hole for their house drain. It's windy, though not cold.

Monday, September 6, 1982—up early, cloudy all day. Got the chain saw all ready to work. Went to wood lot to saw out some lumber I wanted—didn't work very well. Got some firewood and I feel weak today.

Norman Wilkins

Tuesday, September 7, 1982—rainy all day, worked on swamp buggy. Ken Kramer stopped by. He showed me how to put the bolt in at the water pump so it would stay in there. Worked on toboggan sled for snowmobile.

Wednesday, September 8, 1982—rainy all day, went to Glennallen, Sylvia did laundry. Saw Darrel and Frank and had supper at Hoffman's. Talked hunting with Dan B.

Thursday, September 9, 1982—partly cloudy, went to Wasilla, got lumber for a shed for storage and two drums of gasoline for equipment (100 gallons). Got groceries, looked at a tilt trailer. Ken Kramer worked on the swamp buggy.

Friday, September 10, 1982—worked on the buggy, finished welding on sled, Ken helped.

Saturday, September 11, 1982—finished the buggy, got gear ready and drove Allen's trapline trail. Had some troubles on the way in, but got camp set up before dark. Dan flew over, it was a nice day.

Sunday, September 12, 1982—mostly a nice day, a little rain and wind. Tramped all around, saw some ducks and two moose that had hooked their horns while fighting and died together. Found a weather balloon. rain and windy tonight.

Monday, September 13, 1982—Ken and Danny are out here hunting too, with me. Hunted farther out. Ken jumped a caribou. Dan flew over.

Tuesday, September 14, 1982—frosty morning, left camp early, went farther east. Saw nine ducks, a brown thrasher, camp robber, ravens and beaver and bear sign and more moose sign, one trophy caribou and two real nice ones. Nothing that I could get to shoot. Dan flew over and it rained this evening.

Wednesday, September 15, 1982—we hunted even farther from camp. Saw some ducks and a cow moose and one caribou. Very windy. It blew so hard that Danny's tent blew away, maybe 400 yards from where we were camped. It was one of those tents that would roll if it isn't fastened

10,000 Days in Alaska Book One 1978-1989

down right and it just rolled and rolled and rolled until it finally got hung up. The tent that I had, shook, but the wind didn't phase it a bit. Rained in the night.

Thursday, September 16, 1982—wet morning not so windy, Dan flew over again. Went hunting till noon, saw some bear tracks. Left at noon, saw two cow moose on the way out, got stuck and had to winch out of a mud hole. Sunny day.

Friday, September 17, 1982—slept a little late, got started on the storage shed at 10:00 a.m. And had quite a bit of it done by 6:00 p.m. Ate supper and visited Hoffmans. It was really sunny today, 30° in the morning and cloudy tonight. I feel sick tonight.

Saturday, September 18, 1982—worked on the storage shed and hunted a little on the Slide Mountain. Bob Schmidt had some hinges and gave them to me for the door on the storage shed. It was a nice day; visited Dan, Denny, and Charlie T. were all there too.

Sunday, September 19, 1982—worked on the storage shed. Bob and I drove Lake Louise Road, hunting. Then later, Dan and I flew out to John Lake and we slept in his Cessna 185 overnight so we would be legal to hunt in the morning. (It is illegal to hunt the same day airborne.)

Monday, September 20, 1982—up very early, it was a pretty nice day. Stalked a bull moose in a large bunch of cows. We didn't get to see them, we could hear them and the cows didn't pay too much attention to us, but we just never got to see them. Saw four bull caribou, saw nearly a hundred moose on the ground when we got in the plane and took off to leave, Dan circled the area—that's when we saw so many moose. There were about 50 in one bunch and about that many in the other bunch and they were about a mile apart. Salvaged lumber later at Dan's.

Tuesday, September 21, 1982—I have almost all the shelves installed in the storage shed now and started moving things into it. Sylvia went to Glennallen with Bob and Margaret. Blake and Danny stopped by. Later, Henry came home from work and took us out to supper.

Wednesday, September 22, 1982—frosty morning, fine day—fantastic northern lights at night. Moved a lot of gear into the new shed. Bob and

Margaret stopped by for a few minutes. Danny C. left for a California visit. I checked the truck over and serviced and greased it.

Thursday, September 23, 1982—Henry visited this morning, we had a little snow and it melted. Adjusted the clutch on the Cat, helped Max Hoffman clean out the hole that I dug with the Cat for him. Darrel visited in the evening.

Friday, September 24, 1982—got gear ready by early afternoon to go to Delta to hunt Sandhill Cranes and hopefully some geese. Drove up to Glennallen and stayed at Darrel's in the evening. I'm tired tonight, brought Mike, our dog along.

Saturday, September 25, 1982—Charlie, Darrel and I cleaned a bunch of salmon and split them for drying. Darrel and I drove to Delta to hunt on Barney and Scott Hollemback's farm—camped in my tent.

Sunday, September 26, 1982—got up early, we're up at Delta hunting Sandhill Cranes. Scott, the farmer, is hunting with us. The cranes were really flying high today. I only shot one and hit another one hard with b-b shot. Scott got one. We had a good time here today hunting, lots of fun.

Monday, September 27, 1982—up early. One flock of cranes flew almost in range. Then later we tried to stalk some but that didn't work. They spotted us and flew. I bought some hay from Scott and Barney for Hoffman's goats and left Delta early afternoon. Got home at 8:30 p.m.

Tuesday, September 28, 1982—dropped six bales of hay off at Hoffman's place, visited Dan and Patti, Blake and Jackie a few minutes. Built a lean-to on brown trailer. Put away lots of things for winter to make things neater and look better around the cabin. It's cloudy, cool and a little snow and was 20° this morning.

Wednesday, September 29, 1982—snowed all day, warm. Sharpened some knife blades. Loaded a wrecker and pump truck on a lowboy trailer for some people. Winched this equipment on the trailer with the swamp buggy.

Thursday, September 30, 1982—fairly nice day, warmed up and melted some snow. Finished the toboggan sled for the snowmobile to use for trapping this winter.

Friday, October 1, 1982—warm this morning, more snow melted. Did some jobs around the cabin here. Went to Hoffman's and serviced the Cat. Helped Max crib up his septic tank. Sylvia went to Glennallen and then to the Ranch House Days party.

Saturday, October 2, 1982—cool, cloudy, light snow in afternoon and evening. Helped Max finish up his crib and adjusted the clutch on the dozer. Covered up the septic crib and smoothed the lot south of their barn. Henry fed my dogs for me.

Sunday, October 3, 1982—warm and snowing all day. Henry and I went to Lake Louise road to look for a U.S.G.S. survey marker—didn't find it, but we did find a fish & game fingerling raising lake that had feeders out. They raise these fingerlings to transfer to other lakes. Had supper over at Bob and Margaret's this evening. Charlie visited for a few minutes.

Monday, October 4, 1982—helped Dan Billman with his wind generator tower all day. This is quite a job. I'm using the swamp buggy to winch and raise the windmill tower and generator tower that he's going to use it for. It's cloudy and cool.

Tuesday, October 5, 1982—got up early and went to a lake near Gunsight to hunt geese—none flying. Saw one flock of ducks and 58 swans! Helped Dan on the wind generator tower. It was cool and cloudy most of the day.

Wednesday, October 6, 1982—went to the wood lot and cut a medium-sized load, stopped at Hoffman's and drained the water out of the Cat, did some work around the dog yard getting ready for winter. Cloudy and cool.

Thursday, October 7, 1982—it's 18° and snowing this morning. Lots of geese flying east in the valley today. This is their fall migration. They fly mostly down to California, but some stop at different places along the way. Ray from Gunsight wanted the Cat again, but the pony motor carburetor is plugged. Then the carburetor on the chainsaw quit. I did get 1-1/3rd pickup loads of wood. It was a fairly nice day.

Norman Wilkins

Friday, October 8, 1982—went to Gunsight to hunt geese. The lake froze over during the night. Darrel and I went to Delta to goose hunt. Saw two herds of buffalo on a farm. We set out decoys wondering if the buffalo might tromp them or have fun with them but that didn't happen. The geese had all left on the migration. We only saw one crane.

Saturday, October 9, 1982—no geese, none flying. Some hunters killed a buffalo on the farm as they were hunting geese. I bought some grain for Hoffman's goats and straw for my dogs for bedding this winter. I'm having trouble getting the saw fixed. Saw a wolverine and several fox today. It was storming part of the way home. Didn't get home until after 11:00 p.m.

Sunday, October 10, 1982—cloudy with light snow, six to eight inches on the ground. Went to KROA, took the feed that I got at Delta to the Hoffmans and then helped Dan in the afternoon.

Monday, October 11, 1982—went to Dan's but we won't be working on the tower today. Did a few things around here. It was really snowing by noon, still snowing tonight. We had a low of 15° today and a high of 25°.

Tuesday, October 12, 1982—worked on the snowgo most of the day. Charlie brought two dogs for us to take care of for a few days. Very nice day, with 10° for a low and 30° for a high. In the evening, we went down to Lucky and Mary's for movies on the TV.

Wednesday, October 13, 1982—partly cloudy, temperature about the same. Fixed another pair of truck chains and helped Dan with his tower.

Thursday, October 14, 1982—put up 20 feet on the tower today, not much breeze and warmer. Lee Dudley was curious about this tower and stopped to see how we were doing.

Friday, October 15, 1982—we went 20 more feet on the tower—it's finished now. A really nice, sunny warm, day at 33°.

Saturday, October 16, 1982—Dan came down to our place and we loaded some steel for the "Gin"pole to set the generator on his tower. Sylvia and I went to a movie in Glennallen. It was a pretty nice day.

Sunday, October 17, 1982—snowed all day and warm. Took the swamp buggy to Dan's and put up the entire wind generator except the tail vane. Really tired tonight. Lee Dudley made an antenna booster for the radio at our cabin today.

Monday, October 18, 1982—got the tail vane set on Dan's wind generator. He was working up there, 80 feet, getting this work done. I sat in the swamp buggy and worked the winch to get this vane and wind generator up to him. A nice day with highs in the mid 20s and a low just above zero.

Tuesday, October 19, 1982—it's my sister's birthday. Dan and Patti came down to visit and I went with them and drove the swamp buggy back home. They gave us the rear half of a caribou. We like caribou meat and appreciate this. Snowed all day.

Wednesday, October 20, 1982—was a nice day, high 20s, near 0° tonight. Cut up and packaged the caribou that Dan and Patti gave us. Cut up the buffalo liver (I found this liver out in a field up in Delta on the farm—it had been discarded by someone). I'll use the buffalo liver for bait this winter. Visited Bob and Margaret Schmidt and had supper there.

Thursday, October 21, 1982—did a few things around here, my back and also my knee is sore. I hitched up Mac and Oscar on the dogsled, took them for a run, and then visited Hoffmans. Later, I went to Dan's, he was wiring up the wind generator. The weather is much the same today. Henry got back from his job and is home again.

Friday, October 22, 1982—wrote Gordon and asked him to send me some beaver castors from Minnesota. Then I wrote a letter to my mother. An eagle flew right by the cabin. I ran Mac and Oscar and Fluffy on the dogsled again. I did some reshaping work on the gun stock of my 30-06. It was a nice day, 0° to 20°. Alaska dividend checks came.

Saturday, October 23, 1982—beautiful day, below zero to 20 above today. Took batteries to Dan's and drilled a gun stock and sanded it. Visited Hoffmans, bedded the dogs. We hear Sam is back, he's been off on a working job. My back has really been bad for several days.

Sunday, October 24, 1982—went to Lake Louise Junction for propane, then to Jay's on Lake Louise Road and visited these folks for a while. (I park my vehicle there and snowmobile sometimes at Jay's when I'm out trapping). Saw Chris Ronning at Lake Louise Junction. There is a nice restaurant and filling station there. Went home and later went with Sam and Henry to Tolsona Lake Lodge.

Monday, October 25, 1982—Sam and Henry were here for coffee. It's a real nice day, -15° to 10°. Cut some pieces for a ladder I'm making and made a trapping paddle-snow paddle. Paid Blake for a phone bill that we had with him.

Tuesday, October 26, 1982—went to Anchorage, took Shelley's dog, "Bear" to her. Did shopping and stayed at Andy and Connie's overnight.

Wednesday, October 27, 1982—did lots more shopping and was able to leave town before rush hour. Didn't get everything done, but nice to get home.

Thursday, October 28, 1982—slept late, unloaded pickup, took Hoffman's feed to them. Nice day. My back was very sore, put up indoor—outdoor thermometer.

Friday, October 29, 1982—up very early, went with Charlie T. to Anchorage. Got my eyes tested and bought a new knife. Libby Riddles was in town. Gave Charlie a dog, Got back in pretty good time.

Saturday, October 30, 1982—slept kind of late, Charlie and I went to the woodlot, got stuck a couple of times. We got a cord of wood. I sharpened my knife and put linseed oil on a gun stock. Sylvia made Halloween candy and popcorn balls and also knitted.

Sunday, October 31, 1982—high, 5° to -6° today. Did a few things around here, took two dogs to Charlie. He, Sylvia and I got us each a load of wood. Neighborhood kids trick or treated us. I sharpened Blake B's chainsaw.

Monday, November 1, 1982—high, 5° to -10°. Put more linseed oil on 30-06 gun stock. Did several other jobs. Chainsaw is fixed and came in the mail. Charlie, Blake and Jackie had caribou stew here with us for lunch. Sylvia babysat Jessica for a while. I made a fleshing board.

Tuesday, November 2, 1982—warm and clear today. Up early, picked up Charlie T. and went to Glennallen and voted and did laundry. Got Ski-Doo started and sorted some traps and snares.

Wednesday, November 3, 1982—snowed all day. Read some. Blake and Jackie visited and we all went to Lucky and Mary's to see movies. Sam stopped for a minute and James Callahan was here for a bit.

Thursday, November 4, 1982—nice day, pretty warm. Fixed one tarp. Blake and Jackie and I got two loads of wood. Got pretty wet, Snow is getting deep. Sylvia babysat. Put more oil on gun stock.

Friday, November 5, 1982—beautiful day, not cold. Had some problems with Blake's truck, then my truck developed a bad noise. Did get one load of wood home. Chris Ronning hauled it when he pulled me home from the woodlot. Put 30-06 together.

Saturday, November 6, 1982—it was -12° today. Started Henry's Blazer. Had to overhaul my distributor, then found that my motor noise was only a stick stuck in flywheel. Went to "Pollack" days at Tolsona Lodge. Good time and good eats.

Sunday, November 7, 1982—cloudy and warm day, 10° to -16°. Slept late, did things to get ready for trapping: sanded fleshing beam, boiled snares, split wood. Jim Phillips stopped in. James and Jeff ran out of gas. Got them going.

Monday, November 8, 1982—warm, cloudy, light snow. 5° to -5°. Went to Glennallen and registered the snowmobile trailer. Blake went along, we had parts to get. Starter quit. Put one of Henry's in when we got home.

Tuesday, November 9, 1982—worked at trap supplies, did quite a bit of work on Ski-Doo, then loaded it on truck. Had supper at Blake's and Jackie's. Pulled Vern's pickup to Nelchina.

Wednesday, November 10, 1982—went to Jay's and unloaded Ski-Doo and checked out trap trail. Made two sets and pulled Darrel's pickup to

Norman Wilkins

Louise Junction.

Thursday, November 11, 1982—it was 15° to -5° and cloudy. Up early, worked at getting gear ready to go trapping. Helped Henry put throw out bearing in Blazer and transmission in Vern's pickup at KROA. Had supper with the Schmidts.

Friday, November 12, 1982—up early to load trap gear—even then we got a late start. Had to turn around and come back to fix one tongue of snowgo sled that drug on highway. Finished the day getting a load of wood for Blake.

Saturday, November 13 1982—warm today and in the 20s to -5°. Truck starter gave trouble all day, finally got it fixed. Billman's skating party tonight.

Sunday, November 14, 1982—up before dawn and went to Jay's. Parked truck. Had trouble with Blake's snowmobile, It got stuck several times. It was dark at Blue Lake, couldn't find trail to cabin. Siwash camped at Blue Lake, nice night for it. (Siwash is an Alaskan term meaning Indian and "siwashing" is to camp the way the Indians do—with nothing but rifle, fry pan, tea pail, salt, tea, and a little sourdough. Siwashing releases you from the necessity of returning to any fixed campsite.)

Monday, November 15, 1982—broke trail to cabin, then back to Blue Lake and pulled sleds to cabin. Cut a trail to cabin and broke a trail to woodlot. Had a nice evening at cabin, a very nice day.

Tuesday, November 16, 1982—up before dawn, went to woodlot and brought in five loads. Cleaned up cabin, loaded sled and headed out. Saw lots of wolf tracks, mink fox and marten tracks, some moose and caribou tracks. Got home early in the evening.

Wednesday, November 17, 1982—nice sunny day, -20° this morning. Slept late, did some things here then started feeding dry fish to the dogs. Harold and Rachel Dimmick had coffee and then came back for supper. Dan Billman visited in the evening.

Thursday, November 18, 1982—foggy and -30° to -13° today. Worked on some snares and went to Dimmick's for a fine turkey supper. Was home

10,000 Days in Alaska Book One 1978-1989

at 6:00 p.m. then Henry stopped in with our grocery order from Anchorage.

Friday, November 19, 1982—not so much fog and -30° again. High only -15°. Finished 12 snares and took snowmobile to Gunsight to have work done on it. Went to Hoffman's for supper, then sliced some bacon at KROA. Stopped at Bob and Margaret's to get instructions on how to take care of their house while they are gone.

Saturday, November 20, 1982—warmed to -10° today, it was -35° below zero last night. Went to Gunsight, got Ski-Doo, set two traps across road at base of slide Mountain. Went to Dan Billman's and called Nadia, Theresa and Paul's families were there.

Sunday, November 21, 1982—set two traps on Slide Mountain, got gear ready for the trapline.

Monday, November 22, 1982—saw Darrel Gerry before going to cabin. Made a few sets on the way out. Ski-Doo runs poorly when warm. Got there early, cut up some wood and made chain extensions. Saw wolf tracks. 20° to 10° tonight.

Tuesday, November 23 1982—very warm, light snow in the evening, 23° to 10°. Made fox, lynx, and marten sets. Must've been a whole family of lynx near here. Ski-Doo runs badly, Chris and Lloyd flew in for coffee, glad to see them.

Wednesday, November 24, 1982—another warm day, made lots more sets. Caught a silver fox. Ski-Doo runs really badly. Visited Darrel and Lloyd Ronning. Home in time for supper.

Thursday, November 25, 1982—went to KROA for Thanksgiving dinner, had a good time. Stopped at Billman's on the way home. Beverly called while we were there, nice to talk to her. Sam Weaver stayed overnight with us.

Friday, November 26, 1982—went to Jan's and Jay's and worked on Ski-Doo. Seems to work for now. Sherlene, Jay's wife, made tea. Sylvia showed her how to crochet a pillow with yarn. Nothing in traps here.

Norman Wilkins

Saturday, November 27, 1982—sun shines, 10° to -10°. I feel sick today. Had a good trip out here, Ski-Doo ran fine. Very beautiful here at the trap cabin, nothing in the traps. Pack of wolves hunted past the cabin. Cut up stove wood. Almost a full moon tonight.

Sunday, November 28, 1982—ice fog and 15° to 10°. Sore back. Ran some trapline, nothing. Put out two snares and one Marten set. Broke trail in woodlot. Cut up wood and ricked it. Put up fleshing beam in cabin. Beautiful moon tonight.

Monday, November 29, 1982—made wolf, marten, and fox sets today. Reached road early and visited Darrel a few minutes. Saw seven caribou along the road. Ran line here, nothing. Called Beverly.

Tuesday, November 30, 1982—Got Henry and Sam up early for breakfast. Then Dan stopped in about 11:00 a.m., he will get us supplies from town. Didn't get out to Green Acres today. Snowy and warm, Tom and Lisa stopped in to talk land.

Wednesday, December 1, 1982—up at 5:00 a.m. Sam slept here. He had breakfast with us, Henry had coffee. Took Max Hoffman to Glennallen where we got caribou permits. Sylvia did laundry. Tom, Lisa Charlie T. and I looked at the 47 acres for sale.

Thursday, December 2, 1982—20° this evening and it was -20° this morning. Tried to fix Henry's chain, it's worn out. Couldn't reach Bill Johnson on the phone. Henry and Sam filed on their Green Acres 40 acres.

Friday, December 3, 1982—it was -30° this morning and -35° tonight. Did chores and went to Dan's and borrowed his chainsaw. Called Bill Johnson on the land. Charlie T. brought the two dogs back. The truck started okay today.

Saturday, December 4, 1982—warmed up to -20° today. Got Dan's saw sharpened, cut up and stacked wood. Radiator hose on truck ruptured. Dan and Patti took us to KROA for the dance.

Sunday, December 5, 1982—cloudy and -15°. Fixed the radiator hose and got some trapping things together. Visited Lucky and Mary in the

10,000 Days in Alaska Book One 1978-1989

evening.

Monday, December 6, 1982—got things ready to go to trap cabin. Weather is warmer.

Tuesday, December 7, 1982—Henry and Sally came and dropped off two batteries. I got a late start, took Darrel's mail to him. Got one red fox. Found him just as fog settled at dark, lucky! Worked on trap gear, don't feel like sleeping. Warm tonight.

Wednesday, December 8, 1982—bright and very warm today. Ran line near here, re-baited it and scented it. Broke some trail along ridge of Hole Lake. Made fox set on this lake. Broke trail south of cabin, made one fox and Marten set. Saw a cow moose. Can't sleep much.

Thursday, December 9, 1982—slept late, nice warm day. Didn't feel good this morning. Broke more trail and set traps. Red fox thawed out, skinned and stretched him. He had two porky quills in him.

Friday, December 10, 1982—got things ready for the trip out. Saw two moose, had camp robber and rabbit in traps, an owl ate the rabbit. Made one fox set. Caribou had been moving around. Dan Chapel is back.

Saturday, December 11, 1982—cloudy, -10° to 10°. Broke 3 miles on trap trail on Slide Mountain. Set marten and one fox trap. Visited Hoffman's for supper. Sylvia made an apple pie and lots of coffee cake.

Sunday, December 12, 1982—light snow last night and cloudy all day. Temp was -10° to 20°. Cut up some wood and worked on Henry's Ski-Doo.

Monday, December 13, 1982—it's -10°.

Tuesday, December 14, 1982—warm, 20° to -5°. Had a good trip in to the trap cabin. Got two marten and saw a herd of caribou on Blue Lake.

Wednesday, December 15, 1982—nice day, partly cloudy, 20° to -5°. Ran line here and got one mink. Brought to loads of wood in and cut it up.

Thursday, December 16, 1982—very nice day, 10° to -5°. Cut and trimmed a bunch of trees, hauled five loads of wood and cut and stacked it.

Friday, December 17, 1982—cloudy today, 6° to 10°. Trimmed 21 trees eight feet from the ground for next year's wood. Cut and hauled three loads, cut and stacked it.

Saturday, December 18, 1982—loaded up and left for road, checked two traps on way out. Made two sets for rats and one set for marten. Pin came out on sled hitch, lost it. Quite foggy in low places and warm today. Ski-Doo ran well. Tom and Lisa brought our groceries this evening.

Sunday, December 19, 1982—it's -5° today. Sylvia checked Schmidt's house. I went to Dan Billman's and did welding, drilling and sawing. Visited Hoffmans for a while. Took Henry's snowmobile axel to Don McKee to have it turned in his lathe.

Monday, December 20 1982—clear and colder, -10° to -20°. Visited Lee Dudley, Sam and Charley came. Charley brought me dried fish. Sam stayed overnight. We went to Tom and Lisa's to listen to some picking guitar, mandolin and banjo.

Tuesday, December 21, 1982—clear and 12° to -25°. Sam went with Sylvia and me to Glennallen to shop and do laundry. Bought new, hunt, fish, trap license. Called Bill Johnson, he is still in Texas. Beautiful Northern Lights.

Wednesday, December 22, 1982—ice fog most of the day, -25° to -35°. Did not go to cabin today. Got snowmobile part's package. Sylvia knits socks for me.

Thursday, December 23, 1982—nice day, but cold. -25° to -35°. Danny C., Henry, Sam, and Blake all visited. Sylvia went with Rhynell to work on Christmas dinner. I did chores here, cleaned roof, chopped fish etc. Too cold to run trapline.

Friday, December 24, 1982—nice day, -20 to -20°. Loafed all day. Sam, Tator, and Danny C. were here for coffee in the morning—Blake for a few minutes. Sylvia baked a pie and cake and knitted on my socks.

10,000 Days in Alaska Book One 1978-1989

Saturday, December 25, 1982—nice day, -20° all day. Sylvia gave me socks for Christmas. We went to Hoffman's for dinner. Rhynell's husband Ken was there, also Charlie T., Tom and Lisa Smayda, and Dr. Mike and girlfriend. Judy, their dog, is in heat and Mike, our dog, got loose. Called Nadia.

Sunday, December 26, 1982—warm, 0° to -10°. Ran the Slide Mountain line, nothing. Got gear ready for trap cabin line. Did chores and worked on Henry's Ski-Doo. Called Paul and Ruth.

Monday, December 27, 1982—called Theresa and Beverly. Went to Jay and Jan's, parked truck. Took Ski-Doo to Darrel's, then on to trapline. Caribou messed up the rat sets at push ups. Got one mink. Picked up the sled. Looked at some line here. 30°, wind blew snow off trees.

Tuesday, December 28, 1982—40°. Slept late, ran line here, nothing. Got things ready for tomorrow. Skinned and stretched mink.

Wednesday, December 29, 1982—40° today. Made seven sets on the way out to the road. Got two rats. Visited Darrel and got home just at dark. Mike, the dog, is sick.

Thursday, December 30, 1982—fantastic total lunar eclipse at 1:30 a.m., very beautiful with binoculars. Northern Lights running all over sky.

Friday, December 31, 1982—nice day, 0° to 10°. Skinned the two rats. Danny C. and Blake stopped in. Ran trapline and moved a fox set, didn't get anything. Henry stopped in.

Norman Wilkins

Patti and Dan Billman of Alaskan Airventures circa 1980's; Dan Billman looking for color; Patti making home made ice cream for a neighborhood get-together with Norman in background.

Darrel Gerry and Norman Wilkins with the head of the buffalo they bagged on October 19, 1983.

Norman Wilkins

1983—grizzly hunt, buffalo hunt, filing claims

Saturday January 1, 1983—ran trapline here—nothing moving, made two more sets. Worked on Ski-Doo. Cloudy and snowing this evening and 12°. Got a ptarmigan.

Sunday, January 2, 1983—today is foggy. Sylvia helped me get the drive axle in Henry's Ski-Doo. She has the flu. Rested all day.

Monday, January 3, 1983—6° and cloudy with a light snow. Visited Sam and also Lee Dudley today. Went to see Lucky in the evening. Henry stopped by about 10:30 p.m.

Tuesday, January 4, 1983—had to change plugs on the Ski-Doo on the way to cabin. Saw Fox and Cat sign. Remade lots of sets, got three rats. Good trip in. Saw cow and calf moose. Harry Billum up from Mendeltna Springs crossed my trail and went back. Nice day, 6°, -4° this evening. I called Bill Johnson this morning.

Wednesday, January 5, 1983—ran the trapline here. Got one ermine and remade all sets plus one new fox set. Skinned and stretched the three rats and ermine.

Thursday, January 6, 1983—got up early, loaded up and set out. Remade some more sets and made two new sets. Pulled all but one rat set. Got out early and visited Charley Netter. Sylvia is much better now.

Friday, January 7, 1983—Blake visited for a while. We visited Hoffmans and had supper there. Visited Tom and Lisa in the evening; Charlie, Lee Dudley, Dan, Lisa, and Jason came—much mandolin and guitar music. It was -18 to -30° today. The books Nadia sent came.

Saturday, January 8, 1983—slept late, -30° this morning; warmed to -26°. Shoveled out the mailbox and the snow berm that I cross with the Ski-Doo. Overcast today.

At Sunday, January 9, 1983—slept late. Visited Blake, read some. Sylvia crocheted. Nice day, -40° all day. Bright northern lights tonight and -50°. Mike (the dog) slipped his collar and came in the cabin for a little while. After about 20 minutes or so, he begged to go back out, too hot for him in the cabin. He has an insulated house of his own.

Monday, January 10, 1983—warmer today, -30° with lots of ice fog. Read most of the day. Sylvia crocheted.

Tuesday, January 11, 1983—Henry and Craig were here for breakfast. Ran trapline on Slide Mountain and got a marten. Danny C. visited. Sam was here for supper and stayed the night. -30° to -14° and cloudy with ice fog and light snow in the evening.

Wednesday, January 12, 1983—light snow, ice fog and cloudy. It was -25° to -13°. Sam, Henry, and Dan visited. I made a call for a dental appointment, skinned and stretched the marten. Tom and Lisa were here for a few minutes.

Thursday January 18, 1983—it's still cloudy and -26° to -24°. Henry and Sam were here all day.

Friday, January 14, 1983—mostly -10° all day and cloudy with a light snow. Went to see Bill Burch. He wasn't home. Went to Glennallen and did laundry. Dan, Lisa and Jason came here for supper.

Saturday January 15, 1983—cloudy all day, very hard to see to drive on road or trail (white-out conditions). -20° to -8°. Ski-Doo ran poorly (plugs). One rabbit in traps. Alaska Range very beautiful in the light today.

Sunday January 16, 1983—sunny till noon, then cloudy and -10° to 0°. Much spark plug trouble. One camp robber in traps. Reset all traps.

Monday January 17, 1983—fairly nice day, cloudy in the high places. Made one new set. Nothing in the traps. Got home before dark and went to Gunsight Lodge for Ski-Doo parts.

Tuesday, January 18, 1983—slept late, ran trapline on Slide Mountain. Got a marten, saw a cow moose. 10° today. Henry, Sally and Sam visited. Sam brought two books. Did chores here and cut up wood.

Wednesday, January 19, 1983—a real nice day, -10° to 0° today. Cut up wood. Tom, Danny and I measured the land we are planning to buy.

Norman Wilkins

Sam is visiting.

Thursday, January 20, 1983—pretty nice day, 0° to -10°. Henry and Sam were here most of the day. Tom was here for a little while to talk about land. Sylvia and Lisa visited Margaret S. I cut up some wood.

Friday, January 21, 1983—cut up a little wood, -10° all day. Bob S. gave us some venison. He goes to Kodiak Island and hunts deer there and shares some of the meat.

Saturday, January 22, 1983—sunny, -10° most of the day. Ran the trapline here, only some ermine tracks. Sylvia visited Jackie.

Sunday, January 23, 1983—slept late, have the flu. -10° to 10° today. Went to Dan's. Paid for groceries, did some welding. Jerry, Sam, Danny, Tom and Lisa all came to Dan's. Tom and Lisa came here (our place) for a few minutes. We had deer steak for supper and went to Lucky and Mary's for movies and to play pool.

Monday, January 24, 1983—slept late, still sick. Met the mailman—no package. Cut and stacked wood. Visited Hoffmans, wrote more letters and saw a 30 inch bull moose. He still had his antlers.

Tuesday, January 25, 1983—still have the flu. -10° all day. Bob S. cleaned out his freezer and brought some fish for the dogs. Read all day.

Wednesday, January 26, 1983—very nice day, -6° to plus 10°. Visited with Darrel, saw two sharp tailed grouse. Nothing in traps, two or three otter in different places, they followed the snowgo trail for a couple of miles. Wolf, fox and marten track—marten robbed set. Harry B. used trail again.

Thursday, January 27, 1983—light snow, -10° to 10°. Only a camp robber in traps, one marten track.

Friday, January 28, 1983—temperature the same. Fixed all the sets, got out to the road early. Saw three cow moose, and one bull moose along the road. Ran trapline on Slide Mountain. One sprung trap. Got stuck in a deep overflow, used the "come-along" to get out. Bob and Margaret took Sylvia to Glennallen, I came home later.

10,000 Days in Alaska Book One 1978-1989

Saturday, January 29, 1983—a nice day, temp was -8° to -10°. Intestinal flu—read all day and Bob S. brought some water. Someone poached a moose on milepost 135, only took hind quarters.

Sunday, January 30, 1983—temperature about the same, nice. Loafed most all day.

Monday, January 31, 1983—did laundry in Glennallen, got groceries and also lantern gas in Copper Center. Mike and Lynette weren't home. Took Darrel to his place, visited Jay and Sherline and saw their two pairs of breeding silver fox.

Tuesday, February 1, 1983—partly cloudy, -6° to 10°. Sighted in the 30-06 and got water at KROA. Visited Hoffmans and had supper there. Nadia sent a nice knife and two pair of socks for my birthday. Sylvia baked a peach upside down cake.

Wednesday, February 2, 1983—foggy all day, 15°. Henry, Sam, and Gradin visited us. Sylvia went to Jackie's.

Thursday, February 3, 1983—cloudy and 6° to 15°. Ran the trapline here—nothing. Pulled in three sets. Henry and Jerry visited. Peter asked about the land.

Friday, February 4, 1983—mostly cloudy day. Dan B. and I took Leo Zura and Lloyd R. home from Mendeltna Creek. Leo is in the ditch off Lake Louise Road. I shot a Caribou. A moose cow ran out of the dark from the ditch on the way home. I almost hit her with the truck. Sylvia did some baking.

Saturday, February 5, 1983—cut up the caribou, Dan and Patti helped too. Cloudy day, 6° to 15°.

Sunday, February 6, 1983—it's 15° today, and cloudy—2 inches of snow last night. Visited Danny C. Peter came there. Later I went hunting with Bob S., he wanted a caribou. Didn't get a chance at one. Sylvia visited Margaret.

Monday, February 7, 1983—it was cloudy with a light snow and 25°.

Norman Wilkins

Sylvia went to Glennallen with Bob and Margaret to do laundry. Bob got stuck here, then Lee visited us and he too, got stuck. Blake tore up our west drive and I got stuck in there.

Tuesday, February 8, 1983—Very nice day, 10° to 16°. Fox, ermine, and mink tracks. Got two beautiful marten in conibear cubbies. Made two rat sets and saw two moose near Blue Lake. Nice here at the cabin.

Wednesday, February 9, 1983—light snow morning and evening, and cloudy all day. 10° to 18°. Nothing on the line today, skinned and stretched the two Marten and saved two scent glands for lure.

Thursday, February 10, 1983—Up early, picked up some traps on the way out to the road. Remade some sets. Nice trip out. Jay went to the hospital for an operation.

Friday, February 11, 1983—light snow, 10° and cloudy. Ran the line on Slide Mountain and got stuck in deep snow. Ermine sprung one trap that two lynx walked all over! They had scratched up the ground and marked a tree six feet up! They must be breeding. Sylvia baked cookies and visited Jackie.

Saturday, February 12, 1983—a bright day and 20° to 7°. Visited Dan and Patti Billman. Lloyd Ronning stopped there, then we went to see Tom and Lisa Smayda and their new daughter, Laura.

Sunday, February 13, 1983—got the snowgo loaded, put extension chains on some traps and visited Blake. Dan Billman was here this evening. It was -20° to 0° and a bright day. Moose wander through here each evening. Bright, Northern lights.

Monday, February 14, 1983—too cold to run the trapline. Went to Lucky and Mary B's for supper and to play pool. 30° to -10°.

Tuesday, February 15, 1983—slept late, -30° to 0° and a sunny day. Stopped to visit Darrel on the way to the cabin. A mink had eaten a rat out of one of the traps. An owl stole half of a rabbit bait, and one frozen trap failed to catch a fox. Cabin was cold when I got here but was very welcome.

10,000 Days in Alaska Book One 1978-1989

Wednesday, February 16—sunny day and 38° to -3°. Ran the trapline—nothing. Left conibear sets (sprung). Brought other sets in.

Thursday, February 17, 1983—nothing in traps. Pulled all fox and marten traps. Brought Darrel to Hoffman's and home here. He stayed the night. Today it was -30° to -10° and sunny.

Friday, February 18, 1983—sunny, 30° 20°. Called Bill Johnson's brother.

Saturday, February 19, 1983—visited Tom, Lisa and the baby—also Hoffman's. -20° to 20° today. Went to Tolsona with Henry, Doug and Denise. Lots of friends at the lodge, pretty nice day.

Sunday, February 20, 1983—sunny day, -20° to 10°. Tom and I went snowshoeing for a while. Sam, Tater, David and Vern came (Vern to buy a marten). Lisa brought the baby along. Called Beverly from Blake and Jackie's.

Tuesday, February 22, 1983—a warm day and night again. Blake and I went to Glennallen for some lumber for him and to get my wood permit. Sylvia and Jackie did laundry.

Wednesday, February 23, 1983—up early and another beautiful day. Blake and I went to Glennallen for a load of lumber for us. We took his road kill moose to his dad's to cut up. Had supper, and played pool at Lucky and Mary's.

Thursday, February 24, 1983—up early, bright day, a warm, 6° to 20°. Unloaded a load of lumber. (Blake and I went to Glennallen with both trucks and got lumber and unloaded it at home).

Friday, February 25, 1983—bright day, warm, and in the 20s. Covered the lumber pile, took snowgo to Hoffman's and looked for trees to cut. Snow is deep, got stuck a few times.

Saturday, February 26, 1983—mostly nice day, helped Dan and Patti put up a TV antenna, then put one up here. Dan's loaned us a TV.

Sunday, February 27, 1983—nice, sunny day. Bob S. and I went caribou hunting but didn't see any without horns.

Monday, February 28, 1983—nice, sunny day, 6° to in the 20s. Had dental work done in Gulkana.

Tuesday, March 1, 1983—bright sunny, warm day. Stopped at Dan Billman's, loaded his machine and went to trap cabin. Nice trip, very little fur moving. Broke part of a trail north and east to look for beaver prospects. Warm evening.

Wednesday, March 2, 1983—up early, finished breaking trail north and east, then on to the west trail to extend it. Got up on top of the west bench.

Thursday, March 3, 1983—light snow and warm. Loaded up and came out to the road, picked up Darrel and hauled him to Lake Louise Junction and came home.

Friday, March 4, 1983—up early, phoned back and forth, working out house-moving deal with Don Taylor. Visited Lucky and Mary.

Saturday, March 5, 1983—Mary Beaudoin's birthday today, -20° to 20°. 12 visitors. I cut up firewood.

Sunday, March 6, 1983—sunny, -12° to 10°. Cleaned snow off the swamp buggy and my back hurts. Henry visited. We went to KROA to visit Carrol and Vern.

Monday, March 7, 1983—bright, sunny and -20° to 20°. Getting up early these days. Went to Glennallen and got a battery and regulator for swamp buggy and got it running and chained up. Then Don Taylor called to say he would rather use a Nodwell to move the cabin. (A Nodwell is a multi-purpose two-tracked vehicle capable of traversing sand, mud, swamp, and snow.)

Tuesday, March 8, 1983—went to Hoffman's and snowshoed a trail to woodlot to cut logs, then hauled them over to Hoffman's where I load them on the pickup and haul them to our place.

Wednesday, March 9, 1983—bright day, -10° to +20°. Put more trails in and had supper with Hoffmans.

Thursday, March 10, 1983—went to Palmer for groceries and gasoline, the road was dry. It was 6° to 20° today.

Friday, March 11, 1983—bright sunny day, -6° to 20°. Put in more logging trails. Dan Billman ran them with his snowgo. Had supper with Hoffmans, visited Schmidts in the morning.

Saturday, March 12, 1983—trouble with sinus. Today is another bright day, 3° to 30°. Visited Lee Dudley and Sam Weaver. Dan and Jason were there. Rusty? (driving for Tok district), stopped a few minutes. Henry had coffee with us.

Sunday, March 13, 1983—scooped lots of snow. Went to Dan's. (Tom S. had lost Charlie's dog team). Dan flew us to spot them. We found them near Nikolai Lake. Tom caught them. Dan flew the wood lot to look at more trees. Lee Dudley came, Jason went with all of us out to Marie Lake. Took down Dan's Teepee and he flew it home in the airplane. Sunny, 10° to 30°.

Monday, March 14, 1983—another nice day, 5° to 30°. Helped Dan with his sled. Got things ready for getting out logs.

Tuesday, March 15, 1983—up early, 5° to 30°. Sam, Tom, Dan and I got 2-3/4 pickup loads of wood and logs today. Sam, Tom, Lisa, Blake and Jackie ate supper here. We all had a good time. Got 30 logs in.

Wednesday, March 16, 1983—cloudy and warm day. Sam, Tom, Dan, and Darrel helped log. Blake went to town to get three bolts for my chainsaw. 3-1/2 pickup loads of wood, 30 + logs, and Dan and I broke more trails. These friends helping us are all knowledgeable hard working woodsmen. We are glad they are here.

Thursday, March 17, 1983—sunny and -5° to 30°. Got 40 House logs, plus firewood; five pickup loads all together. Trails got soft—was tough snowgo freighting. Sam, Darrel, and Tom worked today. Lisa and baby were here for supper also. Nice evening, though tired.

Friday, March 18, 1983—up early, -5° to 30°. Sam, Darrel, Tom, and

Sylvia and I, got 44 cabin logs. Real nice day.

Saturday, March 19, 1983—got 51 cabin logs hauled, more cut down in woodlot. Some trouble with the snowgo and Dan's sled. Nice day, -10° to in the 30s.

Sunday, March 20, 1983—got two loads, 20 house logs. Easy day—nice easy day. Partly cloudy but nice, 5° to in the 30s.

Monday, March 21, 1983—Sam went home late this morning. Sylvia and I got about six loads of wood in. 0° to 30°, very nice day. Snowgo runs poorly.

Tuesday, March 22, 1983—took Sylvia to Hoffman's place, I went to Dan's—we repaired both wood sleds. I broke more trail to haul in wood. My snowgo runs poorly. Went to Gunsight for plugs and oil. Sunny warm day, -5° to 30s.

Wednesday, March 23, 1983—Sylvia and I got quite a few loads of wood hauled in to Hoffman's today. Used Dan's Arctic Cat (helped him replace a spring on it this morning). Tom brought us to Dan's in the evening. It was -15° to 30°, and a sunny day.

Thursday, March 24, 1983—0° to 30s. Hauled five sled loads of wood in. Tom Smayda and I went to Slana to hunt. I shot a nice bull caribou. Camped overnight, great Northern Lights.

Friday, March 25, 1983—0° to 30s. Tom shot a nice, bull boo this morning. Came home and visited Lucky and Mary in the evening, shot pool and watched TV.

Saturday, March 26 1983—went to Hoffman's to haul wood. We all went to Caribou Creek to get alfalfa cubes and barley from two wrecked semi trucks (for Hoffman's goats), then went to a party at KROA. It was 0° to 30°.

Sunday, March 27, 1983—0° to 30° and partly cloudy. Hauled quite a bit of wood in to Hoffman's. Called Nadia.

Monday in March 28, 1983—0° to 30° and mostly sunny. Finished getting the firewood in and took Dan's snowgo home. Visited Mary and Lucky.

Tuesday, March 29, 1983—sunny day, 0° to 30°. We went with Rhynell H. to Glennallen to do laundry. Charlie T. visited. Henry was here for supper.

Wednesday, March 30, 1983—sunny day, 0° to 30°. Did income tax and went to Billman's and made phone calls looking for power take off for the Cat. Sylvia cut up some caribou.

Thursday, March 31, 1983—15° to 34° and cloudy until noon, then sunny, then partly cloudy. Sylvia cut up more caribou and I worked on the odometer on the truck. Charged TV battery.

Friday, April 1, 1983—sunny day and 16° to 40°. Went with Henry, Sam, and Jerry Lange (Tater) to Glennallen to get Bob Abel out of jail. He was already out. Went to Tolsona, then KROA. Met Jim and Mary there. Lee, Tom, and others had a pick-fest. Got home late. The music was great.

Saturday, April 2, 1983—clear and sunny, 16° to 40°. Hauled small load of wood to Jim and Mary Odden's. Took rear half of a Caribou to Lucky and cut it up on his bandsaw. Hauled a small load of wood home.

Sunday, April 3, 1983—sunny day, 6° to 30s. Good trip to trap cabin. Cut a new change in the trail. Saw a yearling moose calf. Dog musher had camped at north end of Blue Lake. Wolf tracks near cabin. Did a few things here, great to be out here.

Monday, April 4, 1983—16° to near 40°. Light snow this morning, mostly cloudy. Did a few chores, loafed and read mostly.

Tuesday, April 5, 1983—8° to 38°, sunny day. Closed up cabin and went out to road. Saw a few ptarmigan, visited with Darrel Gerry, starter broke on truck. Jay and I talked for a while. Found a nice 2 x 8 in the road ditch. Sylvia's been canning meat.

Wednesday, April 6, 1983—6° to 40s and sunny. Helped clean cabin, scooped snow off brown trailer, lean-to, and storage shed. Split wood.

Sylvia cooked a good dinner we shared with Jay and Sherlene. Sam and Lee II, visited.

Thursday, April 7, 1983—6° to 30s, sunny again. Did things around here. Danny and I went to Lake Louise Junction to get a starter for the truck.

Friday, April 8, 1983—0° to 40° and sunny. Split wood and other jobs. Sylvia stuffed sausage. Visited Hoffmans and Billmans.

Saturday, April 9, 1983—10° to 30s partly cloudy and light snow. Sylvia wrapped steak. Tried to call Bill J., no luck.

Sunday, April 10, 1983—15° to 30°, snow last night, very fluffy. Nice sunny day. Sylvia packaged more meat. Visited around here at Nelchina.

Monday, April 11, 1983—Dan came down and we went to Anchorage. Rented two trucks and loaded building supplies. Finished loading around midnight at George's. Stayed at Denny's. Sylvia made more sausage while we were gone.

Tuesday, April 12, 1983—loaded steel on at Wasilla and went to Dan's. Neighbors, helped unload the trucks. Snowed the last 50 miles to Anchorage, stayed at Denny B's again. Sylvia helped Patti and babysat Jason.

Wednesday, April 13, 1983—got a little shopping done and got plane fuel. Dan let me fly the Cessna 185 from north of Palmer to Snowshoe Lake. Lots of fun, sure enjoyed that—Dan landed the plane. Went home and visited Hoffmans. Glad to be back. Sylvia put more hamburger in freezer.

Thursday, April 14, 1983—cloudy and windy. Helped Dan put rafters on his house. Al Clayton helped too. Went to Tom and Lisa's for supper—they all did some "pickin" (played music).

Friday, April 15, 1983—10° to 35°, cloudy and windy. Helped Dan with rafters and cut up meat.

10,000 Days in Alaska Book One 1978-1989

Saturday, April 16, 1983—snow all day. Helped put visqueen on Dan's housetop, visited with Jim and Mary. Sylvia and I have the flu. Played pool and watched movies at Lucky and Mary's. Got the down payment check for farm.

Sunday, April 17, 1983—pretty nice day, 26° to 30s. Henry, Sam, Tater and I went to Jim and Mary's (Sam stayed), then the Junction, KROA, and to Dan's. In the evening Sylvia and I took Henry and Tater to supper at Tolsona.

Monday, April 18, 1983—another nice day, 10° to 30s. Went to Glennallen, did laundry, then to Dan's and worked on the House.

Tuesday, April 19, 1983—cloudy windy and cool. Helped Dan with his house, still have the flu.

Wednesday, April 20, 1983—some sun, partly cloudy, small snow flurry. Finished the gable ends and most of west side of Roof. Slipped on power cord and banged side of my chin. Called Bill Johnson's brother.

Thursday, April 21, 1983—very nice day with light wind. We got all the steel on Dan's roof. Blake came down and watched TV with us.

Friday, April 22, 1983—15° to 40s and sunny. Finished roof on Dan's house. Went flying and saw lots of swans, some ducks, moose, swamp hawks, two eagles—no bears. Changed oil in truck.

Saturday, April 23, 1983—beautiful day, 20° to 40s. Swans are migrating. Worked on Cat's pony motor carburetor. We took Dan, Patti, Lisa and Jason to dinner at Tolsona Lodge. Called to wish Nadia happy birthday.

Sunday, April 24, 1983—30° to 60°, sunny and warm. Brought the Cat home from Hoffman's place and called Bill J. We are to get land papers ready. Called Bob R., he hasn't found a power take off shaft for Cat.

Monday, April 25, 1983—beautiful day. Called Jake, (Dan's lawyer) about land. Told Tom and Danny. Pulled Lucky's Cat for him.

Tuesday, April 26, 1983—the robins are here. Two eagles perched right outside the cabin in a tree—took pictures. Blake, and Bob Abel visited in afternoon. Visited Tom and Dan B.

Wednesday, April 27, 1983—sunny all day, 31° to 61°. Lisa S. went with us to title office and we met Danny and went to the lawyer's also. Did shopping and Palmer. Put new air filter in the truck.

Thursday, April 28, 1983—partly cloudy, 25° to 53°. Sylvia went with Jackie to Lake Louise Junction. I started with Vern and Darrel to Evergreen Lodge to a meeting. Fan belt broke on Vern's track. Tom's friend, Lou and I measured land.

Friday, April 29, 1983—light rain all day. Went to Wasilla and had lawyer make out purchase agreement on land. Couldn't get the lumber I needed. Lost bucket of oil.

Saturday, April 30, 1983—32° to 52° Sunny and light breeze, snow melting fast. Did a few things around here. Tom and Lisa came down. Sylvia, I, Tom, and Lisa looked at the land, then visited Dan and Patti. Visited Hoffmans. Lee Dudley stopped for a little while and James Callahan was here for a few minutes.

Sunday, May 1, 1983—a beautiful day, 28° to 54°. Fixed the tailgate on pickup and did other small jobs.

Monday, May 2, 1983—cloudy, cool and windy, with a light snow in the evening. It was 28° to 40°. Helped Dan put a second stud wall in his house. Called Johnny Berreth in Tensed, Idaho to buy power take off for our Cat from him—can't find one around here. He sent it to me by air freight.

Tuesday, May 3, 1983—snow flurries. Worked on Dan and Patti's house.

Wednesday, May 4, 1983—partly cloudy. Worked on Dan and Patti's house.

Thursday, May 5, 1983—partly cloudy, 28° to 40°. Went to Glennallen to the doctor to renew our prescriptions. Brought out some lumber for Dan. Built walls upstairs later in the day.

Friday, May 6, 1983—mostly sunny, 28° to 48°. Worked at Dan's until noon; then lucky ran our property line with his transit.

Saturday, May 7, 1983—partly cloudy, some rain mixed with snow, 28° to 40°. Charlie, Tom, Danny and I looked at our land. Potluck picnic at Tom's. Betty Johnson and boyfriend visited Nelchina. Went to Dan's for a movie.

Sunday, May 8, 1983—partly cloudy, 36° to 40s. Danny, Tom, Charlie and I brushed the line while Lucky ran the transit. Visited Hoffmans and helped them get a caribou road kill.

Monday May 9, 1983—nice day, 26° to 50s. Worked on Dan's house, Charlie helped too. Took Bob Abel to a hearing in Glennallen.

Tuesday, May 10, 1983—nice day, 26° to the 50s. Worked on Dan's house, Charlie helped in the afternoon. Went to KROA for supper—it's our anniversary. Called Bill Johnson and then called mother.

Wednesday, May 11, 1983—25° to 50° and a nice day. Two bear hunters got a six-foot bear. Didn't do anything on the house.

Thursday, May 12, 1983—cloudy early in the day but nice later. 25° to 50°. Helped with the house in the afternoon. Dan's hunters didn't get a bear.

Friday, May 13, 1983—cloudy early again and nice later, 30° to 50°. Finished inside walls of Dan's house.

Saturday, May 14, 1983—went to visit Jay and Shirley Hole on Lake Louise Road. They gave me some snowgo skis. Bob Abel bought our supper at KROA. Both rear springs are broken on the truck.

Sunday, May 15, 1983—rained last night, partly cloudy all day. Called and looked around for springs for the truck.

Monday, May 16, 1983—cloudy all day, 29° to 46°. Helped Bob Schmidt a little, then went to Joe Virgin to look at truck springs—no luck. Called Marvin Lange in Idaho. Sylvia did laundry with Margaret in Glennallen. She finished tablecloth blocks and sewed them together.

Norman Wilkins

Tuesday, May 17, 1983—mostly cloudy and a shower, 30 to 40°. Called the lawyer, no luck. Dan and I geared up to hunt Griz. Went flying—poor weather and no bear. A bear has vandalized my trap cabin.

Wednesday, May 18, 1983—cloudy, with rain and snow 30° to 40°. Dan and I hunted from the bluffs on Nelchina River. Went to Glennallen for parts—saw and drill to send to Henry. Called lawyer again, no luck.

Thursday, May 19, 1983—partly cloudy with a very light rain, 29° to 61°. Tried to call Bill. Called lawyer, no satisfaction. Built two sawhorses. Visited Tom and Lisa about land. Bob Abel was here for supper.

Friday, May 20, 1983—partly cloudy, 34° to 60°. Greased the truck and part of the Cat. Finally found button grease head for Cat. Called lawyer, got some satisfaction. Called Bill J. Called about springs for truck.

Saturday, May 21, 1983 partly cloudy, 30° to 50°. Visited Hoffmans, worked on truck, straightened some steel, and finished greasing the Cat.

Sunday, May 22, 1983—cloudy and cool. Took rear springs off the truck.

Monday, May 23, 1983—left early for Anchorage and did some shopping. Stayed overnight with Andy and Connie.

Tuesday, May 24, 1983—finished shopping and got home about six o'clock. Some rain in the pass.

Wednesday, May 25, 1983—cooler with some rain. Went to Glennallen and got springs for the truck. Bob Abel helped with the truck.

Thursday, May 26, 1983—I now have the rear spring replaced. New fan, belts, muffler and adjusted timing—runs great. Helped Bob build torch cart and cut top off car and hauled it to KROA.

Friday, May 27, 1983—cloudy and a light rain all day. Raked dog yard and went to Jay and Sherlene's. Sylvia and Margaret did laundry in Glennallen. I called lawyer, no papers yet. Took Dan B. to Glennallen for car parts.

10,000 Days in Alaska Book One 1978-1989

Saturday, May 28, 1983—Tom and Lee D. came and we tried to survey property line. Made a pack to go to cabin to assess bear damage. Dan flew me out and stayed the night. Bear tore mattress, sleeping bag and cushion. He rubbed four trees leaving blonde hair. He dug the ground up at my old gas cache. (For some reason, bears are attracted to the odor of gasoline.)

Sunday, May 29, 1983—partly cloudy, warm, windy and 69°. Hiked with Dan to his plane on Blue Lake. He left and I came back and built shutters for the trap cabin windows. Hunted griz a while. Griz has rubbed hair seven feet up on trees. Observed a pair of swans and two pair of breeding ducks on my lake.

Monday, May 30, 1983—sunny, then rain, sunny again and 69°. Dug a hole and built outhouse. Built pole floor for porch and set chopping block in ground. Looked for bear at Hole Lake. Saw beaver swimming and the loons are back. Dan came in late in the evening.

Tuesday, May 31, 1983—raining when we got up but soon quit—then we flew to Snowshoe Lake. I came home and did a few things here. We went to visit Allen and Roxanne. Lucky stopped at our place later and picked up his transit.

Wednesday, June 1, 1983—bright and sunny day. Called from Bob's about plywood. Visited Blake a few minutes. Started building pipe rack for pickup. Sharpened one hand saw. Dan Billman stopped by to borrow hole saw. Sylvia visited Hoffmans.

There is a June 2, 1983—real rain! Sylvia went with Margaret in her car and Bob and I drove in our pickup to Wasilla for log siding for him and to get some groceries and tools and log oil for us.

Friday, June 3, 1983—light rain. Helped Dan Billman with his house, then visited Lucky and Mary and also Blake for a little while.

Saturday, June 4, 1983—up early. Bob Abel had breakfast with us, then we went to Glennallen and loaded some 3/4" plywood and unloaded it at home. Visited Hoffmans and picked up some of our wood and took it to Dan's place, then on home. Called Paul for his birthday.

Sunday, June 5, 1983—partly cloudy all day and 60°. Darrell Gerry visited us last night. Small jobs all day. Bob Abel was here for supper.

Monday, June 6, 1983—partly cloudy. Went to Billman's and called lawyer—Bill has signed. Stopped and told Lisa, marked the trees that will be removed from the building site and visited Max and Irene.

Tuesday, June 7, 1983—sunny and partly cloudy. Trimmed more trees. Helped Blake build a storage shed and ate supper with them.

Wednesday June 8, 1983—partly cloudy, calm and 40° to 50°. Blake gave me a 16 foot log for a stringer in our house. We moved his freezer. Sylvia went to Glennallen with Margaret and I cut brush on the road to our property. Pulled a car stuck in loose gravel alongside the highway and got it back on the asphalt.

Thursday, June 9, 1983—mostly cloudy, rainy evening. Cut and piled brush on property. Had supper at Bob and Margaret's. Checked Jim and Mary's house. Wrote Sam.

Friday, June 10, 1983—rained all day. Visited Dan and Patti and visited Hoffmans.

Saturday, June 11, 1983—sunny today. Sylvia and I worked on building site. Went to Lucky and Mary's for supper. Jessica has pink eye.

Sunday, June 12, 1983—worked on a building site. Measured lots today and took the Cat to the parcel and built a road into it.

Monday, June 13, 1983—started digging basement, put some gravel on lane. Frost and 30°. Sunny breezy day, bugs are bad. Sylvia still sick. Earthquake tremor at 9:50 p.m.

Tuesday, June 14, 1983—sunny and a strong breeze. Dug down to the frost on the basement and started on the outhouse. Prepared Bob Schmidt's site for his garage with the Cat. Danny brought Cat power take off from Anchorage. Bob Abel got home from jail.

Wednesday, June 15, 1983—sunny with some showers. Dug more on basement. Cribbed up the outhouse. Frost in gravel in the basement.

10,000 Days in Alaska Book One 1978-1989

Thursday, June 16, 1983—rain in the morning, Dug more in the basement and finished it. Lucky came over with his transit and "shot" the basement. Bob and Kahren Rudbeck arrived here this evening.

Friday, June 17, 1983—Bob Rudbeck was with me all day. We visited around the neighborhood. Went to Glennallen. Lawyer called that papers are ready to sign. Truck has bad seal in transfer case.

Saturday, June 18, 1983—worked on truck. Bob S. took me to Glennallen to look for transfer case seal. Cement came, unloaded it. Beautiful day, Lucky and Mary got their TV antenna dish.

Sunday, June 19 1983—got Father's Day cards from Nadia and Beverly. Worked on basement and piled gravel for cement. Worked on front hubs of truck. Another beautiful day.

Monday, June 20, 1983—Bob Rudbeck drove me in his pickup to Wasilla. We shopped for the house and signed papers for land. Got parts for truck. Nice day, nice trip.

Tuesday, June 21, 1983—up early, Bob Abel went with me to Anchorage to get septic tank, et cetera. Nice trip—got all our shopping done. Mostly nice weather, got unloaded in the evening. Charlie T. stopped to visit about land.

Wednesday, June 22, 1983—beautiful day, worked all day on house basement getting ready to pour cement. Bob Rudbeck helped most of the day. Charlie T. came early to talk about land. Saw a very large eagle.

Thursday, June 23, 1983 another perfect day. Sylvia and I and Bob had the basement ready to pour cement and ate lunch. Started mixing cement at 1:30 p.m. and we were done by 6:30 p.m. Dan Billman Darrell Gerry and Bob S. helped too. We invited everyone to KROA for pizza and beer. Pretty tired tonight.

Friday, June 24 1983—went to Glennallen and bought two beams for the house. Bob and Kahren went along. Henry came out from Slate Creek mine. Visited Hoffmans and Beaudoins.

Norman Wilkins

Saturday, June 25, 1983—hauled lumber to our lot and 28 cement sacks over to Bob S. Henry went back to work. We took Lucky and Mary Beaudoin to dinner at Tolsona Lodge in the evening.

Sunday, June 26, 1983—Bob, Kahren, Jerry Rudbeck and his wife, and Nick and sister stopped to visit. Bob and Margaret visited, Bob Abel helped this afternoon with one wall of the basement. It's a very nice day, sunny, 82° yesterday and in the 70s today.

Monday, June 27, 1983—light rain all day. Bob Rudbeck and Dan Billman helped with basement walls. Sylvia and Bob Abel helped all day. Jerry and Nick helped later. We have all but 20 feet of walls up now. Put up mailbox today.

Tuesday, June 28, 1983—Bob, Jerry, and Nick Rudbeck and Denny Griffith helped finish basement walls and put floor Joists on. Dan Billman brought my ladder and helped put beams up. Beautiful day, happy tonight. Had supper with them at KROA campground. Tom and Lisa brought a cake and we made out a money receipt.

Wednesday, June 29, 1983—up early, worked on basement till 5:00 p.m. then loaded gravel for Bob Schmidt and Allen Farmer. Alan hauled gravel for our lane. Really nice day, bugs were bad sometimes.

Thursday, June 30, 1983—spread gravel in the lane and finished tar coating on basement. Shored up the walls of basement from the inside. Tom brought receipt for his down payment on parcel of land. Visited Lucky and Mary.

Friday, July 1, 1983—put the belt power unit on the Cat and worked at getting sawmill lined up. Lucky and Allen helped. Went to Dan Billman's and borrowed a belt pulley for the sawmill.

Saturday, July 2, 1983—chain sawed some stumps and brush. Chainsaw quit. The Swamp buggy flooded out. I did get the big trailer hauled up to the woodpile. Put a 12 inch pulley on sawmill. Went to KROA campground to visit Rudbecks and Griffith. Another nice day.

Sunday, July 3, 1983—beautiful day. Hauled a big load of wood to our place. Trimmed logs and hauled to sawmill. Took chainsaw to Charlie

10,000 Days in Alaska Book One 1978-1989

Netter and battery to Dan B. to get it charged.

Monday, July 4, 1983—worked on logs for a while, then went to Billman's place for a picnic—had a good time. Visited Hoffmans in the evening.

Tuesday, July 5, 1883—Dan flew Bob, Kahren, Jerry, Betty, Dana and Nick Rudbeck, and Sylvia and me to Kianna Creek to fish king salmon. Nick and Kahren caught fish. Sylvia, Jerry, Dana and Nick lost several. Worked on sawmill in the evening and got water at Bob Schmidt's.

Wednesday, July 6, 1983—Dan B. and Vern B. and wife borrowed hip boots and fish pole. Bob Rudbeck borrowed two pressure canners. Lucky, Sylvia and I got 33 House logs and some lumber sawed. Had supper at Blake and Jackie's. Bob Abel was shooting in the night. Shot two holes in his van.

Thursday, July 7, 1983—another nice day. Took two loads of logs to the mill and hauled 28 logs to our place, also a load of slabs. Hauled Blake's Cat up on the level ground. Hoffmans got more sawdust.

Friday, July 8, 1983—beautiful day, worked early to late. Got lots of logs sided and lumber. Bob S. helped saw. Sylvia and Margaret did laundry.

Saturday, July 9, 1983—got a lot of logs sawed. Saw got hot—may have to get it hammered. Had supper at Lucky and Mary's. Pulled Blake's Cat over on state land. Short shower this afternoon, nice day and 40° by nighttime.

Sunday, July 10 1983—Charlie Netter fixed the vacuum line on my chainsaw. Picked up battery and hip boots etc. at Billman's. Visited Hoffmans, hauled two loads of logs to mill and one load of slabs back. Light rain at 7:00 p.m.

Monday, July 11, 1983—rained all night and day, got lots of rest. Went to Dan's late afternoon. Tried to call George Shaffer, no luck. Dan brought water system Pump down and I welded it. Sylvia and Mary went to see Hoffmans. Mike Dunn and brother to B stopped to pick up saw from Lucky's mill.

Norman Wilkins

Tuesday, July 12, 1983—still rainy. 5.7 earthquake at 6:00 a.m. Went to Dan's, made several phone calls. Hauled the rest of house logs to mill. Hauled two big loads of firewood to our place. Visited Smayda's about land business.

Wednesday, July 13, 1983—Rhynell had picked up roof cement in town for us. Picked it up, and then called Federal Land Bank from Dan's. Hauled a load of wood and put in the pipe from septic to the house. Back filled some dirt around the house and went to KROA for supper. Visited the Rudbeck brothers at KROA campground. Some rain today.

Thursday, July 14, 1983—back filled some more on the basement. Went to Glennallen for materials to insulate pipe to septic tank.

Friday, July 15, 1983—did odd jobs around the building site. Sanded two sill logs. Back filled rest of basement. George Shaffer brought 45 sheets of ½ inch plywood—very nice plywood. Paid him $360. Visited Lucky and Mary.

Saturday, July 16, 1983—sunny day, got nine sill logs on. Took Mike, the dog, over to show him his home to be. Helped Bob Schmidt run some cement.

Sunday, July 17, 1983—put two more sill logs on. Raked and leveled gravel and Cat tracks. Visited Hoffmans. Rain later in the afternoon. Bob Kahren, Jerry and Betty visited in the evening.

Monday, July 18, 1983—rain most of the day, covered the logs and lumber. Did a little nailing. Visited Billmans, Schmidts, Blake and Jackie. Sylvia baked and went to Gunsight with Jackie.

Tuesday, July 19, 1983—light rain several times. Sanded four corner logs and five house logs. Helped Blake drill some bolts. Lisa and her father Joe visited a while.

Wednesday, July 20, 1983—mostly rainy, hard to get logs sanded.

Thursday, July 21, 1983—sanded a few logs. Went to Anchorage with Dan B. Rented truck. Lucky and I drove a loaded truck home. Got back at 3:00 a.m.

10,000 Days in Alaska Book One 1978-1989

Friday, July 22, 1983—Bob Abel was on a rampage. Lucky, Blake and I unloaded the lumber and I drove the truck back to Anchorage and rode home with Dan Billman.

Saturday, July 23, 1983—rainy day. Hauled Bob Abel and his things to Sutton. Picked up Bob Schmidt's lumber at Homesteaders Hardware in Big Lake.

Sunday, July 24, 1983—sanded more logs, very nice day. Went to KROA, had supper and visited. Filled out FLB papers.

Monday, July 25, 1983—Henry and Doug stopped by. Bob S. brought cold water and goodies to the building site. Bob, Kahren and Dana helped us sand logs—we did 28. Beautiful day and hot, 40° at night.

Tuesday, July 26, 1983—Henry went back to the mine, Doug is staying with us. Bob, Kahren and Dana helped with the logs, got 29 sanded today. Dan and Patti brought us a phone message from Nadia this afternoon (we don't have a telephone).

Wednesday, July 27, 1983—perfect weather, though hot. Bob and Kahren helped sand logs. Have 105 done now. Doug put log oil on some of the basement studs. Bob and Kahren treated us to pizza at KROA.

Thursday, July 28, 1983—sunny and hot, some breeze. Sanded 18 logs. Doug went to Tolsona with Bob and Margaret to stay overnight.

Friday, July 29, 1983—sanded six logs, then the rain started. Went to Wasilla and got insurance for the truck. Bought 14, 2x12's for the top plate of house.

Saturday, July 30, 1983—cloudy in the morning, clear later. Sanded four logs and sawed a few. Saw doesn't cut true, heats up. Took a melon over to Bob and Margaret. Got my bison permit today.

Sunday, July 31, 1983—a little rain, but mostly sunny. Finished sanding the logs. We have sawed 143 logs. Re-piled some lumber.

Norman Wilkins

Monday, August 1, 1983—rained all day. Sent certified letter (lease for Boot Lake land) to Division of Lands. Stopped to see some people and returned Dan's tools.

Tuesday, August 2, 1983—very nice day, hauled two big loads of logs to KROA. Jerry R. and Darrel G. helped saw them. Very glad to get them sawed. Called Ken Lewis, he will be out to appraise land Thursday at 10 a.m.

Wednesday, August 3, 1983—beautiful day, put two sill logs on and half the floor. Move the stairs to basement. Helped Bob Schmidt for a while. Measured the distance to Lake—383 feet.

Thursday, August 4, 1983—got some more of the floor on. Ken Lewis didn't show up. Rained at 11:00 a.m. We got some things from Schmidt's garage sale. Visited Lucky and Mary.

Friday, August 5, 1983—finished putting the floor on house. Ken Lewis wants land surveyed before he appraises it. Tom, Lisa, Danny and his dad, Harold and friend Dick visited. We hauled a load of things from Schmidt's garage sale and it rained all afternoon.

Saturday, August 6, 1983—covered the house floor with plastic and bolted stairs to floor joist. Worked at drain field for septic system. Got three sections of pipe in. Went to KROA to see Darrel Gerry.

Sunday, August 7, 1983—finished fourth section drain field. Secured tarps on lumber. Drove pins in Cat track. Moved dogs to new place, got truck ready for a trip. Allen F. and Blake just discovered more log gone. Dan B. stopped and paid share on truck rental.

Monday, August 8, 1983—finished securing things at the building site and finished getting the truck ready. Went to KROA, Hoffman's, and Jim and Mary Odden's to check their place. We are going "outside". Daughter, Beverly is getting married.

Tuesday, August 9, 1983—up early for the trip to the lower 48 for the wedding. Stopped at Schmidt's and Darrel's. Picked up two hitchhikers at Haines Junction. Made it to Whitehorse and slept a little.

10,000 Days in Alaska Book One 1978-1989

Wednesday, August 10, 1983—truck is gobbling oil!! Saw some nice Burl tables and Burwash. Picked up a hitcher, "Bill" at Watson Lake. Lots of road work, saw a coyote. Napped at Fort St. John, and got to Dawson Creek at 6:00 a.m. Left Bill.

Thursday, August 11, 1983—good roads, made it to Regina about 5:00 a.m. Some rain.

Friday, August 12 1983—hot, 90° and winds 30 to 40 MPH. thru Manitoba. Got to Paul and Ruth's at 10:00 p.m. and to bed at 12 o'clock.

Saturday, August 13, 1983—went to the dairy barn on our farm. Saw Rodney and Rose, Kenny and Eva, Tony, Harold and Lorraine. Drove on down to Minneapolis to Beverly and Kevin's. Darrell and Nadia and Laura were there—very hot.

Sunday, August 14, 1983—Hot again here today. Party for Vanessa's birthday at her dad's. Beverly's family and Sylvia and I went to Nadia's for a BBQ, then we all went to the "Pain Reliever" bar. (Sylvia and I drink only pop.)

Monday, August 15, 1983—went with Kevin to help Earl (Caughey) with a flat tire. Measured for a tux for Bev and Kevin's wedding. Called around for a motor for the truck.

Tuesday, August 16, 1983—went to Federal Land Bank in St. Cloud, then to Milaca. Harold Reek wasn't home, then visited friends. Went on to Paul and Ruth's.

Wednesday, August 17, 1983—Paul and Stevie helped us sort out our things in the chicken house. Went to Bridget Shequen's place to get some of our things. Visited some people and walked over the farm. Stayed at Paul and Ruth's.

Thursday, August 18, 1983—nice day, talked with Herald Reek and possible renter. Poor offer of rent. Talked to Butch about motor for truck. Kevin brought suit over.

Friday, August 19, 1983—Hot today. Called Theresa. Went to grooms dinner last night and my sister Virginia and her husband, Don Wink are to come over this evening. They are here from Cedar Rapids Iowa for the wedding.

Saturday, August 20, 1983—got ready for the wedding. Good weather, beautiful wedding, then reception and dance. Everyone had a good time. Went to Ivan and Mary Lou Boulton's for a party—got home (Nadia's) at 2:00 a.m.

Sunday, August 21, 1983—up at 6:00 a.m., went to Holiday Inn to have breakfast with Don and Virginia, then it rained. In the afternoon we went to Ivan and Mary Lou's and Beverly opened presents. Rain quit, then went to Theresa and Earl's for a barbecued steak supper and it rained again in the evening.

Monday, August 22, 1983—sunny all day, cooler. Earl and I went book hunting. Theresa and Sylvia did a little shopping, watched TV, and enjoyed grandkids.

Tuesday, August 23, 1983—sunny in the morning. At noon, Lee and Earl and I picked up Butch and Scott and went to Earl's parents' (Donald and Evelyn) farm in Brainerd to look at a Chevy motor. It didn't run. Got back late.

Wednesday, August 24, 1983—sunny and hot all day. Went to Brainerd and Motley, had supper at Rollins'. Visited Peter Ackermans and stayed at Paul and Ruth's.

Thursday, August 25, 1983—went to the farm, talked to Borders and came back to Paul's. Loaded truck for trip back to Alaska.

Friday, August 26, 1983—left Paul and Ruth's about 8:30 a.m. (Sylvia is staying in Minnesota for a longer visit) Did some shopping, and got to Regina at 9:30 p.m. Got to Saskatoon about 12:30 and napped till 4:00 a.m. Had one rain shower.

Saturday, August 27, 1983—oats are fence post high in the fields around here. Some farmers harvest far into the night. Saw a red fox this morning. Nice sunny day, made Dawson Creek at 6:00 p.m. One rain shower.

10,000 Days in Alaska Book One 1978-1989

Sunday, August 28, 1983—nice dawn, sunny day. Perhaps two dozen porcupines live and dead on the road to Watson Lake. One cross fox, one large black bear. Got to Watson Lake at 9:00 a.m. and got to Whitehorse at 3:00 p.m.

Monday, August 29, 1983—got home about 7:00 a.m. Good to be here. Everything here is okay. Did a few things and visited some people.

Tuesday, August 30, 1983—got things ready to sand logs. Moved some things to our place. Nice most of the day, cloudy and windy in the evening.

Wednesday, August 31, 1983—partly cloudy, trees are in full fall colors now—beautiful. Got six logs sanded, and helped Bob S. and Blake.

Thursday, September 1 1983—40° and cloudy in the morning, 62° and Sunny in the afternoon. Sanded 10 logs.

Friday, September 2, 1983—had some light rain overnight. Sanded logs, and had supper at Blake and Jackie's.

Saturday, September 3, 1983—light snow overnight and some ice, melted soon. Cloudy all day and 40°.

Sunday, September 4, 1983—partly cloudy and 30° to 50°. Helped Tom and Lisa pour cement. Shoveled a little gravel at home. Darrel Gerry gave me a duck stamp.

Monday, September 5, 1983—very nice day, 28° to 50°. Helped Bob S. haul fill for his garage.

Tuesday, September 6, 1983—clear all day, high in the 20s to the 40s. Hauled more gravel to Bob's. Went to Glennallen and notarized the remote parcel lease. Got copies of Pennington Weir claims.

Wednesday, September 7, 1983—20° to 50° and clear. Hauled 30 sacks of cement from Glennallen for Lucky. Loaded and hauled fill dirt for Bob S. Visited Dan and Patti.

Thursday, September 8, 1983—loaded gravel for Lucky, then ran cement on two thirds of his garage floor. Very nice day, highs in the 20s to 50s and clear.

Friday, September 9—cloudy, 32° to 50°. Helped Lucky finish cement in garage. Shoveled dirt at our place. Helped Blake on his house. Hunted moose for two hours. Lucky is sick.

Saturday, September 10, 1983—partly cloudy, 40s to 50s. Lucky has a kidney stone. Helped Jackie with house trusses and cut and piled brush at our place. Hauled a load of water for Lucky.

Sunday, September 11, 1983—partly cloudy, 30° to 52°. Went to the dump, KROA, and Hoffman's. Cut and piled brush, trimmed out a place for the dog yard, and had a turkey supper at Bob and Margaret's. Called Beverly. Sylvia is at her sister, Frances' in Chicago. Nadia and Darrell are home.

Monday, September 12, 1983—mostly sunny, 25° to 52°. Cut more brush and piled and shoveled some dirt. Mixer broke down so didn't get much cement mixed for Tom. Going on a bear hunt with Dan Billman. Flew to a lake near Oshetna River. Saw roughly 50 moose and a Toklat grizzly on a kill. The plane can sleep two people so we didn't have to put up a tent.

Tuesday, September 13, 1983—17° to 42° and cloudy. Dan and I awoke very early this morning and quietly slipped out of the plane. We checked and loaded our rifles and started our stalk towards the place where the grizzly had killed a bull caribou. Soon, a raven flew low and slow over us, sounding its guttural call over and over. It turned back towards the kill sight. We continued in that direction, using the black spruce as our cover. Suddenly there was a partially consumed carcass just a few yards away. We carefully scanned the immediate area and didn't see the bear, but were aware that it may have been warned by the raven and might be near by. We backed up a few yards so we would be able to use our rifles. We then quietly looked over the area and concluded the bear wasn't in the immediate area. Nothing to do but go back to the plane. Dan had flying to do and I sure enough had things to do. We saw lots of caribou on the flight back to Dan's. Later, I helped Tom run cement and Chad Wilson stopped in, great to see him. Bob and Kahren are back with a

10,000 Days in Alaska Book One 1978-1989

new motor in their pickup. Had supper at Bob and Margaret's.

Wednesday, September 14, 1983—cold, 70° to 44° and sunny. Worked on sewer and drain. Called farm insurance and ASCS. Helped Blake some. Rain and snow at dark, heavy snow at 11 p.m. Blake got a road kill moose—I helped him from 1:30 to 3:30 a.m.

Thursday, September 15, 1983—28° to 38°, some snow. Skinned moose, went to Anchorage, visited Connie and Andy until time to pick up Sylvia at the airport (Sylvia her sister Frances, Nadia and Darrell have just returned from three weeks visiting relatives overseas). Got home at 4:00 a.m.

Friday, September 16, 1983—nice day, 22° to 50°. Delivered Bob's 2x4's and went to see Hoffmans. Irene is weaker, she went to hospital. Sylvia and I stayed with Max all afternoon. Tried to trace the spinning wheels. Blake was here for supper.

Saturday, September 17, 1983—clear, 15° to 48°. Hauled three loads of fill dirt, made several phone calls to customs and air freight. Twin moose calves walked very close to me; one fed on his knees 10 feet away. Brought Cat home and did some work with it.

Sunday, September 18, 1983—partly cloudy, 15° to 45°. Sanded six logs, hauled a few loads of things to our place. Lucky turned in some hunters who shot swans on our lake.

Monday, September 19, 1983—cloudy, 38° to 48° and rain in the evening. Finished sanding house logs. Hauled three loads of our things to our place and a load to the dump. Bob S. and I drove Lake Louise Road hunting moose. Visited KROA, Bob and Kahren, and Darrell Gerry.

Tuesday, September 20, 1983—partly cloudy, and rain in the evening. 40° to 50°. Bob S. and I drove Lake Louise Road, then on to Glennallen. I hunted east alone in the afternoon. Got some goose hunting gear ready, got some trap bait bottled. Visited Lucky and Mary.

Wednesday, September 21, 1983—rain all night and all day. Sylvia, me, Bob and Margaret went to Anchorage to get spinning wheels from customs. (Sylvia bought them during her trip and had then shipped here.) Went to KROA. Called Rodney B., then Kevin Volk. Packed hunt gear and visited Dan and Patti Billman.

Thursday, September 22, 1983—cloudy and rain, got to Delta one hour before daylight. Napped one hour, ate breakfast, went to Scott and Barney Hollembeck farm. Good hunting! I shot four crane, Scott and Darrel each got one. Slept in Delta. Bob Abel shot and killed Jack (don't know his last name). Jack was Bob's best friend and he had a 5-year-old son.

Friday, September 23, 1983—freezing rain and snow. Few Sandhill Crane, Darrel and Scott each got a crane. Saw a black bear, chased him and got one shot and missed. Trailed one crippled crane 1- 1/2 miles. Scott shot him at 74 yards. Drove through snow and high winds and got home late. Met veterinarian, Dick Teal—a goose hunter. He lives in Delta Junction.

Saturday, September 24, 1983—windy and light snow. Slept late, Henry slept here. We visited awhile then went to KROA, Billmans and Schmidts and later cut up some wood. Our lake has started to freeze.

Sunday, September 25, 1983—partly cloudy, -2° to 18°. Bob and Kahren visited in the morning. Went to Dan's and then KROA. Went back to KROA for supper and music to celebrate Bob and Kahren buying Danny C's lot, and Jim and Mary back for winter. Saw five otter in Mendeltna Creek. More of the lake is frozen.

Monday, September 26, 1983—mostly sunny, -2° to 18°. Got a pickup tire fixed and changed the oil. Our lake is frozen except a small area—a dozen ducks there. Going to Bob's for his birthday dinner.

Tuesday, September 27, 1983—partly cloudy, 0° to 28°. Moved dogs and houses, moved lumber pile and Sylvia cooked one of the Cranes. Bob Schmidt got a road kill moose calf. We helped with it.

Wednesday, September 28, 1983—cloudy and warmer, up to 28°. Took meat to Billman's meat house, took junk to the dump, helped Ed Farmer take floats off and put skis on his plane. He welded for me. We had supper there, then visited Lucky's and called Kevin and Beverly.

10,000 Days in Alaska Book One 1978-1989

Thursday, September 29, 1983—partly cloudy, 20° to 40°. Burned a pile of brush and moved storage shed to our place. Lucky helped. Took spinning wheel to Dan and Patti.

Friday, September 30, 1983—partly cloudy and warm. Took Cat and pulled our cabin over here—broke down 100 feet from where we wanted to put it. Nice to have it here on our place. The skids started to loosen from under the floor.

Saturday, October 1, 1983—cloudy and warm, snow melts—muddy. Got Cat started and runner back under cabin. Moved, blocked and leveled it. Moved welder, brown trailer etc. over here. Dan and Tom helped. Went to Ranch House for a party.

Sunday, October 2, 1983—snow, then rain and 30°. Covered junk so we can find it after snowfall. Real muddy. Cut up 1/4 pork. Sylvia, Margaret and Bob cut up a calf moose. Darrel, Jim and Mary were here to hunt geese—no geese. Lots of swans using this lake today.

Monday, October 3, 1983—warm all night, cloudy all day. Cut up and hauled some wood and junk. Put up TV antenna. Ground hamburger at Dan's. Dennis Rhodes left a message for Sally here. Henry, Sally and Chris stopped in later. Housewarming for Charlie Netter tonight. He has built a nice log home.

Tuesday, October 4, 1983—very nice day, low of 20°. Moved more wood to our place and moved other things over. Chainsaw quit. Sam came here in the night, slept and had breakfast with us. Visited Hoffmans and KROA.

Wednesday, October 5, 1983—mostly cloudy, 26° to 30°. Fixed cabin door, radio antenna etc. Called Kevin and Beverly about farm, took battery to Billman's to be charged. It tried to snow after dark.

Thursday, October 6, 1983—two inches of snow, cloudy, melted some today. Went to Glennallen and sent power of attorney to Kevin. Help Dan put culvert in and visited Bob and Margaret.

Friday, October 7, 1983—sunny, nice, some wind, and 18° to 30°.

Norman Wilkins

Moved straw over here and built a lean-to for it. Helped Bob S. run some cement. Had supper at Tom and Lisa Smayda's. Dan, Tom, Lee D., Jim, and Mary played music for everyone. Tried to fix TV, didn't work.

Saturday, October 8, 1983—sunny, 1° to 28°. Chris Ronning buzzed our place (flew over and circled in his plane). Did lots of jobs getting ready for winter. Lake froze completely over last night.

Sunday, October 9, 1983—light snow, 14° to 28°. Tried to start swamp buggy, Henry helped. No luck. Will try with propane heat tomorrow. Had supper at Bob and Margaret's. Sylvia did laundry in Glennallen with Bob and Margaret.

Monday, October 10, 1983—cloudy, 20° to 40°. Slept late, tried all day to start swamp buggy with no luck. Jim and Mary brought Sam down to get guns he had stored here. We burned brush piles in the evening then visited Lucky and Mary.

Tuesday, October 11, 1983—40° and raining this morning. Warmed up and was a nice day. 32° tonight. Got a small start on the woodshed. Patti Billman visited Sylvia and we had supper at Henry and Sally's.

Wednesday, October 12, 1983—partly cloudy, 20° to 40°. Tom, Sylvia and I cut property lines preparatory for surveyor.

Thursday, October 13, 1983—cloudy all day and snow flurries, 24° to 30°. Worked on the woodshed. Set poles and framed with poles and trimmed rafters. Sam and a coworker, Greg helped put up heaviest log. Geese and swans are flying above the clouds.

Friday, October 14, 1983—partly cloudy, 20° to 30°. Got rafters on woodshed and half of it sided. Went to KROA for water and to talk to Darrel about going with me buffalo hunting. Shot the .338 to check the sights and visited Hoffmans.

Saturday, October 15, 1983—cloudy, 15° to 28°. Got all the sheeting boards and what roofing I have, on the woodshed. Blocked some wood and called Kevin about the farm.

10,000 Days in Alaska Book One 1978-1989

Sunday, October 16, 1983—cloudy, 15° to 20°. Got gear and truck ready to go buffalo hunting. Tried to saw stove wood, bar on saw failed. Dan Billman. visited. Henry brought an old beer cooler over for storage. Put two handles in axes for Hoffmans.

Monday, October 17, 1983—cloudy, 20°. Darrel and I went to Delta and checked in with Fish and Game and started getting permission from farmers to hunt buffalo. Stayed at Cherokee II. The buffalo tramp down and eat the farmers' grain crops.

Tuesday, October 18, 1983—hunted all day and got permission from more farmers to hunt on their land. Staying at the Silver Fox with Dan and Slick. Al has brought his wife Wendy and two boys from Pennsylvania to live here. Met lots of new people. Didn't see any bison.

Wednesday, October 19, 1983—still snowing here, 0° to 20°. Later it cleared up. We each shot a crane. Darrell probably would've gotten another one but his firing pin broke. Got a nice bull bison after a long exciting chase. It was -10° below zero and dark while we dressed it out. Back to the Silver Fox at 2:00 a.m.

Thursday, October 20, 1983—gave some bison meat to friends here. Checked out with Fish and Game, got home after dark. Had a supper of buffalo hump.

Friday, October 21, 1983—partly cloudy, warm, 30°. Friends came to see bison and take pictures. Hung meat in Schmidt's basement and had supper there.

Saturday, October 22, 1983—partly cloudy, 15° to 25°. Darrel and I took the buffalo cape and hide to get it tanned. Dan came and invited us to their place in the evening. Jim Odden's folks are visiting from Wisconsin.

Sunday, October 23, 1983—cloudy morning sunny in the afternoon 5° to 25°. Cut up buffalo ribs this afternoon and called Kevin again tonight. Talked to Beverly.

Monday, October 24, 1983—partly cloudy, 10° to 25°. Stored some things here and worked on the woodshed. Took some buffalo meat to

Jim and Mary, and to Hoffman's. Called Kevin about the farm.

Tuesday, October 25, 1983—cloudy, light snow, 10° to 20°. Finished the woodshed and visited Lucky and Mary in the evening.

Wednesday, October 26, 1983—mostly cloudy, 10° to 15°. Put weed burner together and soldered radiator on truck. Lots of phone calls. Henry and Sally took us to KROA for pizza. Jim, Mary, Lester (his dad), and Lois (his mother), were there are also.

Thursday, October 27, 1983—cloudy and light snow, 0° to 15°. Had breakfast at Henry and Sally's, Jim Odden and family were there. Tom and Lisa and Lauren were here at our place all day waiting for a man from REA to come and decide where to put electric poles. The man didn't show. Hauled water in the evening. It took REA 16 months to get poles and service to our house.

Friday, October 28, 1983—cloudy, light snow, 16° to 20°. Visited Bob S. and also Henry. Hauled six loads of logs and wood from where we used to live.

Saturday, October 29, 1983—cloudy, more snow—three inches and 20°. Went to KROA, then got Darrel and we cut up buffalo at Bob Schmidt's place. Had supper there, watched movies at Henry's, then took Darrel home.

Sunday, October 30, 1983—bright and sunny, 20°. Got snowgo running. Fixed Sam's saw chain and he patched an overshoe. Nice visit. He left a book with me.

Monday, October 31, 1983—snowed all day, 5° to 20°. Slept late, helped Henry haul water and filled our buckets.

Tuesday, November 1, 1983—cloudy, 6° to 20°. Lucky cut hump and back strap on his meat saw. Andy and Bob visited at Henry's. Dan and Patti visited in the morning. Sylvia babysat in the evening.

Wednesday, November 2, 1983—clear, 10° to 20°. At noon, I took Sam to Jim and Mary's. Jim gave me a part for Coleman lantern. Dan Billman and I got the backhoe home from the claims. Sylvia babysat and

10,000 Days in Alaska Book One 1978-1989

I visited Lucky.

Thursday, November 3, 1983—nice day, 10° to 20°. We still have the flu. Did a few things around here, Sylvia is babysitting.

Friday, November 4, 1983—cloudy, 0° to 15°. The part came for the chainsaw. Fixed the bar and cut some wood.

Saturday, November 5 1983—mostly cloudy, some fog, 3° to 20°. Cut up firewood today.

Sunday, November 6, 1983—cloudy and foggy, 2° to 15°. Cut up more wood. Jim and Sam visited and had supper with us.

Monday, November 7, 1983—cloudy and foggy, 0° to 12°. Went to Glennallen to get the farm papers notarized. Henry got a Steam Jenny and thawed his well.

Tuesday, November 8, 1983—cloudy and 6° to 20°. Chuck Laughlin from the REA came out to talk pole-setting here. Finished sawing up buffalo meat at Lucky's and visited Henry and Sally. Tom, Mary and Sam were there.

Wednesday, November 9, 1983—bright and sunny, 6° to 25°. Tom and I went to REA to sign hookup forms. Trooper Jamie Hall interviewed Nelchina people about Bob Abel.

Thursday, November 10, 1983—partly sunny, 3° to 12°. Finished wrapping buffalo, and put a different starter on the truck. Helped Henry with wrecker, and had beans and cornbread with Henry and Sally.

Friday, November 11, 1983—sunny, 2° to 10°. Took some bison meat to Ed Farmer at KROA. Billmans visited and the Hoffmans, Henry, Sally and Sam were here for supper. Jim and Mary visited also.

Saturday, November 12, 1983—cloudy and warmer, -2° to 15°. Cut up a little wood and Sylvia cooked some dishes for Dan Billman's birthday skating party. Lots of people there, good time.

Sunday, November 13, 1983—cloudy, 6° to 20°. Trouble with truck, battery clamps.

Monday, November 14, 1983—cloudy, 6° to 12°. Cut up the last of the wood from the old place. Sylvia did laundry at Henry and Sally's. Borders called.

Tuesday, November 15, 1983—cloudy and some ice fog, -13° to 8°. Cut and stacked more wood. Tom and Lisa visited this afternoon.

Wednesday, November 16, 1983—cloudy and ice fog with some sun, -11° to 2°. Visited Schmidt's and hauled water. Cut up more wood, had more trouble with the saw.

Thursday, November 17, 1983—mostly cloudy, -10° to 8°. Got ready to go to town.

Friday, November 18, 1983—-6° to 10°. Dan Billman visited early in the morning. We went to Palmer, Wasilla, and Anchorage. Did lots of shopping and business. Got home after 12:00 a.m.

Saturday, November 19, 1983—mostly cloudy with a light snow last night, 0° to 8°. Unloaded supplies. Visited Schmidt's, Dan B., Jim, Mary, and Darrel at KROA.

Sunday, November 20, 1983—cloudy and frosty, -6° to 4°. Sore back, visited Schmidt's and Henry's and Lucky and Mary.

Monday, November 21, 1983—warmed up to 30° during the night. Wind and 30° all day and cloudy. Sylvia went to Glennallen with Mary and Sally.

Tuesday, November 22, 1983—foggy and 20° all day. Jim and Mary visited at noon. We visited Patti Billman, then Lucky and Mary. Jim and Mary stopped in again in the evening.

Wednesday, November 23 1983—cloudy, 8° to 12°. Back is sore. Called surveyor. Harold and Rachel asked us to a reindeer supper.

Thursday, November 24, 1983—cloudy, a very light snow, 2° to 8°. Talked to Dave, another surveyor. Went to Mendeltna lodge for a fine

10,000 Days in Alaska Book One 1978-1989

Thanksgiving dinner.

Friday, November 25, 1983—cloudy, 2° to 8°. Sore back, Sylvia did laundry. Charlie T., Tom and Lisa stopped to visit.

Saturday, November 26, 1983—partly cloudy, 2° all day. Got some trap gear ready.

Sunday, November 27, 1983—pretty nice day, 2° to 10°. Set traps on Slide Mountain line.

Monday, November 28, 1983—nice, partly cloudy day, 20° to 34° with 40 mph winds. Dan Billman and I went to Glennallen to file Affidavit of Labor on gold claims. Got some fox urine from Larry Sieverson.

Tuesday, November 29, 1983—warm and nice though windy, 26° to 36°. Got more trap gear ready and put charger on battery.

Wednesday November 30, 1983—mostly cloudy and warm, 24° to 30°. Ran Slide Mountain line, nothing in it.

Thursday, December 1, 1983—cloudy to partly cloudy, and degrees to 20°. Spent all day trying to get Danny Chapel's cabin deal straightened out. Surveyors had supper here, Ron, Dave and Skip.

Friday, December 2, 1983—overcast, 10 to 16°. Surveyors got started today.

Saturday, December 3, 1983—cloudy, -3° to 10°. Finished surveying around the land. Ron and Dave ate at Tom and Lisa's today.

Sunday, December 4, 1983—cloudy and frost, got quite a bit more surveying done.

Monday, December 5, 1983—cloudy, 6° to 20°. Finished surveying at 11:00 a.m. Visited Bob and Margaret and Hoffmans. Ran the trapline on Slide Mountain but got nothing.

Tuesday, December 6, 1983—cloudy, 6° to 12°. Took snowgo to Dinty Bush's on Lake Louise Road. Gave buffalo meat to Leo Zura, Lloyd

Norman Wilkins

Ronning and Charlie Netter.

Wednesday, December 7, 1983—cloudy and ice fog, 6° 15°. Saw eight moose along Lake Louise Road. Saw coyote, fox, otter, lynx and caribou tracks on the way to cabin. snowgo is sick, had to leave the sled four miles from cabin. Arrived at 2:30, everything fine here.

Thursday, December 8, 1983—cloudy all day, clear in the evening, 0° to 20°. Chinked outside of cabin. Quiet here.

Friday, December 9, 1983—cloudy and ice fog early some sun later, -10° to -16°. Put plastic in windows, made a few sets, and came out to road. Flat tire on truck.

Saturday, December 10, 1983—cloudy, -16° to -5°. Worked on snowgo and door at Henry's for Sally. Hauled water and banked cabin with snow. Sharpened Henry's chainsaw.

Sunday, December 11, 1983—cloudy, -20° to -5°. Took snowgo to Mike McKinley at Eureka and put new carburetor on it.

Monday, December 12, 1983—cloudy, -4° to -17°. Dan visited and told of he and Jim's deer hunting on Kodiak. Sylvia, Sally and I shopped in Glennallen. Got some things for Dan also. We all had supper at Billman's and saw the movie, "Day After" again.

Tuesday, December 13, 1983—cloudy again today, 0° to -10°. Wrote letters and read.

Wednesday, December 14, 1983—cloudy, a little sun, -6° to -16°. Wrote more letters, took water to Hoffmans and sharpened their chainsaw. They gave me some bound, NRA magazines. Irene is weak. Dan and Patti asked Sylvia to stay with their kids a couple of days.

Thursday, December 15, 1983—mostly cloudy with some sun, -20° to -10°. Sylvia is babysitting. I visited Darrel in the evening. Henry and Sally gave us a stone.

Friday, December 16, 1983—cloudy with some sun, -20° to -10°. Went to Hillside Shop. Didn't pick up snowgo, it wasn't repaired.

10,000 Days in Alaska Book One 1978-1989

Saturday, December 17, 1983—cloudy, -10° to -20°. Went to Gunsight and worked on snowgo, brought it home. Jim's, Dan's, Marty and Mike, Kay and Sylvia and I, were at Sally's for some pickin'.

Sunday, December 18, 1983—cloudy, -16 to -6°. Visited Dan's and Jim and Mary's.

Monday, December 19, 1983—nice day, -10° to 20°. Loaded snowgo and went to Dinty Bush's, unloaded and hit the trail. Made new sets and scented others. The snowgo quit on Blue Lake and I walked to the cabin. Got one marten, glad to be here.

Tuesday, December 20, 1983—cloudy, 0° to 10°. Walked back to snowgo, it ran after changing fuel filter. Got a few more sets going. Trails very rough. Skinned marten and did other chores.

Wednesday, December 21, 1983—sunny with a little snow last night, -3° to 10°. Built some conibear boxes and re-chinked inside of cabin.

Thursday, December 22, 1983—sunny, -15° to -5°. Left about noon and made some new sets on the way out. Loaded snowgo, saw three moose along the road. Visited Darrel, then on home.

Friday, December 23, 1983—pretty nice day, -14° to -10°. Ran line on Slide Mountain, got nothing.

Saturday, December 24, 1983—sunny day, -18° to -10°. Water to Hoffmans, nice visit. Visited Sally and Chris and also Billmans. Mary Odden and girlfriend stopped by with goodies.

Sunday, December 25, 1983—warm day, some wind, 0° to 20°. Checked Schmidt's furnace, then went to KROA for Christmas dinner. Haven't felt good all day.

Monday, December 26 1983—pretty nice day, 0° to -10°. Didn't do much, some kind of flu. Charlie and Beth stopped by with Sandhill Crane research report. We visited Lucky and Mary. Later I went to mile 140 and pulled Henry's van out of the ditch. He, Sally, Doug, and Denise hit a small bull moose.

Norman Wilkins

Tuesday, December 27, 1983—cloudy, -20° to 0°. Roger Ford and wife stopped by, talked about his knot book. Sylvia and I installed heating stove that Henry and Sally gave us.

Wednesday, December 28, 1983—nice day, -20° to -10°. Ran trapline on Slide Mountain, nothing. Made a new set and stopped to visit Allen and Roxanne. Allen wasn't home. Got water at Henry's.

Thursday, December 29, 1983—cloudy, ice fog on Heavenly Ridge and Slide Mountain, -26° to -20°. Sore back, and didn't go out to trapline. Denise and Lisa visited us.

Friday, December 30, 1983—nice day, -30° to -25°. Sick today, Sylvia worked on quilt. Charlie T. stopped by.

Saturday, December 31, 1983—cloudy, -25° to -10°. I have the flu, stayed home New Year's Eve.

Henry Johnson, Nelchina Lodge

10,000 Days in Alaska Book One 1978-1989

Top to bottom: Sawing logs for cabin; finished cabin and garage; and view from Scoter Lake looking towards Norman and Sylvia's permanent log cabin.

Norman Wilkins

1984—building permanent cabin

Sunday, January 1, 1984—snowing, 5° to 0°. Zoe, James, and Becky visited. Sally came over and we all went to KROA.

Monday, January 2, 1984—some sun, nice day, 4° to 20°. Loaded the snowgo and went to Dinty Bush's then left to run the trapline. Saw marten track at Blue Lake and the track of a traveling Wolf family near ravine on the trapline.

Tuesday, January 3, 1984—some sun, nice day, 0° to 25°. Sore back, read today.

Wednesday, January 4, 1984—snow last night, and today strong winds, 10° to 20°. I sewed griz rip in my sleeping bag, mixed marten bait, chinked some more in cabin.

Thursday, January 5, 1984—cloudy, 0° to 23°. Nothing on the line, made two marten sets. Saw tracks of two fox. A lot of people are staking at Loon Lake subdivision. Visited KROA, and Henry and Sally—Jim and Mary were there.

Friday, January 6, 1984—nice day, seven inches of new snow, -20° to -10°. Henry and Sally were here for a few minutes. Sylvia did laundry and did some sewing at Sally's—also got water there. Visited Allen and Roxanne.

Saturday, January 7, 1984—sunny, -10° to -5°. Went to Glennallen. Couldn't get wolf urine. Sewed lure, bait bags at Patti Billman's (Dan is in Hawaii). Helped Allen Farmer butcher a road kill moose.

Sunday, January 8, 1984—sunny day, -20° to -17° ran the line on Slide Mountain, nothing—just ermine tracks.

Monday, January 9, 1984—cloudy, bedded dogs, cleaned chimney, and other small chores.

Tuesday, January 10, 1984—pretty nice day, -40° to 25°. Ran line on slide Mountain, nothing again. Dan Billman visited in the morning.

Wednesday, January 11, 1984—mostly sunny and warm, 25°. Ran the line on Slide Mountain—nothing.

Thursday, January 12, 1984—warm and windy, light snow, 34°. Loaded snowgo and went to Dinty Bush's, then left for the cabin. Made rat sets on Rat Lake. Saw marten, fox and lynx tracks. Nothing in traps. Emergency repair trap sled.

Friday, January 13, 1984—warm today and cloudy. Made Fox set for this lake. Checked marten set and made another marten set. Explored for, and cut some new trail. Nailed some more mink and marten boxes.

Saturday, January 14, 1984—foggy all day, 25° to 30°. Sore back, did a few small trap jobs.

Sunday, January 15, 1984—beautiful day. Remade all sets plus three new fox/coyote sets. Got a cross fox, marten and two rats. Left one rat set, skinned fox.

Monday, January 16, 1984—sunny all day, 6° to 20°. Denny Rhodes visited. Ran the line up on Slide Mountain, nothing. Had supper and cut up meat at Allen and Roxanne's, skinned marten and rats.

Tuesday, January 17, 1984—sunny beautiful day. Visited Henry and Sally. Sylvia sewed on a quilt and went to a shower. Made up 18 ounces of marten lure.

Wednesday, January 18, 1984—cloudy and snowy today, -3° to 3°. Visited the Hoffmans, Schmidts, and had supper with Billmans.

Thursday, January 19, 1984—cloudy, two inches of snow last night, -3° to 3°. Did lots of little chores here, cut out parts for 12 marten trap boxes at Lucky's. Mary made a pork chop supper—very good. Tom and Lisa visited this morning.

Friday, January 20, 1984—cloudy, -3° to -6°. Went to Glennallen to get my drivers license renewed and licenses for the truck, trailer, trapping, hunting and fishing. Used snowgo trailer to haul Darrel's machine to KROA.

Saturday, January 21, 1984—cloudy, ice fog, -12° to -10°. Nothing on

Slide Mountain today. Worked on the snowgo and cut wire for marten boxes. Cut ground rod for radio and bedded the dogs. Brought meat home from Schmidts.

Sunday, January 22, 1984—cloudy, foggy, then sunny. -14° to -4°. Nothing in traps, freshened all sets. Saw fox and ermine tracks. Trap cabin is fine.

Monday, January 23, 1984—bright sun, -30° to -20°. Walked to wood lot, four trees blown down.

Tuesday, January 24, 1984—bright sun, clear sky and cold. -40° to -30°. Trimmed the four downed trees in the wood lot, cut into logs and piled them.

Wednesday, January 25, 1984—sunny and clear, -49° to -35°. Cut trap trail south, then west to next ridge.

Thursday, January 26, 1984—mostly sunny, -30° to -15°. Nothing in traps, saw two marten tracks and two moose on the way home. Visited KROA, Lisa Smayda's birthday.

Friday, January 27, 1984—cloudy, light snow, -12° to -5°. Ken Lewis appraised this property today. Ran the line on Slide Mountain, nothing. Saw one ptarmigan.

Saturday, January 28, 1984—nice day, light snow, -16° to -5°. Important business letter came about the farm renter.

Sunday, January 29, 1984—nice day, light snow, -16° to -5°. Visited Hoffman's and Sylvia baked pies and bread.

Monday, January 30, 1984—cloudy, 10° to 18°. Ground 88 packages of moose meat at Allen F.'s. Visited with Sally, Darrel, Tom, Jim, and Mary for a while. Harry Billum was killed this day. I will miss him, he was a fine trapper.

Tuesday, January 31, 1984—sunny, 12° to 18°. Moved some of our things from Nelchina to our woodshed and helped Henry and Sally move some of their things. Henry, Sally, Chris and Darrel were here for supper. Lauren Smayda's birthday.

Wednesday, February 1, 1984—snowed today, 6° to 10°. Got gas for snowgo and truck from Henry. Sylvia went to Glennallen with Schmidts. She baked a cake.

Thursday, February 2, 1984—partly cloudy and above zero all day. Called Mike Philips about Harry Billum. Trapline loop near my trapline.

Friday, February 3, 1984—it was -5° all day with light snow. Eight inches of snow on the trail to cabin. Made one fox set and one snare for lynx—remade most of the rest. Trouble getting up hill at Blue Lake. Got one marten south of cabin.

Saturday, February 4, 1984—0° to 16°. Cloudy, three inches of snow last night, sunshine this afternoon. Put up radio antenna, works well. Skinned marten and cleaned snow off roof again.

Sunday, February 5, 1984—partly cloudy, nice day, -5° to 7°. Made marten set and put up pole for another. Checked snowgo, cleaned snow off outhouse, and set snare for wolf.

Monday, February 6, 1984—bright sun, -5° to 4°. Chris R. flew Dan B. to Hole Lake and we visited for a while in the afternoon. I'll get an early start tomorrow to go out. Put one conibear on pole and made another marten box set farther on trail.

Tuesday, February 7, 1984—sunny day, -10° to -7°. Up early, remade most sets on way out to road. Had to leave small sled half way out. Much deeper snow and many drifts, stuck in snow many times. Flat tire on truck. Stopped and visited Cora at junction and KROA.

Wednesday, February 8, 1984—sunny day, -16° to -4°. Cleaned snow from cabin and woodshed roofs and bedded the dogs. Visited Henry and Sally, Sam, and Jim and Mary. Put belt on Patti Billman's spinning wheel.

Thursday, February 9, 1984—beautiful day, -20° to -5°. Went to see Jim and Mary Odden. We each got a nice pile of wood out to their place and then home with ours after a nice Mexican supper. Lots of neighbors were at the supper and "pickin" after.

Friday, February 10, 1984—sunny day, -16° to -5°. Did very little except cut and piled the wood.

Saturday, February 11, 1984—another perfect day, -14° to 0°. Headaches today. Rested lots. Visited Sally and Chris late in afternoon.

Sunday, February 12, 1984—bright sun, -10° to 10°. Put on new snowshoe bindings. Slept a lot. Saw two flashes in quick succession followed by two roaring, jet-like sounds at about 6:40 p.m. Have no idea what this was, maybe military practice?

Monday, February 13, 1984—sunny and -6° to 10°. Worked on snowshoe bindings again—tried them out. Still sick, visited lucky and Mary.

Tuesday, February 14, 1984—beautiful day, -6° to 10°. Went to lodge and called lawyer about land. Phoned Connie about rug. Got water. Clem borrowed pipe flanger. Bought gas lamp from Jean.

Wednesday, February 15, 1984—partly cloudy, nice day, -16° to 8°. Sent appraisal to Bob R. spent all afternoon trying to start snowgo. Finally got it going.

Thursday, February 16, 1984—cloudy, snow in the evening, -6° to 10°. Moved TV antenna to Henry's and put it up. Had a good supper there.

Friday, February 17, 1984—partly cloudy, -4° to 20°. Put a TV antenna here at home and ran the trapline on Slide Mountain. Nothing on it deep snow. Went to KROA and Tazlina Lodge for lots of good music.

Saturday, February 18, 1984—partly cloudy, 6° to 20°. Visited Allen Farmer, loaded snowgo, and stopped at KROA and Lake Louise Junction. Sled dog team on the road. Parked at Warren's, put up trapline signs. Ran six miles of Harry Billum's old line, found six of Harry's traps.

Sunday, February 19, 1984—cloudy, started to snow at noon, 10° to 15°. Ran traps here, hard to see trail (white out). Saw one fox track, had two

10,000 Days in Alaska Book One 1978-1989

camp robbers in traps. Two inches of snow by evening and windy.

Monday, February 20, 1984—cloudy morning, sunny later, -10° to 0°. Nothing in traps, saw a spruce hen. Good trip out, snowgo quit on road. Saw Mike P. and Charlie Parret at KROA. I told them I picked up Harry's traps and gave them to Mike L. to give them to Harry's wife. Took two books back to Charlie Netter and borrowed three more.

Tuesday, February 21, 1984—sunny, 20° to 6°. Visited Henry and Sally. Got water at Clem and Jean's. Mrs. Hoffman died at 2:00 p.m. today, visited them, and visited Lucky and Mary in the evening.

Wednesday, February 22, 1984—cloudy, some light snow, -10° to 10°. Visited Dan Billman about prospecting Oshetna. Worked at making snowgo skis wider at Lucky's.

Thursday, February 23, 1984—bright sun, -6° to 10°. Finished snowgo skis and installed them. Went to Farmer's and ground the rest of the moose and made sausage with it. Lucky lost his water trailer; it unhooked from his pickup and went into the ditch. I pulled it out of the ditch for him and Allen and I helped get it hooked back up to his pickup.

Friday, February 24, 1984—sunny day, -16° to 10°. Visited Henry, Darrel, and Jim. Loafed all day.

Saturday, February 25, 1984—sunny, then cloudy, -13° to 11°. Chris Rhodes went along when I pulled traps on Slide Mountain. Ski-Doo seems to work well with the wider skis. Got a few things ready to go out to trap cabin tomorrow.

Sunday, February 26, 1984—clear and sunny, 2° to 18°. Loaded Darrel's snowgo at KROA. Parked at Warren's. Ran some of Harry's old line and got a red fox at fox Lake. Everything fine at cabin.

Monday, February 27, 1984—sunny, -4° to 15°. Went to Mendeltna Springs. Found four of Harry's traps. Lost trail at both ends.

Tuesday, February 28, 1984—sunny, then cloudy later in the afternoon, -5° to 5°. Broke lots of trail, tough going. Picked up more of Harry's traps. Explored new north/south seismic—sprung all my traps.

Wednesday, February 29, 1984—partly cloudy, -10° to 5°. Darrel had snowgo belt trouble. Ran lots of trail in Green Acres. Darrel put up some signs. Had coffee with Jack and Jackie Shotyce. Got home late.

Thursday, March 1, 1984—sunny, -10° to 16°. Worked on snowgo.

Friday, March 2, 1984—sunny, -3° to 20°. Visited Warren and Leona at Dinty Bush services, also KROA—Bob and Margaret. Went to KROA Bob Lohman and girlfriend were there and played music with the locals.

Saturday, March 3, 1984—sunny, cloudy near evening and light snow, 10° to 24°. Helped Allen lift up one stud wall on shop. Visited Henry and Sally. Called Beverly and Kevin about farm business from Lucky and Mary's in the evening. Worked on trapping things—we have flu, but not as bad as other people.

Sunday, March 4, 1984—windy last night, sunny today, 20° to 43°. Visited Dan and Patti, also Henry and Sally—Jim and Mary, and Sam were there.

Monday, March 5, 1984—mostly cloudy, 14° to 30°. Helped Henry move out house and other belongings. He gave me a water heater tank.

Tuesday, March 6, 1984 sunny, 16° to 40°. Visited Dan and Patti, went to KROA for boxes, talked to Jim a couple of minutes. Helped Tom with advice on house, worked on snowgo and built two ice chisels. Visited Lucky and Mary.

Wednesday, March 7, 1984—sunny to cloudy, 23° to 36°. Hauled water. Gave Sally an ice chisel. Helped Tom lift a wall into place, loaded meat and hauled it to Billman's freezer. Visited Mary and Jim, Sam was there. Covered seat on snowgo.

Thursday, March 8, 1984—cloudy and foggy, 24° to 40°. Left for trapline. Lots of trouble with snowgo—did get one frozen-in rat trap. Turned around after 12 miles and came back. Sylvia canned seven quarts moose meat.

Friday, March 9, 1984—sunny, snow is settling fast, 22° to 40°. Worked on snowgo all day, no good luck. Allen Farmer and I went down to the Nelchina River to look for burls. Sylvia went with Schmidts to do laundry in Glennallen.

Saturday, March 10, 1984—partly cloudy, 18° to 40°. Took snowgo to Hillside Shoppe. Mike says motor needs work.

Sunday, March 11, 1984—sunny, 16° to 40°. Called Andy Boyle twice about the snowgo. Worked on fur stretchers at Lucky's. Had brunch at Jim and Mary's, with Sally and Henry and Chris. Chris left on plane for Michigan.

Monday, March 12, 1984—sunny, 16° to 40°. Talk to Doug about selling his Yamaha long track, called around also. Shoveled snow from near the basement and went with Henry, Sally and Sam to KROA and Tazlina Lodge.

Tuesday, March 13, 1984—cloudy, 14° to 40°. Shoveled more snow. More calling for snowgo.

Wednesday, March 14, 1984—sunny, 11° to 30°. More calls for snowgo, then shoveled snow from around house. Patti visited, Mary B. and Sylvia went to Glennallen. Bob's stopped by.

Thursday, March 15, 1984—sunny, 6° to 30°. Went to Anchorage, bought new Polaris long track snowgo and did some other shopping. Picked up a rug stored at Andy Boyle's and discussed insulating house. Andy estimates $2200.

Friday, March 16, 1984—sunny, 0° to 30°. Tom and Lisa and Dan Billman visited in the morning. Put some miles on the snowgo. Allen got his Ranger yesterday and he and I went out looking for burls. (A burl is a tree growth in which the grain has grown deformed. Usually found as a rounded outgrowth on the trunk of a tree, it is prized for its beauty and rarity and is sought after by furniture makers, artists, and wood sculptors.)

Saturday, March 17, 1984—sunny, -3° to 30°. Went looking for a bear den, no luck. Helped Tom put up beam in his house. I sure like the new snowgo.

Sunday, March 18 1984—sunny, -6° to 30°. Sylvia went with Schmidt's to Tolsona for Bessie's birthday party. I broke snowgo trail to woodlot north of Hoffman's, visited Max, and helped Jim and Mary with their house logs a little.—ate supper there.

Monday, March 19, 1984—sunny, -3° to 30°. Allen Farmer and I ran his Botley Creek trapline. He had five marten. I brought back a dozen burls. Helped Allen lay out a truss rafter and ate supper there.

Tuesday, March 20, 1984—sunny, 10° to 28°. Dan and Patti were here a few minutes. We got things ready and went to woodlot north of Hoffman's. Got one pickup load of wood. Snowgo works well. Tom and Lisa visited in the afternoon.

Wednesday, March 21, 1984—sunny, -6° to 28°. Dan Billman and I helped Tom put the rafters on his house. Sylvia visited Mary Beaudoin.

Thursday, March 22, 1984—sunny, -10° to 32°. We got two pickup loads of wood cut, hauled to pickup, loaded, hauled it home, and unloaded.

Friday, March 23, 1984—sunny, -5° to 30°. Got two sled loads of wood, then the carburetor came loose on the chainsaw. Got it back together. Helped Tom put purlins on his rafters.

Saturday, March 24, 1984—partly cloudy, light snow in the evening, -3° to 25°. Went to service for Irene Hoffman at Mendeltna Chapel. Put income tax info in mail. Sylvia fixed moose ribs at KROA—went there for bluegrass and old-time music in the evening.

Sunday, March 25, 1984—-7° to 25°. Vern at KROA couldn't remember where big burl was. Mike Philips and Charlie Billum picked up some of my traps. Helped Tom Smayda put roof on his house. Dan Billman helped, also Kim, another girl.

Monday, March 26, 1984—partly cloudy in the morning then sunny. -5° to 40°. Got one pickup load of wood at Hoffman's, it got so warm, the wood trail softened up and I got stuck twice. Bob S. pushed some snow away and I shoveled snow.

10,000 Days in Alaska Book One 1978-1989

Tuesday, March 27, 1984—partly cloudy to sunny, 6° to 47°. We got another pickup load of logs and wood. Broke a wood trail for Dan Billman, scooped more snow off basement. Called surveyor, took a battery to Dan's to charge it. Planned trip to Old Boot Lake with Darrel, Jim and Mary. Tried to chase down some windows.

Wednesday, March 28, 1984—partly cloudy to sunny, 7° to 41°. Got another load of wood and helped Allen Farmer build some truss rafters.

Thursday, March 29, 1984—partly cloudy to sunny, 10° to 30°. Jim and Mary Odden, Darrel Gerry and I went to Green Acres. Jim and Mary will camp and stake a remote parcel beside ours on Old Boot Lake. Darrel and I did some work on our parcels and helped Jim and Mary some. Had a great time.

Friday, March 30, 1984—light snow last night, partly cloudy to sunny, 20° to 35°. Fleshed and stretched furs-Sylvia helped. Scooped more snow off the house. Bob S. pushed some snow here. Sylvia and I don't feel good.

Saturday, March 31, 1984—sunny, 10° to 30°. Shoveled more snow. Got ready to go to trap cabin. Went down on Nelchina looking for more burls. Went to KROA in the evening for good eats and music.

Sunday, April 1, 1984—sunny and windy, 20° to 38°. Sylvia helped scoop snow off basement and then went to Glennallen to do laundry. I came to trap cabin. Saw herd Caribou and moose, no new traps on some of Harry's line, otter sign and new beaver lodge west of springs. Eight inches of overflow on Blue Lake—got stuck, got out easy, everything okay a cabin.

Monday, April 2, 1984—skiff of snow last night, sunny day, 20° to 30°. Went east to headwater lake of Old Man Creek. Did lots of exploring, built marten and mink boxes and added extension chains to traps. Saw cow moose and calf, lots of small birds near Big Spring. Windy in the evening.

Tuesday, April 3, 1984—snow showers, partly cloudy, 10° to 30°. Went to Judd Lake and explored country there. Put up five traps and one marten pole. Cut diamond willow. (Diamond willow is used for carving and making craft objects. The irregularity of shape and color in the grain adds to its appeal.) Explored, build cubby, placed more traps, improved trail–killed a porcupine (Sylvia uses the quills in crafts and Joe and Morey eat them). Saw a fox den on Judd Lake seismic trail south.

Wednesday, April 4, 1984–sunny, 10° to 35°. Up early, worked all morning getting ready to leave cabin and close it up. Ran lots of Harry's line, picked up some more of his traps and hauled all three of sleds out and gear. Snow is soft. Visited Darrel at KROA.

Thursday, April 5, 1984–sunny, 70° to 40°. Unloaded gear. Did 300 mile check on snowgo. Went to Dan's, got battery, and helped stack cedar siding. Pete was there.

Friday, April 6, 1984–sunny, 15° to 34°. Went to Glennallen and registered the plat for this subdivision. Went to Dan and Patti's for potluck supper and music.

Saturday, April 7, 1984–sunny, -5° to 30°. Cut and hauled home a very big burl. Helped Dan Haul in wood, his machine is sick.

Sunday, April 8, 1984–sunny, 0° to 30°. Charlie and Beth stopped in. We took plastic off basement, it's in good shape. Did some trapline work.

Monday, April 9, 1984–sunny, 20° to 40°. Did lots of small jobs.

Tuesday, April 10, 1984–sunny, 10° to 40°. Helped Clem chip holes in ground. Helped Tom haul and install picture window. Fixed rewind on chainsaw.

Wednesday, April 11, 1984–sunny, 10° to 40°. Went to see a lawyer in Anchorage, news wasn't good. Got building materials, groceries etc. Jim and Mary came to visit.

Thursday, April 12, 1984–sunny, 10° to 42°. Talked over lawyer visit with Tom. Power company representative was here. Built a rabbit hutch for Sylvia.

Friday, April 13, 1984–cloudy in the morning then sunny, 12° to 44°.

10,000 Days in Alaska Book One 1978-1989

Did some customizing for trapline on snowgo. Made step for working on house. Repaired sawhorse. Sylvia baked cake for Tom and Lisa's housewarming.

Saturday, April 14, 1984–cloudy morning, sunny afternoon, 18° to 42° .Adzed and sanded sill logs level. Repaired ladder and other odd jobs. Sylvia baked pies this afternoon. Hoping Henry calls tonight. We'll go to Tom and Lisa's housewarming.

Sunday, April 15, 1984–cloudy, then sunny, 15° to 40°. Sylvia and I started on our house, Dan B. came and helped. We got 41 feet of wall up. Tom, Lisa, Jim, Mary, Lee and Bob S. and Margaret visited.

Monday, April 16, 1984–partly cloudy and windy, 10° to 32°. Lots of phone calls and business. Dan helped and we got the rest of the east wall and the south wall up. Picture window is longer than planned, the header is short. Jim and Mary have a longer log and offered it.

Tuesday, April 17, 1984–cloudy and sunny, snow flurries in the evening, 10° to 30°. Went to Jim and Mary's and traded a log. Dan helped put the west wall in. Blake brought two, 2 x 4s back.

Wednesday, April 18, 1984–cloudy, then sunny, 15° to 32°. Finished putting logs in Windows. Re-piled unused logs. Shoveled snow, made several phone calls for materials. Went to KROA and Billman's. Strange pickup in the neighborhood for several days. Allen Farmer visited.

Thursday, April 19, 1984–mostly cloudy all day, we got quite a bit of the plates on the logs. Allen Farmer stopped a couple of minutes. Coyotes were howling.

Friday, April 20, 1984–partly cloudy, 35° to 44°. We took a log back to Jim's and had him two-side it, fine job. Put rest of top plates on house. Building supplies were delivered this afternoon. Clem, Jean, and Ron, helped unload. Swans and geese are flying.

Saturday, April 21, 1984–sunny, 15° to 44°. Dan Billman, Alan Farmer, and Lucky Beaudoin helped with the rafters. A rabbit is making a nest.

Sunday, April 22, 1984–20° to 34°, cloudy, then sunny, a light breeze that shifted to the north and cooler. Lucky helped with 12 rafters. Called Charlie T. to talk about lawyer and plats. Went to Billman's to get some meat we have stored there.

Monday, April 23, 1984—cloudy, then sunny, 42°. It's light outside at 3 a.m. Geese and swans are flying. Finished rafters. Allen, Dan, Ron, and, Blake came over and we put the rafters up in an hour and a half. Jim and Mary stopped in. Everyone stayed to have supper with us.

Tuesday, April 24, 1984—Sunny, 12° to 50°. Allen helped put eight feet of roof on. George Roberson helped for a while and Sylvia and I put four feet of roof on in the evening.

Wednesday, April 25, 1984—partly cloudy, 10° to 40°. Dan helped in late morning and again in late evening. Sheeting and Purlins are on now. Swans are flying, saw a robin, bears are coming out of Dens in the mountains.

Thursday, April 26, 1984—cloudy after 5:30 a.m., 10° to 32°. Allen helped with trim, Dan came down to help but my screws for steel don't work. Sylvia and I put more trim and some hardware cloth on vents.

Friday, April 27, 1984—cloudy, 20° to 46°. Re-stacked the 1 x 8 pine to dry it. Put more screen on eves of house. Waiting for screws to put roof on. Jim and Ted visited and we visited Billmans.

Saturday, April 28, 1984—sunny, 26° to 51°. Geese and swans still going through valley. Dan saw two griz on Nelchina River. Ermine visited us, he has turned brown. Sylvia and I put rafter blocks in and got steel ready. Dan got here with screws at 6:00 p.m. Tom helped and we got 11 sheets on the roof. Went to KROA for supper.

Sunday, April 29, 1984—partly cloudy, 20° to 40°. Dan Billman was held up all day and couldn't help put steel on. Tom was here to help, but we decided to wait for Dan. Sylvia and I put soffit on house, also other things. Saw a pair of canaries and two pair of swans came back to our lake.

Monday, April 30, 1984—cloudy, 25° to 46°. Sylvia and I got some more steel on roof. Andy brought chimney liners. Dan Billman came to help

10,000 Days in Alaska Book One 1978-1989

but it was too windy. George R. visited. Went to KROA with Andy and got home late. Hoffmans had left milk and eggs. Payment on the farm is late.

Tuesday, May 1, 1984—sunny and windy in the afternoon, 29° to 45°. George R. helped put steel on. Finished north side of house. Put plastic on windows. Rhynell and Max visited this morning.

Wednesday, May 2, 1984—light snow early morning, snow showers all day, 25° to 40°. Started building snowgo shed attached to woodshed. Margaret got back, still sick. Lloyd R. and Leo Zura visited. They gave us handmade gifts for our house. These are works of art.

Thursday, May 3, 1984—sunny, 18° to 40°. Finished the addition to the woodshed. Henry, Sally, Sam and Mary arrived very early this morning and had breakfast at 5:30 a.m. at our place.

Friday, May 4, 1984—Sunny, 20° to 40°. Helped Allen put half the roof on his shop. Put snowgo under roof.

Saturday, May 5, 1984—mostly sunny, 24° to 40°. Visited Henry's, got some sand and some small jobs done on house.

Sunday, May 6, 1984—sunny, 20° to 44°. Sylvia did laundry, I beveled some logs. Bob and Margaret had us for supper at KROA.

Monday, May 7, 1984—sunny, 22° to 59°. Went to Wasilla and Anchorage for chimney blocks and upstairs windows. Got back at 9:30 p.m.

Tuesday, May 8, 1984—Sunny, as some clouds and breeze, 26° to 50°. Unloaded blocks and built most of the framing in one end of house. Took Lucky's nails and glue back. Ermine was running around, must have a home here. Lane is drying up.

Wednesday, May 9, 1984—partly cloudy, light shower, 28° to 40s. Finished framing west gable end and started east and. Went to Anchorage in the evening. The little ermine chased vole in yard. Swans on the lake are mated now. If I go down to the lake and imitate their calls, they swim closer and answer call for call. I like to think they are saying to me, "poor imitation" over and over.

Thursday, May 10, 1984—sunny, 30° to 50°. Went to an auction at Elmendorf Air Base. Bought (for $33), a damaged pool table. Andy Boyle got a dozen and a half office machines. Got home late. today was our wedding anniversary.

Friday, May 11, 1984—sunny and windy, 24° to 40s. A bunch of neighbors helped carry pool table into basement. Went to Anchorage and Wasilla for more building supplies, pretty good trip.

Saturday, May 12, 1984—sunny, 20° to 40°. Unloaded lumber and supplies. Visited Lucky, Allen, Henry and Sally. James and Zoe visited us, and then we visited Jim and Mary Odden. Mike a friend of theirs was there.

Sunday, May 13, 1984—sunny, 20° to low 50s. Worked on the house and went to KROA in the evening.

Monday, May 14, 1984—sunny, 24° to 50°. Worked on chimney flue, liners are too big, lots of trouble with them. They may be seconds. It's a 300 mile drive to return them.

Tuesday, May 15, 1984—sunny and windy in the afternoon, 24° to 58°. Laid five more blocks, put some siding on cable end, and Sylvia helped at KROA in the evening.

Wednesday, May 16, 1984—sunny, windy in the afternoon, 24° to 66°. Got quite a bit of siding on east gable end. Sent in subsistence hunting applications. Bob S. brought mason blade for skill saw. Lucky and Blake stopped in.

Thursday, May 17, 1984—sunny and breezy for a while, 24° to 60°. Went to Glennallen, put thimble in chimney and lay three blocks. Finished siding and trim on east end of house. Caribou are in velvet. A large amount of ice went down Nelchina River.

Friday, May 18, 1984—34° to 60°. Light rain in the night, loon on lake this morning. 12 swans today. More ice is gone. Sunny all day. Laid more chimney blocks. Put some siding on west end. Lisa and Lauren S.

visited. Jim Phillips and Rich visited.

Saturday, May 19, 1984—34° to 60°. Light rain early, a few showers until noon, then sunny and hot. Margaret is back in the hospital. We got six more chimney blocks laid. All the soffit is up. Almost half way down on west end with the siding. Ice on lake going fast.

Sunday, May 20, 1984—36° to 65°. Sunny all day, ice went out on our lake. Helped Lucky on his roof today and watched movie, "Mystic Warrior". Visited Henry, Sally and Sam.

Monday, May 21, 1984—30s to 60s. Rainy morning, sunny afternoon. Got some more chimney block ready. Put more siding on west end. Went to Lucky and Mary's to see rest of movie.

Tuesday, May 22, 1984—34° to 50°. Rainy morning, sun in afternoon. Finished gable ends and trim. Six more blocks on chimney. Back is sore.

Wednesday, May 23, 1984—34° to 68°. Sunny, some wind and rain clouds towards evening. Went to KROA, had supper there and visited. Put up seven chimney blocks—almost to attic now. Laid 15 blocks for plenum at the stove in basement.

Thursday, May 24, 1984—33° to 50°. Some sun, showers—a good one in the evening. Laid eight blocks, got to peak. Laid three blocks for the plenum.

Friday, May 25, 1984—33° to 50°. Sunny, one light hail and rain. Built platform for Roof. Sylvia cleaned up the sander dust from logs—eight wheelbarrows. Put four at the loads of dirt on her garden and tilled it. Charlie T., Lisa and Sam visited.

Saturday, May 26, 1984—30° to 48°. Snow showers, some sun. Worked on upstairs windows. Henry and Charlie T. helped put ridge cap on roof. Called Kevin, he called renter. Jeff visited. Picking at Tazlina, supper at KROA. Charlie loaned me *Trailing and Camping in Alaska* by Addison M. Powell. Boy! Is it ever a good one.

Sunday, May 27, 1984—28° to 40s. Three inches of snow, sunny, with snow squalls. James, Zoe and Mike C. visited. Did a little work on the house. Visited Dan B., and Bob and Margaret.

Monday, May 28, 1984—30° to 50°. Partly cloudy. Rudbecks arrived. Finished chimney. Cut joists and framed opening for stairs. James, Mike, Zoe, Becky, Henry and Sally, Sylvia and I, all had supper at Henry's.

Tuesday, May 29, 1984—32° to 40s. Partly cloudy, windy afternoon. Cut out the window holes for basement. I start work every morning at 5:00 a.m. and eat breakfast at 6:00 a.m. We usually have company about 9:00 a.m., have coffee and visit a while, then back to work. Doesn't always work out that way.

Wednesday, May 30, 1984—30° to 50°. Partly cloudy, some rain. Went to Anchorage, picked up rugs for Henry and KROA. Stayed at Candy and Connie's, bought steel for the house.

Thursday, May 31, 1984—40° to 60°. While in Anchorage, went to auction—bought some canvas. Did shopping for the house. Stayed at Andy's.

Friday, June 1, 1984—40° to 60°. Partly cloudy and rainy. Bought some lumber and groceries and got home in afternoon. Truck came home fine.

Saturday, June 2, 1984—30° to 60°. Partly cloudy. Finished last sheet on steel on house. Rudbeck unloaded dozer blade near our lane. We'll use it for loading ramp. Bob helped lay up last of cement block. We all met at Tom and Lisa's to talk about our land contracts.

Sunday, June 3, 1984—30° to 55°. Partly cloudy, light showers and sun. Lots of company. Started work at 4:00 p.m. on ceiling of downstairs.

Monday, June 4, 1984—34° to 60° and cloudy. But on more ceiling. Some visitors. Went to Billman's to get meat from freezer.

Tuesday, June 5, 1984—38° to 60°. Mostly sunny. Put up more ceiling, lowered floor down on plenum. Started raining in evening. Visited Tom to talk about land contract.

10,000 Days in Alaska Book One 1978-1989

Wednesday, June 6, 1984—37° to 50°. Raining this morning, cloudy all day. Put in both upstairs windows and more ceiling. Jim and Mary Odden visited in evening.

Thursday, June 7, 1984—40° to 56° and sunny. Got all but one board on ceiling. Generator gave trouble. We have to use a generator a lot as REA has been slow about getting poles up here.

Friday, June 8, 1984—37° to 50s. Mostly sunny, couple light showers. Called Charlie P. We built walls for interior of house. Bob R. was here for supper. James C. was here. Danny Chappel moved some of his things.

Saturday, June 9, 1984—40° to 60s and partly cloudy. Jim O. got grader blades and chainsaw sharpener. We got some more walls and the stairwell and stairs in. Went to see Jim and Mary.

Sunday, June 10, 84—43° to low 60s. Sunny, light breeze. Put nine sheets plywood on upstairs ceiling. Still have flu. James and Zoe visited.

Monday, June 11, 1984—40° to 50s. Mostly cloudy, some light rain. Finished ceiling upstairs, stair risers and wall framing of bedroom. Visited Lucky and Mary.

Tuesday, June 12, 1984—40° to 60°. Rain and cloudy. Framed closet and framed one window. Visited Max Hoffman and Billmans.

Wednesday, June 13, 1984—40° to high 50s. Put in the rest of window frames except picture window. Jim and Mary took us to Glennallen to a meeting.

Thursday, June 14, 1984—42° to 50°. Put in both entrance door frames. Pothole and frame for wood door or in basement wall. Went to Lucky's to glue extension on picture window frame. Started raining.

Friday, June 15, 1984—40° to 50°. Rained all day and still coming down. Went to Anchorage for more building supplies. Got back late.

Saturday, June 16, 1984—worked on picture window.

Sunday, June 17, 1984—42° to 65°. Beautiful day. Dried out lumber and worked on house.

Monday, June 18, 1984—45° to 70°. Bright and sunny. Worked on house.

Tuesday, June 19, 1984—40° to 60s and sunny. Some clouds and sprinkles. Worked on house. Went to Billman's for meat and visited Jim and Mary.

Wednesday, June 20, 1984—43° to 70s. Light rain in the night, sunny with a few very light showers and some more thunder. Building doors now. Bob and Kahren were here for supper. Bob and I figured yearly payments on our land.

Thursday, June 21, 1984—44° to 72° and sunny. Measured wire and cut electric holes. Stuffed insulation.

Friday, June 22, 1984—46° to 74° and sunny. Went to Anchorage for lumber and electrical supplies.

Saturday, June 23, 1984—44° to 68°. Rain in early morning then mostly sunny. Helped dig the grave and bury Rhynell's husband, Ken.

Sunday, June 24, 1984—40° to low 60s, sunny and windy. Lucky came over and helped wire of the house. Went to a BBQ at Bob Schmidt's.

Monday, June 25, 1984—40° to 60°. No other entry.

Tuesday, June 26, 1984—46° to 50s and mostly sunny. Putting pine paneling, 1"x 8" on walls of house.

Wednesday, June 27, 1984—40° to 48°. Rainy morning, cloudy all day. Still putting up pine paneling in the house.

Thursday, June 28, 1984—36° to low 70s. Sunny, some breeze. Helped Bob Rudbeck pour cement for his hangar. Still sick with flu of some sort.

10,000 Days in Alaska Book One 1978-1989

Friday, June 29, 1984—40° to 60°. Mostly sunny. Wrote a man in Washington about water tanks. Andy called. I went to Anchorage to get urethane materials. Got very little done on house.

Saturday, June 30, 1984—40° to 70° and sunny. Andy Boyle is here spraying at urethane insulation in the house.

Sunday, July 1, 1984—38° to 58°. Cloudy, some light rain. Finished the spraying. Bob Rudbeck unloaded 35 sacks of cement here.

Monday, July 2, 1984—40° to 50s. Rainy, then cloudy. Bob R. worked on kitchen cabinets. Lloyd Griffith and nephew stopped to visit Bob and Kahren. We got urethane trimmed and three sheets of plywood on floor upstairs.

Tuesday, July 3, 1984—40° to 50°. Cloudy and hard rain, some hail—still raining this evening. Lightning and thunder. Worked on kitchen and floor upstairs.

Wednesday, July 4, 1984—44° to 60°. Very little sun, lots of showers—some heavy. Finished floor and quite a bit of walls upstairs. Helped Bob and Kahren raised west wall of hangar. Visited Jim and Mary Odden. Her folks, Bill and Ruth, are there visiting.

Thursday, July 5, 1984—46° to 60s and mostly sunny. Finished putting plywood on walls upstairs and helped Rudbeck raise some walls. Dan Bloomer, CVEA, was here to stake poles for line. Bob and Kahren were here for supper.

Friday, July 6, 1984—46° to 60s. Mostly sunny, some rain last night. Framed wall and chimney upstairs. Helped Bob and Kahren a little bit. Had a salmon supper with them.

Saturday, July 7, 1984—44° to 76° and sunny. Lots of company. Built small bookcase. Went to Tolsona Lodge for BBQ—visited Lucky and Mary. Rain during the night.

Sunday, July 8, 1984—42° to 50s. Cloudy and rainy. Lots of company in the morning. Built one bookcase, put pine on wall around the sink and cupboard. Called Nadia. Rain in the night.

Norman Wilkins

Monday, July 9, 1984—44°, cloudy and rainy all day. Bob and Kahren Rudbeck came to build Sylvia's kitchen. This kitchen is lots of work. Went to Jim and Mary's for potluck supper and music. Her folks, Bill and Ruth, go back tomorrow.

Tuesday, July 10, 1984—40° to 53°. Rain in the night, cleared and sunny, then windy. Finished work in house, lots of visitors. Went with Dan to Kianna Creek. He took some fisherman over in the float plane and brought Peter back. Peter slipped off the float into neck deep water-cold! Brought some meat home.

Wednesday, July 11, 1984—40° to 58° and mostly sunny. Did more finish work in the house. Lots of visitors. Nadia called, visitors from Italy will be here tomorrow afternoon.

Thursday, July 12, 1984—44° to 55°. Mostly sunny, some rain showers at night. Went to Anchorage to meet plane. Ivo, Franca and Mac from Italy will visit for a few days. Borrowed Dan Billman's van to bring them out here to our house.

Friday, July 13, 1984—40° to 60°. Rain last night, sunny and breezy today. We took our visitors to Copper Center to see fish wheels. Fished in Klutina River, didn't land a salmon. Took van back to Billman's.

Saturday, July 14, 1984—44° to 56°. Rainy and cloudy. Helped Bob R. a little bit. Roger and Jo Ford stopped by and took pictures of house. Ivo, Mac and I went fishing at Cache Creek. Water was high, no luck. Visited Tom and Lisa Smayda and family in the evening.

Sunday, July 15, 1984—44° to 52°. Rainy, cloudy, little sun. Took visitors to KROA, then fishing at Billman's. Visited Lucky and Mary in the evening. Lisa Smayda had a baby girl last night at 11:00 p.m.

Monday, July 16, 1984—40° to 50°. Partly cloudy, rainy and windy in the evening. Took Ivo, Mac and Franca to plane in Anchorage. Check prices on some things for the house, got back home in evening.

Tuesday, July 17, 1984—38° to 48°. Rain all night and day. Bob and Kahren worked on our kitchen cabinets. Ate supper with them at

10,000 Days in Alaska Book One 1978-1989

KROA campground.

Wednesday, July 18, 1984—38° to 52°. Partly cloudy, no rain. Worked on house and Cat. Movie and supper at Lucky and Mary's.

Thursday, July 19, 1984—40° to 60°. Mostly cloudy, some showers till noon. Worked on cupboards here till noon. Put up joists at Rudbeck's in the afternoon. Lloyd and Dennis Griffith helped. Supper at KROA in evening.

Friday, July 20, 1984—40° to 60° and partly cloudy. Helped Rudbeck some at their shop, put up rafters and half of purlins.

Saturday, July 21, 1984—42° to 60s. Mostly sunny and hot. Finished Bob's purlins and got the steel on his roof. Met Jerry, Moe, and Liza at Anchorage. They and Dan Billman helped. Bob and Kahren had us all for supper at the Ranch House.

Sunday, July 22, 1984—44° to 60°. Sunny and beautiful day. Worked on house. Bob, Kahren, Jerry, and Moe visited. Gave Henry a TV antenna.

Monday, July 23, 1984—44° to high 60s. Sunny and thin clouds. Worked on house, called escrow account, also C.V.E.A.

Tuesday, July 24, 1984—44° to 65°. Very nice day. Bob built cabinets in the house.

Wednesday, July 25, 1984—44° to 56°. Rained most of the day. Bob Rudbeck worked on Sylvia's cupboards. Charlie T. called us at Billman's.

Thursday, July 26, 1984—43° to 53°. Cloudy and rainy. We worked on cupboards.

Friday, July 27, 1984—46° to 56°. Sunny but lots of clouds and rain to. Bob Rudbeck worked on cupboards. I did some welding for Allen Farmer.

Saturday, July 28, 1984—46° to 53°. Little sun, lots of rain—some heavy. Worked on cabinet doors. Jerry and Moe Liza are visiting the Rudbecks. Henry and Sally had us for supper at Nelchina.

Norman Wilkins

Sunday, July 29, 1984—45° to 55° and mostly sunny today. Put up beams in house. Started pantry shelves. Visited Lucky and Mary, Allen and kids were there.

Monday, July 30, 1984—45° to 61°. Sunny, light breeze. Lots of company. Built reloading bench and cabinet. Put on some inside trim.

Tuesday, July 31, 1984—38° to 58°. Sunny till evening, then cloudy. Worked on pantry and trim. "Pickin" party at Tom and Lisa's.

Wednesday, August 1, 1984—46° to 60s. Cloudy morning, then sunny. Put trim in the house and helped Bob and Kahren a little. Lee D. visited. Welded on PTO device for Allen.

Thursday, August 2, 1984—45° to 70° and sunny. Pretty in the mountains this evening. Put more trim on. Lisa Smayda's dad, Joe, caulked for a while. Lisa and Tom got four rabbits. Allen planed a 4x4 form. Gave me some claws. Very large bear walked the trail by our lake.

Friday, August 3, 1984—46° to 70°. Cloudy morning, sunny afternoon. Helped Bob with his shop door. Put up small beam in bathroom. Move to meat from Billman's to Schmidt's.

Saturday, August 4, 1984—sunny and hot. Stored some lumber. Cut power right-of-way and trees off the area where we'll build the garage.

Sunday, August 5, 1984—56° to 70s and sunny. Worked on truck lights and Cat. Cleaned sawdust and lumber in house.

Monday, August 6, 1984—54° to 70s and sunny. Went to Anchorage. Did paperwork at lawyer's office and a little shopping, then came home.

Tuesday, August 7, 1984—48° to 78°. Hot and sunny, one hard shower. Worked on cats all day, Clem helped. Nadia called.

Wednesday, August 8, 1984—48° to low 70s. Partly cloudy and a few sprinkles. Took Cat over to lodge and helped Clem with sign pole.

Thursday, August 9, 1984—48° to 60°. Partly cloudy. Help Allen work on his wood shop. Another bear has been through twice on the lower trail and through Allen's yard.

Friday, August 10, 1984—44° to 59°. Partly cloudy, rainy in evening. Helped Clem with his sign. Caulked some logs on west side of house. Helped Allen insulate wood shop.

Saturday, August 11, 1984—44° to 64°. Partly cloudy, one heavy shower and some light showers. Helped Allen put in one gable end. Caulked some on our house.

Sunday, August 12, 1984—38° to 65°. Sunny all day. Charlie and Beth, Henry and Sally, and Rhynell visited. Welded on pipe rack. Rolled up visqueen. Finished caulking west end of house with oakum (a preparation of tarred fiber used for caulking or packing the joints of wooden timbers). Made wood tool for tamping it in. Sylvia is sick, but still canned seven quarts of peaches and made two pies.

Monday, August 13, 1984—28° to 60°. Some light frost, sunny day. Went to lawyer and did some shopping for other people and us. Light quake, 5.7.

Tuesday, August 14, 1984—28° to 60s. Sunny, beaut of a day. Got some gear ready for sheep hunting and caulked a little on the house. Visited Jim and Mary in the evening.

Wednesday, August 15, 1984—46° to 82°, hot and sunny. Put plywood on wall in basement near wood chute. Caulked some logs, then helped Bob a little while.

Thursday, August 16, 1984—42° to 70s. Sunny, some haze. Caulked on house and helped Bob Rudbeck. Sylvia oiled some more logs. Visited Billmans and KROA.

Friday, August 17, 1984—40° to 60s and sunny. Helped Bob. Lucky put plastic on house windows. Tried to sight in our rifles, heard that it looked like a bear had messed up the trap cabin.

Saturday, August 18, 1984—42° to 60°. Cloudy, and windy near KROA. We got Bob's rifle sighted in—my scope is no good. We got three rows of plywood on the ceiling of Bob's building. Visited Allen and Roxanne.

Sunday, August 19, 1984—40° to 60s and partly cloudy. Helped Bob and Kahren with ceiling of their shop—finished it. Potluck supper at KROA. There is a fire on our side of Nelchina River near Botley Creek.

Monday, August 20, 1984—40° to 60° and partly cloudy. Shot rifle, had cartridge separation. Got some gear ready and worked on the house. Jim, Mary, Sam, Peter and Eve stopped by. Jim had picked up some .338 shells for me. Visited Lucky about elect easement.

Tuesday, August 21, 1984—40° to 52° and cloudy. Sighted rifle, went to Dan's, worked here, and Chad Wilson visited. Dan flew Bob and me to Terrace Lake.

Wednesday, August 22, 1984—rainy and cooler. Tried to pack up and out of canyon north and west of camp—no go, too slippery. Bob shot a cow boo in evening. Several boo around, whistling—marmot also.

Thursday, August 23, 1984—rainy, snow on peaks. Back very sore till noon. Went exploring east in valley, seeing boo all day—no sheep. Bob called a caribou up close. Red fox close. Saw boo swim lake. Lots of parka squirrels. Rain showers and shifting breeze.

Friday, August 24, 1984—fog. Cooked meal of buffalo and spuds. Rain and fog all day.

Saturday, August 25, 1984—cloudy, foggy, rain, snow, and gusty winds. Dan couldn't fly in. Packed boo to camp. Wind broke pole in tent.

Sunday, August 26, 1984—cleared up, windy and gusts. Packed gear, Dan couldn't fly. Glassed for sheep. Saw two eagles, one raven, one boo. Dried gear. Saw quartz outcrop one quarter mile northwest of Terrace Lake.

Monday, August 27, 1984—sunny and windy, some breeze. Bob saw a griz at end of lake. Dan came in at 3:00 p.m. and picked us up. Some trees blown down here at home. Letters from Nadia.

Tuesday, August 28, 1984—cold and sunny, 18° to 47°. Worked on one door for house. Lucky and Mary visited. Drained Cat.

Wednesday, August 29, 1984—20° to 50° and sunny. Worked on house, got telephone wire spools.

Thursday, August 30, 1984—25° to 44° and cloudy. Worked on house, signed up four NRA members.

Friday, August 31, 1984—sunny, 30° to 53°. Did a little work on the house, helped lucky with his roof in afternoon.

Saturday, September 1, 1984—sunny, 33° to 50°. Helped Lucky finish putting steel on his house roof. Party at Bob and Kahren's shop. James is putting vinyl in kitchen. Mike is helping too.

Sunday, September 2, 1984—32° to 48°. James and Mike put the rest of the carpet in the house. Mike helped with the stairs. Met Les O'Reilly and Eric (?) He came out with Candy to spray that Café Roof.

Monday, September 3, 1984—32° to 46°. Cloudy all day. Lots of visitors. Worked on house.

Tuesday, September 4, 1984—30° to 47° and partly cloudy. Worked on house, lots of company. Kahren Rudbeck's birthday party at Billman's.

Wednesday, September 5, 1984—31° to 50°. Partly cloudy. We put CWF on the gable ends of the house. Bob and Kahren Rudbeck, and Jerry Lica went boo hunting. Bob shot a bull boo.

Thursday, September 6, 1984—28° to 50° partly cloudy. Small shower and rainbow. Went to Anchorage for building supplies for house.

Friday, September 7, 1984—26° to 50s. Sunny and warm. Killed and buried a goat for Hoffmans. Lots of visitors. Didn't do much work on the house. Darrel and I are going goose/crane hunting.

Saturday, September 8, 1984—28° to 50s. Mostly sunny at Delta Junction with an east wind. Shot two crane and two speckled geese. Good time, but tired. Many thousands of crane, some speckled belly and dusky geese, a few mallards and some pintail.

Sunday, September 9, 1984—22° to 60° and sunny in Delta. Fewer birds flying—and flying higher. Got crane and Mallard. Marsh Hawk and raven hunting together observed by Darrel. We are having a good time. Got home late.

Monday, September 10, 1984—31° to 50° and sunny. James put vinyl in the house and Bob hauled gravel.

Tuesday, September 11, 1984—29° to 50° and sunny. Bob Rudbeck and I put Formica on the countertops.

Wednesday, September 12, 1984—24° to 50° and sunny. Loaded some gravel for Rudbeck. Steel hydraulic line sprung a leak.

Thursday, September 13, 1984—30° to 48° and cloudy. Moved cook stove, etc. to new house. Ate and slept there.

Friday, September 14, 1984—30s to 50s and sunny. Loaded gravel, Bob hauled.

Saturday, September 15, 1984—30s to 50s and sunny. Steamed dirt out of radiator of Cat. Doesn't heat so badly now. Clem and Jean had their grand opening party this afternoon and evening. Chad Wilson visited and stayed the night. We had a good time.

Sunday, September 16, 1984—30s to 50s and sunny with rain in the evening. Hauled gravel. Chad left this morning.

Monday, September 17, 1984—30s to 48° and partly cloudy. Dug ditch to bury power line across driveway and yard. Got ready and went to airport in Anchorage and picked up Nadia and Darrell (Breider). Did shopping and came home.

Tuesday, September 18, 1984—34° to 50°. Visited Billman's, KROA, and Odden's. Packed gear to go to trap cabin to hunt moose. Dan Billman flew us out. Cabin in fine shape when Darrell and I got there. Nice to be here.

Wednesday, September 19, 1984—30° to 45°. Mostly sunny, light shower in afternoon. Walked to Hole Lake, drainage to Pristine Lake and the circled back to trap cabin—we are tired.

Thursday, September 20, 1984—34° to 45°. Cloudy and rainy morning cleared up, sunny and windy. Went to Blue Lake, tried to call moose. No luck. Saw a recently used griz trail on west side of Blue Lake. Improved snowgo trail and hunted Hole Lake in the evening with no luck. One marten cubby wrecked. Dan flew us home.

Friday, September 21, 1984—28° to 48°. Nice day, Nadia, Darrell and I went to Anchorage to do research on lode mine. Got back early.

Saturday, September 22, 1984—18° to 42° and sunny. Did some electrical work and went to Margaret Schmidt's memorial services. Had lots of company. Went to "pickin" party at Billman's. Had a good time.

Sunday, September 23, 1984—30° to 45° and partly cloudy. Lucky, Darrell and I worked on connecting up the electricity. Lights in the basement and downstairs tonight.

Monday, September 24, 1984—18 to 44°, nice day. Loaded gravel for Rudbeck—Schmidt, Clem, Henry and me.

Tuesday, September 25, 1984—partly cloudy, 30° to 45°. Dan flew Nadia, Darrell and I to Cog Hill—Shoup Glacier to look at quartz outcroppings. Flew in a white-out—rain, and wind. Made quite a trip. Saw eight or nine mountain goats and caribou, geese and sea otter. Rudbeck started for Minnesota.

Wednesday, September 26, 1984—nice day, took Nadia and Darrell to Anchorage. Darrell did mining research. We went shopping and picked up a freezer for us and bedsprings for Billmans at Red's. Went to a movie and got home late.

Thursday, September 27, 1984—24° to 42° and sunny. Unloaded bedsprings at Billman's place and unloaded the freezer here. Installed underground wire for garage in house, covered logs, leveled gravel and cleaned up a few things for winter. Visited Allan and Roxanne.

Friday, September 28, 1984—25° to 40°. Sunny then cloudy and light shower. Did assessment paperwork at Billman's and lots of jobs getting ready for winter. Visit at Lucky and Mary. Rained all night.

Saturday, September 29, 1984—28° to 40° and cloudy till 4:00 p.m., then sunny. Did not lack for jobs all day. Visited Henry and Sally, called Kevin and Beverly, and talked to Theresa also.

Sunday, September 30, 1984—34° to 50°. Cloudy, then sunny afternoon. Started digging Henry and Sally's basement. We had Sally, Chris, Henry, and Bob Schmidt for supper.

Monday, October 1, 1984—33° to 50°. Cloudy, then sunny. Finished Henry and Sally's basement, then called Kevin about farm business.

Tuesday, October 2, 1984—30° to 45° and sunny. Worked on Cat for five hours at Smayda's. Walked down to Lake, saw some ducks and muskrat. Cleaned dirt off undercarriage of Cat.

Wednesday, October 3, 1984—24° to 40°. Nice day. Andy and Ken Boyle are spraying urethane near here. Got gear ready—Darrel Gerry and I went to Delta to hunt geese. Really lots of smoke in farming area. Stayed at Allen and Wendy's.

Thursday, October 4, 1984—28° to 50° here in Delta—foggy and smoky. Scott Hollembeck hunted with us. No geese or cranes. Stayed at Allen and Wendy's.

Friday, October 5, 1984—28° to 55° and partly cloudy. Some smoke, Darrel got one crane—the only chance either of us had. Saw a few ducks and one small flock of geese. Home by supper time. Called Virginia in Los Angeles, mother is very sick. Cancer.

Saturday, October 6, 1984—30° to 58°. Sunny, windy in the evening. Sylvia and I don't feel well. Went to Ranch House Days at Tolsona Creek. Lucky wired two, three-way switches.

Sunday, October 7, 1984—34° to 50°. Mostly cloudy. Started building east porch on house. Visited Allan and Roxanne. Called Virginia, mother very sick. Called Kevin and renter at farm.

10,000 Days in Alaska Book One 1978-1989

Monday, October 8, 1984—32° to 50°. Partly cloudy. Did some work for Allen Farmer, visited Jim and Mary Odden. Called Virginia and Nadia.

Tuesday, October 9, 1984—30° to 45° and partly cloudy. Lots of swans flying—migrating. Built porch and steps for front of house. Covered Cat for winter and Lee Dudley visited in evening.

Wednesday, October 10, 1984—16° to 40°. Partly cloudy. Built steps on the east end of house. Gave Jim and Mary a rug pad and moved some things into old cabin. Sam and Greg visited and helped move the freezer.

Thursday, October 11, 1984—16° to 38°. Cloudy, then two inches of snow in afternoon. Weather stripped doors, put protection over freezer and some roof on woodshed. Worked at getting ready for winter. Lots of company. Supper at Dimmick's—Arlene's birthday.

Friday, October 12, 1984—16° to 30°. Cloudy, some snow. More work on house. Got most of truck ready for winter. Shot a snowshoe hare. More swans flying, one flock landed in our lake for the night. Visited Allen and Roxanne.

Saturday, October 13, 1984—24° to 32°. Cloudy to partly cloudy. Did odd jobs getting ready for winter and on the house. Helped Henry a little. Visited at KROA.

Sunday, October 14, 1984—20° to 32°. Mostly sunny, clear and bright. Moon tonight. Worked a little on the interior doors. Lots of company. Visited Jim and Mary. Alan and Roxanne and boys visited us in evening.

Monday, October 15, 1984—4° to 18°. Partly cloudy, nice day. Worked on upstairs door and basement door. Allen brought his router over to inlet hinges. Jim and Mary and Sam visited in evening.

Tuesday, October 16, 1984—4° to 20° and sunny. Went to Anchorage, caught plane to Los Angeles and went to hospital to see my mother (Ruby Wilkins). She was sleeping.

Wednesday, October 17, 1984—55° to 75° and sunny. Mom is very sick.

Norman Wilkins

Thursday, October 18, 1984—54° to 74° and sunny. Mom walked a little.

Friday, October 19, 1984—weather is the same. Mother is very ill.

Saturday, October 20, 1984—weather same. Mother worse.

Sunday, October 21, 1984—56° to 76° and sunny. Jerry came to see mother. She is very low today.

Monday, October 22, 1984—weather is the same. Marion flew in from Texas. Mother is the same. I phoned to move reservations back one day.

Tuesday, October 23, 1984—mother is better today.

Wednesday, October 24, 1984—mother is better. Bob H. took me to plane. Got to Anchorage and stayed at Andy's.

Thursday, October 25, 1984—did some shopping and helped Henry load beams got home late afternoon.

Friday, October 26, 1984—4° 18° and sunny. Helped Jim and Mary with their roof.

Saturday, October 27, 1984—sunny and -7° to 19°. Worked all day helping put roof on Jim and Mary's house.

Sunday, October 28, 1984—cloudy in the morning, sunny in the afternoon and -6° to 18°. Helped finish putting Jim and Mary's roof on.

Monday, October 29, 1984—sunny and -18° to 5°. Hung door for upstairs and other odd jobs. Helped unload beams at Henry's. June and Mary and Sam were here. Visited Sam.

Tuesday, October 30, 1984—partly cloudy and -15° to 0°. Worked on chainsaw, went to Glennallen for a doctor checkup. Visited at Mike and Lynette also Allen and Roxanne.

Wednesday, October 31, 1984—mostly sunny, -6° to 8°. Hauled load of wood home, cut and stacked two thirds of it. Lots of Halloween visitors.

10,000 Days in Alaska Book One 1978-1989

Thursday, November 1, 1984—sunny and -8° to 15°. Hauled a load of wood home, cut up and stacked it in the basement. Jim and Mary visited and brought welder home.

Friday, November 2, 1984—Ice fog in morning, sunny afternoon and -6° to 10°. Cut up and put in basement the last load of wood from Hoffman's.

Saturday, November 3, 1984—partly cloudy, -12° to 9°. Put a half pickup load of wood in basement. Helped Allen move a planer-shaper and saw to his shop along with a drum of oil. Allen, Roxanne, the kids and a friend Dave, were here for supper. Cloudy tonight.

Sunday, November 4, 1984—partly cloudy, -9° to 8°. Helped Henry with his basement walls. Jim, Mary, Sam, and Ron helped also. Jim and Mary visited later in the evening. Dave Campbell borrowed some worm meds for Peter's dog.

Monday, November 5, 1984—6° to 12° and partly cloudy. Worked on Henry and Sally's basement. Sent a letter to Rudbecks.

Tuesday, November 6, 1984—12° to 19° and cloudy. Very light snow. Went to vote. Built trap box for snowgo and worked on snowgo trailer.

Wednesday, November 7, 1984—12° to 17°. Cloudy, light snow at night. Worked on basement walls of Sally and Henry's house.

Thursday, November 8, 1984—13° to 17°. Light snow in the morning. Alan visited. Loaded snowgo and went to trapline—Jr. Hunt is trying to take it over. Visited Warren Dawson and also Eddie Farmer. Sylvia and I visited Lucky and Mary in the evening.

Friday, November 9, 1984—12° to 15°. Light snow and cloudy. Called Fish & Game. Ken Lewis picked up some of my traps that Jr. Hunt had set. He ran some of Hunt's line and found set traps. I got more trap gear together. Allen Farmer and I got more gear ready to road trap.

Saturday, November 10, 1984—5° to 12°. Cloudy and light snow. Alan and I put in sets to mile 118. I went to mile 9 Lake Louise Road and put in some sets there. Skating party at KROA. Dan called from KROA, talked to him a little bit.

Sunday, November 11, 1984—it's -20° to -9°. Cloudy and ice fog, clear tonight. Nothing in traps on road line. Put front on plenum on stove. Got water at lodge. Called Virginia.

Monday, November 12, 1984—it's -14° to -4°. Mostly sunny—unusual formation of sun dogs. Nelchina River flooded and stranded four people on south side. Allen and I got one fox. I made sets on Slide Mountain. Jim and Mary visited. Called Nadia and Darrell, ordered snowgo hand warmers.

Tuesday, November 13, 1984—colder, -20° to -12°. Partly cloudy, some sun. Nelchina River running hard. We have some kind of virus. Helped Allen in afternoon. No fur on road line.

Wednesday, November 14, 1984—it's -16° to -5° and partly cloudy. Set more traps north of Old Man Lake—still having trouble with Jr. Hunt. Allen and I set four traps this evening. Helped Henry set camper off.

Thursday, November 15, 1984—mostly cloudy and -6° to 0°. Got one ermine on road line. Stretched some fur. Helped some on Allen's wood shop floor. Called Jr. Hunt.

Friday, November 16, 1984—mostly cloudy with some fog. -16° to -2°. River is still high—Glacier Lake must have dumped. Cut up wood and put in basement. Potluck supper at Nelchina Lodge tonight.

Saturday, November 17, 1984—it's -2° to 8°. Cloudy and ice fog. Ran Slide Mountain, nothing. Made more sets. Allen and family and Jack and Jane visited. Allen and I picked up a red fox this afternoon.

Sunday, November 18, 1984—3° to 6°. Cloudy and ice fog. Allen and I ran west road line, nothing. Cut up lead and stacked in shed. Bob Schmidt got a road kill call. Small bull calf mother didn't want to leave. Got it butchered. Supper at Nelchina Lodge.

Monday, November 19, 1984—cloudy and ice fog, -11° to -4°. Allen and I put out moose gut pile for coyote. Painted the floor of shop, stretched

10,000 Days in Alaska Book One 1978-1989

fox. Sylvia had ladies here doing crafts. We got water at the lodge. Allen and Sylvia and I have some kind of bug.

Tuesday, November 20, 1984—cloudy, fog, snow and wind. -3° to 28°. Nothing in traps off Lake Louise Road. Put in more sets on trail to Cabot. Stopped to visit Darrel, also Jim and Mary.

Wednesday, November 21, 1984—light snow most of day, 13° to 30°. Cut brush and packed a trail to haul wood from shed to house. Shoveled snow. Helped Allen move some shop things. Still snowing this evening, six inches total now.

Thursday, November 22, 1984—cloudy, snow has quit. 20° to 16°. Tom visited. We went to KROA for Thanksgiving dinner. It was very good, lots of friends there. Lee, Jim, Mary and Tom played music.

Friday, November 23, 1984—partly cloudy, -10° to 16°. Ran trapline on Slide Mountain. Got one squirrel, made one set. Divided moose meat. Charlie T., Tom and Lisa, Beth Schmidt, and Kathy, Ron, Lucky and Mary, all visited.

Saturday, November 24, 1984—partly cloudy, -12° to 6°. Cut and stacked wood in the shed. Got old Ski-Doo started. Called mother. Visited Lucky and Mary in the evening. Visited Henry and Sally late afternoon.

Sunday, November 25, 1984—partly cloudy, -14° to -8°. We cut up a pickup load of wood and put it in the basement. Ed and Sandy Farmer and family visited and brought some flour, etc. Allen and Dave visited.

Monday, November 26, 1984—cloudy and clear towards evening, -21° to -9°. Allen and I ran road line and got one marten. One coyote got away. We cut up and stacked more wood in the shed and got water at the lodge.

Tuesday, November 27, 1984—cloudy and foggy, -15° to -10°. Tracks of mink, marten, fox, coyote, otter, and lynx. Made more sets and broke trail to trap cabin. Everything okay, tired tonight. Nothing in traps. Saw caribou along Glenn Highway.

Wednesday, November 28, 1984—cloudy and fog, -20° at night -10° all day. Sore today, also flu. Put new pull rope in snowgo starter. Set small circle of traps near cabin.

Thursday, November 29, 1984—sunny, -17° to -10°. Early start, made lots of sets, nothing in traps. Beautiful sunset, snow covered aspen and spruce—all red and gold the last moments of the sunset. Loaded snowgo at Warren's, and saw four moose along Lake Louise Road, also ptarmigan.

Friday, November 30, 1984—sunny, -18° to -10°. Visited Allen's. Ran line on Slide Mountain, nothing. Visited the lodge and Henry's.

Saturday, December 1, 1984—sunny, -10° to 0°. Took old Ski-Doo to Ed Farmer's to be fixed. Allen, Dave and I got to small loads of wood and some logs out today.

Sunday, December 2, 1984—mostly cloudy, -2° to 10°. Cut up load of wood and stacked it. Allen and I each got a load of wood and some logs.

Monday, December 3, 1984—cloudy, 2° to 12°. Cut a pickup load of wood and stacked it in the shed. Company here all day. Supper at Tom and Lisa's.

Tuesday, December 4, 1984—cloudy, 10° to 70°. Got an early start. From Warren's we saw a red fox cross road. Made a set for him. Stopped for one caribou to cross road. Jr. Hunt had fox in trap. I only had Jay's and squirrels in my traps. Tired tonight, trails are rough.

Wednesday, December 5, 1984—cloudy and some, 18° all day. Flu today ran loop line near here—nothing. Put some extension chains on some traps. Adjusted throttle on snowgo.

Thursday, December 6, 1984—partly cloudy, 10° all day. Went down to Mendeltna Springs—pretty risky. Went to Judd Lake and explored other seismic trails—36 miles. Tired. Allen, Dave, and Pat and Patti Landers visited this evening about Jr. Hunt crowding in on our territory. I hear he already has 275 miles of trapline.

Friday, December 7, 1984—cloudy, 10° all day. Check line on Slide Mountain—nothing. Visited Henry and Sally. Called Virginia from Tom and Lisa's.

Saturday, December 8, 1984—14° to 18°, snowed all day—10 inches. Bright moonlight tonight. Boo on lake today. Visited Allen, finished paying Sally. Put hand warmers on snowgo. Allen plowed out our driveway and yard.

Sunday, December 9, 1984—6° to 0° mostly clear. Moonlight and colder tonight. Allen got four fox. Jim O. visit. Worked on snowgo rewind and also traps.

Monday, December 10, 1984—cloudy, -20° to -10°. Fixed fuel line leak on pickup. Got water at lodge and visited Sally and Henry. Ran line on Slide Mountain, nothing. Made another cat set. Worked on trap repairs. Allen and Dave stopped to borrow aluminum push pins.

Tuesday, December 11, 1984—sunny, -20° to -10°. Stopped at KROA, saw fox on Lake Louise Road, nothing in traps. Very few tracks, a fuel boo near cabin. Only five inches more snow here at the trap cabin. Moon is bright, like daylight.

Wednesday, December 12, 1984—sunny, with sun dogs, -20° to -18°. Ran cabin loop and down by Blue Lake. Nothing in traps. Made four sets, picked up old trap. Repaired an old conibear box and did cabin chores.

Thursday, December 13, 1984—cloudy, -25° to -5°. Ran line, nothing. Made two mink sets at Jud Lake. Track heated up on way home. Clem pulled me from KROA to Nelchina, lost trailer and snowgo at driveway—no damage. Tired but can't sleep.

Friday, December 14, 1984—partly cloudy, -18° to -14°. Worked on truck all day, had it fixed by night. Worked on it at Clem's (at the lodge). There was to be a party at KROA—turned out to be a housewarming for Sylvia and me! Lots of people were there, made us very happy.

Saturday, December 15, 1984—nice day, -20° to -10°. Henry and Sally visited. Underplated the snowgo with heavy aluminum—Allen helped. Helped Allen with a rocking chair. (He later gave me the rocker at Christmas).

Norman Wilkins

Sunday, December 16, 1984—nice day, -10° to 0°. Cut up wood put in basement. Called mother. Had supper at Mary and Lucky's.

Monday, December 17, 1984—nice day, -10° to 10°. Allen and I got wood out to sell and more for wood shop. Worked in wood shop after supper.

Tuesday, December 18, 1984—cloudy, 10° to 16°. Ran Slide Mountain line, nothing. Cut up, split, and put a pickup load of wood in basement. Helped Allen a little.

Wednesday, December 19, 1984—sunny, -10° to 0°. Allen and Ed and I worked in the wood lot. Worked very little in the wood shop. Allen gave Sylvia a food mixer.

Thursday, December 20, 1984—cloudy, then sunny, -18° to -12°. Saw two small moose bulls and some cows. Also some Caribou on the way to Warren's. A few fox and mink track, nothing in traps on way to cabin. Moved some sets.

Friday, December 21, 1984—cloudy, -20° to -10°. A marten at cabin last night—moose feeding near cabin. Saw two otter feeding at Mendeltna Springs. Broke more trail, made more sets, nothing in traps.

Saturday, December 22, 1984—cloudy, -10° to 0°. Water in snowgo fuel system. Fixed up lots of sets. Got one red fox. Saw otter on Judd Lake. Did some exploring, saw two cow and two calf moose. Visited with Lloyd R. at KROA.

Sunday, December 23, 1984—5° to 12°, light snow all day (2"). Called all the kids. Shoveled snow off woodshed roof and also off the storage shed and brown trailer. Supper at Tom and Lisa Smayda's. Mahoney's where there.

Monday, December 24, 1984—8° to 18°, mostly cloudy. Visited around most of the day. Supper at Jim and Mary's.

Tuesday, December 25, 1984—mostly cloudy, -2° to 8°, light snow early in the day. Breakfast at Allen and Roxanne's, Christmas dinner at Tom and Lisa's, visited Henry and Sally in evening.

10,000 Days in Alaska Book One 1978-1989

Wednesday, December 26, 1984—partly cloudy, -2° to 6°. Allen started setting trapline up Botley Creek. Had a marten in a trap on the way home. Took marten to Morey and Joe's. Picked up Ski-Doo at Ed Farmer's. Visited Jim and Mary. Made out trap supply order.

Thursday, December 27, 1984—sunny, -15° to -20°. Nothing on Slide Mountain line. Helped Allen get a load of wood.

Friday, December 28, 1984—sunny, -26° to -31°. Fooled around wood shop a little.

Saturday, December 29, 1984—mostly sunny, -20° to -10°. Did a few odd jobs.

Sunday, December 30, 1984—mostly sunny, -10° to 10°, warm and windy in evening. Worked on traps, visited Ed and Sandy Farmer and had supper at Allen and Roxanne's. Dave is back.

Monday, December 31, 1984—16° to 26°, cloudy, warm, windy. Allen, Dave and I punched in more trapline on east side of Botley Creek. Got two marten. Supper at Ed and Sandy Farmer's, saw New Year in at Nelchina Lodge.

Striking view from the ridge above Scoter Lake

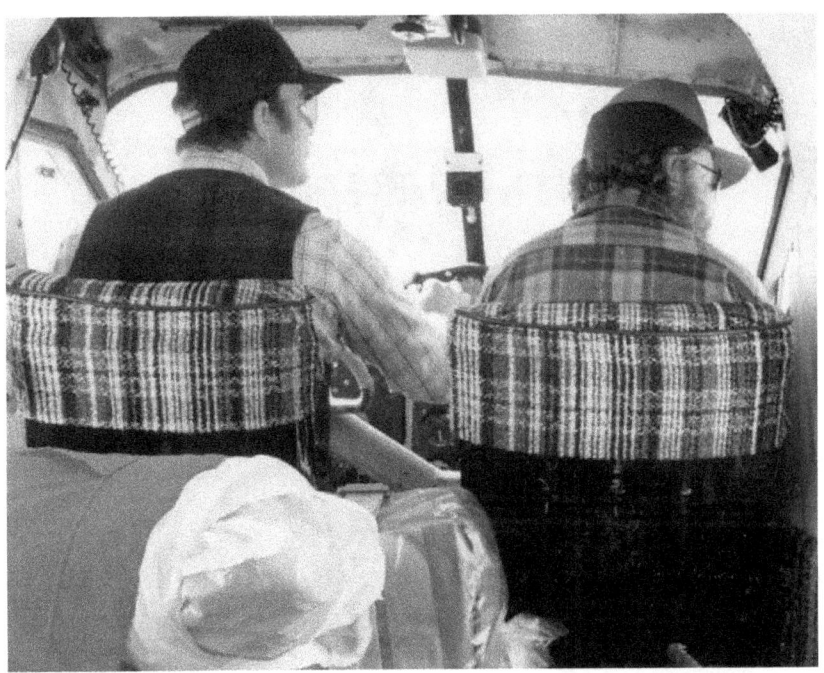

Top: Dan Billman and Norman; Bottom: The Mean Machine (swamp buggy) had articulation that allowed wheels to move independently from each other up and down and from side to side.

Rollogon tires filled with fuel for transport are pulled by the "Mean Machine". Photos taken by Earl Caughey.

Norman Wilkins

1985—prospecting near glaciers, rollogons across tundra

Tuesday, January 1, 1985—26° to 31°, cloudy, light snow and rain at Tazlina and Lake Louise Junction. Allen wants to get wood. Darrell Gerry and I go to Glennallen and Tolsona Lake to work on some trapline things.

Wednesday, January 2, 1985—26° to 10° and cloudy. Tried to run line off Lake Louise Road, nothing. Got into overflow on two lakes. Rat Lake was real bad. Turned around and came home. Henry and Sally borrowed pickup and got groceries for us. Ed Farmer visited.

Thursday, January 3, 1985—10° to 24°, cloudy. Ran line on Slide Mountain, nothing. Pulled some sets. Sore back and sick. Sylvia went with Jean and Sally to Glennallen.

Friday, January 4, 1985—10° and cloudy. Allen, Dave, and I punched more line up the mountain south of Nelchina River on the east side of Botley Creek. Got one marten and two ermine. Tired tonight.

Saturday, January 5, 1985—1° to 0° all day and cloudy. Tom, Lisa and family were here for breakfast. Did some jobs.

Sunday, January 6, 1985—10° to 50°, cloudy, fog, light snow. Worked on some trap things then visited Hoffmans and Lucky and Mary.

Monday, January 7, 1985—no entry.

Tuesday, January 8, 1985—15° to 20°, partly cloudy. Ran Judd Lake part of line. Got nice marten at Rat Lake on way out. Pulled 1-1/2 traps, made four sets and put up two boxes. Eight boo on Blue Lake. Lots of marten track, some fox.

Wednesday, January 9, 1985—warm and cloudy, did some things around here and the shop. Worked on Ski-Doo.

Thursday, January 10, 1985—20° to 25° and cloudy. Allen and I worked on Botley Creek line. Got two marten and three ermine. Land meeting at Alaska House. Jim and Mary here for supper, we went with them to meeting.

10,000 Days in Alaska Book One 1978-1989

Friday, January 11, 1985–22° to 25° cloudy, warm, light snow. Took two marten to Sam's. Helped Allen.

Saturday, January 12, 1985–18° to 26° and sunny. Put headlights in truck. Ran Slide Mountain trapline, nothing. Broke a trail part way up Chain of Lakes east of us. Allen, Roxanne and family, and Dave were here for supper.

Sunday, January 13, 1985–10° to 18° and cloudy. Ran east Botley Creek line. Got three marten and one ermine. Broke more trail and set a lot more traps. Cleared and improved some of previous trail.

Monday, January 14, 1985–2° to 10° and cloudy. Got ready to go to trap cabin tomorrow. Henry butchered a hog.

Tuesday, January 15, 1985–3° to 8°, foggy and cloudy. No fur in traps on cabin line. Unknown snowgo riders have run down my sets. Saw two moose from road, lots of boo in trap area.

Wednesday, January 16, 1985–10° all day, mostly sunny. Kick back and enjoy a day of rest. Went to wood lot, trimmed, cut into logs and stacked two trees.

Thursday, January 17, 1985–4° to 24° and partly cloudy. No fur. Moved some sets, made new sets. Saw fresh lynx track on way out.

Friday, January 18, 1985–10° to 2° and sunny. Dave and I picked up four marten and two ermine and broke more trail on mountain. Barney Anderson broke trail to our line. Jim and Mary flew over us while we were on the mountain. Had supper at Lucky and Mary's. Jim and Mary and Sam visited us.

Saturday, January 19, 1985–cloudy, 2° to 12°. Did snowgo service work. Ran Slide Mountain, nothing. Did some things for trapline.

Sunday, January 20, 1985–cloudy, -1° to 10°. Darrel and I went to Chuck Zimbiki's to get a machine for parts. Sylvia and I went to Jim and Mary's to grind meat.

Norman Wilkins

Monday, January 21, 1985—3° to 14° and cloudy. Got a late start, Allen, Dave and I went to twin Lakes and set 15 to 17 traps.

Tuesday, January 22, 1985—10° all day, mostly cloudy. Five moose along road. Boo along trail to cabin, nothing in traps.

Wednesday, January 23, 1985—10° to 30°, sunny and windy in afternoon. Made six new sets. One marten had been half eaten. Had supper at Jim and Mary's.

Thursday, January 24, 1985—14° to 22° and cloudy. Skinned marten and ermine. Got water at Lodge. Rhynell and Max came with some fresh pork.

Friday, January 25, 1985—2° to 8° and partly cloudy. Did a little service work on snowgo. Sylvia did laundry. Allen, Dave, Jim and Mary, Henry and Lonnie visited.

Saturday, January 26, 1985—10° to 22°, mostly cloudy. Dave ran Twin Lakes line. Allen and I ran Botley Creek and got one marten. Dave got two marten. Visited Jack and Jane and Hoffman's.

Sunday, January 27, 1985—6° to 16°, cloudy morning, sunny afternoon. Built conibear boxes and ran line on Slide Mountain. Made fox set. Two wolves ran line also.

Monday, January 28, 1985—4° to 12° and partly cloudy. Made another set on Slide Mountain. Allen and Dave sold our fur. Called mother.

Tuesday, January 29, 1985—5° to 12°, foggy and cloudy, sun at 3 p.m., beautiful sunset. Some moves and lots of boo, 30 on Blue Lake. Boo tramped some traps. Cut and straightened some of cabin lake trail. Made three rat sets on Rat Lake. Nice to be here, bright moonlit night.

Wednesday, January 30, 1985—0° to 10°, foggy and cloudy. Checked traps at Mendeltna Springs. Otter have moved, nothing in traps. Did some exploring. Must be hundreds of boo near cabin.

Thursday, January 31, 1985—20° to 30° and sunny. Made five sets at Judd Lake and vicinity. Got a marten and ermine, lost a fox. Helped

10,000 Days in Alaska Book One 1978-1989

Darrel at KROA and had supper at Jim and Mary's.

Friday, February 1, 1985—10° to 25°. Ran Slide Mountain, nothing. Jim flew me over Botley Creek in "Rags" (his airplane). Potluck party at Lodge, Sylvia baked a turkey.

Saturday, February 2, 1985—4° to 20° and mostly sunny. Ran Slide Mountain again, then east Botley Creek. Got one marten and two ermine. Took marten to Sam to skin.

Sunday, February 3, 1985—6° to 17°, cloudy, snow in p.m.

Monday, February 4, 1985—6° to 10° and sunny. Mailed fur to Seattle (from Glennallen). Dave and I ran Twin Lakes, got two marten.

Tuesday, February 5, 1985—4° to 10°, snow in the morning then ground blizzard and high winds. Saw moose, hundreds of boo in cabin area. Saw a white yearling on Fox Lake. Extra large marten in conibear. Marked rest of cabin loop.

Wednesday, February 6, 1985—4° to 10°, windy morning, bright sun. Birds ate ermine in trap, otherwise nothing in traps today.

Thursday, February 7, 1985—it's -15° to 5° and sunny. Sore back, did a few light things around here. Tom, Lisa and daughters and Greg Smayda were here for supper.

Friday, February 8, 1985—it's -20° 20 and sunny. Dave and I ran east Botley Creek, got one ermine and one marten.

Saturday, February 9, 1985—still -20° to 0° and sunny. I ran Slide Mountain, nothing.

Sunday, February 10, 1985—temp is -30° to -10° and sunny. Clem went with me to mile 134 to get a road kill boo. We got it butchered. I quartered it, Sylvia cut it ready to grind. Henry and Sally visited.

Monday, February 11, 1985—dropped to -35° to -10° and sunny. Got water at Lodge, visited Henry and Sally. Got eggs at Hoffman's.

Norman Wilkins

Tuesday, February 12, 1985—it's -26° to -10°, sunny and light snow. Visited Tom and Lisa. Sam, Henry, Sally, Sylvia and I got a road kill moose.

Wednesday, February 13, 1985—some sun, light snow and -30° to -14°.

Thursday, February 14, 1985—down to -35° to -14° partly cloudy with sun dogs.

Friday, February 15, 1985—still cold, -34° to -10° and sunny. Dave and I ran Botley Creek and Twin Lake lines.

Saturday, February 16, 1985—it's -32° to -13° and sunny. Nothing on line. Gave moose meat to Dawsons. Lots of Caribou trampled sets and a large pack of wolves killed boo a half-mile from cabin.

Sunday, February 17, 1985—it's -23° to -10 and sunny. Got one ermine on line and made one new fox set.

Monday, February 18, 1985—cold, -31° to -10° and sunny. Sylvia went to Anchorage with Jean and Sally. I worked on traps and chain drags. Lucky welded for me. Allen visited. Called about traps.

Tuesday, February 19, 1985—it's -35° to -12° and sunny. Ran Slide Mountain, nothing. Worked on snowgo. Roxanne mailed trap order.

Wednesday, February 20, 1985—temp is -32° to -6°, sunny then cloudy. Ran twin Lakes line, got one marten. Took moose meat to Dimmick's and visited. They gave us bread.

Thursday, February 21, 1985—partly cloudy and -21° to -2°. Lots of company, skinned and stretched marten. Cleaned chimney, Sylvia went to a painting class.

Friday, February 22, 1985— sunny and -26° to -8°. Did service work on snowgo, bedded dogs, loafed.

Saturday, February 23, 1985—back down to -34° to -7° and sunny. Worked on wolf trap chains. Did lots of visiting.

10,000 Days in Alaska Book One 1978-1989

Sunday, February 24, 1985—it's -25° to -2° and sunny. Made up more trap chains. Did some visiting.

Monday, February 25, 1985—it's -22° to 10° and sunny. Pulled traps on Slide Mountain. Wolves went by Nelchina on the north.

Tuesday, February 26, 1985—8° to 25°, mostly cloudy. Lots of boo in trail. Darrell Gerry is along, got red fox. Skinned fox. Wolves back to kill. Took Darrel's fuel pump apart.

Wednesday, February 27, 1985—15° to 25°, cloudy than sunny. Made a wolf set. Picked up fox and marten traps. Made otter set and did some exploring.

Thursday, February 28, 1985—8° to 25° and sunny. Checked otter set, picked rest of fox and marten traps. Lots of wolves in trail.

Friday, March 1, 1985—it's -10° to 5° and mostly sunny. Dave and I ran Botley Creek and Twin Lakes lines. Got two ermine, pulled traps. Saw cat tracks and wolf tracks.

Saturday, March 2, 1985—sunny and -6° to 19°. Fixed trap sled and sorted traps. Visited Hoffman's and Jim and Mary.

Sunday, March 3, 1985— sunny and -16° to 20°. Freighted gas and beaver traps to cabin. Darrel's secondary clutch broke.

Monday, March 4, 1985—it's -10° to 10° and sunny. Went to Mendeltna Springs and made four otter and four beaver sets. Lots of caribou around. Fine day.

Tuesday, March 5, 1985—it's -10° to 12° and sunny. Then out to Nelchina. Clem welded Darrel's clutch.

Wednesday, March 6, 1985—it's -9° to 16°. Mostly cloudy with a light snow. Went to trap cabin, nothing in traps. Put clutch on Darrel's snowgo. Explored west, south and east to Mendeltna Springs.

Thursday, March 7, 1985—10° to 20°, partly cloudy, eight inches of snow last night. Went east of cabin, new trail, lots of boo. Tolled one group

Norman Wilkins

up to us.

Friday, March 8, 1985—13° to 21°, partly cloudy. Worked on Darrel's snowgo. Went to more lakes east and got in overflow on new trail. Boo don't like to leave snowgo trail. Deep snow. Wolf howl, 11:45 p.m.

Saturday, March 9, 1985—5° to 13°, partly cloudy. Worked on Darrel's snowgo. Finished trail to Judd Lake from the east. Wolves were on trail last night. Saw only a mink and fox track. Thousands of boo in area. Tried to get to Cottonwood Lake—no go.

Sunday, March 10, 1985—10° to 30° and sunny. Loaded up and came home. Darrel was sad to leave.

Monday, March 11, 1985—10° to 39° and sunny. Worked on springs and suspension on my snowgo.

Tuesday, March 12, 1985—11° to 25° and partly cloudy. We went to Anchorage, shopped for snowgo parts and groceries. Left fuel oil barrels at Andy and Connie's. The road was sloppy and sometimes slippery. Jim and Mary came to talk about rat trapping.

Wednesday, March 13, 1985—it's -10° to 20°. Sunny with light snow showers. But no springs on snowgo and worked on tub to make hood fit. Got some gear ready to trap rats. Dave and Allen were here. Plowed snow and settled up on Marten.

Thursday, March 14, 1985—it's -10° to 15° and sunny. Stopped at Benjamin Mary's to make plans for a ratting trip. Left Warren's at noon, less boo on trial. Nothing in traps. Explored west and south, everything fine at trap cabin.

Friday, March 15, 1985—still -10° to 15°, sunny to partly cloudy. Loafed all morning. Went west and south looking for tracks. Saw two marten, two fox and one wolf track. Scattered boo—100 on Blue Lake. One moose near cabin. Pulled otter and beaver sets.

Saturday, March 16, 1985—16° to 24° and sunny. Some of the trail was very drifted over on the way out. Saw marten and fox tracks and quite a bit of boo. Picked up trap at Cat cubby. Stopped at KROA and at Jim

10,000 Days in Alaska Book One 1978-1989

and Mary's. Visited Hoffmans in the evening.

Sunday, March 17, 1985—7° to 30° and sunny. Got my gear ready for rat trapping. John and Sherri Mahoney and family visited. Jim and Mary were here for supper.

Monday, March 18, 1985—0° to 15°, Sunny to partly cloudy. Loaded gear here and at Odden's. Went to "Point of view" lodge at Lake Louise. We got into overflow on Lake Susitna. Got the machines and sled back on firm snow, then tried to find another way off the lake. My machine was having carburetor trouble. Came home for the evening.

Tuesday, March 19, 1985—0° to 20° and sunny. Worked on snowgo most of the day at Jim's. Still doesn't run right.

Wednesday, March 20, 1985—0° to 24° and sunny. Worked on snowgo at home most of the day. It still runs rich. Libby Riddles won the Iditarod this morning. Chris Rhodes stayed overnight.

Thursday, March 21, 1985—9° to 26° and mostly sunny. Took snowgo to Eureka. Tom found a leaking fuel diaphragm. Jim and Darrel visited in the evening.

Friday, March 22, 1985—4° to 30° and sunny. Went to Allen's, he and Dave went to town. Got income tax ready and wrote trap company, Chad, and lots of other letters. Sylvia went with Smayda's to a party for David at KROA.

Saturday, March 23, 1985—0° to 22° and mostly sunny. Loaded gear, went to Jim and Mary's and loaded their gear. Stopped at KROA. Unloaded at Eleven-Mile. Parked truck at Warren's, other snowgos as far as Blue Lake. Lots of boo, one moose near cabin, a few fox and some marten track. Made one beaver and one otter set on Hole Lake and drainage. Broke trail down the drainage to east trail and back to cabin.

Sunday, March 24, 1985—8° to 28° and mostly sunny. Checked sets on Hole Lake—nothing. Went to Mendeltna Springs, made an otter set and went exploring south to lower springs. Saw fox, otter, and marten tracks and lots of caribou—had a fine time.

Norman Wilkins

Monday, March 25, 1985—0° to 25° and sunny. Checked sets on Hole Lake—nothing again. Made two burbot sets. Went to Old Man Lake. Made one rat set, nothing. Made two sets at Beaver Lodge. Saw fewer boo. Saw otter, mink, fox and marten track. Saw an eagle; it was a fine spring day.

Tuesday, March 26, 1985—3° to 22° and sunny. Loaded gear and took the trail out. Shot boo at Fox Lake. Butchered it and went to Old Boot Lake. Then back to the road to Warren's. Had coffee with Leona. Loaded truck and trailer, stopped at KROA. Took Jim and Mary home. Dave and Allen and family were at our place for supper. Dave has a wolf.

Wednesday, March 27, 1985—0° to 25° and sunny. Worked on toboggan sled also the snowgo. Sylvia cut up the boo.

Thursday, March 28 1985—it's -10° to 20° and sunny. Parked at Warren's. Nothing in traps, one 330 was sprung. Picked up three traps from cubbies; lots less caribou around. Did some work on the trapline, it was a fine day.

Friday, March 29, 1985—still -10° to 20° and sunny. Pulled sets on Hole Lake and drainage. Cut drags. Less boo here now (cows). Found some very old trapline signs on Hole Lake drainage, also one wolf track.

Saturday, March 30, 1985—0° to 20° and sunny. Tried to climb west side of Hole Lake following caribou trail but failed. Explored north and east of Pristine and Burbot Lakes. Burbot Lake level down 10 feet. Cut lots of trail on the way to Judd Lake from the west. Built one cubby and two leaning pole sets. Two cow caribou came very near the cabin. Saw one moose, mink, marten and fox track. Very tired tonight.

Sunday, March 31, 1985—temp at -10° to 14° Sunny, cloudy, then light snow in evening. Went to Mendeltna Springs and pulled sets as the water is overflowing the ice. Then went on to sets near Old Man Lake and pulled those. When on out to Warren's. Left the snowgo and sled and visited Jim and Mary. Had supper at Tom and Lisa's—homemade ice cream and good conversation.

Monday, April 1, 1985—still -10° to 12° and sunny. Started letter to Darrel, loafed a lot. Visited Allen and Eddie and then Sam.

10,000 Days in Alaska Book One 1978-1989

Tuesday, April 2, 1985—it's -15° to 14° and sunny. Loafed a lot, visited Lee Dudley and Hoffmans. Allen Farmer visited—showed us some horn slices he was working on.

Wednesday, April 3, 1985—it's -13° to 24°. Sunny then cloudy with light snow in evening. Wrote letters all day. Henry and Chris were here for supper. Lisa and Lauren S. visited in evening.

Thursday, April 4, 1985—temperature is -11° to 17° and mostly sunny. Went to the clinic in Glennallen for medicine. Visited Blake and Jackie, KROA, Hoffman's and Jim and Mary. Took Jim and Mary's grinder back.

Friday, April 5, 1985—it's -9° to 19° and sunny. Ron visited. Allen and Dave borrowed the sketch book. I visited Henry, the Lodge, and Allen's shop. Got gear ready for Green Acres camping trip.

Saturday, April 6, 1985—it's -5° to 25° and partly cloudy. Loaded snowgo and big sled. Went to KROA and met Jim and Mary there. Loaded Darrel's gear. Went to Lake Louise Junction for regular gas for the snowgo. Tim Hurley is running the station. Then to Eleven-Mile Trail, unloaded, then went to Warren's. Loaded my snowgo and back to Eleven-Mile Trail. They had sled loaded and we went to Satiety Lake in Green Acres. Saw a big moose. Darrel has a nice tent we put it up and made camp.

Sunday, April 7, 1985—5° to 30°, light snow, and sunny and cloudy. Loafed around camp. Built a ladder and the main logs for Darrel's cache. Went to Old Boot Lake to see Jim and Mary and my land, then loaded two sled loads of Darrel's things and hauled it out to the vehicles. Finished around 9:30 p.m., went to KROA, then on home.

Monday, April 8, 1985—8° to 35° and sunny. Sylvia went to Anchorage with Jean and Ron. I did chores around here and worked on snowgo. Made some telephone calls.

Tuesday, April 9, 1985—10° to 25°, light snow and sunny. Rudbeck's are here. Called Kevin, renter, and accountant. Our daughter, Beverly is to come up June 11.

Norman Wilkins

Wednesday, April 10 1985—5° to 13° with snow flurries. Clem fixed snowgo trailer tire.

Thursday, April 11, 1985—snow flurries and -17° to 9°. Took Bob Rudbeck to Gulkana to get his plane. He has it parked here at Nelchina right now. Sylvia babysat for Tom and Lisa.

Friday, April 12, 1985—partly cloudy and -5° to 20° Did little work on the left tie rod on the snowgo. Hauled a few loads of wood and put it in the basement. Made homemade ice cream and took Bob and Kahren to Jim and Mary's. Met Mike and Sally and had a good time.

Saturday, April 13, 1985—5° to 30° and sunny. Went to see Hoffmans and broke a trail to the woodlot. Had to use aluminum shovel to level the snow in places.

Sunday, April 14, 1985—it's -4° to 20° and partly cloudy. Clem and I hauled the furnaces from Hoffman's place. Too late to start for the cabin. Sore back, sore stomach, lost my glasses yesterday.

Monday, April 15, 1985—10° to 35° and sunny. Parked at Warren's. Nice trip in. Sun maybe two dozen caribou along with fox, marten, otter and wolf tracks. Marten and caribou have been right up to the door of the cabin. Cut trail from the lake east to Burbot Lake.

Tuesday, April 16, 1985—10° to 30°, sunny in the morning cloudy in the afternoon. Loafed almost all day.

Wednesday, April 17, 1985—8° to 35° and sunny. Marked the trail west and south. Put up two marten boxes and some leaning poles. Cut lots of trap drags, built one cubby, made one 330 conibear leaning pole set. Saw five moose and a sprinkling of caribou. Snow has finally warmed up enough to pack into a trail. A marten robbed some bait from my bait box and dragged it off.

Thursday, April 18 1985—6° to 30° and sunny. Went north of Burbot Lake then west to Near Township corners then north quite a ways. Then I went back and over east to Marsh Lake. I found a live beaver lodge there and saw fox and marten track. I also saw two moose and a few

10,000 Days in Alaska Book One 1978-1989

caribou and found a partially built cabin and some old trap drags near Marsh and Burbot Lakes. Put up more marten boxes and looked for diamond willow.

Friday, April 19, 1985—10° to 25° cloudy, a little sun, light snow. Built a cache and ladder near Blue Lake. Put up another marten box. Did some laundry here.

Saturday, April 20, 1985—9° to 34° and sunny. Emptied lots of things out of cabin and put it up in the cache. Loaded sled and left for the road. Sure dislike closing up the cabin. Warren Dawson is home from the North Slope. We visited and he gave me a muskrat. Then I came on home and later visited Allen's.

Sunday, April 21, 1985—6° to 36° and sunny. Did lots of chores around here and some visiting. Jim, Ed, Sally, Chris, Henry, Lynette, and Daniel were here for supper.

Monday, April 22, 1985—7° to 38° and sunny. Up very early, went to woodlot while the trail was still frozen. Then cut the wood I will haul tomorrow. We are tired stiff and sore.

Tuesday, April 23, 1985—9° to 38° and sunny. Got up early, hauled wood to the pickup while trail was frozen and then cut more. Still stiff in sore—got one load of wood home.

Wednesday, April 24, 1985—11° to 44° and sunny. Unloaded wood. Went to Hoffman's and hauled in enough wood with the snowgo to fill the pickup. Then we cut more wood to haul tomorrow. Called Social Security office.

Thursday, April 25, 1985—11° to 30°, cloudy, snowed most of the day. Hauled 1-2/3 pickup loads of wood home and got water at Nelchina Lodge. Al Smith was here asking about buying the Caterpillar.

Friday, April 26, 1985—19° to 30°. Partly cloudy and windy. Installed Sylvia's kitchen sink.

Saturday, April 27, 1985—26° to 31° and mostly cloudy. Cut quite a bit of wood—broke the side chain and had trouble with sprocket on bar.

Norman Wilkins

Finished hooking up the sink. Jim, Sam, Craig and Dell visited.

Sunday, April 28, 1985–26° to 38° and partly cloudy. Got another cord of wood home and another cord cut in the woods. Broke the chain again.

Monday, April 29, 1985–12° to 42° and sunny. Got a nice big load of wood home and another one cut. Alan F. visited; Sally and Henry had a birthday supper and a gift for Sylvia. Jim and Mary Odden and aunt, Anne brought a bouquet of flowers for Sylvia.

Tuesday, April 30, 1985–10° to 43° and sunny. Hauled another load of wood home and did various odd jobs. Sylvia made a cake and I turned out some ice cream and we went to Jim and Mary's. Geese and swans have been flying daily for quite some time.

Wednesday, May 1, 1985–12° to 42° and sunny. Tried to cut up wood, but the bar on the chainsaw is kaput. Had supper at Lucky and Mary's.

Thursday, May 2, 1985–16° to 44° and partly cloudy. Did a variety of things around here, including the jointer and table saw. Sylvia babysat Lauren and Emily. Alan F. and Jim and Mary visited.

Friday, May 3, 1985–20° to 42° and partly cloudy. Worked on the table saw and filled out Social Security papers. Robins and blackbirds are back in numbers now. Wrote a letter to Bridger Inc. gathered up gear to go with Darrel and Jim and Mary to Lake Satiety.

Saturday, May 4, 1985–22° to 42° and sunny. We all met at KROA and went to Eleven-Mile trailhead, parked and unloaded snow goes, et cetera. Saw four Canadian geese flying. Loaded sleds and had a good trip in. Set up camp and Darrell released the pheasants—they took the trip well. They learned to eat leaves and berries very quickly. It was fun to watch them get settled into their new environment. Put up the two big poles for Darrel's cache.

Sunday, May 5, 1985–24° to 44° and sunny. The pheasants are doing okay. We went exploring on snowgos. There is some overflow now and the trails got rotten in the afternoon. We had some overflow and soft trails out to the trailhead. Darrel treated us to pizza at KROA.

10,000 Days in Alaska Book One 1978–1989

Monday, May 6, 1985—27° to 46° and partly cloudy. Got water at the lodge and worked on the table saw. Brought the generator home from Henry's. Brought the sled home from Hoffmans and tried to call Buscho.

Tuesday, May 7, 1985—Mostly sunny today and I don't feel well. Henry and Sally and Sylvia went to Glennallen to do laundry. I put new valve cover gaskets in the truck and called Buscho—rented the farm to him.

Wednesday, May 8, 1985—30° to 40°, mostly sunny and windy. Re-covered the seat on the truck and sorted and hung traps. Sally and Henry brought ice cream for cake and ice cream.

Thursday, May 9, 1985—24° to 35° partly cloudy and snow flurries. Brought the Ski-Doo home and still don't feel well. Rhynell and Max Hoffman were here for ice cream this evening.

Friday, May 10, 1985—20° to 37° and mostly sunny. Worked on Polaris snowgo. Strengthened tub and built up skegs.

Saturday, May 11, 1985—25° to 39° and mostly sunny. Modified hitch on snowgo to take a ball hitch. Build a rabbit hutch and had supper at KROA.

Sunday, May 12, 1985—25° to 37°, partly cloudy. Felt sick most of the day.

Monday, May 13, 1985—27° to 34°, mostly cloudy with a light snow in the evening. Shoveled a little dirt and other small jobs. Sure don't feel good. Chad and PC Wilson visited in the evening. Coyotes howled a lot last night.

Tuesday, May 14, 1985—29° to 38° and mostly cloudy. Worked on snowgo trailer. Henry, Lisa and girls, Bob Schmidt and Charlie T. visited. Sylvia went to Glennallen with Mary Beaudoin. We had ice cream and cake and music at Tom and Lisa's.

Wednesday, May 15, 1985—30° to 47°, mostly sunny. Went to Palmer and Wasilla shopping. Henry, Sally, Sam and Peter visited. We took Jim and Mary's stove, pipe and dog food to them. Allen and Dave visited in the evening. Two swans landed on the ice down on our lake today.

Thursday, May 16, 1985—30° to 42°, partly cloudy with a light snow during the night. Dan Billman is back. He and Dave Kimball visited us and also Lisa and the girls. I drove small posts around the garden and Allen Farmer gave us a trailer load of dirt. I borrowed his tiller and tilled the garden.

Friday, May 17, 1985—27° to 44°, partly sunny. Worked on the garden fence. Moved some things from the old cabin to the house. Phillip, Arlene, and two of their kids visited us.

Saturday, May 18, 1985—30° to 47°, mostly sunny, some breeze. Finished the fence and windbreaker for garden. Hauled a load of trash to the dump in visited Henry and Sally and Bob Schmidt.

Sunday, May 19, 1985—27° to 34°, cloudy with light snow all day. Hauled some sluice box steel home and started putting some things away upstairs. Sam, Henry, Sally, Chris, Lisa and girls were here for ice cream. Allen, Roxanne and the boys were here later.

Monday, May 20, 1985—28° to 40°, sunny with a little breeze. Went to Glennallen, stopped at six places. Dan Billman, Dave and Rusty were here for supper.

Tuesday, May 21, 1985—34° to 46°, sunny and a very nice day. Did some welding on a toy Allen is building. Visited Henry and Sally.

Wednesday, May 22, 1985—28° to 60°, sunny and warm. Worked on snowgo trailer. Welded the ball hitch on one trap sled.

Thursday, May 23, 1985—33° to 56° and sunny. Finished snowgo trailer. Cut brush and trimmed up some trees. Put in an ax handle and sharpened two other axes. Rachel Dimmick and her daughter and granddaughter's brought us a large amount of mushrooms.

Friday, May 24, 1985—34° to 60°, sunny with a light breeze. Soldered sling swivel on shotgun. Went to Hoffman's and cut and flagged part of a trail to the woodlot. Trimmed up more of our hillside.

10,000 Days in Alaska Book One 1978-1989

Saturday, May 25, 1985—40° to 60° Sunny, a slight haze. Walked down to the river and to old cabin site. No bear tracks, some moose track, a loon was on the lake, lots of ducks too. Sylvia put in more garden and I fixed up a compost box for it. Did lots of jobs around here and had pie and ice cream at Henry and Sally's.

Sunday, May 26, 1985—44° to 54° Sunny, windy and rain. Quite a bit of ice left on the lake. A snowshoe rabbit runs around the yard. Walked trapline on Slide Mountain cutting stumps and logs. Worked on reloading bench. Garden looks good.

Monday, May 27, 1985—40° to 64°, sunny, beautiful day. Hauled a load of dirt from Allen's. Worked on trap dying stove and trimmed up scattered poles. Rhynell and Max visited. Ice is going out on the lake.

Tuesday, May 28, 1985—40° to 54° and partly cloudy—tried to rain. Rhynell and Sylvia went to Anchorage. I built a trap boiling stove, trimmed up some wood and did some odd jobs. The ice is out of the lake.

Wednesday, May 29, 1985—34° to 48°, partly cloudy and windy. Did yard work today and there was a birthday party for Mary Odden.

Thursday, May 30, 1985—34° to 44°, mostly cloudy and very windy. Moved lots of gravel, collected two thirds of a cord of wood. Sylvia is helping out at KROA.

Friday, May 31, 1985—33° to 46°, partly cloudy and very windy with sun dogs in the evening. Did lots of cleaning up outside and moved some more gravel. Pushed Dan Billman's Beaver (plane) back into Snowshoe lake.

Saturday, June 1, 1985—36° to 48°, sunny and still quite windy. Did more cleaning up around here, then went to Warren and Leona Dawson's second anniversary party and had a good time there. Saw to porcupines and several caribou along the Lake Louise Road.

Sunday, June 2, 1985—34° to 58°, partly cloudy, breezy afternoon. Worked on chainsaw today. Hoffmans and Lisa Smayda and her girls visited today.

Monday, June 3, 1985—38° to 60°, mostly clear, windy afternoon. Worked on chainsaw and other jobs.

Tuesday, June 4, 1985—40° to 62°, cloudy and some wind. Went to Anchorage—Social Security exam and did some shopping. Visited Boyle's (Andy wasn't home). Roads were good. I wasn't able to get my tanning supplies.

Wednesday, June 5, 1985—36° to 48°, mostly cloudy, rainy in the evening. Got the chainsaw going, cut and trimmed trees at the lower garden and cut up some other trees. Put zerk in wheelbarrow wheel. Allen visited and I borrowed some STP from him.

Thursday, June 6, 1985—34° to 38°, rainy all day. Mounted reloading equipment, gun rack, coat hooks, and boo horn gun rack. Patti Billman visited.

Friday, June 7, 1985—33° and 38° rainy all day. Lucky ripped a 2 x 4 for me. Sylvia and I planed it into doorstops and installed them. Tom and Lisa visited and so did Dave.

Saturday, June 8, 1985—36° to 46°, rained until evening, then got sunny. Mixed saw bar oil and installed two door latches. Help Dave with his roof in the afternoon and saw bear tracks near his place.

Sunday, June 9, 1985—35° to 50°, partly cloudy. Tried twice to call Bridger Inc. in Utah. Cleared more trees from our view and piled wood and brush. Called Beverly and talked to Kevin too. Visited Tom and Lisa, and also Jim and Mary. I can hear the loons calling from off the lake and can see a moose cow and calf on the opposite side. Young camp robbers are already flying and swans cruise the lakes in pairs.

Monday, June 10, 1985—36° to 56°, sunny and some breeze. Wrote Bridger Inc. and the lawyer in Staples. Carried a cord of Aspen up the hill and loaded it onto the truck then unloaded it onto the woodpile. Hauled a load of brush to the dump.

Tuesday, June 11, 1985—40° to 48°, mostly cloudy and showers. Went to

10,000 Days in Alaska Book One 1978-1989

Anchorage and picked up Beverly at the airport. Showed her some sights as well as some sheep. She got to meet quite a few people around Nelchina; it's great to have her here with us.

Wednesday, June 12, 1985—36° to 41°, rainy all day, cloudy in the evening. Visited with Beverly in the morning. Dan Billman and family are at Crosswind Lake. Coffee with Dave and visited Hoffmans. They gave us some milk. Beverly got to see a young griz on our way home. In evening we went to Beaudoin's to watch movies.

Thursday, June 13, 1985—38° to 49°, partly cloudy and sunny. Went to Lake Louise, stopped at several places. Saw a cow moose and calf. Went to Bob Schmidt's for supper. Tom, Lisa and family and Camille and friend visited in the evening.

Friday, June 14, 1985—33° to 47°, partly cloudy and rain. Went to Valdez. It was nice there all day. Beverly took lots of nice pictures and we talked to a charter boat. It was a fine trip. We also picked some large flat rocks.

Saturday, June 15, 1985—33° to 47°, rainy and cloudy all day. Sorted some of my reloading gear and enjoyed Beverly's company. Rhynell brought milk and cream. Visited Henry and Sally—Dan Billman was there.

Sunday, June 16, 1985—33° to 46°, some rain, some sudden, so on Heavenly Ridge at Slide Mountain. Gunsight Mountain at Eureka had 1 1/2" of white. I put in some rock walk and steel on the outhouse roof. We visited Tom and Lisa and made phone calls from there. Later at Billman's we had a "pickin" party.

Monday, June 17, 1985—33° to 45°, cloudy, some light rain. Went to Glennallen and did laundry then on to Anchorage and met Nadia and Darrell at the plane. Stayed at the Mush Inn with them.

Tuesday, June 18, 1985—34° to 47°, partly cloudy and a few showers. P.D. lease at State office. Took Beverly to the airport, she was going home. While in Anchorage we did some shopping for the prospecting trip and Nadia and Darrell took us out for a nice supper. The trip home was good.

Norman Wilkins

Wednesday, June 19, 1985—63° to 52°, partly cloudy, light showers. Visited Dan, made two wrenches, fixed roof jack on old cabin and started getting gear ready for the prospecting trip. Saw seven swans on the lake in the evening.

Thursday, June 20, 1985—40° to 52°, sunny with rain in evening. Went back and forth to Dan's and finish packing for the trip. Covered Tom's driveway culvert.

Friday, June 21, 1985—weather was fair, went to Dan's and loaded gear into the Beaver and flew over Tazlina Glacier to the Shoup glacier and down it. That area is still buried in snow!! We saw the hopper of an old mill at a mine sticking out of the snow. Landed at an ore loading site of another mine on Shoup Bay. Then flew over Anderson glacier and the Columbia Glacier at 10,000 feet, down Tazlina Glacier, looked at quartz outcrop and landed on Tazlina Lake. Offloaded our gear and Nadia and Dan flew home. Darrell and I packed our gear (4 packs) 2 miles on the way to the outcrop and camped on the side of the mountain. Light rain in the afternoon; saw a few bear tracks, lots of sheep ewes and lambs in the area. Supper, then sleep.

Saturday, June 22, 1985—beautiful day along Tazlina Glacier. The sheep move out on flats of moraine to feed. (Moraine refers to glacially formed accumulations of debris.) We drill gas, etc. up glacier edge, until we can see that we wouldn't get to quartz in the time we had allowed. Tough going. Saw bear track and dung. Back to camp at 10:00 p.m. the sheep were going back up on the mountain to bed down. Beautiful sunset. We are footsore and tired.

Sunday, June 23, 1985—warm, partly cloudy morning. Sheep are going by on both sides of us. One ewe and lamb came on along the trail to within 30 feet of our tent. Darrell got pictures. The plane flew over. We walked up the mountain looking for quartz—nothing. Good view. Then we made two trips packing camp to Tazlina Lake. Partly cloudy and windy afternoon. Set up camp in trees. Saw nice bear track in mud and fox and moose sign. 60 sheep were on the flats. Feet are sore tonight, had a campfire on the beach.

Monday, June 24, 1985—partly cloudy, warmer, breezy. Got a good night's sleep and we're rested today. Camp robbers and squirrel in camp. A raven and also two planes flew over. Saw one small bear track and moose and fox track on the beach. We walked a ways down each beach. Darrell overhauled the camp stove. We miss seeing the sheep. Moved camp a few yards.

Tuesday, June 25, 1985—rain all night and day. Loafed and tended the fire. Another plane and raven flew over. Dan Billman flew us out in the evening. I got started drying out the gear. Nadia has gone back to Minneapolis.

Wednesday, June 26, 1985—37° to 47°, rain all night, lots of rain all day. Went to Glennallen, P.O. check on money order. Organized dredging gear. Theresa called, couldn't reach her back. Called Social Security office about Sylvia's number. Saw a beaver in our lake. Beautiful sunset, fairly heavy showers in the evening.

Thursday, June 27, 1985—39° to 62°, partly cloudy then sunny. Loaded the dredge and gear and went to Dan Billman's. He helped get everything to the site on Cache Creek. We'd dredged until just before supper. Then Darrell, Tom, and I went to Dinty Bush's. Warren gave us a boat. Tom will repair it for our lake. Saw a cow moose and calf and one beaver.

Friday, June 28, 1985—46° to 70°, sunny and hot. Darrell and I went to Cache Creek and dredged all day. Prospects look good. We had an ice cream social at Tom and Lisa's in the evening. Theresa and Earl and family are coming up July 9th of this year.

Saturday, June 29, 1985—48° to 72°, sunny and hot. Darrell and I dredged again today. We are both real tired tonight. Started cleaning up some of the black sand.

Sunday, June 30, 1985—52° to 70° and sunny. Rested all day. BBQ at Jim and Mary's.

Monday, July 1, 1985—53° to 64°, mostly sunny. Dredged all day at Cache Creek, packed the dredge and gear to the road and panned the concentrate.

Tuesday, July 2, 1985—55° to 68°, mostly sunny. Foggy on Thompson Pass on the way to Valdez. Searched old mining claim records, came home and got gear together. Dan flew us to Crosswind Lake (where he has a fly-in, remote cabin). Didn't get any fish this evening.

Wednesday, July 3, 1985—Dan caught a 14 pound, 31 inch lake trout and one small one. Darrell caught one nice lake trout. I had a good one on and lost him. Darrell cooked for us and baked some excellent trout. Dan and Jason flew in late. We fished late, no luck. It's really nice here.

Thursday, July 4, 1985—Dan, Jason, Darrell and I slept late, cleaned up the cabin and flew out to Snowshoe Lake where Dan lives. Later we went to a BBQ and potluck with music and fireworks at Nelchina Lodge.

Friday, July 5, 1985—Darrell and I worked on the swamp buggy and went to Glennallen for parts. We can't get it started.

Saturday, July 6, 1985—50° to 72°, sunny and a beautiful day. Sylvia went to Palmer with Sally. We worked on the swamp buggy but it will not run. Went to Alfred Creek trailhead to see Wimpy Lucas—he didn't show up. Helped Bill and Henry for a while.

Sunday, July 7, 1985—50° to 70°, Sunny, partly cloudy, light rain. Worked on the swamp buggy and Darrell packed up to go home.

Monday, July 8, 1985—50° to 60°, some rain, some sun. Took Darrell to the airport and did shopping in Anchorage. Went to the Social Security office, long day. Theresa, Earl, Darcy and Lee, and Earl's parents, Don and Evelyn arrived from Minnesota. (They drove up the Alaska Highway to get here.)

Tuesday, July 9, 1985—mostly sunny, some light rain. Worked on swamp buggy, then went over to the lodge. Chuck Zimbiki is sawing logs for Henry and Sally.

Wednesday July 10, 1985—partly cloudy and warm. Hurried around and packed gear. Dan Billman flew all of us into Crosswind Lake. Earl, Don and I each caught a small lake trout. Some wind and waves on the lake and it rained in the night.

10,000 Days in Alaska Book One 1978-1989

Thursday, July 11, 1985—70°, and a gentle breeze and sunny in the morning. Theresa, Earl, Evelyn and I didn't catch a fish. We were ready at 2:00 p.m. to leave. Dan flew Earl, Theresa, the kids and I over Klutina ice field and Tazlina country. Saw quartz, goats, sheep, moose (one nice bull), and beaver houses. Lots of salmon on Klutina Lake. Rain in the evening and night.

Friday, July 12, 1985—44° to 56° with rain showers in the morning. Theresa, Earl, Don and Evelyn went to Palmer. Darcy and Lee stayed here with us.

Saturday, July 13, 1985—43° to 56°, mostly rain all day. Cut up some wood for the basement. Helped Chuck Zimbiki saw logs for Henry and Sally. Theresa and Earl and his folks came back from Palmer. Henry helped me try to start the swamp buggy, but no go.

Sunday, July 14, 1985—48° to 64°, sunny and warm. Bill and Henry got the swamp buggy running. We got it geared up and drove it to trailhead and met Wimpy Lucas. Beautiful evening.

Monday, July 15, 1985—warm and sunny. Pulled a load of freight to upper airstrip on Alfred Creek for Dick and Fred. Top-heavy trailer upset on the way. Dick's Willy Jeep has ignition troubles. Got back out to trailhead about 2 or 3:00 a.m. Got four hours sleep.

Tuesday, July 16, 1985—warm and sunny. Theresa, and Don rode with me in the swamp buggy and Earl drove a 3-wheel Honda. Bill Birch built a trail with a D8. I pulled two rollogons of fuel. (Rollogons are used in northern Alaska for transport of materials to and from oil and mine sites. They are also designed to minimize the impact they have on the environment while traversing the tundra with heavy loads.) Henry pulled a large trailer and welder with JD 450. We got to their camp late—quite a trip in. Lance and Dick had flown in earlier they planned to dredge.

Wednesday, July 17, 1985—warm and sunny. Got the fuel unloaded about noon. Picked up Wimpy's trailer at the airstrip, and a wheel fell off of it after a mile or so. Took Dick and Fred out to trailhead. Some Arizona people want me to freight gas for them. They are prospecting upper Alfred Creek.

Thursday, July 18, 1985—warm and sunny. Got geared up and went to Valdez to fish salmon. Visited Chad, Trish, P.C. and Frank Wilson. Stayed at a motel, thanks to Don and Evelyn.

Friday, July 19, 1985—warm and sunny in Valdez. Wilson's and the eight of us went to Pipeline Road. They got 17 humpy salmon. Got home and Rudbecks were here. Dan, Lee, Jim, Sally and her mom, Bud and Chris visited in evening.

Saturday, July 20, 1985—rained all day, 60°. Theresa and family left after breakfast. Leonard and Jerry Berge spent the morning visiting. Dave DeJung brought tools back.

Sunday, July 21, 1985—rainy afternoon. Bud, Sally's stepfather, went with me to haul gas for the Arizonians (Jim, Jim, Bill and Steve) then on down to Wimpy's on Alfred Creek. Saw a cross fox with a limp. She had four pups with her.

Monday, July 22, 1985—40° to 60° and cloudy. Bud and I watched Henry and Bill mine gold for a while. Then we took our time coming out to trailhead. Went to KROA in evening.

Tuesday, July 23, 1985—37° to 58° and mostly sunny. Worked on the swamp buggy near Tahneta. Got diesel fuel.

Wednesday, July 24, 1985—39° to 54°, mostly cloudy with sprinkles. Loaded gravel for Bob Rudbeck in the morning. The pony motor on the Cat didn't want to start in the afternoon.

Thursday, July 25, 1985—mostly sunny, like showers. Worked on digging a basement for the Rudbecks. Left steering clutch on the Cat is slipping. Sylvia's garden is doing great; we are eating out of it.

Friday, July 26, 1985—48° into the 60s, sunny and partly cloudy. Finished digging basement for the Rudbecks. Adjusted steering clutches, and called Kevin about the farm.

Saturday, July 27, 1985—46° to 68° and sunny. Went to upper airstrip on Alfred Creek and brought Fred and Ginny and their gear out to Tahneta with the swamp buggy.

Sunday, July 28, 1985—48° to 74°, mostly sunny. Serviced the Cat. Built road for Tom Smayda and had supper there. Visited Lucky's.

Monday, July 29, 1985—46° to 70°, sunny, with three rain showers. We ran the footing for Bob Rudbeck's basement. Drove the Cat around through Allen's place and pushed out stumps and tore up the tundra on our lower garden spot. Bob and Kahren treated us to pizza at KROA. Lots of friends were there.

Tuesday, July 30, 1985—partly cloudy today. Went to Anchorage to the Social Security office and did some shopping for ourselves and some for Clem and Jean.

Wednesday, July 31, 1985—44° to 60°, rained until mid afternoon. Pulled and stacked roots and stumps from the garden area. Allen and Dave, and later, Lisa Smayda and her daughters were here for supper.

Thursday, August 1, 1985—44° to 60°, partly cloudy and sunny. Pulled roots and leveled more of the garden area. Planned beaching gear for Dan's Beaver. Gave him four, 55-gallon drums for his dock. The Beaver has ignition problems, tried to help with that. I'm not a mechanic, just do as I am told.

Friday, August 2, 1985—46° to 48°, cloudy and rainy. Tried again to help Dan get the Beaver started, no luck.

Saturday, August 3, 1985—43° to 46°, rainy all day. They started drilling a well on Lucky's place. Rested all day. Jim Odden had supper with us. The moon was beautiful on the lake at midnight.

Sunday, August 4, 1985—38° to 66°, foggy morning and sunny the rest of the day. Ran cement for Rudbeck's basement floor. Adjusted brake on pickup.

Monday, August 5, 1985—46° to 60°, partly cloudy with showers in the evening. Loaded fill dirt for our garage at Bob Rudbeck's. Leveled the pad for our garage and built the forms. Started getting everything ready to pour cement tomorrow.

Norman Wilkins

Tuesday, August 6, 1985—34° to 70°, foggy early and sunny the rest of the day. Lucky, Allen, Bob, Chris and I ran cement for garage floor—turned out nice. We loaded fill for Allen and the Ronnings and hauled one load of gravel for Jim and Mary. Beaut of an evening.

Wednesday, August 7, 1985—36° into the 50s, partly cloudy and windy. Put cement sealer on garage slab. Dredged for gold at the gravel pit. Helped Bob and Kahren for a while, then went to Dan and Patti Billman's to watch the movie, "Mother Lode".

Thursday, August 8, 1985—44° to 55°, partly cloudy then rain in evening. Geared up for the trip to Alfred Creek. Someone tried to jump the swamp buggy, burned up points/wiring. Got that fixed. Finished fuel filter on the buggy. Started on pintle hitch adapter.

Friday, August 9, 1985—30° to 50° and mostly sunny. Saw quite a few caribou and a flock of ptarmigan. Lost tools out of the back of the swamp buggy on the way to Alfred Creek, had to backtrack to get them. Visited with all the miners along Alfred Creek and camped at Wimpy's fuel dump. Saw three rams on the way in. Light sprinkle in evening.

Saturday, August 10, 1985—partly cloudy, windy until evening. Looked for sheep, saw a few caribou. Prospected Mouse Creek, found some color on bedrock.

Sunday, August 11, 1985—mostly cloudy, a light rain in evening. Staked two Mouse Creek claims. Climbed the mountain north of Mouse Creek. (Bill tells me there are geodes there). No sheep. Saw one large and two smaller caribou bulls and looked down on three eagles hunting. Found a mineral lick near a saddle at the top. (A saddle is a cleft in the mountain, the lowest point in a ridge.) Saw a mining camp up Flume Creek a couple of miles. Viewing from the mountaintop was worth the climb. Light rain in the evening. I decided to drive out to the road—got home at 10:00 p.m. Andy is staying at our house while he is putting in urethane insulation for some other people around here.

Monday, August 12, 1985—39°, light rain early and partly cloudy. Formed apron for garage footings and for the arctic entrance and porch of the house. Visited Lucky and Mary. Tried to call Jim Rudbeck.

10,000 Days in Alaska Book One 1978-1989

Tuesday, August 13, 1985—44° to 56°, light rain, partly cloudy in the evening. Ran cement for apron and footings. Lots of company for supper.

Wednesday, August 14, 1985—34° to 60°, partly cloudy, light shower then sunny. Worked on front idler yoke on the Cat all day. Called Jim Rudbeck in the evening.

Thursday, August 15, 1985—38° into the 50s and partly cloudy. Took one link out of the right side of the Cat track. Removed belt pulley and put on counterweight. Charlie Trowbridge and three friends visited us. Later we visited Oddens. David D. saw a black bear on our lake.

Friday, August 16, 1985—38° to 50°, cloudy, hard shower. Cut up some wood and tried to fix chainsaw bar oiler. Bob Rudbeck and I cut a large culvert in two.

Saturday, August 17, 1985—37° into the 50s, mostly sunny. Lucky tried to dig our culvert in for a well—too much frost. We did get Rudbeck's culvert dug in with a backhoe. Hauled a culvert home to Lucky. Went to a party for Charlie and Beth at Smayda's.

Sunday, August 18, 1985—39° to 60°, partly cloudy. Tried to dredge out gravel from Bob's well. No luck. Helped Lucky put in his culvert well. Bob Rudbeck took me flying. Flew over the trap cabin—it looks okay! Saw 11 cow moose, no calves. Did some chores around home.

Monday, August 19, 1985—38° to 58°, partly cloudy in the morning, sunny in the afternoon. Tried to find Cat parts all morning. Put CWF on gable end of house in afternoon. Call Jim Rudbeck in the evening about our farm.

Tuesday, August 20, 1985—37° to 54° and cloudy all day. Bob and Kahren went to Anchorage so I rode to Tahneta with them and drove the swamp buggy home. Later, went to Jim and Mary's. Lester and Lois are going with John to Fairbanks tomorrow.

Wednesday August 21, 1985—38° to 48°, cloudy all day, rain late afternoon. Worked with Allen at Hoffman's place putting footings and posts in for the deck on the apartment they are adding. Our renter called, and I went over to lucky in Mary's to call Kevin about the farm. We all visited a while. Rhynell is building the apartment which will be on top of a log garage.

Thursday, August 22, 1985–36° to 47°, cloudy and rainy all day. Allen gave me a moose horn button. Sliced it, started polishing it. Helped Allen with an outhouse for Henry.

Friday, August 23, 1985–38° to 50°, cloudy, sunny, light rain. Put up one beam, one plate, and the stairs at Hoffman's apartment.

Saturday, August 24, 1985–36° to 60°, sunny all day. Built a boom to go on the Cat bucket to lift logs on Rudbeck's house. Went to Billman's and Hoffman's.

Sunday, August 25, 1985–35° to 55°, cloudy in the morning and sunny in the afternoon. Went to Billman's, took tires to Clem to mount on rims and helped run a little cement at Lucky's—had supper there.

Monday, August 26, 1985–38° to 58° and sunny all day. Allen and I went to Rhynell's and put up the rest of the joists for the deck, one beam, and six posts.

Tuesday, August 27, 1985–29° to 56° and sunny. Sylvia answered Billman's phone (took calls from their flying clients). Allen and I put up a lot of decking at Hoffman's place.

Wednesday, August 28, 1985–28° to 60°, sunny. Finished decking on the south side and the east side at Hoffman's. My back is really hurting these days.

Thursday, August 29, 1985–29° to 50°, cloudy most of the day. Welded up the beaching gear for Dan's Beaver and took it to him. Called Al Eckes and got the name of the hospital.

Friday, August 30, 1985–38° to 48°, mostly cloudy, light showers. Allen and I finished up the deck at Rhynell's. Put the repair parts on Cat in the evening.

Saturday, August 31, 1985–35° to 51° and mostly cloudy. Framed up the south wall for Rhynell's house. Allen went moose hunting and Sylvia helped me at Rhynell's.

Sunday, September 1, 1985—44° to 56°, rainy cloudy morning, sunny afternoon. Dug a hole with my Cat in the bank at Tom and Lisa's for their well house.

Monday, September 2, 1985—36° to 55° and sunny. Allen and I finished the north wall and several people came and helped stand the two long walls up.

Tuesday, September 3, 1985—34° to 50°, mostly cloudy, windy, rain at dark. Put dirt in dozer blade for the loading dock. Went to Rhynell's to check the walls because it was quite windy.

Wednesday, September 4, 1985—early rain shower. Put up the east wall.

Thursday, September 5, 1985—30° to 52° and sunny. We got the west wall up today. Did 1-1/2 hours of Cat work for Sally. Jim and Mary Odden visited in the evening. A flock of old squaw ducks was on our lake.

Friday, September 6 1985—26° to 52° and mostly cloudy. Cut parts for rafters at Rhynell's and moved gravel at Rudbeck's with the Cat. Hydraulic control arm broke. Called FHA in Brainerd Minnesota.

Saturday, September 7, 1985—30° to 56°, sunny beautiful day. Built 13 rafters at Rhynell's. Rebuilt control rods for the hydraulics on the Cat.

Sunday, September 8, 1985—46° to 56° and mostly cloudy. Built five more rafters and put them up. Hoffmans got their pump put in the well casing. Henry got his basement poured and Bob Rudbeck troweled it.

Monday, September 9, 1985—34° to 48°. Mostly cloudy, showers with hail. Hard rain last night. We got half the plywood and one row on the roof. Got storage tank, pump, pressure tank, and lights from Lucky and Mary.

Tuesday, September 10, 1985—33° to 46° some sun, some rain. Finished sheeting Rhynell's house. Put visqueen on windows. Loaded gravel at

Rudbeck's. Jim, Mary, and Greg visited. Packed gear for Sandhill Crane goose hunt.

Wednesday, September 11, 1985—34° to 48° and mostly sunny. Loaded gear in Odden's Blazer and went to Delta. Took care of some business for other people, sized up goose flights and got camp set up. No cranes.

Thursday, September 12, 1985—24° to 50° and sunny. Got permission to hunt. I got two speckled geese, Mary got one teal. Jim got one goose (two wounded) and one duck. Cranes were flying like crazy—couldn't sneak up on them.

Friday, September 13, 1985—26° to 56°, mostly sunny. Mary got a spruce hen. We didn't get under the geese or the cranes. Broke camp, lost two dogs for a while and came home.

Saturday, September 14, 1985—35° to 47°, several showers, some sun. Bob Rudbeck and I loaded and hauled 16 loads of fill and gravel. Built road to his culvert at spring. The Cat broke down. Henry and Sally and Bob and Kahren had supper here with us at our house.

Sunday, September 15, 1985—37° to 50°, partly cloudy and windy. We got the gravel in and around Bob's well and spread some gravel at our place. Piled black soil and Peat at Allen Farmer's. Saw a big, bull moose in Lucky's driveway. Henry helped me fix the Cat hydraulic drive.

Monday, September 16, 1985—28° to 40° and sunny. We loaded and hauled seven loads of black dirt for Lucky and four loads for me. From Allen's pile, three for him and one for Bob. Sylvia and I spread subsoil and quite a bit of one a load of dirt.

Tuesday, September 17, 1985—18° to 38° and sunny. Visited Billmans and Hoffmans in the morning and Sylvia spread more dirt at home. Pulled roots in the garden and hauled five Cat bucket loads of dirt to the garden—the pin came out on the track and I had trouble getting it back in. Had supper at Lucky and Mary's.

Wednesday, September 18, 1985—18° to 40°, sunny to cloudy. Finished hauling five more loads of dirt to lower garden. Did a little bulldozing work for Allen and Lucky. Allen and I went to moose hunting in the afternoon. Allen shot a nice bull close to dark. Got it gutted and we walked out in the dark.

Thursday, September 19, 1985—26° to 44° and cloudy. Allen and I went to moose kill—54 inch spread. We hunted for and hour, then Eddie Farmer and Bob Rollins showed up to help skin and quarter the moose (9 pieces). Hauled it to the road with the Ranger then the truck to Allen's and hung it in the garage. Allen gave me ribs from his half. I'm happy. Did yard work in the evening.

Friday, September 20, 1985—28° to 36° snow in the night, cloudy morning, and sunny afternoon. Allen, David, Dave and I went boo hunting on Lake Louise Road—nothing. Saw an eagle. Went to milepost 120 in the evening to hunt a small bull. Another excited hunter (pals were late) delayed us. Saw cow and calf, no small bull.

Saturday, September 21, 1985—14° to 34° and sunny. Put end soffits and trim on Rhynell's house. Borrowed Allen's road drag for our lane. Andy Boyle (the guy who insulated our house) and a friend came out from Anchorage. They brought us a fresh crab and a chair.

Sunday, September 22, 1985—27° to 37°, cloudy, snow and rain. Got tar paper and 25 sheets of steel along the north side at Rhynell's. Formed up a garage floor for Allen. Andy got stuck at Henry's—used swamp buggy to pull him out.

Monday, September 23, 1985—27° to 41°, foggy till noon, sunny afternoon. Poured Allen's garage floor in the morning. Got the rest of the steel on at Rhynell's in the afternoon. Covered Allen's concrete with plastic. Really tired and sore these days.

Tuesday, September 24, 1985—31° to 34°, foggy, rain, snow. Helped Rudbeck move his rafters. Raining at Rhynell's so didn't work on their house. Scattered five yards of dirt on our garden and visited Billmans.

Wednesday, September 25, 1985—28° to 34° and sunny. Put boom on Cat and unloaded Rudbeck's log's from the semi, then started putting them on the basement.

Thursday, September 26, 1985—24° 34° cloudy morning, sunny

afternoon. Got most of the logs on Bob's house. Rebuilt the boom on the Cat—long hard day. I'll be glad when it's done. Nearly a full moon tonight, just beautiful reflecting off the lake.

Friday, September 27, 1985—26° to 49°, a beautiful sunrise reflected in the lake. Partly cloudy, windy in the afternoon. Finished placing logs and I did two hours of dozer work for Henry. Didn't get much done on Bob's house. A tree almost went down on Sylvia's rabbit hutches.

Saturday, September 28, 1985—26° to 54° another pretty sunrise, warm and sunny. Slow getting started on Bob's rafters but got them up and sheeted today. They took everyone who helped to KROA for pizza. Still some ducks on the lake. Full moon tonight.

Sunday, September 29, 1985—28° to 46°, cloudy, windy, some sun. Got steel on Bob's roof. Moved Andy's house trailer and brought my fuel tank home. Moved big trailer out by the road and worked on the lane. Loaded furnace. Dan Billman and Patti and Jason helped. They stayed here for supper. The moonrise was beautiful.

Monday, September 30, 1985—44° to 48°, sunny and partly cloudy. Worked at Rhynell's. Allen and I got nine ducks here on our lake in the evening. He got two mallards, two scoters and I got five scoters.

Tuesday, October 1, 1985—30° to 32° and partly cloudy. Worked at Hoffman's. Got one duck in the morning and Allen and I got six ducks in the evening.

Wednesday, October 2, 1985—30° to 32°, snow in the morning, rain and cloudy all day. Worked at Rhynell's, then visited Lucky and Mary and paid them for pump tank and some other things.

Thursday, October 3, 1985—31° to 34° and mostly cloudy. We worked on Rhynell's house and finished the soffits. Put on more T-111 and trim. Poured cement pad for furnace. Swans are migrating.

Friday, October 4, 1985—24° to 35° and sunny. More work on Hoffman's house. We pulled Dan's Beaver out of the water using the beaching gear I built for him.

10,000 Days in Alaska Book One 1978-1989

Saturday, October 5, 1985—16° to 36° and sunny. Worked on the garden: cut, chopped, shook roots out of dirt, burned stumps and brush, spread three yards of dirt. Ducks are still on the lake—90% of it is already frozen over. The Northern Lights are spectacular with their reds and greens. Very tired tonight.

Sunday October 6, 1985—26° to 30° and cloudy. Finished cleaning the cut Aspen from our south slope and burned it. Welded three hitches on snowgo trailer and sleds. It's snowing just after dark.

Monday, October 7, 1985—24° to 33° and cloudy. Got 1 inch of snow. Rain in the morning and in the evening. Went to Anchorage shopping and to do business. Got bath and building supplies and was back home by 1:15 a.m.

Tuesday, October 8, 1985—26° to 40° and sunny. Worked seven hours at Hoffman's and later got two ducks (scoters) on our lake. Jim and Mary brought greenhouse material from Billman's and had supper with us.

Wednesday, October 9, 1985—24° to 34° and cloudy. Went to Jim and Mary's, but it's a bad morning to fly the trapline, so they helped us with our arctic entry—got one wall up. Dan helped too.

Thursday, October 10, 1985—22° to 36° and cloudy. Got the rest of the logs up and plate on our arctic entry. Allen helped. Cranes are flying and there are still a few ducks on our lake.

Friday, October 11, 1985—30° to 33° and cloudy. Allen helped us and we got the steel on the entry roof. We got the news that Beverly had a baby boy, his name is Tyler. Geese rested on the lake and we saw a coyote. Many geese and swans are flying down the valley. Jim and Mary left their dog, Nellie with us and went on vacation. Dan Billman left for Hawaii.

Saturday, October 12, 1985—17° to 34° and sunny. Put on fascia, soffit, screen, some flashing and of most of the gable ends for the arctic entry. Most of the lake is frozen. Some ducks haven't left yet. Called Beverly from Lucky's. Rhynell and Max were here with rabbit food, chainsaw parts and flashing.

Sunday, October 13, 1985–12° to 30° and sunny. Finished flashing trim, framed door and windows and put the rest of the siding on. Changed spark plugs and soldered radiator on truck. Dyed traps all day. Put away lumber for winter.

Monday, October 14, 1985–20 to 30° and sunny. Still dying traps. Worked at Rhynell's and worked on several jobs getting ready for winter.

Tuesday, October 15, 1985–16° to 30° and sunny. Finished deck and put in chimney and three windows at Hoffman's. Went to prospecting class (Leo Mark Anthony).

Wednesday, October 16, 1985–20° to 28°, cloudy with a light snow. Worked at Rhynell's. Darrel Gerry is back from his trip. We visited until 2:00 a.m. he borrowed my snowgo trailer, his broke down near Chistochina.

Thursday, October 17, 1985–24° to 28°, a light snow all day. Felt sick all day. We put up snowgo lean too on storage shed. The hill going down to Lucky's is very slick. Went and got water today.

Friday, October 18, 1985–20° to 24°, snow all day, six inches now. Put glass in the two windows of the arctic entry. Sylvia went to Anchorage with Rhynell. The starter on Rhynell's pickup quit so they will stay in town tonight.

Saturday, October 19, 1985–12° to 18° and cloudy all day. Hauled furnace from Lucky's to Rhynell's. Worked until 5:30, then loaded logs and took them to Allen's mill. Had supper at Allen's. Sylvia and Rhynell got back.

Sunday, October 20, 1985–cloudy and -7° to 6°. Helped Allen haul logs home and worked a while at Rhynell's. Put anti-freeze in Swamp buggy.

Monday, October 21, 1985–4° to 12° and cloudy with a dusting of snow. There has been a fox around our place, Allen shot at him when he was over there. Tried to call fox near Moosey Boo (a long time home in the area). Worked at Rhynell's.

Tuesday, October 22, 1985–8° to 10°, cloudy with a light snow. Worked at Hoffman's, then worked on setting up our waterworks at home in the evening.

Wednesday, October 23, 1985—4° to 14°, cloudy than sunny. Hung the door, vapor barrier and did some other things at Rhynell's. Went to a course on prospecting at Glennallen.

Thursday, October 24, 1985—mostly cloudy, snow in the evening and -14° to 4°. Helped Allen saw logs. Eddie helped us. Hauled two loads of water to our place and hauled another load of logs for Allen.

Friday, October 25, 1985—cloudy and light snow, -13° to 4°. Worked at Rhynell's. Killed two rabbits.

Saturday, October 26, 1985—cloudy with a light ice fog, -9° to 8°. Worked at Rhynell's again today. Allen didn't work today. Lucky and Mary were here for supper. Did some waterworks and plumbing planning.

Sunday, October 27, 1985—sunny and -13° to -2°. Worked at Rhynell's and got lots done. Allen took the day off. Beautiful full moon.

Monday, October 28, 1985—sunny and -10° to 2°. Went to Anchorage and did business and shopping. Stopped at Andy and Connie's and went to their neighbor who gave us a davenport and chair.

Tuesday, October 29, 1985—sunny and -16° to 6°. Worked at Rhynell's, then went to prospecting class in Glennallen. While I was on my way home from the class, I saw a meteor burning up as it entered the atmosphere.

Wednesday, October 30, 1985—sunny and -12° to 4°. Worked at Rhynell's. Ordered 2-750W eliminators/Lanegan's. Cut up some wood at home.

Thursday, October 31, 1985—sunny, and again it's -12° to 4°. Worked at Rhynell's. Sylvia and I have some kind of flu. Some of the neighborhood kids came trick or treating. I ordered some long johns and mailed claim location notices. Sent Earl his cap.

Norman Wilkins

Friday, November 1, 1985—sunny and -14° to 0°. Worked at Rhynell's, then cut up more wood at home. Boiled oil out of trap chain and sharpened chain on the chain saw. Visited Henry and Sally.

Saturday, November 2, 1985—mostly cloudy, -8° to 4°. Cut and stacked wood in shed and put small load of wood in basement. Went to Lake Louise Junction to get propane. Visited at KROA.

Sunday, November 3, 1985—sunny, -12° to 6°. Put 1 1/2 loads of wood in the basement and stacked more wood at the shed. lost gas cap. Did a few other odd jobs and visited Allen and Lucky. Lisa and the girls visited here.

Monday, November 4, 1985—cloudy, ice fog, -8° to -10°. Worked on trap gear and other odd jobs. Allen came over and visited.

Tuesday, November 5, 1985—it was -8° all day and mostly cloudy with ice fog again. Worked at getting in wood for Hoffmans and started gluing chair.

Wednesday, November 6, 1985—it was -14° to -4° and sunny all day at our place, but at Hoffman's they had lots of ice fog. We got more wood cut and stacked. Tanning supplies came.

Thursday, November 7, 1985—ice fog early then sunny with some light breeze. -22° to -6°. Allen and I cut more wood at Hoffman's. Called Andy about Sears tool sale.

Friday, November 8, 1985—it's -22° to -6° and sunny. Went to Hoffman's late and helped more with getting up wood. Sylvia started cutting up moose front quarter that Allen brought over.

Saturday, November 9, 1985—cloudy and -12° to 2°. Went to Allen's, didn't have all the fittings to put pump in the spring well. Worked on getting trapping gear ready.

Sunday, November 10, 1985—6° to 12°, cloudy, starting to snow tonight. Set a few traps on Eleven-Mile Trail today and Hoffmans visited. We went to see Lucky and Mary. I can't find my block and tackle to help Lucky pull the pipe from his well.

10,000 Days in Alaska Book One 1978-1989

Monday, November 11, 1985—18° to 22° and sunny. Helped Lucky try to pull the pipe from his well. It was frozen at 90 feet. Cut up more wood and put it in our basement and stacked more at the woodshed.

Tuesday, November 12, 1985—6° to 18° and cloudy. Boo on Lake. Did some wiring at home. Lucky had 70 feet of ice in his well. Clem thawed it and we had the pipe pulled and back in by 2:00 a.m. in the morning.

Wednesday, November 13, 1985—it's -10° to -6° and sunny. Tom and girls visited. Made some sets on Slide Mountain and stopped at Henry's and also Lucky's on the way home.

Thursday, November 14, 1985—it's -18° to -6° and sunny got my trap gear ready and tried to grease the truck at Nelchina. The chimney cleaner came, but the chimney is too dirty to use it—must punch out creosote.

Friday, November 15, 1985—down to -22° to -10° and sunny. Worked on chimney again, still has creosote in it. Did more wiring and mounted fire extinguisher. Made phone calls from Tom's. Henry, Sally and Chris visited in the evening.

Saturday, November 16, 1985—colder, -24° to -6°, sunny, then cloudy. Finished cleaning the chimney. Picked up five Helfrich 750w traps. Got buffalo hide from Ray—he'll mount it for $100.00. Welded swivels at Lucky's.

Sunday, November 17, 1985—today it's -12° to -2° and sunny. Ran the lined on Slide Mountain—nothing. Made some new sets and adjusted skis on snowgo. Went to KROA for supper.

Monday, November 18, 1985—sunny and -14° to -2°. Didn't feel good this morning. Got trap gear ready. Finished dying wolf traps. Put different radiator in truck. Cut and stacked more wood. Hoffmans and Dave Kimball were here on errands.

Tuesday, November 19, 1985—it's -12° to -2° and sunny. Lots of boo on Lake Louise Road. Parked at Warren and Leona's. Had a red fox in the first set checked, nothing else. Trail is very rough (five inches of snow). Brought everything out of the cache. Put in a new pipe and stove, clean snow off the roof and banked snow around cabin. Outhouse was leaning badly. A bear has been here, he pulled off the T-shirt I had nailed to the door. (It was well-worn and unwashed, put up for man-scent to repel bears.) No damage to the cabin.

Wednesday, November 20, 1985—it's -16° to -6° and sunny did a few things here, loafed a lot.

Thursday, November 21, 1985—sunny and -12° to 0°. Lots of trouble trying to pull sled in this rough country. Made two wolf sets and fox and marten sets. Saw lynx, wolf, fox and marten tracks. Lots of boo around. Stopped at Hoffman's and Jack and Jane's on the way home.

Friday, November 22, 1985—sunny and -10° to 2°. Worked at Rhynell's and cut and stacked wood at home. Joe and Peg Virgin stopped in with my medicine on the way home. Put hinges and doors on some kitchen cupboards.

Saturday, November 23, 1985—sunny and -14° to -2°. Started work on the ceiling at Hoffman's. Put on a few more cupboard doors at home.

Sunday, November 24, 1985—sunny and -10° to -2°. Worked at Rhynell's again and put more cupboard doors on here at home.

Monday, November 25, 1985—it's -8° to 0° and sunny. Ran the trapline on Slide Mountain—nothing. Made one new set. Worked at Rhynell's in the afternoon. Got truck ready in the evening. Ground points on fox drags.

Tuesday, November 26, 1985—it's -10° to 4° and cloudy. We went to Anchorage for tools, supplies, building material, repairs and groceries. Very windy, 50 to 70 mile an hour gusts.

Wednesday, November 27, 1985—cold continues, -13° to 6°, cloudy and frosty. Worked at Rhynell's and later on the cupboard doors at home.

Thursday, November 28, 1985—it's -10° to -4°, cloudy and ice fog. Unloaded lumber. Worked on sled. Went to Tom and Lisa's for Thanksgiving—had a fine dinner. Max and Rhynell were there too. Did little electrical work at home in evening.

10,000 Days in Alaska Book One 1978-1989

Friday, November 29, 1985—it's -8° to 8°, cloudy and ice fog. Didn't feel well so didn't go out on the trapline. Worked on trap gear in the morning and made one set at the dump. Cleaned our chimney and visited Henry and Sally in the afternoon. Ordered some things from Dennis Kirk catalog.

Saturday, November 30, 1985—it's -14° to -10° and cloudy with patchy ice fog. Saw three bull moose, some cows and some caribou along Lake Louise Road. Saw one set of new fox tracks and some marten tracks on the way in to the trap cabin. Boo had sprung one wolf trap.

Sunday, December 1, 1985—colder again, -25° to -15°, cloudy. Sorted traps and split wood. Trail too rough and too cold to set traps. Read a lot.

Monday, December 2, 1985—today it's -10°, partly cloudy and colder down in the flats. Eight boo walked up to the cabin in early morning while I was outside. Made two sets east of Blue Lake (overflow). Had one marten on the west ridge. Nothing in traps on the way out. Made a few new sets.

Tuesday December 3, 1985—it's -22° to -20° and cloudy. Nothing in the set at the dump. Put on more ceiling at Rhynell's. Sally and Henry visited in the evening. Skinned and stretched marten.

Wednesday, December 4, 1985—temp dropped to -26° to -6° and partly cloudy. Worked until mid afternoon at Rhynell's. Didn't get around to hauling water again today.

Thursday, December 5, 1985—mostly cloudy and -5° to -10°. Ran Slide Mountain, got a nice marten. Started tanning pelts. Henry came over so we hauled two loads of water each. Skinned and stretched marten until late.

Friday, December 6, 1985—mostly cloudy and -10° to -4°. One boo killed—other small groups crossing highway. Worked at Rhynell's and then on fur and tanning in evening.

Saturday, December 7, 1985—it's -20° to 10° and sunny. More boo on the road. Worked again at Hoffman's. Checked sets at dumps—nothing.

Sunday, December 8, 1985—it's -10° to 4°, cloudy with a very light snow in the evening. Worked for Rhynell. A cow moose crossed the road near Sam's. Took two marten off boards in the evening. Sylvia is working with her rabbit pelts.

Monday, December 9, 1985—warmer, 45° to 16° and mostly cloudy. Worked at Rhynell's and later tanning pelts.

Tuesday, December 10, 1985—25° to 40°, cloudy and windy. Ran trapline on Slide Mountain. No fur, only camp robber and squirrel. Had to remake all sets. One wolf track on upper trail.

Wednesday, December 11, 1985—put a small load of wood in the basement and killed seven rabbits. We work at tanning the pelts. Tom, Lisa and the girls visited.

Thursday, December 12, 1985—20° to 14°, partly cloudy. Tried to go to the trap cabin but too much overflow on lakes. Came home. Had a blowout on one of the trailer tires. Clock movements came (for clocks Sylvia and I are making). Still tanning pelts.

Friday, December 13, 1985—10° all day, cloudy and foggy. Went to Palmer to get supplies to make clocks and for sewing skins. Lost muffler and blew heater hose. It was sunny in Palmer.

Saturday, December 14, 1985—4° to 6° and cloudy all day. Slept late. Allen Farmer and family visited. Put new muffler on truck. Clem fixed two tires for snowgo trailer. Worked with pelts and made a rat stretcher. Split and put a small load of wood in the basement.

Sunday, December 15, 1985—6° to 0°, partly cloudy. Parked at Eleven-Mile. Found I had an eagle caught by one toe in a trap. Threw a coat over it and released it. It wasn't injured. Had a marten in one trap at the north end of Blue Lake. Saw lots of boo. Remade many sets. Skinned marten out through the mouth.

Monday, December 16, 1985—9° all day and cloudy. Made a few sets on the west and south slope but didn't finish. Trail is very rough, much overflow on the trail east of Blue Lake.

Tuesday, December 17, 1985—10° to 0° in partly cloudy. Left trap cabin early and went to Jaw Lake making sets, then out to the road. Someone is using my marten boxes. One marten at my box—their trap.

Wednesday, December 18, 1985—6° to 10°, cloudy and some snow. Worked at Rhynell's and visited Allen's. Fleshed a beaver pelt.

Thursday, December 19, 1985—20° to 34°, cloudy and some breeze and rain. Allen and I worked at Rhynell's. Got heater motor going in the pickup. Helped Allen install pump in his well. Sylvia started sewing a fox fur cap. We had shaggy mane mushrooms Sylvia had raised.

Friday, December 20, 1985—28° to 30°, cloudy and foggy. Worked at Rhynell's. Didn't feel well in the afternoon. Cleaned pitch out of three pelts. Sylvia is still sewing on the fox fur cap.

Saturday, December 21, 1985—20° to 35° and cloudy. Allen and I worked at Rhynell's. Nadia and Darrell sent VCR tapes with movies on them. Stretched one marten and Sylvia finished Allen's fox fur cap. Jim and Mary Odden returned home tonight.

Sunday, December 22, 1985—20° to 32° and cloudy (at the trap cabin). Parked at Eleven-Mile trail, no fur in sets. One camp robber. One bull boo calf in wolf trap. He was small, easy to release. Three fox had worked frozen sets.

Monday, December 23, 1985—at trap cabin it is 22° to 35°, windy, cloudy, rain, and snow. Nothing in sets. Fresh wolf tracks. One cow moose, fewer boo. Whoever had started trapping on Twelve-Mile Trail has pulled his traps. Four inches of wet snow here.

Tuesday, December 24, 1985—rained all night and snow, then rain in the early morning and cloudy later. Called Nadia and Theresa. Visited Allen and then Mary Beaudoin and later Henry and Sally. Clean snow from several roofs. Skinned marten and carried fur tumbler into the basement. John, Jim and Mary Odden visited. Went to KROA for supper. Visited lots of neighbors.

Norman Wilkins

Wednesday, December 25, 1985—8° all day and cloudy. Allen Farmer plowed our driveway. We visited Hoffmans on the way to KROA for Christmas dinner. Had a good time, gave Charlie Netter a jump to start his pickup.

Thursday, December 26, 1985—8° to 15° and mostly cloudy. Allen and I worked at Rhynell's. Back aches tonight.

Friday, December 27, 1985—8° to 20° and mostly cloudy. Spent the day working at Rhynell's.

Saturday, December 28, 1985—18° to 24°, partly cloudy and a light snow early. Worked at Hoffman's. Moon is almost full.

Sunday, December 29, 1985—10° to 20° and mostly cloudy. Ran trapline on Slide Mountain. Most sets frozen with marten tracks over them. Did get one marten in cubby set. Visited Lucky and Mary in the evening.

Monday, December 30, 1985—6° to 10°, cloudy, frosty, patchy fog. Worked until noon at Rhynell's. Allen had chest pains—I went with him to Glennallen Hospital. He's back this evening.

Tuesday, December 31, 1985—9° to 14° and cloudy. Allen and I didn't work at Rhynell's today. I wired two outlets in the living room and converted the clothes dryer into a fur tumbler. The VCR Nadia and the rest of the kids sent arrived today. Went to New Year's celebration at Nelchina Lodge.

Neighbors, Kahren and Bob Rudbeck

10,000 Days in Alaska Book One 1978-1989

Norman gears up for a hunting trip.

Norman Wilkins

1986—exploring old mines, staking claims at Nelchina

Wednesday, January 1, 1986—it's -4° to 2°, cloudy and some sun. Worked at Rhynell's. Got one rat on our lake and skinned him.

Thursday, January 2, 1986—0° to 8°, snow all day, four to five inches. Worked at Rhynell's.

Friday, January 3, 1986—10° to 26° and snowing today, eight inches total. Some breeze in evening. Lucky plowed our lane and I worked on Rhynell's house and shoveled a little snow at home. Electricity was off in evening.

Saturday, January 4, 1986—24° to 28°, cloudy. Worked at Rhynell's. Allen Farmer was here for supper. Borrowed Rhynell's VCR connector to hook up the VCR we got from the kids. Watched some movies.

Sunday, January 5, 1986—8° to 15° and mostly sunny. Went to see Chuck Zimbiki. He sliced some birch into Clock slabs for me. Ran Slide Mountain trapline, but got nothing.

Monday, January 6, 1986—10° to -6° and mostly sunny. Bull boos on the lake this morning. Got ready to go to the trapline and visited Dave K. Had supper with Oddens and did some work for our crafts.

Tuesday, January 7, 1986—0° all day and sunny. Parked at Warren's, talked to Phil. Got a silver fox with red tinge on fur. Someone had shot it in the trap. Trap cabin is fine. Snowgo suspension broke. Wired up the spring and continued on. Skinned the fox. Marten had eaten a camper robber out of conibear.

Wednesday, January 8, 1986—0° to -4°, mostly sunny. Dinged up the suspension and got gear ready to leave tomorrow. Did chores around the cabin. Nice and peaceful here.

Thursday, January 9, 1986—it's -5° to 5°, sunny and breezy. Got one marten and one ermine. Made two wolf sets and two fox sets. Saw a mother lynx with two young ones east of Judd Lake. Fewer caribou now. Visited at Farmer's. Tom came over to get things stored here.

10,000 Days in Alaska Book One 1978-1989

Friday, January 10, 1986—mostly cloudy, -12° to 0°. Worked at Rhynell's. Fish and Game left a front quarter of a road kill moose for us (they do this for seniors around here).

Saturday, January 11, 1986—it's -6° to 9°. Cloudy and light snow in evening. Allen and I put glass in the last picture window at Hoffman's.

Sunday, January 12, 1986—mostly sunny and -6° to 6°. Ran Slide Mountain trapline. Several marten tracks, got one. Pulled a slide suspension out of snowgo—broken welds in two places. I welded them up. Skinned and stretched one marten and one ermine.

Monday, January 13, 1986—10° to 8° and mostly cloudy. Worked at Rhynell's trimming out windows. I skinned out and stretched a marten. Dave Kimbel visited.

Tuesday, January 14, 1986—11° to 60°, cloudy and some ice fog. Worked at Rhynell's doing more finish work. Turned marten pelt on board in evening. Sore back tonight. Lee D. and Jim and Mary Odden visited.

Wednesday, January 15, 1986—2° to 10° and sunny. Put slide suspension back under snowgo. Ran Slide Mountain trapline and got another marten, a small one. Hauled water for the house. Borrowed Allen's meat grinder. Jim and Mary stopped in to bring us some of Mary's home made, fresh bread, Jim gave me some lynx scent.

Thursday, January 16, 1986— sunny and -8° to 0°. Parked at Warren's and ran the Judd Lake loop. Made two new sets. Saw some wolf tracks and got a mink near the trap cabin. Tired tonight. Skinned out the mink.

Friday, January 17, 1986—cloudy, light snow and -12° to -2°. Rested all day.

Saturday, January 18, 1986—it's -10° to -2°, cloudy and a light snow. Made more sets on the west-south loop of the trapline. I hit a snow covered hump of grass that threw the snowgo off the trail and ran an old dead spruce tree (leaning just right) into the headlight mounting on the center of the cowling. I was already standing up and simply stepped off the machine before the pole got to me. I cut it up with my little bow saw and tramped the snow down to get back on the trail. Some of the pole didn't come out of the cowling, but that didn't hamper the operation of the machine. Made more sets as far as Burbot Lake. Had to cut through some downed trees. Nothing in traps. No marten tracks. Two fox tracks and some boo around.

Sunday, January 19, 1986—it's -15° to -3°, mostly sunny and ice fog out at Lake Louise Road. Nothing in traps. Visited Darrel at KROA. Ron and his family and Jack Shotice were there. Allen Farmer visited us in the evening—he shot two wolves Saturday.

Monday, January 20, 1986—temp is -60° to -4° and partly cloudy. Worked at Rhynell's, then went with Jim and Mary to Glennallen for Air Force radar site informational meeting.

Tuesday, January 21, 1986—today it's -20° -4° and mostly sunny. Worked at Rhynell's. Did a few things for Don and Mildred, whose house burned. (Our own home burned to the ground in 1965 and we know how devastating that can be.) Worked on headlamp holder for the snowgo.

Wednesday, January 22, 1986—it's -6° to 2° and mostly cloudy with some light snow. Worked at Hoffman's part of the day, then worked on snowgo holder. Later, Tom and I went to Lake Louise Junction got our hunting licenses.

Thursday, January 23, 1986—sunny and -4° to 3°. Fish and game called for us to pick up three road kill caribou. Tom Smayda and I each got one, Bill Birch, the other. Put headlight holder back on snowgo. Ran Slide Mountain line—nothing. Sylvia cut up the caribou today. Allen Farmer and family visited us in the evening.

Friday, January 24, 1986—it's -4° to 0° and sunny. Two boo on lake this morning. Later, I went east from our lake hunting them but didn't see any. Got snowgo, fuel, and gear ready. Visited Henry and Sally. Rhynell and Max stopped by. Allen borrowed a chain tool.

Saturday, January 25, 1986—it's -2° to 11° and cloudy. Didn't feel well in the morning. Later Tom and I tried hunting caribou east of our lake. No luck. Found one bull antler. Later we drove to milepost 131 but found no shootable boo. Built stake for softening pelts. Not feeling well tonight. Sylvia went over to visit Tom and Lisa.

Sunday, January 26, 1986—12° to 5°. Cloudy, six to eight inches of snow last night. Parked at Warren's. No fur in traps, nothing moving. Very few boo out here.

Monday, January 27, 1986—5° to 10°, cloudy and some light snow. Made more sets and one new fox set. No fur moving. Very few boo—none with horns nor big enough to shoot.

Tuesday, January 28, 1986—2° to 8°, cloudy and light snow. Worked at Rhynell's. Sent in an order to Van Dyke's catalog.

Wednesday, January 29, 1986—3° to 9°, cloudy and ice fog with light snow. Worked at Rhynell's. Mailed in an order to Northern Hydraulics. Went to see Jim and Mary but they weren't home.

Thursday, January 30, 1986—it's -4° to 4° and cloudy. Worked at Rhynell's, then had supper at Jim and Mary's.

Friday, January 31, 1986—4° to 12°, sunny beautiful day. Worked at Rhynell's, then went to a birthday party at Smayda's for Lauren.

Saturday, February 1, 1986—10° to 19°, nice day, but I didn't feel well. Didn't go to work. Saw legal boo on lake, tried for them but couldn't get close enough. Allen got a gray female wolf in trap. Tom and Lisa had seen it, Allen killed it and brought it to show me. It appeared to be one that Ed shot at last week—it had a bullet hole in its hind leg. Went to a potluck clam chowder supper and music at KROA for my birthday.

Sunday, February 2, 1986—10° to 18°, sunny and a light breeze. Henry, Sally and I went boo hunting on snowgos. No luck. Had supper at their place. Back hurts.

Monday, February 3, 1986—10° to 14° and sunny worked at Rhynell's all day.

Tuesday, February 4, 1986—it's -5° to 2° and mostly cloudy. Worked at Rhynell's today.

Wednesday, February 5, 1986—2° to 12°, cloudy and ice fog. Worked at Rhynell's. Chris R. got stuck at Henry's. I pulled him out.

Thursday, February 6, 1986—5° to 22°, mostly cloudy, some breeze and light snow. Worked at Rhynell's. We don't see many caribou these days. A cow moose is feeding near Sam's.

Friday, February 7, 1986—20° to 34° with snow all day—large flakes. Helped Allen shovel snow off sawmill roof. Borrowed a sheet of plywood from Allen. I shoveled snow here at home. Planned and worked on the bathroom. Lucky and Mary plowed our driveway and visited for a while.

Saturday, February 8, 1986—24° to 28°, cloudy with more snow. Worked more on our bathroom. Lucky plowed more snow for us and Lucky and Mary were here for supper.

Sunday, February 9, 1986—3° to 10°, sunny most of the day and cloudy by evening. Spent more time working on our bathroom. Went to Hoffman's place to get some of my work things and tools. Sylvia and I both feel sick this evening.

Monday, February 10, 1986—10° to 22° and a sunny day. Three moose walked down by our lake this morning. Worked on our bathroom. Henry and Sally visited and Tom and his daughters came by also. I took a half inch pipe nipple to Lucky to get it shortened.

Tuesday, February 11, 1986—10° to 23° and mostly cloudy. Ran Slide Mountain trapline. Pulled a snare and three traps and remade sunsets. Fixed a package for Darrell Breider (Nadia's husband). Sylvia has made a beaver skin trapper's hat for him. Henry and I made a deal. Allen and I ground a deeper notch in meat grinder.

Wednesday, February 12, 1986—3° to 20° and sunny. Parked at Warren's. Saw moose browsing, boo track, and wolf, fox, coyote and lynx track. Remade all sets and pulled some. Judd Lake trap was gone, someone had taken it. Got a nice extra large marten south towards springs. Several marten near trap cabin and a coyote at Burbot Lake—made set. Lots of overflow going into Rat Lake. Cabin was fine.

10,000 Days in Alaska Book One 1978-1989

Thursday, February 13, 1986—5° to 22° and sunny. Loafed and did a few chores around here at the trap cabin. Skinned the marten and read a book—just enjoyed the day.

Friday, February 14, 1986—10° to 26° and sunny. Got an early start. Forgot my sunglasses at the cabin. Didn't get any fur—remade sets. Saw three moose and a small bunch of boo. Got home early and stopped at Hoffman's. Called Mike Lanegan from Lucky's.

Saturday, February 15, 1986—6° to 19° and sunny. Worked on sewer lines in the house here at home. Five caribou bulls crossed our lake—didn't hunt them. Tom has snowgo trouble.

Sunday, February 16, 1986—0° to 21° and sunny. Tom asked me to haul his snowgo home. I took him up on the shoulder of Slide Mountain on my snowgo and replaced his drive chain. He drove his snowgo back to the highway. Lucky made some special saw cuts for me and I nailed the rest of the boards above the tub surround in the bathroom.

Monday, February 17, 1986—temp went from -20° to 20° and sunny. Took eight marten to Glennallen to ship to Hudson Bay in Winnipeg. Visited Dave. Jim and Mary Odden, and John Wood were there. Allen and Roxanne and family had supper with us.

Tuesday, February 18, 1986—it's -20° to -5° and sunny. Worked on our linen closet. Lucky sawed out the door for it. I put a new water pump on our truck in Lucky's garage. We had supper there and watched a movie.

Wednesday, February 19, 1986—still cold, -25° to -2° and sunny. Worked on our water lines and on hooking up pump and pressure tank. Got some more fittings from Lucky. Arlene Brooks' brother from Palmer visited. We called Beverly and Kevin and talked about the offer on our farm.

Thursday, February 20, 1986—it's -10° to -1° and sunny. Worked on water lines. Ran trapline on Slide Mountain—no fur. Tom S. and girls visited in the afternoon and also evening.

Friday, February 21, 1986—sunny, cloudy, light snow and -22° to 0°.

Worked on linen closet and hunted caribou.

Saturday, February 22, 1986—it's -20° at home and 22° in Anchorage. We went to Anchorage and attended a fur auction at noon, then did our shopping all afternoon. Went to another fur auction in the evening and after that, Andy and I went to the Legion Club. Bought six beaver at $10.00 each.

Sunday, February 23, 1986—it was 23° in Anchorage today, -16° here at home this evening. Before we left town this morning, we did some shopping and went to another fur auction. Bought one coyote, two red fox, two cross fox and eight beaver. Then we did more shopping and got home at 7:15 p.m.

Monday, February 24, 1986—it's -23° to -5° and mostly sunny. Rhynell stopped by early. I worked on the plumbing and installed door and drawer pulls. Went boo hunting, but saw nothing legal.

Tuesday, February 25, 1986—sunny and -20° to -3°. Made several phone calls to Minnesota about farm business. Did more plumbing and water system work. Soldered a leaking joint.

Wednesday, February 26, 1986—it's -10° to 0°, cloudy with a light snow. Did some plumbing. Called George Stanos (about selling the farm). Started tanning five fox pelts. Hunted caribou with no luck. Pulled my traps on Slide Mountain. Visited Jim and Mary Odden—brought home a cross fox to tan for them.

Thursday, February 27, 1986—cloudy and -6° to 6°. Visited Max Hoffman and hauled one load of water. Hunted boo. Pack of wolves on this side of the river.

Friday, February 28, 1986—breezy and partly cloudy, -16° to -4°. Parked at Warren's. Picked up marten and fox sets, got one nice male marten. Made one wolf set and picked up one set. Saw one moose and lots of track, but few boo track. Saw wolf, fox and marten tracks. Some snowgos have been following my trapline. Saw seismic from along west side of Burbot Lake, will investigate later. Overflow on ice is humping six feet high.

10,000 Days in Alaska Book One 1978-1989

Saturday, March 1, 1986—it's -10° to 12°, sunny and windy in the morning, cloudy and breezy in the afternoon. Picked up wolf set from west trench. Made a wolf set at crooked Tree east of Rat Lake. Made two more wolf sets. Visited KROA and Hoffmans.

Sunday, March 2, 1986—it's -6° to 8°, cloudy and a light snow. Borrowed two fox stretchers from Allen. We have four fox drying now—broke four others this morning. (To break a tanned fur, one has to pull it inside out and while damp, pull it back and forth over a shaped board to make the skin soft and pliable.) We cut clock slabs from a spruce log in the afternoon.

Monday, March 3, 1986—sunny and -10° to 10°. We worked with four fox and two coyote pelts. Borrowed three pair of hinges from Lucky. Allen was sick so we didn't work at Rhynell's.

Tuesday, March 4, 1986—it's -17° to 10°, sunny beautiful day. Allen and I worked at Rhynell's.

Wednesday, March 5, 1986—temp was -20° to 10° with bright sun. Worked at Rhynell's. Sylvia started work on Lucky's hat. Jim and Mary stopped by to pick up their tanned fox skin. Rhynell was with them.

Thursday, March 6, 1986—-20° to 4° and cloudy. Worked at Rhynell's. Sylvia and Rhynell went to Glennallen to do laundry.

Friday, March 7, 1986—it's -5° to 7°, mostly cloudy with a light snow. Worked at Rhynell's on the kitchen cupboards. Max is recovering nicely.
Saturday, March 8, 1986—temp dropped. -60° to 10°, cloudy and light snow. Worked at Rhynell's. Sylvia finished sewing Lucky's fox hat and we took it to them this evening.

Sunday, March 9, 1986—it's -10° to 5°, cloudy with a very light snow. Worked with tanning. Ran trapline and checked wolf traps. Two traps were sprung by moose. No wolf sign. Very little other fur tracks. Harold and Rachel Dimmick visited and had supper with us.

Monday, March 10, 1986—sunny and a nice day with temps at -10° to 50°. Worked at Rhynell's building kitchen cupboards.

Norman Wilkins

Tuesday, March 11, 1986—sunny and -12° to 22°. Worked at Rhynell's until noon. Allen took Roxanne to the hospital—baby is ready. Worked on Sylvia's sewing table-she is sewing a beaver hat. Jim got a new Ski-Doo long track.

Wednesday, March 12, 1986—it's -10° to 17° and sunny. Tom got a road kill calf moose. We took our truck to get it. Lots of meat was ruined. Hauled a load of water for ourselves and for Allen. Roxanne had a baby girl—Ellie Marie. Worked more on Sylvia's sewing table.

Thursday, March 13, 1986—0° to 30 is and sunny. Went to Anchorage and bought craft supplies and some lumber. Visited Dimmick's and went to see Farmer's new baby.

Friday, March 14, 1986—60° to 30° and sunny. Work a half day at Rhynell's. Lots of visitors. Jim Odden got a wolf. I helped him skin it and we finished at 2:30 a.m.

Saturday, March 15, 1986—Jim, Mary, and I went to the trap cabin. We saw fox and wolf tracks and did some exploring. Saw a beaver lodge that appeared empty.

Sunday, March 16, 1986—10° to 25° and sunny. Explored north on new seismic and west and east from there. Saw two ptarmigan, fox tracks and some caribou. Made an otter set on Hole Lake.

Monday, March 17, 1986—0° to 25° and sunny. Left early, nothing in otter set. Saw fox and marten track. Went to Judd Lake—only found one rat push-up. Made set, no luck. Ken Lewis from Fish and Game landed in his plane to check us out. We did some looking for push-ups, then out to Warren's and home.

Tuesday, March 18, 1986—0° to 25° and sunny. Allen and I worked at Rhynell's on the cupboards all day.

Wednesday, March 19, 1986—0° to 25°, cloudy with a light snow and sunny in the evening. Worked at Rhynell's—hung cupboards. Sylvia reworked two fox hats. I worked on beaver pelt and cut up pork to grind. Got a letter from Jerry—mom is pretty sick.

10,000 Days in Alaska Book One 1978-1989

Thursday, March 20, 1986—60° to 24°, sunny and breezy. Worked at Rhynell's. Sylvia ground and packaged 100 pounds of sausage. Mother is very sick, I phoned Jerry.

Friday, March 21, 1986—18° to 26° and sunny. Worked on cupboards at Rhynell's and later visited KROA. Broke beaver pelt. Beaver pelts are open, but the process is essentially the same as for closed pelts.

Saturday, March 22, 1986—10° to 22°, cloudy then sunny in the afternoon. Worked on Rhynell's cupboards and worked more on beaver pelt.

Sunday, March 23, 1986 day—it's -10° to 10°, sunny and some breeze. Sent off some tool orders. Parked at Eleven-Mile to check traplines. Had a red fox by the toe in a wolf trap (Helfrich 750w). Laid a sack over its head and released it, as fox season is over. Saw fox, marten and mink tracks on Seismic Trail north of Burbot Lake while I was looking for more trail. Saw several groups of boo. Got to the trap cabin early, nice to be here.

Monday, March 24, 1986—sunny and -10° to 20°. People are running dogs on my trapline. Pulled the Rat Lake wolf trap. Went to Boot Lake where Jim and Mary are logging for their cabin. Saw four moose and more boo.

Tuesday, March 25, 1986—partly cloudy today and -10° to 32°. Hauled some of our logs for the garage down to the sawmill and two-sided 21 of them. Sawed some of Allen's logs for lumber. Allen pushed snow off garage floor and widened our lane. Four caribou cows crossed our lake.

Wednesday, March 26, 1986—10° to 22° cloudy and snow in the afternoon. Worked at Rhynell's all day.

Thursday, March 27, 1986—0° to 18° and mostly sunny. Put in Formica counters at Rhynell's and put a top on the vanity at home.

Friday, March 28, 1986—8° to 18° and sunny with some breeze. Installed Walnut trim in Rhynell's kitchen. She gave me a book on working iron.

Saturday, March 29, 1986—3° to 12°, a little sun and snow. There is ash in the air from the Mount Augustine eruption. Worked at Rhynell's. Sylvia sewed two ladies pillbox fur hats. Went to a party at KROA. Roger and Joe Ford visited.

Sunday, March 30, 1986—it's -10° to 2° and mostly sunny. Didn't feel well in the morning but went to trap cabin. Nothing in traps. Enjoyed being out there.

Monday, March 31, 1986—temp dropped to -24° to 14° and sunny. Loafed until the temperature got to 0°. Saw wolf, fox and marten tracks. Pulled the rest of the wolf traps and the one snare. Visited Allen and Roxanne.

Tuesday, April 1, 1986—it's -20° to 11°, partly cloudy, hazy with ash in the air. Sylvia and Mary Odden went to Glennallen to do laundry. Morey Second Chief went also. Worked at installing vanity top and sink in the bathroom. There was a meeting at Atlasta House on land use, C.R. Basin.

Wednesday, April 2, 1886—6° to 20°, hazy and sunny. Worked on income tax. Hoffmans, Henry and Sally, Allen and Kyle visited. Sylvia has the flu. Sanded one beaver hide.

Thursday, April 3, 1986—10° to 21°, hazy, sunny, light snow. Rhynell and Max, Tom S., and daughters, and Jim and Mary visited. Did some work with beaver pelt and sent in two orders and letters. Hauled two small loads of water and phoned my brother Jerry, Nadia and Beverly.

Friday, April 4, 1986—10° to 20° with a light snow all day. Sore back. Worked on vanity, small table saw and beaver hide.

Saturday, April 5, 1986—0° to 24° with a light snow all day. Sore back again. Worked in the basement, put some plywood on part of a wall. Built craft table and cupboard. Tom, Lisa and girls, Allen and Dave visited.

Sunday, April 6, 1986—it's -4° to 4°, cloudy, breezy and light snow. Max and Rhynell visited. Rhynell is tanning rabbit pelts here at our place. We worked on drawers and doors for cupboards. Built power tools stand. Cut out lower jaws from some boo skulls.

10,000 Days in Alaska Book One 1978-1989

Monday, April 7, 1986—cloudy, light snow, breezy and -6° to 3°. Allen came over with a message. Did some electrical wiring and worked on sander.

Tuesday, April 8, 1986—it's -10° to 10° in a partly cloudy. Worked on cool room. Finished it except for door jamb and door. Finished sander and mounted vise. Bob Schmidt died today, also Lee D.'s father. Visited Roxanne and kids, Allen came home late.

Wednesday, April 9, 1986—temp dropped to -20° to 6° and sunny. Loafed a lot. Called weatherization people.

Thursday, April 10, 1986—Put up some shelves in basement and mounted buffering unit on bench.

Friday, April 11, 1986—it's -10° to 30° and sunny. Rhynell and Max were here to work on pelts. I felt sick all day. Did some sanding on horn buttons. Allen visited and borrowed a pump.

Saturday, April 12, 1986—still -10° to 24° and sunny with a light snow. Worked on bear claws. Tried engraving a moose horn slab. Went to Hoffman's to bring a doe rabbit home.

Sunday, April 13, 1986—-5° to 30°, light snow then sunny. Visited the sons and daughters of Bob Schmidt. Worked on bear claws. Went down on the Nelchina River and cut a load of spruce burls. Visited Henry and Sally and ordered clock works.

Monday, April 14, 1986—20° to 36° and sunny. Went to get teeth cleaned. Don't feel well today. Worked on claws. Jim and Elaine brought some things here to store.

Tuesday, April 15, 1986—-6° to 34° and sunny. Attended memorial service for Bob Schmidt at Mendeltna Chapel and lunch at KROA. Checked rat trap and worked on a few claws. Talked to Kevin about sale of farm.

Wednesday, April 16, 1986—-6° to 34° and sunny. Worked at Rhynell's. Tired and sore tonight.

Norman Wilkins

Thursday, April 17, 1986—0° to 34° and sunny. Max Hoffman is in the hospital. Visited Allen's, Mary B., Jim and Mary Odden and worked on bear claws. Pulled rat trap.

Friday, April 18, 1986—12° to 25°, sunny and breezy here at the trap cabin. Went to lake on Mendeltna Springs, then followed snowgo track west of trench. It was blown over (with snow) on top and I lost it. Saw otter, marten and fox tracks.

Saturday, April 19, 1986—10° to 24°, sunny, cloudy, some lights snow. Saw fox and marten tracks. Closed trap cabin for the summer. snowgo is making a strange noise. Elaine M. gave Sylvia a lot of things that had belonged to Bob Schmidt.

Sunday, April 20, 1986—12° to 37° and sunny. Henry and I helped Elaine close up her house. She stored some of her things here and gave us a lamp and chair. Sylvia gave her a fox hat. Mary (don't know last name) bought a cross fox hat from Sylvia. I hauled water from Allen's and worked on bear claw necklace.

Monday, April 21, 1986—12° to 40° and sunny. Worked on diamond willow and made some jigs for lamps and clocks.

Tuesday, April 22, 1986—16° to 37°, light snow in the morning and sunny the rest of the day. Worked on craft projects. Rhynell visited. Allen and Dave borrowed VCR movies. Called Nadia and Rollins' from Smayda's.

Wednesday, April 23, 1986—20° to 39°, sunny and light snow. Went to Anchorage for craft supplies. Stopped at Andy's—Mike Callahan was there. Got home just at dark.

Thursday, April 24, 1986—16° to 38°, sunny and some breeze. Worked on beaver hoops and unloaded lumber and plywood. Allen, Dave and I sawed (two-sided) 58 logs and a few boards. Took a chair to Oddens.

Friday, April 25, 1986—17° to 36°, sunny and some breeze. Worked on electrical, snowgo, and clocks. Max came home from the hospital. They had supper here.

10,000 Days in Alaska Book One 1978-1989

Saturday, April 26, 1986—10° to 33°, mostly cloudy with snow flurries and breezy. We worked at Hoffman's and later I worked on a clock.

Sunday, April 27, 1986—16° to 39° and cloudy all day. Worked on a lamp and a slab for Mary Beaudoin. Tom, Lisa and girls were here for supper.

Monday, April 28, 1986—14° to 42° and mostly sunny. Snow really melted today. Saw two marsh hawks and one unknown. Worked on Clocks and lamps. Carol Adkins had ordered a beaver hat for Vern's birthday. We took it to KROA and pizza.

Tuesday, April 29, 1986—24° to 47°, sunny and warm. Snow is going fast. Saw more marsh hawks. Swans are coming back. Worked at Hoffman's and visited Dimmicks. Harold was gone. Worked on Clock slab.

Wednesday, April 30, 1986—22° to 46°, sunny and warm. Worked at Rhynell's and later on a clock slab at home. Eleven eagles were eating on Allen's bait pile. Lots of ravens around.

Thursday, May 1, 1986—26° to 46° and partly cloudy. Left some burls with Chuck Zimbiki to be sawed. Went to Glennallen to do laundry and get craft materials. Notarized warranty deed for farm. Took Max Hoffman to hospital.

Friday, May 2, 1986—24° to 48° and mostly sunny. Worked on clock slabs—routing and sanding. Experimented with decoupage. Sylvia is making Eskimo dolls with fur garments. Max Hoffman is home from the hospital. Lots of ravens, eagles, and marsh hawks around. Geese and swans are migrating.

Saturday, May 3, 1986—30° to 40° and cloudy. Sylvia and Rhynell took craft items to bazaar at Glennallen. Sylvia sold a doll. I worked on diamond willow for Rhynell's house and on lamp and clock slabs. Visited Henry and Sally in the evening.

Sunday, May 4, 1986—20° to 42° and partly cloudy. Hauled a load of water and whittled on diamond willow for lamps. Hooked up vanity sink. Sylvia worked with goat and boo hides. Vacuumed up the dust in basement.

Monday, May 5, 1986–31° to 44°, mostly sunny. Carved on lamps and worked on snowgo. Helped Allen saw logs. Dave and Steve were there. Lisa stopped by with messages and had coffee with us.

Tuesday, May 6, 1986–26° to 43° and sunny. Did some more cane and lamp carving. Put up two shelves in Sylvia's sewing room.

Wednesday, May 7, 1986–24° to 42°, sunny and some breeze. Allen and I laid carpet at Rhynell's. Finished cleaning and sanding a diamond willow cane. Griz got into Peter's dog food.

Thursday, May 8, 1986–25° to 42°, sunny and breezy. Laid more carpet and put baseboard on all but one room. Did some labeling on willow cane.

Friday, May 9, 1986–26° to 40° at mostly cloudy. Put sealer on burl clock slabs and did other odd jobs. Mounted Whetstone grinder on board. Did some whittling.

Saturday, May 10, 1986–25° to 40°, cloudy light snow and flurries then sunny. Finished laying carpet and installing baseboard trim. Called my brother Jerry Wilkins. Jim and Mary Odden visited.

Sunday, May 11, 1986–30° to 36°, snow, cloudy, breezy. Made some drawings on jawbone sled and whittled on diamond willow. Put sole savers on Mukluks and L.L. Bean boots. Laced beaver pelt into willow hoop.

Monday, May 12, 1986–34° to 47° and mostly sunny. Installed sink and started putting up rain gutters at Rhynell's. Phoned mother.

Tuesday, May 13, 1986–30° to 46° and mostly sunny with a small shower. Helped Allen in the morning. Went to the woods in the afternoon and got a small load of firewood and four garage logs.

Wednesday, May 14, 1986–30° to 44° and mostly sunny with a breeze. We got two loads of logs and wood. Had lots of chain saw trouble.

10,000 Days in Alaska Book One 1978-1989

Sanded one diamond willow.

Thursday, May 15, 1986—30° to 45°, sunny and breezy and evening. Got more wood and 20 more logs today. Lots more trouble with chainsaw. Had supper at Steve and Karen Mailey's

Friday, May 16, 1986—26° to 42° and cloudy with some breeze. Steve Mailey helped me get two loads of wood and logs. Called Paul this evening.

Saturday, May 17, 1986—30° to 47°, heavy snow until noon (three inches) then sunny. Worked some on lamps and visited Allen and Lucky. Had supper at Tom and Lisa Smayda's.

Sunday, May 18, 1986—27° to 44° with snow flurries then mostly sunny. Unloaded, cut up, and stacked wood. Went to see Hoffmans. Jacked-up and leveled our old cabin. Sore back.

Monday, May 19, 1986—34° to 50° and sunny. Seven boo crossed lake. Started cleaning old cabin. Sharpened tines on Rhynell's tiller. Hooked up temporary wiring to garage.

Tuesday, May 20, 1986—38° to 50°and sunny then plenty in the evening. Cleaned up old cabin and fixed up a bench for it. It will be my woodworking shop. Took trash to dump. Changed oil in truck. Sylvia cleaned house and tilled garden.

Wednesday, May 21, 1986—36° to 51° and partly cloudy with a shower. Cleared a place for the old cabin. Started getting Cat ready. Put fertilizer and lime on big garden.

Thursday, May 22, 1986—38° to 53° and sunny, then cloudy. Started Cat and hauled gravel from Lucky's to make a pad for the wood shop. Back is very sore.

Friday, May 23, 1986—40° to 54° and sunny with a light shower. Moved old cabin and leveled it, then did other odd jobs. Dan Billman is back. He and Don visited.

Saturday, May 24, 1986—30° to 56°, sunny and breezy. Blocked windows from Allen Farmer. Built lean-to on east side of woodworking shop. Lisa Smayda and her girls, and Roger and Jo Ford came and visited. We went over to see Hoffmans, and Dan Billman and Don.

Sunday, May 25, 1986–32° to 57°, sunny and cloudy. Moved storage shed. Took our refrigerator to Allen's to sell and bought a small electric refrigerator and a tap and die set from him. Dan and Don and Andy Boyle came by our place. Pumped water at the greenhouse. Visited KROA in the evening.

Monday, May 26, 1986–42° to 48°, cloudy and light shower. Moved brown trailer and lots of stuff to the house. Hauled another load to dump. Got doors out of dump and put them on lean-to the shed. Allen gave us overhead garage door. Edge of our lake is thawing–a few ducks were down there. Allen and Dave came over in the evening.

Tuesday, May 27, 1986–42° to 52°, shower, sunny, rain. Worked on machine shed at Hoffman's. Tom brought sealer and tried it out. Put straw in shed and put spikes away. Ice has started to go out on our lake.

Wednesday, May 28, 1986–38° to 56°, sunny with a light breeze. Finished putting logs in wall at Rhynell's. Dan Billman visited and so did Mary Odden. Worked on wall of lean-to. My back is really bad.

Thursday, May 29, 1986–40° to 57°, sunny, some breeze. Ice is going fast on our lake. Saw some caribou bulls. Put up quite a few rafters at Rhynell's. Hung door on lean-to and cleaned up lumber pile and trash.

Friday, May 30, 1986–40° to 56°. Sunny, partly cloudy, breezy to windy in the evening. Brought gas pump home. Moved different things around here and cut up a bunch of slabs. Max and Rhynell were here for supper. Dan Billman visited in the evening. Ice is out on the lake. Quite a few pairs of ducks and an eagle flew by the house.

Saturday, May 31, 1986–40° to 53°, sunny, cloudy, light rain. Built porch on woodworking shop. Hauled a huge load of trash to the dump and salvaged a pickup topper and gas pump. Sylvia is sick. Went to the clinic at Glennallen in the morning and then to Rhynell's.

Sunday, June 1, 1986–34° to 42° and rainy all day. Arranged and organized woodworking shop. Stacked two thirds of a cord of slab wood. Visited Allen and Lucky.

Monday, June 2, 1986—34° to 43°, sunny and windy. Worked until noon at Rhynell's. Allen's feet hurt and it was cold and windy. Hauled some gravel and landscaped near outbuildings. Dug two birch trees for lucky. He will replant them.

Tuesday, June 3, 1986—33° to 40°, cloudy, some breeze. Tried to work at Hoffman's, but too windy and cold. Did some dozer work at home and two-sided some logs at Allen's.

Wednesday, June 4, 1986—36° to 59°, sunny and light breeze. Worked at Rhynell's. Did more dozer work at home. Helped Dan Billman get his Beaver float plane back in the lake. We then flew over Nelchina and Nelchina River, Old Man Lake and back to Snowshoe Lake where Dan lives. Saw moose, caribou, swans, eagles, ducks and beaver houses. Patti and the kids are home now.

Thursday, June 5, 1986—42° to 57°, sunny and windy in the evening. Raked and smoothed dozer work. Mounted second sander. Sanded clock slabs and put sealer on a few. Henry and Sally visited.

Friday, June 6, 1986—44° to 59°, sunny and windy again in the evening. Slept late, then helped Lucky pull his well pump and put in a larger one. John Johnson helped us. I put more sealer on a lamp and on more clock slabs. Raked more of the yard and driveway.

Saturday, June 7, 1986—37° to 57°, Sunny, cloudy, breezy. Put a double window in south side of woodshop. Hauled six loads of gravel and got most of it spread. Loaded and piled more peat for Allen. Called my son Paul and his family.

Sunday, June 8, 1986—38° to 48°, sunny, gusty winds. Put another window in the woodshop. Weatherization representative was here. Hauled water. Peeled and drove in some garden posts. Patti Billman brought us some lake trout fillets.

Monday, June 9, 1986—36° to 44°, sunny, cloudy, light rain. Put steel on roof for Rhynell—got some three-sided logs from her. Cleaned up some more around here. Swans are back on the lake.

Tuesday, June 10, 1986—38° to 48°, sunny, cloudy, light rain—hail on Lake Louise Road. Worked on garden fence. Went to Dr. and got prescription refilled. Cut 30 pieces of diamond willow and peeled 10 of them. Visited Dawson's. Went and got propane at Lake Louise Junction.

Wednesday, June 11, 1986—37° to 54° and partly cloudy. Did some Cat work for Allen, then went over to Henry's and put in four more hours there with the Cat. Henry gave me some electric motors.

Thursday June 12, 1986—40° to 63° and sunny. Did more Cat work for Henry—he gave me a truck frame. Hauled stumps to dump. Peeled more diamond willow. Sylvia went to Anchorage with Rhynell. Shoveled and wheelbarrow landscaped on east side of house.

Friday, June 13, 1986—42° to 67°, sunny and some breeze. Things are getting dry. Did more yard leveling and spread more dirt. Laid a plastic hose to the lake. Took pump and generator down to the lake. Put new handle in wheelbarrow. Rudbecks came by for breakfast.

Saturday, June 14, 1986—44° to 66° and partly cloudy. Went to Wasilla. Stopped at Ron's, cached a check and did some shopping. When we got home, and Dan and Patti Billman asked us to go to Crosswind Lake with them—we did. Fished a little in the evening, beautiful sunset. Saw a swimming moose, three beaver houses and a few swans from the air.

Sunday, June 15, 1986—44° to 68° and partly cloudy. Dan and his daughter, Lisa caught three lake trout (one 12-pounder) between them. His son, Jason caught two grayling. We saw 17 swans and three geese. Dan let me fly the beaver on the way home.

Monday, June 16, 1986—48° to 68°, partly cloudy, raindrops, some breeze. Thunder in Chugach Mountains. Hooked up water pump but it doesn't have enough pressure to push water all the way up the hill to the house. I did get some work done on the lower garden. Allen and I fished in the evening. I got one rainbow trout.

Tuesday, June 17, 1986—48° to 70° and partly cloudy. Dan Billman brought us some grass seed. Fixed a door at Schmidt's and brought some garage windows home. Lucky checked three submersible pumps for Allen and I took two beaver pelts in hoops to Allen's yard sale.

Wednesday, June 18, 1986—15° to 60° partly cloudy, one shower. Tried to fix submersible pump. Helped Allen saw logs and hauled a load of water. Henry and Sally took Sylvia to KROA. Dan and I got our gear together and flew out over a lot of the Chugach Mountains looking for black bear. Saw one black bear so we landed on the southwest side of Tazlina Lake. Slept in the plane (not allowed to hunt the same day we fly). A cow moose got a little belligerent this evening. Maybe she had a calf nearby.

Thursday, June 19, 1986—40° to 60°, partly cloudy and windy in the evening. We glassed for bear from Hig Hill. Saw one black, far away, late in the afternoon. A little later, I saw a grizzly feeding on last year's berries about 125 yards away. He fed off farther, so we stalked him to observe his feeding for a while, and then continued on to the plane. After we were airborne, we saw a small black bear within a short distance of the trail we had just taken to the plane. Saw several moose today.

Friday, June 20, 1986—44° to 52°, cloudy, had a good rain today. Worked on lamps. Seeded the lawn, leveled and moved dirt, and hauled some gravel. Stripped down a furnace. Sweet corn is tasseling.

Saturday, June 21, 1986—44° to 54°, mostly sunny with some breeze. Unloaded and placed gravel in walkway, then went to Hoffman's to do laundry. Started stripping a trailer there. Hauled a load of pole cutoffs for Rhynell. We all went to KROA for pizza.

Sunday, June 22, 1986—36° to 44°, cloudy, some breeze and hail. Worked on tearing the body off trailer and built a handle for Rhynell's push mower.

Monday, June 23, 1986—38° to 54°, cloudy and rain. Finished cleaning up the trailer at Mendeltna dump. Worked on woodshop. Helped Allen deliver a refrigerator and airplane fuel tanks to Billman's.

Tuesday June 24, 1986—40° to 53° partly cloudy. Made a call (from Hoffman's) to try and sell the belt pulley for Cat. Painted the inside walls of the woodshop. Put down more grass seed and hauled a load of gravel.

Wednesday, June 25, 1986—39° to 62° and sunny most of the day. Unloaded the gravel and built a rock and gravel front walk. Drove in some more garden posts. Dug in a drywell barrel for basement drain. Henry gave us a washing machine. I fixed up a fuel barrel for Dan's Crosswind cabin. They stopped to pick it up this evening.

Thursday, June 26, 1986—44° to 64° and sunny. Hauled water for the house, and hauled five loads of logs to sawmill. Cleaned up and leveled more of our backyard. Allen and I cut up two loads of slab wood. Sylvia and I stacked our load.

Friday, June 27, 1986—52° to 72°, sunny, and some wind in afternoon. Sawed and two-sided a large pickup load of logs for the garage we plan to build. Did a bunch of other small jobs around here. Started hooking up Lucky's pump at the lake. Rhynell and Max visited and also Jim and Lynn came by.

Saturday, June 28, 1986—48° to 70°, sunny with a windy afternoon. Finished two-siding our logs at Allen's. Lucky helped wire the pump at the lake to the generator. Sylvia got the garden and some of the lawn watered. Lisa and her girls and Rhynell visited. Went to Billman's and borrowed a sander—Dan, Della, and Monica from Wisconsin were there, and also Billy from Grizzly Lake.

Sunday, June 29, 1986—50° to 72° and sunny to partly cloudy. Hauled lumber home from the sawmill. Helped Lucky lower mast. Max and Rhynell were here and Rhynell helped with the garage logs—we did 21 blocks. Lisa Smayda and her girls visited.

Monday, June 30, 1986—50° to 70°, mostly sunny and some breeze. Sanded six logs. Dan Billman came to take us salmon fishing at Kiana Creek. Dan, Della, Monica, Jason, Lisa and Sylvia went also. I caught a 42 inch king salmon. We got five kings and numerous reds between us.

Tuesday, July 1, 1986—44° to 62° partly cloudy and some showers. Went to Dan Billman's and used the telephone to call the lawyer. Sanded 16 logs. Sylvia watered the lawn and garden.

10,000 Days in Alaska Book One 1978-1989

Wednesday, July 2, 1986—48° to 72° and mostly sunny. Sanded logs and painted half of the floor or on the wood shop. Dan, Della and Monica visited.

Thursday, July 3, 1986—50° to 76°, sunny and hot. Sanded logs and did dozer work for Henry, Lucky and Allen. Hauled a load of black dirt to Dan Billman for his lawn.

Friday, July 4, 1986—52° to 78°, sunny with an afternoon shower. Sanded more logs and finished painting woodshop floor.

Saturday, July 5, 1986—48° to 76° and mostly sunny. Sanded logs all day. Henry and Sally borrowed truck tube. We visited Max Hoffman and then Dan, Della and Monica at Jim and Mary Odden's.

Sunday, July 6, 1986—50° to 72° and partly cloudy. Sanded 27 logs. Mike Callahan and his girlfriend Shirley, and mother Annie visited us. Sylvia has been doing Smayda's chores. Gave Mike C. a lamp and a hooped beaver (beaver pelt stretched on a hoop).

Monday, July 7, 1986—47° to 60°, cloudy with a few sprinkles. worked on Rhynell's woodshed. Came home and sanded a few more logs. Did some dozer work for Allen after supper. He gave me a barrel of used oil.

Tuesday, July 8, 1986—44° to 64° partly cloudy. Worked on Rhynell's woodshed again. Lucky and I drove two pins back in Cat track. Watched a movie at Lucky and Mary's.

Wednesday, July 9, 1986—45° to 61°, partly cloudy with a light shower. Put steel on Rhynell's woodshed roof and sanded 12 logs at home. Loaded some wood for Andy and Connie.

Thursday, July 10, 1986—44° to 54° and three. Drove to Anchorage, and did business and shopping and left wood with Andy and Connie. He gave me Thermax, paint, tubes etc.

Friday, July 11, 1986—45° to 60°, partly cloudy with a light sprinkle in the evening. Started tearing down a chicken house at Hoffman's. Sanded logs at home. Windows for the house came this evening.

Saturday, July 12, 1986—44° to 55°, cloudy, rainy in the afternoon. Henry and I put it seven windows. Dan, Della and Monica visited in the evening.

Sunday, July 13, 1986—42 and 48°, rained all day. Put in two casement windows and stopped in others. Helped Mark, Henry and Jim carry large window down to Sam's place. Lots of visitors today.

Monday, July 14, 1986—45° to 60°, cloudy during the day and sunny towards evening. Stopped in more windows. Installed door in arctic entry and made a run to the dump. Allen borrowed a 3/4" drive socket set.

Tuesday, July 15, 1986—34° to 61° and partly cloudy. Worked down at Allen Farmer's. Put on T 1-11 siding. Removed deck from house. Called Nadia.

Wednesday, July 16, 1986—44° to 64° and partly cloudy. Finished the siding on Allen's house and spent the rest of the day working on Lloyd Ronning's house. Visited Jim and Mary Odden.

Thursday, July 17, 1986—46° to 76°, mostly sunny. Still working on Ronning's roof, really tired tonight.

Friday, July 18, 1986—50° to 71° partly cloudy. Finished Ronning's roof. Put roof on lean-to at Lake Louise Junction.

Saturday, July 19, 1986—58° to 70° and partly cloudy. Sanded rest of logs. Dan Billman visited. Allen brought tools back—we visited at his place in the evening.

Sunday, July 20, 1986—48° to 58° and cloudy with a good rain all afternoon. Loaded quite a bit of peat for Allen and moved Lucky's gas barrel. Dug some trees for Allen. Cleared and leveled a site for Dave DeJung's garage.

Monday, July 21, 1986—43° to 59° partly cloudy. Worked on our basement windows and picture window. Helped Allen haul two loads of logs. Called lawyer.

10,000 Days in Alaska Book One 1978-1989

Tuesday, July 22, 1986—42° to 54° and partly cloudy. Trimmed door upstairs. Built door. Put trim on outside of picture window. Called Nadia. Visited Dan and Patti.

Wednesday, July 23, 1986—42° to 58° and partly cloudy. Finished picture window, hung door, and put doorstops on frame. Dan, Della, and Monica visited this afternoon. Sanded a few sill logs for garage.

Thursday, July 24, 1986—48° to 59° and mostly cloudy with a light shower. Finished sanding logs. Visited Max and Rhynell. Hen and ducklings are feeding on the lake.

Friday, July 25, 1986—44° to 54°, partly cloudy with a shower in the evening. Put down sill logs for garage. Finished driving posts for garden and burned a large brush pile.

Saturday, July 26, 1986—40° to 48° with rain showers. Put up logs on garage. Snow on the mountains to the south.

Sunday, July 27, 1986—38° to 61°, sunny partly cloudy. Lucky helped put the big beam up over garage door—we used the Cat. He helped put logs on west wall and one third of the east wall. Really tired tonight.

Monday, July 28, 1986—36° to 62° and sunny. Sanded the rest of the logs. Called lawyer—land sale closed. Dan, Patti, Sylvia and I flew to Prince William Sound (Shoup Glacier) looking at quartz outcrops to prospect—saw many. Two men were right where we want to go. My back is very bad.

Tuesday, July 29, 1986—38° to 70°, mostly sunny, strange haze for two days. Allen helped on east wall of garage. Called Darrell from Billman's and had supper there.

Wednesday, July 30, 1986—38° to 64°, sunny and hazy. Worked on garage wall. Allen and Chris helped in the afternoon—Dave for a while too. Finished walls. Stacked left over logs, swept floor and cleaned up cutouts. Nailed the cull lumber on top of logs to protect from rain.

Thursday, July 31, 1986—36° to 52°, cloudy with a light rain. Went to Palmer. Lawyer made the check out wrong—straightened that out. Went to Wasilla for plywood and then to Anchorage for steel roofing. Got some groceries in Palmer and was home about 8:30 p.m. Very little rain here.

Friday, August 1, 1986—42° to 58° and partly cloudy. Made a jig for building rafters—Dan Billman helped. Got one end rafter done and started on another.

Saturday, August 2, 1986—44° to 64° and sunny. But top plates on garage. Built one rafter and cut gussets. Dan Billman and his friend Dan, helped part of the afternoon.

Sunday, August 3, 1986—34° to 62°, sunny and windy. Lucky helped nail and glue garage rafters—got them all done. Harold and Rachel Dimmick were here for supper.

Monday, August 4, 1986—8° to 62°, sunny and partly cloudy and breezy. Got things ready to start putting roof on garage. Nadia, Darrell and Laura arrived at 11:00 p.m.

Tuesday, August 5, 1986—40° to 52° or cloudy rain and hail. Darrell, Lucky, Bob R., Allen and Curt all helped put up rafters and three quarters of the plywood sheeting.

Wednesday, August 6, 1986—partly cloudy, finished roof on garage. Packed gear for prospecting trip and visited Billman's.

Thursday, August 7, 1986—mostly cloudy. Loaded gear, went to Billman's and called the Bureau of Land Management about land status. Headed for Valdez. Nadia, Laura and Sylvia followed in the car. Laura doesn't feel well. Hired a helicopter to take us up Shoup Glacier and landed at old stamp mill. Nadia took VCR movies. She went back to Valdez and they all went on a cruise to the Columbia Glacier—had quite an adventure (tour boat became trapped in icebergs calving off of Columbia Glacier—took eight hours to break free). Darrell and I explored around old stamp mill at Cameron-Johnson. Set up camp—had trouble with propane stove. Some light rain. Very interesting here. Saw three ptarmigan, two parka squirrels and two hoary marmots.

Friday, August 8, 1986—rained all day. Darrell fixed a shelter at mill site.

I loafed and read. Rain quit in the afternoon. We started around the shoulder of the mountain to the north. Then Darrell's knee bothered him. Saw a black bear feeding. We are hoping for better weather tomorrow. There are lots of small flowers—blues and yellows and a few white ones. We got about three quarters of an inch of rain. Streams are running strong and there is a continuous roar from the waterfall.

Saturday, August 9, 1986—foggy and rain. Made our way across the snowfield and climbed up to the glacier at the head of waterfall. Looked over the mine portal. We could see a one-lunger lead compressor, cook and bunkhouse, all caved in, and a small track for ore cars along with much machinery, dynamite, et cetera. Looked for the mother lode outcrop. Saw several outcrops. Some had been dynamited in the past. Roped across glacier and snowfields to look over another area. Saw goat tracks here, and a ptarmigan. Awful lot of slick rock and snow. Climbed back down. Somewhat disappointed and tired tonight.

Sunday, August 10, 1986—rained all night, cloudy and foggy and rained most of the day. Went north and found old claims and many outcrops of quartz. Took samples and staked three claims. Rambler Camp had a ball mill. Two claims were probably Tuscarora. We didn't see Rambler tunnels or Olson tunnel. The one outcrop we staked is really long. Saw several ptarmigan and parka squirrels—and the marmots whistle at us.

Monday, August 11, 1986—rain. Sun tried to shine for a few minutes, then more fog and rain. We staked two claims on Johnson Creek below the mill site. Saw bear track. Darrell collected some samples from the creek. Made out location and filing papers. Finished second book. Didn't feel very well this afternoon. Darrell has sinus problems.

Tuesday, August 12, 1986—rainy and foggy. Loafed around camp until 11:00 a.m., then started breaking camp. Len Paur copter pilot arrived at noon. He looked over the mill site and flew us up to the mine area. We spotted two large outcrops. He flew us through a snowstorm over the mountain to Shoup Glacier then past Cliff Mine and on to Valdez. We filed claims, had lunch and went home.

Wednesday, August 13, 1986—partly cloudy, 34° to 44°. Did some things around home then some dozer work for Dave J. Drained the dozer and cleaned dirt off. Called Knik lumber. Darrell called Bill again and Dan Billman visited in the evening.

Thursday, August 14, 1986–30° to 50° partly cloudy. Left early for Anchorage and left my truck at Wasilla. Rode to Anchorage with Nadia, Darrell and Laura. Went to USGS. State Lands Office and also did some shopping while we were there. Bought materials for garage in Wasilla. Visited Billmans in the evening to make plans for staking near Nelchina Glacier.

Friday, August 15, 1986–34° to 49° and partly cloudy. Dan flew Nadia, Laura, Darrell, Sylvia and I out to stay overnight at Crosswind Lake and go fishing. Darrell got a lake trout and Nadia caught five nice grayling—one was a 17-incher. Really nice here, so very quiet.

Saturday, August 16, 1986–34° to 50° partly cloudy and windy in the afternoon. I caught a four pound lake trout. Beautiful day. Dan flew us out to Snowshoe Lake and we drove home from there. Once home, painted 17 sheets of plywood and Allen brought over a nice mess of rainbow trout. Tom stopped in for a few minutes.

Sunday, August 17, 1986–34° to 61°, sunny all day. Darrell got gear ready to stake claims at Nelchina Glacier. I finished screwing down steel on the roof of garage. Drilled entrance hole for electric wires in garage. Hewed a flat place on the wall to mount a breaker box and painted 17 sheets of plywood a second time.

Monday, August 18, 1986–35° to 51° at partly cloudy. Light shower, rained in the night. Chris Ronning flew Dan Billman, Lisa, Darrell and I to Nelchina Glacier. We staked seven, 40 acre, state claims on a huge outcrop. Saw two ewe sheep and lambs. Took samples to be assayed.

Tuesday, August 19, 1986–34° to 46° and snowing out to 4500 feet this morning. Very nice day. Staked three more claims—ten in all. Prospected a large area. Pulverized and panned many rock samples. Chris Ronning flew us home in the evening. Had supper at Dan and Patti's.

Wednesday, August 20, 1986–35° to 54° and sunny. Went to Hoffman's for C.W.F. Worked on garage soffits, trim and electricity. Rhynell borrowed a steel clamp from me. Butchered rabbits. Tired tonight. Patti brought claim location notices.

Thursday, August 21, 1986—38° to 48° and mostly sunny. Darrell and I went to Mouse Creek, got stuck on the way. Made camp at mouth of Mouse Creek on Alfred Creek. Saw a few caribou and did some panning for gold—didn't find much.

Friday, August 22, 1986—34° to 46°, light rain and cloudy. Panned a little for gold on the way out to highway—made it out with little trouble. Started putting ceiling in garage and took Darrell fishing for rainbow trout in the evening.

Saturday, August 23, 1986—24° to 41°, Sunny, cloudy. Finished ceiling and garage and put in the installation and floor in the attic along with one window and some wiring. Darrell treated us to pizza at KROA.

Sunday, August 24, 1986—40° to 60°, sunny and partly cloudy. Put two windows in the garage and did some electrical wiring on the garage and on the woodshed. Darrell sorted ore samples and went fishing once. He and I went fishing together later. He caught two small rainbows. Sylvia did laundry.

Monday, August 25, 1986—35° to 55° and mostly cloudy. Darrell and I put the ceiling in the arctic entry and cut plywood and primed it for the basement.

Tuesday, August 26, 1986—40° to 54° and partly sunny. Left early to take Darrell to the plane to go home (Nadia and Laura left a few days ago). I brought back more material I needed for the garage. Took a tomato plant to Lucky and Mary's.

Wednesday, August 27, 1986—44° to 58°, mostly sunny summer breeze. Started on the garage chimney. Dan, Della, and Monica Zappa helped in the afternoon. In evening we watched a movie at Lucky and Mary's. The tree leaves have turned yellow and red.

Thursday, August 28, 1986—30° to 50°, sunny cloudy and rainy. Finished masonry work on the garage chimney. Lucky and I went to Glennallen. I got permits to go hunting. The mountains are beautiful with color.

Norman Wilkins

Friday, August 29, 1986—30° to 54°, sunny and partly cloudy. Put T & G pine paneling on gable end of garage. Lisa Smayda and daughter visited in the evening.

Saturday, August 30, 1986—36° to 52°, sunny and partly cloudy. Put attic window in garage. Built man door and frame—put on trim.

Sunday, August 31, 1986—34° to 51°, Sunny, cloudy, light rain. Put more pine on gable end, and chimney flashing on garage. Went to Black Powder Rondy at McKee's. Hauled two loads of drain field rock for sewer line. Hauled garbage and visited Hoffmans. There was a bald eagle on our lake today.

Monday, September 1, 1986—34° to 50°, mostly cloudy, some light rain. Finished door and hung it. Landscaped gravel over sewer drain field. Called Theresa from Rudbeck's.

Tuesday, September 2, 1986—34° to 50°, partly cloudy, light rain. Went to Anchorage to get a garage door, more building materials and a water hauling tank.

Wednesday, September 3, 1986—34° to 54° and mostly sunny. The leaves are so beautiful. Took Hoffman's feed to them and took seven tires to Warren Dawson. Didn't see any moose. Jim Odden's folks and Mary visited. Finished north Gable end and siding today.

Thursday, September 4, 1986—34° to 60°, sunny beautiful day. There was a small fire near the Nelchina Glacier. Put trim on and window in north gable end of garage. Got garage ready to put CWF on. Did some electrical wiring and Sylvia worked on some of the painting and staining.

Friday, September 5, 1986—31° to 63° and sunny. Worked more on the electrical wiring, staining, painting and CWF. Went to see Hoffmans and Billmans

Saturday, September 6, 1986—20° to 60°, sunny beautiful day. Worked on the garage on the house—put linoleum in the arctic entry floor. Visited Henry and Sally in the evening.

10,000 Days in Alaska Book One 1978-1989

Sunday, September 7, 1986—36° to 52°, cloudy and breezy in evening. Worked on garage, arctic entry, and put a clean-out riser on septic tank and a thick 4 x 8 sheet of Thermax.

Monday, September 8, 1986—34° to 50°, cloudy, sunny, and breezy. Installed trim on inside of garage. Lucky helped me start putting the big door up. Called Nadia from Billman's. Flew with Dan to Moore Lake—saw swans, ducks, beaver and moose. Trap cabin looked fine from the air.

Tuesday, September 9, 1986—30° to 48°, cloudy and sunny, light rain at night and snow at 3600 feet. Finished garage door. Steve and Karen Mailey were here for supper.

Wednesday, September 10, 1986—30° to 60°. Went to Anchorage and shopped for more garage materials, groceries, a mattress and dog and rabbit feed—ran into the Rudbecks while we were there.

Thursday, September 11, 1986—26° to 57° and sunny. Installed garage door opener and cleaned garage. Painted floor and stained trim. Painted step on the wood shop. Visited at KROA in evening.

Friday, September 12, 1986—30° to 57° and a sunny beautiful day. Visited Allen and Henry. Sylvia painted the garage door. I wired outside light and outlet on garage and storage shed.

Saturday, September 13, 1986—34° to 60° and sunny. Darrel Gerry and I went to Delta Junction—arrived at 5:30 a.m. and put out our goose decoys. No birds flying until evening. Some cranes came fairly close. The 1500 others were very high. Visited with friends there and slept on the floor at Allen and Wendy Bakers.

Sunday, September 14, 1986—Frost in the morning. Later, temp got up to 54° and sunny. Up early, one flock of geese, and none on pond. Went exploring. Saw more geese and cranes but they were out of range. Came home late.

Monday, September 15, 1986—36° to 63°. Sunny day, slept late. Put tung oil on inside garage walls and wired the button control for the garage opener. Sylvia painted the inside of the garage door.

Tuesday, September 16, 1986—38° to 62°, is that a cloudy in the evening. Sylvia mowed the lawn and watered it. I Dozed trees and made a gravel pad where we will build a greenhouse.

Wednesday, September 17, 1986—34° to 54°, sunny and cloudy. Worked on electrical wiring all day. Dan Billman came by. Visited Della and Mary O.'s mother, Ruth in the evening.

Thursday, September 18, 1986—34° to 52°, cloudy, partly cloudy. Worked with electrical fixtures then moved black dirt and gravel with wheelbarrow and landscaped. Saw a cow moose feeding in the lake. The bugs are bad. Sylvia picked lots of cranberries.

Friday, September 19, 1986—30° to 51° and cloudy. Worked again on the electrical wiring then hunted for two hours. Did some more landscaping and lime and ashes. Watched a home video movie by Greg from the Bureau of Land Management at Henry and Sally's in the evening.

Saturday, September 20, 1986—40° to 60°, rain and cloudy in the morning, sunny towards evening. Worked on the garage, then went moose hunting—no luck. Found a moose jaw and dog skull. Chopped roots and made a panel for the garage electrical service box. Lisa and her girls were here, then Della, Ruth, Lois, Mary and Monica came over later. Sylvia has the flu.

Sunday, September 21, 1986—30° to 52° and mostly sunny. Took pump out of the lake and cleaned it. Brought generator home. Cleaned telephone cross arms and prepared them for greenhouse footings. Allen Farmer visited. Helped Rudbeck unload floats. Made ice cream at Monica Zappa's birthday party over at Billman's.

Monday, September 22, 1986—22° to 46°, cloudy with a light rain. Moved steel pile and put roof over it. Put rear door in storage shed and cleared a rear entryway to the shed. Put more lumber in attic of garage. Greg brought Dall Creek video and showed it to Les, Lois, Jim and Mary Odden, Ruth Looney, Sam Weaver and another lady friend of Mary's.

Tuesday, September 23, 1986—28° to 35°, cloudy and very windy, 30 to

10,000 Days in Alaska Book One 1978-1989

50 mph. Dan flew us to Lake Number One near Prince William Sound to hunt goats. Too windy—too windy also to go to Clarence Lake to hunt caribou. Put scope on .338 and sighted it in.

Wednesday, September 24, 1986—10° to 34° and partly cloudy. Placed and squared footing for greenhouse. Hauled a load of crushed rock for greenhouse, plus several odd jobs. Kahren and Sylvia did laundry in Glennallen.

Thursday, September 25, 1986—4° to 33°, partly cloudy and a light breeze. Chinked some of the arctic entry and then did a little Cat work around here. Did some dozing for Allen, then dug a septic system for him. Dan, Mike Walsh, and I flew to Clarence Lake to hunt. Saw a few moose—one bull.

Friday, September 26, 1986—4° to 32° Sunny, then cloudy in the evening. Missed one bull caribou in the morning, shot another at noon and packed it the short way to the lake. Ate lunch and flew to Snowshoe Lake. We saw lots of caribou, some big bulls. Saw some moose on the way home. Tried to find repair for Dan's rifle—no luck.

Saturday, September 27, 1986—26° to 34°, cloudy with a light snow. Hauled a load of water from Hoffman's and helped Allen Farmer.

Sunday, September 28, 1986—31° to 40°, snowy and cloudy. Helped Allen Farmer with his septic system. Shot five ducks on our lake. Had pizza at KROA.

Monday, September 29, 1986—34° to 44° and cloudy. Ice is gone from the lake. Dan Billman and Allen Farmer came by. Started putting up lean-to on storage shed.

Tuesday, September 30, 1986—32° to 48°, sunny then cloudy with a light rain in the evening. Finished roof and put most of the boards on the north side of lean-to. Put electric trolling motor on canoe and hunted ducks on our lake—they are spooky now. Managed to get one scoter duck. Motor drove the canoe so hard at the landing, I capsized in shallow water—big joke on me. Dan Billman visited in the evening.

Wednesday, October 1, 1986—36° to 38°, cloudy, foggy and rain. Moved a few loads of gravel with the wheelbarrow. Moved Blake's house to blacktop for Allen to move. I hear the geese and swans are flying.

Thursday, October 2, 1986—35° to 38°, cloudy, foggy, rain. Finished siding on the lean-to and wheeled more gravel. Stacked lumber and set posts for driveway fill. More geese flying.

Friday, October 3, 1986—36° to 40°, cloudy and foggy. Charlie Trowbridge visited in the morning. I returned Rhynell's tiller and brought 25 telephone cross arms home. Ole delivered a propane tank. Bob and Kahren came over to watch "Dallas" at our place.

Saturday, October 4, 1986—25° to 40°, mostly sunny with some breeze. Charlie and Beth visited in the morning. Sylvia finished cutting up boo today. I finished retaining wall for our circle drive and loaded black dirt for me and for Allen—and pushed up more for him.

Sunday, October 5, 1986—25° to 40°, sunny beautiful day. Cleaned the chimney. Put canvas cover over the Cat and reattached TV wire. Worked on snowgo bearings. More swans flying. Lucky put his garage door opener in.

Monday, October 6, 1986—12° to 30° and partly cloudy. Re-piled used lumber, trimmed trees, cleaned up, and adjusted garage door. Jim and Mary brought a barrel stove to us. Hunted ducks—got four. Lake is half covered with ice, 1/4" thick.

Tuesday, October 7, 1986—18° to 32° and cloudy. Made a makeshift lean-to over used lumber. Set up garage stove. Put in new copper tubing to water heater and to gas stove. Allen moved Blake's house. Sylvia and Kahren did laundry.

Wednesday, October 8, 1986—23° to 32°, snow in the night, cloudy to partly cloudy. Made propane regulator brackets. Started framing garage workbench. Visited Hoffmans. Lucky planed some boards for me.

Thursday, October 9, 1986—24° to 34° and cloudy. Worked on garage bench, wired outlets, and cut some shelves.

Friday, October 10, 1986—36° to 54°, cloudy, high winds. Eight trees blew down here. Built two large cupboards for the garage. Hauled some gravel. Allen borrowed my truck. Rainy and windy tonight. This wind is an offshoot of a typhoon South China Sea.

Saturday, October 11, 1986—40° to 45° and partly cloudy. Repaired Jim and Elaine's greenhouse. Cut up some trees and put up a cupboard. Shot six ducks from the canoe on our lake. All the ice is out now. Moved some things from storage shed to the garage.

Sunday, October 12, 1986—32° to 45°, mostly cloudy and windy in the late afternoon. Covered at greenhouse soil. Built doors for lumber shed. Pulled swamp buggy over near a large tree. Tied a rope to re-anchor the rabbit hutches.

Monday, October 13, 1986—36° to 46°, partly sunny, cloudy and rain in the evening. Parked swamp buggy. Built cupboard for welder supplies. Put trim on other cupboards. Large flock of swans rested on our lake. They were tired from fighting a head wind. Dave DeJung helped me haul three loads of gravel and stayed here with us for supper.

Tuesday, October 14, 1986—30° to 45° and sunny. Built the bedroom and bathroom doors. Leveled and packed the gravel that we hauled last evening. Visited Jim and Mary Odden. Tom and his girls visited us.

Wednesday, October 15, 1986—20° to 40°, sunny, and light rain and partly cloudy in Anchorage where we shopped today. Got lots of supplies for winter and to finish building. Stopped at Andy and Connie's.

Thursday, October 16, 1986—22° to 32° in mostly sunny. Loaded tools and welder and did some welding for Rhynell. Then I did the prep work to put skirting around her ATCOs.

Friday, October 17, 1986—8° to 24° and mostly cloudy. Allen and I worked at Rhynell's and skirted ATCOs, them we sided the woodshed. Bob and Kahren were here at our place tonight for duck supper and to watch TV.

Saturday, October 18, 1986—9° to 26° and cloudy. Installed attic ladder in garage. Put up radio aerial to the house, wood shop and also the garage. Hauled water and did some other jobs.

Sunday, October 19, 1986–22° to 24° with a light snow all day. Did a lot of small jobs. Smayda family visited. I looked at phone installation at Rudbeck's.

Monday, October 20, 1986–24° to 28°, a light snow and occasionally cloudy. Rotated tires and put new leaf in spring. Welded door or on truck. Visited Lucky and Mary.

Tuesday, October 21, 1986–34° to 40°, sunny nice day. Went to Glennallen on business and did jobs around here in afternoon.

Wednesday, October 22, 1986–20° here at Nelchina and 46° in Anchorage. We went there shopping and got most of what we needed. Saw two moose cows, one calf and a large owl after dark on the way home.

Thursday, October 23, 1986–20° to 28°, some snow and cloudy all day. Unloaded our shopping from yesterday and I worked four hours at Hoffman's. Arlene Dimmick visited us and Jim and Mary Odden came by too.

Friday, October 24, 1986–24° to 30° and cloudy. Worked at Rhynell's closing up the machine shed. Sylvia did laundry and helped Bob and Kahren. They came over later to watch Dallas.

Saturday, October 25, 1986–22° to 28° and partly cloudy. Worked at Hoffman's. Brought material home to build machine shed doors. Worked on those for six hours. I don't feel well tonight.

Sunday, October 26, 1986–8° to 22° and sunny. Worked on Hoffman's doors again and helped Rudbeck get plane into hangar. Worked on snowgo. Bob, Kahren, Jim and Mary Odden were here for supper.

Monday, October 27, 1986–11° to 25°, partly cloudy and breezy in the afternoon. Spent another four hours on Hoffman's doors and did he electric wiring. Allen and Roxanne and their family were here for supper.

10,000 Days in Alaska Book One 1978-1989

Tuesday, October 28, 1986—3° to 13°, mostly sunny and breezy and evening. Took one door to Hoffman's and brought more lumber home to finish the last door. Ran telephone wires in our house and helped Allen start logs for the addition on his house.

Wednesday, October 29, 1986—it's -6° tonight, partly cloudy and foggy. Finished the last of Hoffman's doors. Helped Allen in the afternoon. He bought supper at Nelchina.

Thursday, October 30, 1986—it's -5° to 5°, cloudy and ice fog all day. Tried to fix my trolling motor. Fixed the brushes in Dan's sander. Helped Allen with log wall of his addition that he is putting up.

Friday, October 31, 1986—it's -10° to 8° and cloudy. Hung all four doors on the machine shed at Hoffman's. Took five hours. Still more work to finish them. The neighborhood kids were here for trick-or-treating.

Saturday, November 1, 1986—10° to 21° and mostly cloudy. cleaned quite a bit of the storage shed today and helped Allen with his logs in the afternoon.

Sunday, November 2, 1986—12° to 24° and partly cloudy. Finished cleaning the storage shed and putting the snowgo together. Built jack stand for snowgo and visited the Smaydas.

Monday, November 3, 1986—10° to 26° and cloudy. Plumbed in the heating stove hot water loop/cold water to hot water heater. The pipe threader set was very useful.

Tuesday, November 4, 1986—10° to 26° and cloudy. Finished plumbing and hauled a load of water from Lucky and Mary's. Voted in Glennallen. Bought two, Manning No. 9's (a type of wolf trap). Visited Darrel Gerry at KROA.

Wednesday, November 5, 1986—12° to 25° and cloudy. Visited Allen. Lucky gave me a steel tube to make traps setters. We got the phone hooked up. I built two sets of traps setters. Jim and Mary Odden visited.

Thursday, November 6, 1986—6° to 19° and sunny. Went with Lucky as he pulled his pickup to Anchorage with Blake's pickup. We had troubles with the first hitch and had to fashion a second one. Did shopping in town.

Friday, November 7, 1986—it's -5° to 5° and sunny. Oil in snowgo cylinder had to be dried out with ether before it would start. Worked on trap setter for Helfrich traps—first try failed, so I started over with another idea. Lisa Smayda and her daughters and Greg visited. Allen Farmer and Tracy visited. Gave Allen trap setter. Jerry Lica and his friend, Harold are staying at Rudbeck's place.

Saturday, November 8, 1986—cloudy and -10° to 6°. Worked on the snowgo and the trap setter. My back is very sore. Allen Farmer came over to get a needle and thread to recover his snowgo seat. Called the fire chief in Motley Minnesota. Henry, Sally and Sam brought a VCR over to record a movie for us.

Sunday, November 9, 1986—10° to 19° and cloudy. Helped Allen put up rafters on his addition. Did some more work getting ready to go trapping.

Monday, November 10, 1986—11° to 19° and cloudy. I got my trap gear together and made a few sets on Slide Mountain—very little sign. Many trees blown down. Trail is rough due to very little snow. Allen Farmer visited in the evening. I gave him a doghouse.

Tuesday, November 11, 1986—14° to 24° and cloudy. Made four fox sets and six marten sets on 13-Mile Trail. The trail was so rough I came home. Welded on the snowgo trailer. Allen visited in the evening.

Wednesday, November 12, 1986—5° to 12°, partly cloudy event and sunny. Sylvia and I both don't feel well. Worked on trap chains and thumb warmer on snowgo. Cleaned chimney. Allen stopped in—he got a fox.

Thursday, November 13, 1986—2° to 3°, cloudy, ice fog and frost. Worked at servicing truck all day. Had a good supper at Odden's tonight. Smayda's stopped there after supper was over and we all had pecan pie and homemade ice cream.

Friday, November 14, 1986—2° to 15° and partly cloudy. Fixed throttle on truck and other odd jobs. Went to Hoffman's to bring in the mail and packages for Max.

Saturday, November 15, 1986—10° to 20° and partly cloudy. Worked at Hoffman's a half day on machine shed doors. Went to an ice skating party at Snowshoe Lake today and a pot luck at KROA in the evening. Nothing in the trap at the dump.

Sunday, November 16, 1986—0° to 12° and mostly sunny. Ran trapline on Slide Mountain—got a male marten, skinned and stretched it. Visited Tom and Lisa and family, and altered a pair of ski poles for Lauren. Allen borrowed my trap boiling stove and pot. Beautiful moonlit nights.

Monday, November 17, 1986—0° to 9° and sunny. Went to the Eleven-Mile Trail and Lake Louise Road. Set traps to end of Seismic Trail and took Judd Lake Trail to 13-Mile Trail. Nothing in traps. Made a few sets, one wolf set. Saw fox, marten and wolf tracks. Caribou on Lake Louise Road.

Tuesday, November 18, 1986—it's -10° to 2°, Sunny, colder, breezy. Started hanging bedroom and bathroom doors. Painted ski poles for Lauren Smayda. Hauled a load of water from Lucky's place. Jim Odden was over and we talked trapping. Mary came by after her hobby class.

Wednesday, November 19, 1986—sunny, colder and -20° to -8°. Worked a little on the basement and welded on snowgo trailer. Philip and Arlene visited. Allen brought the trap boiler back. I dyed some snares.

Thursday, November 20, 1986—sunny, partly cloudy and -24° to -14°. Hung dining room blinds and put doors on bathroom vanity. Started cleaning wood shop. Dyed some traps. Lisa Smayda and daughters visited.

Friday, November 21, 1986—temp is -22° to -12°, Sunny, partly cloudy. Checked trap and snares at dump. Worked on some traps and equipment. Got a 2 x 6 from Rhynell and the snares I ordered from Thompson came. Allen brought over a thermometer to test.

Saturday, November 22, 1986—still -22° to -8°, Sunny, cloudy, light snow. Allen's thermometer was 6° colder. Tom borrowed a half inch drill.

Sylvia baked bread again today and I started marten boxes, dyed snares and traps. We made trim for two doors.

Sunday, November 23, 1986—it's -8° to -5°, cloudy skiff of snow. Ran Slide Mountain trapline with no luck. Saw one fox track. Set one wolf snare. Dyed some fox traps and built eight marten boxes.

Monday, November 24, 1986—it's -17° to -7° and cloudy with 2 inches of snow. I don't feel well today. Split and put two wheelbarrow loads of wood in the basement. Visited Henry. Allen and Kyle visited us in the evening. Mailed abstract to lawyer in Little Falls. Saw six boo on our Lake today—one nice bull.

Tuesday, November 25, 1986—it's -7° to 2°. Snowed all night and most of the day—we have 6 inches accumulation. Lucky plowed our snow. I shoveled snow and dyed and repaired traps. Sylvia cleaned and baked.

Wednesday, November 26, 1986—very light snow and -10° to -2°. Saw caribou on and near the road on the way to Eleven-Mile Trail. Ran the trapline and remade all sets. Made one wolf set at drainage below the two lakes. Stashed some traps where drag and trap lean along trail. Saw an owl, a spruce hen, boo. Ermine, rabbit and fox tracks. Nothing in sets. Nothing moving. Talked to Paul Shitari, just this side of Lake Louise Junction. Trail is still rough and difficult.

Thursday, November 27, 1986—down to -37° to -19°, cloudy and cool. Tom, Lisa and family, and Allen and Roxanne and their family were all here for Thanksgiving dinner. We had a great day. Rudbecks called.

Friday, November 28, 1986—it's -8° to 10°. 2 inches more snow last night and cloudy today, fog in the evening. Did some small jobs for Rudbecks and visited with Allen. Allen got a road kill call for a moose calf. Dave, Allen, and I went to salvage the ham and shoulder.

Saturday, November 29, 1986—10° to 16°, clouds, fog and son. Sunset on the clouds over the mountains was very beautiful. Allen and I went to mile 134 to get the moose calf carcass, but it hadn't frozen yet. I cut out some parts for a garage ladder and shoveled some snow. Allen got a red fox at the campground. Henry's kids, Denise, Doug and Shelley are visiting him.

10,000 Days in Alaska Book One 1978-1989

Sunday, November 30, 1986—8° to 10° and cloudy. Put wood in basement and finished garage ladder. Allen plowed our snow, then Allen and I worked on his "under the seat" box for his snowgo. Jim and Mary Odden visited us in the evening.

Monday, December 1, 1986—it's -3° to 5° and cloudy. Ran trapline on Slide Mountain with no luck. Went exploring east and south of our lake. Allen and I went to Chuck Zimbiki's for snowgo plugs and a belt. Tried to fix windshield on snowgo.

Tuesday, December 2, 1986—cloudy and -6° to 4°. Took chairs back to Allen and hauled a load of water from Lucky's. Put ladder on garage roof. Got trap gear ready.

Wednesday, December 3, 1986—cloudy and -5° to 0°. Saw two moose and lots of Caribou on Lake Louise Road. Parked at Eleven-Mile Rd—no fur in traps. Saw fox, coyote, marten and wolf tracks. Made trail set for wolf. Made coyote set near Blue Lake. Marten near trap cabin. Moved food and kitchen utensils back into trap cabin. Really nice here, no bear trouble.

Thursday, December 4, 1986—cloudy, some fog, -5° to -2°. Rested all day.

Friday, December 5, 1986—it's -2° to 8°. Made sets west and south along bench. Saw fox and otter track. Cut a quarter mile of trail and made sets east to Burbot Lake. Nothing in traps. Rough trail—water table is low. Very little ice in drainages. Many exposed rock in lakes and on their bottoms! Set otter snare in trench.

Saturday, December 6, 1986—6° and mostly cloudy. Ran line down the drainage to Mendeltna Springs. Made sets. Fox walked all over one set. Marten wouldn't go up pole at another. Had something large at trap at crossing—it ran off with drag, tangled it up and popped jaw out of trap. Saw a 40" inch bull moose and two cows and a calf.

Sunday, December 7, 1986—2° to 8° and cloudy. Ran the line on Slide Mountain—nothing. Saw marten and fox tracks, one dead Boo. Made fox set. Allen Farmer got a male gray wolf. Skinned it in our garage this evening.

Monday, December 8, 1986—4° to 11° and cloudy. Tried to extend trapline on Slide Mountain. Reached upper Seismic, and no fur tracks. Saw an eagle on a boo carcass. Set trap at moose calf road kill and another at boo kill. Saw a moose calf licking salt from off roadway.

Tuesday, December 9, 1986—33° to 25°, cloudy and light rain horn. Checked set at mile 133. Allen checked sets at campground and chopped conibear and box out of overflow near bridge. Nothing in sets at boo kill. Put a snare in trail east of our lake. Repaired conibear and made a mink set down by lake. Put more wood in basement.

Wednesday, December 10, 1986—31° to 39° and cloudy. Boo on road to Eleven-Mile Trail. Got a half mile with snowgo and broke suspension spring. Returned home and repaired the snowgo. Cleaned snow off of some roofs and visited with Lee D. at Nelchina. Visited Jim and Mary in the evening.

Thursday, December 11, 1986—34° to 22°, partly cloudy and warm. Boo on Lake Louise Road. Saw wolf and fox track. Made Lynx and wolf sets. Remade lots of other sets. Had to go back three miles for my coat (lost it along the way). Sled came unhooked many times. Got female marten at Blue Lake and had a camp robber and raven in traps. Skinned the marten.

Friday, December 12, 1986—8° to 10° and cloudy. Went west and south in trench. Made cubby sets and redid all others. Saw more wolf and marten tracks, but nothing in traps. Went to Blue Lake, then east several lakes. Checked sets and made new ones. Trail got too rough to break anymore. Real tired tonight.

Saturday, December 13, 1986—8° to 15°, cloudy and fog. Nothing in traps on the way out. A marten had twisted himself out of one trap. Stretched marten in the evening.

Sunday, December 14, 1986—15° to 19°, cloudy and foggy. Slept late, then visited Tom and Lisa and Henry's. Made two wolf sets east of our lake. Ran Slide Mountain trapline and got one female marten. Eagle is still feeding on boo. Started rebuilding snowgo sled ski. Henry, Sally

10,000 Days in Alaska Book One 1978-1989

and Chris were here for supper.

Monday, December 15, 1986—15° to 27°, windy, cloudy, skiff of snow. Went to Glennallen. Sylvia went to the doctor and did laundry and we did shopping. Finished welding on snowgo sled. Had trouble with broken propane fittings. Visited at KROA late into the evening.

Tuesday, December 16, 1986—20°, partly cloudy and foggy some of the day on our lake. Got trap gear ready and fixed propane line. Wrote letters. Allen got a wolverine on Slide Mountain. Sylvia babysat the Smayda girls.

Wednesday, December 17, 1986—4° to 10° and mostly cloudy. Allen and I went looking for lynx on Mendeltna Creek with no luck. Nothing on Slide Mountain—made three new sets.

Thursday, December 18, 1986—10° to 20° at partly cloudy. Parked at Eleven-Mile. Lured and baited all sets. Made two sets at Judd Lake. Got a silver cross fox. A wolf pack left fresh tracks at Blue Lake. Made a marten set near the lake. Saw five boo lying on the lake ice near cabin. Quite a few boo in the area. Here at the trap cabin, I split wood, melted snow for water and skinned the fox. Read, and listened to the radio.

Friday, December 19, 1986—8° to 20°, foggy, cloudy, and foggy again. Went west and south. Saw wolf, marten and fox track but nothing in my traps. Made a wolf set on the way to Blue Lake. Went east past Burbot Lake. Got a nice silver, red cross fox. Made more sets—fox and marten sets at the north end of Burbot Lake. Lured all the sets. Skinned fox.

Saturday, December 20, 1986—10° to 18° and cloudy with some breeze. Up early, got traps and bait ready and went to Hole Lake. Made cubby at lower and. Some boo on Pristine Lake. Made a marten set in big trees in south drainage of Pristine Lake. Went to lake on Mendeltna Springs—saw lots of wolf track. Set a wolf snare and made one set on lake at once set at upper cut. Made a mink set downstream from lake. Water level is very low. The wolves had been chewing and playing with sticks—ripping and tearing chunks of dead wood from upright willows. Tired tonight and don't feel well. Nothing was in traps today.

Sunday, December 21, 1986—it was 0° all day. Slept late, nothing in traps today. Went to line at lower end of Mendeltna Springs and made a marten set. Did some exploring—kept losing the sled—laid it over the snowgo. Made Fox set near the junction in the drainage. Some people there were freighting. building materials into the subdivision. Found some snowgo bogeys in the trail left them on a pickup at Eleven-Mile trail head. Fleshed and stretched the two cross fox this evening. Beverly called.

Monday, December 22, 1986—it's -10° to -6°, cloudy and an ice fog. Tried to run traps east of our drainage but broke steering on snowgo and got lost in the fog. Got the snowgo home. Jim and Mary brought their sled down to our place to put handle warmers on and do some welding on it. I rebuilt snowgo steering—finished about 2:45 a.m.

Tuesday, December 23, 1986—still -10° to -7°, cloudy and more ice fog. Ran traplines around here—nothing. Visited Henry and Sally. Allen stopped in to look at maps. Sylvia and I visited Lucky and Mary in the evening.

Wednesday, December 24, 1986—it's -10° to -6°, cloudy and ice fog. Visited Allen. Got trap gear ready and put two sled loads of wood in the basement and another in the garage. Had supper at Odden's—good time.

Thursday, December 25, 1986—0° to -5°, cloudy, light snow, ice fog. Had Christmas dinner at Smayda's. Oddens were there too.

Friday, December 26, 1986—temp is -5° to 12° with a light snow—three inches. Nothing in the traps around here. Got water at Hoffman's.

Saturday, December 27, 1986—it's -10° to 8°, cloudy, sunny, cloudy. Saw three moose on Lake Louise Road. Went in on 13-Mile. Got one marten, re-lured and baited all sets. Broke trail along Mendeltna Springs—tough going.

Sunday, December 28, 1986—8° to 10°, sunny then cloudy. Checked sets west and south—nothing. Boo stepped in one set. Put up one marten box. Put a short trapline in near beaver pond west of springs. Made three sets.

Monday, December 29, 1986—0° all day, cloudy, sunny then cloudy.

10,000 Days in Alaska Book One 1978-1989

Went to Hole Lake and Pristine Lake. Went part way on North Seismic. Got a cross fox and skinned it. Put up two marten boxes and made a fox set.

Tuesday, December 30, 1986—it's -5° to 10°, cloudy, sunny, cloudy. Nothing in traps on the way out to truck. Made a fox set and moved a fox set. Jim brought fur to send to Winnipeg. Stretched fox and marten.

Wednesday, December 31, 1986—8° to 18°, light snow and cloudy. Ran traplines around here—nothing. Made one fox set at the east end of our lake. Had business to do in Glennallen: notary, ship fur, Blazo, laundry, etc. had supper with Jim and Mary.

Norman Wilkins

Norman and Sylvia Wilkins

Top: Norman Wilkins at a campfire. Bottom: Pregnant caribou killed by wolves; the calf was eaten, leaving the rest of the carcass largely untouched.

Norman Wilkins

1987—ore samples, crane hunting, goose hunting

Thursday, January 1, 1987–14° all day, cloudy and ice fog. Slept late, then built four marten platforms for 120 coni traps. Got ready to go out again. Visited Lucky. People were skating on the lake today. Phoned mother.

Friday, January 2, 1987–10° to 2°, cloudy with some fog. Went in at Eleven-Mile. Boo had sprung wolf trap in trail set. Wolves went through later. Made some sets along Mendeltna Springs and got a nice male marten at Beaver Lake (west). Made set at Hole Lake near top of abandoned beaver lodge. Extended line there and made one set. Nothing in other sets.

Saturday, January 3, 1987–0° to 3°, cloudy, sunny, then cloudy again. Ran line east and north. Nothing in traps. Extended line north. Made two new sets. Skinned marten.

Sunday, January 4, 1987–0° to 10° and cloudy. Got a marten over towards Hole Lake (120 on leaning pole). Nothing in other traps. Baited and lured all sets. Remade wolf sets. Junior Hunt isn't trapping north of Old Man Lake. Jim and Mary took Sylvia to KROA. Stretched one marten and skinned and stretched the other one.

Monday, January 5, 1987–14° to 24°, cloudy, light snow. Nothing in traps here. Broke snowgo ski, welded it and got trap gear ready. Allen Farmer visited. Sylvia's gone to glass class. Called Nadia.

Tuesday, January 6, 1987–20° to 30°, cloudy, breezy, light snow. Picked up some traps off 13-Mile Trail. Went to Old Boot Lake, everything okay there. Got a ball for hitch from Allen. Went to dump.

Wednesday, January 7, 1987–12° and sunny. Allen plowed our snow (got 4 inches last night). Got more traps ready and build more marten boxes. Got fox urine from Simons.

Thursday, January 8, 1987–24° to 20°, cloudy, snow—white out. Broke trail and made sets on Nine-Mile above Old Man Lake and west. Lots of boo on Blue Lake and in that vicinity. Saw a young bull moose still with horns. Saw one fox and one marten track. Don't feel well tonight.

10,000 Days in Alaska Book One 1978-1989

Friday, January 9, 1987—8° to 15°, sunny and partly cloudy with light snow last night. Went west and south to Mendeltna Springs. Saw five moose feeding. Made two otter and one mink set at beaver dam. No fur. Saw two moose near Beaver Lodge Lake and lots of boo. Found one dead caribou. Marten didn't go in box set.

Saturday, January 10, 1987—it's -5° to -12° and sunny. Ran line east and north. Boo had sprung lots of sets. Lots of moose in the area also. No fur in traps. Saw only mink tracks. Felt sick this morning.

Sunday, January 11, 1987—sunny and -20° to -12°. Ran line out to pick up—no fur. Remade some sets. Lots of drifted snow. New skis are here for snowgo. These moonlit nights are simply beautiful.

Monday, January 12, 1987—dropped to -32° to -36° and sunny. Rested all day. Tom Smayda and girls brought over some things to store here. Jim and Mary Odden visited in evening.

Tuesday, January 13, 1987—still -36° to -24°, sunny and partly cloudy. Worked some on trap gear. Tom Smayda brought some canned goods to store here while they are in Hawaii.

Wednesday, January 14, 1987—it's -26° to -10°, sunny and partly cloudy. No fur. No tracks on line here. Moose stepped in Manning wolf trap. Bent it up pretty badly. Put wood in basement and one load at garage. Put skis on snowgo. Butchered a road kill boo, Allen helped.

Thursday, January 15, 1987—cloudy and -18° to -1°. Sylvia cut up and packaged four quarters of boo. I made new wire grill for snowgo and did service work. Straightened out Manning trap.

Friday, January 16, 1987—it's -10° to 1° and partly cloudy. Finished 18 marten boxes. Rebuilt hold-down on snowgo trailer. Got trap gear ready. Hauled load of water from Hoffman's.

Saturday, January 17, 1987—0° to 5° and partly cloudy. Saw 12 moose along Lake Louise Road and some marten wolf and fox tracks. The wolf, marten and fox were close calls. Made three new marten sets on Nine-Mile overflow on the lake at Mendeltna Springs. Nothing in traps. Nice

Norman Wilkins

to be at the cabin.

Sunday, January 18, 1987—it's -2° to 10°. Had a marten in a fox set at end of west-south line. Went west to trail Allen put in. Went southeast from Mendeltna Lake and made fox set east across from Beaver Lodge. Went southeast and made one marten set. Did quite a bit of exploring. Snowgo suspension broke where I welded it last year. Skinned marten.

Monday, January 19, 1987—10° to 20° and cloudy. Nothing on line. Saw some fox and wolf tracks and looked over cubby under large spruce.

Tuesday, January 20, 1987—10° to 60° and partly cloudy. Left cabin early, nothing in traps. Moved fox set on Judd Lake Trail and picked up wolf trap north of Judd Lake. Visited Allen and Roxanne for supper and stretched one marten.

Wednesday, January 21, 1987—20° to 31°, cloudy and breezy. Visited Allen and brazed the broken places in the suspension on snowgo. Dan Billman phoned.

Thursday, January 22, 1987—22° to 32° mostly cloudy and breezy. Ran line here—nothing. Explored some. Pulled some traps and got gear ready.

Friday, January 23, 1987—20° to 23° and cloudy. Parked at Eleven-Mile. There were boo in the road. Got one marten on Nine-Mile Trail. Made three wolf trail sets. Got one beaver on Mendeltna Creek. Suspension broke again on snowgo. Skinned marten and beaver.

Saturday, January 24, 1987—0° to 8° and sunny. Nothing on line near beaver pond. Came out to fix snowgo. Jim Odden came down to braze the broken parts. Allen Farmer and Dave Kimball visited.

Sunday, January 25, 1987—sunny and -2° to 10°. Finished repair of snowgo parts and installed them. Now I'm sick with the flu.

Monday, January 26, 1987—it's -3° to 9° and mostly cloudy. Still have the flu.

Tuesday, January 27, 1987—0° to 7° and partly cloudy still sick, Mary

10,000 Days in Alaska Book One 1978-1989

Odden brought some medicine.

Wednesday, January 28, 1987—mostly cloudy and -2° to 0°, light snow in the evening. Still sick.

Thursday, January 29, 1987—temp is -10° to 17° and mostly cloudy with a light snow. Still have the flu, Jim and Mary Odden visited.

Friday, January 30, 1987—down to -23° to -11° partly cloudy at a light snow. Got trap gear ready and put some wood in basement.

Saturday, January 31, 1987—it's -10° to 0°. Some sun, cloudy, light snow. Went to Copperville to pay for airline tickets at the travel agent. Stopped at Chuck Zimbiki's for snowgo spark plugs. Visited Jim and Mary Odden and stayed for supper there. Mary had made a birthday cake for me.

Sunday, February 1, 1987—cloudy and -5° to 5°. Parked at Eleven-Mile Trail. Made a boo hide, gut pile set with snares on Nine-Mile Trail. Nothing in sets today. Pulled some traps.

Monday, February 2, 1987—0° to 5° and partly cloudy. Went west and south, pulled one fox set. Moved wolf trap to near boo carcass. Ran line west of Mendeltna Springs—no fur. Did some exploring.

Tuesday, February 3, 1987—it's -5° to 5° and sunny. Ran lines east and north—no fur—some fox tracks. Boo sprung some sets. Saw wolf tracks on lots of the trail today. Went north of Burbot Lake to creek drainage coming from "V" Lake. Follow low ridge west to unnamed lake and on up drainage, around bend and back west. Put up three marten boxes north of Burbot Lake.

Wednesday, February 4, 1987—still -5° to 5°, sunny and cloudy. Nothing on line out to truck. Lost sled and had to go back to get it. Visited at KROA. Allen brought me a birthday cake.

Thursday, February 5, 1987—temp about same, -9° 0° and partly cloudy. Ran lines around here—nothing. Some wolf track on Slide Mountain. Jim Odden helped me load and unload two old snowgos. Smayda family got back from Hawaii.

Friday, February 6, 1987—mostly cloudy and -8° to 3°. Smayda family visited and picked up their "freezables" that were stored here while they were on vacation. Went to Hoffman's for a load of water.

Saturday, February 7, 1987—it's -4° to 12° and mostly cloudy. More caribou are down on the lake today. Put three slide loads of wood in basement. Phoned my brother Jerry Wilkins and also Dan Billman.

Sunday, February 8, 1987—8° to 18° and partly cloudy. Really beautiful this morning with the sun on the mountains. Took three dog houses to Darrel Gerry at KROA and visited Hoffmans.

Monday, February 9, 1987—5° to 10° and partly cloudy. Got trap gear ready. Jim and Mary Odden were here for supper.

Tuesday, February 10, 1987—5° to 10° and cloudy. Parked at Eleven-Mile. Boo in the road again. No fur on line. Much overflow on springs and lake.

Wednesday, February 11, 1987—it's -5° to 10° and sunny. Ran line east and north. No fur. Boo wrecked one of my traps. Broke trail to Grayling Lake. More wolf tracks and some fox and marten tracks. Put up marten boxes and improved trail.

Thursday, February 12, 1987— still -5° to 10° and sunny. Went exploring north and west of Burbot Lake. Try to go up "V" Lake drainage but it was tough going. Saw fox and marten track and lost my mitts off snowgo. Made two fox sets and improved more trail. Beautiful day. Much overflow from "V" Lake drainage into lake.

Friday, February 13, 1987— temp is -15° to 0° and mostly sunny. Ran line out to Lake Louise Road—no fur. A marten had tripped conibear in box. Trap bound up and failed to catch marten. Warren D. and Tom stopped to visit. Sylvia went with Mary Odden to get plane tickets. Had supper at Odden's.

Saturday, February 14, 1987—it's -10° to 8° and mostly sunny. Ran lines around here—and. Picked up traps north of lake and visited Smayda's. Allen stopped in. Phoned Vanessa.

10,000 Days in Alaska Book One 1978-1989

Sunday, February 15, 1987—still -10° to 12° and mostly sunny. Worked on income tax records.

Monday, February 16, 1987—cloudy with a very light snow and -8° to 10°. Visited Jim and Mary Odden, Karen Mailey and Hoffmans.

Tuesday, February 17, 1987—it's -5° to 10° and mostly sunny. Jim Odden went with me on the line. Lots of boo and moose—no fur. Picked up traps on Nine-Mile. Hung up traps along Mendeltna Springs. Jim went home and I came to the trap cabin and hung up traps.

Wednesday, February 18, 1987—0° to 12°, cloudy, and some light breeze. Ran line pulling traps. No fur east and north. Boo had sprung some traps. Camp robber and raven in two traps. Retraced exploring trail—didn't find my mitts. No new fur tracks but lots of moose and boo.

Thursday, February 19, 1987—10° to 18° and partly cloudy. Ran line west and south but no fur. One raven. Pulled traps all the way to road. Several camp robbers in conibears. Several moose, lots of boo.

Friday, February 20, 1987—10° to 22° and mostly cloudy. Ran Slide Mountain. No fur, picked up traps. Rinsed out trapping box on snowgo and mixed gas. Tom and his girls visited. Talked to another surveyor (Gulkona).

Saturday, February 21, 1987—10° to 24° and mostly sunny. Russ Hoffman looked at big trailer. Got some things ready to go on our trip. Had supper with Oddens.

Sunday, February 22, 1987—18° to 22° and cloudy. Allen plowed some snow from in front of the big trailer. Buyer for trailer backed out of the deal. Jim Odden flew me out over my trapline—and his.

Monday, February 23, 1987—left home early for Anchorage. Renewed remote parcel lease. Stayed at Andy and Connie's and visited Mike and Shirley—they took us to the airport.

Tuesday, February 24, 1987—flew to Seattle/Frisco/Kona Hawaii. Patti Billman met us and took us to their house in Waimea.

Norman Wilkins

Wednesday, February 25, 1987—Patti took us to south of the Big Island to sightsee and go shopping. Dan worked.

Thursday, February 26, 1987—Sylvia and I used Billman's car and went to Kohala. Saw a reconstructed village and visited a real estate agent. Talked about building, and houses for sale. Beautiful scenery on the drive back.

Friday, February 27, 1987—Dan is off work because of rain. We all went flying in Cessna 72—saw wild pigs, ranches, farms, bull whale, cow and calf and other whales, porpoises, boats and a canoe race.

Saturday, February 28, 1987—went to a park on east side of the island for a picnic.

Sunday, March 1, 1987—Dan and I flew to Mouliki Island and Met Bill and Nora. We sighted whales on the way over. Lots of wind and turbulence and surf. Saw fishing boats and tugboats pulling barges and cruise ships. We visited the leper colony and saw head and horns of axis deer. We flew near Hilo on the way back.

Monday, March 2, 1987—Dan and I looked at lots of property and spent some time at the airport.

Tuesday, March 3, 1987—up at 4:00 a.m. Dan and Patti took us to Hilo Airport. We caught a plane to Honolulu, then to Los Angeles. Jerry met us there and took us to his place.

Wednesday, March 4, 1987—went to Hemet and visited mother.

Thursday, March 5, 1987—visited mother. Cousin Jack and wife Bev came from near Phoenix, Arizona. We had a nice visit. Mother went to Doctor.

Friday, March 6, 1987—up early, Jerry and Mary took us to the L.A. airport and we caught a plane to Minneapolis. Nadia and Beverly and their families met us at the airport. We stayed at Nadia's.

Saturday, March 7, 1987—made lots of business calls, did some shopping

10,000 Days in Alaska Book One 1978-1989

and went to a birthday party for grandson, Lee Austin. It was a good time.

Sunday, March 8, 1987—did some more shopping and then went to the Science Museum and Omni theater that was fun.

Monday, March 9, 1987—went to Beverly and Kevin's and visited there. Called a lawyer about land sale. Brother Jerry called in the evening—mother passed away during the night.

Tuesday, March 10, 1987—spend the day with Beverly and family and went out for supper in the evening. Jerry called about funeral for mother. (she had told me she wanted me to see her alive, and after she was gone, it was not important).

Wednesday, March 11, 1987—babysat for Beverly while they went out and did some business and Kevin took us to Theresa's at noon.

Thursday, March 12, 1987—tried to trace insurance for mobile home that had burned.

Friday, March 13, 1987—Kevin Brought income tax papers over for us. Earl and Theresa drove us to Paul and Ruth's in Staples. Steve was real glad to see us. Mother was buried today.

Saturday, March 14, 1987—did some visiting and made lots of phone calls pertaining to principals of land contract and Sale.

Sunday, March 15, 1987—made a lot more phone calls today, finally reached the last person. Visited friends. Went to cemetery. Saw Earl's folks, Don and Evelyn Caughey while we were there.

Monday, March 16, 1987—borrow Paul and Ruth's car. Made lots of phone calls in the morning. Visited Harry and Neva McCoy, then Taymond and Clara Hanson. Jim and Arlene R. came to see us for supper.

Tuesday, March 17, 1987—Paul and Ruth and Steve drove us down to Theresa and Earl's. Later we went to Beverly's, then on to Nadia and Darrell's for supper and stayed overnight.

Wednesday, March 18, 1987—Darrell drove us over to Beverly is. We looked at a house for investment with Kevin and stopped to get my eyes tested.

Thursday, March 19, 1987—looked at properties with Kevin and stayed the night at Nadia's.

Friday, March 20, 1987—did some last minute shopping then caught our flight to Denver/LA/Seattle/Anchorage. Warm day, nice to be headed home.

Saturday, March 21, 1987—up early, did shopping in Anchorage, then headed home. Great to be back, Stove has burned up all our propane.

Sunday, March 22, 1987—sunny and warm. We are trying to thaw out sewer. It froze while we were gone. Allen visited. Went to lucky and Mary's, visited with them and added up cost of house.

Monday, March 23, 1987—15° to 40° and sunny. Called surveyor and called Palmer account in Staples. Did some things around here. Helped Jim and Mary with logs and visited at KROA Went to Old Boot Lake.

Tuesday, March 24, 1987—15° to 40° and mostly sunny. More boo on Lake. Jim and I picked up two Mannings that were on Allen's line. One had a cross fox in it. Visited Roxanne and Henry and Sally.

Wednesday, March 25, 1987—20 to 25°, sunny and partly cloudy. Bob and Carmen visited. Skinned cross fox. Loaded snowgo and parked at Eleven-Mile. Saw lots of caribou and one moose. Pulled one wolf trap and three snares. Explored for new trail. Saw two fox and one marten track. Wolves had made a boo kill on Eleven-Mile Trail. They ate everything except some hide and two hooves. Everything at trap cabin is fine. Glad to be here.

Thursday, March 26, 1987—0° to 30° and sunny. Left the cabin at noon and went to explore Grayling Lake country. Some marten and fox track and lots of boo and one moose. At Old Beaver Dam, I put up one marten box and cached another one along with a trap and a double long, # 2 spring. Left 1-1/2 coil and drag on the next lake. Lots of overflow on the lake where "V" Lake Creek comes in. Several snowgos have crossed east and west over my Trail about 1 mile north of Burbot Lake. Lots of large pingos east of Blue Lake.

Friday, March 27, 1987—0° to 40° and sunny. Went to Beaver Dam at Mendeltna Creek and picked up two 330 conibears. Cached marten box at Harry's old set. Went east from drainage and found cat trail. Followed it northeast and marked it at larger opening. Lost it 1/2 to 3/4 of a mile from Eleven-Mile Trail. Went to Hoffman's to pick up a load of water in the late afternoon.

Saturday, March 28, 1987—12° to 30° and mostly sunny. Went to Old Boot Lake to help Jim and Mary put up a log cabin.

Sunday, March 29, 1987—10° to 30° and mostly sunny. Put up the logs today.

Monday, March 30, 1987—10° to 30° and mostly sunny. Bob and Kahren came in to visit at Old Boot Lake.

Tuesday, March 31, 1987—10° to 30° and mostly sunny. Worked on Jim and Mary's cabin and cleaned some brush along property line.

Wednesday, April 1, 1987—5° to 30° and mostly sunny. Cleared more brush along property line. Tom, Lisa and their girls came in. All of us brushed lines in the afternoon. Jim and Mary finished brushing late evening. I came home and stopped at KROA to talk to Darrel about his 40 acres. Some snow today.

Thursday, April 2, 1987—0° to 30° and mostly sunny. Phoned lawyer, Rested all day.

Friday, April 3, 1987—12° to 30° and cloudy. Went out to Old Boot Lake and helped Jim and Mary put up end logs on their cabin.

Saturday, April 4, 1987—10° to 32° and mostly sunny but windy in the evening. Put up the rafters today. Put plywood on and framed in the door. Broke camp and came home. Rip, Jim's dog, rode out to the road on my machine.

Sunday, April 5, 1987—14° to 36°, sunny and breezy. Dust blew off the river across west end of our lake. We babysat Laura and Emily today and went to KROA to pick up a rabbit hutch. Called surveyor. Jim and Mary visited.

Monday, April 6, 1987—12° to 37° and sunny. Did some things around here, made lots of phone calls and rested a little. Bob and Kahren helped unload the rabbit hutch. Visited Allen and Roxanne in the evening.

Tuesday, April 7, 1987—12° to 31°, sunny with some breeze. Went to the bank in Palmer and did some business. Sighted a marsh hawk on the drive home.

Wednesday, April 8, 1987—14° to 34°, Sunny, cloudy. Got gear ready to go to trap cabin and put some slabs in the basement. Visited Darrel at KROA and later, Jim and Mary Odden about surveying Old Boot Lake.

Thursday, April 9, 1987—14° to 25°, Sunny, cloudy, breezy. Saw a wolf track in the vicinity of Rat Lake on the way to trap cabin, and a fox and mink track near the cabin. Saw two moose feeding near the cabin this evening.

Friday, April 10, 1987—15° to 35°, sunny and cloudy with 3 1/2 inches of heavy, wet snow. Cut up and hauled several loads of wood for us. Ravens are calling a lot.

Saturday, April 11, 1987—15° to 35° and partly cloudy. I brought in more wood—got stuck. Covered the woodpile with a tarp and ringed more trees. I have one small pile of wood in the lot I still need to get.

Sunday, April 12, 1987—16° to 35° and mostly sunny. Put up three marten boxes on the way to Beaver Lodge. Saw a counterclockwise snow devil (a small, rotating wind that picks up loose snow instead of dirt, much like a dust devil). Put 330 and poles at outlet at Beaver Dam. Put 330 and poles in the drainage south of Beaver Lodge Lake. Cut some trail. Went to Green Acres, Jim and Mary were here about the surveyor.

Monday, April 13, 1987—14° to 41° and partly cloudy. Visited Rudbecks. They furnished pizza dinner here. Serviced snowgo. Looked over traps and ore samples. Jim and Mary brought papers to send to surveyor. Jim and Mary and Bob and Kahren were here for ice cream.

Tuesday, April 14, 1987—16° to 44° and mostly sunny. Visited Rudbecks. Nadia called again about our claims and lawyer for them. Chris Ronning was killed at 8:50 p.m. this evening in a rollover accident with his pickup. He was a really good friend.

Wednesday, April 15, 1987—18° to 36° and mostly sunny. Henry borrowed water hauling tank. Visited Tom and Lisa. Allen Farmer got some two inch plastic pipe from me.

Thursday, April 16, 1987—14° to 44° and mostly sunny. Put two sled loads of slabs and wood in the basement. Shoveled some snow from greenhouse area.

Friday, April 17, 1987—20° to 30° with a light fluffy snow most of the day. Loafed around the neighborhood all day.

Saturday April 18, 1987—18° to 36° and mostly sunny. Put up six sheets of plywood on our basement walls.

Sunday, April 19, 1987—18° to 34° and mostly sunny had Easter dinner at Rudbeck's place. Jerry and Moe and Jim and Mary were there too. We all had a good time.

Monday, April 20, 1987—16° to 39° and sunny. Wrote letters/US General order. Jim Odden and Rudbecks visited in the evening.

Tuesday, April 21, 1987—18° to 38° and sunny. We went with Jim Odden to Chris Ronning's funeral.

Wednesday, April 22, 1987—24° to 36° and partly cloudy. Went to Old Boot Lake. Surveyors have started to work.

Thursday, April 23, 1987—22° to 42° and mostly sunny. Did laundry and shopping in Glennallen and worked on snowgo.

Friday, April 24, 1987—26° to 44°, sunny and cloudy. Worked on snowgo.

Norman Wilkins

Saturday, April 25, 1987—22° to 40° and sunny. Went to Anchorage early to do some shopping and to go to Mike and Shirley's wedding. Got home late.

Sunday, April 26, 1987—20° to 36° and sunny. Rudbecks had a birthday party supper for Jim Odden and for Sylvia at their place. Bud and Jerry (Sally's mother) arrived for Sally and Henry's wedding.

Monday, April 27, 1987—18° to 42° and sunny Allen and I went fishing and got a mess of rainbow trout—saw a bald eagle. Cut up trail bait. Bud, Jerry, and Chris visited. Allen was here for supper.

Tuesday, April 28, 1987—15° to 40°, sunny and then cloudy. Hung two doors upstairs and installed knobs and doorstops and installed two more doors downstairs.

Wednesday, April 29, 1987—27° to 47° sunny and breezy. Sylvia's birthday. Went to Glennallen on business. Henry, Bud, and Sam borrowed generator.

Thursday, April 30, 1987—32° to 44°, sunny and cloudy. Hauled a load of water from Hoffman's. Had several visitors.

Friday, May 1, 1987—28° to 49°, sunny with a light breeze. Andy, Connie and family along with Mike and Shirley C. stayed overnight at our place. We all went to Henry and Sally's reception. Saw lots of people we hadn't seen in five years.

Saturday, May 2, 1987—28° to 48° and mostly sunny. Visited all day. Saw quite a few caribou bulls going west on the lake.

Sunday, May 3, 1987—27° to 46°, sunny and then sprinkles. Did some more visiting and we had some company here too.

Monday, May 4, 1987—30° to 45°, mostly cloudy with a light rain and some snow. Rudbecks and I went fishing. We got a mess of grayling trout through the ice.

Tuesday, May 5, 1987—32° to 48° and mostly sunny. Worked on the Cat

10,000 Days in Alaska Book One 1978-1989

and Bob and Kahren came over here to watch a movie.

Wednesday, May 6, 1987—26° to 44° and cloudy. Worked on the gas water pump. Bud and Jerry visited.

Thursday, May 7, 1987—25° to 40°, snow, rain, cloudy. Worked on Homelite water pump. It pumps water. Started work on lawnmower. Tom borrowed water tank and truck.

Friday, May 8, 1987—30° to 43°, mostly cloudy and several showers. Did very little here at home. Well driller is working at Smayda's. Sylvia and Kahren went to rummage sales. Lisa and the girls visited in the afternoon.

Saturday, May 9, 1987—27° to 45° and sunny. Worked on lawnmower and the few other small jobs.

Sunday, May 10, 1987—31° to 41°, snow in the morning, and sunny in the afternoon. Worked on a caribou Jaw sled for Allen. Rudbecks and Sylvia got back this evening. They had been in Anchorage getting supplies and stayed overnight.

Monday, May 11, 1987—28° to 46° and mostly sunny. Went to Wasilla for building materials—mostly for the greenhouse. While I was there I picked up a few things for Allen Farmer.

Tuesday, May 12, 1987—30° to 49°, cloudy, misty and showers. Cut and painted plywood for basement and unloaded the truck. Allen Farmer and Rudbecks visited.

Wednesday, May 13, 1987—34° to 46° and partly cloudy to cloudy. Finished painting the plywood and greenhouse door. Started on the rabbit hutch foundation.

Thursday, May 14, 1987—34° to 49° and mostly sunny. Rebuilt rabbit hutch and put it on foundation. Kahren and Bob came over to watch a movie.

Friday, May 15, 1987—34° to 43° and mostly cloudy. Several showers. We don't feel well today. Worked at landscaping the old dog lot.

Norman Wilkins

Saturday, May 16, 1987—36° to 47° with lots of showers. Finished landscaping the dog lot. We went to a party at KROA in the evening. Swans are courting—eight here.

Sunday, May 17, 1987—38° to 57°, sunny with some breeze. Put a lock on the door at Hoffman's. Visited Jim—he needed some pipe fittings. Visited Lucky and Mary in the evening.

Monday, May 18, 1987—26° to 50° and mostly sunny but windy. Grubbed out three stumps and built north wall of greenhouse. Panned some gravel at Smayda's well. Went for a pie and a movie at Rudbeck's.

Tuesday, May 19, 1987—30° to 51° and mostly sunny but windy in the afternoon. Walls of the greenhouse are framed up and I started on the rafters. Allen gave me some T-111 pieces for the greenhouse. All the ice has gone out of the lake. Lonnie G. wants the big trailer.

Wednesday, May 20, 1987—34° to 54° and sunny. Worked on the greenhouse and started some dozer work at Smayda's—2-1/2 hours.

Thursday, May 21, 1987—36° to 52° and partly cloudy. Built more rafters, felt sick all day. Dan Billman is back from Hawaii.

Friday, May 22, 1987—34° to 53° and mostly cloudy. Worked on the greenhouse. Dan Billman helped put up the truss rafters and headers.

Saturday, May 23, 1987—26° to 48° and partly cloudy. Worked on the greenhouse and dozed another 2 1/2 hours at Smayda's. Visited Dan Billman and had supper at Allen Farmers.

Sunday, May 24, 1987—26° to 50°, sunny than partly cloudy. Finished framing the greenhouse through. Dan Billman and done helped put fiberglass on the roof this afternoon. Had supper at Dan's. The Mailey family was there too. We borrowed the movie, "Walks Far Woman".

Monday, May 25, 1987—26° to 50° and mostly cloudy and breezy. Put more fiberglass on the greenhouse. Had dinner at Rudbeck's and Lisa and the girls came by to visit.

10,000 Days in Alaska Book One 1978-1989

Tuesday, May 26, 1987—38° to 48°, partly cloudy and windy. Worked on the greenhouse. Dan Billman was here for supper. Phil and Arlene and two cousins visited us in the evening.

Wednesday, May 27, 1987—28° to 50°, light showers. Went to Anchorage to do some shopping for materials and supplies. Saw lots of boo and some moose between here and mile 118.

Thursday, May 28, 1987—27° to 52°, partly cloudy and breezy. Helped Dan with some repairers on his plane all day. Sylvia tilled the garden and picked up trash along the road.

Friday, May 29, 1987—32° to 60° and sunny. Helped Dan Billman put his Beaver in the water. Did more bulldozer work at Smayda's. Built an electric wire reel and ran wire to the lake for our water pump.

Saturday, May 30, 1987—38° to 61°, Sunny, cloudy, shower in evening. Went to a health fair in Glennallen. Picked up some trash along the highway. Visited KROA. There was a community ball game at the gravel pit near State Camp—I didn't go.

Sunday, May 31, 1987—40° to 46° and rained most of the day. Worked on greenhouse all day and made a trip to the dump.

Monday, June 1, 1987—40 to 51° and rainy. Beautiful sun on the mountains in late evening. Worked on the greenhouse. Built a stand water pump and put it in the lake. Didn't get any water pumped. Allen Farmer visited. Two swans swam up to Sylvia and I while we were down at the lake.

Tuesday, June 2, 1987—40° to 45° rained all night and day. Worked on the greenhouse. Electric breaker is not 220 type for water pump.

Wednesday, June 3, 1987—40° to 50° rain showers and cloudy. Worked a little on the greenhouse. Hooked the water pump up across the road at that greenhouse. Switch breakers for the pump here and it worked. Finished digging basement garage for Smayda's.

Thursday, June 4, 1987—40° to 45° rain showers all day. Finished a diagonal bracing in greenhouse. Dan Billman went with me to mile 15 on Lake Louise Road to get a load of dirt. Then we finished filling our garden beds with dirt.

Friday, June 5, 1987—42° to 60° and mostly sunny with one rain shower. Went to Anchorage for building materials—got almost everything.

Saturday, June 6, 1987—40° to 57°, and rainy all day, nice in the evening. Worked on lawn spreader and on the greenhouse. Alan and Roxanne and family were here for supper. Beverly called about divorce.

Sunday, June 7, 1987—34° to 47° cloudy, breezy in the evening. Worked on greenhouse, garage, wiring, garden fence and lawn seeding. Talked again to Beverly.

Monday, June 8, 1987—34° to 54°, mostly sunny and breezy. Allen gave me a bolt bin and drawers—got them painted today. Took him a lamp kit. Sylvia put tomatoes in greenhouse.

Tuesday, June 9, 1987 33° to 59°, sunny and windy. Built cabinet for steel drawers and mounted bolt bin to wall. Painted it and the fertilizer spreader—and toolbox. Did some lawn work and Sylvia did a large wash.

Wednesday, June 10, 1987—30° to 50°, cloudy with a light breeze. Went to Palmer for supplies.

Thursday, June 11, 1987—37° to 57°, partly cloudy with sprinkles. Visited Lloyd Ronning. Dan Billman and Patti stopped in for coffee. Helped Dan with his dock. Started cleaning the wood shop. Jim Odden was here for supper.

Friday, June 12, 1987—34° to 44° rained all day. J.M. took up dining room carpet and put down new. Re-stretched other carpet. Rudbecks were here for supper.

Saturday, June 13, 1987—35° to 45° and raining most of the day. Sorted nuts and bolts and put them in the bolt bin. Dan and Don visited. Bob and Kahren came over to watch a movie.

Sunday, June 14, 1987—35° to 43° and raining again today. Built drawers and doors for workbench in the garage. Helped Bob Rudbeck move a furnace.

Monday, June 15, 1987—37° to 47°, light rain to partly cloudy. Worked on a variety of jobs.

Tuesday, June 16, 1987—40° to 56°, sunny and windy. Mounted scope on .22 rifle. Ran wire to the greenhouse and hooked it up. Wrote to Weaver for scope knob cover.

Wednesday, June 17, 1987—33° to 53° and partly sunny. Painted cupboards, workbench, drawer and doors. Varithaned canoe paddles and some other things. Put two more sections of pipe on sewer system.

Thursday, June 18, 1987—40° to 52°, sunny, windy in the evening. Worked on garage, canoe paddles, rabbit hutch, hay dryer (we dried lawn clippings for the rabbits). Visited Allen's. He gave us some broken window for the glass.

Friday, June 19, 1987—38° to 50°, Sunny, then cloudy and breezy. Spent some time straightening up the shop in the garage.

Saturday, June 20, 1987—36° to 64°, sunny, then cloudy in the evening. Put spare tire mounting in truck bed. Varithaned another canoe paddle. Put rung in ladder. Worked on clothesline, truck light and tailgate.

Sunday, June 21, 1987—40° to 70°, sunny, then cloudy in the evening. Helped Tom S. run cement for garage. Finished fixing clothesline and applying varithane to canoe paddles.

Monday, June 22, 1987—46° to 50°, cloudy, a clearing in the evening. Shoveled some gravel, then put up shelves in basement. Put some plywood on walls and ceiling. Cut off shotguns stock. Did some electrical work.

Tuesday, June 23, 1987—44° to 60°, sunny and then breezy in the evening. Dressed up gravel around outhouse. Target shot the .22. Put up ceiling in basement and did some more wiring. Had supper at Rudbeck's.

Wednesday, June 24, 1987—46° to 54° and cloudy. Did a lot of small

Norman Wilkins

jobs around here then hauled a load of water from Lucky's.

Thursday, June 25, 1987—40° to 60° and mostly sunny. Varithaned a cupboard in the basement. Seeded the grass, sorted fishing gear and borrowed Billman's mower.

Friday, June 26, 1987—34° to 54°, mostly cloudy then breezy and evening. Did more Varithaning. Transplanted two fair-sized spruce trees with the Cat. Allen Farmer and his sons stopped by to show us their 38 pound king salmon.

Saturday, June 27, 1987—34° to 54°, mostly sunny, windy. Found my lost log chain. Made a silkscreen board for Denise Johnson. Started putting handles in two shovels. Sylvia watered the two transplanted trees.

Sunday, June 28, 1987—36° to 58°, mostly sunny then cloudy and breezy in the evening. Finished the two shovel handles. Finished silkscreen board and went to a local ballgame. Spike bull moose fed on water plants in our lake.

Monday, June 29, 1987—46° to 64°, mostly sunny and windy. Made greenhouse stakes, worked on trolling motor, sorted tools and bolts and repaired joiner fence. Dan and Jason visited. Took silkscreen board to Denise and visited with Henry.

Tuesday, June 30, 1987—44° to 66°, sunny with a breezy afternoon. Mosquitoes have been here for a week or so now. Did some small projects and worked on the Cat. Rudbeck's and Quests (John and Joan) visited in the evening.

Wednesday, July 1, 1987—46° to 70°, sunny, then cloudy and breezy late. Changed oil in cat. Transplanted a spruce tree and made a dumb run. Lots of people here today for ice cream.

Thursday, July 2, 1987—50° to 66° and partly cloudy. We went to Palmer and also Wasilla for house building supplies.

Friday, July 3, 1987—50° to 71° and sunny. Painted plywood for the basement and finished wiring switches for the pump down at the lake.

10,000 Days in Alaska Book One 1978-1989

Shoveled dirt, etc.

Saturday, July 4, 1987—48° to 70° and partly cloudy. Worked on house doors, greenhouse water barrels, wood chisel and adz's, and many small jobs. Sylvia doesn't feel well.

Sunday, July 5, 1987—50° to 62°, lots of rain, but sunny in the evening. Finished the plywood on basement ceiling. Got lawn mower running but it needs more work. Sylvia is not entirely well yet.

Monday, July 6, 1987—40° to 51°, cloudy and rain. Worked on shelving in the house. Dan and "Red" stopped over for movies.

Tuesday, July 7, 1987—40° to 60° and sunny. Worked on the house and lawn mower. Helped Dan Billman fix a leaky float on his plane.

Wednesday, July 8, 1987—46° to 61°, sunny and then rainy in the evening. More work on the lawn mower and hauled a load of water. Went with Dan Billman and kids to Kianna Creek king salmon fishing. Sylvia and I had supper with Billmans.

Thursday, July 9, 1987—46° to 62° and sunny. Put up some bookshelves and sorted books and magazines. Sylvia mowed the lawn. I put on the lime and fertilizer and some grass seed and shoveled some dirt.

Friday, July 10, 1987—45° to 55°, cloudy and rainy. I don't feel well today, didn't do much.

Saturday, July 11, 1987—45° to 55°, cloudy and rainy. Built door for cool room. Started making a dehydrator for Sylvia. Rhynell and Max Hoffman visited.

Sunday, July 12, 1987—41° to 49°, cloudy and rainy. Finished the dehydrator. Sylvia butchered rabbits and re-planted some lawn.

Monday, July 13, 1987—42° to 54°, mostly cloudy and showers. Did lots of odd jobs. Nadia and Darrell got here about supper time. Nice to have them.

Tuesday, July 14, 1987—43° to 57°, Rained all night and into the afternoon. Mostly clear by evening. Visited Billmans. Worked some on the cool room door and spent time visiting with Darrell and Nadia.

Wednesday, July 15, 1987—40° to 65° and mostly sunny. I didn't feel very well today. Worked on rabbit food storage. Fired up the swamp buggy and drove it up near the garage. Nadia, Darrell and I hiked up on Slide Mountain to look for fossils.

Thursday, July 16, 1987—45° to 62° and mostly sunny. Got some swamp buggy parts at the dump. Worked on swamp buggy all day.

Friday, July 17, 1987—40° to 64° and mostly sunny. Went to Anchorage to look at dry suits for dredging.

Saturday, July 18, 1987—45° to 66° and mostly sunny, windy in the afternoon. We all went to Crosswind Lake and stayed at Dan Patti's remote cabin. Caught lake trout.

Sunday, July 19, 1987—45° to 68°, sunny, beautiful day. Caught more lake trout—very enjoyable here. Eagle robbed trout carcass from Gulls. There are good cooks in this group, the fish were fabulous.

Monday, July 20, 1987—45° to 74° and sunny. Dan flew us out to Snowshoe Lake in the morning. Did a few things around here and seeded more grass. Nadia and Darrell took Dan, Patti and the kids, Sylvia and I to KROA for pizza. Darrel Gerry gave me a nice photo of a wild Canadian goose and with a bunch of goslings under her wing—it was taken on Potter's Marsh.

Tuesday, July 21, 1987—48° to 68°, mostly sunny all day, shower in the evening. Dan flew all of us up Nelchina River, the glacier, Barnett Creek, and over Heavenly Ridge. We saw a black bear and cub, around 20 or more moose (mostly bulls—some big ones) and looked over the claims and the trailed leading to them. Later, I put a door knob on the lean-to door. Made ice cream for a fine supper at Billman's.

Wednesday, July 22, 1987—44° to 55°, partly cloudy and rainy afternoon. Worked on our gear to go to the claims. Nadia left to catch a plane home early in the morning. Visited Allen at the store and also Rudbecks.

10,000 Days in Alaska Book One 1978-1989

Thursday, July 23, 1987—40° to 60°, partly cloudy to sunny then one shower in the afternoon. Packaged an antenna, Allen Farmer' dogsled, and a beaver skin to be tanned and mailed them in Glennallen. Worked more getting gear together. Darrell took us to supper at KROA.

Friday, July 24, 1987—40° to 62° and partly cloudy. Cut down a few more trees near the garden, and called Beverly and later Nadia (she has gone back to Minneapolis). Worked on the swamp buggy. Darrell went trout fishing twice. Called State geological survey in Fairbanks.

Saturday, July 25, 1987—45° to 62°, cloudy and rainy. Worked on a swamp buggy and our gear. Visited Allen Farmer. Went to Billman's for a camp stove. Sent in two orders.

Sunday, July 26, 1987—48° to 66° and sunny. More work on swamp buggy and gear. Finished in the afternoon.

Monday, July 27, 1987—40° to 70°. Up early, drove swamp buggy to Goober Lake trailhead and put on the chains. Saw a Toklat sow grizzly bear and twin clubs a mile before Goober Lake. The trail down the mountain to Nelchina River is steep and slanted, with sharp turns around trees. Took some exploring to find trail to, and up the river. Ran river bars, many crossings. Came across Mike Meekin and lady wrangler with pack string camped on river. Went on up river. They came after, riding double, looking for five horses—found them. We had a tough time trying to find a way through brush and glaciated bedrock. Finally camped on an "island". Set up camp in a nice place and ate supper at 11:00 p.m. Windy and cool here. Broke gas filter off in the brush. Saw griz and moose tracks. River is running strong. Glacier is calving. We are tired tonight.

Tuesday, July 28, 1987—sunny, hot, cooler and cloudy in the evening. Glacier calves more ice once in a while. Up early, packed work gear in to claims. Brushed two lines and set two claim corners. Saw more griz tracks. Read a little and then looked swamp buggy all over. Breezy here, bugs are bad.

Wednesday, July 29, 1987—high of about 60, partly cloudy and breezy. Put up more posts on our claims. Broke rock and panned. Glacier makes lots of strange noises and calves lots of ice into the river. We use glacier ice in our cooler. Saw tracks of a small bear up on the mountain. Darrell took a bath in a pool of rocks—flushed some rock ptarmigan.

Thursday, July 30, 1987—mostly cloudy, one rain showers while we were panning gold. Keep losing shotgun shells out of elastic holder. Spent morning looking for 1980 cached rerod stakes. Dan flew over in the evening. Sun shining on mountain and glacier was fantastic. Glacier calved more bergs and the river is higher with lots more ice in it.

Friday, July 31, 1987—30 is to 64° and partly cloudy. We were up early and went to No. 1 claim. Saw two ewes and two lambs, took pictures. Renewed claim notices. Most of our work was claim evaluation work. Chisel is Dull now. Glazier is noisy and river higher. Did lots of high climbing. My pack was heavy. Came across another old claim stake. There were small grayling in all the pools in the glaciated bedrock. Took a new route back to camp. It was a long day—real tired tonight. Hope John gets here tomorrow. Saw more moose track. Sheep lick at minerals that the water carries out of the rock. More ice in the river.

Saturday, August 1, 1987—up early, nice day. Rained just after we got back to camp and all through supper. We had been at the airstrip only a few minutes and Mike Meekin flew John Wood in here in a Super Cup. An hour later, he was back, bringing Dan Billman. John worked hard on our claims, taking samples and evaluating our prospects. It was another very long, hard day. Saw a mother ptarmigan and chicks on the way back to camp. John and Dan got their tents set up before it rained. When the glacier calves into the river in sounds like someone has thrown gasoline on a fire—such a roar. Ptarmigan were clucking around our tent just at dawn.

Sunday, August 2, 1987—sunny and breezy. John and Darrell hiked up to the west outcrop. Took "79" samples. Found one fouler and two Canadian "80" claims stakes. Dan and I picked and Panned. Meekin flew Dan and John out. Darrell and I started packing—we will leave in the morning.

Monday, August 3, 1987—mostly cloudy. A packed gear into the buggy. We knew the trail better and made good time going down river—it is 1 foot deeper than when we came in. Tough going sometimes. Just got in the trees and the O-ring on the power steering reservoir poohed out. Fixed that and put in more oil. The Swamp buggy handled climbing up the mountain very well. Uneventful ride from Goober Lake to trail head. Ran down the road a ways to sling mud off the tires then removed the chains and came on home. Found an eight foot, 4x4 post along the road. Got home at 7:00 p.m. and went to the lodge for pie and ice cream. Allen Farmer, Ellie and Kyle brought over some things to our place late in the evening.

Tuesday, August 4, 1987—partly cloudy. It washed the chains that were on the Swamp buggy. Shortened and repaired them. Remounted the large fuel filter on a new bracket onto the buggy. Put camp gear away and took Dan's gear back to him—visited there in the evening

Wednesday, August 5, 1987—62°, partly cloudy and windy. Left to take Darrell to the airport at 4:00 a.m. Did a little shopping in Anchorage and got home in the early afternoon. Worked on the Swamp buggy and Sylvia Varithaned bookshelves. Visited Dan and Patti in the evening.

Thursday, August 6, 1987—38° to 60° and mostly sunny. Worked on bookshelves in the house. Put doorstops on the cool room door. Visited Lucky and Mary—he planed some boards for my cool room shelves.

Friday, August 7, 1987—40° to 52° and mostly cloudy. Made some phone calls, did some business, went to Glennallen on more business. Finished shelves in the cool room. Went to a "dump" meeting at KROA.

Saturday, August 8, 1987—40° to 64° and mostly sunny. Did some service work on the pickup truck and went to a potluck birthday party at Henry Johnson's. Lots of people were there.

Sunday, August 9, 1987—40° to 67° sunny and hazy in the evening. Talked to Jerry Lica about snow plow. Put different gas tank on lawnmower and did other odd jobs. sighted the .338 rifle. Visited Billmans. Jim and Mary Odden visited us in the evening. Called Beverly.

Monday, August 10, 1987—44° to 68°, sunny and partly cloudy in the evening. Sawed a big burl—it's no good—very disappointed. Sylvia mowed the lawn and I worked on the mower and chainsaw. Cut brush and brought tiller up the hill. Dan, Chuck and Jason visited.

Tuesday, August 11, 1987—40° to 66° and sunny. Sylvia Cut brush and I did a bunch of small jobs and put the chainsaw back together. Visited Billmans in the evening.

Wednesday, August 12, 1987—48° to 58°, sunny and then cloudy. Called around about plane tickets to go to the lower 48—Nadia found some. Did more small jobs. Tom and Lisa came to visit.

Thursday, August 13, 1987—44° to 59°, sunny event showers. Dan Billman and I ran tests on some ore samples. Sylvia is picking lots of mushrooms. Blueberries are starting to ripen.

Friday, August 14, 1987—38° to 55°, cloudy and showers all day. Prepared assay samples for shipment. Sawed some trim for greenhouse. Visited Harold and Rachel Dimmick in the evening.

Saturday, August 15, 1987—38° to 50°, cloudy and rainy all day. Measured and cut trim for the inside windows downstairs. Went to KROA for a little while in the evening.

Sunday, August 16, 1987—38° to 55°, Sunny, then showers. Cut more trim and installed some around windows. Went to a potluck supper and music at Smayda's.

Monday, August 17, 1987—42° to 54°, mostly cloudy with some showers. Visited Allen Farmer about hunting. Worked a little more on the trim and got one window frame ready on the arctic entry. Went with Bob Rudbeck to Glennallen to get subsistence permits to take moose and caribou.

Tuesday, August 18, 1987—38° to 59°, sunny and then cloudy. Installed more trim. Beth T. and baby, and Tom and his daughters, visited. Tom gave us some mushrooms and we gave him some lettuce. We went to Beaudoin's to see "Clan of the Cave Bear". We took them some lettuce and zucchini. There was a moose cow and calf down on our lake tonight. It was a beautiful evening.

10,000 Days in Alaska Book One 1978-1989

Wednesday, August 19, 1987—38° to 50°, mostly cloudy and rain showers. Helped unload Charlie Trowbridge's lumber. Got one large overhead shelf put up in the garage. Sylvia oiled the trim in the house and picked mushrooms.

Thursday, August 20, 1987—36° to 56° and sunny. Finished overhead shelves and painted them. Started north door for storage shed. Allen Farmer, Roxanne and the family and her mother, Karen were here for supper.

Friday, August 21, 1987—34° to 60° and sunny. We had frost this morning. Tried to do a few small jobs. Sylvia mowed the lawn and dressed out eight rabbits. Charlie Trowbridge visited. Motor burned out on the 10-inch saw. Jerry and Mo Lica, Jerry, Betty, Bob and Kahren Rudbeck, were here in the evening to watch a movie.

Saturday, August 22, 1987—34° to 62°, sunny beautiful day. Helped Charlie T. with his storage building. Went to a potluck and BBQ at Billman's in the evening. Some water skied and used the sauna. Darla "Red" is visiting Rudbeck's.

Sunday, August 23, 1987—34° to 66°, sunny, hot and buggy. Helped Charlie again with the building. Bob Rudbeck and I flew a tent to Shallow Lake and set it up. Went for pie and conversation at Nelchina lodge.

Monday, August 24, 1987—36° to 66° and sunny. Got gear ready to go hunting. Jim Shelton dug our spring site deeper with track backhoe. Bob Rudbeck flew Kahren, Darla and I too Shallow Lake (4 miles south of Eureka). We packed our gear ¼ mile in to the tent site. Beautiful evening, some ducks on the lake. Glassed lots of moose east and south of the lake just at dusk.

Tuesday, August 25, 1987—26° to 70° and sunny. We were up before the sun, had a quick breakfast. I spotted a paddle bull moose near the east end of Shallow Lake and shot him. A cow and heifer were with him. Another cow and heifer came by while I was butchering him. Bob, Kahren and Darla helped me pack him to lake shore. We covered the meat with a space blanket to help keep it cool. Then back to camp for lunch and a nap. There was another bigger bull that Bob didn't see, so he didn't get to shoot. While we were glassing for moose, we spotted Allen Farmer in his Ranger traveling across the valley from one of their kill sites. We went out for the evening to hunt south and east of Shallow Lake—no moose.

Wednesday, August 26, 1987—33° to 70° and sunny. Bob and I leave camp at first light and hunt north, east, south and back to Shallow Lake. Didn't see a moose. We did scare up a medium sized bull caribou. Dennis flew over. We decided to break camp and go home. Hung meat in garage.

Thursday, August 27, 1987—48° to 62°, sunny, then cloudy with a hard shower. Cut up the moose today. Jim, Mary and Carol stopped in and helped finish cutting and wrapping. Philip, Arlene and daughter came over for meat and fresh vegetables we can't store.

Friday, August 28, 1987—56°, mostly clear, fog in low places. Went to Boyle's in Anchorage—Andy drove us to the airport. Took a nonstop Sun Country flight over Valdez, Whitehorse, Fort Nelson, Saskatoon, Fargo and on to Minneapolis-St. Paul. Nadia and Darrell met us and drove us to Beverly's house. Met a lady on the plane (Diane Barbour). She sat in our row on the plane.

Saturday, August 29, 1987—hot and breezy here. Went shopping in the morning. Tyler fell out of his wagon and cut his forehead.

Sunday, August 30, 1987—sunny day. Nadia, Darrell, Teresa and family were all here at Beverly's for a BBQ'd moose dinner on the patio. We had a fine time. Bev's friend Dan was there.

Monday, August 31, 1987—mostly sunny. When shopping and visited Ivan and Mary Lou. Paul and Teresa called. A squirrel electrocuted itself on a transformer and knocked out electricity. Squared up some business with Kevin.

Tuesday, September 1, 1987—sunny today. Theresa and family picked Beverly and us up and we all went to the Minnesota State Fair. Saw livestock, machinery and exhibits. The grandkids had lots of fun on the rides. Later we had pizza at Beverly's and then over to Theresa's to stay the night.

10,000 Days in Alaska Book One 1978-1989

Wednesday, September 2, 1987—visited at Theresa's all day.

Thursday, September 3, 1987—sunny and hot. Went shopping for snowgo and chainsaw parts. Paul and Theresa and Nadia and their families were at Beverly's in the afternoon. We had a good barbecue supper. Packaged the plow levers Paul brought down from Allen Rollins.

Friday, September 4, 1987—sunny today. Nadia drove us to the airport. Our flight took us over Brandon, LeRounge, Manitoba, Lesser Slave Lake, Fort Nelson, Watson Lake, White Horse and Valdez. Andy met us at the airport. We did some shopping in Anchorage and then came home. There has been a freeze here. Leaves on the trees are beautiful and the moon over the mountains and on our lake is a sight to see. Everything was fine here at home.

Saturday, September 5, 1987—28° to 50° and sunny. Painted cabinets and did some other odd jobs. Got rock salt from Oddens and visited Ed Farmer at KROA and then Billman's. Sylvia worked on goat skins.

Sunday, September 6, 1987—33° 54° and mostly sunny. Sylvia fleshed the goat skins yesterday and two fox today. I fleshed one beaver and skinned one muskrat. They are all in tanning solution. I put up one cabinet in the wood shop. In one cabinet I put the grease guns and oil.

Monday, September 7, 1987—33° to 54° mostly cloudy, rainy evening. Put cold air intake in outside wall of cool room. Got some crane hunting gear ready and visited Henry. Called Dan and Scott and Delta. Cleaned distributor cap on truck.

Tuesday, September 8, 1987—34° to 45° and mostly sunny. Finished putting together my gear to hunt cranes in Delta. Darrel Gerry and I left in the afternoon for Delta Junction. There was construction on the road, it was rough. Lots of snow in Isabel Pass area. Got to Hollenbeck's just before 10:00 p.m. Slept on straw in Scott's barn.

Wednesday, September 9, 1987—30° to 40°, light rain, fog, low clouds. Hunted pond and field nearby. We got nine cranes there on Scott's farm. Cleaned the birds at Scott's. Many thousands of cranes were flying in the evening. Great crop of grouse and spruce hens. Sharp tail grouse are on the increase here. We rented a cabin from Slic (Silver Fox Roadhouse) and visited with Al, Wendy and Mike.

Thursday, September 10, 1987—30° to 40°, low clouds. Slept too late. Saw sharp tail grouse, then three wolves where we planned to hunt cranes. Went to Small Lake—No geese or crane. Drove around a while up/tried to find a pothole (grain around it), then asked Steve H. to hunt his farm and access to Gerstle River. Parked on one end of the field and had only walked 100 yards down the trail to the river when we came to an area where a cow moose had been shot. A 6 foot grizzly was on the moose. She had cubs. She stood up, looked at us, popped her jaws, ran a little closer towards us and stood up again. I talked to her. Darrel and I started backing up the trail. Sounded like there were more bear in the brush on our right. We worked our way out of there, back to back. Glad the confrontation didn't get more serious. Drove back close to where we had flushed the Canada's and saw crane landing. Barely got in a position to shoot when thousands flew up. When they came over and the shooting started, they got confused and flew near us again. We got five cranes—had a fantastic shoot. Cleaned the birds including the spruce hens we got earlier. Saw quite a few geese flying. Stopped to tell about the griz incident to the land owner. There was rain changing to snow at Isabel Pass. Got home and to bed at 2:30 a.m.

Friday, September 11, 1987—34° to 40°, rain and cloudy. Visited Rudbecks. Cleaned shotgun and tried to dry out gear and get things ready to go again. Jim Odden, Rudbecks and Smayda's girls were here for a roast crane supper. Lisa Smayda is sick.

Saturday, September 12, 1987—34° to 45°, partly cloudy, rainy night. Got gear ready to go to Delta. Jim Odden came down and we picked up Darrel Gerry and went on to Delta Barley Farms area. Stayed at Al and Wendy Bakers.

Sunday, September 13, 1987—snow in the night, wind and snow on and off most of the day. Lots of crane and some geese flying—we just weren't under them. We got two grouse. Stayed at Dan and Slic's that night.

Monday, September 14, 1987—27° to 40°, beautiful day. Went to Tanana—no cranes flying so we went to Delta Barley # II and drove trails to Tanana River. Jim shot a sharp tail ruffed grouse and spruce hens.

10,000 Days in Alaska Book One 1978-1989

Loki, his dog, retrieved them. We didn't find any geese or cranes there. Went to Steve H. farm and shot two cranes there and some sharp tailed grouse. Lots of other hunters. We did some exploring. Earlier in the day, Darrel laid his shotgun on the tire of a blazer and it got run over. We ate supper and drove home. Arrived here at 4:00 a.m.

Tuesday, September 15, 1987—25° to 40° and sunny. Slept, rested and dried out gear. Sylvia is working with pelts. I shot a spruce hen in our lane and visited Dave D, Rudbecks and Smaydas.

Wednesday, September 16, 1987—28° to 44°, cloudy heavy, wet snow turned to a light snow. Rudbecks, Jim Odden and Sam visited. Dug the potatoes—350 pounds and 80 pounds of rutabagas. Brought in the rest of the cabbage and cauliflower. Phoned Theresa and called several people in Cordova about goose hunting. Went to Billman's place in the evening to help Dan Pull the Beaver floatplane out of the lake.

Thursday, September 17, 1987—29° to 34° cloudy, rain, snow. Helped adjust coils on shop door. Worked on beaver pelt. Rested a lot. Phoned Charlie Trowbridge.

Friday, September 18, 1987—30° to 40° and mostly cloudy. Got swamp buggy ready for winter. Started boiling traps. Hauled a load of water from Lucky's. Jean Campbell's son Ron visited us.

Saturday, September 19, 1987—31° to 48°, cloudy then sunny in the evening. Boiled traps and repaired some of them. Washed and cleaned duck decoys. Patched smoke leak in the house stove. Bob and Kahren came over to watch a movie and have ice cream with us. Charlie Trowbridge left maps of the Cordova area with Lisa Smayda for me.

Sunday, September 20, 1987—35° to 45° and cloudy. Put a roof jack on greenhouse for a chimney. Worked at breaking a beaver pelt. Ed Farmer visited. Serviced the truck.

Monday, September 21, 1987—28° to 52° and sunny. Put silicone and trim on greenhouse. Lisa Smayda and her girls and Karen M. and boys visited. We went to Smayda's to see Charlie Trowbridge.

Tuesday, September 22, 1987—23° to 39°, cloudy then windy in the evening. Went to Anchorage to get lumber and supplies. Visited Andy and Connie. Got home around 9:30 p.m. Saw a moose in the road this morning.

Wednesday, September 23, 1987–34° to 44°, cloudy, showers, then Sun. Unloaded the truck. Sylvia mowed lawn. I did trap repair and dying. Dan and Patti were here for supper. Jim Odden stopped in. Did book work on claims.

Thursday, September 24, 1987–26° to 42°, cloudy and showers. Built cabinet for canning jars, dyed more traps and put new anchor cords on duck decoys. Visited Dan and Patti and went over to KROA.

Friday, September 25, 1987–34° to 38° and cloudy. Did lots of things necessary to be ready for winter. Charlie, Beth, Beth's brother Paul, Charlie II, Lauren and her sister visited us. I took camo parka material over to Lisa to sew. Shot nine ducks on our lake from canoe. Bob and Kahren were here to watch TV in the evening.

Saturday, September 26, 1987–34° to 38°, cloudy and partly cloudy. Got some trap bait ready and put wolf droppings and fox urine in Ziploc bags. Cleaned up a bit in the garage. Took a zipper over to Lisa Smayda. Went to Allen's and got truck chain. Allen, Bob and Kahren Rudbeck, and I hunted ducks on our lake. Shot 18 and lost one. Allen got one, and wounded one. Bob got five. We cleaned them at bob's. I shot one duck straight overhead from canoe and made another shot with right-hand only to the extreme right. Allen did a fine job keeping the canoe upright.

Sunday, September 27, 1987–20° to 36° and mostly sunny. Some ice this morning. Jim and Eilene Manning are back for a visit. We visited Jim and Mary Odden, KROA, and took Joe and Morey Second Chief a couple of ducks. Visited Lucky and Mary in the evening.

Monday, September 28, 1987–24° to 37° and mostly cloudy. We had lots of visitors today and did lots of visiting ourselves. I sanded some on beaver pelt and weather stripped the greenhouse door.

Tuesday, September 29, 1987–30° to 42° and partly cloudy. Went to Anchorage to do some shopping. Left locks with Danny Griffith.

10,000 Days in Alaska Book One 1978-1989

Stopped at Andy's. Had supper and a visit with Chad and Trish Wilson, Charles, Criss, Pici.

Wednesday, September 30, 1987—30° to 42° and mostly sunny. Finished our shopping—bought a tiller and mower. Came home and tried on camouflage parka Lisa Smayda is sewing for me. Bob, Kahren, Jim Odden and Darrel (by telephone) got together and planned grub and gear list for our upcoming goose hunt in Cordova.

Thursday, October 1, 1987—28° to 34°, cloudy, rain, snow. Packed and loaded gear into Bob's pickup to go to Cordova. Put the canoe on Jim Odden's Blazer. Lisa finished my camo parka. Hauled a load of water from Hoffman's.

Friday, October 2, 1987—snowed in the night. Shopped in Copper Center on the way to Cordova. Rained all the way from Thompson pass to Valdez. Ferry left at 7:30 p.m. Arrived at Cordova 1:30 a.m.

Saturday, October 3, 1987—it's 1:30 a.m. in Cordova with a light rain. Charlie Trowbridge met us and took us to his place and fixed us a breakfast. We went to our rented Forest Service cabin at mile 20 on the Copper Road and unloaded our gear. Randy Phipps came to the cabin and led us on a goose hunt. Saw some ducks, jumped a goose—knocked it down. It got up and flew away. Much water, brush and very heard walking. Tore muscles in my legs. Everyone is complaining about their legs. Jim shot four ducks in the evening. We got pretty wet today. Grateful to have a cabin and roof over our heads to dry out.

Sunday, October 4, 1987—up early, hunted dry slough. I missed a widgeon. Went to Cordova, shopped, and went to Hartley Bay. Bob Rudbeck and I each shot a teal. Charlie Trowbridge hunted with us. Talked with Ron and Mary Stephens about hunting. They let us use their freezer. Beautiful sunny day.

Monday, October 5, 1987—up at 5:00 a.m. every morning. Warm here. Went to mile 24 and heard geese. A 40-inch bull moose came along while we were stalking the geese. Kahren got him on the camcorder. Bob Rudbeck jumped eight geese and knocked two down. 60 geese flew up a quarter mile ahead of Jim Odden and me. Jim tried to get to where they went down (landed), but ran into a lot of bear sign on a creek. He turned and walked straight out to the road. I pass shot a hen mallard while I was walking out. We went on out to the road across the Copper River Flats to Million Dollar Bridge over the Copper River at mile 49. Looked at Childs and Miles glaciers and fish counting camp. Saw a flock of geese at mile 37 bridge. We were hunting ducks on the way back to the cabin when Randy Phipps overtook us. He and Diane had shot a sow griz and a 2-year-old Cub. He asked for the canoe. We ate supper and went to help skin the bears. They were on a small stream. We followed it about 1 1/2 miles. Saw lots of beaver sign. Got the bears skinned out and were back to the road in two hours. Saw large, wet bear tracks across the road near the bridge that goes across Aliganik River. Tired tonight.

Tuesday, October 6, 1987—40° to 45°, a few showers, then partly cloudy. I felt sick in the morning. Went to Hartney Bay. Put out decoys; saw a few ducks, no shots. Jim got four ducks jump shooting. Darrel got one. Bob got a dusky goose, two buffle heads and one teal. Bob, Kahren and I had put out decoys near mile 37 bridge and were just leaving at dark when geese came over. Put the boat in to get the geese that Bob got. Got back to cabin late.

Wednesday, October 7, 1987—40°, quite a few showers, cloudy and breezy. Up at 5:00 a.m. again—hunted dry slough. Jim got a mallard. Jumped several other bunches and didn't get any. Had lunch and hunted out to mile 49 then looked at Miles Lake to see if geese were flying. All unsuccessful stalks for ducks. We didn't put out decoys at mile 37. Geese slipped in and landed. When we walked up the road, they flew up and landed out on a bar in the river. It was dark by then.

Thursday, October 8, 1987—went to mile 37. Geese flew up in two groups and another group flew over. Darrel got one, Jim got one and lost one in the river. Bob got one that sailed way out on the flats. I saw it and went down and picked it up. We hunted at mile 25 with no luck. Raining and blowing. Packed up and went to Cordova, did some shopping and got on the ferry to go back to Valdez.

Friday, October 9, 1987—arrived in Valdez at 1:30 a.m. It was raining. There was blowing snow at Thompson pass. Got home at 5:00 a.m. Nadia called at 9:00 a.m. She and Darrell split. Dan Billman came over for breakfast. We sorted our gear at Rudbeck's. Later Jim Odden and

10,000 Days in Alaska Book One 1978-1989

Darrel Gerry, Bob and Kahren and I tried for ducks on our lake. They got some ducks. Jim and Darrel shot from canoe.

Saturday, October 10, 1987—28° to 42° and mostly sunny. Didn't do much today, my knee is sore. Two spruce hens were in the yard. I shot one and the other one flew into the wood shop window. Ate the one I shot for supper.

Sunday, October 11, 1987—28° to 36°, mostly cloudy with a skiff of snow. Loafed most of the day, visited Rudbecks.

Monday, October 12, 1987—24° to 34° and cloudy. Vented gas water heater out basement wall. Visited Allen and Roxanne. Allen and friend Greg used my canoe and hunted ducks. Bob and Kahren were here for supper.

Tuesday, October 13, 1987—20° to 34°. Sunny—our lake is almost frozen over. My back is very bad and knee is very sore. Took Allen's meat grinder home. Didn't do much all day.

Wednesday, October 14, 1987—18° to 34°, cloudy handsome breeze. Six swans are on the lake ice. The lake opened up some today. Replaced the window in the wood shop that the spruce hen broke. Covered D4 with tarp. Put tires and tarps up on a shelf in garage. Put mower and tiller in lean-to. Beth and Charlie Jr. were here for supper.

Thursday, October 15, 1987—22° to 30° snow in the night and most of the day. Lake opened up a little more. 30 to 35 swans rested on the lake. My back is real bad. Allen and Roxanne and family were here for supper.

Friday, October 16, 1987—12° to 30°, sunny then cloudy. Cleaned the chimney on the house. Put 3/4" plywood over sewer line. Visited Ed Farmer and KROA. Phoned in an order to D. Kirk catalog.

Saturday, October 17, 1987—14° to 30° cloudy, a son, cloudy. Took two snowgos to Ed Farmer. Charlie, Beth, and Charlie II visited.

Sunday, October 18, 1987—18° to 28°. Cloudy and some snow. Put away some gear and worked on truck. Henry helped too—Sam was with him. We visited and Charlie came and visited.

Monday, October 19, 1987—18° to 30°, cloudy, foggy, some snow. Stock market crashed. Worked on truck, hauled water. Visited Trowbridge. Jim Odden was here for supper.

Tuesday, October 20, 1987—22° to 34°, cloudy, and rain. Wet snow on the way in to Anchorage—road was slippery to King Mountain. Did lots of shopping and had supper with Danny and Adie Griffith. Was home by 11:00 p.m.

Wednesday, October 21, 1987—26° to 36°, mostly cloudy and breezy. Visited Allen Farmer. We picked up road kill coyote pup. Allen went to Glennallen with us. Sylvia did laundry. Allen sealed bear skull and hide at Fish and Game.

Thursday, October 22, 1987—30° to 42° and mostly cloudy. Made some picture frames and got parts ready for plenum door. Charlie and Beth visited.

Friday, October 23, 1987—33° to 40°, rain and snow. Went to bank on business in Palmer. Got truck tires and insurance. Last 50 miles were slippery on the way home.

Saturday, October 24, 1987—10° to 23° at mostly sunny. Put a new rotor and distributor cap on the truck and new parts in the carburetor on the chainsaw. Ed Farmer and Charlie Trowbridge visited. We heard some geese or swans fly over.

Sunday, October 25, 1987—24° to 30° and sunny. Visited Allen, cut up some wood, put hinge and latch on stove plenum. Sylvia sewed mukluks. Muskrat push-up on lake.

Monday, October 26, 1987—10° to 22° and cloudy. Worked on snowgo dolly. Called around about goose hunting.

Tuesday, October 27, 1987—12° to 22°, cloudy with fluffy snow. Replaced snowgo brake pucks and worked on snowgo sled and snowgo dolly.

10,000 Days in Alaska Book One 1978-1989

Wednesday, October 28, 1987—18° to 24°, cloudy with 6 inches of fluffy snow. Built trap box for snowgo. Allen Farmer visited. Jim and Mary Odden and Charlie and Beth and Charlie Jr. (Trowbridge) were here for supper.

Thursday, October 29, 1987—10° to 21° and cloudy. Worked on trap box and snowgo dolly. Jim Odden's dog Loki was here. Jim came to get him.

Friday, October 30, 1987—12° to 60° and cloudy. Worked on the pickup and visited Charlie. Split and loaded a pickup load of wood and put it in the basement.

Saturday, October 31, 1987—9° to 14° and cloudy. Finished putting wood in the basement. Neighborhood kids were here for treats.

Sunday, November 1, 1987—9° 28°, cloudy with a light snow. We made lots of frames for Sylvia's wildflowers. She sewed a cover for the snowgo and some ditty bags.

Monday, November 2, 1987—18° to 22° and a mostly sunny. Put a lockset on the east door of house (kitchen). Went down to Allen Farmer's and took pictures of an eagle. Charlie Trowbridge visited. Worked on trap gear. Sylvia is framing flowers.

Tuesday, November 3, 1987—10° to 20°, cloudy with some fog. Helped Charlie Trowbridge hang a door on his storage shed. Haven't felt well all day. Visited KROA in evening.

Wednesday, November 4, 1987—10° to 16°, cloudy and foggy. Visited Allen Farmer, he gave me a trap. Tuned and dyed some traps. Charlie Trowbridge came over and visited.

Thursday, November 5, 1987—16° to 18°, cloudy and foggy. Saw wolf and fox tracks at Mendeltna dump. Visited Jim and Mary to get measurements to make a stretcher for my wolf pelts. Build my stretchers and dyed more traps.

Friday, November 6, 1987—8° to 18° and sunny—beautiful day. Worked on marten boxes and snowgo sleds. Visited Allen and Roxanne in evening.

Saturday, November 7, 1987—6° to 10°, mostly sunny, nice day. Hauled water from Hoffman's. Worked on snowgo sleds and built a new box for toboggan sled. Allen stopped in with a message from Eddie.

Sunday, November 8, 1987—12° to 20°, cloudy with a light snow. Worked at getting ready to trap. Stopped at the lodge for a few minutes. Allen Farmer stopped by—someone carried off his barrel stove.

Monday, November 9, 1987—14° to 20°, cloudy and a light snow. Worked more with my trap gear. Visited Lucky Beaudoin. Allen Farmer and his family visited us. Set two traps in each dump after 12:00 a.m.

Tuesday, November 10, 1987—14° to 19° and cloudy. Nothing in the traps. I don't feel well. Got more gear ready for trapping. Went to see "Pop Wagner" perform at KROA in evening. He has quite the reputation as a singer, picker, fiddler, lasso twirler, poet and funny guy. We enjoyed visiting with friends while we were there.

Wednesday, November 11, 1987—14° to 20° and cloudy. There was a vole in one of my traps. Saw a coyote cross the road near RCA site. Set traps up on Slide Mountain. Saw coyote, fox, marten and boo tracks. Did more trap work. Charlie helped move Ski-Doo into garage. He borrowed my Polaris to move some things to his storage shed. Visited Allen Farmer in the evening and went over the map of his trapline north and east of Slide Mountain.

Thursday, November 12, 1987—12° to 16° snow and cloudy. Ran Allen's line to his trap cabin. Made a few fox and marten sets. Made one wolverine set at his old cabin and one wolf set on the trail to the backside of Slide Mountain. Lots of overflow/creeks running. Saw numerous boo tracks and three moose cows at Allen's cabin. Found a couple of his traps.

Friday, November 13, 1987—10° to 12° and cloudy. Nothing in the dump traps. Coyote pulled wax paper off trap. Took jugs off Ski-Doo motor. Got ready to go out on trapline tomorrow. Lisa and the girls visited and Charlie Trowbridge came by.

10,000 Days in Alaska Book One 1978-1989

Saturday, November 14, 1987—12° to 14° and partly cloudy. Got three inches of snow last night. Worked around here. Lee D. called in the evening. He had seen a cross fox traveling with what he thought was a trap on its foot. I found that the tracks near Jim Bowden's place. Allen Farmer plowed our snow. I pulled Charlie Trowbridge out of the ditch he stayed to visit in the evening.

Sunday, November 15, 1987—3° to 10° and cloudy. It's not my trap that the fox is in—maybe it wasn't a trap he saw on the fox's foot. Went to Tom and Lisa's in evening. Beth, Charlie, Lee D., and Jim and Mary Odden played music.

Monday, November 16, 1987—3° to 16° and partly cloudy. Checked all sets near here. Didn't go to Eleven-Mile Trail as I didn't feel well. Tried to run sets on Slide Mountain. A half mile from home, the bearing broke on the snowgo. Had a spare part and replaced it. 12 caribou went west on our lake today.

Tuesday, November 17, 1987—15° to 20° and mostly sunny. Had a raven and a magpie in my dump traps. Saw a cow moose and a number of caribou near Lake Louise Road. Went in on 13-Mile Trail. Made three wolf sets, four fox and set two marten boxes. Saw wolf, fox, and mink tracks. Two creeks were not frozen. Lakes aren't well frozen yet. Jim Odden came down to weld some of his gear.

Wednesday, November 18, 1987—15° to 26° and sunny. Put another trap in dump and hung a snare. Nothing on Slide Mountain. Made marten set. One marten wouldn't go up pole. Put a load of wood in the basement. Help Allen Farmer put two large windows in his addition.

Thursday, November 19, 1987—18° to 28° light snow and cloudy. Allen and I checked traps at the dump. He had an ermine and a coyote—gave them to me. The coyote pup was real fat. Helped Allen move a stove and toilet. He and the boys were here for a movie. He treated us to milkshakes.

Friday, November 20, 1987—14° to 16° cloudy and of them funny in evening. Nothing in the traps at the dumps and the snare was knocked down. Got gear ready to go on the line tomorrow. Skinned ermine.

Saturday, November 21, 1987—6° to 9°, cloudy and foggy. Went north on Allen's line and made more wolf sets, one marten set and one fox set. Got a pretty red fox. Quite a few boo were there.

Sunday, November 22, 1987—it's -3° to 6° and mostly cloudy. Started wiring another light in the garage and got some more trap gear ready. Nothing in traps along the road. Trowbridge family and Henry and Sally visited us. Lucky and Mary Beaudoin were here for supper.

Monday, November 23, 1987—it's -3° to 12° so and cloudy. Set traps on Cache Creek Loop. Caribou trampled some sets. Nothing on Slide Mountain line. Dave DeJung visited.

Tuesday, November 24, 1987—had a light snow overnight, partly cloudy today and -6° to 10°. Ran Lake Louise line. Made two marten sets—nothing in sets. Saw a bull moose and lots of caribou on the road. Saw a black/dark cross fox close to Nine-Mile trail. Charlie, Beth and baby visited. Worked on Jim Odden's snowplow mounting until 1:30 a.m.

Wednesday, November 25, 1987—3° to 14° and cloudy. Nothing in traps along the road. Starter on the truck quit. Took rewind off snowgo. Had supper with Smaydas.

Thursday, November 26, 1987—8° to 12° and partly cloudy. Worked on the truck, then went to Henry and Sally's for dinner. Denise and Sam and Chris were there too. Came home and got the truck starter fixed.

Friday, November 27, 1987—10° to 14°, cloudy, then snowed after dark. Serviced the snowgo and got gear ready to run a trapline. Rudbeck's electricity has been shut off. Got CVEA to turn it back on. Their house would have frozen up if I hadn't noticed the power was off. Didn't haul water today.

Saturday, November 28, 1987—15° to 20°, cloudy, seven inches of snow. Hauled a load of water from Hoffman's. Moved one trap at State Camp dump and picked up two of mine and one of Allen's. Alan plowed our snow.

Sunday, November 29, 1987—2° to 10°, mostly cloudy then a flurry of snow in evening. Ran Allen's trapline. Two marten had moved. Saw

10,000 Days in Alaska Book One 1978-1989

lots of boo. No fur in traps.

Monday, November 30, 1987—11° to 8°, cloudy and flawed. Nothing on Slide Mountain line. Worked on my truck. Charlie Trowbridge brought over a pecan pie Beth had baked. He worked a little on his dogsled. Allen and Roxanne and the kids brought nachos, pop and a movie.

Tuesday, December 1, 1987—3° to 15° and mostly cloudy. Saw two 40-inch moose bulls face to face on Lake Louise Road along with cows and calves. Lots of boo too. One Wolf crossed the road in front of me. Got a nice buck mink and an ermine. Lots of overflow. Build a snow bridge over a creek. Allen Farmer came over to use the shop to rebuild his snowplow blade.

Wednesday, December 2, 1987—8° to 14°, cloudy with a light snow. Went to Anchorage for supplies. Brought back a bunch of stuff for Charlie. Saw quite a few moose and caribou along the road.

Thursday, December 3, 1987—it's -2° to 10°, cloudy and foggy. Went to Glennallen to do laundry and pickup medicine. Rudbecks got back.

Friday, December 4, 1987—8° -9°, mostly sunny. Ran Allen's trapline. Got a marten near the road. Moved some traps and set others. Skinned mink and ermine.

Saturday, December 5, 1987—colder, -15° to -5° and mostly sunny. Skinned and stretched marten. Took Sylvia and her mounted and framed flowers to Tazlina Lodge to sell at a bazaar. Checked traps along the road—nothing. Got lots of rest today.

Sunday, December 6, 1987—it's -10° to -4° and cloudy. Started to run Slide Mountain line but broke front slide strap and spring on snowgo. Fixed strap, went out and finished line—nothing. Got trap gear ready to go again. Met Charlie Trowbridge and his dog team on the trail. Tom, Lisa and girls were out on their snowgo to cut a Christmas tree.

Monday, December 7, 1987—it's -5° to 0°. Parked at Eleven-Mile. Nothing on line. Made Helfrich wolf set near a downed tree on the trail east of Judd Lake. Made a fox set half way between marten boxes west of lake in hole. Made marten set just south of lake on north-south Judd

Lake Trail. Saw lots of marten and fox track. Baited and set several sets. Saw a number of moose and caribou. Tough breaking trail to my trap cabin. Cabin is okay. Split wood, cleaned snow from roof and carried everything in from cache. A marten has been here at the cabin. Blue Lake is covered with overflow.

Tuesday, December 8, 1987—sunny and -15° -4°. Went east to Burbot Lake. Rode through 50 yards of overflow on one small lake, and didn't get stuck. Burbot Lake is unsafe. Made sets south and west of cabin and broke trail west for a ways. Made fox set on my lake.

Wednesday, December 9, 1987—mostly sunny and -12° to -10°. Went to set Mendeltna loop. Saw a red fox at Fox Lake. Hit it with the second shot at 60 yards with a .22 revolver. Tried to trail it, but lost it in a maze of other tracks. Set Helfrich at corner at long drainage. Broke loop back to Mendeltna Springs Lake. Made lots of sets—beaver are gone from small dam. Got stuck once—tough breaking trail. Saw lots of fox sign. Set Helfrich trap on hump between Blue Lake and the turn off to my cabin. A real nice day. Tired tonight.

Thursday, December 10, 1987—it's -12° to -5°. Ran line back out to truck at road—nothing. Made more sets. Truck boiled over on the way to Warren's (froze up). I got it thawed out. Saw a lot of moose and caribou along the road towards home. Dan Billman pulled in to our place and will stay with us for a few days.

Friday, December 11, 1987—still -11° to -4° and partly cloudy. Rudbecks visited in the morning. We tightened Dan's alternator belt and went to his place and looked at his Arctic Cat. Visited Mary Odden. Chopped bait. Dan took us over to Nelchina for pie and ice cream.

Saturday, December 12, 1987—it's -4° to 4°, cloudy with three inches of snow in the night and another inch today. Dan and I went to the dump and picked up one trap. Went to Steve Malley's then to Chuck Zimbiki's, then Blackie Z. Frank Z. was there. Back to Chuck's, picked up pistons and jugs for Ski-Doo. Dan will take them to a shop in town. Visited Art Wikle and KROA. When to Smayda's for community group music in the evening.

Sunday, December 13, 1987—2° to 4°, cloudy with a fine snow. Ran

Allen's trapline. Got a cross fox on Cache Creek Trail. Remade all sets and made one new one. Pulled the one he caught the fox in. Something got in a marten set and ran off after chewing up brush.

Monday, December 14, 1987—temp is -14° to -20° and sunny. Dan Billman left after breakfast. I service my snowgo and did a few other small jobs. Visited Charley and Beth and went to Lucky's for a load of water.

Tuesday, December 15, 1987—colder, -28° to -16°, sunny and cloudy. Sylvia took some crafts to Tazlina. Charlie Trowbridge and I went up Lake Louise Road. We checked a wolf set and made two fox sets and hunted ptarmigan. Charlie got one bird.

Wednesday, December 16, 1987—some sun and -12° all day. Parked at Eleven-Mile. Nothing in traps. Made a fox set off trail south of Cross Road Lake. Made a marten set south of there near the turnaround. Remade lots of sets. Saw marten and fox tracks, lots of moose and boo. Sore shoulder tonight.

Thursday, December 17, 1987—it's -5° to 6°. Cloudy, white-out, light snow, breezy evening. Got a big male marten southwest of the trap cabin. Nothing on line to Burbot Lake. Went east setting traps to the last one. Went to upper end of Burbot Lake made two sits there. Did chores here and skinned marten.

Friday, December 18, 1987—cloudy with some white-out and -10° to 5°. Nothing in traps. Made loop up Mendeltna Springs and made it more sets. Very tough going. Came home. Bob and Harvey came over to watch a TV show. Called John Wood, Nadia and Chuck Z.

Saturday, December 19, 1987—-2° to 22°, cloudy with a light snow. Got gear ready to trap tomorrow. Made out a bunch of location notices and talked to Dan about claims. Went to KROA for a Christmas party.

Sunday, December 20, 1987—-8° to 2°, partly cloudy and sunny. Ran Allen's old trapline. Got one female marten. Set two traps for wolverine, one for marten and one snare for fox. Broke trail north of Allen's cabin to meat pole. Saw a well-used wolf trail out there. Pulled traps on Slide Mountain.

Norman Wilkins

Monday, December 21, 1987—it's -8° to 8° and cloudy. Ran the loop on Allen's old trapline. Wolverine is still in this vicinity. Picked up three more traps. Went to Glennallen and filed mining claim location notices and did lots of other business. Charlie Trowbridge and family visited—Charlie worked on his sled. I skinned and stretched marten.

Tuesday, December 22, 1987—it's -10° to 22°, Sunny, cloudy. Ice fog on Lake Louise Road. Bob and Kahren went with me today. I pulled wolf trap—nothing in other traps. Saw a wolf track between 7th and 8th mile. Didn't see any ptarmigan to hunt. Rudbeck's filmed moose and caribou. I serviced the snowgo, and checked traps at the dump. Charlie worked on his dogsled in my garage.

Wednesday, December 23, 1987—22° to 28°, cloudy, foggy and breezy. Ran Allen's trapline, no fur. Made two wolf sets past Allen's cabin. Wolves on trail 1 mile from highway. No luck finding trail north to Mendeltna Springs. Neighborhood Christmas carolers were here. Truly nice of them to do that.

Thursday, December 24, 1987—30° to 22°, cloudy with a light snow. Rested most of the day. Made stretcher boards for fox and marten front legs. Visited Allen Farmer. Went to Jim and Mary Odden's for supper. John O. and Charlie Trowbridge and his family were there. Steve Malley stopped later.

Friday, December 25, 1987—10° to 8° and cloudy. Had a fine Christmas dinner at Smayda's. Charlie, Beth and baby were there. We had a really good time.

Saturday, December 26, 1987—it's -4° to 4° and cloudy. Ran the short loop on Allen's trapline—nothing. Saw some wolf tracks and made a wolf set where a wolverine got caught in a marten trap. Got ready for tomorrow and checked trap at dump. Charlie Trowbridge stopped to pick up some of his things.

Sunday, December 27, 1987—8° to 0°, cloudy with a light snow and some white-out. Saw several moose along Lake Louise Road but nothing in traps along the road. Parked at Eleven-Mile. Took care of all traps on the way in to cabin. Got a marten at the lake in a hole. Got a cross for fox at four corners east of Judd Lake Trail. Two marten didn't go up leaning poles. There was a rabbit in one set—a marten ate it. Birds got bait out of the box at Blue Lake. Marten investigated but didn't touch trap. Had a fox by one toe—he got away. Missed two other fox and one trap didn't fire. Everything is fine here at the cabin. Skinned fox and marten.

Monday, December 28, 1987—stayed at -5° all day. Ran trapline east and north of Blue Lake. A marten ate squirrel out of fox set. Got a red fox on hump at Burbot Lake. Made a wolf set on the hump before seismic starts. Made a fox set north on seismic. Baited all sets out to Big Lake (on way to Grayling). Put one fox set up on the bank a little ways. Not much fur moving out here.

Tuesday, December 29, 1987—temp is -10° to -2°, cloudy, some sun in the afternoon. Ran Mendeltna Springs Loop. Got a red fox at east corner of south end. Nothing else in traps. Made some new sets. Saw caribou and moose. Skinned fox.

Wednesday, December 30, 1987—colder, -15° to -8° and mostly cloudy. Put fox and marten on stretchers. Ran loop on Allen's line—nothing. Wolves have been through here, but the wolverine hasn't shown up. Went to a meeting at KROA. Turned the pelts on stretchers.

Thursday, December 31, 1987—14°, cloudy and foggy. Worked on Ski-Doo snowgo. Went to Rudbeck's for supper then over to the Nelchina lodge. Henry and Sally hosted a New Year's party. Had a very good time.

Top: Tom and Lisa Smayda with Charlie, Cora and Paul Trowbridge. Bottom: David, Kyle and Allen Farmer (Norman with back to camera).

10,000 Days in Alaska Book One 1978-1989

Top: Charlie Trowbridge at cabin on Woods Creek (names of visitors listed on back of door date back to the '50's. Bottom: Ralph Fuson and Jeff Routt, two of Norman's hunting buddies.

Norman Wilkins

1988—moose hunting, caribou hunting

Friday, January 1, 1988—it's -8° to -2° fog early, cloudy later. Went to the dump and picked up trap and tried out the critter call. Drove a few miles of road looking for caribou—season is open. Then home and took the snowgo east. Saw a few, no chance to shoot. Did trapping chores.

Saturday, January 2, 1988—still -8° to 0°. Partly cloudy, fog in places. Ran Allen's trapline, no fur. Made new fox snare set. Wolves were howling over a period of a couple hours. Searched more for whereabouts of wolverine.

Sunday, January 3, 1988—dropped to -20° to -18° and partly cloudy. Visited Trowbridge family and Rudbecks. Allen Farmer, Tom B. (brother-in-law), Bob R. and I hunted caribou. I got a young boo. Sylvia and I skinned and quartered it. Bob and Allen also each got boo. Charlie, Beth, and baby were here for movies in the evening.

Monday, January 4, 1988—still at -20° to -16° and mostly sunny. Sylvia worked with caribou meat. I finished working on the Ski-Doo snowgo. Put Polaris snowgo into the garage for service work I will do tomorrow.

Tuesday, January 5, 1988—it's -18° to -14° and partly cloudy. Worked on Polaris snowgo and Sylvia cut meat.

Wednesday, January 6, 1988—warmed to -16° -12° and partly cloudy. Saw lots of moose and boo. Parked at Eleven-Mile. Boo hunters had followed my trail a few miles. No fur moving, nothing but squirrel and camp robbers in my traps. Seemed a little colder on Blue Lake. Ice on Fox Lake sank and overflowed. Nice day, everything fine here at the cabin.

Thursday, January 7, 1988—0° all day and mostly cloudy. Went to Hole Lake and down that drainage. Made a marten set at a big spruce on other side of Creek. Nothing east of Burbot Lake. Got a marten on seismic going north but nothing in other sets. Went north from Big Lake. Made a fox and marten set and broke trail up the hill. Saw marten and one fox track. Made otter set north of Burbot Lake and made a mink set at lower end of Burbot Lake. I could see where the mink had been going in and out under the ice. Lake level is ten feet lower now.

10,000 Days in Alaska Book One 1978-1989

Skinned marten back at cabin. The sunset this evening is full of bright reds and it's beautiful on the snow and trees.

Friday, January 8, 1988—it's -10° to -8° and colder than that in the lower elevations. Slept late. Did Mendeltna loop, lots of overflow, well frozen. Broke trail to Beaver Lodge Lake and made marten sets and one otter set at lake outlet. Made combo fox and marten set just up from Mendeltna Lake. Moved and remade a fox set at Little Round Lake. Made a marten set north of Judd Lake Trail. When it was time to go home, my truck didn't start. I got a jump from passersby. Stopped at KROA to see Darrel, he loaned me a battery, mine is dead.

Saturday, January 9, 1988—still -10° to -2° and partly cloudy. Hauled a load of water from Lucky's. Visited Allen Farmer family. Charlie Trowbridge visited. Took battery out of swamp buggy and put it into my truck. Chopped trap bait.

Sunday, January 10, 1988—partly cloudy and -8° to -4°. Went to KROA. Sylvia did laundry. Darrel and I went to Tazlina Lake on our snowgos on the KROA trail. Part of it is the old Mendeltna Trail. Visited an old cabin site—cabin is falling down. Saw some old Indian campsites—dug outs where they stored salmon. Some fox, marten, lynx and wolverine tracks.

Monday, January 11, 1988—stayed at -4° and partly cloudy all day. Ran Allen's old trapline out to the far meat pole. Circled around and found a trail going northeast. Broke trail two miles to small lake. Made two marten sets out there and made a wolverine set at sharp turn on old trail. Saw some moose. Wolf tracks at small lake—here I turned around. No fur in traps. Beautiful out in that country. Late afternoon sun was beautiful on the basin surrounding Old Man Lake. I could see where Charlie Trowbridge ran his dogs out that way.

Tuesday, January 12, 1988—it's -4° all day and cloudy. Ran Ski-Doo for a while/3 miles. Visited Jim and Mary and picked up salmon heads for trap bait from Darrel Gerry. Chopped bait for trapline and pulled together other gear. Jim and Mary visited in the evening. They need insulation for an outside drainpipe and we have some we don't need.

Wednesday, January 13, 1988—temp is -12° to -10° and partly cloudy.

Moose and boo along Lake Louise Road. No fur in traps. Wolves on Judd Lake Trail for a short ways before junction with Eleven-Mile Trail. One fox looked over sets at Blue Lake. Nothing much is moving, colder at lower elevations.

Thursday, January 14, 1988—still around -10° all day and -15° at night. Sunny day. Ran line east and north, no fur, just one porcupine and squirrel. Put up more marten boxes and made a fox set at opening at top of hill. Made more mink sets and improved the trail some. A plane has landed on Big Lake to the north. Shot a spruce hen. Wolves have been at outlet of creek from "V" Lake. I missed seeing a marten set at big tree across Hole Lake drainage. Northern lights are out.

Friday, January 15, 1988—colder, -20° to -8° and mostly cloudy. No fur. Made a wolf set in their trail coming onto Judd Lake Trail from the west. My truck didn't start again, got a jump from surveyors.

Saturday, January 16, 1988—it's -14° to -8°, mostly cloudy with ice fog. Visited Trowbridge and Smayda. Trowbridges and Hoffmans came to see us in the afternoon.

Sunday, January 17, 1988—cloudy with an ice fog and -11° to -9°. Worked on Ski-Doo snowgo all day.

Monday, January 18, 1988—foggy all day with temps at -15° to -5°. Worked on Ski-Doo snowgo and also the Polaris. Got bait and traps ready. Rudbecks came by, we visited with them for a while. Allen and Tom came to visit.

Tuesday, January 19, 1988—it's -5° to -3°, cloudy with a light snow. Ran Allen's old trapline. Pulled a marten set under leaning spruce tree. Got small marten before Small Lake. Broke trail from Small Lake to Mendeltna Springs crossing. Got large marten at box on Blue Lake. Made fox set between Small Lake and barrels in swamp—left side going out.

Wednesday, January 20, 1988—temp is -10° to 0° and mostly sunny. Skinned two marten. Ran line east and north. Made wolf set in snowgo trail and a wolf pee post set near mouth of "V" Lake Creek. Got a small marten in box near beaver dam between small lakes. Made a marten set going up the hill. Went north to Grayling Lake Creek. Saw one fox and one marten track and wolf also. Put up a marten box across creek in Hole Lake drainage. Skinned today's marten this evening.

Thursday, January 21, 1988—8° to 16°, cloudy with a light snow in the afternoon. Made two fox sets between Mendeltna Springs and Small Lake. No fur in traps. Lots of boo on trail along Slide Mountain. Several moose along trail. Visited Ed Farmer in the evening.

Friday, January 22, 1988—6° to 12°, partly cloudy and fog. Did some snowgo work and took my Ski-Doo to Chuck Zimbiki. He changed jets until it was running right. Allen and Tom visited, borrowed a movie.

Saturday, January 23, 1988—8° to 11° and partly cloudy. Went to Jim and Mary's to get groceries they had picked up in town for us. Went to Ed Farmer's and put a new thermostat in truck. Rhynell replaced defective gloves. Mixed snowgo gas and repaired snowgo trailer. Fleshed and stretched three Martin. Smayda family visited this evening we had a good time.

Sunday, January 24, 1988—10° to 14°, cloudy with a light snow. Parked at Eleven-Mile—freighted four, 5-gallon containers of snowgo gas, and 1, 5-gallon Blazo in to near Blue Lake. One fox very attracted to "passion scent". No fur in traps. Made two marten sets west on Nine-Mile Trail.

Monday, January 25, 1988—it was -8° all day and cloudy with three inches of snow in the night. Did a few trap chores. Helped Max Hoffman with chimney cleaning, then hauled a load of water from there. Went to a birthday party at Allen Farmer's.

Tuesday, January 26, 1988—it's -10° to 0° and mostly cloudy. Helped Allen Farmer build a display island for his store. Got trap gear ready.

Wednesday, January 27, 1988—colder, -24° to -15° and sunny. Worked with furs, pitch removal. Allen brought snowgo parts.

Thursday, January 28, 1988—still cold, -34° to -20° and sunny. Put snowgo recoil back together on Polaris. Visited Trowbridge's.

Friday, January 29, 1988—sunny and -33° to -20°. Moonlit nights.

Worked on income tax. Crossbeak birds were feeding in spruce trees in front of our house. Jim and Mary Odden and Bob and Kahren Rudbeck were here for supper. Allen and Roxanne stopped and visited.

Saturday, January 30, 1988—it was -31° and cloudy. Loafed all day.

Sunday, January 31, 1988—partly cloudy with a light snow and -8° to 4°. No fur—one fox track south and west of Mendeltna Springs. Broke trail part way to Brush Hill. Covered gas cans at my gas cache with garbage bags. Everything is fine here at the cabin. Split wood and melted snow.

Monday, February 1, 1988—it's -15° to -5°, sunny, more moonlit nights. Ran line east and north. One fox had jumped trail to the east. Got an otter in 330 coni set in small drainage ditch just north of Burbot Lake. Mink are running all drainages. Pulled mink sets as season is over. Nothing in other sets. Wolf set in trail on North Big Lake was frozen in six inches of overflow. Pulled that trap.

Tuesday, February 2, 1988—temp is -22° to -5° and sunny. Ran trapline up to and including Judd Lake Trail and Nine-Mile. Made marten set just west of Nine-Mile on Judd Lake Trail. No fur today. Saw some boo and fox tracks and flushed a spruce hen.

Wednesday, February 3, 1988—sunny and cloudy with a light snow and -12° to -6°. Visited Rudbecks. Worked on snowgo. Charlie I and Charlie II visited. Had supper at Odden's.

Thursday, February 4, 1988—it's -6° to 0°, cloudy with a light snow. Sylvia and Mary Odden and I went to Glennallen on business. Skinned and fleshed the otter.

Friday, February 5, 1988—cloudy with a light snow and -6° to 2°. Worked on snowgo. Sharpened skinning and fleshing tools. Lisa and the girls visited.

Saturday, February 6, 1988—cloudy, sunny. Went to Ed Farmer's, parked and went exploring for wolf tracks on the seismic trails east and north. No luck. Came home and geared up to go out tomorrow. Visited Bob Rudbeck and Buttons (visiting from Minnesota).

10,000 Days in Alaska Book One 1978-1989

Sunday, February 7, 1988—sunny and -8° to 2°. Parked at Eleven-Mile and picked up and hung up traps as far as Little Round Lake on Judd Lake Trail. Saw two marten, two fox and some otter tracks today, covered 53 miles. No fur.

Monday, February 8, 1988—sunny with some breeze on the way to the cabin and -10° to 5°. Flushed a flock of Ptarmigan and a spruce hen. Saw caribou and moose tracks in several places. Saw two fox tracks—and a red fox had come by the cabin and down the trail to Blue Lake and was waiting in the trap there. She is a pretty one, and minus one toe—probably the fox that left a toe in my trap here on the lake near the cabin. There is three inches of new snow here. I cleaned snow off the roof, skinned the fox and did chores around here. Broke a handle in my axe. Broke trail over to creek at base of Brush Hill.

Tuesday, February 9, 1988—dropped to -20° to -10° clear sunrise but then cloudy all day. Made a wolf set (Helfrich) on trail below Hole Lake. Pulled and hung up two traps on east loop. Marten tracks on high ground before Big Lake. Made lever pole set with snare in otter trail near 330. Made 330 otter set at south end of Burbot Lake.

Wednesday, February 10, 1988—it's -15° to 0° and sunny. Just as I drove out onto Blue Lake, a male otter was traveling up the other side of the lake "porpoiseing" in a moose trail. Shut off the snowgo and pulled a .22 from scabbard. Ran out on the lake and drilled him just in front of the ears with the first shot. Made a wolf set near Small Lake and saw more spruce hens and two moose. Picked up one of Charlie's dog booties. Skinned otter, fleshed it, washed it and put to dry. Alan and Tom stopped to visit.

Thursday, February 11, 1988—sunny and cloudy at -9° to 3°. Serviced snowgo and put a new handle in my ax. Visited around the neighborhood. Allen brought over a movie.

Friday, February 12, 1988—sunny, cloudy towards evening and -5° to 9°. Ran Ski-Doo to Odden's and around Cache Creek loop. It ran okay. Put three sled loads of wood in our basement and hauled a load of water. Visited Rudbecks and Buttons. They were here in the evening to watch "Dallas".

Norman Wilkins

Saturday, February 13, 1988—it's -3° to 6°, cloudy with a breeze in the evening. Max and Rhynell visited. Worked on the snowgo.

Sunday, February 14, 1988—3° to 9° and mostly cloudy with a light snow in the evening. Finished putting new bearings and the drive and chain case on snowgo. Went to a birthday party for Lee D. and Darrel G. in the afternoon.

Monday, February 15, 1988—3° to 9°, snow, clearing then snow again. Bob Rudbeck and Buttons went with me to my trap cabin. They only got a little ways from Nelchina when Bob's snowgo refused to pull his sled and load. We loaded essentials on our machines and went on. I had a cross fox on Allen's old line. Buttons took pictures of this fox. They made burbot sets on Mendeltna Springs and Blue Lake. I ran the line to the east. A marten had been around a set but it was frozen so I missed him. The cabin is in fine shape. Bob fried us a good halibut supper. I think Bob and Buttons are having a really good time.

Tuesday, February 16, 1988—it's -5° to 5°, cloudy and snow all day. Buttons tended the Burbot lines, but got no fish. Bob and I ran line east and north—no fur. Can't find wolf trap near inlet on the Big Lake/lots of overflow. Bad snow conditions to see or travel. Remade lots of sets. Hurt my back early in the morning.

Wednesday, February 17, 1988—0° to 8°, cloudy and a light snow. No fur, no fish on lines. Got stuck several times on the way out. Picked up Bob's sled on the way home. Rudbecks and Buttons were here for supper.

Thursday, February 18, 1988—20° to 30°, snow, breezy and cloudy. Used heating pad a lot today. Jim Owen has gotten a wolf. "Bumped" garage and greenhouse to slide off snow. Visited Rudbecks and Charlie Trowbridge.

Friday, February 19, 1988—22° to 34°, partly cloudy and snow. "Bumped" the house roof and snow slid off. My back is better today. Went to Glennallen on business. Rudbecks, Buttons, Doolies and Inger were here to watch the Winter Olympics and Dallas. Mailed in an order to Northern Hydraulics for a metal detector.

10,000 Days in Alaska Book One 1978-1989

Saturday, February 20, 1988—6° to 9°, sunny, breezy and then cloudy. My back is still a little sore. Put the last cross fox on a stretcher and fleshed it. Phoned Beverly—Nadia was at her place.

Sunday, February 21, 1988—temp is -24° to -9°, sunny then cloudy. Worked on snowshoes, watched Olympics and visited Smaydas.

Monday, February 22, 1988—it's -10° to 0°, mostly cloudy. Went to Odden's and picked up some things they had gotten for us in Anchorage. Got snowgo and the gear ready to go out on the trapline again tomorrow. Rudbecks and Buttons were here in the evening to watch the Olympics.

Tuesday, February 23, 1988—it's -10° to 20° mostly sunny and cloudy in the evening. Left home at 10:00 a.m. Trail was good except where it was drifted (windy in the afternoon). Unbroken trail was tough going—went off the trail a few times. Pulled lots of fox and marten sets. Saw three fox and eight marten tracks. Got one ermine. A marten also came to the set. Saw caribou and moose. My back is very sore and I'm tired.

Wednesday, February 24, 1988—15° to 25°, mostly sunny, blowing snow in open areas. Saw quite a few marten tracks—all seem to be going east. Wolf track crossed my trail west of Big Lake. Hunted for trap. Snowshoed from trail to creek. Sprung all fox and marten traps. A female marten broke wire/trap to limb/found dead.

Thursday, February 25, 1988—15° to 31°, mostly sunny and windy. Trail badly drifted in open areas. No fur. Saw more fox and marten tracks. Pulled the fox and marten sets except one marten I missed. Made a wolf set just north of Mendeltna Springs.

Friday, February 26, 1988—20° to 29°, mostly sunny. Borrowed Allen's meat grinder. Tried to start Cat—diesel motor wouldn't turn over.

Saturday, February 27, 1988—10° to 20°, cloudy and snow. Took Allen's meat grinder back. Borrowed his Reddy Heater. Got the Cat started and into the garage. Took Allen's heater back and borrowed his elect impact wrench. Called John Wood about Nelchina claims.

Sunday, February 28, 1988—20° to 30° and sunny. Buttons and I worked on the Cat—got the head off. Bob, Kahren and Buttons were here for supper. Alan and Tom stopped by and Jim and Mary Odden, along with Paul, Fran and their son Paul from Montana came over. They brought pie and ice cream. We all had a real nice time.

Monday, February 29, 1988—10° to 31°, sunny beautiful day a breeze in the morning. Windy in the mountains. Worked on the Cat all day. Lots of people were in and out all day. I didn't feel well most of the day.

Tuesday, March 1, 1988—7° to 30° and sunny. Worked at putting the Cat back together. Buttons helped a lot. He knows those Cat engines and construction equipment.

Wednesday, March 2, 1988—10° to 27° and mostly sunny. Worked on the Cat again today and hauled water.

Thursday, March 3, 1988—18° to 26°, cloudy with a light snow. Took marten fur to Lanegan's in Glennallen and shipped them with Margaret Scott. Sylvia did laundry. Later we had pizza and visited at KROA.

Friday, March 4, 1988—10° to 24° and sunny. Worked on the Cat all day. Buttons came over and set the tappets. He and Bob had supper with us.

Saturday, March 5, 1988—10° to 20° and sunny. Finished working on the Cat, then cleaned the garage. Visited Smayda's today.

Sunday, March 6, 1988—10° to 20°, fog, cloudy, light snow. Loafed and rested all day. Visited Allen's and Beth.

Monday, March 7, 1988—20° and sunny. Nothing in wolf or otter traps. Saw some fox and marten tracks. Several moose near trail. Only fell off trail a few times. I need nine boxes between meat pole and Mendeltna Springs. One box south of beaver house and 120 at beaver house. Cleaned snow off cabin roof and woodpile.

Tuesday, March 8, 1988—5° to 20°, cloudy morning, sunny afternoon. Went east and north to Big Lake. Wolves have been near inlet. One wolf has two toes missing from its right front foot and one from its left front foot. Some fox tracks and lots of marten tracks east of cabin. Saw

10,000 Days in Alaska Book One 1978-1989

lynx tracks near Burbot Lake. Saw one fresh otter track near Big Lake. Moved two boxes and raised some others. Hunted for that missing wolf trap.

Wednesday, March 9, 1988—0° to 25°, mostly cloudy, windy. Wolf tracks for a mile east of Blue Lake. Nothing in traps. Picked up a Manning north of junction of Judd Lake and Eleven-Mile trails. Fell off trail a few times—one bad one. Light conditions were bad at times. Snowshoe gang messed up lots of the trail. Windy and snowy this evening. Moose on our lake.

Thursday, March 10, 1988—29° snowy and cloudy, 4 inches of snow last night. Visited Rudbecks. Started building marten boxes. Lucky plowed our snow.

Friday, March 11, 1988—24° to 32°, Sunny, partly cloudy then windy in the evening. Worked on marten boxes and the snowgo. Shoveled a little snow.

Saturday, March 12, 1988—23° to 30° and partly cloudy. Put a sled load of wood in the basement. Visited Oddens and Mary's mother, Ruth. Played trivia game at Rudbeck's in the evening.

Sunday, March 13, 1988—20° to 30°, sunny and partly cloudy. Up early, went to Smayda's and helped put up a rafter on their garage. Went to a skating party on Snowshoe Lake.

Monday, March 14, 1988—10° to 23°, cloudy with a light snow in the evening. Worked on trapping gear. Beth and Charlie Jr. visited and also Kahren. Then Bob Rudbeck came over.

Tuesday, March 15, 1988—20° to 22°, cloudy with snow. Waited until late then started out on trapline. I could see snow coming so I returned. Went to visit Harold and Rachel Dimmick. Repaired old sorrel boots with silicone.

Wednesday, March 16, 1988—17° to 21°, cloudy with a light snow. Mended moccasins and oiled boots. Allen Farmer visited.

Thursday, March 17, 1988—10° to 16°, cloudy and snowy. Did research on gold areas. Went to a birthday party and music for Charlie Trowbridge at Smayda's.

Friday, March 18, 1988—10° to 18°, cloudy, light snow, then sunny. Visited at KROA. Studied geology books. Rudbeck's were here to watch Dallas in the evening.

Saturday, March 19, 1988—4° to 22° and sunny. Got as far as the ridge past Allen's cabin—stuck many times. Trail is completely drifted over. Picked up wolf traps and a snare and came home. Saw a cow moose with a collar on her.

Sunday, March 20, 1988—12° to 26°, sunny and then cloudy. Knee is sore, put heat on it.

Monday, March 21, 1988—22° at home and 10° here at the cabin. Parked at Eleven-Mile and went to Mendeltna Springs. Ran the line to a half mile past meat pole. Picked up two wolf traps. At one wolf set, a caribou had run off with the trap after breaking the rivet. I heard a plane and later a shot (from Marie Lake perhaps?) while I was putting up eight new marten boxes on that line. I put up one box south of Beaver Lodge Lake and picked up and cached the two 330 coni there. Saw fox, marten and moose tracks. Had good luck getting up meat pole hill. It was a long hard day. I'm real tired tonight—so hungry I ate everything in sight.

Tuesday, March 22, 1988—0° to 15°, cloudy morning, Sunny afternoon. Went east and north. Real hard to see the trail. Cleaned snow off the two wolf traps and hung up a 330 at south end of Burbot Lake. Saw fox, otter, marten and mink tracks. Tough going off trail.

Wednesday, March 23, 1988—0° here at the trap cabin and 26° at home. Mostly cloudy today. Put up one marten box and tended the wolf traps. Got home early. Visited Charlie Trowbridge and Allen Farmer.

Thursday, March 24, 1988—20° to 29° and mostly sunny. Hauled a load of water from Hoffman's and visited Rudbecks. Tom and Kim Huddleston and their kids visited us and borrowed some movies.

Friday, March 25, 1988—20° to 26°, snowing most of the day. Visited Charlie Trowbridge and read a lot. Went to KROA for Art and Bonnie

10,000 Days in Alaska Book One 1978-1989

Winkle party.

Saturday, March 26, 1988—0° to 26° and sunny. Loafed and read.

Sunday, March 27, 1988—2° to 25° and sunny. Visited Oddens and later Trowbridges came over to visit with us.

Monday, March 28, 1988—it's -2° to 15° at the trap cabin. Left home late and parked at Eleven-Mile. A plane has landed on Blue Lake. Nothing in my traps. Went east and north to Big Lake. Hunted for that wolf trap again with no luck. Hung Helfrich in a tree near north end of the hump north of Burbot Lake. Picked up three, 330 conibear traps from Burbot Lake to Big Lake. Moved marten box south 150 yards from hump. Cleaned snow from cabin roof and cache.

Tuesday, March 29, 1988—0° to 24°, cloudy and then sunny. Picked up seven wolf traps and two, 330 coni south at Beaver Lodge. Cut poles for beaver trapping. Had a chili supper at Rudbeck's.

Wednesday, March 30, 1988—18° to 32°, cloudy and sunny. Jim Odden and I went to KROA and up Mendeltna Creek (on snowgos) looking for beaver lodges to trap. Got into some overflow. Then we went west to Tawawe Lake, made a set there, then west again to Upper Lake above Snowshoe Lake (on east/west seismic) and made another set. We got into lots of deep overflow going south to Snowshoe Lake. Jim has been getting Burbot from Snowshoe Lake. Smayda family visited us in evening.

Thursday, March 31, 1988—14° to 32° and partly cloudy. I helped Allen Farmer a little and salvaged some paneling out of the trailer he is taking apart. Lucky decided he could use it for storage—we were ready to take it to the dump.

Friday, April 1, 1988—12° to 31°, partly cloudy then a light snow in the evening. I checked the two beaver sets, both were sprung. One setting pole was chewed off. Reset them. Made two Burbot sets. Bob and Kahren came over to watch Dallas.

Saturday, April 2, 1988—18° to 36°, sunny, cloudy. Visited Rudbeck. Lisa and the girls came here to our place. Didn't do much, I had a headache all day.

Sunday, April 3, 1988—17° to 27°, sunny, cloudy. Cut and cached two drags on the way to check the two beaver sets. Had a beaver in each set. Skinned them both and began fleshing one pelt. No Burbot in sets. Took the two beaver carcasses to Morey and Joe Second Chief. They are well thought of native folks and have seen many winters. It is very interesting to listen to their life stories. Stopped at KROA.

Monday, April 4, 1988—2° to 28° and partly cloudy. Went to Jim Odden's. We didn't get anything at the first lodge but we did get a beaver at the second lodge. Went on to Old Man Lake outlet to hunt otter—no otter. Came back via Army Trail. Finished fleshing yesterday's beaver.

Tuesday, April 5, 1988—it's -1° to 28° and mostly sunny. Visited Charlie Trowbridge and Rudbecks. Charlie and I went to mile 111 on the Glenn Highway. I bought a Ski-Doo Alpine. It needs work, so I took it to Chuck Zimbiki to work on. Went to Allen Farmer's also.

Wednesday, April 6, 1988—10° to 26°, sunny then cloudy and a light snow in the evening. Went to Jim Odden's. Checked to the two sets alone, no beaver. Adjusted sets a little. Pulled burbot sets, no luck. Saw boo on trail and mink tracks. Worked on salting pelts. Bob and Kahren were here for coffee. Sylvia doesn't feel well.

Thursday, April 7, 1988—8° to 32° and sunny. Sent off Sears and US Gen. catalog orders. Cleaned the salvaged plywood. Went for supper and music at Smayda's.

Friday, April 8, 1988—1° to 26° and cloudy. Ran the beaver traps and then helped Allen and Lucky take mobile home off of trailer frame. Went to KROA to a wedding party.

Saturday, April 9, 1988—8° to 28°, light snow and cloudy. Got chain saw ready, hauled a load of water and later visited Allen Farmer. Sylvia boiled meat from animal skulls.

Sunday, April 10, 1988—16° to 37° and sunny. Loafed most of the day. Visited Lucky and Mary in the evening.

10,000 Days in Alaska Book One 1978-1989

Monday, April 11, 1988—20° to 40°, sunny, windy. Got a late start. Parked at Eleven-Mile, had to repair sled hitch (I had the spare bolts with me). Left sled at "Y" and went to Mendeltna Springs downstream to beaver lodge. Made a baited conibear set. Picked up the 120 coni at the bad glacier spot. Picked up the #4 Montgomery also. Saw some otter and fox tracks. Put some screw and roofing nails in the cabin roof. I saw a spruce hen a few feet from the trail and a cow boo with a collar on her neck along the highway. The Eagles are back and hunting. Wolves are howling south of cabin at 11:00 p.m.

Tuesday, April 12, 1988—20° to 40°, sunny and windy. Went north of Burbot Lake and picked up Helfrich 750 W. Checked beaver set and trimmed trees along the trail. Cached mink box and trap south of Mendeltna Lake. Painted cabin roof camouflage. Beautiful sunset this evening.

Wednesday, April 13, 1988—16° to 35°, sunny and breezy. Cut up and stacked four loads of wood I had sledded into the cabin. Covered the wood pile with a tarp. Did various other small jobs around the cabin. My back and right knee a really sore tonight. I've used 4/10 of a cord of wood at the cabin this winter.

Thursday, April 14, 1988—10° to 35°, sunny, windy later in the afternoon. Cleaned up the cabin and moved lots of gear to storage barrels up at the cache. Put four, 5-gallon cans of mixed gas up there also. But shoveled snow from around the cabin, boarded up windows, cleaned out the ashes from the stove, and put a bucket over the stovepipe. Checked beaver sets and picked it up—this lodge must be empty. Saw quite a few ravens. Mendeltna Creek is flowing faster and opening up. Got home in good time. Tom Smayda and the girls came over. Tom needed rods to put tension on his garage door spring. Saw two moose today.

Friday, April 15, 1988—24° to 36°, cloudy, windy, sunny. Went to Glennallen and mailed tax forms. Sylvia did the laundry. When we got back, I went out and pulled the two beaver sets—nothing in them. Rudbecks came over to watch Dallas. I wrote to Tanner about our lost beaver.

Norman Wilkins

Saturday, April 16, 1988—22° to 38°, sunny, some wind. Bob Rudbeck and I went up the Army Trail to an area west of Mendeltna Dump. We were looking for wood to cut for fuel (and we hauled some trash to the dump).

Sunday, April 17, 1988—28° to 36°, sunny with some breeze. Went to KROA to watch Ski-Touring. Mary Odden took 1st, Bob Rudbeck 2nd, David Adkins 3rd. Rudbecks visited in the evening.

Monday, April 18, 1988—16° to 40°, sunny then cloudy. Bob Rudbeck and I went up the Army Trail again and cut down dead, standing trees for wood. Later I did a few small things around here and visited Harold and Rachel Dimmick.

Tuesday, April 19, 1988—18° to 42° and sunny. Bob and I went back and cut some more dead trees. Visited Allen Farmer and sharpened some saw blades. Allen, Roxanne, David and Ellie were here for supper.

Wednesday, April 20, 1988—26° to 37°, sunny and cloudy. Took a bear carcass and boo offal to the dump. (Offal refers to the entrails and internal organs of a butchered animal.) Unloaded a barrel of diesel fuel. Started sawing out picture frame material.

Thursday, April 21, 1988—24° to 30°, cloudy with snow. Went to Glennallen to pick up order and do some other business. Odden's stopped in with things they got for us in Anchorage.

Friday, April 22, 1988—24° to 44° and sunny. Tom Smayda, Lue Stewart and I went to Eureka. We took the trail to Goober Lake and on to Nelchina River and right up the Nelchina Glacier with our snowgos—wonderful trip. It would have been a good day to go to Valdez over the ice field.

Saturday, April 23, 1988—22° to 44°, cloudy and sunny. Cut up three sled-loads of wood and put it in the basement. Did a lot of cosmetic fixing on the Ski-Doo.

Sunday, April 24, 1988—22° to 34°, cloudy and windy. Built a plywood box for ice auger. Visited Allen (he gave me some snowgo parts). Allen and Dave came over to look at catalogs.

Monday, April 25, 1988—28° to 39°, sunny and windy. Allen Farmer and I went south of Eureka towards Goober Lake, then east to one of his hunting camps. We picked up his tent and a can of gas. Visited Ralph Pike and KROA.

Tuesday, April 26, 1988—30° to 44°, sunny to partly cloudy. Got up late. Allen Farmer came over and we visited. Did some small jobs around here. Went and visited with Rudbeck's. Bob and I went to see the wood trail. Bob and Kahren were here at our place for pizza and shortcake.

Wednesday, April 27, 1988—30° to 46°, mostly sunny. Snow is melting fast. Did some small projects for the garage. Allen Farmer gave me some quarter inch dowling and cut some up for me. Went over and watched a movie at Rudbeck's.

Thursday, April 28, 1988—30° to 46°, sunny then cloudy with a light rain in the evening. Painted tool box and ice auger box. Organized woodshop. Started building rolling cabinet for tools.

Friday, April 29, 1988—31° to 48°. Sunny, cloudy by evening. We had visitors, then I helped Bob Rudbeck get his trailer ready to go to the woods. We got a jag on the pickup and a load on the trailer, cut up, home and unloaded. Went to KROA for supper.

Saturday, April 30, 1988—30° to 40°, cloudy, sunny, light snow. Built a cabinet for my tool boxes and put one coat of paint on it. Bob Rudbeck went to the woods this evening alone. Went to a party at KROA. Dan Billman is back—took him to McKee's where his van had quit and pulled it back here.

Sunday, May 1, 1988—24° to 40° snow and sometimes some sun. Helped Dan B. try to find mechanical trouble with his van then went to his place, then KROA, then back home and painted the tool cabinet.

Monday, May 2, 1988—23° to 41° and sunny. Worked on snowgo and chainsaw. Hauled a load of water from Max Hoffman's. Rudbecks were here for supper.

Tuesday, May 3, 1988—26° to 42° and partly cloudy. Sylvia and I went

Norman Wilkins

early to the wood lot on Army Trail. Sylvia got sick from the tree dust on the first load—she is allergic to it. We got two loads into the woodshed. Did a bunch of other jobs this afternoon.

Wednesday, May 4, 1988—27° to 43° and cloudy. Brought one trailer and two pickup loads of wood home—along with some for Rudbecks. Sylvia stayed home. Visited Allen Farmer. Got the garden tiller ready for the season.

Thursday, May 5, 1988—31° to 44° and mostly sunny. Went to Anchorage to do business and shopping. It was a good trip. Saw sheep on Sheep Mountain.

Friday, May 6, 1988—33° to 43° and partly cloudy. Put casters on tool cabinet and built a tray for screws. Built a rack for packages at the mailbox. Visited Allen Farmer. Rudbecks were here to watch Dallas.

Saturday, May 7, 1988—34° to 44° cloudy. Painted and put up the rack for mail packages. Built another tray and did a few other small jobs. Roger and Jo Ford visited us. Saw eagles at the dump.

Sunday, May 8, 1988—31° to 49° and partly cloudy. It's Mother's Day. Did lots of small jobs. Rhynell and Max, and Tom and Lisa and their family were here. We visited Rudbecks for a few minutes too. Some ducks and swans are here, as the lake slowly opens up.

Monday, May 9, 1988—33° to 52° and cloudy to partly cloudy. Worked on the Polaris snowgo and the snowgo trailer. Sylvia did some planting in the greenhouse.

Tuesday, May 10, 1988—32° to 54° and partly cloudy. Worked on snowgo. Cut up some wood around here and did other small jobs. More ice is going out on the lake and there are more swans and ducks.

Wednesday, May 11, 1988—30° to 57°, sunny then cloudy and windy. Did a bunch of small jobs, and then went to KROA to meet Chuck and pick up snowgo parts. Hauled a load of gravel to fill in low places around here. More ice is gone from the lake. Visited Allen Farmer.

Thursday, May 12, 1988—37° to 57° and partly cloudy. And in small jobs around here, then went to Glennallen for parts and to take care of other business.

Friday, May 13, 1988—30° to 47°, cloudy with a light rain. Did some measuring for building materials. Took acetylene and oxygen tanks to Dan Billman. Sylvia went to Anchorage.

Saturday, May 14, 1988—32° to 44°, cloudy and rainy. Some sun in the Matanuska Valley, then snow and rain near the pass on the way home from Big Lake where we bought some lumber.

Sunday, May 15, 1988—30° to 40°. 1 inch of snow, cloudy, then rain. Wrote letters and unloaded pickup. Sylvia bought a recliner in Anchorage.

Monday, May 16, 1988—30° to 43°. Rain, cloudy, then sunny. Worked on Sylvia's new chair. Worked on snowgo. Borrowed Allen's electric impact wrench.

Tuesday, May 17, 1988—26° to 45°. Sunny, cloudy, then showers. Put up most of F8 fiberglass windbreaker on south side of garden. Hauled two loads of wood up to the wood shed and cut it up. Jim and Mary Odden stopped in—they will take the fur to the tannery.

Wednesday, May 18, 1988—34° to 45° cloudy and rainy. Finished with the wood from over by the garden—put it in the wood shed. Put up the rest of the fiberglass sheets. The ducks are carrying on with their frantic courtship. Put fittings on air tank and visited Allen Farmer.

Thursday, May 19, 1988—32° to 42°, snowed all night, rain then sunny in afternoon. Worked on Polaris snowgo all day. I am almost finished now. Every spring I prepare snowgo and trap gear for the next season. Dan Billman was here for breakfast. Beth Trowbridge and baby visited.

Friday, May 20, 1988—35° to 46°. Sunny then a rain shower. Dan rode with me to Big Lake. We visited with his mother and Loyd (Red). Dan's plane was tied up there. He flew it home to Snowshoe Lake. I bought the building materials in Wasilla. It was a good trip all around. Saw quite a few caribou from mile 118 to here.

Saturday, May 21, 1988—34° to 50°, sunny with occasional rain showers. Started building a fiberglass windbreak around strawberry bed.

Sunday, May 22, 1988—36° to 55°, sunny that some rain. Finished windbreak except for door. Put snowgo in shed, battery in truck. Jim and Elaine Manning got here from Michigan.

Monday, May 23, 1988—35° to 45°, cloudy with light showers. Visited with Jim and Elaine Manning. Tuned the motor on lawnmower. Mannings were here for supper.

Tuesday, May 24, 1988—37° to 47°, mostly cloudy and some light rain. Went to Copper Center looking for some people with a dryer—didn't find them. No one had tomato plants to sell either. Had supper at Odden's.

Wednesday, May 25, 1988—35° to 54° and mostly sunny. Helped Jim unload a Stove and did some small jobs. Got ready to go bear hunting with Dan Billman. We flew past my trap cabin to Big Lake north of Burbot Lake. Found the lost wolf trap and carried it to a spruce tree and cached it. Flew over Slide Mountain by way of Allen's cabin, then over to Tazlina Lake. Saw caribou and moose and some sheep on the mountains on the east side of Tazlina Lake. Flew through the saddle east and landed on Small Lake, not having seen any bear. There were beaver and nesting ducks on this lake. Slept the night in the plane here. It is illegal to hunt the same day we are airborne.

Thursday, May 26, 1988—30° to 50°, sunny then rain in the afternoon. Up early, walked north and east glassing for bears. Spotted what look like a griz, but when we got closer, we couldn't find it. We did watch a black bear sow with cinnamon on its back (possibly a small griz sow) for two hours. She had two small cat-sized cubs. Then back to plane, ate, and flew home in the rain. Saw a Toklat griz sow and dark cub on a sandbar on the Nelchina River below us at the mouth of Cache Creek. Landed at Snowshoe Lake, unloaded gear and went home. Rained hard for a while this evening. Dan called later. He and Don Culp and I flew to Dan's cabin at Crosswind Lake.

Friday, May 27, 1988—got up early and went fishing. Dan And Don each got two nice lake trout. Fried them up for lunch and went back out to fish again. Don caught another nice one. Ate supper and headed out. Dan let me fly the beaver during the level flight home. Unpacked and put away my gear.

Saturday, May 28, 1988–36° to 56° mostly sunny with a light rain very early in the morning. Finished the bagger for the mower. Took some garbage to the dump and brought back some lumber, steel and small stuff. Made up a clamp for the light and extra heavy 50 foot extension cord. The gas water pump quits at Manning's well.

Sunday, May 29, 1988–38° to 58° and cloudy. Put a roll of roofing on two lean-tos. Put the water pump in down at the lake. Doug and Denise J. visited. Roxanne, Jackie and kids visited. Stopped at Rudbeck's a few minutes.

Monday, May 30, 1988–37° to 45°, cloudy and a light rain. Worked on snowgo sleds and small jobs. Charlie, Beth and Little Charlie visited. Went to a birthday party with cake and ice cream for Little Charlie, Tom, and Mary Odden at Smayda's.

Tuesday, May 31, 1988–34° to 45°, cloudy and rainy that Sun. Worked on snowgo sleds. Went to Dan Billman's, borrowed some paint and discussed places to prospect. Made some phone calls to Cold Foot. Allen Farmer visited. Charlie Trowbridge asked me to look over his road and building site project.

Wednesday, June 1, 1988–34° to 44° and snowed down to 3400 feet on the mountains–rain here in the early morning, lots of clouds, some sun later. Did several small jobs and took three tires and wheels to Tom Huddleston to mount.

Thursday, June 2, 1988–36° to 44° rain all day. It quit around 6 p.m. and we got a little sun. I was over at Dan Billman's for a while and later he came over here to sharpen some drill bits. Mike Shelton came to talk about gold mining on our claims. Cal Gilchrist came here to talk about fixing Bob Herring's truck.

Friday, June 3, 1988–30° to 50°. Sunny, then partly cloudy and later a hard rain and hail in the evening. I built a road from the garden to the lower road and improve our boat landing area with the D4 Cat. Cut up the house trailer frame and cut off the axle. Pretty nearly have the axel ready to weld onto an 8 foot trailer. Hauled a load of water from Beaudoin's.

Saturday, June 4, 1988—34° to 64°, sunny with a light breeze. Most people in the neighborhood picked up after the storm—many truckloads of windblown trash at Mendeltna dump. Worked on trailer in the evening.

Sunday, June 5, 1988—44° to 58°, partly cloudy to cloudy. Put the axle under my trailer. Dan came over and we went to the dump and his place for materials for his floating dock. Did some cat work for Allen Farmer. Dan and Jason came down to do some engraving and to borrow some movies.

Monday, June 6, 1988—42° to 52°, cloudy with rain in the evening. Worked on Dan's dock all day. Lorraine Hanson from Minnesota called. They start their trip tomorrow. We'll meet them at the airport in Anchorage on the 14th.

Tuesday, June 7, 1988—42° to 56° and mostly sunny. Worked on Dan's dock again all day today. Took Leo Zura to the fish wheel at Copper Center. No salmon in the wheel. It was nice to visit with Leo. A cow moose fed along the far side of the lake and a bull caribou swam across it and trotted west along the far shore.

Wednesday, June 8, 1988—sunny today. Helped Dan get his van to Nelchina, and then we worked on his dock. Drilled some steel at Allen's on his press. Four caribou bulls were near our greenhouse.

Thursday, June 9, 1988—48° to 72° and sunny. Worked on Dan's floating dock all day. Lots of visitors. Dan helped in the late afternoon. We visited Smayda family in the evening.

Friday, June 10, 1988—47° to 70°, sunny and cloudy. Worked on the dock, then helped Bob Rudbeck pour a cement foundation—we had a small crew. Bob took us all to KROA for pizza.

Saturday, June 11, 1988—47° to 70°, sunny then cloudy. Worked on the dock and later ran around the neighborhood looking for 7/8 inch steel

10,000 Days in Alaska Book One 1978-1989

drill—no luck.

Sunday, June 12, 1988—46° to 57° and mostly cloudy. Rain shower in the evening. Went to Dan's and worked on the dock, then helped him with his van in the evening.

Monday, June 13, 1988—47° to 70°, sunny beautiful day. Worked on the dock and later on Dan's van.

Tuesday, June 14, 1988—46° to 68°, sunny then cloudy on the way to Anchorage. Did lots of shopping while in town and picked up Harold and Lorraine Hanson at the airport. The sun came out and we had a nice drive back to our place. Saw a moose on Palmer flats and three sheep on Sheep Mountain.

Wednesday, June 15, 1988—44° to 50° rained most of the day, one hard shower. Visited with Harold and Lorraine all day and went over to the Rudbeck's in the evening.

Thursday, June 16, 1988—42° to 66° and partly cloudy. We drove up to Lake Louise Road looking for wildlife. No luck. Harold and Lorraine took lots of scenery pictures. Later Harold and I went to Max Hoffman's and got a load of water. We saw a large coyote on the way.

Friday, June 17, 1988—42° to 54°, partly cloudy and a shower in the night. Walked around the neighborhood with Harold, and went to Jim and Mary's fish wheel. Filleted five red and one king salmon, barbequed one red salmon. Mark Hines has a fish wheel nearby and gave us a king and we filleted it. Got back home about 12:30 a.m.

Saturday, June 18, 1988—44° to 48°, cloudy and rainy. Rudbecks, and Lisa and her girls visited here. We are having a great time with the Hanson's. In the evening we went over to Dan and Patti's. Dan came home with a new motor in the Beaver.

Sunday, June 19, 1988—37° to 42°, cloudy, foggy, rain all night and day. Loafed, slept in, visited with Harold and Lorraine. Nadia called, it's Father's Day.

Monday, June 20, 1988—36° to 50°, cloudy, rainy then sunny in the late afternoon. Visited Rudbecks. Dan stopped in, tested washing machine (bad motor). Beautiful evening.

Tuesday, June 21, 1988–38° to 60° and partly cloudy, windy and breezy in the evening. Stripped the washer. Went to Dan's and he flew Harold, Lorraine, Sylvia and I on a two hour flight over the trap cabin and west. We saw caribou and a big bear. Then we flew south over the Nelchina River and glacier and then over the ice field and down to Tazlina glacier. Saw lots of dall rams, ewes and lambs. Then we went on to Kianna Creek–no salmon there–none at Mendeltna either. We flew up the Nelchina River and saw a grizzly sow on a gravel bar below the confluence of Cache Creek. It was a beautiful flight. Later I went to the dump and hauled a load of water from Hoffman's. Visited with Darrel Gerry at Nelchina.

Wednesday, June 22, 1988–42° to 52° and partly cloudy. Rain in the afternoon. Got ready to take Harold and Lorraine to their flight leaving Anchorage. We did some shopping, had supper with them then went to the airport. Stopped at Andy Boyle's to visit, them went on home.

Thursday, June 23, 1988–36° to 47°, cloudy and rain. Did some small jobs. Dan came over and we went back and worked on his boat dock. I am building it for him.

Friday, June 24, 1988–40° to 54°, mostly cloudy with some light rain. We got enough sun to paint the floating dock. Dan and I worked on it most of the day.

Saturday, June 25, 1988–42° to 58°, partly cloudy with some light showers. More work and painting on the dock–Dan and Lisa were here a lot. A moose is standing in the lake.

Sunday, June 26, 1988–42° to 50°, cloudy, breezy, light rain. Sylvia and I worked on Dan's dock all morning. Later we took two watermelons to a ballgame at the gravel pit across from State Camp. There was a cookout after the game.

Monday, June 27, 1988–42° to 48°, cloudy and rainy all day with some sun later. Worked on the dock all day. Visited Tom H. in the evening.

10,000 Days in Alaska Book One 1978-1989

Tuesday, June 28, 1988—40° to 58° and sunny. And worked on the dock all day—mostly at Billman's. Had supper with Steve and his sons, Ian and Caleb Malley.

Wednesday, June 29, 1988—44° to 66° and sunny. Got the dock halves assembled and loaded on the floats of the beaver. We flew out to Crosswind Lake. Saw a cow moose and her twins in the water of Old Man Lake. We got the frame bolted together and Dan had to leave to fly some clients. I put the rest of the dock together. We put the transom in it when he came back and took it on a trial run.

Thursday, June 30, 1988—42° to 54°. We stayed overnight at Crosswind. Dan and Jason went fishing and caught two lake trout. We got one anchor in the lake bottom and the dock tied off. Dan flew Jason and I out along with some clients. Hard rain at home this evening.

Friday, July 1, 1988—42° to 60°, partly sunny, very light showers. Started working on our dock here. Visited KROA in the evening.

Saturday, July 2, 1988—44° to 70° and partly cloudy. Built my dock and put it in the lake at our landing. I don't like it—should have built it square or nearly so.

Sunday, July 3, 1988—44° to 73°, sunny, partly cloudy in the evening. Worked on Sylvia's picture frames and a gate for the strawberry patch.

Monday, July 4, 1988—48° to 56°, sunny, cloudy and rainy. Had a Fourth of July picnic with Rudbecks at Mendeltna.

Tuesday, July 5, 1988—48° to 57°, sunny, rain shower, cloudy. Allen and Cal stopped by, wanted me to go to Allen's claims, but my back is sore so I didn't go. Made and hung strawberry garden gate for Sylvia. Dan and Jason Billman visited.

Wednesday, July 6, 1988—44° to 64°, rain in the night, mostly sunny all day. Went to Glennallen on business then stopped at KROA and later at Billman's.

Thursday, July 7, 1988—42° to 60°, mostly sunny, cloudy in the evening. Worked on trailer for Swamp buggy. Sent in a bid to G.S.A.—snowgos and miscellaneous.

Friday, July 8, 1988—47° to 57°, cloudy, rain in evening. Worked on trailer again, cutting and welding. Visited Rudbecks in the evening.

Saturday, July 9, 1988—48° to 60°, sunny and some showers. Loafed a lot. Worked on trailer. Chad Wilson and Jane showed up in the evening. They will camp on Lake Louise.

Sunday, July 10, 1988—50° to 62°, sunny, showers. I went to Lake Louise and went out with Chad and Jane in their whaler boat. It was sunny all day on the lake. We had a great time. Chad water skied and we all fished—no luck with the fish. In the evening, Allen and Roxanne took us all to Eureka for supper. We had a great time and lots of fun with Kyle and Elli.

Monday, July 11, 1988—48° to 58°, mostly cloudy, and rainy. Painted trailer. Dan Billman visited. Got a load of water at Max Hoffman's. Phoned Fred Marolf about small "bug" building.

Tuesday, July 12, 1988—50° to 68°, sunny, partly cloudy, heavy rain late afternoon. Cut out the floor and sides for trailer and painted them. Tom H. came over for a lawn mower I gave him. Dan Billman offered a chance to fish crosswind.

Wednesday, July 13, 1988—48° to 65°, rain, partly cloudy. The metal detector I ordered a long time ago finally came—built an armrest for it. Visited Allen Farmer. Sylvia and I had supper at Kim and Tom's.

Thursday, July 14, 1988—50° to 65°, cloudy, some sun. Went to Anchorage, to State Lands about claims. Stayed overnight at Chad Wilson, had a nice visit.

Friday, July 15, 1988—66° and partly cloudy here at home. Chased around Anchorage doing shopping. Denny B. couldn't load us. We were tired when we got home.

Saturday, July 16, 1988—52° to 72°, mostly sunny, smoky from distant forest fires. Visited Allen Farmer. Worked on wiring the trailer. Went to the dump for some parts. Hanson's sent us copies of the pictures they

10,000 Days in Alaska Book One 1978-1989

took while they were here.

Sunday, July 17, 1988—54° to 68°. Sunny, cloudy, smoky, a light rain. Went to the dump and cut the fenders off a Chevy Luv to put on the trailer. Built brackets for taillights on the trailer. Visited Billmans.

Monday, July 18, 1988—50° to 70°. Sunny, smoky. Worked on trailer. We took some of Sylvia's etchings to KROA to sell. Visited there and at Billmans.

Tuesday, July 19, 1988—49° to 71°, sunny, smoky. Worked on trailer all day. Put in the bed and sides on it along with several different steel parts and painted them.

Wednesday, July 20, 1988—49° to 66°, mostly cloudy. Lots of rain in the evening. Visited Allen Farmer. Worked on the trailer and went to the dump and cut the rear end and tranny off a Ford Maverick. Allen and I went to Glennallen to see a fella by the name of Roy (lives near Copper Center).

Thursday, July 21, 1988—40° to 49°, rain all night and day. Put fenders and tailgate irons on the trailer and went to the dump again.

Friday, July 22, 1988—40° to 46°, cloudy and rain most of the day, mostly cloudy in the evening. Painted rails for trailer. Put new fuel pump on truck. Messed around with the metal detector.

Saturday, July 23, 1988—40° to 54°, mostly cloudy with some sun in the afternoon. Visited Allen and the Rudbecks. cleaned up some steel and painted a little on the buggy. Dan Billman and Jason visited. Herb S. brought Tony here. Tony has a 6x6 in deep water on little Nelchina River. He needed to be pulled out. I got the "mean machine" ready so we can go in the morning.

Sunday, July 24, 1988—partly cloudy. Left early with Tony. Went to Little Nelchina campground and up river about a mile or a mile and a half above Old Man Creek. Tony and Curt had a GI 6x6 stalled in deep water. I winched it up on a gravel bar or where they could dry it out and get it running again. Got back home mid afternoon.

Monday, July 25, 1988—38° to 64°, partly sunny, rain in the morning. Moved gas tank filler pipe on Swamp buggy. Couldn't get D4 started. Had supper at Rudbeck's.

Tuesday, July 26, 1988—42° to 66°, mostly sunny, rain in the night, light shower this evening. Can't get the Cat started, the pony motor won't run. I cut off and lowered vise stand. Tony came to ask me to pull their 6x6 to where they can get it repaired. It is a diesel and they bent some rods when it went into the deep water. My buggy has a high speed miss—Allen is working on it.

Wednesday, July 27, 1988—46° to 63°, sunny. Worked on Swamp buggy most of the day. Allen Farmer helped. Darrel Gerry brought his folks, Marsha and Ralph to visit with us. They are interesting people.

Thursday, July 28, 1988—44° to 64° cloudy in the morning and sunny in the afternoon. Took the Swamp buggy up little Nelchina and pulled Curt and Tony's 6x6 down to Old Man Creek. They will repair it at Overland Trail. Saw a mother duck and 10 ducklings on the river. Saw two boo go 40 feet up a nearly vertical gravel bank. Brought a load of Curt and Tony's gear out to our place. (They will try to get my distributor on the swamp buggy fixed).

Friday, July 29, 1988—38° to 58° with alternating sun and rain showers. Put heavy aluminum heat reflectors over the mufflers on the swamp buggy. Repaired the hooks on two of the buggy chains. Tony and Keith came with a three wheeler and a plan to go in to where the 6x6 is and repair the engine. Kurt plans to be here late in the evening. Hauled a load of water from Hoffman's and visited with Max and Rhynell. Frank was there helping Rhynell.

Saturday, July 30, 1988—46° to 60°, partly cloudy. Sanded on swamp buggy. Tried to get pony motor going, compression is low, no luck. Allen Farmer brought a trailer over to do some welding on it. While he was here, he leveled the gravel around the yard.

Sunday, July 31, 1988—48° to 66° and sunny. Painted the swamp buggy camouflage and worked on the legs for our dock on the lake. Smayda ladies, Beth and Little Charlie, Tom H., and Alan Farmer were here. I gave Roxanne an old ladder.

10,000 Days in Alaska Book One 1978-1989

Monday, August 1, 1988—46° to 60° and partly cloudy. Dan Billman visited in the morning. Went to Palmer and Wasilla for steel, welding rod and some other things. Saw a small group of dall sheep on the way. It was raining around Palmer.

Tuesday, August 2, 1988—44° to 60°, partly sunny, rained in the night and again this evening. Sheldon tried to dig our spring deeper. I welded some more on the dock and made a new ball hitch arrangement for the pickup.

Wednesday, August 3, 1988—40° to 56°, partly cloudy, some rain. Went to Glennallen, did laundry, shopping, visited KROA and Billmans. Darrel Gerry and his folks had just gotten in from Old Boot Lake. Beth and little Charley visited in the evening.

Thursday, August 4, 1988—39° to 64° and sunny. Worked on the swamp buggy, went to the dump, and worked on trailer hitches. Ate supper at Nelchina Lodge.

Friday, August 5, 1988—38° to 56°, partly sunny. Went to Wasilla to look at a pickup truck, I didn't buy it. Went to an auction house hoping to find a freezer, none there like we want. Came home early.

Saturday, August 6, 1988—41° to 51°, cloudy, rainy. Took Allen's tow bar back. Adjusted the distributor on swamp buggy. Put tarp hooks on trailer box.

Sunday, August 7, 1988—40° to 50°, cloudy, rainy. Visited Billmans. Shoveled some gravel and started adapting a tent trailer for the swamp buggy. Allen and Tom visited.

Monday, August 8, 1988—40° to 51°, cloudy, rainy. Worked on tent cover for trailer and started getting gear ready to hunt sheep. Shoveled some more gravel.

Tuesday, August 9, 1988—40° to 58° and mostly sunny. Drove the swamp buggy to Alfred Creek trailhead and put the chains on there. Saw two boo and lots of other hunters. Got part way and adjusted the brakes. Went down Alfred Creek a ways and discovered I had a broken right rear bearing. Took wheel off, put it back on and limped all the way back home—over 60 miles today in the buggy. Got home at 10:00 p.m. Saw two nice boo bulls on the way out. Some sheep are back there.

Wednesday, August 10, 1988—36° to 54°, mostly sunny, cloudy in the evening. Worked on the swamp buggy bearings. Gave Jeanne Herring the money to repair their pickup. Went to Anchorage to get buggy bearings. Couldn't find Danny Billman. Couldn't find a pickup or freezer to buy either.

Thursday, August 11, 1988—46° to 60°, hard rain last night, mostly cloudy all day. Got the new bearings on the rear hub of the buggy. Repaired the gear case cover.

Friday, August 12, 1988—40° to 54°, partly cloudy, showers in the night. Cleaned and replaced the grease in the final drives on the swamp buggy. Waterproofed the tent over the trailer. Sylvia planted runners from strawberries.

Saturday, August 13, 1988—39° to 52°, mostly sunny, light rain in the night. Waterproofed the big tent and repaired camp cot. Serviced the buggy and truck. Shoveled some gravel. Allen Farmer visited in the evening. Lucky's Ranger is broken down on the trail. I offered my welder to fix it.

Sunday, August 14, 1988—44° to 56° and mostly sunny. Alan and Lucky came over. We loaded my welder and went to trailhead near Gunsight. Went off the highway to near old roadhouse and unloaded the welder to work on Allen's Ranger and trailer. David and Allen Farmer, Lucky Beaudoin and I went down Squaw Creek Trail several miles until we got to Lucky's Ranger. Allen re-welded the right axle and hub and Lucky left to go home. Allen and I rode around with the Ranger for a while, then made camp.

Monday, August 15, 1988—34° to 60°, sunny, windy in the evening. Walked up a creek bed into the Syncline Mountains. Explored both forks of the creek. Found three old ram skulls and one younger ram skull and horns along with one ewe skull with one horn. We saw one small bunch of sheep with four rams that were at or near 3/4 curl. None were legal. Pretty tired when we got back to camp. David walked six miles—pretty good for a youngster his age. We had a wiener roast for supper.

Tuesday, August 16, 1988—26° here on squaw Creek, up to 63°, sunny and warm. Glassed for sheep on the way to trail head. Didn't see any legal rams. Allen shot ptarmigan with a pellet gun. I cleaned them. We met a father and son on the trail hunting boo on 3-wheelers. Found a buck knife in the trail. We stopped the father later; the knife belonged to his son. We loaded up our equipment, headed out and stopped to have pie at Gunsight. Unloaded hunting gear at home and started unloading the trailer parked here.

Wednesday, August 17, 1988—42° to 62°, sunny, windy in the afternoon. Put away and straightened some gear. Painted some 2 x 4's. I'll use them to hang shovels and other things.

Thursday, August 18, 1988—32° to 64°, sunny in the morning cloudy in the afternoon. Put up the painted 2 x 4's, then worked on the D4 all morning. Allen Farmer didn't come, I was expecting him. Went to Glennallen and did some shopping and the laundry. Later I worked on the Cat some more. Allen and the kids stopped here in the evening—they had been hunting.

Friday, August 19, 1988—40° to 60° and partly cloudy. Finished up a few things that needed to be done to get ready to go hunting. Worked on magneto for the Cat, still no spark. Sylvia went to Copper Center in the "seniors" car. The Billman family had us over for supper. Mary Odden and a young English man who is on a bicycle ride from the tip of Argentina all the way to Anchorage were also there.

Saturday, August 20, 1988—38° to 55°, cloudy to partly cloudy. Visited Farmers. Got some gear ready for sheep hunting. Helped Allen build up his tandem axle trailer here at our place. Visited a little with Charlie Trowbridge.

Sunday, August 21, 1988—34° to 50°, cloudy and rain. Allen came over with Larry and Heather Severson. They had breakfast with us. Loaded our gear in the swamp buggy and trailer and went down Squaw Creek Trail. Larry and Heather hunted alone. Allen and I didn't see any rams, but saw some boo bulls, one with a nice rack. Allen didn't shoot as pack was far. Got stuck and winched our way out on the way to Eureka. The mud was almost to the top of my hip boot when I stepped out of the buggy. Had a heck of a time getting the boot out of the mud.

Monday, August 22, 1988—38° to 55°, cloudy then sunny. Rode to Eureka with Roxanne and drove the swamp buggy back home. Welded up one rear wheel and did some other small maintenance work. Some of Allen's gear got wet so I dried it out for him. Dan and Patti and Jason Billman were here for supper. Allen and some of the kids visited later.

Tuesday, August 23, 1988—34° to 56° and partly cloudy. Allen Farmer and family were here for coffee. Cal Gilchrest visited also. Tried to fix a windshield wiper on swamp buggy but had no luck. Got some gear ready to moose hunt. Charlie and I moved his freezer over here. They are moving to Cordova for now. Greg flew Allen around the Goober Knob area looking for moose, but only saw three bulls. Sylvia and I babysat the kids while they were flying. There's a heavy snowstorm south in the mountains. With the sun shining on it, it is very beautiful—a real attention getter. I took two pictures.

Wednesday, August 24, 1988—36° to 56°, mostly sunny. Tried to locate a bull moose near our place in our own little valley. Found a moose skull and 32 inch horns. Charlie Trowbridge saw a small bull on his land. Allen Farmer and Darrel Gerry visited in the evening.

Thursday, August 25, 1988—38° to 57°, mostly cloudy with some showers moving through. Hunted for the small bull seen just to the east of us. Burned a bunch of paper. Put another return spring on the clutch in the truck.

Friday, August 26, 1988—39° to 52°, mostly cloudy, some sprinkles. Hunted moose around here, then Allen and I went to Moosey Boo looking for one too. Beth and Charlie are moving to Cordova for a while, there was a party at Odden's.

Saturday, August 27, 1988—partly cloudy. Allen called and got us out of bed. We loaded gear on his truck, hooked up my trailer, and went to his place. There we loaded the four-wheel-drive ATV. We picked up Cal Gilchrest on the way to Site Road. Unloaded at trailhead and glassed three moose. We unloaded the Ranger and ATV and drove in to Small

10,000 Days in Alaska Book One 1978-1989

Lake and made camp. Saw some nice boo and some other hunters. Harry, Chris and Dave hauled out a bull boo. Allen went off to see Pat Lander and friend. Cal and I went hunting, found a spike fork and tried to stalk within shooting range, but failed. Saw a two or three-year-old bull and cow too far away to stalk that day. Saw a bull boo walk by tree stand (12'). Cooked supper, glassed for more moose, no luck. Allen took the ATV into a valley to the south and saw nice boo bulls there.

Sunday, August 28, 1988—light frost in the morning but warm and mostly sunny the rest of the day. Cal and I found the little spike fork and a cow near the same area. We made a successful stock to 150 yards. The bull was lying down in the brush with just his head out. Cal made three shots from a rest and missed. The bull and cow got up and he started running, I nailed him in the head with the .338 Magnum. Butchered him out and went to camp. Allen came in later after killing a bull boo. We brought the moose to camp and went up the small valley after Allen's boo. It wasn't an easy pack to get this boo to where we had to leave the ATV. Got back to camp, loaded up and headed for trailhead. Loaded the truck and stopped at Eureka for hamburgers. Got home late. Cal found out later his rifle sights were off.

Monday, August 29, 1988—36° to 50° and sunny. Hung all the meat in our garage. Geared up again and Cal and I took my buggy from his place to the "burn". We camped overnight. Didn't see a moose, but saw three teal.

Tuesday, August 30, 1988—frost in the morning then up to 50° and sunny. No moose here, so we went on towards the river to end of trail and camped. Did lots of walking and glassing. Saw no moose; one moose was in the area.

Wednesday, August 31, 1988—rain. No moose. Saw six teal. Packed up camp and came home. Unloaded and put gear out to dry.

Thursday, September 1, 1988—30° to 46°, mostly cloudy, rain, snow, hail. Cal and I road hunted. Sylvia cut up a lot of the moose.

Friday, September 2, 1988—28° to 56° and sunny. I cleaned the trailer, Sylvia cut up more moose. Went to KROA in the evening. Got some gear ready to go goose and crane hunting. Elaine Manning called—Jim

Norman Wilkins

had a heart attack.

Saturday, September 3, 1988–30° to 65° at Delta Junction, cloudy at home, rain in Glennallen and sunny north of Summit Lake. Did a little shopping in Delta Junction, then drove out the Alaska Highway to Sawmill Road and down to Barney and Scott Hollenbeck's farm. Scott and I checked his gut pile dump. A bear had been feeding on it. No luck hunting sharp-tail here, so we went to Scott's "40". I got two birds near there, saw a few geese. Visited him and the Baker family. Al is "fly out" hunting. Did a lot of glassing for geese and crane, but not much luck. Lots of hunters out and about looking for moose and grouse as well as crane and geese. Slept in the truck.

Sunday, September 4, 1988–46° to 65°, spotty rain than mostly sunny. Went over to the AG Project II. Talked to Steve Holcomb who farms at the end of the road. Saw other hunters who were road hunting, but saw no cranes while I was working the fields. About a thousand cranes rode the thermals up and left the area on their flight south. Stalked a small flock of geese with no luck. Three small flocks wanted to set down in this field, so I carried my decoys out to this blind and set up. Soon, a federal Fish and Wildlife team of officers checked my gun for a plug and my license and duck stamp. My stamp wasn't signed, but the one officer allowed me to sign it. No luck with the geese. It was windy in the afternoon. Clouds in the sky are very beautiful this evening. This is the second year the grasshoppers have been hard on the crops. The grassy weed foxtail is spreading fast in the farming areas.

Monday, September 5, 1988–45° in Delta with a light rain and 50° at home. I only saw one flock of 16 geese, so I left for home early. Visited the Baker's for a few minutes. Someone had thrown away four cranes and six geese at the roadside trash barrels. Maybe they had spoiled. I saw a black bear carry one away–the meat won't be wasted. Just got down the Richardson Highway 20 miles or so and a Japanese couple had rolled their car. I helped there for a few minutes. Injuries didn't seem serious. Drove up the Denali Highway and walked out on some hills looking for ptarmigan. No luck. Headed for home. Drove through intermittent showers from Glennallen all the way home. Unloaded my gear and took Sylvia to KROA for pizza. Then we stopped at Jim and Mary's, but they weren't home, so we stopped at Billman's. Jim's folks were visiting there, so we got to see Lester and Lois.

10,000 Days in Alaska Book One 1978-1989

Tuesday, September 6, 1988—30° to 50° and sunny. Allen helped me clean out the grey trailer. I did some other odd jobs and Sylvia picked two gallons of cranberries.

Wednesday, September 7, 1988—25° to 48° and mostly sunny. There was a skim of ice on the lake this morning. Worked on the gray trailer and put some paint on it. Went moose hunting in the afternoon, found one, sex unknown. Went back out hunting in the evening. Saw two cars belonging to hunters that were in that spot. Sylvia picked two more gallons of cranberries.

Thursday, September 8, 1988—23° to 50° and sunny. I road hunted moose and later, Cal and I hunted near the gravel pit. Started to pump water in the culvert at the spring. I hunted ducks on our lake, got six. Tried to spot a bull moose in the evening. Sylvia picked another two gallons of berries.

Friday, September 9, 1988—21° to 51°, Sunny, cloudy, breezy evening. Visited Cal Gilchrist in the morning. He got a 35 1/2 inch bull moose just at dark last night. Started thawing the permafrost where the 4' x 10' culvert stands on end using a 20' x ½" galvanized pipe and water pressure from the pump in the lake. 8' of pipe "washes in" in two minutes. Sylvia picked four gallons of cranberries today.

Saturday, September 10, 1988—34° to 49° intermittent sun and rain. Got the culvert in deeper—still need to go another 4 feet down. Borrowed Jim Odden's pump but it wouldn't start. Rebuilt the carburetor on my pump and will try it tomorrow. Sylvia went with Mary Beaudoin to a BBQ at Eureka.

Sunday, September 11, 1988—20° to 52° mostly sunny, cloudy evening. My pump doesn't work, so I gave up trying to wash in the big culvert. Tested for frost near the lake with half-inch pipe under water pressure. Found ice at 6 feet. This could be a place to put in a short culvert. Took Jim Odden's pump and hose back to him. Shot a spruce hen and a squirrel for supper with BB gun. Went to the dump, put some gear away and tried to call Beverly.

Monday, September 12, 1988—34° to 48° and cloudy. Did a bunch of small jobs around here. Visited Allen. Patti Billman called; Dan had struck a rock with the Beaver and had been out overnight on a lake. He got the Beaver to their home on Snowshoe Lake. We rushed down with the pickup to help get the beaching gear on the Beaver and pull it up onto the shore so repairs could be made tomorrow.

Tuesday, September 13, 1988–28° to 42° partly cloudy and some showers. One float on Dan's plane has four compartments with large rips in them. Dan, Patti and I spent most of the day doing the repairs. Sylvia canned nine quarts of cranberry juice.

Wednesday, September 14, 1988–28° to 50° and mostly sunny. Went to Snowshoe Lake and helped Dan get the Beaver back in the water. Visited Allen. Removed heater motor from the truck and a lubed it, then did some other small jobs. Allen got some movies in the evening.

Thursday, September 15, 1988–24° to 50° and sunny. Dug out and cleaned up a stump along our lane. Hauled a load of water from Hoffman's. Sylvia dug potatoes; I carried them down into the pool room. They yielded very well.

Friday, September 16, 1988–30° to 50°, cloudy, sunny, beautiful day. Got gear ready to go to Clarence Lake and repaired Allen's pack sack. Allen came over, we went to Billman's and Dan flew us to Clarence Lake. We saw lots of moose, both bulls and cows along with some caribou a few miles from the lake. Allen and I each got two grayling for supper. A small plane and two hunters flew in and camped.

Saturday, September 17, 1988–warm, rain shower at daylight. Hot in the cabin. Warmed fish and spuds for breakfast. Hunted up the hill in back of the cabins. A cow and calf moose were there, boo also. Glassed lots of moose, bulls and cows—some large bulls 2 1/2 to 5 miles from Camp. Came in at noon and had a hot lunch. Crossed the creek and headed towards four small bulls that were just east of the old trap cabin put up by Elmer Saman in 1932. We just got started when I spotted a 50-inch bull on the hill behind the cabin in the tallest of the willows. Allen decided to try for him—that was about the time the bull took off at a fast walk hot on the trail of the cow and calf we had seen in the morning. We gave up the stalk and continued east. Those bulls went east also. We saw lots more moose and boo, at least five large bulls in one bunch.

10,000 Days in Alaska Book One 1978-1989

Four of them were trying to get the cows from the bigger bull. We explored the old trap cabin, lots of old stuff there. It was his #4 line cabin nine miles east of his headquarters cabin on Gilbert Creek. We saw some grizzly tracks and spent time glassing moose and boo. Some beaver are in the creek. The airplane hunters that camped near us must have gotten their caribou. They've left. Another plane landed and three people fished. Some spotty showers this evening. Alan is out fishing right now for a trophy—or our supper.

Sunday, September 18, 1988—hard frost last night and ice on smaller ponds. Loafed around glassing moose and boo. Allen counted over 150 at one time on the hill back of the cabin. More people flew in and fished for Grayling. Allen caught more and released all but one Grayling. We packed our gear and cleaned the cabins. Dan came and flew us out to Snowshoe Lake. Rudbecks were here at our place watching TV when I got home.

Monday, September 19, 1988—34° to 44° with wind in the night and most of the day. Looked over the job of getting Darrel's camper put on my truck. Serviced lower part of my pickup. Parked swamp buggy and pulled two stumps. Cleaned up around the 16 foot trailer. Emptied oil out of old tank.

Tuesday, September 20, 1988—32° to 36° and cloudy. Shot a spruce hen in the morning. Jacked up the D4 and put boards under the track and finished up a variety of other jobs. Beaudoins brought over our tanned otter skins.

Wednesday, September 21, 1988—34° to 42°, low clouds and rain all day. Didn't do much except to make a box for magazines.

Thursday, September 22, 1988—32° to 38°, rain, cloudy. I can see snow down lower on the mountains. Put more finish on the magazine box. Trimmed a small spruce tree for wood.

Friday, September 23, 1988—34° to 44° and mostly sunny. Called people at Delta about crane and goose hunting. Spent all day getting a hunt together and gear ready for it. Sylvia put fertilizer and lime on the Garden and tilled it. Our hunting party (Jim and Mary, Darrel, Dan and I) left for Delta in the night.

Norman Wilkins

Saturday, September 24, 1988—34° to 42° and mostly sunny. We stopped up for a pee call about 25 miles out of Delta around at 3:30 a.m. Jim's dog Loki got out with us. He ran right in front of an Alaska Pipeline truck and was killed instantly. Jim and Mary were grief stricken. Darrel, Dan and I felt a big loss too. Loki was an excellent, well trained lab hunter. He was so well mannered and nice to be around. We went on to Delta, camped and cooked breakfast, then returned home. Dan, Darrel and I headed back to Delta later and arrived late in the night and camped in a farm field.

Sunday, September 25, 1988—another nice day. We got three cranes this morning, no geese flew close. Went to Delta II in the afternoon and shot five spruce hens. We camped in a field and slept in the van.

Monday, September 26, 1988—another nice day—we overslept!! The morning flight was about over when we went out but we did get one crane while making coffee. Darrel made a stalk on some geese. Dan and I were to ambush them. They flew over Dan but he didn't get any killed. Then Darrel flushed up some cranes. We didn't get any of those either as they missed us flying out. One young crane came back right over the top of us and we got him. We broke camp, got gas and visited Wendy Baker and sons. Then Dan and Darrel had a few drinks at the bar. After that we headed home. Snow, ice and sloppy through the pass, but dry here at home when I arrived at 4:30 a.m.

Tuesday, September 27, 1988—20° to 40° and sunny all day. Some clouds and breezy in the evening. Straightened out my gear and rested a lot. Cal Gilchrest visited. I gave him a rabbit. Patti brought over some gear. Went to visit Jim and Mary Odden in the evening.

Wednesday, September 28, 1988—20° to 36°, partly cloudy and breezy. Went to Dan Billman's. Blackie Zimbiki flew with us out to Crosswind Lake. We moved and covered boats at Blackie's place. The wind made it tricky beaching the plane. We went to Billman's cabin and moved boats higher and winched the pontoon boat out of the water. Then we came back to Snowshoe Lake and saw a 36 inch bull moose near Cache Creek. Lots of swans are staging for their flight south. We put the beaching gear on the Beaver, pulled it out of the water, and parked it for the winter. Loaded Dan's runabout on its trailer and parked it. Came home and

10,000 Days in Alaska Book One 1978-1989

Sylvia and I got our dock out of the water and attached legs to it. Alan and Roxanne had us over for supper. When we got back home, I went up on the roof and repaired the TV lead wire.

Thursday, September 29, 1988–20° to 38° and mostly sunny. We were out early and went shopping all day at Palmer and Anchorage. Got home early in the evening.

Friday, September 30, 1988–20° to 38°, sunny beautiful day. Did some small chores around here. Sylvia went to Glennallen in the senior's car. Allen, Roxanne and family were here for supper.

Saturday, October 1, 1988–18° to 36° cloudy with a very light snow. Cut up some pole wood, put some in the basement and at the garage. Built metal sides and bottom for wood chute and trimmed more wood. We went to KROA for music and potluck.

Sunday, October 2, 1988–2 inches of snow in the night, cloudy, sunny afternoon. No luck hunting for spruce hens. Hauled trash to the dump. Covered the Cat. Watched a movie at Rudbeck's.

Monday, October 3, 1988–16° to 32°, rainy, cloudy and rain and fog. Put oxy/acetylene bottles on cart. Cut and welded fenders for a trailer (out of an old, leaky oil storage tank). Allen's G.I. Buddy, Greg, I think his name is, crashed his plane while landing at Eureka. Allen was aboard but no one was hurt.

Tuesday, October 4, 1988–34° to 38° rain, fog, cloudy, small amount of sun. Worked on turn signals for truck. Finally took the truck to Tom H. and he fixed the lights.

Wednesday, October 5, 1988–34° to 40°. Off and on rain, clouds and sun. Made a carrying case for the metal detector. Built a five-gun, gun rack in the closet near the kitchen door.

Thursday, October 6, 1988–34° to 36°, cloudy, sunny, breezy. Dan Billman visited. Cut up and wheeled some pole wood to garage. Back is sore. Jim and Mary bicycled over and stayed for supper.

Friday, October 7, 1988–24° to 43° partly cloudy, Sunny, windy and cloudy in the evening. Trimmed up wood around here and did some paperwork for our claims. Bob Rudbeck and I took the camper off Darrel's truck and put it on mine. Then we loaded Darrel's truck onto Bob's big trailer. Bob hauled it to KROA. Dan Billman was here for supper and we worked on our affidavits of labor on our claims.

Saturday, October 8, 1988—24° to 40°, mostly sunny here at home. Cleaned Darrel's things out of the camper and loaded it with our gear. We are taking meat, berries and Beth's bicycle to Beth and Charlie in Cordova. We'll do some shopping for them on our way. The mountains are beautiful and the beaver are getting their feed piles up for winter. Ran into rain and slush before Thompson pass. It was raining in Valdez (continuous, varying intensity). Had supper, much too early to sleep. The ferry doesn't leave until tomorrow morning.

Sunday, October 9, 1988—temperature in the 40s with intermittent rain. Got on the ferry at 7:30 a.m. Had a nice trip to Cordova. Saw sea ducks, two whales, seals, sea otter, and some boats hunting deer near Cordova. Got off about 1:45 p.m. Charlie and Beth greeted us. We went to their place and visited for the rest of the afternoon.

Monday, October 10, 1988—light to medium rain all the time. Up early, drove out to the road looking for geese, saw three flying. Randy Phipps and I met back at Ten-Mile pull off after meeting him while he was running his otter line/live trapping. We followed the tree line south to get up on some geese at the sand bars on the creek flood plain. We jumped two flocks of nine and seven but didn't get a shot. Randy went west to stalk them again. They flushed wild—an airboat was running around. I went to 37 mile. It was all changed, went onto 41 mile. There I saw some geese flying and also some ducks. I heard geese at mile 23 just at dark. My alternator started to fail. Got about two miles from Charlie's, called him and he came to lead me home in the dark. We put a charger on it for the night. Slept well, rained all night.

Tuesday, October 11, 1988—temperatures in the 40s, rain and then windy later, one peek at the sun. Left town at daylight and stalked the spot where I heard geese at mile 23 with no luck. Trooper Jim Cavin was waiting for me when I got back to the road. Darrel's license plate was still on the camper. He was nice about it. I took Darrel's license plate off. Couldn't locate any geese. Went in to Cordova and picked up federal

10,000 Days in Alaska Book One 1978-1989

and state duck stamps for Charlie Trowbridge. He and I went out to Ten-Mile after he got off work. We walked down a row of trees hoping for pass shooting, and no luck. Had a good supper and nice visit with Charlie and Beth. Sylvia doesn't feel very well this evening.

Wednesday, October 12, 1988—temperature in the 40s with intermittent showers. Went to N.A.P.A. store and bought new alternator and install it on the truck. Drove out to mile 23 and Salmon Creek. Glassed geese in some jointed grass. Stalked them and got one. Water was very close to the top of my hip boots. Legs were tired when I got back to the pickup. Took pictures and drove out to 37 mile. Saw lots of ducks, no geese to shoot. Clean the goose on the way back to town. Had a good supper and some ice cream. Intermittent rain during the night.

Thursday, October 13, 1988—still in the 40s, clearing and sunshine. Randy Phipps took Charlie and me down Eyak River to boxcar slough. We saw a collared goose. Went upstream two or three miles and hunted geese there. First Flock got up wild. Charlie and Randy went east and Charlie got a goose out of a flock there. Later and other Flock flew over them and Randy got one. I heard the shots and saw it fall. Then we went back to Eyak River to Lydic slough and saw some geese. Randy stalked them, got a long shot, no luck. We saw lots of beaver sign.

Friday, October 14, 1988—40s, intermittent rain. Went to landing where Randy keeps his boat. He and Diane were just leaving to tend otter traps. They were late; he had two eagles in soft catch traps. They released the eagles unhurt. He didn't get any otter. He and I went down to Eyak River to Lydic slough and up to the goose area. Quite a few geese there. When we put out the decoys, it was raining fairly hard. Later Randy did a stalk on a flock of geese. They flushed wild. Later we gave it up and went back to the boat landing. I had coffee with Randy, then drove out to the road to 23 mile and Salmon Creek. No geese there. Went back to McKinley Lake Trail and walked in to McKinley Lake. No geese. I stopped at a grassy slough on the way back and hunted mallards. Got six nice fat ones. Went out to the truck and drove towards town. Pulled off in a gravel pit and cleaned the ducks. On the way in to town, I saw three geese land near the road, but there was lots of traffic and no place to pull off so I didn't hunt them. Went on into town and to a great roast goose and moose shish kebab supper at Randy and Diane's. We put the ducks in the freezer where Charlie works. And we put the decoys out to dry.

Saturday, October 15, 1988—temperatures in the 40s, cloudy, not raining. Had coffee with the Trowbridges, then loaded up and went to the ferry. Bought tickets and got on right away. Beth and Little Charlie came to see us depart. Saw two dusky geese fly through the harbor area and a flock of 70 geese just as we reached Prince William Sound proper. Just east of where the Columbia glacier water and icebergs and enters Prince William sound (lots of bergs), a small (30 feet?) Diesel powered boat had engine trouble. It would go a while, then quit, then broach again to the waves. The ferry we were on, "Tustimina" stood by in case the people on the boat needed rescue. Help came in the form of a powerful, though not large, boat. Last we saw them; they were traveling together towards Valdez. We disembarked at Valdez. Gassed up and inquired at lumber hardware about goose hunting. Saw geese and mallards. Wind was very strong. Saw a coyote or a small wolf cross the road. Got home at 9:15 p.m. It's 6° and we had two inches of snow on the ground.

Sunday, October 16, 1988—4°, mostly sunny. Rudbecks stopped by for a few minutes. I cleaned our things out of the camper and phone some friends. Visited Smaydas.

Monday, October 17, 1988—10° to 20°, fog, partly cloudy. Put some of the hunting gear away and made some calls about insurance and also mining claims.

Tuesday, October 18, 1988—12° to 22° and cloudy to partly cloudy. Went to Glennallen—forgot it was Alaska Day!! Magistrate's office was closed so I couldn't file assessment work papers. Sylvia did laundry.

Wednesday, October 19, 1988—12° to 24°, cloudy, light snow. Helped Allen Farmer build a three-wall, galvanized chimney and install it. Left hip came loose in socket.

Thursday, October 20, 1988—we went to Wasilla, had teeth cleaned and one filled. Stayed at a hotel overnight.

Friday, October 21, 1988—Sylvia went to the doctor in Palmer, got home early. Went to have chili, music and ice cream at Odden's. Lots of fun.

10,000 Days in Alaska Book One 1978-1989

Saturday, October 22, 1988—14° to 24° snow, sunny, cloudy. Caribou are going west on our lake. Saw one big bull with no horns. He acted like he didn't feel well. Saw three other really nice bulls. Mary Beaudoin visited. Rested my hip a lot today. Sylvia worked with her flowers today and I wrote letters. We went to Gilcrease's for a visit in the evening and exchanged movies and yarns.

Sunday, October 23, 1988—14° to 26°, cloudy with a very light snow. Rested my hip all day. Cleaned and oiled guns and watched the caribou down on the lake. Barking dogs sure worry the boo. Sylvia fixed a moose roast and we had the Tom Huddleson family here for supper. Then Tom and Lisa Smayda and their girls came over. We all visited, watched TV, and ate peach upside down cake.

Monday, October 24, 1988—8° to 26° and cloudy. Still lots of boo migrating west. Sylvia helped cut paneling into pieces to be used for tracing patterns. I boiled and dyed traps all day. Back is troublesome.

Tuesday, October 25, 1988—10° to 17°, cloudy with a light snow. Slept late. Built a fire in the woodshop stove. Made a pattern and started cutting out Sandhill Crane silhouette decoys. Went to a potluck supper at the new grade school. Lots of people came in Halloween costumes.

Wednesday, October 26, 1988—10° to 14°, cloudy with a light snow. Nadia called. A marten has been back through the yard again. Cut out more crane silhouettes. Had pie at Rudbeck's. Sylvia a roasted one of the mallard ducks from Cordova, it was excellent.

Thursday, October 27, 1988—8° to 22°, cloudy, sunny then cloudy. More caribou are going west across our lake. Took some alpine snowgo parts to Chuck Zimbiki. Went to Glennallen and filed the assessment work papers for our gold claims. Visited Mike Lanegan sporting goods. Stopped at KROA and left Darrel's camper topper with him. Tom and Emmy were here to look at the Ski-Doo 340 I have for sale.

Friday, October 28, 1988—6° to 26°, cloudy, foggy. Split and loaded three loads of wood and put it in the basement. Tom Smayda and Emily came over to visit. Tom helped with a load of wood.

Norman Wilkins

Saturday, October 29, 1988—18° to 28°, cloudy and ice fog. Tom Smayda and girls came over to borrow muffin tins. We went to the schoolhouse for a bake sale. I worked on the hood of the Ski-Doo Alpine.

Sunday, October 30, 1988—10° to 22°, sunny most of the day. Ice fog in the evening. Did some work on the truck and got the Ski-Doo started. Visited Smayda's and brought our meat home from their freezer. Had supper at the Rudbeck's, Mary and Jim Odden were there too.

Monday, October 31, 1988—12° to 20°, cloudy and some ice fog. Jim and Mary Odden, and Allen Farmer were here for lunch. I sorted nuts, bolts and screws all afternoon and split some cut off stumps.

Tuesday, November 1, 1988—8° to 12° is, ice fog and cloudy. Cal Gilchrist came over and showed me how to repair the Alpine hood with fiberglass. had a headache all day.

Wednesday, November 2, 1988—it's -7° to 0°, ice fog through Tahneta pass, then sunny. Windy near Palmer. We went to Anchorage for parts and repairs. I bought two snowgos, a 3-wheeler and a new drill press.

Thursday, November 3, 1988—still -7° to 6°, sunny but fog near here. Up early, went to Palmer and loaded the Ski-Doo and the Hondo 110 3-wheeler and got home before noon. Put the drill press together, it looks good in the garage.

Friday, November 4, 1988—6° to 11° and cloudy all day. Did more repairs on the Alpine hood. Cal Gilchrest stepped in for a few minutes. Painted inside of the hood, primed the outside and put one coat on. Allen Farmer and Clayton visited. Made a holder/tray for steel bits at the drill press. Worked on topographical maps of the Delta farming area where we hunt cranes and geese. I have lots of the farms plotted on the maps.

Saturday, November 5, 1988—0° to 5° and cloudy all day. Built a fire in the garage and the wood shop. Painted the hood for the Alpine (second coat). Tom and Lisa and the girls visited for a while. Sylvia and I finished cutting out the crane decoy silhouettes, then we cut out 40 picture frames and started several more.

10,000 Days in Alaska Book One 1978-1989

Sunday, November 6, 1988—5° to 12° cloudy all day. Lots of frost on the trees. Cut out more frames for Sylvia's projects. Worked on hood for Nordic. Jim Odden came over and did some repair and service work on his Chevy S10.

Monday, November 7, 1988—6° to 12° and cloudy. Went to Wasilla and Palmer and shopped for snowgo repair parts and picked up four drums of gas. There were some boo along the road as far as mile 120. Got back early in the evening and unloaded the gas.

Tuesday, November 8, 1988—10° to 12° and partly cloudy. Checked over two of the snowgos. Went to Glennallen and voted. Sylvia did laundry. Placed an order at Sears, had pizza in town, visited at KROA and gave Darrel a map. Picked up some snowgo parts from Chuck Zimbiki at KROA. Made out and planned craft orders.

Wednesday, November 9, 1988—it's -5° to 5° and mostly sunny. Got trapping gear ready to go in the morning. Sylvia helped take paint off the Ski-Doo Nordic hood. Cal Gilchrist brought instruments for Polaris and some movies. Sylvia gave him some of our movies.

Thursday, November 10, 1988—mostly sunny and -5° to 10°. Ran trapline to ridge north of Allen's cabin. Made two wolf sets and four fox sets. Caribou tracks everywhere. Wolves had a boo kill along the trail. Couldn't discern any marten tracks. Squirrels had been in Allen's cabin and made a heck of a mess in it.

Friday, November 11, 1988—sunny and -8° to 2°. Loaded snowgo and went to Eleven-Mile trail. Unloaded there and went to 13-Mile and broke trail and set seven marten and three fox traps. Saw a moose and quite a few caribou. One spruce hen sat under a marten box. When I got back to the track and loaded it, I went to see Warren Dawson. He gave me some of his fresh pork he had raised. Stopped in to visit Lloyd Ronning and see if he had some Polaris parts I needed. Lloyd told me several interesting stories about some of the early people who have lived around here.

Saturday, November 12, 1988—2° to 10° and cloudy. Kahren's dad Barney is weak. Worked on snowgo and helped Bob get ready so they can fly "outside". Welded up the muffler for Alpine. Kahren brought over things from her refrigerator. Jim and Mary Odden brought back my generator and visited with us for a while.

Sunday, November 13, 1988—2° to 5°, cloudy with a light snow. Went to Ed Farmer's, parked, unloaded snowgo, and made sets east and north to Four Corners. Saw wolf sign there (pee posts) and made two sets. Some fox track and one mink. Visited Darrel at KROA. Jim and Mary Odden were here or for a duck supper and we made homemade ice cream.

Monday, November 14, 1988—2° to 6° and partly cloudy. Worked on muffler/Cowling/windshield for Alpine. Got gear ready to go to my cabin on the trapline. Cal Gilchrist came to visit and borrowed some movies. Then Allen and Tom came to borrow some movies. Made a mink cubby from a white plastic bucket.

Tuesday, November 15, 1988—17° at home and 5° here at the trap cabin and mostly sunny. No fur in traps. Saw wolf/fox/marten tracks. Set all marten boxes except the one at Blue Lake. Made 2 sets at rat push-ups there at Blue Lake. Boo are scattered out here. Light snow, rough trails, upset sled many times. Good luck following trail for first time this winter. Two marten boxes were knocked off trees. Some of the springs are still running well. Cabin is in good shape. Squirrels have pulled chinking out of logs. Clean snow off the roof.

Wednesday, November 16, 1988—0° to 8° snowed until mid afternoon them some sun. Loafed most of the morning. Split wood, checked over the snowgo, shoveled snow up around the base of the cabin and made the marten sets near the cabin.

Thursday, November 17, 1988—it's -2° to 7°, cloudy, sunny more snow. Two inches accumulation since I got here. Tried to go east from Blue Lake. Lots of shallow overflow. Got as far as the first lake. One box had been knocked down and was frozen in the ice. There was open water going into the lake so I decided not to cross to the trail on the other side. Cached a Manning and three, 330 conibear, white bucket and 120 conibear at the tree with the mink box in it. Came back to Blue Lake, nothing in the rat push-ups. Left sled on lake and cut one troublesome tree from the trail back to the cabin. Split wood, gassed up the snowgo and cleaned ice from the undercarriage. Made a fox set near the bump north of Blue Lake. Lost fox scent and fox pee when I upset the snowgo on the way back from the first lake.

Friday, November 18, 1988—it was -13° at the cabin when I left and 5° here at home. Sunny day. Got two rats from the push-ups. Made a wolf set at lone tree on little lake. Made a fox sets on Fox Lake and a wolf set nearby on trail. Made a fox sets south of marten box near upper Mendeltna Springs. Nothing in marten sets on the way to Allen's cabin. No fur period! A wolf had been at boo kill. It was hunting south. I made a set south of Cache Creek for it. Real tired and back hurts tonight.

Saturday, November 19, 1988—partly cloudy and -8° to 5°. Went to Eleven-Mile on Lake Louise Road, (after going to Evergreen Lodge for the lady hauling mail. She had run out of gas and wanted her hubby to bring gas from the junction.) nothing on that line. Saw fox and wolf tracks. Then went to the line back of Ed's at Mendeltna. Nothing in those traps, but saw more fox and wolf tracks. They just wouldn't go in my sets. Made a trail set for wolf just west of mink box set. Called Ed Vogel for Polaris parts. Dave DeJung called asking how to flesh muskrats. Found one of Allen's traps he had lost track of.

Sunday, November 20, 1988—0° to 10°, light snow all day. Took Alpine parts to Chuck's place. Found a Colt Polaris hood along the highway. Gave it to Lloyd Ronning. Gave Kahren's presents to Lloyd, Leo, and Charlie. Sylvia gave them cranberry sauce. Found the muffler I lost, it is ruined. Visited KROA. Hauled a load of water from Max Hoffman's. Checked Jim Odden's light in pantry and well. The light is to prevent the well from freezing. I am watching their place while they are gone.

Monday, November 21, 1988—it's -4° to 10°, cloudy with snow in the afternoon and evening. Slept late. Put a new water pump on the truck and soldered a leak in the radiator. Sanded on the Nordic hood. Worked with the claim papers. Dave DeJung brought trap boiling stove back and had supper with us.

Tuesday, November 22, 1988—8° to 10°, cloudy and snowed all day, 4 1/2". Cleaned chimney on the house. Plowed our snow with Odden's Blazer and worked on snowgos. Cal Gilchrist came over to borrow some

TV tapes. We had him here for supper. Nadia called this evening and it is still snowing.

Wednesday, November 23, 1988—7° to 10°, cloudy and some snow. Put two coats of paint on the Nordic hood. It's finished. Rebuilt and recovered the seat on the long track. Mixed gas for tomorrow. Got three more inches of snow.

Thursday, November 24, 1988—it's -15° to -4°, a mostly cloudy and some fog. Parked at Eleven-Mile. Got a red fox and female marten at the first two sets and picked up all the traps on that line. Went to Ed's place and ran that line. A boo had sprung a fox trap, then a fox walked all over that area, then went down the trail to a mink set, looked it over and went farther down the trail to one of my wolf sets and got caught in a Manning #9. Ruined the wolf set. I went on to 4 Corners, followed the tracks of two wolves for over a mile. The male peed on stump and he stepped each side of the trap. I went on north looking for marten tracks with no luck. Lost my new mitts in Ed's yard and had to go back and get them. Skinned out one fox and the marten. The one fox has a poor pelt. I'll see if Jim Odden wants it. Our son Paul called on Thanksgiving.

Friday, November 25, 1988—temp is -20° to -16°, cloudy and lots of ice fog. Got trap gear ready. Cleaned and boiled a wolf and a fox trap. Visited Allen Farmer and Lucky and Mary. Pulled Ski-Doo Nordic into the garage. Tom, Lisa and girls brought over some pie and visited in the evening.

Saturday, November 26, 1988—cloudy, then sunny and -26° to -22°. A coyote came out on the west end of our lake for a short time. Now I keep the 06 near the door. Went to Allen's and looked at how the coils are wired on his Nordic. Worked on the wiring, dash, skis, clutch sheaves and switches. Cut a finger today.

Sunday, November 27, 1988—it's -15° to -11° and sunny. Worked on Nordic skis, spindles, welding and lots of painting. Trying to glue the track separations together. Tom and Lisa came over and did some copying at Rudbeck's. Allen came over and borrowed some movies. Lee D. visited for a while.

10,000 Days in Alaska Book One 1978-1989

Monday, November 28, 1988—mostly sunny and -20° to -12°. Called land office about claims and did paperwork. Worked on the Nordic dash, some fiberglass work, built a skeg (A skeg is a small, flat appendage located along a vessel to stabilize it.) and got the motor to fire. Built a box for the rear and mounted a tail light.

Tuesday, November 29, 1988—temp is -6° to 6°. It snowed all day. Went to Glennallen on business about the mining claims and to pay the light bill. I picked up an order from Sears at the Post Office and a package to Rudbecks and a large envelope for Billmans. Plowed out our snow (six inches) and plowed Lucky and Allen's driveways. Steve Malley brought over his snowplow from off of his Ranger and did some welding and drilling on it.

Wednesday, November 30, 1988—-5° to 6° and mostly sunny. Plowed Jim and Mary's driveway then went on to Ed Farmer's and plowed snow. Came back home and loaded the snowgo and went back to Ed's Farmers and ran the trapline there. Remade two fox sets, one mink and one wolf. Saw two fox tracks on the line. Came home and got gear ready to run the north line.

Thursday, December 1, 1988—2° here at home. Started for the trap cabin pulling the sled behind. Only got a quarter of a mile after leaving the highway before I had to unhook it. Just too much trouble to pull in the deep snow. Put personal gear on snowgo and continued on. Boo had sprung wolf sets, trap setter handles are slipping off the trap levers. Got a beautiful male marten at the second vertical box on the trail that leads from the meat pole to Mendeltna Springs. Nothing else in traps. Saw moose cow and calf, caribou and fox tracks. There was overflow on Mendeltna Springs, Fox Lake, Blue Lake and the drainage above Blue Lake. Snow is deep, though there is less here at the cabin. Cleaned the snow off the cabin roof and from the undercarriage of the snowgo. It's -11° here and dropping to -20 and colder.

Friday, December 2, 1988—it's -10° to -5°, snowed all day. Skinned the marten when it thawed out, then ran the trap loop near the cabin. I got one nice, dark male and one light colored male marten. Split a supply of wood. It took a lot of wood to warm the cabin last night. Easy to heat it today. I need to re-chink the logs. The marten I got today were thawed enough to skin before bedtime (took me an hour to do it).

Norman Wilkins

Saturday, December 3, 1988—10° at the cabin and 14° at home. Remade some sets and skirted most of the overflow areas. The spring near the gas drums had thawed and I had to find a new crossing. The trail was really miserable to stay on. The fog rolled in when I got to brush Hill (meat pole hill area). From there on, white-out conditions were bad most of the time and the trail was a struggle. Got stuck many times. Got stuck on steep hill across from home and again near the culvert. I was wore out and disgusted when I got home.

Sunday, December 4, 1988—warmed up to 22° and got breezy last night, dropping to 0° this evening, but it was mostly sunny all day. Plowed the snow out of the yard. Tom Smayda and his girls came and visited with us. We went over to the lodge for a while. I took the cover off the snowgo chain case and it looks okay, but there is a noise in there somewhere. Thawed the marten pelts and put them on stretchers.

Monday, December 5, 1988—temp is -12° to -14°, clear and sunny. Plowed snow for Lloyd Ronning, Charlie Netter, Leo Zura and Max Hoffman. Worked on my Nordic snowgo.

Tuesday, December 6, 1988— colder, -24° to -20°, sunny and cold. Went to Wasilla and Palmer for truck and snowgo parts. Lots of boo between here and mile 118. Saw a spike bull moose and a few cows on the way to town. Saw a large coyote near the road just outside of Sutton. Talked to John Mahoney who now works for Safeway store. Visited Cal for a few minutes.

Wednesday, December 7, 1988—temp is down, -32° to -18°, sunny and cloudy. Took the head and jug off the LT Polaris motor. Lots of carbon and both rings were stuck. Cleaned everything very well. Put new rings, pin and wristpin bearing. New top end gaskets. Now it sounds fine. Serviced it.

Thursday, December 8, 1988—it's -6° to -2°, at 5 inches of snow last night, cloudy today. Put muffler and temperature sensor on truck. Shoveled snow here and plowed Cal's, Jim Odden's, Farmer's, some of Hoffman's and most of ours.

Friday, December 9, 1988—still -6° to 8°, cloudy and ice fog. Ran the trapline north of Ed Farmer's. Saw one wolf track and one old fox track. I could see that there had been caribou in that area. Remade all sets and added a wolf set. Snowgo motor wanted to overheat because of the poor trail conditions and new ring job. Pushed the snow from in front of the woodshed and all along the driveway up to the house.

Saturday, December 10, 1988—6° to 30° and cloudy. Continued trying to get Everest snowgo started. Finally got plugs and cylinders dry enough to start. Replaced the wood supply at the garage. Allen Farmer brought his snowplowing blade over to weld it and stayed to visit. I went Hoffman's and got a load of water. Mary Beaudoin brought some movies she had taped. Cal Gilchrest, Mary and Philip brought some movies back along with some they had taped and borrowed more of ours. Cal bought a nice-looking Jeep pickup yesterday.

Sunday, December 11, 1988—25° to 30° and mostly cloudy. Worked on Nordic snowgo and went to Chuck Zimbiki's for some parts. He's bummed out over working on the Alpine. Sylvia left some of her crafts at Tazlina bazaar. Stopped at KROA and gave Darrel a pair of snowgo boots. Jim Odden called in the evening.

Monday, December 12, 1988—12° to 15° and cloudy. Tried to run Slide Mountain line to my cabin. Made a set for wolverine where one came into a marten set last year. Boo messed up one wolf set. Wolves had been on the trail. Saw lots of places where they had peed—including the old boo kill. I moved a Manning to a little tree they had peed on. Snowgo gave me lots of trouble, probably overheating. Started taking the motor apart tonight. Asked Chuck Z. what to do. Allen and Ellie came over to borrow a couple of movies.

Tuesday, December 13, 1988—0° to -8° and sunny. Took the jug off snowgo and honed it. Shortened end gap on one ring and put everything back together. The diaphragm was leaking and it wouldn't start. Put different parts in the diaphragm and it still leaks. All in all a pretty exasperating day.

Wednesday, December 14, 1988—20° to 10°, mostly cloudy, 1 inch of snow in the night. Went to chucks and got snowgo parts. Put two fuel pumps together. The carburetor on Nordic is giving me trouble.

Norman Wilkins

Thursday, December 15, 1988—20° to 22°, cloudy, fog, light snow. Tried to get the carburetor adjusted on the Nordic. Borrowed Allen's carburetor off his Nordic. It worked okay, that means I must need more new parts. Borrowed Allen's impact wrench and still couldn't get the clutch apart to service it.

Friday, December 16, 1988—31° most of the day, cloudy, snow, breezy and fog. Allen Farmer and I went to get school teacher's car out of a snow berm. Allen and Kyle had breakfast with us. Shoveled lots of snow and cleaned some off the roof. Went up on the peak of the house to check TV wire. Worked on the Ski-Doo and the Nordic. Nadia called.

Saturday, December 17, 1988—12° all day, sunny. Ran trapline north of Mendeltna. Made two sets, saw fox and marten track, but no fur. Took Nordic and carburetor to Chuck Zimbiki. Problem seems to be wrong sized butterfly on throttle shaft. Checked things at Odden's place, some pop is frozen and a water jug.

Sunday, December 18, 1988—4° to 8° and mostly cloudy with some fog. Visited Smayda's. Pulled a Polaris colt into the garage and worked on it. Wrote out some Christmas cards. Tom Smayda came over and looked at my garage door opener. Lisa and the girls visited with Sylvia.

Monday, December 19, 1988—10°, cloudy, very light snow. Went to Cal Gilcrease for snowgo part/wrong size. Lots of boo along the road. Worked on Polaris Colt all day, rebuilt muffler for it. Got too much exhaust from welder motor. Phoned Big Lake to get some snowgo parts.

Tuesday, December 20, 1988—14° all day and cloudy. Woke up with my back hurting badly. Didn't do anything all day. Public nurse, Karen Martenek, gave us our flu shots. Mary Beaudoin came over for her shot. Lee D. came by for some trail information.

Wednesday, December 21, 1988—4° all day, cloudy and fog. My back is still bad. Worked on Polaris today: cleaned fuel pump and put on a new filter and fuel line, aligned skis and started building a bracket to mount coil and cleaned the fuel tank. Carol, Mary Odden's friend, stopped by and wanted Odden's driveway plowed out. Sylvia went with Smayda's to a Christmas program at the chapel.

10,000 Days in Alaska Book One 1978-1989

Thursday, December 22, 1988—10° all day, foggy. Plowed snow at Odden's for Carol and also plowed out Ed Farmer's and here at home. Then I worked on the Polaris Colt; it's nearly done.

Friday, December 23, 1988—it's -10° clear and cold. Parked truck and trailer at Slide Mountain trail. Some marten had crossed the trail and I made two sets for them. Many wolf tracks on the snowgo trail. Wolves did not use my pee post set on either side of old boo kill. Broke trail out to Small Springs. Saw a few fox track. Nothing in marten boxes. Took two hours to get back to the truck. The wolves had been on the trail while I was out there. Lots of caribou using that country out there too. Saw a spike moose bull and a cow near our place. Some people are hunting caribou already—season opens January 1. Flushed some spruce hens that had buried themselves in the snow along the track trail. James and Zoe Callahan called us this evening.

Saturday, December 24, 1988—colder, -26° to -10°, Sunny, cloudy in the evening. Rested a lot. Tom Smayda gave me some brake fluid so I bled and filled the brake system on the Polaris Colt. Allen Farmer visited in the evening.

Sunday, December 25, 1988—temp is -8° to -12°, sunny, cloudy. Went to Smayda's for Christmas dinner. Tom and I went to Odden's to help Carol get her pickup started. Father Mike (priest) and a Sister were there for dinner also. Weld-repaired the air shroud for the 250 Polaris Colt.

Monday, December 26th, 1988—it's -10° 20°, ice fog, sun, and then cloudy. Ran trapline north of Ed Farmer's. Moved mink box north near crossing for a marten set. No fur, just one squirrel. Visited KROA, Darrel Gerry, and Charlie Netter. Sylvia and I went to Lucky and Mary's with some sweets. I borrowed Lucky's electric staples. Put air shroud on Polaris Colt and started to mount hood but didn't get lights hooked up.

Tuesday, December 27, 1988—still -10° to -4°, cloudy and ice fog. Worked on the lighting on the Polaris Colt. There are some problems to find and fix. Tom Smayda came over to borrow some electrical spray. Called Chuck and talked to him about the wiring.

Wednesday, December 28, 1988—saw a little sun, then cloudy with light snow and fog. -4° to 12°. Visited Allen and Roxanne. Our Ski-Doo

Nordic was there, brought it home. Went to Lucky's for a load of water. Got taillights and half the headlights working. Switch is bad on one side.

Thursday, December 29, 1988—it's -4° to 0°, very little sun, cloudy with lots of ice fog. Ran trapline to cabin. Had nothing in the wolverine set. Made two wolf sets. Met two lost Blue Lake snowmobilers and directed them to another trail. (They had been out to the last meat pole hill earlier). Remade three fox sets and one wolf set near Fox Lake. Got a dark marten just past Fox Lake. Saw one nice big moose on Mendeltna Springs Lake. Made a rat set on Blue Lake. Overflow has ruined the other push-up. A mink had torn the top out of a new rat push-up. There were many marten tracks between Blue Lake and my trap cabin. A marten has been here at the cabin and stole three rats I had for bait. He also tore a hole in the plastic window but didn't go inside. Ran the short loop near the cabin. Had a mink in a conibear box leaning pole set. He was hanging close enough to the snow that a marten ate about half of him. Split wood but didn't clean snow off the cabin roof, just too tired. Skinned the marten later. Will tan the ½ hide at home.

Friday, December 30, 1988—it was -15° during the night, -10° in the morning and -2° at home. Ice fog all day. Checked mink set on east drainage, then started home. Rat trap was sprung. Nothing in traps on way home. Saw a beautiful ptarmigan fly up from near the trail. Stopped at wolverine set and picked up that trap. Got home at 2:30 p.m., rested, and then put the marten on a stretcher.

Saturday, December 31, 1988—it's -3° to 10° and mostly cloudy. Went to Ed Farmer's and ran the trapline there. No fur. Stopped at KROA. Ron and Greg were there with their families. Came home and took the Polaris Colt for a test ride. It's running fine. Tom H. came over and took the Everest for a ride. Visited Allen to offer him a snowgo to hunt boo in the morning. Went to Nelchina in the early evening. Some neighbors and people we know were there. Then went on to KROA and visited with Darrel and Ron and Greg. The Northern Lights are really bright tonight.

10,000 Days in Alaska Book One 1978-1989

Norman with wolf—1988

Norman Wilkins

1989–incident with a wolf

Sunday, January 1, 1989—cloudy all day and 12° to 20°. Alaska Fish & Game had a one day caribou hunt today. I shot a boo east of our lake and Sylvia got the whole animal cut up for grinding today. Allen came over just at dark and asked Sylvia to baby sit Elli while he and I walked quite a ways trailing a wounded caribou (the caribou are migrating, this animal had been shot somewhere east of us). We never did catch up to it. Enjoyed having the little kids around.

Monday, January 2, 1989—mostly sunny and -2° to -12°. Worked on the Nordic all day. Kim came over to borrow movies. Cal G. borrowed a sausage book and some movies.

Tuesday, January 3, 1989—sunny and then overcast with light clouds in the afternoon. Temperature was -22° to -16°. I reworked a new windshield for the Nordic. It is mounted and fits well. Went to Glennallen and turned in the harvest cards for boo hunt and the lower jaw of the one I got (the DNR will want to pull a tooth to determine the age of the animal). Got part of snowgo parts order from Chuck Z. Checked Odden's house. A unique and interesting sliver of a moon rise over the mountain to the South at 8:28 a.m. this morning. It was beautiful. Tom Smayda and family visited in the evening.

Wednesday, January 4, 1989—sunny with high clouds in the afternoon, -20° to -18°. Took the Nordic for a trial run. This carburetor needs more repair. Loafed and then took recoil starter off the Polaris LT. Cleaned it and put it back on. Tom H. had a headlight bulb that I could make work on the Nordic.

Thursday, January 5, 1989—mostly sunny with a beautiful sunrise, -10° to -18°. Ice crystals in the air today. Made one carburetor out of two and got the Nordic running then I built two risers to make the skis contact the snow more firmly. Fixed the turn signal on the truck.

Friday, January 6, 1989—cloudy and -20° to -10°. Took the snowgo springs over to Allen. Nordic wouldn't start and I had to pull it home. He brought the school bus here and we rebuilt and repaired the mirror frame on the driver's door. I hauled trash to the dump.

10,000 Days in Alaska Book One 1978-1989

Saturday, January 7, 1989—mostly cloudy and -4° to 8°. Ran the line north of Ed Farmers. No fur, no tracks. Visited Darrel at KROA. Charlie Knetter came in later. Shoveled snow out of berms at schoolhouse for snowgo trail. Checked Odden's place. Cal G. stopped for a minute. I had sledded wood to the garage.

Sunday, January 8, 1989—cloudy, ice fog, snowy and -5° to 4°. Took the Ski-Doo Nordic carburetor apart. Diaphragm is kaput. We put six small sled loads of wood in the basement about one cord maybe. Caribou still spend time on our lake. I wonder if they feel safer when resting out in the open.

Monday, January 9, 1989—partly cloudy with some snow, -8° to -5°. Had to change plug in snowgo. Put a # 3 double long spring at wolverine set. Made a new wolf set. Missed one marten set. Broke suspension spring on snowgo south of Meat Pole Hill. Got a cross fox in set at upper Mendeltna Springs. Built a fire at the cabin and ran the loop here. Had a large male marten in set where mink had been half eaten. Split wood and cleaned snow off roof. Can't skin animals—forgot glasses at home!

Tuesday, January 10, 1989—cloudy with an ice fog, -10° to -4°. Got one rat from push-up on Blue Lake. Left trap, poles, ice chisel at beaver house. Uneventful trip out. boo had been on trail and one fox out near highway.

Wednesday, January 11, 1989—cloudy and breezy, 16° to 23°. Went to Glennallen and renewed driver's license, cashed some checks and picked up some snowgo parts at Chuck's. Cal stopped by for his parts and some movies. Took the cover off the Alpine seat.

Thursday, January 12, 1989—16° to 14°, cloudy and snow. Mary G. returned one carburetor kit and picked up another one for me. Put new spring on Polaris LT and put used diaphragm in fuel pump. Ran line north of Ed's. Made a fox set and two traps. found a boo rib cage in grassy swamp. Also a trail side fox set with a boo hoof—this just south of marten box. Moose had sprung one wolf trap and ruined the wolf trail where I had that trap. I tried to arrange tracks to fit trap. Had camp robber and squirrel in marten sets. Got most of the gear ready to go to cabin.

Norman Wilkins

Friday, January 13, 1989—cloudy then sunny, snow ended. -5° to -12°. Did some things here, hauled a load of water from Hoffman's place, got bait ready for trapline and put up Ski-Doo "for sale" sign at Eureka. Dropped off snow flap material at Cal's and visited a while.

Saturday, January 14, 1989—cloudy with some snow and -16° to -6°. Tom Smayda came over for a couple of garage door spring adjustment rods. Put carburetor kit in the two, HR 40 A carburetors. Nordic won't run on either one and getting worse.

Sunday, January 15, 1989—snow, sunny then cloudy and -6° to -12°. Found the Nordic trouble. One carburetor isn't quite right and one plug wire comes out of coil. Cal came over to help. Then I went down on our lake and east—nothing. Fur is feeding on the gut piles. I chopped out three sets of small horns and brought them home. Plowed out Jim Odden's and checked their house then visited at KROA. Plowed out our place.

Monday, January 16, 1989—mostly cloudy with some falling ice crystals. -18° to -10°. Got a few things ready for trapline. Rebuilt and recovered the seat for the Alpine. Put up snowgo "for sale" sign at Nelchina Lodge and phoned in an ad to KCAM radio.

Tuesday, January 17, 1989—sunny and -25° to -20°. Bill Granger, a friend of Chuck Z. called about the ad. They came over and he drove the Nordic and bought it. I made and welded hooks on two pelt hangers. Dave DeJung and a friend, Brian visited here looking for beads to sew on a fur hat.

Wednesday, January 18, 1989—mostly sunny and -36° to -20°. Lots of boo on our lake. Allen, Roxanne and Elli visited quite awhile. I put up track lights over the kitchen island and checked Odden's place (they are visiting relatives down in the lower 48). Cal brought back movies and borrowed a few more.

Thursday, January 19, 1989—mostly sunny and -43° to -30°. Went over to Smayda's and picked up a letter and fire extinguishers. Worked on my trapping note book. Allen, Tom and Kim H. came over to borrow movies.

10,000 Days in Alaska Book One 1978-1989

Friday, January 20, 1989—partly cloudy and -36° to -20°. Ice fog across the river. Some boo on the lake. Lots of ravens feeding on gut piles out on the lake ice. Checked Odden's place, replaced bulb in well. Visited the Malley family. Made a fox set a short way up Slide Mountain Trail. Organized goose and crane hunting information material. Steve, Karen, Ian and Caleb Malley were here for supper and brought pecan pie.

Saturday, January 21, 1989—sunny and -40° to -30°. Tom Smayda and Charlie Trowbridge visited in the morning. We went over to Smayda's to see Beth and Little Charlie and Cora Elizabeth, then back over here in the evening to make homemade ice cream.

Sunday, January 22, 1989—sunny with ice in the air and -48° to -34°. Checked Odden's place—more beer is frozen, hope they get home soon. Checked fox set along the road. Charlie Trowbridge brought his pickup over and changed the thermostat on it in our garage. Our plumbing vent is full of frost and I brought it down to thaw out. Loafed most of the day. Saw two boo out on our lake. The ravens feed no matter how cold it is.

Monday, January 23, 1989—cloudy light snow, clear in the late afternoon and -25° to -15°. Slept late, wrote a letter, then loaded snowgo and sled. Went to Mendeltna and ran that line. Lots of fox track, more than earlier in the season. a fox almost went in one set. Made a new fox set at natural pee post. Got a marten in a coni box set on snow out near the wolf sets. Moose had sprung two trail sets for wolf. Visited KROA and Darrel Gerry. Checked fox set at Slide Mountain trail head—nothing. Gassed truck at home and mixed snowgo gas and refill the Polaris LT.

Tuesday, January 24, 1989—cloudy with snow in the afternoon and -20° to -10°. Skinned marten. Got a call to look at the Ski-Doo Everest I had for sale. Had a hard time getting it started, plus the O-rings that hold the windshield on had shrunk in the cold and broken and the windshield broke at the bottom. I trimmed it and put it back on. Primed the carburetor and it started. The guy didn't show up. Plowed part of Rudbeck's drive. Went to an ice cream party at Smayda's. Jim and Mary Odden got back this evening.

Wednesday, January 25, 1989—some sun, cloudy and snow. -10° all day. Jim and Mary Odden were here for breakfast. Fred Rungee visited and bought the Ski-Doo Everest. Jim took his plow and blazer home. Rudbecks got back and came over for supper. Cal, Mary, and Phillip also visited in the evening. Bought chances on snowgo and loaned movies.

Thursday, January 26, 1989—cloudy, ice fog, light snow and -20° to -10°. Waited until it 11:00 a.m. to start on trapline. Wolves had been on the trail. Had a young male wolf in the set at the old boo kill. Saw movement through the brush just before I got there. Quick looked at the area then went on down the trail and caught up to him. He bared his teeth and turned and I went over him. He ran back south on trail after I gave him a glancing blow with a hatchet on his head. Then I grabbed the .22 rifle and ran down the trail, pulling a muscle in my leg. Lobbed two shots at him and missed. Unhooked sled, turned snowgo around and caught up to him in about a quarter of a mile. He ran off the trail when I got to him so I pinned him with the snowgo, loaded the .22 and shot him in the head. Cleaned the snow off him and put him in a gunny sack. Loaded him in the sled and started for home. (this is a pretty raw account of killing a wolf. I didn't enjoy having things get to this stage, but the problem was there and the wolf deserved the quickest death I could administer under the circumstances.) Cached a bunch of Bait at the place where I caught the wolf. Picked up the trap with his foot still in it and came on home. Jim Odden came over after supper and helped skin him—took us two hours. Mary visited with Sylvia. Froze the pelt for tannery. The wolf is a real nice gray.

Friday, January 27, 1989—cloudy at first, -25° to -38° with ice fog, snow then sunny with sun dogs. (A sun dog is a common bright circular halo seen around the sun. It is an atmospheric optical occurrence associated with the refraction of sunlight by small ice crystals.) Went to Glennallen and did laundry, sealed wolf hide, paid electric bill, bought stamps at post office and visited at KROA and also Jim and Mary Odden. Shoveled snow out of snowgo trail near schoolhouse.

Saturday, January 28, 1989—ice fog all day and -42° to -32°. Visited David DeJung and Rudbecks.

Sunday, January 29, 1989—ice fog, clearing overhead in the afternoon and -38° to -30°. Sold chances for prizes/American trapper, to Henry and Sally Johnson. Tom, Kim and family came over to visit and borrow TV tapes. Tom and Lisa Smayda visited in the evening and brought ice cream and adjusted Sylvia's sewing machine. (Celebrating birthdays with good friends is something we do a lot.)

Monday, January 30, 1989—ice fog, clear and sunny. -45° to -30°. Many boo on our lake all day. A cow moose is browsing around here. Went to see the Rudbecks and sold two raffle tickets. Tom H. wasn't home. Lisa Smayda and the girls visited while Kahren was here. I sorted more pictures today.

Tuesday, January 31, 1989—sunny and -45° to -30°. Visited Tom Smayda. Two cow moose and one calf are browsing near by. Lots of caribou are crossing the lake; some are coming up our hill and going north. I did some trapping information research and organization. Hooked up a 20,000 BTU propane heater in the basement. Harold and Lorraine Hanson from Minnesota called and Sylvia's sister, Francis Collins from Chicago called.

Wednesday, February 1, 1989—sunny slight ice fog early in the morning and evening. It's -45° to -28°. Sorted pictures and did some reading. Back hurts real bad. The Smaydas, Oddens and Rudbecks all came over for ice cream and pecan pie to celebrate my birthday.

Thursday, February 2, 1989—sunny, some ice fog. It's -48° to -30°. Walked down to Allen and Roxanne's for coffee and snacks. Loafed all day. Red sunrise and sunset.

Friday, February 3, 1989—sunny and -43° to -22°. Didn't do much all day. Fred Rungee came and paid for the snowgo. I helped him arrange his load and we visited. Went to Odden's for a nice supper.

Saturday, February 4, 1989—sunny and -38° to -18°. Bob and Kahren were here for brunch. Kahren and went with us to KROA. I ran the trapline north—no fur. Boo had messed up all good sets. Picked up the marten sets. Had a two-year-old cow in a Manning. She was real feisty so I called Fish & Game from KROA. Mike Roscovius came out and I led him to the boo. It would rear up and strike and try to rush us with its horns. By the time we got it down, it was dark. Heck of a time getting trap off and rope cut to release the animal and not get injured ourselves.

Sunday, February 5, 1989—sunny and -30° to -10°. Put new diaphragms in snowgo fuel pump and got ready to go to the trap cabin. On the way to the cabin, many boo had been on the trail and cut it up so bad it is troublesome to travel. Had a cow boo in a Manning at fork in the trail. Tied her head to a tree and loosened cable clamps on both ends to get the trap and cable off and unwrapped from her leg so I could turn her lose. Nothing else in my traps. Saw wolf turds in the trail and fox, marten, mink, otter and ermine tracks. A spruce hen flew up from beside the trail and showered me with snow. Saw lots of moose tracks but didn't see any. Sprung all marten sets and cleaned five inches of snow off cabin roof.

Monday, February 6, 1989—sunny frost coming out of trees and -20° to 0°. Stiff and sore this morning, loafed and read all day.

Tuesday, February 7, 1989—sunny and partly cloudy. It's -15° to 0°. Frosty fuel in bottom of snowgo engine, trouble getting it started. Picked up sets east of Blue Lake. Made fox set at upper Mendeltna Springs and just below Meat Pole Hill. Made wolf set at a pee tree (Helfrich). Saw a moose on Allen's lake and more spruce hens. No fur in traps. Boo sure wrecked trail. Visited with Tom Smayda just as I reached the highway. He was out skiing.

Wednesday, February 8, 1989—sunny and cloudy and it's -10° to 6°. Ran line north of Ed Farmer's. Lots of boo and moose tracks and two fox. No fur. Made wolf set near where boo was caught. Remade fox sets. Took carburetor apart on snowgo but couldn't see anything wrong with it. Hauled a load of water from Lucky's.

Thursday, February 9, 1989—mostly sunny and -2° to 13°. Fired up snowgo and went to Allen's but he wasn't home. Loafed most of the day. Allen visited in the afternoon, then Cal, Mary and Philip stopped in.

Friday, February 10, 1989—cloudy and fog, 7° to 10°. Repaired two Alaska # 9's and took them and two Helfrich and some snares to Cal. Cal and I went to the end of his trapline and made four sets at wolf pee posts and hung three snares near some boo bones. Saw a couple of fox tracks. Came home, got ready and went to Glacier View School for a potluck supper and drawing for a new Yamaha snow machine. Didn't win the snow machine but we did win a rag doll door prize.

10,000 Days in Alaska Book One 1978-1989

Saturday, February 11, 1989—partly cloudy and 10° to 19°. Went with Rudbecks to the clinic in Glennallen and had our blood tested for cholesterol levels. Had lunch and went shopping in town, then came back home. Changed clothes and ran the wolf sets on the east side of Slide Mountain—no wolves. Returned the trap I caught the wolf in and am boiling it tonight. Saw wolf, marten, moose and caribou tracks.

Sunday, February 12, 1989—mostly sunny, 9° to 19°. Went down on our lake to the east end and made a trail set and a pee post set for fox. Loaded snowgo and left Sylvia at KROA. Ran line north of Ed's. Just got started and shot three ptarmigan. Saw two marten and one fox track but no fur. Went west to see beaver lodge on the lake there. Lodge looked abandoned. Visited KROA and worked with my trap gear in the evening.

Monday, February 13, 1989—fog, then sunny. It's 9° to 12°. Ran line at Cal's. Wolf stepped on edge of one trap and a boo sprung another. Made one trail set and hung another snare. Someone had crossed trail. Allen Farmer gave me a 330 conibear. Nothing in the two fox sets on our lake. Hauled three loads of wood and put in the basement. Shoveled snow and built up the sled trail along the house. We cleaned the chimney, it needed it. Serviced the snowgo. Shaved caribou hair for trap sets and put it in plastic bags. Called Sam Agaur about snowgo recoil. Cal G. has motor mount problems.

Tuesday, February 14, 1989—Fog, sunny and -7° to 3°. Cal G. borrowed a few things to fix his snowgo. Ran line to cabin. Other machines have been on much of the trail. No fur. A fox looked at one set. Moved south wolf trap to north of natural crossing at a broken off tree wolf pee post. Saw quite a few moose on the long ridge today. One cow with calf didn't want to run off. Made an otter set on Mendeltna Springs Crossing. Very fresh wolf track on the way to Fox Lake. Remade wolf set there. Forgot aluminum shovel so I won't trap beaver this time. Got to cabin real early. Nice here. Broke a spring on snowgo.

Wednesday, February 15, 1989—fog, then sunny. It's -10° to 6°. Loafed until noon, then went east to the north end of Burbot Lake. Made a gang set for otter at the north end and one otter set at the south end. Saw some fresh fox tracks and old otter trails. Stiff and sore and sick with a head cold and flu.

Norman Wilkins

Thursday, February 16, 1989—fog then sunny and it's -10° to 5°. Feeling really sick with the flu. Got the dishes done and left cabin about 11:30 in the morning. Ran trapline home. Saw fox, marten and wolf tracks. Also saw quite a few moose and lots of fresh caribou tracks. Got home a little after 3:00 p.m.

Friday, February 17, 1989—fog, sunny, -10° to 10°. Put a new spring on snowgo, loaded it up and went to Cal's and ran trapline there. Reset two traps that boo had sprung. Made one new set. Saw four moose—one was huge. Came home and then left Sylvia at KROA while I ran the trapline north of Ed Farmer's. Remade one fox set. Made one new wolf set with dog pee on post, then broke trail two miles west. First lake has beaver lodge. Second lake has rat push-ups. Found a # 3 Victor with chain grown into a tree. Gave Darrel some Delta pictures.

Saturday, February 18, 1989—fog then sunny. -9° to 9°. Checked the two fox sets here—nothing. Mixed gas and put oil in truck, etc. Cleaned snow off greenhouse then had lunch at Rudbeck's. Loafed in the afternoon.

Sunday, February 19, 1989—fog, sunny, -8° to 4°. Went visiting at Warren and Leona's, Jim and Mary Odden's, then went to see Lloyd Ronning. He gave us a package of halibut.

Monday, February 20, 1989—sunny and it was -10° to 10°. Checked line at Cal's. Had a caribou in a Manning. Roped it and got it turned loose. Went on down the drainage and made a set. Had a nice lunch at Cal's, then went to Ed Farmer's. Ran that line. People had been on it and had gotten stuck many times. It was torn up and wolf trap was sprung. I saw a moose calf lying down very near the trail. It didn't move either time I went past it—no sign of the mother. Stopped at KROA to find out about snowgos on trapline. Darrel tells me they were from Wolverine Lodge. I assume he told them about that trap trail.

Tuesday, February 21, 1989—sunny to partly cloudy and -10° to 10°. Started out on Slide Mountain trapline. Had a very large light gray male wolf in an Alaskan No. 9 at the first natural pee post north of East West game trail. He was caught tightly by his rear foot so I took lots of pictures. He howled. I dispatched him, sacked him and checked my other traps and then came back home. Took more pictures in the heated garage and skinned him in the evening. Smayda's came over and Dave DeJung came to visit.

Wednesday, February 22, 1989—partly cloudy, snow in the evening, -10° to 15°. Nothing in traps all the way to cabin. Some fox and marten tracks and one otter track at south end of Blue Lake. Shoveled snow and chiseled two holes, but found no entry to the beaver lodge. Ice is very close to bottom of lake. Went east and checked otter sets, but no fur. Did a few small chores. Reset the boiled trap where I caught the big wolf. Hung two snares, one in pee tree and one directly east across trail.

Thursday, February 23, 1989—mostly sunny and -10° to 12°. Had a light skiff of snow during the night. Broke a trail off Burbot Lake to the "knob" north of the lake. Bad overflow east of Blue Lake. Had to break new trail part way back to the cabin trail, then shoveled snow over bare ice at beaver house. Took a 330 Coni and set it for otter at the south end of Blue Lake. Picked wolf trap at Fox Lake and picked several fox traps on the way home. Set Manning at "mound" wolf pee post. Had to go past it to find big drag for trap, then came back and made set. A teacher and some parents were out skiing with school kids.

Friday, February 24, 1989—mostly cloudy and -10° to 12°. Went to Cal's and ran his trapline. The overflow had broken a hole in the ice and flooded two of our traps. Quite a deal to get them and the three snares out. We picked another trap in a high-risk spot. The water was tearing down the drainage at a fast rate. Will try later to go down and get the lower trap. Tried to run line north of Ed's but snowgo wouldn't start so reloaded it and brought it home. Eventually found a bare wire. Smayda family was here for coffee and a visit. They are fun.

Saturday, February 25, 1989—10° to 26° and mostly cloudy with "flat light". Ran trapline north of Ed's. A fox had put a paw on pan of trap but didn't spring it. Moose calf I had seen earlier curled up alongside the trail is now dead. Went exploring north and then the west to Mendeltna Creek. Found another No. 3 trap. I marked with blue tape where marten cross the trail. At home, I got some trap gear ready, serviced snowgo and then welded a new ice chisel and a broken 330 Coni.

Sunday, February 26, 1989—12° to 20°, sunny with a light breeze. Built a metal skinning gambrel and set of hooks and a tie off cleat for pulley rope. Allen Farmer and kids came over to visit. We made homemade ice cream and Sylvia fixed a spaghetti supper.

Monday, February 27, 1989—sunny and -12° to 12°. Started out to run the Slide Mountain trapline, but snowgo quit running 100 yards up the trail from the highway. I hitched a ride home with Bill, then came down to Cal's and got him to drive my truck and help get the machine loaded. He pulled it out to the highway. I pulled the fox and wolverine traps—no wolves in traps. I wired a wolf carcass in some small spruce trees and set two Manning there. Boo had sprung one trap. I reset it a few feet away and then set one Manning at a pee tree near main wolf crossing. A small pack of wolves crossed the line.

Tuesday, February 28, 1989—mostly sunny and -12° to 10°. Loaded snowgo and went to Chuck's. We found a circlet had come loose and scored cylinder liner. Flywheel side bearing and seal is bad. I did a few things to a 250 Colt so I can use it on the trapline and cleaned some marten pelts.

Wednesday, March 1, 1989—mostly sunny and -10° to 12°. Left early for Anchorage to get snowgo parts, repair/gasoline (4 drums), get groceries, fabrics, see Dr. and pick up prescriptions. Saw lots of moose and caribou along the road.

Thursday, March 2, 1989—snow, wind and -6° to 6°. Took furs to Glennallen to ship and be sold in Winnipeg. Got the Wolf No. 2 sealed at Fish and Game. Sylvia did laundry. Paid electric bill and visited KROA. It was windy with drifting and blowing snow.

Friday, March 3, 1989—partly cloudy to cloudy, windy with snow and blowing snow. Temp was -10° to 4°. Ran the line north of Ed's. Kicked snow off of one wolf set and picked up fox traps. Took ½ of a lower jaw (incisor teeth) and a leg from a bull moose calf for game biologist to determine its age and state of health. The 250 Colt runs poorly at half throttle. Ran east side of Slide Mountain wolf traps. Nothing there. Change the setting of intermediate jet needle on the Colt 250 and test drove it. It seemed okay.

Saturday, March 4, 1989—mostly sunny and breezy, -12° to 2°. I unpacked bandsaw. It has much freight damage. Loafed for most of the day. Beth Trowbridge, Charlie II and baby Cora visited for a while in the evening.

Sunday, March 5, 1989—mostly sunny with a light breeze and -22° to 6°. Rechecked damage to bandsaw. Loafed again most of the day and had supper at Odden's in the evening. Lee D., Smayda family, Beth and kids, Mailly family were there also.

Monday, March 6, 1989—mostly sunny and -24° to 6°. Caribou have been passing by literally on both sides of the house. Saw one cow and calf in front of picture window. Tried to straighten out bandsaw problem over the phone. Cal visited and also Allen and son David.

Tuesday, March 7, 1989—sunny and -26° to 6°. There was a 75% solar eclipse this morning. Made a phone call again about the bandsaw. Put three sled loads of wood in the basement. Dave J. visited. I visited Smaydas and Lisa and the girls came here.

Wednesday, March 8, 1989—mostly sunny and -24° to 7°. Went to Palmer and Anchorage to get snowgo repairs/also bandsaw/sausage/maps, etc. Lots of boo still being killed on the highway. Stopped at Cal's on the way home.

Thursday, March 9, 1989—sunny and -33° to 6°. Put recoil starter on Colt this morning—pretty cold on the fingers. Took snowgo and sled to trailhead on the east side of Slide Mountain. Wolves had been on the trail near top of grade and at Cache Creek. Snowgo trail wreckers had been on trail north of Four Corners. Saw fox and marten and ptarmigan tracks but nothing in traps. Came home, then went to Cal's and we ran that line. Lots of boo and one moose. Wolves haven't been back. All the overflow has been frozen over by this cold spell. The wolf trap we had down there was barely frozen in. Bob Rudbeck brought Sylvia's mirrors. Odden's picked up the dog food and glue we picked up for them while we were in town.

Friday, March 10, 1989—sunny and -23° to 16°. Went to Chuck's and worked on L. T. snowgo. Got it back together and it sounds great, but there is a rumble still to find in the drive train. Ran the trapline north of Ed's. Wolves had been on south half of it but they didn't go near my sets.

Saturday, March 11, 1989—sunny and -22° to 19°. Built a fire in woodshop and we put the bandsaw together. It's working this evening. Visited Allen and kids after supper. Roxanne was working up at Eureka and the family was at home.

Sunday, March 12, 1989—sunny and -60° to 20°. Made some adjustments and repairs on both snowgos. Put different tire and wheels on snowgo trailer. Allen came over and borrowed some tools and paint. It was a beautiful day.

Monday, March 13, 1989—It's -6° to 18° and a sunny beautiful day. Fantastic red Northern Lights last night. A pack of wolves have been on the south end of Slide Mountain trail. They made a kill or two nearby. I made a wolf set at a natural pee post tree on the west side of trail about two thirds of the way up the hill on a gentle grade. Saw a moose calf and a spot where a pair of traveling fox were hunting and breeding along with some marten tracks. Remade all the otter sets. They were badly drifted in. Snowgo ran pretty well. Northern Lights were out again tonight. Peaceful and quiet here at the trap cabin. Real fine standby boiled supper.

Tuesday, March 14, 1989—sunny and -10° to 28°. Another beaut of a day. Broke a trail to woodlot, scooped snow off cache and picked up one fox trap on the way home. Lots of marten track between Mendeltna Springs and Meat Pole Hill. Boo have been on the trail, I saw a few. Got home early. Cal borrowed a tape.

Wednesday, March 15, 1989—sunny and -4° to 32°. Went to Ed's and ran the trapline. Nothing. Watched Joe Runyon cross finish line to win the Iditarod. Rudbecks and Lisa Smayda visited. Took chain case apart, cleaned it and put it back together.

Thursday, March 16, 1989—8° to 30° and sunny. Took a wolf leg, a moose leg and a lower incisor, lower jaw to Alaska Fish and Game biologist while Sylvia did laundry. (Alaska Fish and Game asks for these animal parts in order to glean information from them.) Did some business at Glennallen sporting goods, then ran the line at Cal's. Nothing. I shot two ptarmigan and did a few little things around here.

Having some problems with the bandsaw blade tracking on the wheels.

Friday, March 17, 1989—sunny at trap cabin and -3° to 10°. No wolves have ran on the line. Otter came on to south end of Blue Lake and went around 330 coni set that was mostly drifted in. The ice pingo on trail east is getting bigger and more treacherous. (A pingo is a mound of earth-covered ice. In some places under the tundra, water flows in dead of winter. As it freezes, it pushes up through the tundra, sometimes reaching several feet high depending on temperature and water flow.) I passed by a moose calf on one side of trail and cow on the other side—boy did she have her ears back and the hackles up. Very protective of the calf this one!! Saw boo track but none in sight. A spruce hen flew up from beside trail and there were marten tracks I marked with blue tape. The marten box I planned to chip out of the ice is completely covered with overflow now. Picked up ice chisel and took it to cabin.

Saturday, March 18, 1989—It's -2° to 22° here at home with a light snow this morning. Setting in the afternoon. Picked up a Manning at Lone Tree south of Blue Lake. Quite a few moose between Mendeltna Springs and Meat Pole Hill. I'm seeing ptarmigan tracks quite often. No wolves in traps. Set the Manning I picked up today at a 12 foot lone spruce just north and west of Cache Creek and hung a snare 30 feet west of trap in wolf trail. Worked on gear case and ordered new chain and sprockets. Partly disassembled the bandsaw and installed a shim to align the wheels for the blade.

Sunday, March 19, 1989—cloudy in the morning and sunny at the afternoon and -2° to 25°. Started getting rifle ready to sell. Made a fiberglass repair on the "hard" gun case. Ran trapline at Ed's. No wolves. Hung two snares for wolves. Ski touring and party at KROA. I wasn't feeling well so didn't stay long at KROA.

Monday, March 20, 1989—2° to 22° and sunny, clouding up in the evening. Still feeling sick. Nadia called. Mary B. and Tom H. visited. Put a sled load of wood in basement. Hauled Darryl's freezer to woodshed on my sled and did a few other small things. Visited Lisa Smayda and Allen and Roxanne a little while in the evening.

Tuesday, March 21, 1989—8° to 24° cloudy. Went to Glennallen, Tazlina and Copper Center for income tax, shopping, parts and to pick up a deep freeze at Sears. Took garbage to dump, shot rifle, hauled load of water and mixed gas for snowgo.

Wednesday, March 22, 1989— 12° to 30° cloudy. Ran Slide Mountain wolf traps. Nothing. Wolves had chased a boo--much fur and blood. Followed the trail 150 yards where the boo had continued on. Straightened up some things on the garage bench.

Thursday, March 23, 1989—12° to 37° and partly cloudy. Went to Glennallen for snowgo parts with no luck. Changed jets in LT Polaris and finished working on the bandsaw. Cal, Mary and Philip brought a pie and visited in the evening.

Friday, March 24, 1989—16° to 37° and partly cloudy. Dave D. J. went with me on the Slide Mountain trapline. Didn't get any wolves. Tracked the wolf/boo chase I saw yesterday even farther. Pretty soon no more blood. I hung a snare in that trail. Did some things around here. Oddens had us and Smaydas over for supper.

Saturday, March 25, 1989—22° to 34° with a light snow, cloudy and sunny. Ran line north of Ed's. Wolves had been on north end, but didn't go in the sets. Had a boo in the snare in the wolf trail. Then I went to Cal's and ran that trapline. A plug failed in his snowgo so I came back to his garage and got another plug. Saw some boo in that area. Pulled the wolf traps and the snare. Rudbecks came over for supper and movies.

Sunday, March 26, 1989—2° to 23° and sunny. Checked colt snowgo. It has a broken fan shroud. Loafed most of the day, then went to KROA for an Easter dinner and potluck.

Monday, March 27, 1989—2° to 5° here at the cabin. Sunny, breezy and plenty cool on the trail. Lots of moose east of Meat Pole Hill. Fox and mink tracks. Wolves have been at the head of Mendeltna Springs. Snowmobilers widened out the trail and ran over wolf trap. Pulled otter sets and wire-tied 330 Coni and pole to small tree near ditch at the north end of Burbot Lake. Had soup for lunch and then repaired the broken stump stool.

Tuesday, March 28, 1989—it's -20° to 10° (at home). Cleaned up and put away things at the trap cabin and closed it up. Hauled two small loads of wood into the cabin and pulled the 330 coni at south end of Blue Lake. Pulled and put a 330 coni and pole in tree at Mendeltna crossing. Explored Lake along trail. Nothing in traps. Put perfume on small lone tree in overflow area. Talked with Tom Smayda at school ski hill. Right knee sure hurts.

Wednesday, March 29, 1989—it's -20° to 12°. Went to Anchorage and shopped for craft materials, went to the Social Security office, and took bandsaw to Frt. Co.

Thursday, March 30, 1989—sunny and -12° to 18°. Ran trapline north of Ed's. Wolves had consumed boo. Picked wolf traps. Gathered more wolf pee. Worked in woodshop.

Friday, March 31, 1989—sunny ad -12° to 26°. Ran Slide Mountain and picked up all wolf traps and snares. No fur. Put some new parts LT snowgo. Saw a big moose and lots of boo traveling west on our lake.

Saturday, April 1, 1989—a mostly sunny, beautiful day. -2° to 30°. Went to KROA to watch the ski touring races. Dave DeJung came over to visit, then later Roger and Jo Ford visited.

Sunday, April 2, 1989—8° to 33° and sunny. We got four packages of Sylvia's crafts ready to mail to the kids in Minnesota. Made a tool to adjust open sites on a rifle. Visited Allen and Roxanne in the evening.

Monday, April 3, 1989—10° to 34° and sunny. Got gear ready and went north and west of Ed's to trap beaver. Didn't find the run out from lodge. Then the wind had blown the snow level on Rat Lake and I couldn't find the push-ups. A fox had dug up two push-ups and they were frozen over. Cut push-up markers and poles for beaver trap/wolf drag. Shoveled snow off some roofs here at home and unloaded a half cord of wood Allen had cut and brought here for us. Allen came over in evening and borrowed some movies. Saw an Eagle today and also saw a sharp tailed grouse at the junction north of Ed's.

Tuesday, April 4, 1989—9° to 32°, sunny then cloudy. Allen brought a half cord of wood. Cut it all up today and sharpened chainsaw. Lisa and Emily visited. I went to Chuck's for Snowgo repairs. Picked up Darrel and one of KROA's machines on the way. Cal and family visited, brought back some tools and borrowed a socket. Brought another half load of wood late.

Wednesday, April 5, 1989–21° to 31° cloudy them partly sunny towards evening. Visited Rudbecks then cut up the load of wood. Put two new bearings in snowgo gear case. Allen brought another half load of wood and we cut and ricked it. He brought yet another load before dark.

Thursday, April 6, 1989–12° to 34° and sunny. Cut up and ricked the half cord of wood then Allen and Roxanne and Ellie brought another half cord. We fixed lunch for them and we all cut and ricked the load. I did some other odd jobs, then Rudbecks came over to use the saber saw. In the evening Allen brought over a full cord of wood—we have a total of four cords now.

Friday, April 7, 1989–4° to 33° and sunny. Cut up and ricked the last cord of wood. Made a rack for the brad point wood drill bits. Hip is sure sore. Visited Allen and borrowed some envelopes.

Saturday, April 8, 1989–3° to 33° and sunny. Went down to our lake and explored the area to the east looking for caribou horns. Only found one, but saw some cows and calves. Beverly called to talk. Fooled with gun, scabbards, and snowgo. Adapted the router to a junk saw table.

Sunday, April 9, 1989–7° to 34° Sunny, then cloudy in the evening. Visited Smayda's and signed each other's Alaska dividend applications. Put a switch and plug in the router table. Finished some woodcraft patterns and repaired a dresser drawer. Rudbecks visited. Saw three eagles at boo gut pile on Lake. Tall coyote there late evening. Allen called and I went down. He had trouble finding caller tape. I shot a few times at the coyote, then Allen found tape. Too dark then to use it. Allen gave me a Tillotson snowgo carburetor. Allen taped a "screaming rabbit" call for me.

Monday, April 10, 1989–22° to 42° Sunny then cloudy. Went to mile 133 on the Glenn Highway, parked, and ran the trail to little Nelchina/Crooked Creek. Saw fox and wolf tracks as far as Old Man Creek. Lots of boo and moose at Little Nelchina. Disappointed no ptarmigan and no boo horns. Finished dresser drawer and got another

10,000 Days in Alaska Book One 1978-1989

half cord of wood from Allen.

Tuesday, April 11, 1989—22° to 42°. Sunny then partly cloudy in the evening. Allen brought over a full cord of wood and we cut it all up/put five sled loads in the basement and stacked the rest in the woodshed. Lisa Smayda visited a couple of times today. Allen Farmer was here for lunch. I modified the bandsaw to take 93 1/2 inch long blades and sharpened the chainsaw.

Wednesday, April 12, 1989—26° to 43° and mostly sunny. Nadia called. Worked in the wood shop all day. Made wheel cutting jig and cut out parts for wheelbarrow planter. Cut out "table center hearts". Allen's Ranger broke down.

Thursday, April 13, 1989—16° to 43° and sunny. Snow is shrinking every day. We went to Anchorage for crafting supplies and did some other shopping and got a VA blue card. Saw moose and caribou. Boo killed at mile 99. Ran into Dan's mother and Red in the Fred Myer store. Stopped at Pinnacle Mountain RV park to inquire about leaving crafts on consignment.

Friday, April 14, 1989—18° to 41° and sunny. Worked on the wheelbarrow planters all day. Built another jig for putting them together.

Saturday, April 15, 1989—20° to 42° and sunny. Snow is still melting fast. Put more planters together and cut a few more parts. Built some bins for parts and rearranged woodshop. Cal G. and Philip visited. Lloyd Ronning visited. I went with Cal to the dump; he had seen mirrors that someone had thrown away. We can use these in our craftwork.

Sunday, April 16, 1989—18° to 40° cloudy and then sunny. Worked on more planters. We have 25 put together now. Went to Jim and Mary Odden's for supper. Carrol was there.

Monday, April 17, 1989—28° to 40° and mostly cloudy. Worked in the woodshop all day.

Tuesday, April 18, 1989—16° to 40° and mostly sunny. Went to

Glennallen on business and to do laundry. Stopped at Chuck's for snowgo parts. Flamed all the wheelbarrow planters and sold two. Visited Allen and Roxanne in the evening and Fred Rungee stopped in to see us for a few minutes.

Wednesday, April 19, 1989–24° to 42° and mostly sunny. Had breakfast with Allen, then we went to highway camp and took the trail up Slide Mountain looking for horns. Allen found a set of nice bull boo horns at a wolf kill. We saw a porcupine and two ptarmigan. Beaut of a view from up on top of Slide Mountain. Worked on the router table and sharpened the 3/8" rounding bit. Went to Pat Landers and loaded two house trailer axles on the snowgo trailer and brought them home. Made a number of calls about cedar planters. Saw six eagles circling.

Thursday, April 20, 1989–30° to 46° and mostly sunny. Worked in the woodshop all day. Visited KROA in the evening. Mount Wrangell belches steam. The first of the geese and swans are flying. 3000 Sandhill Cranes have been seen in Palmer.

Friday, April 21, 1989–20° to 50°, sunny/cloudy with a light rain in Palmer and Anchorage. Got craft materials, tools, and a tire fixed. Sold two wheelbarrows and left some others at a couple of places. Got an order for planter boxes. Saw some swans near Palmer and Sylvia saw two swans here at home. Lots of boo near mile posts 133–135.

Saturday, April 22, 1989–33° to 43° partly cloudy. Piled and stickered cedar lumber. Built a wide heavy-duty sawhorse, nail box, bandsaw blade holder, small nail and brad wall rack, and put a new switch on the bandsaw.

Sunday, April 23, 1989–30° to 40° and mostly cloudy. Built five duck-nesting boxes. Made a miter for splitting cutouts on the bandsaw. Tom, Lisa and the girls came over with a pie and some ice cream mix and we watched TV in the evening.

Monday, April 24, 1989–34° to 40° and cloudy all day. Worked in the woodshop all day and Allen and his son David visited us in the evening.

Tuesday, April 25, 1989–36° to 46° and mostly cloudy with some rain. Took Honda 110 to Chuck Z. for a tune-up. Hauled a load of water from

10,000 Days in Alaska Book One 1978-1989

Hoffmans and worked in the woodshop. Jim brought a box of drywall screws for me from Glennallen. Jim Odden's birthday party was at Rudbecks today.

Wednesday, April 26, 1989–30° to 50° and sunny. Built 10' x 4' planter boxes. Cal G. came over for some steel and Mary Beaudoin visited Sylvia. Beautiful day, swans flying west and evening grosbeaks are here.

Thursday, April 27, 1989–30° to 53° and mostly sunny. Worked on cedar planters all day and got sixteen of them put together. Harold and Rachel Dimmick visited for lunch and to use the phone. Nice to see them again. Did some service work on the truck.

Friday, April 28, 1989–33° to 43° and mostly sunny here. Some wind and cloudy in Palmer and Wasilla where we delivered some planters, sold a wheelbarrow, and bought some lumber and craft supplies. Saw an eagle on a boo carcass along the road. Went to Allen's yard sale and to KROA. Snow and ice on the lake is going fast.

Saturday, April 29, 1989–25° to 48° and partly cloudy. Felt cool to us. Built cedar planters all day. Sylvia's sister Frances called to wish her a happy birthday and Lisa Smayda gave her a nice apron.

Sunday, April 30, 1989–32° to 54° and a sunny beautiful day with robins singing. Finished planter boxes and cut and sanded some cedar blocks. Serviced truck. Dan and Patti Billman visited. They needed some rubber hose also. Went to KROA and had pizza.

Monday, May 1, 1989–34° to 54° and partly cloudy. Loaded up cedar boxes and took them to Nancy Lake. Sold two wheelbarrows there and cut some diamond willow nearby. Took care of some business and shopping we had to do in Glennallen, then worked on the Honda 3-wheeler at Chuck's. Gave him some Arctic cat parts. Allen Farmer visited in the evening and we watched caribou on the mountains far to the south.

Tuesday, May 2, 1989–40° to 56° and sunny. Lots of visitors today. Peeled eight pieces of diamond willow and we built four hanging cedar planters for Lisa Smayda.

Wednesday, May 3, 1989—36° to 55° and mostly sunny clouding up in the evening. Drilled drain holes in cedar boxes. Borrowed Allen's air compressor and blew dust out of several motors. Repaired tire on a wheelbarrow and started changing motor on table saw.

Thursday, May 4, 1989—30° to 46° and partly cloudy. Finished putting different motor on table saw and sharpened the blade, now it works great. Sylvia went to Anchorage with the Rudbecks. I took one barrel pump apart and re-did gaskets and put a new hose on the other barrel pump. Sanded more cedar blocks.

Friday, May 5, 1989—29° to 46°, had a light snow overnight and it's partly cloudy. Packaged some cedar blocks and Lisa and Emily Smayda visited. Worked on diamond willow and return some things to Allen. Took trash to dump. More ice is gone from our lake.

Saturday, May 6, 1989—30° to 44° and mostly cloudy. Worked on diamond willow. But an extension cord on the table saw and rigged a dust chute for it. Tom Smayda borrowed my extension ladder and came back over later for ideas to correct a mistake. Sounds like the ice is going out on the Nelchina River.

Sunday, May 7, 1989—30° to 50° and mostly sunny. Worked in the wood shop and then went to visit Dan Billman and to get some steel from him. Rudbecks were here for a while.

Monday, May 8, 1989—33° to 48° and raining all day. Spent all day in the woodshop building jigs for crafts. We had Dan Billman here for supper and the Smayda family came over for homemade ice cream.

Tuesday, May 9, 1989—30° to 48° rain and snow all night. Ground well covered with snow in the morning. Allen and I started work on the tandem axle trailer. A very wet eagle sat on top of a spruce tree on the hillside near the house for quite awhile. Five swans were down on the lake.

Wednesday, May 10, 1989—34° to 42° and mostly cloudy with some rain. More ice is gone from the lake. An eagle is hunting on our hillside. Welded mounting brackets for springs on the tandem axle trailer. Cut out plywood killer whales for crafts with the bandsaw. Took Sylvia to

10,000 Days in Alaska Book One 1978-1989

Eureka for an anniversary dinner and visited Harold and Rachel Dimmick on the way home. Made hangers for hanging baskets in the greenhouse.

Thursday, May 11, 1989—33° to 40° back to 30° cloudy, rain, hail, and snow. Built a cedar wheelbarrow planter. Lisa and Emmy Smayda visited. Started converting the gray box by rebuilding the lid. Snow on the ground tonight. Rudbecks came over to use the bandsaw to make a wooden race car for Brian and stayed to watch TV with us.

Friday, May 12, 1989—30° to 45°. Sun came out and melted lots of the 8 inches of snow we got overnight. Finished rebuilding the lid for the gray box. My sander gave up the ghost. Helped Dan Billman move Rudbeck's cedar cabin to his new land. He had helped load a doghouse I wanted to haul to Darrel at KROA. We went to a baby shower for Mary Odden at KROA.

Saturday, May 13, 1989—34° to 44°, cool cloudy and breezy all day with some sun in the afternoon. Helped Jim and Elaine Manning get unpacked and moved into their house.

Sunday, May 14, 1989—30° to 42°. Mostly cloudy, windy in the afternoon. Welded up a welding table and welded two bases for steel posts to hold yard sale signs. Lettered the signs and mailbox. Mannings visited. More ice is gone from our lake. The rabbits run and frolic all around the house and a little finch stunned itself flying into the window. Nadia and Theresa called mother. The scoter ducks are back on our lake.

Monday, May 15, 1989—30° to 41°, cloudy, snow, rain. Bolted yard sales signs on posts. Made an apparatus to fill small torch bottles with propane. Split 3/4" cedar lumber on the bandsaw and cut some animal cutouts from it. Cut out some mug tree bases. Lisa and Emmy visited and so did Jim and Elaine Manning.

Tuesday, May 16, 1989—34° to 45°, cloudy, sunny, partly cloudy. Worked in the wood shop all day using the bandsaw and working on cup trees. Chuck Z. stopped by for Honda parts list and Jim Manning came over to use the phone. Ice is out of the lake. Beautiful in the mountains this evening.

Norman Wilkins

Wednesday, May 17, 1989—30° to 50° and sunny getting cloudy in the evening. Put pump in lake and put up three duck nesting boxes. Made two signs for selling the trailer. Did some craft work. Visited Farmer's, and Jim and Elaine came over for homemade ice cream.

Thursday, May 18, 1989—32° to 47° and mostly sunny. Took old axle from under 16 foot trailer. I have trouble with the axle mounting. Went to Glennallen for some acetylene and picked up the 3-wheeler at Chuck's. Lisa and the girls came over and took rides on it. Even Sylvia rode it. Sanded on rear rack in the evening.

Friday, May 19, 1989—30° to 44° and cloudy with a light rain. Went to Nelchina school to listen to Doug (Digger) Beaudoin give his presentation on fossils and hunting for them. A dozen of us went up to a slide area and found some fossils. Allen drove his Ranger and I took my 3-wheeler and we had lunch while we were up there. A winter killed cow moose is close to the trail.

Saturday, May 20, 1989—34° to 60° and sunny with a light breeze. Worked at putting the tandem axles under trailer. Worked on the rear rack on my 3-wheeler and did a little fishing, then got water at Max Hoffman's. Sylvia planted potatoes, peas etc.

Sunday, May 21, 1989—42° to 46° and cloudy. Rain in the evening. Worked on the trailer all day and got both axles welded onto the frame. Went to get Allen to help but he had other plans. Coyotes sang a chorus on the riverbank across the lake. Two eagles tried to catch ducks down at the west end of our lake. One eagle actually landed in the water. Lisa Smayda and the girls visited in the evening.

Monday, May 22, 1989—34° to 42°, snow in the night, rain and cloudy all day. Worked in the wood shop. Dan Billman visited. Put a headlight and rack on the 110 Honda and built a house for the thrush.

Tuesday, May 23, 1989—34° to 44° with light rain and snow getting sunny in the afternoon but still cool all day. Worked on single trailer axle. Allen came over and we looked for tires and rims, then Dan Billman drove in with his new Suzuki 4x4 ATV. We went down to the lake (pump motor had quit) and brought the motor up to the garage. My

10,000 Days in Alaska Book One 1978-1989

Honda upset backwards near the top of the hill and broke the lens and bulb in the new headlight. Pump motor is shot. Made some hanging baskets for Sylvia and took two duck boxes to the boat landing. Lisa Smayda and daughters were here for supper and TV.

Wednesday, May 24, 1989—36° to 48° and mostly sunny. Took the canoe and paddled down the lake and put up two duck nesting boxes. I saw a moose feeding while I was down there. Worked on crafts in the wood shop all day, then visited the Odden's. Mary's mother Ruth is here for the arrival of Odden's baby. Saw two more moose this evening.

Thursday, May 25, 1989—36° to 54° and mostly sunny. Finished repairing the single axle. Glued wood figures to towel racks and Varithaned the bases of mug trees. Cut up fuel storage tank to make fenders to put on tandem axle trailer. Sure have lost interest in rebuilding the trailer.

Friday, May 26, 1989—33° to 56° and mostly sunny. Worked on tandem axle trailer all day, Allen Farmer helped. Started getting things ready for the yard sale tomorrow. We are real tired tonight.

Saturday, May 27, 1989—34° to 53°, cloudy and partly cloudy towards evening. Long hard day with the yard sale but sold some things.

Sunday, May 28, 1989—35° to 54° and partly cloudy then rain, then sunny. Sold a moose horn and a battery and probably a trailer axle. Mannings bought the freezer and we bought a few things from Mannings.

Monday, May 29, 1989—38° to 57° and sunny turning to cloudy and rainy in the evening. Sold some more stuff today. Jim and Elaine took the freezer. We are tired tonight. A cow moose and twin calves are hanging around the south shore of our lake.

Tuesday, May 30, 1989—44° to 54° and partly cloudy. Moved some of the unsold items back into storage. Delivered some planter boxes to Nancy Lake Nursery and sold some to a lady at Tazlina. She wants a retainer wall planter built.

Norman Wilkins

Wednesday, May 31, 1989—40° to 54°, partly cloudy and very windy. The moose cow and calves are still across the lake. I redid the gaskets in the fuel transfer pump. Jim and Elaine borrowed the Rototiller.

Thursday, June 1, 1989—40° to 55° and mostly sunny. Went to Anchorage and got a new motor for the pump, plus others shopping and got lumber to make more cedar planters. Sheep were on the mountains in the Sheep Mountain area. Stopped and helped a fellow with wheel problems. (I keep a full tool box in the pickup.)

Friday, June 2, 1989—36° to 52° and mostly sunny. Unloaded the truck and picked the trash along "our mile" of highway today. Dan Billman treated us to lunch at Nelchina. Built a stand for the submersible pump and had supper at Jim and Elaine's.

Saturday, June 3, 1989—38° to 54° and mostly sunny. Went to Glennallen for the health fair, then left a bunch of tires and wheels at Warren and Leona Dawson's where we had coffee and cookies. Phil stopped in while we were there. Then we went on to Naomi's at Lake Louise and left some crafts for her to sell. Went down to Allen's and tried to take pictures of the cow moose and calves.

Sunday, June 4, 1989—40° to 57° partly cloudy and sometimes a light shower. But submersible motor and pump together, rewired it and put it in the lake. It works fine Sylvia watered everything. We build her a four foot planter and also the planter for the retaining wall for the lady in Tazlina. Straightened up the garage and did some yard work.

Monday, June 5, 1989—40° to 52° and partly cloudy and cool. Quite a few moose are hanging around and an eagle sits in one tree across the lake often. Jim Manning was here for help several times. Built two cedar goose planters. Allen and the kids visited in the evening.

Tuesday, June 6, 1989—40° to 55° and partly cloudy with a very light shower. Built seven Swan planters. Nancy Lake called and wanted three, 3' x 4' planter's so we built them to. Had supper at Nelchina Café.

Wednesday, June 7, 1989—frost in the morning but up to 60° and mostly sunny the rest of the day. A cow and calf moose were on the highway. Lisa and the girls brought a new sander over for me and I gave her a yardstick. She likes Swan planters. Did odd jobs most of the day and visited Jim and Elaine.

Thursday, June 8, 1989—36° to 64° and sunny. Caribou waded out in the lake again today. Worked at crafts most of the day, then rotated tires on the pickup and visited KROA.

Friday, June 9, 1989—42° to 54°, cloudy then sunny with some breeze. Worked on crafts all day. Having some sinus trouble.

Saturday, June 10, 1989—34° to 52°, cloudy, and sunny, a light rain. Worked on crafts all day. Sylvia mowed the lawn, motor is weak. Mannings visited and so did Roger and Jo Ford.

Sunday, June 11, 1989—40° to 58° and mostly sunny. Did lots of visiting around the neighborhood, and very little craft work. Lots of scoters at mud flat on lake and also two Swans. Small graylings are jumping.

Monday, June 12, 1989—44° to 60° and sunny. Went to Tazlina Trading Post and mounted planter on the retaining wall. Went to Copper Center and cut diamond willow along Copper River, peeled some of it this evening. Dan Billman and Jason and Mike Sheldon were here for supper.

Tuesday, June 13, 1989—40° to 64° and mostly sunny. Peeled the rest of the diamond willow. Submitted a bid to make a large planter for Tazlina River Trading Post and got the job. Lisa Smayda and the girls visited in the afternoon. Hauled trash to the dump and visited with Mannings. Got truck ready to go to Anchorage.

Wednesday, June 14, 1989—44° to 38°, cloudy and rain. Went to Anchorage and did lots of shopping and did some business in Palmer. Got most of what we need. Wind and rain on the way home.

Thursday, June 15, 1989—38° to 56° Sunny most of the day with a shower in the middle. Worked with lumber and some odd jobs and started preparations for the Tazlina Trading Post job. Pulled tree out from in front of a house. Took a swan planter with flowers in it to KROA.

Norman Wilkins

Friday, June 16, 1989—36° to 54° and sunny. Used grader blades and welded forms to make the flower bed planter for Tazlina Trading Post. Lisa and the girls visited and later we went to Billman's (Patti is here now). Mike has built a landing strip and has cleared a large area for Dan. Visited Odden's and family. My two wolves are back from the tannery-they did a fine job on them.

Saturday, June 17, 1989—36° to 60° and sunny. Loaded tools and lumber and went to Tazlina and built and installed the 28 foot flower planter. Stopped at KROA for pizza. Clem and Jean are out from Manker Creek.

Sunday, June 18, 1989—46° to 58° and sunny with a shower in the afternoon. Unloaded tools from a truck. Sylvia mowed Rudbeck's lawn and I did a little work on the truck. After that I did a few things in the wood shop.

Monday, June 19, 1989—40° to 66°. Sunny, then cloudy and some light showers area did made a shop jade for cutting lengths of dowling. Started on Alaska clocks. Cal G. is back from vacation and stopped here and visited for quite a while.

Tuesday, June 20, 1989—52° to 64° and mostly sunny. Worked more on the Alaska clocks and helped Sylvia haul corn to the garden to transplant. Visited Dan Billman. Bart Bartly's horses (Snowshoe Lake) got this far from home. Hauled a load of water from Hoffman's and visited Tom Smayda. The thrush family eggs may have hatched today. Sylvia saw them flying away with something in their bill several times.

Wednesday, June 21, 1989—50° to 62° and mostly sunny, then windy in the late afternoon. Did a little work in the wood shop and other odd jobs. Put a screen door together and installed it. Beautiful evening.

Thursday, June 22, 1989—37° to 57° and mostly sunny. Put up planters under roof overhang. Put the dock in the lake and did some work in the wood shop. Lisa Smayda's folks, Joe and Shirley visited us. Cal G. stopped by and later we went over to Mannings.

Friday, June 23, 1989—40° to 52° and cloudy, showering in the Palmer area. Went to Anchorage and looked at several cars with no luck. Did some shopping and bought two drums of gas. Went to Wasilla and Palmer looking for vehicles. Put our crafts in two new places and saw a coyote at mile 106.

Saturday, June 24, 1989—38° to 49° and partly sunny. Built two cedar wheelbarrow planters. Helped Jim Manning hook up his water heater, dryer and stove to LP gas. Started sawing out more Alaska clocks. Joe, Lauren and Emily visited in the evening. A squirrel tried to get into the Flicker nest box while the Flicker was in it.

Sunday, June 25, 1989—36° to 53°, mostly cloudy, rainy in the night and a light shower. Snow on Chugach Mountains. Cut out clocks on the bandsaw today, then went to a potluck supper at Smayda's. We met some new neighbors, the Bartley's.

Monday, June 26, 1989—44° to 56°. Worked mostly in the wood shop today. Eagles are still hunting ducks on the lake and the drakes are chasing the hens again. Perhaps they will try another hatch.

Tuesday, June 27, 1989—caulked the tandem trailer, roof and also the woodshop chimney. Finished cutting out the Alaska clocks and made some wooden cutouts for Elaine. Started two "gifts" signs. Had Jim and Elaine over for supper and called the Rudbecks.

Wednesday, June 28, 1989—44° to 66° and sunny with a light shower. Visited Smaydas. Billman's visited. Borrowed Darrel's propane refrigerator and worked in the woodshop the rest of the day. Flickers are out of nest box.

Thursday, June 29, 1989—50° to 70°. I built a small flat basket for Elaine to try painting and sanded the split cedar pole and built flowerbeds at west and of the house for Sylvia. Visited Joe at Smayda's and he was over here too. Mannings brought their friends, Cliff and wife from Haines to visit in the evening. Sylvia was feeling sick most of the day.

Friday, June 30, 1989—48° to 66° and partly cloudy. Worked on the Alaska clocks all day except for helping Kim H. get their car going. We had a pretty hard shower in the late evening and a golden light came from Slide Mountain to the north. It shone on the freshly washed spruce trees and gave everything a strangely beautiful color. What a beautiful evening this has turned out to be.

Saturday, July 1, 1989—48° to 60°, sunny and three thundershowers. Worked on Alaska clocks, Jim visited in the afternoon and went to a potluck supper at Nelchina in the evening.

Sunday, July 2, 1989—44° to 56°, sunny and showers. Worked more on the class then took crafts to Tazlina Lodge and visited at KROA. Took Prototype of wooden basket to Elaine. Eagle is hunting the ducks.

Monday, July 3, 1989—48° to 72° and sunny. A beaut of a day. Lisa Smayda's parents visited. Poured epoxy on six clocks. It didn't work out the best. Got ready for a trip to McCarthy.

Tuesday, July 4, 1989—50° to 70° and sunny. Got up early and picked up Joe and Morey Second Chief and went to CRNA joined group of people and we went to Chitna and had breakfast, then on to McCarthy. Stopped to see fish wheels in Copper River. We crossed the river at McCarthy on the cable trans they have there, then took a van to Kennecott Lodge. Walked around old mine buildings, ate and slept at the lodge.

Wednesday, July 5, 1989—some of the people are weak and have trouble getting back to river crossing and the van had a flat tire. We also saw a young moose cross the road. Mark, our driver, saw two more Kennecott Railway spikes lying in the road. Stopped at KROA and had pizza.

Thursday, July 6, 1989—48° to 73° and sunny. Sylvia mowed our lawn and Rudbeck's and also watered the garden. Hose sprung a leak, I fixed it. Weeded three rows in the garden. Visited Mannings. Helped Allen get furnace at Mannings and visited with Allen and Cal. Worked on the truck. Visited Billmans. Nice breeze tonight.

Friday, July 7, 1989—50° to 74°, sunny, light breeze, beautiful day. Worked on some more clocks. Smoothed up cycle tracks in front of our place and put fuel pump on truck. Put snowgos away. Visited Dimmicks, Cal and Mary G. Lisa Smayda gave us a nice lot of red salmon cleaned and filleted. Rudbecks got back about 11:30 p.m.

Saturday, July 8, 1989—46° to 74° and sunny with a light breeze. Mary

10,000 Days in Alaska Book One 1978-1989

Odden and Kara took us to the fish wheel on Tok Road. We got 31 salmon. Shared the fish with KROA, Bartley's, Mannings, Odden's and Cal Gilcrease. Odden's were here for roast salmon. Sylvia canned salmon late into the night.

Sunday, July 9, 1989—49° to 78°, sunny and hot! Sylvia canned salmon all night, finished this morning—85 pints. Worked on towel stands for Elaine's class. Took Odden's canner back and the can sealer to Billmans. Hauled a load of water from Hoffman's place and visited Mannings.

Monday, July 10, 1989—50° to 81° and sunny with some breeze. Worked in the wood shop all day. Fiberglassed corners on coolers.

Tuesday, July 11, 1989—48° to 79° and sunny with some breeze. Beth T. and Charlie Jr. and Cora were our morning visitors. Louisiana Joe and the Mannings visited in the afternoon. Worked in the wood shop in between times. It's real dry; Sylvia waters the lawn and garden often.

Wednesday, July 12, 1989—51° to 75°, sunny, then cloudy in the evening. Worked in the wood shop. Visited a long time with Louisiana Joe. Mounted new tire on a wheelbarrow. Sylvia watered the lawn again and painted the edges of some clocks.

Thursday, July 13, 1989—48° to 70° and partly cloudy. Worked in the wood shop. Charlie Trowbridge visited and Joe came over too. There was an ice cream party at Smayda's in the evening. We had a good time.

Friday, July 14, 1989—46° to 68° and the partly cloudy, then breezy towards evening. Worked in the shop again. Buried a "dead man" anchor in the dirt on the rise by highway.

Saturday, July 15, 1989—48° to 66° and mostly cloudy with a nice shower. Worked at refinishing clocks. Put some baskets together and cut out more parts. Painted the edges of more clocks. Helped Rudbeck lift off his pickup topper. Elaine Manning visited for a while.

Sunday, July 16, 1989—46° to 66° and mostly sunny. Worked in the wood shop all day, Sylvia helped too. Lisa Smayda and her folks and the girls came over to visit. I gave the girls a ride on the 3-wheeler. We went over and visited with the Mannings in the evening.

Monday, July 17, 1989—46° to 64°, rain in the night, cloudy, then sunny. Worked in the wood shop all day, coffee at noon and supper later at Smayda's. Sylvia went with the senior's car.

Tuesday, July 18, 1989—45° to 68° and a sunny, beautiful day. Cut out cat-shaped napkin holders. Poured epoxy on six clocks. Moved trailer to my "dead man" out by the road. Brought Freezer home from Jim Manning.

Wednesday, July 19, 1989—45° to 65° and mostly cloudy. Worked in the wood shop. Louisiana Joe stopped by for a visit. I gave him a diamond willow cane. Put more sealer on the moose pellets (for the clocks). Lisa, the girls, and her parents came to watch home movies on our VCR. We went to visit the Bartleys at Snowshoe Lake. Sylvia heard noises in the chimney of the garage. It was a golden eye duck that had gotten trapped in there. Got it out and released it unharmed. They go down there expecting to build a nest as they do in trees. I had to make wire mesh screens to keep them out of the chimneys.

Thursday, July 20, 1989—45° to 58° and cloudy with light sprinkles of rain. Worked in the wood shop and on the faces of clocks. Shoveled dirt at boat dock. Delivered napkin holders. Visited Lucky and Mary Beaudoin.

Friday, July 21, 1989—partly cloudy during the day with showers in the evening. Finished filling in the holes at the dock and seeded grass. Finished getting more clocks ready and poured the epoxy, also poured epoxy over flowers on a board. Worked on cup trees after supper.

Saturday, July 22, 1989—46° to 58° with rain in the night. Partly cloudy all day. Worked on mug trees all day. Visited Louisiana Joe. Mannings walked through the yard. Went to Odden's for pie and ice cream. Sylvia mowed the lawn and cleaned the house.

Sunday, July 23, 1989—45° to 52° and cloudy all day. Spent the day working on the clocks. Took three clocks to KROA to sell and got things ready to go to Wasilla tomorrow.

Monday, July 24, 1989—43° to 54°, partly cloudy and rain in the

10,000 Days in Alaska Book One 1978-1989

Matanuska Valley. Went in to get Sylvia an eye test. A dry left eye is the problem. While there, we did some shopping.

Tuesday, July 25, 1989—43° to 64°, heavy rain during the night but a sunny beaut of a day. Stripped and stacked lumber overhead in the garage. Visited Mannings for lunch. Cut out, drilled, sanded, sealed and put one coat of paint on four snowy owl clocks.

Wednesday, July 26, 1989—43° to 63° and mostly sunny. Resanded and painted owls and worked with some antlers. Split scrap ¾ inch on bandsaw. Visited Smaydas, we had supper there. Had a nice visit, made ice cream, and took it with us. Sent in an order to Gander Mountain for shoes.

Thursday, July 27, 1989—43° to 67° and mostly sunny. Nothing went well today. Made a few antler spacers for bear claw necklaces.

Friday, July 28, 1989—45° to 72°, sunny and hot. Sanded log and Burl slices. Cal G. and family visited. Put a new fiberglass bottom on ice cream mixer and ordered binoculars from Cabela's catalog.

Saturday, July 29, 1989—43° to 63° and partly cloudy. Worked on slabs for a while. Hauled a load of water from Hoffman's and returned a ladder for Max Hoffman to Lucky Beaudoin. Joe and Tom visited. Sold the tandem axle trailer to a guy named Fred. We went to a pot luck supper in honor of Joe and Morey Second Chief.

Sunday, July 30, 1989—46° to 66° and a sunny, beautiful day with a little light rain. Cleaned latex and sanded owl clocks. Cleaned the wood shop and made a prototype wall ski rack. Joe, Shirley, Lisa and her daughter were here for supper, then we took homemade ice cream and rhubarb cake to Odden's neighborhood party.

Monday, July 31, 1989—45° to 65° and partly cloudy with a few drops of rain. Helped Lincoln Smith fix his van. Sylvia went to Glennallen while I worked in the wood shop all day on blanket racks and ski racks and helped Roxanne with some electrical problems (water pump had locked up in well). Sent another order to Miesel Hardware. Kahren came over and said she would buy two clocks. Shot another squirrel today. Mother duck and her brood spend lots of time feeding on the lake. Darned squirrels try to chew holes in the house trying to get inside.

Tuesday, August 1, 1989—42° to 65° and mostly sunny. Worked on crafts all day, mostly on the Alaska clocks. Cut out some parts for quilt racks and visited KROA in the evening.

Wednesday, August 2, 1989—48° to 56° and mostly cloudy, much rain in the night and showers in the day. Worked on Alaska clocks. Sylvia picked currants near Nelchina Mendeltna dump.

Thursday, August 3, 1989—42° to 62° with lots of rain and showers and some sun in between. Worked on Clock boxes and quilt racks. Lisa Smayda and her girls visited and had lunch with us. Sylvia painted seven Alaska clock edges black.

Friday, August 4, 1989—48° to 65° with rain in the night and a sunny breezy day. Sylvia painted pipeline and rivers on Alaska clocks. I worked on quilt racks and ski racks. Sylvia mowed the lawn. The last of the 1" x 6" lumber has been split.

Saturday, August 5, 1989—49° to 68° and sunny. Worked a little on quilt racks then went to Glennallen to get sheep tags and on to Lincoln and Ann Smith's place where I walked to Klutina River and cut diamond willow. Had a BBQ salmon supper with them.

Sunday, August 6, 1989—49° to 71° and a sunny beautiful day. Drew a plan for making a moose coat rack. We got yesterday's diamond willow all peeled. Jim and Elaine visited and later we went to visit Cal and Mary Gilcrease. Saw a swan on the lake this evening.

Monday, August 7, 1989—43° to 63° and mostly sunny. Worked in the wood shop on quilt racks. There are many squirrels this year, shot another one today.

Tuesday, August 8, 1989—35° to 62° and mostly sunny with much fog on the lake in the early morning hours. Put five quilt racks together. Helped Jim Manning haul a heavy heater to the dump. Went to KROA and shot rifle, but it was too windy to target shoot. Stopped at Steve and Karen Malley's.

10,000 Days in Alaska Book One 1978-1989

Wednesday, August 9, 1989—49° to 62° and partly cloudy. Put another quilt rack together. Dan Billman came over and we fixed the trailer hitch on his motorhome. Made some cardboard boxes for Alaska clocks. Sylvia put epoxy on six boards of wildflowers. Watered grass at boat dock. Gave woodworking magazines to Lucky and visited Henry about the Alfred Creek Trail. Dan brought the hitch back and drove the swamp buggy around.

Thursday, August 10, 1989—43° to 69° and mostly sunny. Had to put a little fence around the newly planted grass at the dock. Shot two more nuisance squirrels. Sylvia picked strawberries. Built a ball trailer hitch on the 3-wheeler. This was sure a beaut of a day.

Friday, August 11, 1989—45° and mostly sunny. Flamed one quilt rack and painted basic gray on 47 crane decoys. Sylvia canned beets and Swiss chard. Lisa Smayda and her girls visited.

Saturday, August 12, 1989—49° to 74°, sunny and hot. Sylvia went with Lisa and Karen M. and picked a gallon of blueberries. I stained one quilt rack, made a pattern for a musical baby buggy and cut four out. Shot another squirrel.

Sunday, August 13, 1989—50° to 74° and sunny, turning partly cloudy in the evening. Put finish on a quilt rack and did some more work on the musical baby buggies. Watered the new seeding at the dock down by the lake. Visited with Lucky and Mary and went to a wedding shower were for Dave and Wilma at Nelchina.

Monday, August 14, 1989—48° to 66° and a sunny beautiful day with a light shower in the night. Put polyurethane on quilt rack. Built axle for 3-wheeler trailer and got the box for it pretty far along. Allen and his kids visited in the evening. The moon is nearly full and when it first came up, the reflection of yellows, reds and pinks made the lake look like it was on fire.

Tuesday, August 15, 1989—in the 30s to 70° and sunny, a beautiful day. My back is very bad. Touched up the finish on a quilt rack and worked a little on the 3-wheel trailer and put one coat of paint on it. Lisa and the girls, Jim and Elaine M., Dan and Patti B., and Cal and Phillip G. all visited today. We visited Rudbecks in the evening.

Norman Wilkins

Wednesday, August 16, 1989—temperature in the 30s up to 66° starting out sunny, to cloudy in the evening. Sanded the musical baby buggies. hauled water, went to the dump, KROA and Billmans. Traded the swamp buggy for Dan's quad runner Suzuki ATV and trailer and 30 logs. There were sun dogs out today, strange for this time of year.

Thursday, August 17, 1989—49° to 66° and partly cloudy. Went to Palmer, Wasilla, and Anchorage for crafts, supplies, groceries etc.

Friday, August 18, 1989—46° to 56° and mostly cloudy with a sprinkling of rain. Finished ATV trailer, camo painted it and the bigger ATV trailer. Put epoxy on four Alaska clocks. Lloyd Ronning stopped by to visit.

Saturday, August 19, 1989—56° to 66° and partly cloudy. Worked on ATV trailer and we had lots of company today. Lauren and Emily Smayda stayed here with us while their parents went on an E.M.T. run to Eureka, /Willow/Crooked Creek 3-wheel ATV accident.

Sunday, August 20, 1989—48° to 52° and cloudy with lots of rain and low clouds. Made a pattern and cut out three quilt racks that will display two quilts each. Darrel Gerry bought 1-1/2 x 1-1/2 steel tubing for ferules on crane decoy stakes. I cut 25 of them to length with the hacksaw.

Monday, August 21, 1989—41° to 61° and mostly sunny. Worked on ferules for crane decoy stakes. Cut 1-1/2" long pieces from 1-1/2 x 1-1/2 lightweight tubing. Drilled a hole in it, then drove a square punch into a die clamped in the vice to square hole in the tubing. Now it will accept quarter inch carriage bolts to hold the decoy after the stake is driven into the ground.

Tuesday, August 22, 1989—30° to 60° and sunny with clouds in the evening. Went to a BBQ at Billman's place, it was windy there. Lots of neighbors and good food. Worked on quilt racks and Sylvia put epoxy on more wildflowers.

Wednesday, August 23, 1989—30° to 61°, sunny, cloudy, rainy in the evening. We had lots of company today. Put the three double quilt racks

10,000 Days in Alaska Book One 1978-1989

together.

Thursday, August 24, 1989—30° to 56° and mostly cloudy. Finished four snowy owl clocks and four Alaska clocks. Dan Billman laid the Mean Machine front ½ on side and came over to weld the universal yoke. Dimmicks visited to get some papers signed for their grandkids. Rudbecks needed gun parts. Cal G. and I plan to hunt moose. Went to KROA and put up Clocks. Sold 3-wheeler trailer to Darrel Gerry. Rush to get gear ready and find drop ball hitch.

Friday, August 25, 1989—34° to 52° and cloudy with sprinkles on rain all day and evening. Loaded ATV's onto truck and trailer and went to Cal's, but forgot my sleeping bag. Went to Little Nelchina River and saw a few boo and 1 cow moose. Picked up a lower jaw bone from a moose cow kill and also one boo antler. Cal went out just at dark and shot a 3-prong bull moose—butchered it and got back to camp—late to sleeping bag.

Saturday, August 26, 1989—up early, cooled out the meat, and fixed a sandwich for breakfast. Took down the tent, loaded up and headed for Cal's place. Everything went fast—good trail. The Suzuki ATV air filter plugged up and it ran poorly. Unloaded the meat at Cal's. He gave me some ribs and I came on home. Leaned up my gear and the air filter. Sylvia packaged the ribs. Allen Farmer visited. I fixed the ATV trailer tail gate so it will stay closed. Allen and I went to mile 118 looking for bull moose.

Sunday, August 27, 1989—40° to 62° and sunny, cloudy in the evening. Went up on Slide Mountain with the ATV. So many leaves on the brush, it was hard to see any distance—or any moose. Picked up a lower jaw from a cow moose. Machine didn't run right, so I checked a few things, but found nothing definite. Did some painting and modifications on the meat trailer. Gave Steve Malley another electrical entrance pipe. Someone (Bill?) came to see about the 110 Honda. Bob and Jerry Rudbeck came to look through the Cabela's catalog.

Monday, August 28, 1989 - Allen and I went to Glennallen.

Tuesday, August 29, 1989—40° to 52°, some sun, clouds, light rain. Allen and I loaded our ATV's and gear, picked up Cal G. and his son

Norman Wilkins

Phillip and went in on Goober Lake Trail to Matanuska Creek and set up camp there. Saw a nice meat bull there, but didn't hunt him right away because our noise scared him off. Saw two grizzly and several moose and some boo with the spotting scope. I picked up a boo horn and a moose lower jaw. Where I slept was very uncomfortable.

Wednesday, August 30, 1989—40° to 60°, cloudy then sunny. Stalked a fork horn bull and a cow, but lost them in the brush. Back to camp and had dinner and loaded up gear. Three, Suzuki quad tracks went past our camp. We went out to trail head. Saw 12 sheep (one was a ¾ curl ram), some moose, and boo. Spent a lot of time spotting game. Got home in time for supper and called Teresa on her birthday.

Thursday, August 31, 1989—30° to 54° and mostly sunny. Worked on snowgo trailer and irons for 4x6 3/4" plywood to load ATV. Allen visited and Jim Manning came by too. Had trailer tire fixed at Nelchina and took ATV to Little Nelchina and up hill. Found the river bluff trail and went down it two miles. Saw trapping signs, three old camping sites, one wolf dropping and one cow moose. Got home just at dark.

Friday, September 1, 1989—40° to 51°, mostly cloudy and windy. Up early and road hunted, then home for breakfast. After that went to Eleven-Mile Trail on Lake Louise Road. Unloaded 4-wheeler and went close to Old Boot Lake. Walked the mile to Jim and Mary's cabin. Everything is OK there. Found one set of boo antlers and two very small ones. Stopped at KROA, then home for supper. Sylvia went with me to Roundhouse gravel pit. A yearling cow moose and its mother were there. Tried to spot moose but no luck. Much traffic. Sunshine on the snow in the mountains at east fork of Matanuska Creek was beautiful.

Saturday, September 2, 1989—degrees to 54°, be and sunny. Went looking for bull moose where Allen Farmer cuts firewood with no luck. The mean machine broke down so I helped Dan Billman with it. Cut and put metal tops on Sandhill Crane decoy stakes. Beth Trowbridge and kids were visiting Smayda's so we went over there too.

Sunday, September 3, 1989—30° to 51° and partly cloudy. Road hunted moose, then home for breakfast and worked on a new child toy. Made a jig and made six toys. Got the idea from a toy Beth Trowbridge had gotten for her son. Went north on the seismic west of Cache Creek.

10,000 Days in Alaska Book One 1978-1989

Took the Suzuki and trailer. A creek stopped me about the time I started seeing tracks. Then I turned my knee a little so I went home for supper. Then put anchor of chain for Suzuki and bed of pickup. Chad Wilson phoned in the evening.

Monday, September 4, 1989–28° to 47° and mostly cloudy. Breezy in the evening. Worked on crafts then went looking for moose, came back and worked in the wood shop some more. Visited the KROA and looked for moose but no luck.

Tuesday, September 5, 1989–34° to 60°, cloudy then sunny. I'm stiff and sore this morning. Painted stakes for crane decoys. We had lots of company today. Got a little work done with the crafts and road hunted for moose after supper with no luck. Very beautiful sunset this evening.

Wednesday, September 6, 1989–43° to 57° and cloudy, rainy, and partly cloudy. I saw two cow moose while road hunting in the morning and in the afternoon I did more craft work. We had some visitors and then I went to the dump, then to Billman's and Odden's and did some more road hunting. Saw one moose (sex unknown).

Thursday, September 7, 1989–44° to 61° and cloudy. Today I road hunted, painted on the crane decoys, went to the dump and over to KROA.

Friday, September 8, 1989–40° to 56° cloudy to partly cloudy. A fellow, I think his name was John, came and pumped the septic tank. Sylvia painted the red on the rest of the crane decoys. I got gear ready to go hunting. Lincoln Smith came over about 5:30 and we took the ATV's down the power line to the BLM trail (my trapline trail). His machine was running poorly, then it quit after the worst mud hole. We met Dave DeJung and Lucky Beaudoin on their ATV's on the way out. Dave with a moose. We saw moose tracks and lots of bear pooh. Got our tent up just before dark. There are beaver in these two lakes. Slept well this night.

Saturday, September 9, 1989–up early, very foggy and damp. Hard to hunt. Fog blew off later and Lucky and Dave came in over the trail past our camp. Lincoln hunted north on a steep hill. The beaver are building their feed piles now. I took my ATV up on High Hill to the south. A bear had killed a big bull boo. No moose, so I went north. Dave had just seen a 24" bull moose and cow. We went back but couldn't find them again. We went west exploring a trail we had not been on before. I came back and found Lincoln back in our camp in the tent. He had found two moose horns. Had a bite to eat and went north and east to lower trail but didn't see any moose.

Sunday, September 10, 1989—up early, warm day, no fog. Hunted south and east as far as where we had left Lincoln's ATV. I found three moose horns on the way back but no moose to shoot at! Had a bite to eat and a plane flew over. Later, Lincoln and I hunted north of camp on a couple of hills. No luck there either. Back to camp, packed up and Lincoln rode with me down to his machine. We couldn't get it started so I pulled him and it all the way to the road. Then on home and drove his pickup to trailhead and loaded his ATV and gear and he brought me back home. Had just finished supper when Mike and Shirley Callahan called and came over to visit. Bob Rudbeck was over for a few minutes too.

Monday, September 11, 1989—40° to 54° and mostly sunny. Adjusted the ball hitch on ATV trailer and put a different bolt in the ball for the ATV. Mike and Shirley didn't leave until late morning. Lincoln picked up the quilt racks today. Started a tow strap for ATV and rewound cable on ATV. Tom S. and Lucky B. got bull moose today. Went road hunting in the evening? Saw a forest fire north of Barnette Creek and reported it. Loaded ATV for morning. The 3/4" plywood broke in the middle and the ATV didn't come over backwards—Lucky me! Jim Odden called in the evening to talk hunting. Planned to go to John Johnson's early in the morning to hunt moose.

Tuesday, September 12, 1989—40 to 56° and partly cloudy, beautiful day. I was up long before daylight and went to John Johnson's. Only saw a moose cow and two calves. I stopped at KROA on the way home and later built a new loading ramp and worked on some camping gear. Went up to Lake Louise Road in the evening but only saw one cow and calf moose, a spruce hen and a snowshoe rabbit.

Wednesday, September 13, 1989—34° to 49°, rained in the night, cloudy then sunny. Cal went with me in on Old Man Creek Trail. 3 1/2 miles down the trail I shot a 42 inch bull moose. Butchered him out and was across the swamp and home by 5 p.m. there were two cows that we saw with him. One shot put him down and one coup de grace. Picked up a small armload of caribou horns that were in the area. The ravens and camp robbers were impatient for us to leave so they could feast. Bob and Kahren helped hang the huge pieces of moose in the garage.

Thursday, September 14, 1989—34° to 46°, cloudy to partly cloudy. Sylvia cut and packaged moose ribs. I strengthened loading ramps and got gear ready to go sheep hunting. Washed ATV and trailer. Chad W., P.C. and Jim S. stopped in and later in the evening, I visited their camp on Lake Louise. Lisa Smayda and her girls visited. I stopped at KROA and Darrel and I talked goose hunting.

Friday, September 15, 1989—33° to 42°, rained in a night with a few snowflakes, cloudy to partly cloudy. Snow line is working its way farther down the mountain sides. Loaded the ATV and went to Gunsight Trail to Squaw Creek and went to Caribou Creek Overland Trail and took it for a ways. Saw no game except for sheep up on Sheep Mountain (a no hunting area). Did some exploring. Trail was real greasy on the way in, but had dried quite a bit on the way out. I saw Lucky and Allen Farmer and sons who were on their way out. Rudbecks invited us to a spaghetti supper at Nelchina. Washed the Suzuki when I got home.

Saturday, September 16, 1989—20° to 42° and mostly sunny. Went to KROA and helped Darrel with the roof on the new dining room. That Eagle still hunts ducks every day.

Sunday, September 17, 1989—29° to 34° snow in the night and snow all day. Fixed up a spare wheel and tire for trailer. Got gear ready to go crane hunting at Delta. Darrel Gerry can't go. Jim Odden is going. Moose swam our lake this morning. Saw a large beaver down in the lake this morning too. Still snowing. Got gear ready and road to Delta Junction with Jim Odden and dogs. Took ATV and got to Scott's late. He let us sleep in the mobile home.

Monday, September 18, 1989—frozen ice here at Delta Junction. Up early, saw six Cranes. Jim shot two sharp tailed grouse. Many cranes flying high in evening. Saw five geese. Started home. Billman and Darrel caught us near Donnley Dome. Late night again, slept in Billman's Winnebago.

Tuesday, September 19, 1989—light freeze, windy, lots of Northern

Lights. The same six cranes landed a half-mile away. Stalked them, they got up wild—no other birds. Somebody has leased lots of the farm and charges $40 a day to hunt. We all sat around after breakfast, then Jim Odden and I came home. Real tired tonight.

Wednesday, September 20, 1989—28° to 38° and mostly sunny. Dan Billman was here for breakfast and picked up his swamp buggy repairs. We pulled the water pump from the lake—fitting had already frozen and broken. Filled 20 plastic buckets with dirt for sweet corn next year. Went to look at a pickup for sale near Copper Center and visited KROA.

Thursday, September 21, 1989—40°, cloudy, rain then fog in the late afternoon and evening. Went to KROA and helped Darrel Gerry with new roof. Saw a few ducks flying.

Friday, September 22, 1989—39° to 42° and partly sunny. Helped Darrel again with the new roof at KROA. Rudbeck's are over to watch Dallas, this being Friday night.

Saturday, September 23, 1989—29° to 40° cloudy and rainy evening. Worked on the KROA roof again today. Most of the plywood is on now. Smayda's visited in the evening. Sylvia cut up more of the moose meat.

Sunday, September 24, 1989—30s to 40s, and some rain and fog. Went to Palmer and to the Wasilla area and bought a cab-over camper for the pickup. Stocked it with gear and food to go to Delta.

Monday, September 25, 1989—sunny today. Picked up Darrel at KROA. Vern fired him last night. We fixed rear camper lights in Glennallen and went to Delta Junction, he inquired at Fish & Game and ASCS/farmers and friends for permission to hunt farms. Saw geese on Saylor's Lake, but couldn't get permission to hunt there. Saw more geese just before dark and heard some cranes just at dark. Stopped at Hollembeck's and gave owl clock and some other gifts to Ruby H.

Tuesday, September 26, 1989—30s to 40s, vivid Northern Lights in the night. Clouded up and started raining about 8:00 a.m. and rained all day. Chased around trying to find where the birds were flying. About 3 p.m. they started flying over Bremmer's and Hollembeck's. We put up goose and crane decoys but none flew within range. A few showed interest in the decoys. Many thousands were flying high to the west of us along the mountains. Saw a couple of flocks of geese and also a herd of buffalo on Carlson's. Slept in Scott's old mobile home and visited with Scott and Ruby for a while in the evening.

Wednesday, September 27, 1989—30s and 40s, a clear and cloudy spells. No birds flying early. Went to Delta for gas, oil and propane. Saw cranes on Delta II project. Looked for places to hunt next year. Saw sharp tails, spruce hens, ravens, marsh hawks, cranes and swans flying in the evening. Stalked cranes with no luck. Scott drove us around looking for shooting. I shot a sharp tail with a 3" B.B. mag. Ha! Scott chased a herd of buffalo and then two moose with his pickup. (The buffalo were in his grain field. They cause a lot of crop damage.)

Thursday, September 28, 1989—30s and 40s, very foggy in the morning. We heard geese and cranes to the south. Found them on Thuringer's farm and Darrel got one crane there. We hunted and stalked bird until early evening, then loaded up and started for home. Darrel had some housekeeping and shopping to do. Got back just at dark.

Friday, September 29, 1989—31° into the 40s and foggy. Went to Palmer and picked up crafts, and did some shopping, then went to Jim and Mary Odden's for supper and later to KROA to a community meeting.

Saturday, September 30, 1989—30s to 40s, and fog and cloudy. Did some visiting and small jobs and helped Darrel a little moving. Helped David DeJung with his garage walls. Shot two spruce hens. Sylvia made 50 pounds of breakfast sausage from the moose meat.

Sunday, October 1, 1989—30s to lower 40s, cloudy then a hard rain and sunny. Worked on camper all day. Sylvia ground and packaged hamburger all day.

Monday, October 2, 1989—30° to 42° and partly cloudy. Attached a step under the door of the camper. But some tar on the roof and caulked a few possible leaks. Got some hunting gear together, and shot a few spruce hens as they appeared in the yard. Jim didn't get vehicle reservations made on the ferry east for October 6 and by today, only one space was left for his (Jim's) vehicle. We were happy for the good luck.

Norman Wilkins

The Oddens are good hunters and fun to be out with.

Tuesday, October 3, 1989—20° to 39° and mostly sunny. Built a step to get into camper and other small jobs on it. Sylvia cleaned it out. Visited Smayda's. Shot a spruce hen, hauled a load of water, and tried to see Darrel but he wasn't home.

Wednesday, October 4, 1989—30° to 38° and partly cloudy with some wind. Visited Billmans, Oddens and Darrel and Matt at Snowshoe Lake. Worked on furnace in the camper and spent the rest of the day working on the truck and camper. Sylvia started loading the camper. Billmans are to come over to do some gold claim paperwork.

Thursday, October 5, 1989—nice day. Loaded gear and food into camper. Jim Manning went with us to Glennallen. Made one false start, had to come back and get a sleeping pad for Darrel Gerry. Did some shopping and ran some errands in Glennallen and Copper Center. Filed assessment affidavits for claims. Met Oddens at Copper Center Laundromat. Sylvia had fixed chicken and potato salad and we had a picnic on the way to Valdez. Saw Mike Callahan at his guard post. Got on the ferry and left for Cordova at 4:00 a.m.

Friday, October 6, 1989—it was raining when we arrived at Cordova at 9:30 a.m. went to Charlie and Beth's place on Main Street. Had breakfast and rested all day, it was raining hard with gusty winds all day long. Went to Charlie's office and looked at an aerial photo of Egg Island.

Saturday, October 7, 1989—still raining hard here in Cordova. Ate breakfast and got gear ready to fly out to Egg Island. I forgot to pack a shovel and tent stakes and my .338 rifle got put on the plane by mistake. Steve Ranney flew us out to Egg Island in a Cessna 180 on wheels (Darrel, me, Charlie, Jim O. and two dogs—Nellie and Tigre). Steve flew us out in two trips. He landed us on the beach and we packed the quarter mile inland, set up camp and went hunting. Charlie got a mallard and widgen and I got two teal with one shot. Jim O. got six ducks. We walked and hunted getting familiar with the island. Saw Canada/dusky and snow geese.

Sunday, October 8, 1989—sun and light rain. Jim Odden and dogs and I went to a blind. I shot one goose on the way. Jim and I shot six geese this morning. Darrel shot one white front. He's not hitting well with his Marlin bolt-action 10 gage. Charlie Trowbridge got four geese. Geese are flying down and using Egg Island, thousands are resting here.

Monday, October 9, 1989—Charlie and Jim each got one goose. Very few are flying today, but it's a beautiful, blue, bird day. Went back to camp, fixed breakfast and packed our gear out to the airstrip on the beach. Did some beachcombing until the plane came to pick us up and take us back to Cordova Airport. Our wives met us there and we all went to Charlie's for supper.

Tuesday, October 10, 1989—pretty nice day. Went out Copper River Highway looking for hunting, then back for breakfast. Then we drove to Million Dollar Bridge (wives and kids also), had a lunch at Child's glacier. Darrel and I hunted on the way back to town with no luck. We stopped and listened for resting geese several times. Jim Odden got two ducks. Had a good supper at Beth's.

Wednesday, October 11, 1989—froze last night but today is a sunny day. Jim, Darrel and I went to mile nine and hunted south. No luck hunting geese, saw a few flying and also some ducks. Lots of beaver around here. Went back to the house and fixed lunch at noon. Went to McKinley Lake and the afternoon. Jim Odden shot a spruce hen. Then he hunted Alleganik Slough. Darrel and I hunted to Copper River and back to town with no luck.

Thursday, October 12, 1989—sunny and breezy. Up early again. Charlie went with us this morning until 11:00 a.m. but we had no luck. Darrel and I went to the U.S. Forest Service and talked to Keith Giezentanner, the wildlife biologist there about building goose nesting islands. In his office he has mounted moose horns that measure 77 inches. We hunted out as far as Allganik Slough and explored more places. Glassed five cow and one small bull moose out on the flats from high rocky observation place. Odden's dog Tigre cut his foot. Back in town we looked at and '84 Chevy pickup S walling const. will be selling Dec. 1. Diane and Randy Phipps were at Charlie and Beth's for supper in the evening. They have bought a 26 foot bow picker boat (Aleut Splendor).

Friday, October 13, 1989—freezing in the morning then became a warmer, beautiful sunny day. Windy Over on Copper River and Delta we drove out past the airport but didn't see any geese and only a few ducks. Went to Hartley Bay where there were hundreds of mallards, but we didn't shoot as we couldn't retrieve them. Packed up our gear and went to the Fish and Game office to look at Steve Ranney's atypical moose horns on display there. While we were there, some hunters brought in goat horns to be registered and measured. Talked to Diane P. She works at F & G. She gave us permission to go to the slip on the city docks and look at their boat and invited me to come in December to hunt deer. Said goodbye to Trowbridge family and got on Ferry and started out. Lots of sea otter in the harbor. After going west for a while, we saw more otter and some sea lions lying on a channel marker buoy. A coast guard helicopter circled our ferry. Two state D.O.T. workers from above Million Dollar Bridge were also on the ferry. Landed at Valdez, gassed up the truck and headed out of town to Lowe River. Listened for geese and made coffee, then drove on home. Arrived around 11:00 p.m. and Darrel slept in the camper.

Saturday, October 14, 1989–10° to 28°. Mostly sunny and the lake is frozen over. Darrel had breakfast with us and helped unload gear from the camper and then I drove him home. After that, Sylvia and I started taking the camper off the pickup truck. Tom Smayda came by and helped us. While we were gone, Mannings had done some shopping for us (canned goods) so we went over and picked it up. Put away lots of gear. Jim and Mary Odden stopped by the evening with more geese. Very thoughtful of them.

Sunday, October 15, 1989–32° to 42°, mostly cloudy and windy in the afternoon. Shot a spruce hen. Built a wood chute from a road sign. Visited Dennis G. at Rudbeck's. Split and put two pickup loads of wood in the basement. Smayda and Malley family's we're here for coffee. Called Beverly and her family.

Monday, October 16, 1989–20s to 30s today and snow. Went to Darrel's and loaded two pick-up rear ends and brought them back to my place to try to make one good one. It didn't work, there was too much of a difference in years between them. Darrel is calling Ron Sopko to try to find one in the Mat-Su valley.

Tuesday, October 17, 1989–30° to 34° with 4 inches of wet snow. Went to Oddens, and Rudbecks and Darrel and I put in a large window in the S.E. corner of their house. Got some work done in the shop today.

Wednesday, October 18, 1989—24° to 28°, cloudy with three to four more inches of snow. Took Darrel Gerry to Glennallen and did laundry and looked at some places he might like to live. We also looked for a rear end for his truck. Stopped at KROA for pizza. Darrel took care of his dogs and came home with us. Sylvia's sister Frances called this evening with the news that their mother, Stefania Kolenc, passed away in Yugoslavia. We called Paul and Beverly and Teresa called us. Rudbecks plowed our lane.

Thursday, October 19, 1989—20° to 25° and mostly cloudy with some snow. Got a call that Warren Dawson of Lake Louise passed away Tuesday night of a massive heart attack. Sylvia and I went to the service held for Warren at Lake Louise Lodge. I fixed the left front turn signal and mounted a ball hitch on the front bumper of the pickup. I will miss Warren.

Friday, October 20, 1989—20° to 24°, snow, fog, cloudy. Took Darrel to Wasilla to buy a rear end for his pickup. Visited Ron and Elli. Ron sold me some gasoline. Picked up oxygen at welding shop. Some people were having trouble driving the highway today. Got home very late.

Saturday, October 21, 1989—18° to 20°, cloudy and some snow. Worked with the rear end for Darrel's pickup. Sure is rusty and tough to install. Hauled a load of water from Beaudoin's.

Sunday, October 22, 1989—partly cloudy and -4° to 17°. Loaded the acetylene torch and some tools and went to Mendeltna and installed the rear end under Darrel's truck. Got that done and wheels on it. No breaks or driveshaft/emergency etc. discovered the anti-freeze was frozen, so pulled his truck to Nelchina and put it in Rudbeck's shop to thaw out.

Monday, October 23, 1989—10° to 17° with more snow. 12 inches on level now. Got Darrel started off. Put ATV in the shed and brought the snowgo out. Shoveled snow off the camper and began to straighten out some messes and organize things around here. Cleaned 12 gauge and .338. Manning's came and visited for a few minutes in the evening.

Norman Wilkins

Tuesday, October 24, 1989—10° to 20° and mostly sunny. Put a pickup load of split wood in the basement. Worked in the wood shop the rest of the day.

Wednesday, October 25, 1989—10° to 21° and mostly sunny. Straightened up more things around here and planed 28 boards. Started making more sewing blocks. Darrel was here for supper, we hauled the old truck axle away.

Thursday, October 26, 1989—3° to 10° and mostly sunny. Loaded the snowgo and went to trapline trailhead and went over near Allen's cabin. Saw tracks of a large wolf pack, ptarmigan, three fox tracks and some moose and caribou. When I took the west trail around past beaver lodges, I came upon grizzly tracks coming onto the trail. I followed a ways to find a turnaround and came upon his bed right in the trail. He had gone on. I turned around and went back to the north-south trail. Didn't get to the big hill where the caribou kill and horns are. Picked up Sam at his driveway and brought him to Nelchina.

Friday, October 27, 1989—4° to 12° cloudy with a little snow. Lucky Beaudoin brought over a red fox he had picked up off the highway. I skimmed it and froze it. Cut out some patterns and some 3/4" pine puffins and later worked on mounting a scope on my .338 rifle.

Saturday, October 28, 1989—10° to 17° and cloudy with a light snow. Put more wood in the basement and worked in the wood shop. Elaine brought over a couple of craft orders.

Sunday, October 29, 1989—12° to 22° and mostly cloudy. Some caribou are going west on our lake. Allen Farmer and family are back home. Their well is frozen. Worked in the wood shop. Smayda family visited in the evening.

Monday, October 30, 1989—10° to 20°, cloudy, misty, freezing rain. Worked in the wood shop and did other odd jobs. Allen Farmer visited. Ruth Midgett asked me to cut out wood snowmen for her.

Tuesday, October 31, 1989—18° to 20°, cloudy and foggy. Spent all day on the phone about our will and applying for Social Security benefits. Went to a Halloween party and potluck supper at the Nelchina

10,000 Days in Alaska Book One 1978-1989

elementary school.

Wednesday, November 1, 1989—12° to 20° with fog and then rain in Anchorage. Lots of ice on the road on the way to Anchorage. Once there, we went to the lawyer and got started doing our wills, after that we did some shopping. Stayed overnight at Andy and Connie Boyle's. Went to Sheep Creek and bought a used gas cook stove.

Thursday, November 2, 1989—32° and raining in Anchorage. Finish the rest of our shopping and drove home. The roads were pretty good until we came through the pass where they were very icy. An older couple had slid into the ditch and wrecked their car but were not hurt. It was 25° here at Nelchina.

Friday, November 3, 1989—22° to 30° and a cloudy with a light snow. Finished unloading the truck (Tom Smayda helped us get the stove off). Put away some things. Cut out some dinosaurs and drew out helicopter "bank" (pattern for children—they like dinosaur banks also).

Saturday, November 4, 1989—25° to 30° and cloudy with some snow. Built a fire in the garage so Sylvia could clean up the cook stove we bought. I finished one moose coat rack and gave it to Matt and Marie along with a baby carriage and wooden bear. I cut out more wood with the bandsaw. Cal G. visited. He left two rifles here are with me for safekeeping while he goes "outside". Allen Farmer visited in the evening.

Sunday, November 5, 1989—11° to 20° and sunny and cloudy and sunny again. Worked in the woodshop. Put sole saver on Sylvia's boots. Went to the dump and tried to sight in my .338 rifle. It doesn't shoot well. Cleaned the chimney. Smayda's visited

Monday, November 6, 1989—10° to 4° at a cloudy with 1 inch of snow. Worked in the woodshop, but didn't feel well much of the day. Allen stopped in and Kahren came over to have Mickey Mouse cut out.

Tuesday, November 7, 1989—it's -10° to -5° and mostly cloudy. Worked in the woodshop. Went to Hoffman's for water—sill cock there was frozen. Came back and went to Lucky Beaudoin's and got water there. Mary gave me two movie tapes. We visited Oddens and later Sylvia went to a painting class.

Wednesday, November 8, 1989—it was cloudy all day clearing up later and -12° to -14°. Worked in the woodshop. Jim Manning came over to saw a board. He took the things they had stored at our place back to his home. Dan Billman called and I went to his place and tested the antifreeze in the swamp buggy. It tested at -32° to -37°. Ted G. and Mary Odden stopped by for a few minutes. Rudbecks left for the winter.

Thursday, November 9, 1989—partly cloudy with some ice fog and -24° to -18°. Worked in the woodshop. Ruth Midgett visited and left some rolls.

Friday, November 10, 1989—mostly sunny and cool. Jim Manning visited in the morning. I built a fire in the woodshop and did some work in there. Allen Farmer and his son David came over in the evening to borrow some movies.

Saturday, November 11, 1989—sunny and -40° to -25°. The ice has shrunk a lot on the lake and now there is overflow in the snow. Worked in the woodshop. A string broke that Sylvia had hung dinosaurs on and nine of them broke. Smayda's visited in the evening.

Sunday, November 12, 1989—sunny and -40° to -25°. Put all of our tool and appliance manuals in a three ring notebook. A spruce hen flew into our dining room window and killed itself. Beth Trowbridge called from Cordova.

Monday, November 13, 1989—sunny and -30° to -20°. Mounted scope on rifle for wolf hunting. Allen Farmer and Ellie visited. Went to lodge for hamburgers and pie. Didn't do much today.

Tuesday, November 14, 1989—cloudy with some ice fog in the distance and a breeze from the west. It's -31° to -19°. Took the old gas cook stove out of the house and put another used one in its place. Visited Jim Manning late in the afternoon. Darrel Gerry called in the evening.

Wednesday, November 15, 1989—mostly cloudy and -13° to -9°. Fixed the seal on the oven door. Worked in the wood shop. Jim Odden came here for a goose supper. Lisa Smayda and girls were here to visit in the evening. Sylvia has gone to a painting class.

10,000 Days in Alaska Book One 1978-1989

Thursday, November 16, 1989—cloudy and -5° to 2°. Got some trapping gear ready and worked in the wood shop. Allen Farmer came over to get some cement nails. Jim and Mary Odden and daughter came over to borrow power tin snips. Dan Billman's nephew had a problem with his Jeep that seemed to fix itself.

Friday, November 17, 1989—10° to 20°, cloudy, foggy and breezy. Worked in the wood shop, then took some crafts to Ruth Midgett's to take to the Kenny Lake Bazaar.

Saturday, November 18, 1989—10° all day and sunny. Shot the trapline rifle at home, then Sylvia and I went to the dump and shot some more. Got it fairly well sighted in. Kurt and his cousin and Henry and Sally came to use the dump while we were there. We went to KROA to visit, then came home and worked on crafts.

Sunday, November 19, 1989—mostly sunny and -10° to 5°. Worked in the wood shop and cleaned the barrel and refinished the stock on my 30-06.

Monday, November 20, 1989—1° to 5° and cloudy with light snow. Sylvia went on to senior citizens bus and I put a load of wood in the basement and worked in the wood shop. Ruth Midgett stopped by.

Tuesday, November 21, 1989—clouds and snow with temps. at -5° to 10°. Visited with Allen and worked in the wood shop. Sylvia painted crafts again today.

Wednesday, November 22, 1989—5° to 12° and cloudy with four inches of snow. Up early and went to Anchorage. Bought "moose dick", the goose getter. Couldn't find the man with the pickup truck for sale. Did other shopping and got home at 8:00 p.m.

Thursday, November 23, 1989—10° to 0° and cloudy and foggy. Beverly and Theresa both called. We went to Nelchina Lodge for a Thanksgiving dinner, visiting, and music. John Odden was there and we talked prospecting. I phoned Dan Billman when I got home and we agreed to offer John a partnership in our gold ventures.

Friday, November 24, 1989—4° to -4°, cloudy, fog, sunshine, cloudy and ice fog. Went with Jim and Elaine to pick up a road kill boo. It had been smashed. I saved the horns and two front legs for bait. Worked in the wood shop. Allen Farmer visited. Jim, Mary, Kari, John Odden, and Colleen were here for supper. John is interested in doing the geological work on our claims. We offered him a partnership.

Saturday, November 25, 1989—ice fog all day and -4° to 0°. Sylvia did laundry at Nelchina and painted crafts. I put sealer on 29 ski holders. Jim and Elaine Manning had us over for supper. Henry borrowed a water tank. Charlie Trowbridge and Sam and two sons stayed here for the night.

Sunday, November 26, 1989—some fog, then sunny with temps at -20° to -15°. Lots of company for breakfast, then we hauled three loads with the snowgo from Charlie's storage shed to our garage. I put urethane on ski racks. Henry brought the water tank back, then I hauled us a load of water.

Monday, November 27, 1989—it was -10° all day and sunny. Worked in the wood shop on crafts, then went to a baby shower for Kim Huddleston's baby, Charles.

Tuesday, November 28, 1989—it was -19° to -18° and partly sunny with ice fog in the mountains to the south and a light snow in the evening. Worked in the wood shop all day.

Wednesday, November 29, 1989—temperature at -8° to 8° and cloudy with a light snow and some fog. Put urethane on a quilt rack and did a few small jobs and Sylvia painted. Visited at the lodge.

Thursday, November 30, 1989—today it's -4° to -8° and cloudy. Urethaned another quilt rack and got things ready for the Glennallen bazaar. Allen and Roxanne Farmer visited and did a bunch of Christmas shopping at our place. Smayda's visited and bought two dinosaur banks.

Friday, December 1, 1989—cloudy and -5° to 10°. Worked in the wood shop, cut out seven dinosaurs and got crafts ready for the bazaar in Glennallen. Jim and Elaine stopped by. Jim and Mary Odden stopped for a piece of Velcro to use on a baby cap.

10,000 Days in Alaska Book One 1978-1989

Saturday, December 2, 1989—10° and cloudy all day. Sylvia went with Jim and Elaine to the Legion Hall in Glennallen today and sold some crafts. I worked on dinosaur banks all day. Charlie Trowbridge stopped to pick up some things he had stored in our garage and stayed for supper and to visit.

Sunday, December 3, 1989—10° to 15° and cloudy with a little fog and light snow. we had coffee over at Nelchina and then worked in the wood shop.

Monday, December 4, 1989—14° all day and cloudy. Started setting traps along Slide Mountain. Saw two female marten and some fox tracks and possibly wolverine tracks (couldn't be certain) but no wolves. I only went as far as the first meat pole. Snowgo ran poorly.

Tuesday, December 5, 1989—10° and cloudy. Tom and Lisa came over to watch a ski movie they had. We went to Glennallen to shop and do laundry. Saw Darrel Gerry.

Wednesday, December 6, 1989—4° to 14° and cloudy with ice fog. Worked in woodshop all day making wooden people, rocking horse toy and dinosaur banks. The Smayda family brought us a small, decorated Christmas spruce tree. Very thoughtful of them. Their daughters got a kick out of that. They wanted to be sure we had a Christmas tree.

Thursday, December 7, 1989—6° to -4° and sunny with some light breeze. Worked in the wood shop most of the day. Allen Farmer and I went out and tried to call foxes. I had hoped to shoot one with the new 10 gauge. No luck though.

Friday, December 8, 1989—it's -8° to -4° and sunny. Put side plates on some dinosaur banks. Kim came over to borrow VCR tape. We took two dinosaurs to Manning's, then went to Oddens for supper.

Saturday, December 9, 1989—it's -12° to -4° and cloudy with ice fog. Put side plates on six dinosaurs. Ran trapline. No fur, set two more Mannings.

Norman Wilkins

Sunday, December 10, 1989—5° to 11° and snow fell most of the night and day to 12 inches. Took Allen to Moosey Boo. He plowed Jack and Jayne out, then I pulled his Ranger and trailer home and he plowed us out. I gave him some gas, oil, Heet, and $50.00. Packed three dinosaur banks to send to Trowbridge's at Cordova.

Monday, December 11, 1989—14° to 26° and mostly cloudy. Shoveled snow off the wood shop, lean-to, storage shed and lean-to, brown trailer, woodshed, camper and pickup. Repaired canvas mukluks and some other small jobs. Took six dinosaurs to Allen and Roxanne and visited in the evening.

Tuesday, December 12, 1989—14° to 29° cloudy with a gusty breeze in the evening. Made out Christmas cards in the morning and visited Huddleston's in the afternoon and wrote two long letters. Clayton and Ruth Midgett came to buy some crafts. Leo Zura was found dead by Lucky and Lloyd. Cleaned the house chimney.

Wednesday, December 13, 1989—22° to 28° and snowed most of the day to three inches. Worked in the wood shop for Ruth M. Hauled a load of water. Helped pull a fuel truck at Moosey Boo—he had slid to the side of the driveway. Got water at Max's and looked at the work Allen did at the store. He brought some money for supplies. Got ready to go to Anchorage. Sylvia is enrolled in decorative "tole" painting class.

Thursday, December 14, 1989—17° this morning and mostly cloudy today. Went to Anchorage to the Social Security office and to the lawyer to sign our wills. Left the quilt rack I made for Billman's Christmas gift with Dan's mother, Faye. Got most shopping done.

Friday, December 15, 1989—10° all day and cloudy. Put the 2 x 10s in the basement to dry and unloaded materials we had picked up for Allen at his store. Cut out and sanded and sealed three brontosaurus dinosaurs. Had supper with Allen and Ellie at the lodge. Oddens, Lee D. and Smaydas played music at the lodge.

Saturday, December 16, 1989—10° to 14° and cloudy with light snow in the night. We haven't had any ash from the Mount Redoubt eruption yet. (Once in a while the wind carries ash from the eruptions. It can damage people's respiratory systems, ruin engines, paint on vehicles—the list goes on and on.) Cut out and sanded and sealed two more dinosaurs. Jim Odden was here repairing a ski on his snowgo.

Sunday, December 17, 1989—12° all day, cloudy and snowy. Tried to run the trapline. Made one marten set and got almost to top of hill and got stuck. The steering column had worn thin and I pushed on it, it almost broke off. Man handled a turnaround in the trail and got it home. Repaired broken windshield and started fixing it—found a worn out bearing on the secondary clutch. Ruth Midgett came to get more wooden cutouts.

Monday, December 18, 1989—16° all day with a fairly steady snow stopping at about three inches. Alan and Elli came over and borrowed a sawhorse. Worked on snowgo windshield again. Drew out a pattern for a red fox candleholder centerpiece. Went with Sylvia and senior citizens for a Christmas party and gift exchange.

Tuesday, December 19, 1989—5° to -1°, cloudy and snow. Lucky Beaudoin came over and plowed out our lane again. Put new bearings on snowgo and ran trapline. No fur. Everything is under 16 inches of snow. Awfully tough to break trail, plus the motor ran badly. I was lucky to get the line run. Nadia sent a nice package. Did a little work in the wood shop.

Wednesday, December 20, 1989—clouds and light snow and -10° to 0°. Helped Allen Farmer hang garage doors. Mike Callahan and a friend visited. Mike left Christmas gifts for us. We went to a kids Christmas program at the school and later I did some more work in the wood shop. Allen broke a finger late in the evening.

Thursday, December 21, 1989—cloudy with a light snow and -5° to -1°. Worked in the wood shop and made some 1-1/4" dowels to cut into checkers. Cut out fox candleholders and put side plates on more dinosaurs. Neighborhood Christmas carolers were here this evening and sang carols for us.

Friday, December 22, 1989—cloudy, sunny then cloudy again and -5° to -1°. Worked in the wood shop. Put sling swivels on 10 gauge. Kim brought movies back and Elaine Manning visited.

Norman Wilkins

Saturday, December 23, 1989—16° to 24° and cloudy with a light snow. We visited around the neighborhood (took presents around) then had supper at Smaydas. Worked a little on the snowgo and broke and packed some trails around home.

Sunday, December 24, 1989—8° to 24° cloudy and snow in the evening. Helped Allen with his snowgo windshield and did a load of laundry at Nelchina. Sylvia cleaned house. We took a couple of presents to the Malley boys and had a Norwegian holiday supper with Oddens. Lloyd Ronning and Kurt's cousin were there. Lloyd brought pictures and told stories.

Monday, December 25, 1989—18° to 24°, cloudy, fog, cloudy. Smayda family, Mannings, and Darrel Gerry were here for the excellent Christmas dinner Sylvia fixed. We had lots of good conversation and really enjoyed the day.

Tuesday, December 26, 1989—4° to 12°, cloudy, sunny then cloudy. We saw a few caribou down on our lake. There has been lots of overflow down there for several days now. Loafed most of the day.

Wednesday, December 27, 1989—7° to 12° and mostly cloudy with light snow and fog. Shoveled a little snow at the mailboxes. Visited the Huddlestons. Sylvia went with the senior van. Theresa called and we talked to Darcy and Lee.

Thursday, December 28, 1989—8° to 15° and cloudy with ice fog and snow. Ran the trapline but no fur. Wolves had gone west up Cache Creek. Got back home and Tom Huddleston came by to visit for the rest of the afternoon. We went to their house for a ham supper.

Friday, December 29, 1989—4° all day, cloudy, then on Sunday. We put four loads of wood in the basement. Jim Odden borrowed our water hauling tank. I visited Allen Farmer and gave him some rug pieces to use for weather stripping on his garage doors, then I went, picked up the water tank and went to Hoffman's and got a load of water for our place. Sylvia pumped it off. Temperature is at -8° and dropping this evening.

Saturday, December 30, 1989—it's -14° in the night and up to 4° today.

10,000 Days in Alaska Book One 1978-1989

Slept late. Put two sled loads of wood in the basement. Changed sparkplugs in the snowgo and adjusted its tie rod. Tried to phone a man about a plow truck. Jim and Elaine came over and we went to the lodge where Sylvia was visiting Mae.

Sunday, December 31, 1989—it's -26° to -20° and mostly sunny. Slept late and loafed all day. Had Elaine Manning here for lunch. Tom H. visited in the afternoon. Went to Nelchina Lodge for a New Year's Eve party and pot luck snacks. Lots of people we knew where there and we had lots of fun. Clouded over at midnight and temperature dropped to -26°.

Norman and Sylvia Wilkins at their log home near Nelchina

Norman Wilkins

A gathering of Nelchina residents at the home of Jim and Mary Odden.

10,000 Days in Alaska Book One 1978-1989

Norman Wilkins

Norman Wilkins

For more information about the author and his wife,
Or to learn where to get additional copies of this book,
go to www.10000daysinalaska.com.

10,000 Days in Alaska by Norman R. Wilkins
is a three-book, documentary journal series.
To contact the publisher,
email Nadia Giordana
at
iinadia@msn.com
or
nadiagiordana99@gmail.com

Cloud 9 Publishing

THE ROAD NOT TAKEN

Two roads diverged in a yellow wood,
And sorry I could not travel both
And be one traveler, long I stood
And looked down one as far as I could
To where it bent in the undergrowth;

Then took the other, as just as fair,
And having perhaps the better claim,
Because it was grassy and wanted wear;
Though as for that the passing there
Had worn them really about the same,

And both that morning equally lay
In leaves no step had trodden black.
Oh, I kept the first for another day!
Yet knowing how way leads on to way,
I doubted if I should ever come back.

I shall be telling this with a sigh
Somewhere ages and ages hence:
Two roads diverged in a wood, and I—
I took the one less traveled by,
And that has made all the difference.

—Robert Frost

www.ingramcontent.com/pod-product-compliance
Lightning Source LLC
Chambersburg PA
CBHW062039080426
42734CB00012B/2508